TRUST, AUTHORITY, AND THE WRITTEN WORD IN THE ROYAL TOWNS OF MEDIEVAL HUNGARY

UTRECHT STUDIES IN MEDIEVAL LITERACY

41

TRUST, AUTHORITY, AND THE WRITTEN WORD IN THE ROYAL TOWNS OF MEDIEVAL HUNGARY

Katalin Szende

BREPOLS

British Library Cataloguing in Publication Data

A catalogue record for this book is available from the British Library

D/2018/0095/205

ISBN 978-2-503-57881-1

e-ISBN 978-2-503-57882-8

DOI: 10.1484/M.USML-EB.5.114658

ISSN: 2034-9416

e-ISSN: 2294-8317

Printed in the EU on acid-free paper

Contents

Acknowledgements ix
Abbreviations xi
List of Figures and Tables xv

Introduction 1

On This Volume 1
Trust and Authority 5
Literate Mentalities 16
European Frameworks 20

1. Setting the Scene 25

Whose Literacy? Urban Development and Urban Society in Medieval Hungary 25
Pragmatic Approaches to Pragmatic Literacy 44
Sources and Scholarship 49

2 In the First-Person Plural: Civic Literacy and Communal Identity 61

Royal Charters and Urban Identity 62
The Beginnings of Civic Literacy 67
Civic Literacy and Places of Authentication 72
Formulae and Community 84
The Municipal Seal: The Matrix of Identity 87
Communal Concerns: The Contents of Early Municipal Documents 107
Conclusions: Trust in Charters 115

3. From Charters to Books and Back 121

The Institutionalisation of Writing Offices 121
Municipal Books as Instruments of Civic Governance 134
The Material of Town Books: The Use of Paper in Administration 140
The Contents of Municipal Books: Thematic Differentiation 148
Miscellaneous Books 149
Financial Registers 157
Court Books and Judicial Administration 164
Municipal Books for Property Administration 176
Town Books and Testamentary Practice 181
Outlook 1: The Beginnings of Pragmatic Literacy in Craft Guilds 185
Outlook 2: Town Chronicles and Municipal Literacy 189
Conclusions: Trust in Municipal Books 197

4. Language and Literacy 203

Language on the Research Agenda 203
Why Not Monolingual? 206
Areas of Urban Life Where Language Became an Issue 218
Administration and Justice 218
External Relations 223
Trade and Accounting 225
Pastoral Care and Preaching 229
Medieval Urban Language Use in the Light of Sociolinguistic Research 234
Conclusions: Trust in Language 244

5. "*in cartula scribere faciat*" – The Uses of Writing between Christians and Jews 249

Legislation on Jews and Literacy – A Chronological Overview 250
Records of Urban Administration as Sources on Jewish-Christian Coexistence 259
Normative Legislation – Local Statutes 259

Administering Justice 262
Real Estate and Moneylending 266
Conclusions: Trust in Writing between Christians and Jews 279

6. From Charters to Archives 287

Variations on Archives 288
The Advent and Advantage of Civic Archives: Storage and Safekeeping 292
Binding Records: The Example of Sopron 306
Using Civic Archives 314
Conclusions: Trust in Archives 318

Final Conclusions 323

Appendices 335

Appendix 1: Gazetteer of Names of Towns in the Medieval Kingdom of Hungary Discussed in the Book 336
Appendix 2: Regnal Years of the Kings of Medieval Hungary 339
Appendix 3: Documents Issued by Civic Authorities in Hungary, (1244) 1255-1305 340
Appendix 4: Earliest Mentioning of Municipal Notaries (up to 1400) 352
Appendix 5: The Earliest Preserved Charters of Bishops' Towns (Issued by the Municipality) 357
Appendix 6: Municipal Books Started before 1500 359

Bibliography 365
Index 407

Acknowledgements

The medieval city is daughter to the written word – writes Paul Zumthor. As a grateful daughter, however, she has returned more to her parent than what she had received, generating an immense amount of writing, pragmatic, scholarly, and literary alike. My first word of thanks goes to those named or unnamed scribes, notaries, and town clerks whose writings have provided the sources for the present inquiry.

Naturally, I am grateful to just as many of my contemporaries for their inspiration and support. A broader scholarly context will be offered in the introductory chapter of the volume, but I wish to thank already at the outset Anna Adamska and Marco Mostert for introducing me to the conceptual framework of medieval literacy, and to the academic network pursuing its study. My everyday working environment, Central European University, a unique example of academic integrity and resilience, and its Department of Medieval Studies in particular, has been the other source of encouragement. From among my colleagues the warmest thanks are due to Zsuzsa Reed, a keen scholar of textual studies, who offered invaluable help in improving the clarity and fluency of this work. László Kontler, Gábor Klaniczay, and János M. Bak were most supportive readers of my work and gave me reassuring confirmation concerning its intellectual setting. I am also grateful to the students attending my palaeography courses over the years, who directed my attention to a variety of documents that I otherwise would not have noticed.

My work was supported by two more research projects in which I currently participate: the Hungarian Atlas of Historic Towns (NKFI K 116594) and the MTA 'Lendület' Hungarian Economic History Research Group (LP2015-4/2015, Principal Investigator: Boglárka Weisz). Many of my friends and colleagues at other institutions have given extremely helpful comments and corrections. Bálint Lakatos (also member of the 'Lendület' research group) was a most meticulous reader of an earlier version of the manuscript, and provided me with precious comparative material from his rich data collection on seigniorial and market towns. László Veszprémy suggested important further readings and inspired the outlook on urban historiography. Juraj Šedivý (Univerzita Komenského, Bratislava) offered his generous support on literature from Slovakia, his photos from Levoča, as well as his insights gained from his extensive work on the archival and epigraphic record.

I am grateful to my colleagues at all those institutions that provided access to their collections and gave permission to reproduce images from their materials. Special thanks go to Judit Benda and Péter Farbaky (Budapest History Museum), László Szende and Gábor Tomka (Hungarian National Museum), György Rácz and Krisztina Arany (National Archives of Hungary), Péter Dominkovits (Sopron Municipal Archives), Suzana Miljan (HAZU, Zagreb), Michal Duchoň (Archív Mesta Bratislavy), and Mária Hajduová (Archív Mesta Košice). Krisztina Arany and Judit Majorossy were extremely helpful in collecting the images and checking the data in the Appendix, and András Vadas has offered his kind and efficient assistance with maps and graphs, and compiled the Index.

I have benefitted from the opportunity provided by the European History Seminar at the Institute of Historical Research (University College London) to present a summary of my argument in November 2017. Feedback from the audience and the organisers of the event, Miri Rubin and Patrick Lantschner, and particularly from Susan Reynolds and Martyn Rady, who helped me refine my terminology and broadened my perspective.

An earlier version of Chapter 4 as well as Chapter 5 were parts of edited volumes published by Brepols and Ashgate (now represented by Routledge), respectively. I owe thanks to both publishers for agreeing to reprint these texts here in modified form. The exact references to the earlier versions can be found at the beginning of each chapter. The publication of this volume was skilfully overseen by Guy Carney and the Brepols team.

Finally, but most importantly, I owe the greatest gratitude to my family, my parents, my husband Finn-Einar, and my five children, particularly Nóra, for helping me through difficult moments with their trust, patience – and love.

Abbreviations

AMB	Archiv Mesta Bratislavy.
AMK	Archiv Mesta Košice.
Anjou-oklt.	*Anjou-kori oklevéltár* [Charter collection from the Angevin period], ed. Gyula KRISTÓ, László BLAZOVICH, Ferenc PITI, Ferenc SEBŐK *et al.*, 48 vols. (Budapest and Szeged, 1990-2017).
AO	*Anjoukori okmánytár* [Cartulary of the Angevin period] 7 vols, ed. Iván NAGY, Gyula TASNÁDI NAGY (Budapest, 1878-1920).
BFL	Budapest Főváros Levéltára
BTM	Budapesti Történeti Múzeum.
BTOE	*Budapest történetének okleveles emlékei / Monumenta diplomatica civitatis Budapest*, 1, *1148-1301*, ed. Albert GÁRDONYI (Budapest, 1936); 3, *1382-1439*, ed. Lajos Bernát KUMOROVITZ (Budapest, 1987).
CDCr	*Codex diplomaticus regni Croatiae, Dalmatiae et Slavoniae* 18 vols, ed. Tadija SMIČIKLAS *et al.* (Zagreb, 1904-1990).
CDES	*Codex diplomaticus et epistolaris Slovaciae*, ed. Richard MARSINA, 2 vols. (Bratislava, 1971, 1987).
CDH	*Codex diplomaticus Hungariae ecclesiasticus ac civilis*, ed. Georgius FEJÉR, 11 vols. in 48 parts (Buda, 1829-1844).
CEU	Central European University, Budapest.
Csáky	*Oklevéltár a gróf Csáky család történetéhez* [Cartulary to the history of the Count Csáky family], ed. László BÁRTFAI SZABÓ (Budapest, 1919)
DF	Collection of photographs of documents prior to 1526 (in MNL OL).
DL	Collection of original documents prior to 1526 (in MNL OL, unless another archive is mentioned in the reference).
DRH	*Decreta Regni Hungariae – Gesetze und Verordnungen Ungarns 1301-1457*, ed. Ferenc DŐRY, György BÓNIS, Vera BÁCSKAI (Buda-

	pest, 1976: *Magyar Országos Levéltár kiadványai*, 1, *Forráskiadványok* 11).
DRMH	*Decreta Regni Medievalis Hungariae*, 1 *(1000-1301)*, trans. and ed. János M. BAK, György BÓNIS, James Ross SWEENEY, second. edn. (Idyllwild, 1999); 2 *(1301-1457)*, trans. and ed. János M. BAK, Pál ENGEL, James Ross SWEENEY (Salt Lake City, 1992).
EFHU	*Elenchus Fontium Historiae Urbanae*, 3.2, ed. András KUBINYI (Budapest, 1997); 3.3, ed. Paul NIEDERMAIER (Bucureşti, 2005).
ELTE	Eötvös Loránd Tudományegyetem, Budapest.
FEJÉRPATAKY	*Magyarországi városok régi számadáskönyvei* [Old account books of Hungarian towns], ed. László FEJÉRPATAKY (Budapest, 1885).
HÁZI, *Sopron*	*Sopron szabad királyi város története*, ed. Jenő HÁZI [The history of the free royal town of Sopron], vols. 1.1-7, 2.1-6 (Sopron, 1921-1943).
HAZU	Hrvatska Akademija Znanosti i Umijetnosti, Zagreb, Arhiv.
HO	*Hazai okmánytár – Codex diplomaticus patrius*, ed. Arnold IPOLYI, Imre NAGY, and Dezső VÉGHELYI, 8 vols. (Győr and Budapest,1865-1891).
IVÁNYI, *Bártfa*	*Bártfa szabad királyi város levéltára, 1319-1526* [The archives of the free royal town of Bardejov], ed. Béla IVÁNYI (Budapest, 1910).
IVÁNYI, *Eperjes*	*Eperjes szabad királyi város levéltára (Archivum liberae regiaeque civitatis Eperjes), 1245-1526*, ed. Béla IVÁNYI (Szeged, 1931).
JAKAB *Oklt*	*Oklevéltár Kolozsvár története 1. kötetéhez* [Cartulary to vol. 1 of the History of Cluj], ed. Elek JAKAB (Buda, 1870); *Oklevéltár Kolozsvár története 2. és 3. kötetéhez* [Cartulary to vols. 2 and 3 of the History of Cluj], ed. Elek JAKAB (Budapest, 1888).
LAKATOS, *Adattár*	LAKATOS, Bálint Péter, "Hivatali írásbeliség és ügyintézés a késő középkori magyarországi mezővárosokban, okleveleik tükrében" [Official literacy and administration in late medieval market towns of Hungary as reflected in their charters] (unpublished PhD dissertation, ELTE Budapest, 2013), 2, *Adattár* [Gazetteer].
MES	*Monumenta Ecclesiae Strigoniensis*, ed. Ferdinandus KNAUZ *et al.*, 4 vols. (Esztergom, 1874-1999).
MHJ	*Magyar Zsidó Oklevéltár – Monumenta Hungariae Judaica*, ed. Ármin FRISS, Ferenc KOVÁTS, Fülöp GRÜNVALD, Jenő HÁZI *et al.*, 18 vols. (Budapest, 1903-1980).
MMB	Štátny archív v Prešove, pracovisko Archív Bardejov, fond Magistrát mesta Bardejov.
MMBB	Štátny archív v Banskej Bystrici, fond Magistrát mesta Banská Bystrica.
MMBŠ	Štátny archív v Banskej Bystrici, pracovisko Archív Banská Štiavnica, fond Magistrát mesta Banská Štiavnica.

MMG	Štátny archív v Prešove, špecializované pracovisko Spišský archív v Levoči, fond Magistrát mesta Gelnica.
MMKK	Štátny archív v Prešove, pracovisko Archív Poprad, fond Magistrát mesta Kežmarok.
MMKa	Štátny archív v Banskej Bystrici, pracovisko Archív Zvolen, fond Magistrát mesta Krupiny.
MMKr	Štátny archív v Banskej Bystrici, pracovisko Archív Kremnica, fond Magistrát mesta Kremnica.
MMM	Štátny archív v Bratislave, pracovisko Archív Modra, fond Magistrát mesta Modry.
MMNB	Štátny archív v Banskej Bystrici, pracovisko Archív Kremnica, fond Magistrát mesta Novej Bane.
MMP	Štátny archív v Prešove, fond Magistrát mesta Prešov.
MMTT	Štátny archív v Trnave, fond Magistrát mesta Trnava.
MMŽ	Štátny archív v Žiline, fond Magistrát mesta Žiliny.
MMS	Štátny archív v Prešove, fond Magistrát mesta Sabinov.
MMSNV1	Spišská Nová Ves – Štátny archív v Košiciach, pracovisko Archív Spišská Nová Ves, fond Magistrát mesta Spišskej Novej Vsi.
MMTr	Trenčín – Štátny archív v Trenčíne, fond Magistrát mesta Trenčína.
MNL OL	Magyar Nemzeti Levéltár Országos Levéltára, Budapest.
MNM	Magyar Nemzeti Múzeum, Budapest.
Ofner Stadtrecht	*Das Ofner Stadtrecht: Eine deutschsprachige Rechtssammlung des 15. Jahrhunderts aus Ungarn,* ed. Karl MOLLAY (Budapest, 1959: *Monumenta Historica Budapestinensia* 1).
OSzK	Országos Széchényi Könyvtár, Budapest.
PT	*Das Preßburger Protocollum Testamentorum* 1410 (1427)-1529, 1, *1410 (1427)-1487*, and 2, *1488-1529*, ed. Judit MAJOROSSY and Katalin SZENDE (Köln and Wien, 2010- 2014: *Fontes rerum Austriacarum: Fontes Iuris* 21.1-2).
QGSÖ	Sopron Város Történeti Forrásai – Quellen zur Geschichte der Stadt Ödenburg.
RA	SZENTPÉTERY, Imre, *Az Árpád-házi királyok okleveleinek kritikai jegyzéke – Regesta regum stirpis Arpadianae critico-diplomatica* (Budapest, 1927).
REGSLOV	*Regesta diplomatica nec non epistolaria Slovaciae*, ed. Vincent SEDLÁK, 2 vols. (Bratislava, 1980-1987).
SVL	Magyar Nemzeti Levéltár Győr-Moson-Sopron Megyei Levéltár (MNL GyMSML) Soproni Levéltára/
TKALČIĆ	TKALČIĆ, Ivan Krstitelj, *Monumenta historiae liberae regiae civitatis Zagrabiae metropolis regni Dalmatiae, Croatiae et Slavoniae,* 11 vols. (Zagreb, 1889).
TT	*Történelmi Tár.*

UBB	*Urkundenbuch des Burgenlandes und der angrenzenden Gebiete der Komitate Wieselburg, Ödenburg, und Eisenburg*, ed. Hans WAGNER, Irmtraut LINDECK-POZZA, Erich REITER, and Leo PRICKLER, 5 vols. (Wien, Köln, and Graz, 1955-1999).
UGDS	*Urkundenbuch zur Geschichte der deutschen in Siebenbürgen,* ed. Gustav GÜNDISCH, Carl WERNER, and Franz ZIMMERMANN, 9 vols. (Sibiu, Köln, Wien, and Bucharest, 1892-1991).
USML	*Utrecht Studies in Medieval Literacy.*
VEML	Magyar Nemzeti Levéltár Veszprém Megyei Levéltára.
VMMS	*Výsady miest a mestečiek na Slovensku* [Privileges of towns and market towns in Slovakia], 1, *(1238-1350)*, ed. Ľubomír JUCK (Bratislava, 1984).
Zichy	*A zichi és vásonkeői gróf Zichy-család idősb ágának okmánytára* [Cartulary of the elder branch of the Count Zichy family] 11 vols, ed. Imre NAGY *et al.*, 11 vols. (Pest, then Budapest, 1871-1915).
ZsO	*Zsigmondkori oklevéltár*, ed. Elemér MÁLYUSZ, Iván BORSA, Norbert C. TÓTH, *et al.*, 12 vols. (Budapest, 1951-2017).

List of Figures and Tables

Fig. 1	Trust: a semantic map. Taken from: G. HOSKING, *Trust: A History* (Oxford, 2014), p. 29. Reproduced by permission of Oxford University Press.	8
Fig. 2	Counties and county seats in the kingdom of Hungary, *c.*1300.	28
Fig. 3	Newly chartered settlements in the kingdom of Hungary up to 1300.	30
Fig. 4	The eastern wall with the Torah ark of the medieval 'old synagogue' in Sopron. The system of vaulting follows the practice observed in house chapels in Regensburg. Photo: Zoltán Bolodár. Reproduced with permission.	34
Fig. 5	Mining towns in medieval Hungary (map prepared by András Vadas).	38
Fig. 6	The most important towns and trade routes in medieval Hungary.	40
Fig. 7	Buda, Pest, and Óbuda as separate communities in the First Military Survey (Josephinische Landesaufnahme), Coll. XIV, Sect. XX, 1782-1785. Reproduced with the permission of the Institute of Military History, Budapest.	43
Fig. 8	Dancing couple and a jester, painting presumably based on literary models in a burgher's house in Buda, Táncsics Mihály utca 24. Fresco in the collection of the Budapest History Museum. Reproduced with the permission of the Budapest History Museum.	45
Fig. 9 a-b	Slate tablet with German writing samples on both sides from the Carmelite friary of Buda, Kapás u. 3. Excavation of Judit Benda, Budapest History Museum. Reproduced with the permission of the Budapest History Museum.	47
Fig. 10	Slate tablet with the name of Chajjim Katz, an inhabitant of the fourteenth-century *Platea Iudaeorum*, Buda, Szt. György tér.	

Excavation of András Végh, Budapest History Museum. Reproduced with the permission of the Budapest History Museum. 49
Fig. 11 Charters of privilege received and early municipal documents issued by settlements in medieval Hungary, up to 1320. 70
Fig. 12 Town plan of Pécs, showing the cathedral, the Chapter district and the civic part of the town. Designed by Tamás Fedeles, drawn by András Kikindai. The Hungarian version of the Fig. was published in FEDELES, "*Eztán Pécs tűnik szemünkbe*", p. 49. Reproduced with the permission of Tamás Fedeles. 76
Fig. 13 An official document issued by the community of Sopron, probably written by Stephen of Harka, 5 February 1329 (MNL OL DL 2523). Reproduced with the permission of the National Archives of Hungary. 78
Fig. 14 A pair of chirographed documents issued by the municipality of Buda, 29 November 1392 (MNL OL DL 39270 and DL 100250). Reproduced with the permission of the National Archives of Hungary. 82
Fig. 15 Images showing the dorse. The fragments of the seals show that both halves were sealed with the smaller municipal seal before cutting the copies apart. The notes on the dorse show the customary marks of the collections where the documents ended up. Reproduced with the permission of the National Archives of Hungary. 83
Fig. 16.a-b Both sides of the matrix of the double seal of the *Latini* of Esztergom. The original design presumably dates from the 1220s-1230s; the extant piece was restored to the community in the 1240s or 1250s, after the Mongol invasion. Reproduced with the permission of the Hungarian National Museum. See front cover for colour image. 89
Fig. 17 Charter issued by the mayor and council of Esztergom with a perfectly preserved imprint of the double seal, July 1265 (MNL OL DL 76145). Reproduced with the permission of the National Archives of Hungary. 90
Fig. 18. The imprint of the double seal of Buda. The insignia were originally given to Pest in the 1230s and taken over by Buda on royal order together with the charter of Pest in the late 1240s. This imprint was preserved on a document issued in 1292. MNL, Veszprém County Archives XVI.1 T191 (DF 229 963). Reproduced with the permission of the Veszprém County Archives. 91

Fig. 19 The seal of the *Latini* of Fehérvár, imprint from a document issued on 16 March 1270. (MNL OL DL 83 130). Reproduced with the permission of the National Archives of Hungary. 92
Fig. 20 The seal of the town of Vasvár on a document issued on 14 February 1414 (MNL OL DL 92434). Vasvár was protected by earthwork fortification in the eleventh to thirteenth centuries, but was never encircled by stone walls. Reproduced with the permission of the National Archives of Hungary. 92
Fig. 21 The seal of Kremnica on a document issued on 17 July 1331 (MNL OL DF 250 152). Drawing by Anna Grüll, reproduced with permission. 93
Fig. 22 The seal of Nová Baňa. The matrix is kept in the Hungarian National Museum; its earliest extant imprint is on a charter issued on 29 January 1348 (DF 237 060). Reproduced with the permission of the Hungarian National Museum. 93
Fig. 23 Charter sealed by eight Hungarian towns endorsing the marriage contract between princess Hedwig and William, duke of Austria, 20 March 1381 (Österreichisches Staatsarchiv, Wien, Haus-, Hof- und Staatsarchiv, Urkundenabteilung, Familienurkunden, 242.1). Reproduced with the permission of the Österreichisches Staatsarchiv. 96
Fig. 24 Imprint of the of the municipal seal of Sopron, endorsed by king Charles I in 1340 on a document issued on 15 March 1389 (MNL Sopron Archives of Győr-Moson-Sopron County, DL 276). Photo: József Kücsán. Reproduced with the permission of the Sopron Archives. 98
Fig. 25 Illuminated grant of arms featuring the coat of arms of the town of Košice depicted on the charter issued by King Sigismund, 31 January 1423 (Archív Mesta Košíce, Archivum secretum C2, MNL OL DF 269 164). Photo: Judit Majorossy. Reproduced with the permission of Archív Mesta Košíce. 100
Fig. 26 Grant of arms to Pressburg issued by King Sigismund on 9 July 1436 (Archív Mesta Bratislavy, Nr. 1436, MNL OL DF 274 282). Reproduced with the permission of Archív Mesta Bratislavy. 102
Fig. 27 First page of a book of sermons copied by Liebhart Egkenfelder, vice-notary of Sopron, notary of Pressburg, *c.*1425-1450 (Budapest, Library of the Hungarian Franciscan Province, Múz. 1, Esztergom bequest). Photo: Zoltán Fáy. Reproduced with permission. 128
Fig. 28 Sixteenth-century copy of the *Ofner Stadtrecht*, so-called Cromer-Handschrift, formerly owned by Leonhard Cromer, notary of Košice († 1582). On the lower part of this page, un-

der the heading "*Von des Stadtschreiber schreiblon*" begins a detailed list of the notarial tariffs for preparing various documents (ELTE University Library, Collection of Manuscripts and Rare Books, No. B 31). Reproduced with the permission of the ELTE University Library. 132

Fig. 29 Index of entries in the first *Protocollum testamentorum* of Pressburg, indicating the name of each testator and the page number where their last will begins (AMB, Nr. 4.n.1, f. 2r). Photo: Judit Majorossy. Reproduced with the permission of Archív Mesta Bratislavy. 139

Fig. 30 List of house owners in Sopron, compiled in German in a paper booklet in 1379. The names are listed together with the sizes of the plots owned by them. The list begins with the Jewish house owners in column 'a' and proceeds afterwards in topographic order from the lower half of column 'b'. (SVL DL 240; MNL OL DF 201 873). Reproduced with the permission of the Sopron Archives. 143

Fig. 31 Distribution of the products of the Hader paper mill in Nuremberg, an enterprise founded by the Stromer family. Map prepared by Lore Sporhan-Krempel, reproduced in IRSIGLER, "Papierhandel", p. 311. 146

Fig. 32 Entries on proscribed persons in the second municipal book of Banská Štiavnica, inscribed in 1434-1436. The names of those persons who were forgiven for their crime were crossed out (MNM 61.54.C, f. 188v). Reproduced with the permission of the Hungarian National Museum. 151

Fig. 33 Image of the Calvary from the second town book of Banská Štiavnica, 1432, attributed to the illuminator Valentin Gobil. The image faces the oath of the town judge and the first verses of the Gospel of St John (HNM, Medieval Department, 61.54. C). Reproduced with the permission of the Hungarian National Museum. 155

Fig. 34 A page from the 'Great Linen Register ' of Bardejov. The pages show the deliveries of unbleached linen by various persons and the payments by the town to them. Note the finger pointing to an addition in the left margin (MMB Kníhy 1510, pp. 67-68). Photo: Sándor Gyarmati. Reproduced with permission. 163

Fig. 35 Promissory letters in the *Gerichtsbuch* of Sopron by priests serving in the town. The entry crossed out was written by Valentinus de Chepreg, chaplain of the hospital chapel, in faulty Latin. (SVL DL 3796, pp. 426-427). Reproduced with the permission of the Sopron Archives. 171

Fig. 36 A page from the Pressburger Satzbuch, showing house owners and the encumbrances on their properties in the Schöndorfergasse, one of the suburban streets of Pressburg. Repaid charges as well as former owners were crossed out (AMB, Nr. 4 I 3, f. 56r). Photo: Judit Majorossy. Reproduced with the permission of Archív Mesta Bratislavy. 180
Fig. 37 Distribution of last wills per decade in Pressburg. Designed by Judit Majorossy, in: PT 1, p. 20. 183
Fig. 38 Two pages from the guild book of the German butchers' guild of Buda. The left page contains contributions in wax and some monetary transactions, the right page shows rental payments for meat stalls (*pank*) in the common meat hall (BFL XV. 5. No. 8, ff. 26v-27r). Reproduced with the permission of the Budapest City Archives. 187
Fig. 39 Wall chronicle on the southern wall of the porch in the parish church of Levoča, *c.*1500. Photo: Juraj Šedivý. Reproduced with permission. 193
Fig. 40 Reconstructed view of the Jews' Street (*Judengasse*, present-day Új utca) of Sopron with its two synagogues. Drawing by János Sedlmayr. Reproduced with permission. 268
Fig. 41 Credit contract between the town of Pressburg and Yosepp von Himberg and his son-in-law Moyse, 13 December 1426, with cuts indicating repayment (AMB Listine Nr. 1000) Photo: Judit Majorossy. Reproduced with the permission of Archív Mesta Bratislavy. 272
Fig. 42 Sopron, *Gedenkbuch*, agreement between Thomas Dresinger, councillor, and the Jewish moneylender Kassariel concerning a loan, 19 April 1497. The creditor acknowledges the fulfilment of the conditions in Hebrew script on the bottom of the page on the right side. (SVL DL 3797, f. 43r). Reproduced with the permission of the Sopron Archives. 273
Fig. 43 Architectural changes of the town hall complex in Pressburg from the thirteenth to the seventeenth century. Reproduced from: HOLČÍK, *Bratislavská radnica*. 294
Fig. 44 The three subsequent medieval town halls in Sopron. Map A.3.3, in: JANKÓ *et al.*, *Sopron*. Cartography: Péter Banyó. Reproduced with permission. 297
Fig. 45 The town hall of Bardejov seen from the west. Photo: Béla Zsolt Szakács. Reproduced with permission. 298
Fig. 46 a-d The distribution of documents by different issuers in the town archives of Sopron, Pressburg, Prešov, and Bardejov up to 1437. Graphs prepared by the author on the basis of the respective editions or inventories of archival holdings. 300

Fig. 47	Archives cabinet in the town hall of Bardejov. This is the only purpose-made furniture for any civic archives surviving in its original place in the medieval kingdom of Hungary. Photo: Béla Zsolt Szakács. Reproduced with permission.	303
Fig. 48	Spine and binding of the first municipal book of Sopron started in 1390 (SVL DL 2988). Photos by the author. Reproduced with the permission of the Sopron Archives.	309
Fig. 49	The Main Square of Sopron, with the possible image of the buildings on its northern side. The building in the middle, with a tower in the back yard by the town wall, was the second town hall. Drawing by János Sedlmayr. Reproduced with permission.	310
Fig. 50	Binding of the *Burgerbuechl und Ächtbuchl* (SVL DL 3830). Photo: Zsolt Kálócz. Reproduced with the permission of the Sopron Archives.	312

Table 1	Some characteristics of the various scribal hands in the guild book of the German butchers of Buda (based on J. NÉMETH, "Lateinische Relikte").	228
Table 2	Loans taken out by the town of Pressburg from Jewish and Christian creditors, 1360-1500 (compiled by F. KOVÁTS).	270
Table 3	Correlation of town history, archival bindings and chancery development in Sopron.	307
Table 4	Appearance of innovations in administrative literacy in various town types, up to the mid-fifteenth century.	327

Introduction

On This Volume

What constitutes a city (or town)? This is the most frequently asked question among urban historians. By now it has become obvious that, "recognizing the multifunctionality of urban communities over time", no single overarching definition can do justice to the complexity of urban existence in the past millennia.[1] Among the high number and variability of possible answers and criteria, however, a refreshing point of consensus is that cities and towns are settlements with a higher density of population concentrated on their territory than in the surrounding countryside. This density had several distinctive consequences, including the need for increased communication and administration, both of which led – with great variation – to the introduction of writing to various fields of urban life. The ways in which this happened have stimulated a long series of historical inquiries, including the present one.

The present volume guides its readers through the history of using the written word for pragmatic, mainly administrative purposes (as distinct from religious and scholarly matters) in the royal towns of medieval Hungary. After the first chapter, which sets the overall scene for urban literacy in medieval Hungary, the subsequent ones address, step by step, new forms of writing and communication that necessitated a re-negotiation of acceptance and trust in these forms. Chapter Two presents the formation of civic literacy: the beginnings and gradual broadening of issuing authentic documents by urban authori-

[1] P. Clark, "Introduction", in: *The Oxford Handbook of Cities in World History*, ed. P. Clark (Oxford, 2013), pp. 1-29, at p. 4. For the difficulties of a standard definition medieval towns see the erudite study by F. Irsigler, "Was machte eine mittelalterliche Siedlung zur Stadt?", in: *Miscellanea Franz Irsigler: Festgabe zum 65. Geburtstag*, ed. V. Henn *et al.* (Trier, 2006), pp. 472-486.

ties, including the emergence of the authentic seals and sealing practice of urban communities. Chapter Three discusses the appearance of the first professional notaries in municipal service and the chanceries where they worked. This provides the background for exploring the launching and increasingly specialised use of municipal books as an effective way of creating and storing documents in the urban context. It also makes a short detour to follow the introduction of paper as a new writing material that revolutionised administration. Chapter Four investigates language use in oral and written form, and the appearance of various vernaculars in urban life and administration. Chapter Five deals with the specific issue of trust in writing in the context of Jewish-Christian contacts. Finally, Chapter Six sums up the question of storage, safekeeping, and information retrieval in town archives of medieval Hungary.

The chronological scope, indicated as 'medieval' in the title, is delineated by the dates of the surviving documents to be analysed. Although in some respects, for instance regarding the legislation on Jews, it goes back to the period immediately following the foundation of the Hungarian state around the turn of the first millennium CE, the bulk of the urban material discussed here dates from the mid-thirteenth to the mid-sixteenth century.[2] In other words, this means focussing on phenomena of the late Middle Ages, because of the small number of sources pertaining to the earlier periods. By and large the volume stops just before the next important innovation, printing, entered the realm of pragmatic literacy.[3] In fact, since my main point is to explore the circumstances and impact of the initiation of new methods in administrative literacy that took place at different points in time, the chronological frame shifts from one chapter to the other.

As for the geographic focus, 'Hungary' also deserves a brief comment. The territory of the Carpathian Basin that once constituted the spatial framework of the Hungarian kingdom, is now shared between no less than eight different countries, each of which has its own perception of its medieval past and its

[2] P. ENGEL, *The Realm of St. Stephen: A History of Medieval Hungary, 996-1526* (London, 2001). See also the regnal years of the kings of Hungary in Appendix 2.

[3] Sporadically, printing entered the documentary material already in the second half of the fifteenth century, in the form of printed letters of indulgence. An example from Pressburg from 1480 was issued to "*honesta Agnes de Posonio*" (AMB Oddelenie knižničných fondov = Régi Magyar Nyomtatványok 6), see the image at http://typographia.oszk.hu/html/uk/nyomdak/confessionale_uk.htm (last accessed: 20.05.2018). Otherwise the question why the introduction of printed forms to urban administration took so much time after the invention of printing would deserve separate research.

own tradition of researching it. The present volume embraces the extent of the medieval polity, since both the network of towns and the royal policy concerning them used this as its framework. A short overview of urban development in medieval Hungary is given in Chapter One, which also introduces the concept of royal towns and explains why the present research concentrates on these.

Linguistic and cultural complexity characterises urban literacy on all levels, from the basic to the most sophisticated, an issue that will be discussed in several chapters throughout the work. Let me just mention here one of the most basic problems, town names. Readers from the region are familiar with the fact that most settlements have two or three, and sometimes even more names. These names may reflect changes in population, political power or cultural connotations. For instance, Bratislava, the modern-day capital of Slovakia, had at least five historic names in four different languages before arriving at the present one: Brezalauspurc / Preslava, Posonium, Pozsony, Pressburg, and Prešporok (leaving aside the very short-lived twentieth-century Wilsonovo). In this book, the name Pressburg will be used.[4] In case of counties (regional administrative units), however, the medieval Hungarian names will be applied, because the modern divisions often differ from the historic territories of the counties.

Some chapters of this volume grew out of papers given at conferences between 2001 and 2015, and some were published as separate articles between 2004 and 2016 in English, German, Hungarian, and partly even in Czech and Polish translations. When the idea of creating a summary publication of these in a uniform language emerged and was generously embraced by the editors of the *Utrecht Studies on Medieval Literacy* (USML) series, I was surprised to discover that over all these years, even if I answered the calls of various conference organisers and devised my papers to fit into the general agenda of the given meeting or session, I have been, in fact, working on various aspects of the same theme. The framework of 'trust and authority', to be discussed below

[4] These names are used, in an original and ingenious way, as titles of a multi-volume history of the town, edited by J. Šedivý *et al.*, the first volume, entitled *Brezlauspurc*, was published in 2012. Following the usage of Engel, *The Realm of St. Stephen*, for simplicity's sake the place names will be used in their current forms; a gazetteer of the varieties of historic names can be found in Appendix 1. In the case of Bratislava, where the modern name is a creation of the twentieth century, the German name Pressburg will be used. In the case of Budapest, which was united from Buda, Pest and Óbuda in 1873, the constituent parts will be named using the historic (pre-1873) forms; in the case of Székesfehérvár, the medieval form Fehérvár will be used instead of the modern form where the context allows this.

and followed up in the conclusions of the individual chapters, not only bound these studies together, but it also necessitated re-thinking and extensive re-writing. In many of the chapters new and more systematically arranged data were added, references were updated, and a new Introduction and Conclusion were written. I *trust* my readers (an asymmetrical relationship, as it will be explained later) that they will find this narrative framework convincing and helpful.

My personal interest in the topic goes back even earlier than the date of the first conferences on literacy that I attended: to my undergraduate years in the late 1980s under the guidance of András Kubinyi (1929-2007), one of the best experts of Hungarian archival material, urban and otherwise. In the first decade of my working life, in the 1990s, employed by the Museum of Sopron, I regularly worked in the municipal archives conveniently placed in the town hall next to the museum. Sopron has the best preserved medieval town archives in the territory of present-day Hungary, a gold mine for research on civic literacy. This fact explains why so many of the examples used in this volume refer to Sopron's rich archival holdings. The 1990s was, furthermore, an exciting time when, making use of new opportunities after the fall of the Iron Curtain, we established the series of *Sopron Város Történeti Forrásai – Quellen zur Geschichte der Stadt Ödenburg* (Sources on the History of the Town of Sopron) with the essential contribution of the prominent German linguist and my former teacher in German palaeography, Professor Károly (Karl) Mollay (1914-1997), and the then director of the Sopron Archives, Éva Turbuly. The aim of the series has been, first and foremost, to publish previously unedited medieval and early modern municipal books of this free royal town.[5]

Another publication project of a municipal book, accomplished together with my one-time graduate student, now friend and colleague, Judit Majorossy, was the editing of the first *Protocollum Testamentorum* of Pressburg, one of the main sources for her PhD dissertation as well as (previously) mine.[6] I have

[5] Individual volumes of the series will be quoted throughout the volume, where relevant. All the volumes published until 2008 are available on-line at https://library.hungaricana.hu/en/collection/mltk_megy_gyms_sopm_svtf/ (last accessed: 20.05.2018).

[6] *Das Preßburger Protocollum Testamentorum 1410 (1427)-1529*, ed. J. Majorossy and K. Szende, 1, *1410 (1427)-1487* and 2, *1488-1529* (Köln and Wien, 2014: *Fontes rerum Austriacarum: Fontes Iuris* 21.1-2), henceforth: PT; J. Majorossy, *Church in Town: Urban Religious Life in Late Medieval Pressburg in the Mirror of Last Wills* (unpublished PhD dissertation, to be published in 2018 by CEU Press – CEU Medievalia); K. Szende, *Otthon a városban: Társadalom és anyagi kultúra a középkori Sopronban, Pozsonyban és Eperjesen* [At home in town: Society

been particularly glad to see that my interest in urban literacy and its social uses have been carried further by my students at the Department of Medieval Studies of Central European University (CEU). Besides Judit Majorossy, let me mention the names of Ágnes Flóra, Károly Goda, and Mária Lupescu Makó, who have contributed to various volumes of the USML series, as well as Sándor Gyarmati, János Incze, Márta Kondor and Olha Kozubska-Andrusiv, who have also elaborated topics relevant for the broader context of this work.

Working on urban literacy has gained new dimensions and perspectives in my academic life by becoming part of the USML community. This was a direct result of a workshop organised at CEU in 2001 by my colleague Gerhard Jaritz on *The Oral History of the Middle Ages*.[7] This was when I first met Anna Adamska as a participant of the workshop, and when we discovered our shared interests. This encounter has been followed by an invitation to Utrecht in the same year and countless other meetings, many of them organised or facilitated by Anna and her husband and true academic companion, Marco Mostert. All these occasions have furthered my work with new insights and inspiration, in an ever-growing network of like-minded scholars. Finally, my interest in the use of languages and ethnic diversity follows from my teaching practice at CEU as well as my family life, where the parallel use of various languages is not an academic interest but part of daily reality. I am very grateful for all this inspiration.

Trust and Authority

Let me proceed by explaining the broader conceptual framework of this volume, starting with a seemingly far-fetched example. There are very few texts in Hungarian history, and presumably in medieval Europe in general, that would show so clearly how trust in writing – writing under the king's name and seal – could be used and abused in a political conflict situation. One of these comes from the time of the Mongol invasion of Hungary in 1241-1242, which stands out in popular memory as well as in learned historiography as one of the worst cataclysms in the history of the country. As an eyewitness, Master

and material culture in medieval Sopron, Pressburg and Prešov] (Budapest, 2004: *Társadalom- és Művelődéstörténeti Tanulmányok* 32).

7 Published as: *Oral History of the Middle Ages: The Spoken Word in Context*, ed. G. Jaritz and M. Richter (Budapest and Krems, 2001: *Medium Aevum Quotidianum: Sonderband* 11 – *CEU Medievalia* 3).

Roger, at that time canon of Oradea, later archbishop of Split, describes, that the enemy was fierce and cunning beyond any measure. However, one element in their ruthless advance strikes the reader as unexpectedly shrewd, and very different from their usual style of warfare. When the 'Tartars' divided the booty after their landslide victory at Muhi in April 1241, and they found the king's seal with his chancellor who fell victim to the Mongols in the battle:

> *Et fecerunt scribere per quosdam clericos Hungaros, quos adhuc ad vitam servaverant, maioribus omnibus et popularibus per totam Hungariam existentibus sub nomine regis multa varia ficticia litterarum sub hac forma: "Canum feritatem et rabiem non timeatis, nec vestris de domibus vos movere audeatis [...]". Hec fuerunt littere per quosdam Hungaros, qui iam eis adheserant, destinate, qui me ac totam Hungariam destruxerunt. Nam* tantam illarum certitudini litterarum fidem dedimus, *quod, licet omni die contrarium cernentur, [...] ob hoc ad sciendum rumores nuncios mittere nullatenus poteramus, contrariumque credere nequibamus.*

> And they made a few Hungarian clerks, whom they left alive, write letters in the name of the king to the nobles and commoners living in Hungary with these words: "Do not fear the ferocity and madness of the hounds and do not dare to leave your houses [...]". This letter was carried around to the addressees by some Hungarians who had joined the Tartars. This ruined me [Master Roger – K.Sz.] and all Hungary, because *we gave credit to the truth of the letter* and, although we beheld the very opposite every day, we could not send out scouts to ascertain the truth.[8]

The unconditional acceptance by "nobles and commoners" of the kingdom of the fake letters produced by the Mongols testifies that by the mid-thirteenth century this means of communication had already set firm roots in Hungary, and even a nomadic enemy was aware of its potential. The main subject of my inquiry here, however, is not the king's authority and his chancery, but a group of settlements that were emerging and gaining importance around the time of the Mongol invasion and in the decades of recovery after the great crisis: the royal towns of the kingdom.

One of my aims in this volume is indeed to offer a summary of empirical information, qualitative and quantitative data on when and how various practices of communication and administrative literacy, chanceries, and archives

[8] *Master Roger's Epistle to the Sorrowful Lament upon the Destruction of the Kingdom of Hungary by the Tartars*, trans. and annotated by J.M. Bak and M. Rady (Budapest and New York, 2010), Ch. 31, pp. 190-193.

appeared in the royal towns of medieval Hungary, and what roles they played in urban life. This set of information on who committed certain issues to writing, and where, has not been systematically collected and made available to Hungarian and international scholarship so far.[9] However, if the series of questions should be joined by the most intriguing one, that of 'why?', a broader conceptual framework, indicated by the main title of the book, *Trust and Authority*, should prove to be helpful. By placing my study in this framework, I intend to reach out beyond the details of places, names, and documents, and offer some points of reference to the understanding of the driving forces of medieval societies in general, and urban communities in particular.

Trust is a concept with multiple meanings and a rich history. As Geoffrey Hosking, the author of the most recent historical study on the subject remarked: "Trust is one of the most pervasive – and perhaps for that reason least noticed – aspects of social life" (Fig. 1).[10] It would be fully justified to apply here the proverbial starting clause: "Already the ancient Greeks ...",[11] and follow up the development of this concept in ancient, medieval, early modern, and modern political thought up to the present. Thankfully, this challenging task has been taken care of by a recently published volume of essays that provides new foundations for exploring this concept in its full philosophical and political complexity.[12] Let me therefore restrict my survey here to those points that may have relevance for my own exploration of medieval civic literacy.

[9] For the historiography of Hungarian urban literacy see the references in Chapter 1, as well as B.P. LAKATOS, *Hivatali írásbeliség és ügyintézés a késő középkori magyarországi mezővárosokban, okleveleik tükrében* [Official literacy and administration in late medieval market towns of Hungary as reflected in their charters] (unpublished PhD dissertation, ELTE Budapest, 2013, to be published as B. LAKATOS, *Mezővárosi oklevelek: Települési önkormányzat és írásbeliség a késő középkori Magyarországon, 1301-1526* [Documents from market towns: Local self-governance and literacy in late medieval Hungary] (Budapest, 2018: *Magyar történelmi emlékek: Adattárak – Monumenta Hungariae historica: Elenchi*).

[10] G. HOSKING, *Trust: A History* (Oxford, 2014); ID., "Trust and distrust: A suitable theme for historians?", *Transactions of the Royal Historical Society* 16 (2006), pp. 95-115 (quotation from p. 95); U. FREVERT, "Vertrauen – eine historische Spurensuche", in: *Vertrauen: Historische Annäherungen,* ed. U. FREVERT (Göttingen, 2003), pp. 7-66.

[11] On the practical aspects of human interaction see S. JOHNSTONE, *A History of Trust in Ancient Greece* (Chicago, 2011); in the framework of ideas and political thought: S. JOHNSTONE, "*Pistis* and citizens in ancient Greece", in: *Trust and Happiness in the History of European Political Thought*, ed. L. KONTLER and M. SOMOS (Leiden, 2018), pp. 371-390.

[12] *Trust and Happiness in the History of European Political Thought.*

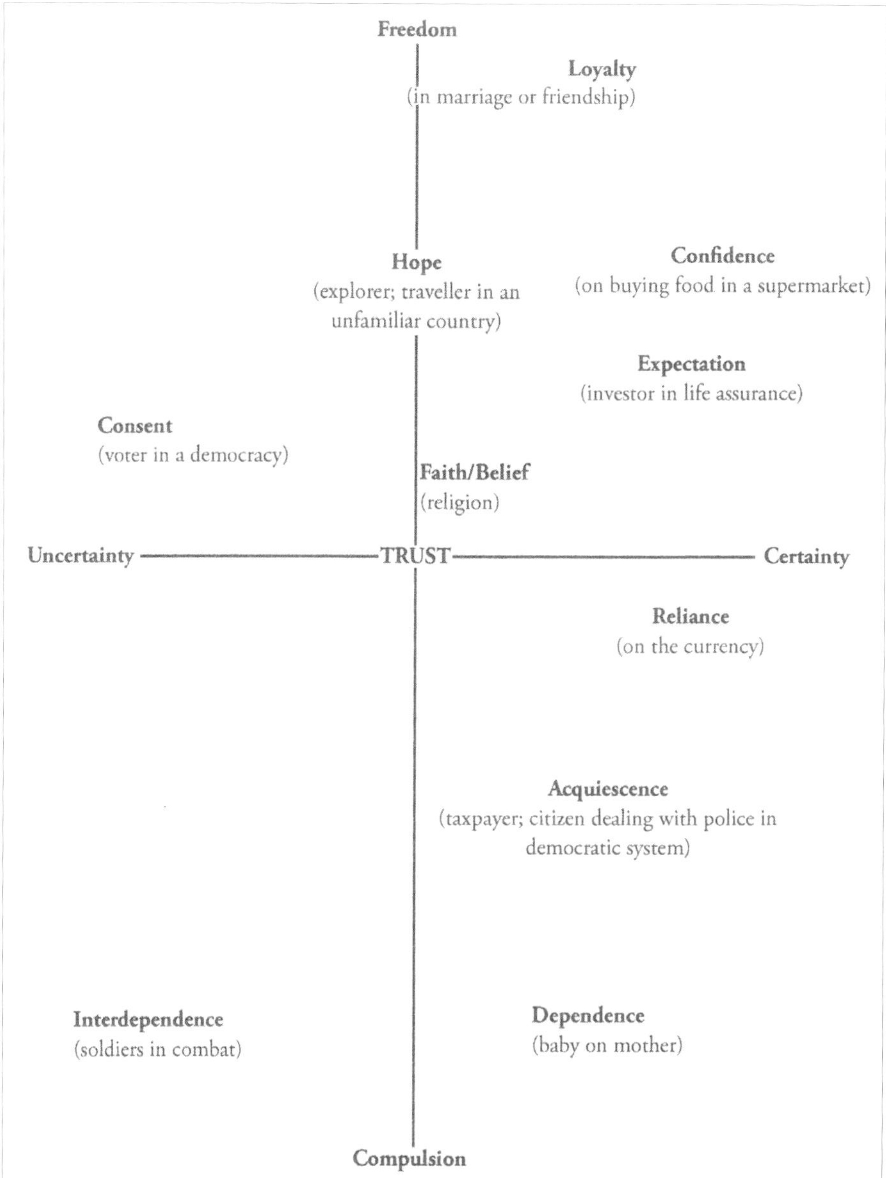

Fig. 1 Trust: a semantic map. Taken from: G. HOSKING, *Trust: A History* (Oxford, 2014), p. 29. Reproduced by permission of Oxford University Press.

The prime field where trust belongs is probably moral philosophy, with Annette Baier's famous essay on "Trust and antitrust" being the first port of call for most of us outside the hard core of philosophy and the social sciences. Baier and many others explore the moral and emotional dimensions of trust, as well as its risk factors, both in the context of personal relationships and of institutional examples. They point out, among other things, the unequal power-relation between truster and trusted, and emphasise the importance of trust and caring especially for the value systems and motivations of women.[13]

In sociological terms, trust has been defined as a "combination of cultural practices" comprising "matters as different as loyalty, cooperation, security, and courage".[14] Niklas Luhmann (1928-1998), the author of the first monograph dedicated to the subject published, presumably not by coincidence, in 1968, examined the role of trust in the framework of his social system theory. In his effort to explain the workings of the 'modern' world of the twentieth century, he has pointed out that an increasing level of complexity in social relations can only be managed with an increasing need for trust – in other words (as the original German title of his essay sums it up), trust is a "mechanism for reducing social complexity".[15] In the terminology of economists, this would roughly correspond to 'reducing transaction costs'.

One generation later a new cohort of thinkers, most notably Anthony Giddens and Adam B. Seligman took up the question of trust and offered a re-interpretation, combining the sociological and philosophical agendas. A common feature in their otherwise very diverse views is a combination of personal and institutional elements. In Giddens's words, "trust is a crucial phenomenon of personality development [...] directly linked to an early sense of achieving

[13] A. Baier, "Trust and antitrust", *Ethics* 96.2 (Jan. 1986), pp. 231-260. See also her 1991 Tanner Lectures "Trust", delivered at Princeton University in 1991: http://tannerlectures.utah.edu/_documents/a-to-z/b/baier92.pdf (last accessed: 20.05.2018). In more general terms, see e.g. the entry "Trust" by C. McLeod in: *The Stanford Encyclopedia of Philosophy*, https://plato.stanford.edu/entries/trust/, first published Mon Feb 20, 2006; substantive revision Mon Aug 3, 2015, last accessed: 20.05.2018.

[14] D. Weltecke, "Trust: Some methodological Reflections", in: *Strategies of Writing: Studies on Text and Trust in the Middle Ages*, ed. P. Schulte, M. Mostert, and I. van Renswoude (Turnhout, 2008: usml 13), pp. 379-391, at p. 391.

[15] N. Luhmann, *Trust and Power* (Chichester, 1979); original German title: *Vertrauen: Ein Mechanismus der Reduktion sozialer Komplexität* (Stuttgart, 1968). See also, on the applicability of his system theory to medieval contexts: R. Schlögl, "Historiker, Max Weber und Niklas Luhmann. Zum schwierigen (aber möglicherweise produktiven) Verhältnis von Geschichtswissenschaft und Systemtheorie", *Soziale Systeme: Zeitschrift für soziologische Theorie* 7 (2001), pp. 23-45.

ontological security".[16] At the same time, both of them allow also for a more general understanding and refer to Luhmann's system-based approach, although in a limitative way: "trust enters into social interaction in the interstices of system, or at system limit, when for one reason or another systematically defined role expectations are no longer viable", says Seligman;[17] whereas Giddens states in his *Modernity and Self-Identity* that "various forms of dependency – or to put the matter less provocatively, trust – are fostered by the reconstruction of day-to-day life via abstract systems".[18]

With all the interpretive potential of the concept of trust for modern individuals or societies (that is, contemporary to the authors of the essays quoted above), to what extent can this narrative be transferred to the analysis of premodern times? Representatives of modern social sciences often neglect the relevance of a historical perspective behind their ideas. Seligman, for instance, bases his claim that "the problem of trust first emerged in modern society" on the assertion that "in pre-modern societies, the 'fit' between persons and their roles is very close and strong". In such a situation, in his view, 'familiarity' or 'confidence', two of his other concepts, made it unnecessary to develop trust, a relationship more prone to taking risks of asymmetrical dependency.[19] However, this rigid and generalising image of pre-modern societies as a single category does not stand the test of closer inquiry.

Conversely, as Dorothea Weltecke has repeatedly pointed out, 'familiarity' and 'confidence', as elements of traditional behavioural patterns, could not have developed without the initial trust in those institutions (in the sociological sense of the word) that were created and fostered by various communities.[20] The usage of medieval Latin sources – an issue to be considered in detail in the following chapters – underlines this statement. The equivalents of trust: *fides* (*creditiva*), *fidelitas*, *fiducia*, or (*con*)*fidentia* appear as guiding principles of human relationships in a wide variety of contexts.[21] At the same time, Selig-

[16] A. GIDDENS, *Modernity and Self-identity: Self and Society in the Late Modern Age* (Stanford, 1991), p. 3.

[17] A.B. SELIGMAN, *The Problem of Trust* (Princeton, 1997), p. 25.

[18] GIDDENS, *Modernity and Self-Identity*, p. 176.

[19] Quotation from the review of SELIGMAN's *The Problem of Trust* by J. GRONOW, *Acta Sociologica* 41.2-3 (1998), p. 181. Cf. also the criticism in HOSKING, "Trust and distrust", p. 107.

[20] D. WELTECKE, "Gab es 'Vertrauen' im Mittelalter? Methodische Überlegungen", in: *Vertrauen*, ed. FREVERT, pp. 67-89, at p. 88.

[21] HOSKING, *Trust*, p. 66; P. SCHULTE, "Friedrich Barbarossa, die italienischen Kommunen und das politische Konzept der Treue", *Frühmittelalterliche Studien* 38 (2004), pp. 153-172, elaborates on several general points of the concept.

man's claims for trust being important "in the interstices of system or at system limit" may well apply to various transitional periods with their own changes over time. It is in this context that I intend to use trust as an analytical tool in this volume.

A particular form of such interstices – or rather radical limits and changes in the system of communication – was the appearance of new media. The transition between orality and writing was one of the most important of these, but there were also plenty of other instances when new media for securing rights of individuals or communities, and new bodies claiming authority to promulgate these appeared. Such transitions indeed interrupted customs of 'familiarity' or 'confidence', and took place repeatedly at different times, depending on historical periods, localities, communities, and social strata. The pioneering article on "The consequences of literacy", the combined work of a social anthropologist and a literary historian published in 1962, opened completely new perspectives in international scholarship on the fact how different modes of communication, and especially the "widespread and habitual recourse both to the recording of verbal statements and then to the dissecting of them" changed human history.[22]

It is worth noting here that a Hungarian social historian and palaeographer, István Hajnal (1892-1956), approached the history of writing and literacy from the viewpoint of its impact on society already in the 1930s.[23] His discovery was that the diffusion of charters and the recourse to writing not only depended on the participation of broad strata of society, but it also fundamentally changed human relations and social development. His novel approach to 'pragmatic literacy' *avant la lettre* could have revolutionised the study of palaeography, diplomatics, and the history of administration, had it been discovered by Euro-

[22] J. GOODY and I. WATT, "The consequences of literacy", *Comparative Studies in Society and History*, 5.3 (Apr. 1963), pp. 304-345, at p. 345.

[23] His early work focused on the Hungarian royal chancery: I. HAJNAL, "Die Kanzlei König Bélas IV", *Ungarische Rundschau* 5 (1916-1917), pp. 26-62; he then turned to a broad comparative approach. See for instance I. HAJNAL, "Le rôle social de l'écriture et l'évolution européenne", *Revue de l'Institut de Sociologie* (Bruxelles), 14.1-2 (1934), pp. 23-53, 253-282; ID., "Írásbeliség, intellektuális réteg és európai fejlődés" [Literacy, intellectual stratum and European development], in: *Évkönyv Károlyi Árpád születése nyolcvanadik fordulójának ünnepére* [Yearbook on the eightieth anniversary of Árpád Károlyi's birth] (Budapest, 1933), pp. 183-214, or his short essay "Racionális fejlődés és írásbeliség" [Rational development and literacy], in: *A Bécsi Történetkutató Intézet Évkönyvve* [Yearbook of the Hungarian Historical Institute in Vienna] (Wien, 1932), pp. 1-6.

pean scholarship in his own time.[24] Sadly, the pre- and post World War II history of Central Europe did not allow any wide dissemination of his works. He died six years before the above-mentioned study by Goody and Watt was published; his work was only re-discovered in Hungary in the 1980s, and it received broader recognition from the 1990s onwards when he was posthumously given the Széchenyi prize.[25] Although by that time international scholarship had moved beyond the scope of Hajnal's discoveries, his writings offer valuable insights into the social uses of writing even today.[26]

Further differentiation in the process of media change was conceptualised in German scholarship by the use of the terms *Verschriftung* and *Verschriftlichung*, in a collection of studies on media change, referring by the latter to a gradual increase of fields where the written word gained ground; however, the English terms proposed to indicate this difference: 'scripting' and 'textualisation' have not been generally embraced by historical scholarship as viable alternatives for the term 'literacy'.[27]

Research on the role of trust in writing and written agreements as part of this trend has brought much new understanding in recent years to the relationship between social development and literacy. Such inquiries are relevant for any historical period since the introduction of writing. Franz-Josef Arlinghaus, one of the pioneers of this research has convincingly pointed out that "not the content, but the possibility to refer to a written document may be seen as the

[24] His internationally best known work is his *L'enseignement de l'écriture aux universités médiévales* (Budapest, 1954: *Studia Historica Academiae Scientiarum Hungaricae*; second revised edition 1959). The Hungarian translation of this work only appeared half a century later: *Írásoktatás a középkori egyetemeken* (Budapest, 2008).

[25] A broad selection of Hajnal's studies was published in Hungarian (unfortunately with no reference to literacy in its title, and without a full bibliography) as I. HAJNAL, *Technika, művelődés* [Technology, culture], ed. and commented by F. GLATZ (Budapest, 1993); see further: I. ROMSICS, *Clio bűvöletében: Magyar történetírás a 19-20. században – nemzetközi kitekintéssel* [Enchanted by Clio: Hungarian historiography in the nineteenth and twentieth centuries, from an international perspective] (Budapest, 2011).

[26] E.g. L. VESZPRÉMY, "On the margins of book and charter palaeography, the dating of some Hungarian manuscripts from the eleventh to the thirteenth century", in: *Dating Undated Medieval Charters*, ed. M. GERVERS (Woodbridge, 2000), pp. 193-206, esp. p. 193; K. PÉTER, "Az egyszerű ember, az oklevelek és a levéltárak a 16-17. századi Magyarországon – háromszáz éves visszatekintéssel" [The common people, the charters and the archives in Hungary in the sixteenth and seventeenth centuries – with a look back to the preceding three hundred years] *Történelmi Szemle* 53 (2011), pp. 335-349, at pp. 335-337.

[27] See, e.g. the editors' introduction in: *Verschriftung und Verschriftlichung. Aspekte des Medienwechsels in verschiedenen Kulturen und Epochen*, ed. C. EHLER and U. SCHAEFER (Tübingen, 1998: *ScriptOralia* 94), pp. 1-9, at pp. 4-5.

core element of trust in writing".[28] Challenging and reasserting trust may have been on the agenda whenever new forms and genres of writing appeared, be it a change in material or conceptual sense.

Before proceeding to the empirical agenda of the present volume, another important conceptual question needs to be addressed: what was the relationship between trust and authority in pre-modern communities or personal contacts, and how did trust in writing enter this discourse? The authors of the sociological studies on trust quoted above point out that trust usually implies an asymmetrical relationship, with one of the parties, the 'trusted' having a stronger position, a higher authority than the 'truster'. In this equation, the primary function of trust is to stabilise the authority of the trusted, but it also secures the position of the truster. In Giddens's words,

> An individual who vests trust in others or in a given abstract system, normally thereby recognises that she lacks the power to influence them significantly. Yet, the vesting of trust can also generate new capacities.[29]

In the context of medieval society and politics, Geoffrey Hosking emphasises that "the concept and practices of trust [...] were channelled far more through religious belief and religious institutions" than they were in more recent periods.[30] In other words, with Christianity constituting the civilisatory framework, the highest authority directly concerned with salvation, and therefore superior to any secular power, belonged to the Church. This authority manifested itself not only in spiritual and moral issues, but also in judicial matters (consider the long-standing practice of ordeals[31] and the wide-ranging authority of canon law over laypersons), and in governance. The issue of the religious legitimisation of medieval rulership with the *Dei gratia* or similar formulas of the *intitulatio* appears in the administrative literacy of all medieval polities from their very inception.[32]

[28] F.-J. ARLINGHAUS, "Point of reference: Trust and the function of written agreements in a late medieval town", in: *Strategies of Writing*, pp. 277-299, at p. 277; ID, "Rituelle und referentielle Verwendung von Schrift: Textgebrauch in der spätmittelalterlichen Stadt", *Frühmittelalterliche Studien* 38 (2004), pp. 393-413.

[29] GIDDENS, *Modernity and Self-Identity*, p. 193.

[30] HOSKING, *Trust*, pp. 67-68.

[31] R. BARTLETT, *Trial by Fire and Water: The Medieval Judicial Ordeal* (Oxford, 1986).

[32] Cf. J.M. BAK, "Legitimization of rulership in three narratives from twelfth-century Central Europe", *Majestas* 12 (2004), pp. 43-60.

At the same time, on the local level much trust was vested in the parishes as the ideal amalgamation of ecclesiastical institutions and hubs of social security. The eminent medievalist Susan Reynolds points out the element of trust in horizontal, community-based relationships as sources of internal solidarity as well as in vertical relationships between different social strata: "lay society [...] combined acceptance of inequality and subordination with a high degree of voluntary cooperation".[33] As will be discussed in later chapters, subordination and co-operation were both highly relevant for the emergence and maintenance of the practices of literacy.

The political scientist and historian Charles Tilly in his posthumously published introduction to an unfinished survey of world history from 7000 BCE to the present developed the concept of 'trust networks' for "an ever-present form of commitment-maintaining connection" that have "crucial importance [...] for the texture and efficacy of systems of rule" due to their interactions with both cities and states, leading in the long term to the preponderance of the latter over the former in world history. Under 'commitment' he understands "operation of ties that facilitate mutual recognition and coordination".[34] Tilly adopts an extremely broad view of 'trust networks' by including among those fully or partially "kinship, local solidarities, or religion as well as neighbourhoods, communities, voluntary organisations, and ethnic groups". Despite the admittedly broadly generalising character of this work, his emphasis on the intertwined character of cities, states, and trust networks, and pointing out the dynamics of trust and authority is worth our attention.

Tilly's categories were refined and adopted to conditions in the cities of Europe between 1000 and 1600 by the Flemish medievalist Wim Blockmans. He pointed out that "community building in the first stage of urban growth rested essentially on personal ties, formalised by oaths of loyalty" which later "needed to organise themselves as public institutions". Blockmans offers a comparative typology of six types of trust networks that appeared over time in autonomous urban communities. These all differed from the kinship-based

[33] S. Reynolds, "Trust in medieval society and politics", in Ead., *The Middle Ages without Feudalism: Essays in Criticism and Comparison on the Medieval West* (Ashgate, 2012), No. IX; Ead., *Kingdoms and Communities in Western Europe, 900-1300* (Oxford, 1984), pp. 77-78, 332. On trust in parishes, see also Hosking, *Trust,* pp. 67-68.

[34] Ch. Tilly, "Cities, states, and trust networks: Chapter 1 of *Cities and States in World History*", *Theory and Society: Renewal and Critique in Social Theory* 39.3 (2010), see http://escholarship.org/uc/item/3565d2n4 (last accessed: 20.05.2018). See also Ch. Tilly, *Trust and Rule* (Cambridge, 2005), pp. 85-88.

model of the countryside and fitted better the urban social fabric: first, private associations of merchants (*hanses*); secondly, public authorities of local merchant clans and associations who formed sworn communes and administered justice on the basis of testimony by trustworthy citizens; thirdly, guilds and confraternities of artisans; fourthly, joint-stock companies of international merchants; fifthly, party clans of urban nobility; and sixthly, a new officialdom of secular and clerical elites or experts, the loyalties of which reached beyond the urban realm in the interest of the state.[35]

Oaths can indeed be considered as links between trust and authority – swearing an oath of loyalty to the community reinforced ties to a common goal, be it subversive or collaborative. Members of town councils, whose contribution to various administrative innovations will be discussed in the following chapters, were also called *jurati*, that is, 'the sworn ones' – but so were often even leaders of villages. Oaths played a major part in administering justice and occupied a liminal position between orality and literacy. Their text was written down (often in municipal books discussed below), and could be controlled. However, they had to be uttered aloud and making a mistake could result in losing the case;[36] furthermore, there could be a distinction concerning the preconditions of the validity of the oath according to the ethnic and religious affiliation as well as the gender of the person(s) taking it.

Blockmans's lucid analysis of the "transition process from personal ties to institution building" shows the "limit of the efficiency" of such trust networks in the medieval urban context. It also demonstrates the versatility of the concept of 'trust' for modern research – which also has its limits. In Blockmans's use of the term, 'trust network' and 'institutionalisation' are mutually exclusive: he concludes by stating that by the fifteenth century most cities had grown too big and complex to be ruled by trust networks; therefore institutions and officials took over instead. This specific interpretation of 'trust' differs from the interpretation of many previously quoted authors who argue for the development of institutions as the result of accumulation of trust.

The theoretical approaches offered by the social sciences, and the broad-ranging historical overviews surveyed above will be used to frame the inquiries that follow. Questions such as how Blockmans's typology of trust networks

[35] W. Blockmans, "Inclusiveness and exclusion: Trust networks at the origins of European cities", *Theory and Society* 39 (2010), pp. 315-326.

[36] Reynolds, "Trust in medieval society", pp. 9-10; L. Kolmer, *Promissorische Eide im Mittelalter* (Kallmünz/Opf., 1989: *Regensburger historische Forschungen* 12), pp. 233-246.

corresponds with the development of the written record and with the eventual extension of trust in writing will be considered. It will also be worth observing whether there was regional variation in the appearance of these types of networks in different parts of Europe. Blockmans admittedly focused only on the earliest and most urbanised regions of the continent, the Low Countries and Italy. Towns in Central and East Central Europe may provide us with different patterns, with a lower level of urbanisation. However, before turning to the region of our investigation, let us focus our attention on research traditions on 'writing', the supposed object of trust.

Literate Mentalities

Raising the issue of trust in writing would not have been possible without a long series of systematic inquiries into the development of various forms of writing and literacy in the Middle Ages. Seeking the very roots of this interest in writing and its trustworthiness, one may go back as far as the practice of testing the authenticity of individual documents while they were still actively in use. Lorenzo Valla's criticism of the Donation of Constantine was only the tip of the iceberg, as examining the authenticity of documents produced as evidence in court cases or presented for transcription and confirmation was routinely carried out by the relevant authorities. As the histories of diplomatics and palaeography describe, seventeenth-century debates about the rights secured by medieval charters led to the development of these disciplines as fields of scholarly study. The works of Mabillon and the Bollandists have been amply analysed in this context.[37] Applying modern methods of testing resulted in identifying an astonishingly high number of documents, particularly before the mid-thirteenth century, that were outright forgeries or where the contents had been tampered with.[38]

Ongoing and very industrious research in modern German scholarship gathered around such workshops as the MGH and the *Regesta Imperii*; in the post-World War II era, they provide a certain link between nineteenth-century academic traditions and modern scholarship. Through the entangled histories of the Holy Roman Empire and East Central Europe, their work is connected

[37] L.E. BOYLE, "Diplomatics", in: *Medieval Studies: An Introduction*, ed. J.M. POWELL (Syracuse, NY, 1992), pp. 82-93.

[38] M. MOSTERT, "Forgery and trust", in: *Strategies of Writing*, pp. 37-60.

in many ways with the region under scrutiny here. German research indeed represents tradition as well as innovation. The renowned *Konstanzer Arbeitskreis für mittelalterliche Geschichte* put the theme of "law and literacy" on the agenda at its meetings at Reichenau in 1975 and 1976. The editor of the resulting volume, Peter Classen, was aware that "*das Thema mag auf dem ersten Blick ungewöhnlich erscheinen*" ("the topic may at first sight seem to be unusual"), and indeed, these meetings addressed many novel questions, such as the transition from oral to written administration, that became central to later research on the development of pragmatic literacy.[39]

The results of the *Arbeitskreis* conferences, however, did not immediately reach international scholarship. For most of the academic community, a completely new scene was set by Michael Clanchy's revolutionary monograph, *From Memory to Written Record*, on the seemingly less-than-exciting subject of the birth of administrative literacy. The volume was originally published in 1979, it appeared in a second edition 1993, and, exceptionally among academic monographs, it was reissued in a third revised edition after 34 years, in 2013.[40] As one of its early reviewers formulated, "it charts the way in which literate modes became more and more acceptable among the politically influential".[41] This statement shows how much the present enquiry is also indebted to Clanchy's approach. His arguments for questioning 'trust in writing', and showing evidence for the reluctance displayed to accept written testimony, are equally relevant. Besides his many valuable statements, perhaps the title of his second part, "The literate mentality", became the most influential, starting an avalanche of publications on that very same subject.

From 1986 onwards, a special research project was initiated at the University of Münster in Westfalia, the *Sonderforschungsbereich "Träger, Felder und Formen pragmatischer Schriftlichkeit im Mittelalter"* ("Carriers, fields and forms of pragmatic literacy in the Middle Ages"), led by Hagen Keller. Their international colloquium in 1989, published in book form in 1992, can be considered revolutionary for the field. The leader of the project offered a broad definition of 'pragmatic' literacy:

[39] *Recht und Schrift im Mittelalter*, ed. P. CLASSEN (Sigmaringen, 1977: *Vorträge und Forschungen* 23), p. 7. See, e.g. R. SCHNEIDER, "Schriftlichkeit und Mündlichkeit im Bereich der Kapitularien", *ibid.*, pp. 257-279.

[40] M. CLANCHY, *From Memory to Written Record. England 1066-1307*, third edition (Oxford, 2013).

[41] Review by A.G. MOLLAND in: *Isis: A Journal of the History of Science Society*, 71.3 (Sept. 1980), p. 258.

> *Als pragmatisch verstehen wir dabei alle formen des Gebrauchs von Schrift und Texten, die unmittelbar zweckhaften Handeln dienen oder die menschliches Tun durch die Bereitstellung von Wissen anleiten wollen.*
>
> We consider as 'pragmatic' all forms of the use of writing and texts, which serve an action with an immediate purpose, or that aim at furthering human action by the presentation of knowledge.[42]

The numerous sub-projects accumulated an interest in a wide range of fields from religious orders to princely chronicles, schoolbooks and broadsheets, using source materials from the entire range of the Middle Ages.[43] From the urban milieu the attention of the project members extended to the structure of norms in town laws (Gerhard Dilcher) as well as the administration of Italian city communes (Hagen Keller).[44] In the continuation of the project, particularly the codices of customary law commissioned by urban magistrates or private persons were scrutinised.[45]

Parallel to German research, French scholarship also paid increased attention in the last few decades to the social uses of writing. Fertilised by anthropological approaches, Olivier Guyotjeannin and Roger Chartier have implanted the concept of pragmatic literacy in the traditionally strong fields of diplomatics and manuscript studies,[46] Most recently Paul Bertrand explored the production of documents and the changes in their layout and their script ("*écrits dits pragmatiques*") during the 'documentary revolution' of the late thirteenth and early fourteenth centuries. Concerned with both the quantitative increase and thematic broadening of the range of documents, Bertrand explicitly states that

[42] *Pragmatische Schriftlichkeit im Mittelalter. Erscheinungsformen und Entwicklungsstufen. Akten des Internationalen Kolloquiums, 17.-19. Mai 1989*, ed. H. KELLER, K. GRUBMÜLLER, and N. STAUBACH (München, 1992), quotation from p. 1.

[43] The yearly reports of the project were published from 1988 onwards in the journal *Frühmittelalterliche Studien.*

[44] *Pragmatische Schriftlichkeit*, pp. 9-20, 21-37.

[45] R. SCHMIDT-WIEGAND, "Rechtsbücher als Ausdruck pragmatischer Schriftlichkeit: Eine Bilanz", *Frühmittelalterliche Studien* 37 (2003), pp. 435-475.

[46] From his numerous studies see for instance O. GUYOTJEANNIN, "'*Super omnes thesauros rerum temporalium*': Les fonctions du trésor des chartes du roi de France (XIVe-XVe siècles)", in: *Écrit et pouvoir dans les chancelleries médiévales: Espace français, espace anglais,* ed. D.J. GUTH (Louvain-la-Neuve, 1997), pp. 100-131; O. GUYOTJEANNIN and O. MATTÉONI, "Écrire, décrire, ordonner: Les actes et la légitimité du pouvoir à la fin du Moyen Âge", in: *La légitimité implicite: Actes des conférences organisées à Rome en 2010 et en 2011 par SAS en collaboration avec l'École française de Rome*, ed. J-PH. GENET, 2 vols. (Paris, 2015), 1, pp. 299-316; R. CHARTIER, *Inscrire et effacer: Culture écrit et littérature (XIe-XVIIIe siècle)* (Paris, 2005).

his work is "*un essai d'histoire sociale*", in which he uses the methods of diplomatics, palaeography, and codicology as means, and not ends. Bertrand also arrives, apparently through deduction independent of the sociological considerations summarised above, to the concept of 'trust in writing', and the mutual interdependence of the credibility of a document and the authority of the institution that issued it.[47]

The third extremely impactful research initiative that served as a direct inspiration for the current volume started as a Pioneer Project in 1996 at the University of Utrecht and has been going on for more than twenty years. It has created the Medieval Literacy Platform and published close to forty volumes in the USML series under the leadership of Marco Mostert.[48] Its research community approaches medieval communication in the broadest sense of the word, also beyond the pragmatic aspects, branching out to images, orality, and materiality as elements of the communication process (e.g. USML 8, 12, 20, 23). It has produced introductory volumes and bibliographies for classroom use on undergraduate and graduate levels (USML 1, 2, and 6).

In the last decade, the Utrecht team has chosen urban literacy as one of their main foci. After a workshop in Brussels in 2008 and a series of sessions at the International Medieval Congress at Leeds between 2007 and 2009, two important and wide-ranging volumes were published which will be discussed below.[49] In the "provisional synthesis" derived from this extensive work, Marco Mostert has shown that practices of pragmatic literacy developed in step with the increasing complexity of economic relations. This applies to the use of written records among all groups of society, but especially in the urban context, the settlement type where – as has been already pointed out – the greatest density and variety of people had to be accommodated.[50]

[47] P. Bertrand, *Les écritures ordinaires: Sociologie d'un temps de révolution documentaire (1250-1350)* (Paris, 2015), quotation from p. 15; 385. On trust / credibility, see pp. 360-365. An English translation will be published in USML in 2018.

[48] See https://medievalliteracy.wp.hum.uu.nl/home-2/utrecht-studies-in-medieval-literacy/list-of-volumes/ (last accessed: 20.05.2018).

[49] The materials of the Brussels workshop were published as *New Approaches to Medieval Urban Literacy*, ed. G. Declercq, M. Mostert, W. Ysebaert, and A. Adamska (Brussels, 2011), the papers of the Leeds sessions were included in the volumes of *Writing and the Administration of Medieval Towns*, ed. M. Mostert and A. Adamska (Turnhout, 2015: USML 27) and *Uses of the Written Word in Medieval Towns*, ed. M. Mostert and A. Adamska (Turnhout, 2015: USML 28).

[50] Mostert, *Medieval Urban Literacy: Questions and Possibilities*, http://medievalliteracy.wp.hum.uu.nl/wp-content/uploads/sites/34/2013/01/Medieval-Urban-Literacy.pdf (last accessed: 20.05.2018).

At the end of this section, a very inspiring volume of the USML series needs to be highlighted, entitled *Strategies of Writing: Studies on Text and Trust in the Middle Ages* (USML 13). This collection of studies, based on a conference under the same title, takes up the issue of trust in writing in a much greater complexity than any previous works. The authors discuss questions such as

> Are medieval texts trusted only because of their contents? Are some contents more trustworthy than others? Does writing as a medium engender trust irrespective of the contents of the written text? [...] What was considered to constitute a breach of trust?[51]

An additional point to be considered here is the authority and authenticity, or in other words, the legal status (*Beweiskraft*), of certain texts as official documents. Most of the studies are not based on urban sources, but still contain useful points. The most directly relevant piece is Arlinghaus's already quoted article which "explores how written documents began to attain an independent, 'autonomous' status of 'trustworthiness' in political discourses". According to the study, texts can enter as a "third party" in a case between two litigants, two political allies, or two business partners. "What is gained in this triangular type of communication is a kind of common ground".[52]

European Frameworks

The previous section presented a brief and sketchy diachronic overview of the most influential research trends on medieval literacy from the seventeenth century to the present, in which the present work can be situated. Here I change the viewpoint to a synchronic one and place my work in today's international scene. The present volume deals first and foremost with medieval Hungary, but does not intend to do so in isolation, therefore it needs to identify similar studies in other countries of the Continent. The bulk of such a survey has already been completed by Marco Mostert, in his above-mentioned overview ranging from Dubrovnik in the south to Novgorod in the north, Britain in the west and

[51] Quoted from the blurb on the back of *Strategies of Writing*.

[52] ARLINGHAUS, "Point of reference", pp. 278-279. The first quote is taken from the review by J. HEROLD in *The Medieval Review*, 10.05.17, https://scholarworks.iu.edu/journals/index.php/tmr/article/view/17031/23149 (last accessed: 20.05.2018).

seventeenth-century Russian towns in the east.[53] This range shows that there are plenty of studies, mostly devoted to a single town or groups of towns. But is this also the case for the more immediate neighbourhood of the Carpathian Basin, the region of (East) Central Europe?

A couple of decades ago the answer to this question could not have been entirely affirmative, and especially not for works available for an international readership. For instance, Britnell's early and remarkably wide-ranging overview jumps from Western Europe to the Far East without even attempting to include, in broad terms, the eastern half of Europe. In fact, the easternmost European locality discussed in that volume is Lübeck; otherwise the European chapters of the book are mostly devoted to the British Isles and France.[54] Another region of Europe that is very well provided with studies on the development of administrative literacy, autonomy, and identity is that of the Italian city-states. These studies can also be used as eventual comparisons, but rather for the sake of contrast than as parallels.[55]

It is mainly due to the results of the research community gathered around the USML, and the personal incentive of Anna Adamska and Marco Mostert, that research on pragmatic literacy expanded beyond the traditional focus on Western Europe. Having recognised that much of the research done on the peripheries is not readily accessible for international scholarship because of language barriers, notable efforts have been made by them to improve this situation. Thankfully, by now out of the almost forty volumes published in the USML series on literacy, alphabetisation, and the use of the written word in medieval Europe, a considerable share has been devoted to Eastern and Central Europe, some of the volumes concentrating entirely on this region.[56]

The collected volume on *The Development of Literate Mentalities in East Central Europe* with its 28 studies on medieval and early modern Poland, Ru-

[53] See n. 44, above.

[54] *Pragmatic Literacy, East and West, 1200-1330*, ed. R.H. BRITNELL (Woodbridge, 1997).

[55] See, e.g. the studies of H. Keller, mentioned above; TH. BEHRMANN, "The development of pragmatic literacy in the Lombard city communes", in: *Pragmatic Literacy*, ed. BRITNELL, pp. 25-41; P. SCHULTE, *"Scripturae publicae creditur": Das Vertrauen in Notariatsurkunden im kommunalen Italien des 12. und 13. Jahrhunderts* (Tübingen, 2003: *Bibliothek des Deutschen Historischen Instituts in Rom* 101).

[56] A. ADAMSKA, "Intersections: Medieval East Central Europe from the perspective of literacy and communication", in: *Medieval East Central Europe in a Comparative Perspective: From Frontier Zones to Lands in Focus*, ed. G. JARITZ and K. SZENDE (London, 2016), pp. 223-238.

thenia, Bohemia and Hungary is one of the best examples.[57] Closely related to trust in writing, studies by Tomasz Jurek and Jiři Kejř discuss the probative value of charters.[58] The two recently edited volumes on urban literacy (USML 27 and 28) also offer additional materials on Central Europe. Poland is represented by Andrzej Janecek writing on Ruthenia as well as Anna Adamska, Paweł Kras, Jakub Wysmułek and Agnieszka Bartoszewicz. Their English-language studies transmit the results of very prolific local research communities. Bartoszewicz has also completed a thorough survey of urban literacy in medieval Poland, a volume that may be considered the closest parallel and a valuable point of reference for the present study.[59]

Research on the lands of the Bohemian crown is more sporadically represented in the USML volumes (mainly in USML 9). There are important research communities in the Czech Republic connected to the Prague City Archives, the Brno City Archives and the University of Ustí nad Labem that have not only published valuable source material such as municipal books, but have organised an international symposium discussing the research and edition of such archival fonds.[60] Among the projects closely related to the Central European region, the *Index librorum civitatum*, housed by the Martin-Luther-Universität Halle-Wittenberg needs to be mentioned here; the project also extends to some areas of modern-day Poland with significant German archival heritage.[61]

Historiography and recent research trends from Hungary will be discussed in detail in the next chapter. Let me just mention briefly here that the volumes

[57] *The Development of Literate Mentalities in East Central Europe,* ed. A. ADAMSKA and M. MOSTERT (Turnhout, 2004: USML 9). A. ADAMSKA, "Orality and literacy in medieval East Central Europe: Final prolegomena", in: *Oral Art Forms and their Passage into Writing*, ed. E. MUNDAL and J. WELLENDORF (Copenhagen, 2008), pp. 69-84.

[58] T. JUREK, "Die Rechtskraft von Urkunden im mittelalterlichen Polen", in: *The Development of Literate Mentalities*, pp. 59-91; J. KEJŘ, "Die Urkunde als Beweismittel im Gerichtsverfahren im mittelalterlichen Böhmen", *ibid.*, pp. 51-58.

[59] A. JANECZEK, "Urban communes, ethnic communities, and language use in late medieval Red Ruthenian towns", in: *Uses of the Written Word*, pp. 19-35; A. ADAMSKA, "Away with the Germans and their language? Linguistic conflict and urban records in early fourteenth-century Cracow", *ibid.*, pp. 65-85; A. BARTOSZEWICZ, "Urban literacy in small Polish towns and the process of 'modernisation' of society in the later Middle Ages", in: *Writing and the Administration*, pp. 149-182; A. BARTOSZEWICZ, *Urban Literacy in Late Medieval Poland* (Turnhout, 2017: USML 39).

[60] *Stav a perspektivy zpřístupňování středověkých a raně novověkých městských knih* [The state and perspectives of accessing medieval and early modern municipal books], ed. L. SULITKOVÁ, M. HRUBÁ, and V. ZÁBRANSKÝ (Ustí nad Labem, 2010).

[61] http://www.stadtbuecher.de/ (last accessed: 20.05.2018).

of the USML series also contain articles pertaining to the territory of the medieval kingdom of Hungary, both by authors from Slovakia and from the Transylvanian part of modern-day Romania.[62] Such publications, besides making available new results, are also important for fighting the political biases and misconceptions often spread from outside the academic circles. For further contextualisation and conceptual extension beyond the area of primarily Latin literacy, but staying in the neighbourhood of the Carpathian Basin, works on the Romanian principalities and medieval Serbia offer valuable possibilities of comparison.[63]

It is in this spirit of integrating questions and research experiences from the eastern half of the continent into the framework of European development that a small piece of the overall picture, the use of writing in the towns of medieval Hungary, is presented in the following chapters.

[62] D. Zupka, "Communication in a town: Urban rituals and literacy in the medieval kingdom of Hungary", in: *Uses of the Written Word*, pp. 341-373; M. Lupescu Makó, "Spoken and written words in testaments: Orality and literacy in last wills of medieval Transylvanian burghers", *ibid.*, pp. 271-297; Á. Flóra, "'*Laborem circumspecti domini notarii*': Town notaries in early modern Transylvania", in: *Writing and the Administration*, pp. 313-335.

[63] M. Goina, *The Uses of Pragmatic Literacy in the Medieval Principalities of Moldavia and Wallachia* (unpublished PhD dissertation, CEU, Budapest, 2009, available at https://sierra.ceu.edu/search?/aGoina/agoina/1%2C2%2C3%2CB/frameset&FF=agoina+mariana&2%2C%2C2 (last accessed: 20.05.2018); Đ. Bubalo, *Pragmatic Literacy in Medieval Serbia* (Turnhout, 2014: USML 29).

Chapter 1

Setting the Scene[1]

Whose Literacy? Urban Development and Urban Society in Medieval Hungary

To set the scene for the birth and expansion of civic literacy in the Carpathian Basin, and to see the people behind the parchment (or the paper), one needs to get acquainted with the emergence of cities and towns in this territory. It is important to bear in mind that this region was sparsely inhabited and joined the community of Christian states only around the turn of the first Millennium. Accordingly, urban development also started relatively late, and in a protracted and subordinate way. To give a summary of this development in a nutshell, one can divide it into two phases, the watershed being the mid-thirteenth century, when a series of new processes were set in motion.[2]

In the period prior to those decades, various 'old centres' existed, among which early royal seats took pride of place. Esztergom and Székesfehérvár both fulfilled secular and ecclesiastical functions alike, while Óbuda, the northern part of present-day Budapest, served as a secondary royal residence at the

[1] Some parts of this chapter were previously published in: K. SZENDE, "Towns and the written word in medieval Hungary", in: *Writing and the Administration,* pp. 123-148.

[2] A. KUBINYI, "'A magyar várostörténet első fejezete'" ['The first chapter of Hungarian urban history'] in: *Társadalomtörténeti Tanulmányok: Studia Miskolcinensia 2,* ed. CS. FAZEKAS (Miskolc, 1996), pp. 36-46. J. LASZLOVSZKY, "Frühstädtische Siedlungsentwicklung in Ungarn", in: *Burg – Burgstadt – Stadt: Zur Genese mittelalterlicher nichtagrarischer Zentren in Ostmitteleuropa,* ed. H. BRACHMANN (Berlin, 1995), pp. 307-315; K. SZENDE, "Was there a bourgeoisie in medieval Hungary?", in: *The Man of Many Devices, Who Wandered Full Many Ways ... Festschrift in Honor of János M. Bak,* ed. B. NAGY and M. SEBŐK (Budapest, 1999), pp. 445-459.

crossing of the Danube. All three cities were situated fairly close to each other, in the so-called *medium regni*, the centre of the realm.[3] It needs to be mentioned at the outset that, unfortunately, the destruction of the municipal archives of all the royal seats *in medio regni* (Esztergom, Fehérvár, Óbuda, Buda, Pest, and Visegrád) leaves a lacuna that can only partially be filled and which inevitably distorts some of our research results.

The set of bishop's seats included altogether fourteen settlements by the middle of the thirteenth century, including two archbishoprics (Esztergom and Kalocsa),[4] whereas in the secular administration over fifty county seats with their earthwork fortifications and adjoining suburban markets played the central role. In nine cases out of twelve, the bishop's seats were at the same time centres of secular administration, that is, seats of royal counties *(comitatus,* Hung. *megye)*, but this was not a necessary combination. Nevertheless, there were about five times as many counties as bishoprics, so the county seats formed the most extensive network of central places in the first centuries of Hungarian statehood (Fig. 2). This system was complemented with many other places of weekly markets as secondary centres, often near specialised villages of craftsmen or the seat or monastery of a powerful family.

It was in these partly administrative, partly military, and partly commercial settlements that new settlers or immigrants (termed in the sources as *hospites*, literally 'guests') moving to or within the country had to find their place. The loosely arranged structure of the various forms of early centres in fact made the newcomers' integration much easier: they were able to settle in a group of their own without upsetting any existing arrangements or having to contend with a strong demand for adaptation to a common administrative body. On the whole, the early phase of urbanisation in Hungary up to the early thirteenth century

[3] *Medium Regni: Medieval Hungarian Royal Seats,* ed. G. BUZÁS (Budapest, 1999); *In medio regni Hungariae: Régészeti, művészettörténeti és történeti kutatások "az ország közepén"* [Archaeological, Art Historical and Historical Researches "in the Middle of the Kingdom"], ed. E. BENKŐ and K. OROSZ (Budapest, 2015).

[4] L. KOSZTA, "Püspöki székhely és városfejlődés" [Episcopal seats and urban development], in: *Kelet és Nyugat között: Történeti tanulmányok Kristó Gyula tiszteletére* [Between East and West: Historical studies in honour of Gyula Kristó], ed. L. KOSZTA (Szeged, 1995), pp. 233-272; I. PETROVICS, "The cities and towns of medieval Hungary as economic and cultural centres and places of coexistence: The case of Pécs", *Colloquia* 18 (2011), pp. 5-26; L. KOSZTA, *A kalocsai érseki tartomány kialakulása* [The formation of the archiepiscopal province of Kalocsa] (Pécs, 2013), English summary at pp. 146-150; ID., "Byzantine archiepiscopal ecclesiastical system in Hungary?", in: *A Kárpát-medence, a magyarság és Bizánc – The Carpathian Basin, the Hungarians and Byzantium*, ed. T. OLAJOS, SZ. KOVÁCS, and P. SZABÓ (Szeged, 2014: *Acta Universitatis Szegediensis Opuscula Byzantina* 11), pp. 127-143.

was a basically autochthonous process, in which immigrant populations played only a minor role. The emergence of urban autonomy and institutionalised internal administration, however, was strongly influenced by the presence of the various ethnic groups, especially those of western origin.[5]

Archaeologists often distinguish between a 'pre-urban' development phase of old cultic, administrative, and trading centres and an 'urban' phase of more modern towns.[6] I would be reluctant to subscribe to this terminology, since the early centres also fulfilled proper urban functions in their own environment and in their own time. However, it would be appropriate to call them 'pre-literate', since reading, writing, and written administration played a very minor role, if at all, in their internal life and external connections. This was one of the features that changed gradually but significantly in the second phase of medieval urban development, which led to the emergence of 'fully-fledged towns'.[7]

The reigns of Andrew I, his son Béla IV, and their successors brought about new ideas and, consequently, new attitudes and arrangements in all fields of life, including state and local administration. These were part of the overall structural changes of society, which affected practically every inhabitant of the kingdom, from peasants to nobles, as well as the urban population and those people who were to join their ranks from other social strata.[8] As one of the instruments to achieve these changes, the kings granted an increasing number of charters of privilege to towns, confirming existing development and promoting new sites. Such charters were not unknown to the royal chancery before the

[5] K. Szende, "Von der Gespanschaftsburg zur Stadt: Warum, wie – oder warum nicht? Ein möglicher Weg der Stadtentwicklung im mittelalterlichen Ungarn", in: *Stadtgründung und Stadtwerdung: Beiträge von Archäologie und Stadtgeschichtsforschung,* ed. F. Opll and Ch. Sonnlechner (Wien, 2011), pp. 375-405; on the system of early centres: A. Végh and K. Szende, "Royal power and urban space in medieval Hungary", in: *Medieval Urban Form in Comparative Perspective: The Contribution of the Historic Towns Atlas*, ed. A. Simms and H.B. Clarke (Farnham, 2015), pp. 255-286, esp. pp. 257-260.

[6] A. Simms, "Paradigm shift: From town foundation to town formation", in: *Städteatlanten: Vier Jahrzehnte Atlasarbeit in Europa*, ed. W. Ehbrecht (Köln, Weimar, and Wien, 2013), pp. 217-233, with further references.

[7] J. Šedivý, "Deutschsprachige Beurkundung im Donaugebiet des mittelalterlichen Königreichs Ungarn", in: *Urkunden und ihre Erforschung: Zum Gedenken an Heinrich Appelt,* ed. W. Maleczek (Wien, 2014: VIÖG 62), pp. 247-265, at p. 248 writes in a similar vein about "*auf Oralität beruhende* illitterati-*Kultur*".

[8] These changes are described extensively in J. Szűcs, *Az utolsó Árpádok* [The last Árpádians] (Budapest, 1993), esp. pp. 223-276, and summarised in Engel, *The Realm of St. Stephen*, pp. 101-123.

Fig. 2 Counties and county seats in the kingdom of Hungary, *c.*1300.

Vel'ký Šariš
ABAÚJVÁR
ZEMPLÉN
UNG
Uzhgorod
Abaújvár
Zemplín
BEREG
Beregovo
Szabolcs
Tisza
MÁRAMAROS
SZABOLCS
Satu Mare
SZATMÁR
DOBOKA
KRASZNA
Crasna
Bihor
BIHAR
Dăbâca
Cluj
KOLOZS
Turda
TORDA
SZÉKELYFÖLD
Zărand
ZARÁND
KÜKÜLLŐ
Cetatea de Baltă
Arad
ARAD
Alba Iulia
SZÁSZFÖLD
Sibiu
FOGARAS
SZÁSZFÖLD
Timişoara
TEMES
FEHÉR
KRASSÓ
Caraşova
Danube
0 50 100 150 200 km
MJ

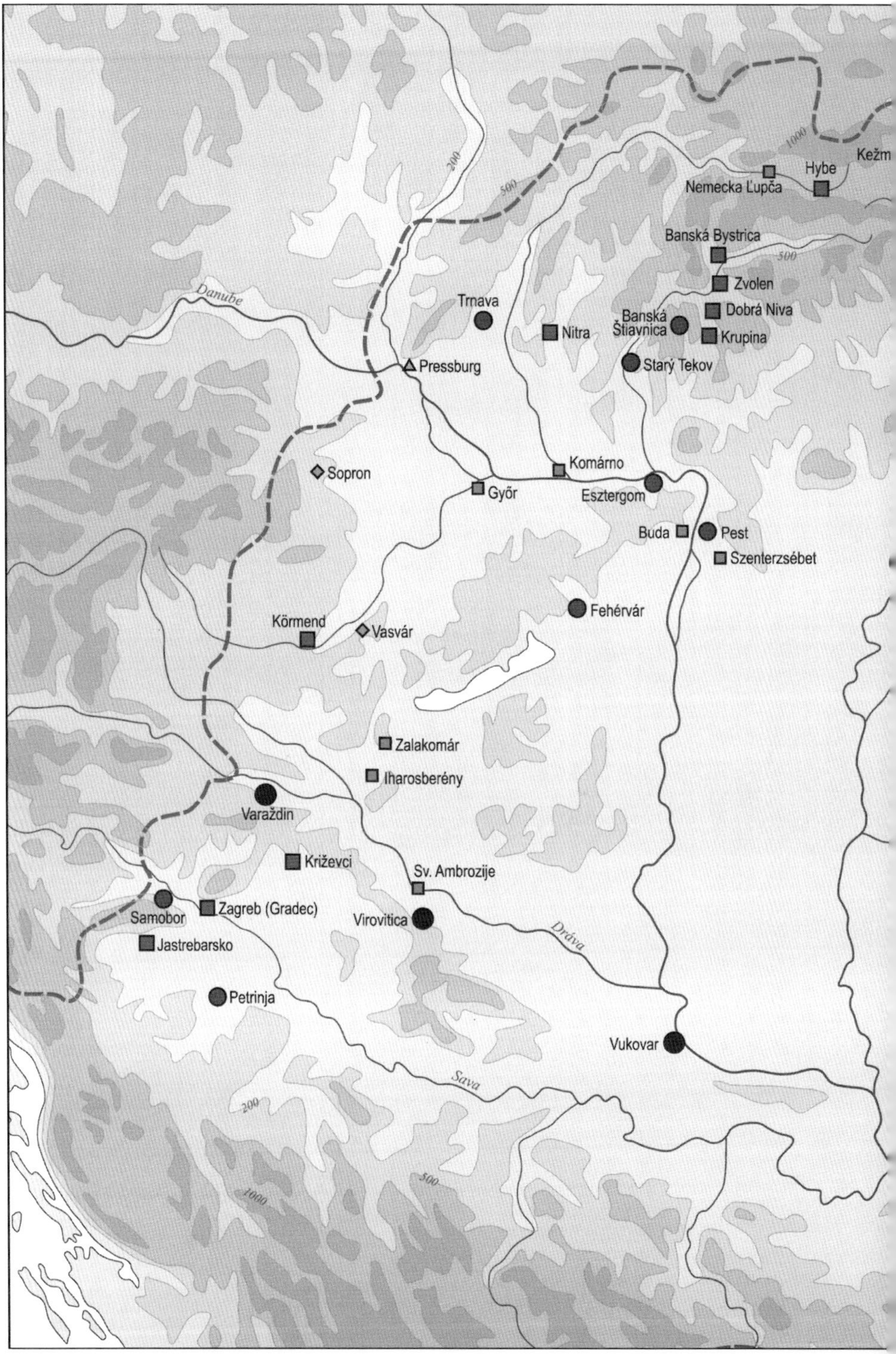

Fig. 3 Newly chartered settlements in the kingdom of Hungary up to 1300.

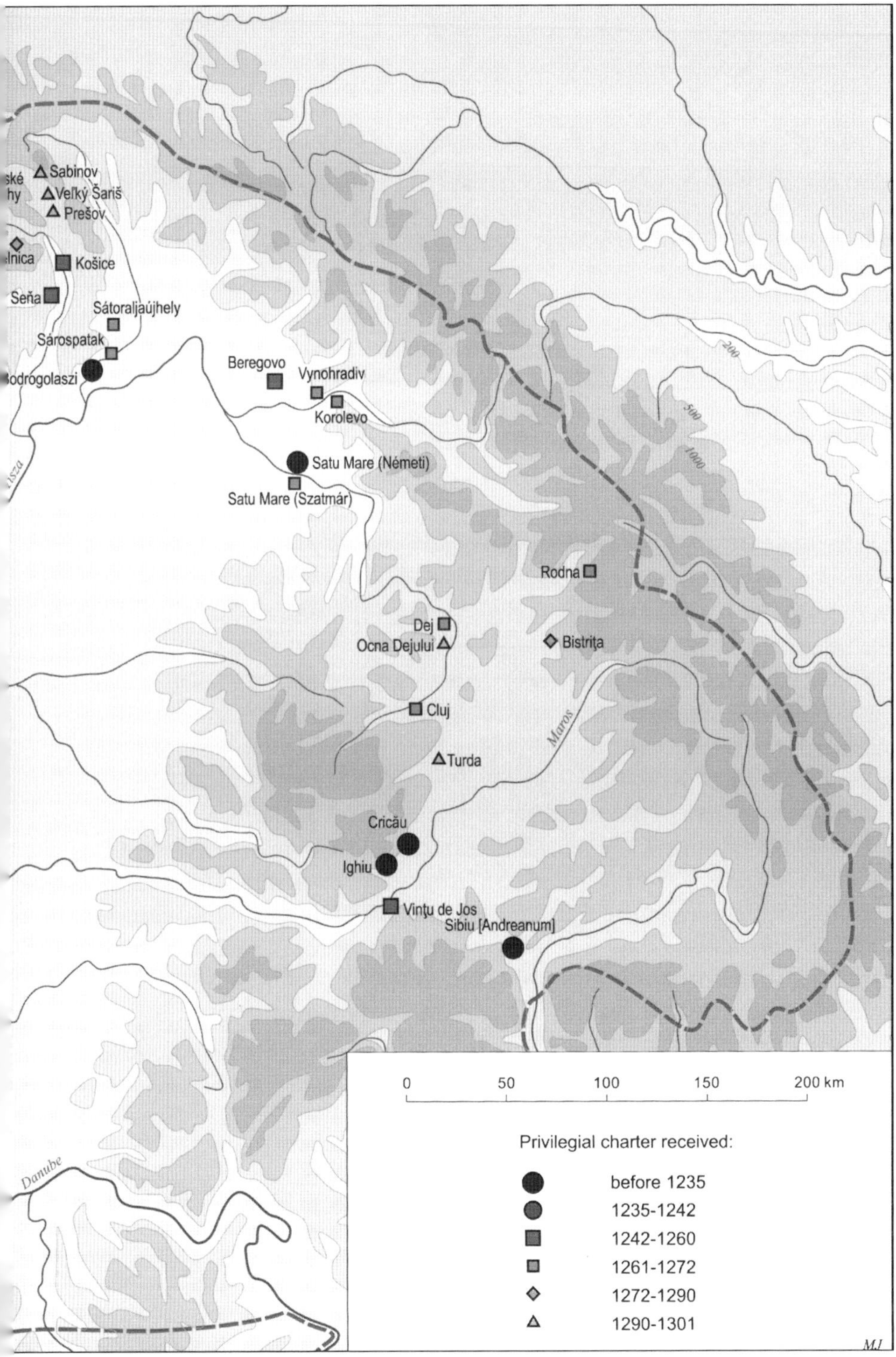
Sabinov
Veľký Šariš
Prešov
Košice
Seňa
Sátoraljaújhely
Sárospatak
Beregovo
Vynohradiv
Korolevo
Satu Mare (Németi)
Satu Mare (Szatmár)
Rodna
Dej
Ocna Dejului
Bistrița
Cluj
Turda
Maros
Cricău
Ighiu
Vințu de Jos
Sibiu [Andreanum]
Danube
200
500
1000
0
50
100
150
200 km
Privilegial charter received:
before 1235
1235-1242
1242-1260
1261-1272
1272-1290
1290-1301
MJ

Mongol invasion (1241/1242) either, but from the 1240s their number increased and embraced settlements all over the kingdom. The consequences of the appearance of these essential written documents in the urban context will be discussed in detail in Chapter 2.

The kings' measures carried the strongest weight in those places where the local conditions and demands for long-distance trade favoured the emergence of new central places. Such were, for instance, the towns of Bardejov, Prešov, Košice, Levoča and Sabinov in the north-east of the country, members of the later alliance named Pentapolis.[9] All of them were characterised by a mixture of indigenous and immigrant, Hungarian, Slavic (Slovak), and German populations. A great advantage of the newly established settlements was that they did not have to comply with the special prerogatives of already existing administrative entities, but could establish their own administration according to the latest norms. Other new towns, like Beregovo, Vynohradiv and Sátoraljaújhely, which were geared towards the eastern trade, lost their importance in the long run (Fig. 3).

Many of the rights secured for the 'new towns' were also included in the royal charters given to the *hospites*. The charters can be understood as contracts between the settlers and the ruler, with rights and obligations for both parties. In their entirety, however, the privileges given to towns did not follow one single external pattern, but were created with respect to the local conditions and often absorbed elements of local customary law. The eclectic character is even more apparent in case of the statutes and law codes that were compiled in the major towns during the fourteenth and fifteenth centuries. Hardly any explicit references were made to any foreign city as a model, either in the vicinity or further away. Particularly conspicuous is the absence of references to Magdeburg Law, which played such important and diverse roles in urban development in Central and Eastern Europe during the 'Eastward Expansion' (*Ostsiedlung*). The settling process in the royal towns of Hungary (with the exception of Bardejov) was significantly different from that of the *locatio* practised, for instance, in Silesia and in large parts of Poland, because no provisions were made for a settling agent (*advocatus* or *scultetus*); such a form of settling was only used in Hungary to establish villages, some of which devel-

[9] I.H. Németh, *Várospolitika és gazdaságpolitika a 16-17. századi Magyarországon: A felső-magyarországi városszövetség* [Urban policy and economic policy in Hungary in the sixteenth and seventeenth centuries: The alliance of Upper Hungarian towns], 2 vols. (Budapest, 2004).

oped later into smallish market towns in the northern and north-eastern parts of the kingdom.[10]

An essential element of the charters of privilege was to secure the freedom of movement to and from the given settlements. With this measure, the rulers recognised the need to rely on continuous immigration to maintain or increase the population of the newly chartered centres in these thinly populated lands. This welcoming attitude had a beneficial influence on the arrival of new settlers both from within the country and from abroad. Among the earlier arrivals, the *Latini* (Romance-speaking people) were most frequently mentioned; from the thirteenth century onwards, the majority of foreign newcomers were Germans.[11] They settled in greatest numbers not only in the southern territories of Transylvania (as mentioned above), in the Spiš region (Zips, Szepesség) in the north-east, and the western fringes of Hungary (Sopron, Pressburg, Kőszeg), but also in Buda, the most significant new settlement. Italians, too, had a considerable presence, and the ranks of the Jewish communities were also regularly supplemented by new members coming from the west, for instance from Regensburg (Fig. 4).[12]

The old royal residences could not retain their former importance. By the beginning of the fourteenth century, Buda had undoubtedly become the capital city of the kingdom, not only concerning its administrative and commercial functions, but presumably also due to its number of inhabitants. The town was

[10] A. Körmendy, "Mittelalterliche *aedificatio terrae* im Lichte der ungarischen Historiographie", in: *Historiographical Approaches to the Medieval Colonization of East Central Europe*, ed. J. Piskorski (Boulder, 2002: *East European Monographs* 611), pp. 145-177. The distinction between the zones of the Neumarkt-Magdeburg law, the various German, Bohemian and Moravian local laws, and the South German law (Bavaria, Austria and most of the Carpathian Basin) is clearly shown on the map "The development of German law cities" in: P.R. Magocsi, *Historical Atlas of Central Europe*, cartographic design by G.J. Matthews (Seattle, 1993), pp. 40-41.

[11] E. Fügedi, "Das mittelalterliche Ungarn als Gastland", in: *Die deutsche Ostsiedlung des Mittelalters als Problem der europäischen Geschichte*, ed. W. Schlesinger (Sigmaringen, 1975: *Vorträge und Forschungen* 18), pp. 451-490, reprinted in id., *Kings, Bishops, and Burghers in Medieval Hungary* (Aldershot, 1986), Chapter viii.

[12] K. Szende, "Traders, 'Court Jews', Town Jews: The changing roles of Hungary's Jewish population in the light of royal policy between the eleventh and the fourteenth centuries", in: *Intricate Interfaith Networks in the Middle Ages: Quotidian Jewish-Christian Contacts*, ed. E. Shoham-Steiner (Turnhout, 2016), pp. 119-151; E. Spekner, *Hogyan lett Buda a középkori Magyarország fővárosa? A budai királyi székhely története a 12. század végétől a 14. század közepéig* [How did Buda become the capital of medieval Hungary? The history of the Buda seat from the end of the twelfth to the mid-fourteenth century] (Budapest, 2015: *Monumenta historica Budapestinensia* 17).

Fig. 4 The eastern wall with the Torah ark of the medieval 'old synagogue' in Sopron. The system of vaulting follows the practice observed in house chapels in Regensburg. Photo: Zoltán Bolodár. Reproduced with permission.

established in the late 1240s by royal order on a well-defendable hilltop overlooking the Danube ferry site across to Pest. In the first century of its existence, Buda's autonomy was restricted by the royal appointment of rectors instead of locally elected judges, but the twelve-strong council operating alongside them always represented local interests and power relations. Although the presence of the king's treasury and minting house on the northern side of the hilltop can be traced back to the first half of the thirteenth century, the establishment of a stable royal residence on the southern cliffs took place, partly because of dynastic changes, only during the fourteenth and fifteenth centuries.[13] In the meantime, two other sites gained importance as temporary royal residences: Timişoara from 1315 to 1323 and Visegrád from 1323 to the 1410s. However, these fairly small settlements,

[13] See the studies by E. Spekner, M. Rady, K. Magyar and A. Végh in: *Medieval Buda in Context*, ed. B. Nagy, M. Rady, K. Szende and A. Vadas (Leiden, 2016); A. Végh, *Buda, Part 1, Up to 1686* (Budapest 2015: *Hungarian Atlas of Historic Towns* 4).

which were not easily accessible from many parts of the kingdom, could not compete with Buda's geographically determined central significance.[14]

Among the burghers of Buda, as indicated above, the Germans were the most significant. They benefitted from their manifold connections to cities of the Holy Roman Empire along the Danube and beyond (Passau, Regensburg, Nuremberg, Vienna). From the fifteenth century onwards, most of the new arrivals were Hungarian, which resulted in the balance shifting in their favour. The Italians, mostly Florentines and Venetians, although smaller in number, played a crucial role in linking Buda to the Mediterranean world; there was also a route through Zagreb in Slavonia and Senj in Dalmatia towards the Adriatic.[15]

Contacts were not, however, one-sided: Buda did not simply adopt, but rather adapted and transformed elements of the newcomers' culture. A good example of this is the reference to Magdeburg law, the most widespread urban legal system in Central and Eastern Europe, in the *Ofner Stadtrecht*, the law book of Buda (the German name of Buda was *Ofen*).[16] This source, compiled in several instalments between 1403 and the early 1440s, contains extremely valuable information on trust in writing and will be often quoted in the rest of this volume. According to the law book's first chapter, the legislation in Buda "*mit helet in etlichen dingen oder stugken Maidpurgerischen rechten*" ("complies in some parts and pieces with Magdeburg law").[17] However, hardly any articles were copied directly or verbatim: Magdeburg was mentioned rather as a point of reference that imbued the articles of local customary law with widely recognised authority. From a literary point of view, the most significant part of the book is the prologue, which summarises, in rhythmical prose with rhyming

[14] I. PETROVICS, "The fading glory of a former royal seat: the case of medieval Temesvár", in: *"The Man of Many Devices..."*, pp. 527-538; *The Medieval Royal Town at Visegrád: Royal Centre, Urban Settlement, Churches*, ed. J. LASZLOVSZKY, G. BUZÁS, and O. MÉSZÁROS (Budapest, 2014).

[15] A. VÉGH, "Buda, the multi-ethnic capital of medieval Hungary", in: *Segregation, Integration, Assimilation: Religious and Ethnic Groups in the Medieval Towns of Central and Eastern Europe*, ed. D. KEENE, B. NAGY, and K. SZENDE (Farnham, 2009), pp. 89-100.

[16] *Das Ofner Stadtrecht: Eine deutschsprachige Rechtssammlung des 15. Jahrhunderts aus Ungarn*, ed. K. MOLLAY (Budapest, 1959: *Monumenta Historica Budapestinensia* 1); K. GÖNCZI, *Ungarisches Stadtrecht aus europäischer Sicht. Die Stadtrechtsentwicklung im spätmittelalterlichen Ungarn am Beispiel Ofens* (Frankfurt am Main, 1997).

[17] *Ofner Stadtrecht*, cap. 1, p. 58.

clauses, contemporary ideas on the common good – a potent concept in the urban milieu – and the virtues that should characterise the town's leaders.[18]

The new towns that developed in the mid-thirteenth century also included mining towns. The emergence of these was not simply a consequence of new times: they catalysed the changes themselves. Due to the discovery of silver, copper, and gold ores, Hungary took an increasingly active role in the European economy in the late thirteenth century, orienting itself to the West after centuries of emphasis on eastern and southern connections. The exploitation of these resources necessitated the establishment of several new settlements in Upper Hungary and Transylvania; it is questionable though, to what extent each of these had an urban character, since mining as a 'rural industry' was bound to the occurrence of minerals and not to other factors of urban growth. The most important ones among them, however, were definitely towns: Rodna, with written mining statutes from as early as 1270; Banská Štiavnica, chartered before the Mongol invasion (probably in 1238, with statutes borrowed from Jihlava in 1249/1280); Banská Bystrica which received the privileges of the former in 1255; and Kremnica which was established later (1328). Several other mining towns were owned by the kings or queens; and there were smaller ones which belonged to private landowners. With Hungary providing about one-third of Europe's silver production and at least 80 per cent of the gold until the Age of Discoveries, the importance of the mining towns and their contribution to the wealth of their respective regions can hardly be overestimated (Fig. 5).[19]

As we shall see in the following chapters, civic literacy experienced its first great boom in the fourteenth century. This rise is connected to an intensive phase of urban development. After an extensive and truly spectacular wave of urbanisation in the thirteenth century, the decades following the 1320s saw steady consolidation. Hungary's Angevin kings, Charles I and Louis I, as well as Sigismund of Luxembourg, recognised the economic potential of towns and took measures to strengthen them. Sigismund, a ruler of the broadest European

[18] *Ofner Stadtrecht*, pp. 35-40. A. KUBINYI, "A budai jogkönyvről".

[19] F. IRSIGLER, "Die Bedeutung Ungarns für die europäische Wirtschaft im Spätmittelalter", in: *Sigismund von Luxemburg: Ein Kaiser in Mitteleuropa,* ed. M. PAULY and F. REINERT (Mainz, 2006), pp. 25-34; *Banské mestá na Slovensku* [Mining towns in Slovakia], ed. R. MARSINA (Martin, 1990); B. WEISZ, "Mining town privileges in Angevin Hungary", *The Hungarian Historical Review* 2 (2013), pp. 288-312; B. WEISZ, "A bányaváros mint önálló várostípus a 14. században" [Mining towns as a separate town type in the fourteenth century], *Bányászattörténeti Közelmények* 19 (2015), pp. 31-57.

horizons (also elected King of the Germans in 1410 and subsequently Holy Roman Emperor in 1433), consolidated the system by keeping only the most lucrative cities and towns under direct royal control, while donating or pledging the others to the nobility.[20]

At the same time, the foundations of the institutional handling of urban affairs were laid down. From the 1440s, towns were occasionally invited to attend the diet, and a special court of appeal, that of the Master of the Treasury (*magister tavernicorum*), the 'tavernical court', was designated for the seven (later eight) most important merchant towns. These were the so-called free royal towns: Buda, Pressburg, Sopron, Trnava, Košice, Bardejov, Prešov, and after 1498 also Pest. As part of the pragmatic co-operation between the towns and their rulers, the kings chartered and involved in their plans those towns that could provide them with secure incomes, offer safe and appropriate places for lodging and diplomatic meetings, supply military support, and procure reliable information. This pattern of mutual expectations characterised the relations between crown and town under the reign of Matthias Corvinus and the Jagiellonian kings, Wladislas II and Louis II, until the fall of the medieval Hungarian state.[21]

With the exception of mining towns, the late medieval towns in the Carpathian Basin were geared first and foremost to commerce (Fig. 6). Privileges to hold annual fairs were given by Louis I to all important towns on the borders located on major trade routes, as well as to Buda and Zagreb. Beginning in the early fifteenth century, this development was complemented by the growing significance of a new land route of Levantine trade, arriving from the Balkans at Sibiu or Braşov, then passing through Cluj, Oradea, and Košice and across the Carpathians, to reach Cracow. For the west-bound trade, Pressburg and Sopron had similar significance, especially until the 1460s. The preponderance

[20] K. SZENDE, "Between hatred and affection: Towns and Sigismund in Hungary and the Empire", in: *Sigismund von Luxemburg*, pp. 199-210; J. INCZE, "The pledge policy of king Sigismund of Luxembourg in Hungary (1387-1437)", in: *Money and Finance in Central Europe during the Later Middle Ages*, ed. R. ZAORAL (Basingstoke, 2016), pp. 87-109; J. INCZE, "'Bound by pledge': Bártfa (Bardejov) and king Sigismund's policy of pledging towns", *Annual of Medieval Studies at CEU* 19 (2013), pp. 83-94.

[21] Š. MERTANOVÁ, *Ius tavernicale: Studie o procese formovania práva tavernickych miest v etapach vyvoja tavernickeho súdu v Uhorsku (15-17. stor.)* [Ius tavernicale: A study on the development of the law of tavernical towns in the period of the formation of the tavernical court] (Bratislava, 1985).

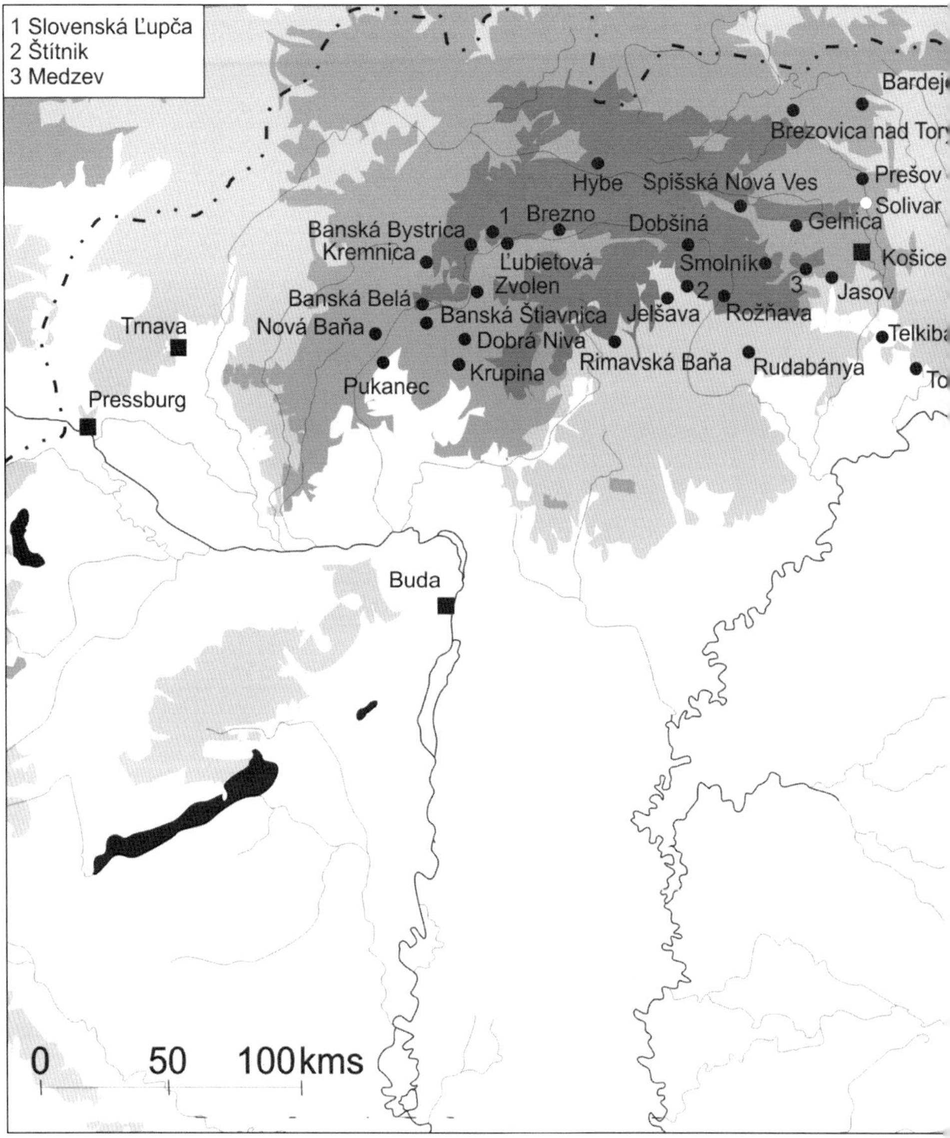

Fig. 5 Mining towns in medieval Hungary (map prepared by András Vadas).

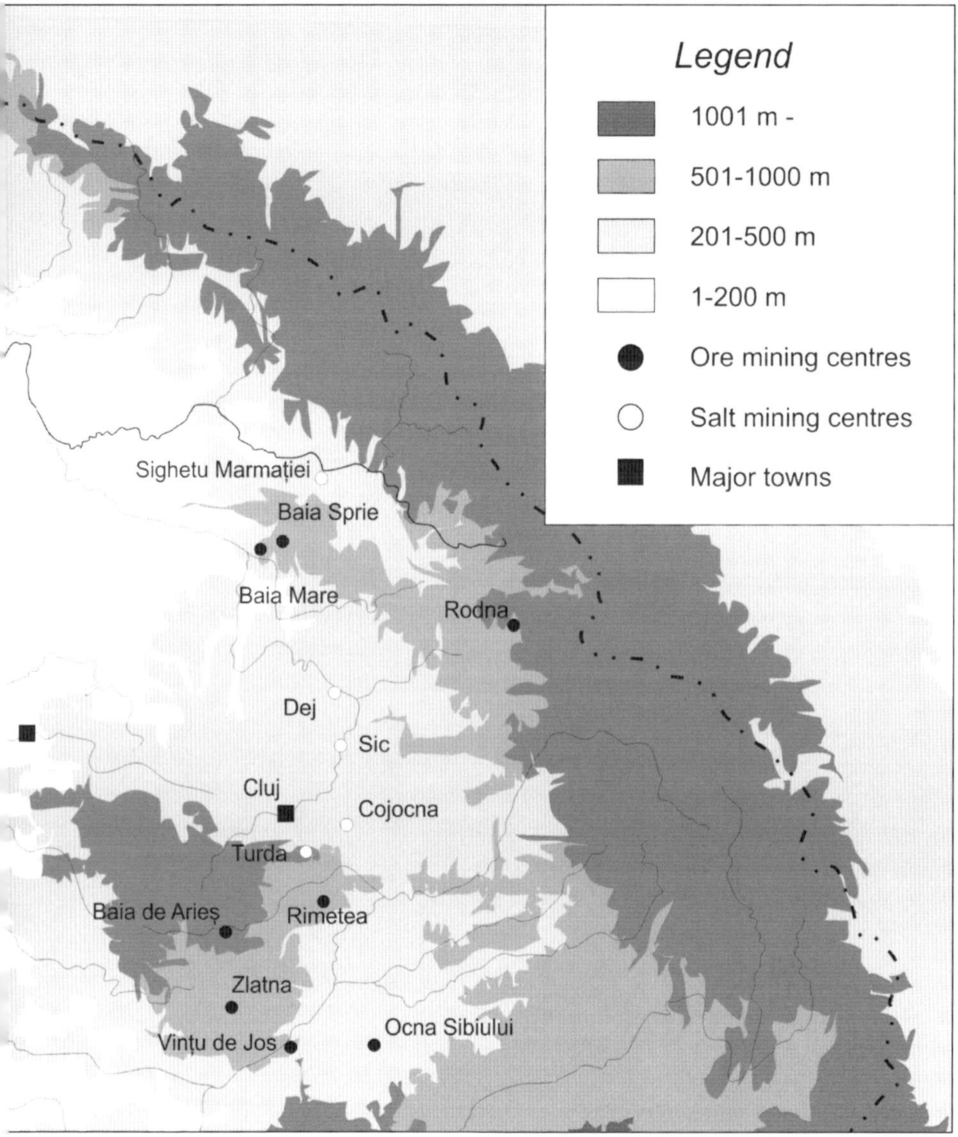
Legend
1001 m -
501-1000 m
201-500 m
1-200 m
Ore mining centres
Salt mining centres
Major towns
Sighetu Marmației
Baia Sprie
Baia Mare
Rodna
Dej
Sic
Cluj
Cojocna
Turda
Baia de Arieș
Rimetea
Zlatna
Vințu de Jos
Ocna Sibiului

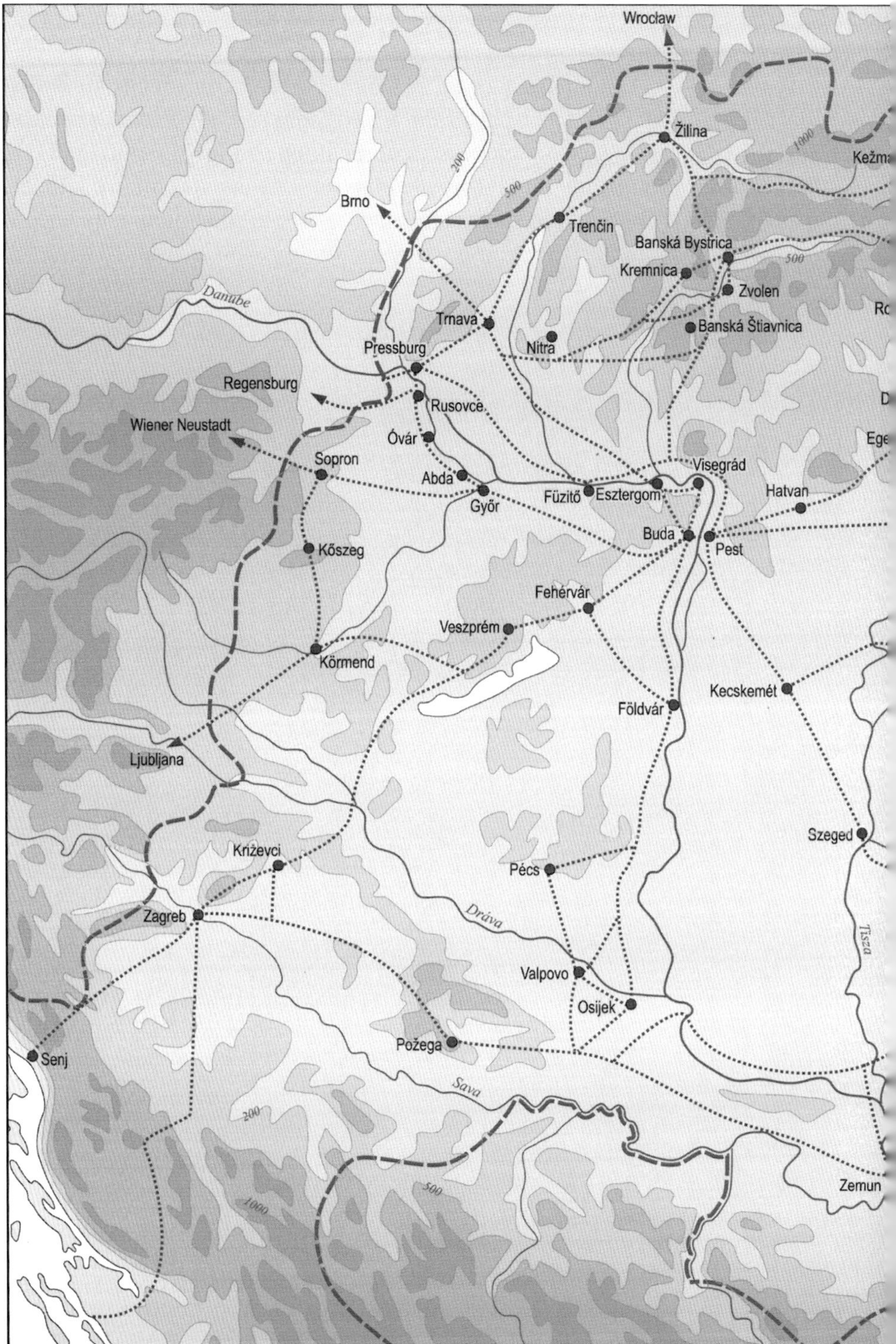

Fig. 6 The most important towns and trade routes in medieval Hungary.

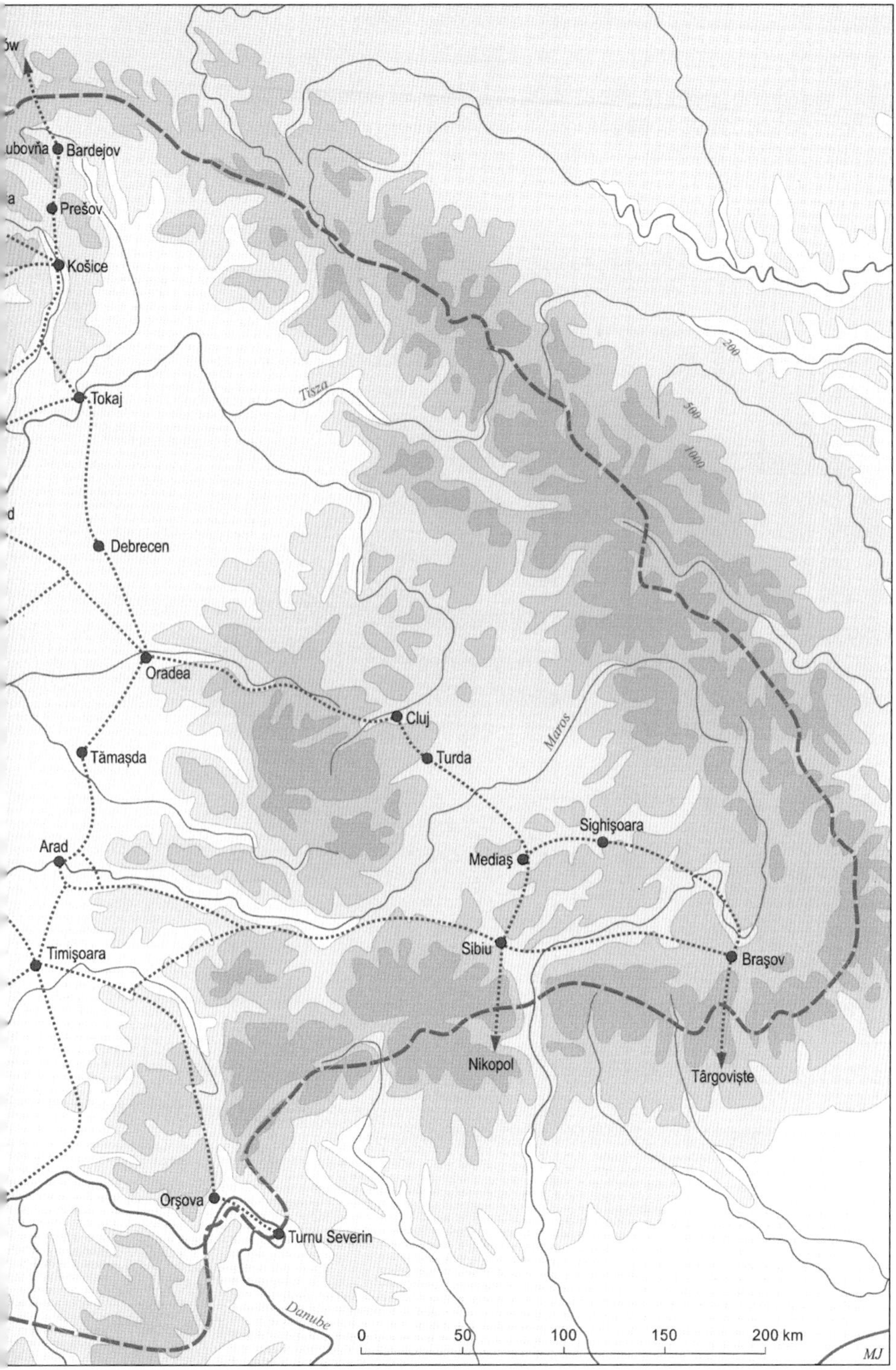
Bardejov
Prešov
Košice
Tokaj
Tisza
Debrecen
Oradea
Cluj
Turda
Tămașda
Maros
Arad
Sighişoara
Mediaş
Timişoara
Sibiu
Braşov
Nikopol
Târgovişte
Orşova
Turnu Severin
Danube
200
500
1000
0
50
100
150
200 km
MJ

of trade was combined with relatively low levels of craft production, sufficient for provisioning the towns and their hinterland, but hardly more.[22]

The most important novelty in the urbanisation of the fourteenth and fifteenth centuries was undoubtedly the increasing number of market towns (*oppida*; *Märkte* or *Marktflecken* in German), the spread of which completed the process of the development of a hierarchically structured urban network in the Carpathian Basin. Their main function was to act as secondary centres of distribution for commercial goods; however, they may also have functioned as central places of primary importance for their hinterlands in regions without 'proper' towns, especially in the central agricultural areas of the country. Many of them also participated in the specialised production of agricultural commodities, such as wine and livestock (mainly cattle and horses). This was all the more significant, because these were the main export goods of Hungary besides precious metals.[23]

Such settlements in private (seigniorial) landownership can be found in several countries all over Europe, not only in the eastern half of the continent.[24] For the assessment of market towns that fulfilled significant urban functions, the late András Kubinyi devised a method of calculation based on ten different criteria including administrative, economic, and ecclesiastical central functions, and geographic centrality. He also included a cultural phenomenon, the number of students attending foreign universities from the given settlement, which indeed (with some provisos) reflects the importance of a town in the

[22] Zs.P. Pach, "Hungary and the Levantine trade in the fourteenth-seventeenth centuries", *Acta Orientalia Academiae Scientiarum Hungaricae* 60.1 (2007), pp. 9-31; K. Szende, "Towns along the way: Changing patterns of long-distance trade and the urban network of medieval Hungary", in: *Towns and Communication*, 2, *Communication between Towns*, ed. H. Houben and K. Toomaspoeg (Lecce, 2011), pp. 161-225.

[23] E. Sárosi, *Deserting Villages, Emerging Market Towns: Settlement Dynamics and Land Management in the Great Hungarian Plain, 1300-1700* (Budapest, 2016), pp. 21-24, 131-156; L.Sz. Gulyás, *Mezővárosi önkormányzat a középkori Hegyalján* [Self-government of market towns in the medieval Hegyalja region] (Budapest, 2017), pp. 11-23.

[24] V. Bácskai, "Small towns in Eastern Central Europe", in: *Small towns in Early Modern Europe*, ed. P. Clark (Cambridge, 1995), pp. 77-89; for comparison see T. Scott, "Kleine Städte, keine Städte: Das so genannte 'urbane Netz' in Südwestdeutschland im ausgehenden Mittelalter", in: *Minderstädte – Kümmerformen – Gefreite Dörfer*, ed. H. Knittler (Linz, 2006), pp. 181-200, and further articles in both volumes.

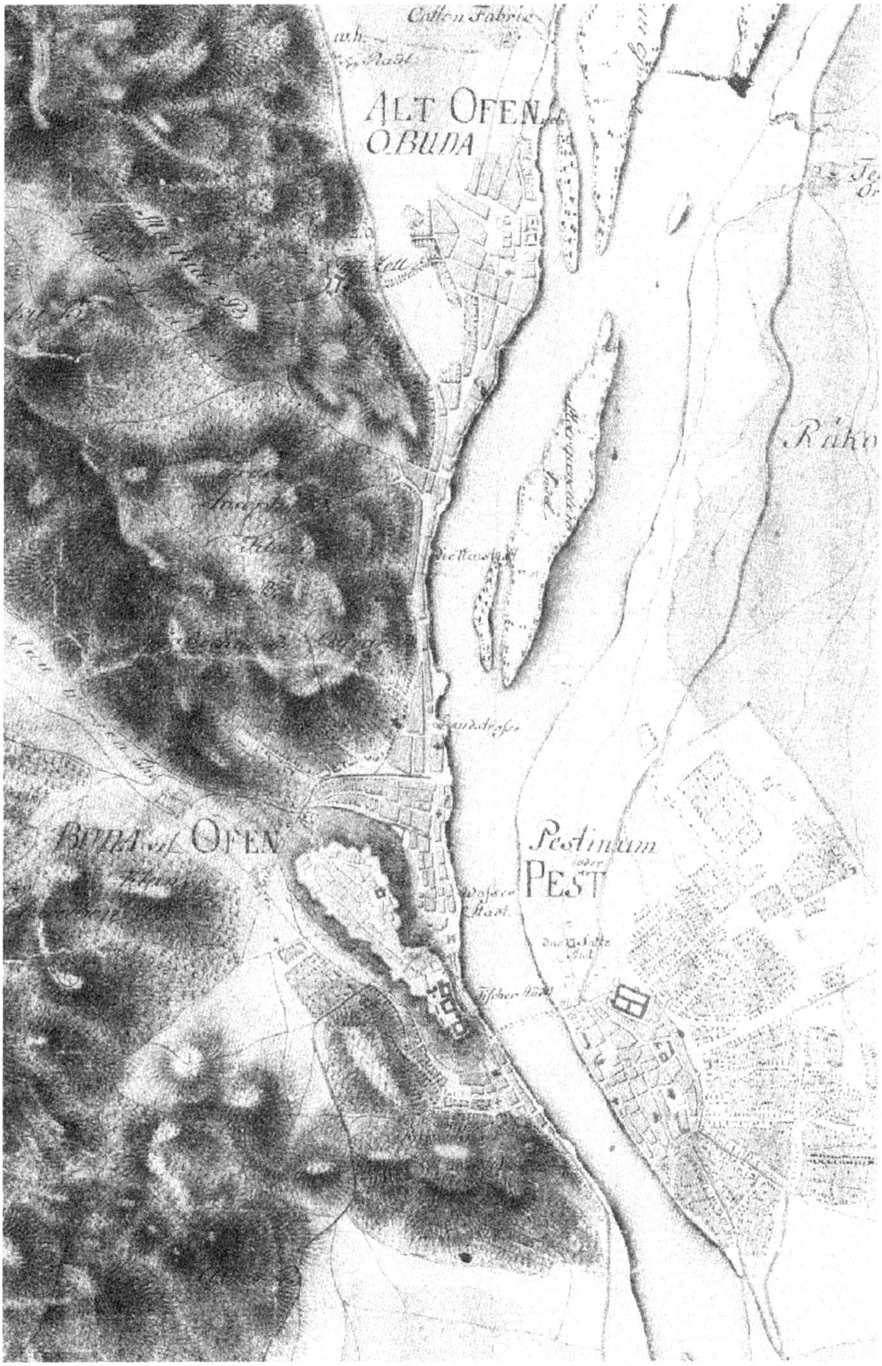

Fig. 7 Buda, Pest, and Óbuda as separate communities in the First Military Survey (Josephinische Landesaufnahme), Coll. XIV, Sect. XX, 1782-1785. Reproduced with the permission of the Institute of Military History, Budapest.

network of 'central places'.[25] In recent years, one of Kubinyi's last disciples, Bálint Lakatos, has completed the survey and used this as a background to his comprehensive analysis on the administrative literacy of private towns and market towns. His work, soon to be published, complements the present one on royal towns. This is a significant step forward, since – as Lakatos has convincingly shown – by the late Middle Ages many of these small communities also appear as issuers of documents and start to develop their own internal administration, like their bigger counterparts did a couple of centuries earlier. In the second half of the sixteenth century, even some smaller market towns started keeping municipal books as well.[26]

To sum up the late medieval situation in numbers, the urban network of the kingdom of Hungary (apart from Croatia and Dalmatia) at the beginning of the sixteenth century consisted of about 150 settlements that housed between 5 and 10 per cent of the population of the kingdom. This hierarchically structured system of central places included free royal towns, mining towns, the Saxon towns of Transylvania and Spiš, sixteen episcopal sees (including two archbishoprics), as well as a growing number of seigniorial towns or market towns in the private ownership of the king, the queen, or other private lay and ecclesiastical landowners. The urban appearance of the royal towns was beyond doubt, even if their population was fairly small, between 2000 and 7-8000 inhabitants; the agglomeration of Buda with its twin-town Pest and the older Óbuda housed a population of at least 15,000 (Fig. 7).

Pragmatic Approaches to Pragmatic Literacy

In medieval Hungary, as István Hajnal has already pointed out almost a century ago, literacy was confined to a great extent to legal and pragmatic issues, in towns and in other social contexts alike; or at least this is the segment that has come down to us to the greatest extent.[27] As we shall examine in

[25] On the peregrination, see A. KUBINYI, "Städtische Bürger und Universitätsstudium in Ungarn am Ende des Mittelalters", in: *Stadt und Universität im Mittelalter und in der frühen Neuzeit*, ed. E. MASCHKE and J. SYDOW (Sigmaringen, 1977: *Stadt in der Geschichte* 3), pp. 161-175. On the definition of central places based on a set of ten criteria, see A. KUBINYI, "Városhálózat a késő középkori Kárpát-medencében" [The urban network of the Carpathian Basin in the late Middle Ages], *Történelmi Szemle* 46 (2004), pp. 1-30.

[26] LAKATOS, "Hivatali írásbeliség", forthcoming as B. LAKATOS, *Mezővárosi oklevelek*.

[27] On other aspects of the use of the written word, see in general E. MADAS, "Írás, könyv és

Fig. 8 Dancing couple and a jester, painting presumably based on literary models in a burgher's house in Buda, Táncsics Mihály utca 24. Fresco in the collection of the Budapest History Museum. Reproduced with the permission of the Budapest History Museum.

greater detail below, the materials of the town archives consist almost exclusively of charters of privilege, statutes, judicial records, deeds and other documents on property transactions, and various accounts. The correspondence with the ruler, with other towns, and with the neighbouring noblemen is also centred on legal and economic affairs. Wherever archival materials of smaller communities or (very rarely) of private persons within the towns have come down to us, they also bear witness to litigation or economic activity.

This concentration on pragmatic matters, however, may be seen in a positive light: "The use of writing in daily life (pragmatic literacy) is considered

könyvhasználat a középkori Magyarországon, 1000-1526" [Writing, books and their uses in medieval Hungary], in: E. Madas and I. Monok, *A könyvkultúra Magyarországon a kezdetektől 1800-ig* [Book culture in Hungary from its beginnings to 1800] (Budapest, 2003), pp. 11-88, esp. pp. 54-57.

more important for the development of literate mentalities than the use of literate behaviour in matters religious or scholarly".[28] Nevertheless, the almost complete lack of references to literary works that flourished in towns of other European regions in the late Middle Ages shows the limitations of research possibilities on literate behaviour in medieval Hungary. Very few such works like town chronicles or praises of towns (*laudes urbium*) have come down to us (on these see Outlook 2 in Chapter 3), let alone poetry, drama, and other literary genres that were cultivated in the vernacular, and mostly in oral form.[29] In some rare instances evidence furnished by archaeology or art history can help us fill the gaps. For example, judging from an exceptionally preserved depiction featuring a dancing couple and a jester painted in the style of the Viennese Neidhard frescoes in one of the Buda burgher's houses,[30] motifs of courtly literature were not unknown to the urban elites in Hungarian towns either (Fig. 8).

Outside the pragmatic sphere, these limitations apply especially to secular literacy. In practically every town there existed a rich and varied tradition of ecclesiastical literacy, which is only seldom considered in its urban context. Liturgical books and collections of sermons are almost exclusively investigated in the context of intellectual history, theology, or codicology, with little regard to their lay audiences. When comparing the surviving material with items mentioned in last wills and inventories, one can see that, unfortunately, much of the original stock fell victim to destruction for various reasons, be it religious intolerance, changing liturgical practices, wars, or neglect. The lack of legal significance further weakened the chances of survival.[31]

A telling and probably typical example in this respect is that of the hospital chantry in Sopron, from which three inventories have survived from the 1570s and 1580s, the time of the local breakthrough of Lutheranism. Within eleven

[28] Preface to ADAMSKA and MOSTERT, *Literate Mentalities*, p. 3.

[29] On the logic of the survival of literary works, see I. HORVÁTH, "Magyar versek: mi veszett el?" [Hungarian poems: what has been lost?], in: *Ghesaurus: Tanulmányok Szentmártoni Szabó Géza hatvanadik születésnapjára* [Ghesaurus: Studies for Géza Szentmártoni Szabó's sixtieth birthday], ed. I. CSÖRSZ RUMEN (Budapest, 2010), pp. 83-98.

[30] See *Neidhartrezeption in Wort und Bild*, ed. G. BLASCHITZ (Krems, 2000: *Medium Aevum Quotidianum, Sonderband* 11).

[31] Cs. CSAPODI and K. CSAPODINÉ GÁRDONYI, *Bibliotheca Hungarica: Kódexek és nyomtatott könyvek Magyarországon 1526 előtt* [Codices and printed books in Hungary before 1526], 1-2, *Fönnmaradt kötetek* [Surviving volumes] (Budapest, 1988, 1993), 3, *Adatok elveszett kötetekről* [Data on lost volumes] (Budapest, 1994); for a case study, see the section on books in SZENDE, *Otthon a városban*, pp. 223-231.

Fig. 9 a-b Slate tablet with German writing samples on both sides from the Carmelite friary of Buda, Kapás u. 3. Excavation of Judit Benda, Budapest History Museum. Reproduced with the permission of the Budapest History Museum.

years, a fair number of liturgical vestments and three manuscripts out of the original four had disappeared or were crossed out from the third list compared to the first one.[32] However, the remaining pieces, together with the scrutiny of other written records, for instance last wills of townspeople who had ordered the copying or illumination of liturgical books, can provide insight into lay and ecclesiastical interaction in the social uses of the written word. An excellent example of such an approach is Juraj Šedivý's monograph on the literacy of the Pressburg Collegiate Chapter.[33]

Finally, one must also keep in mind that literacy in towns was not restricted to parchment and paper. Other forms and material manifestations of writing on stone, wood, clay, or metal were integral parts of the same intellectual framework. One just needs to think of the inscriptions on tombstones, church bells and baptismal fonts, which are also seldom regarded as witnesses of the alphabetisation process. Šedivý's above-mentioned book is pioneering in this respect, too: as part of his account, he presents the epigraphic remains as yet another form of the chapter's written culture.[34]

New archaeological excavations in Buda, the medieval capital, also underline the importance of non-parchment or paper-based writing. For instance, during the excavation of the Carmelite Friary in the north-eastern suburb, slate tablets with fragments of German words were found, showing educational practice and testifying to the fact that these friars were part of the German province of the Carmelites (Fig. 9).[35]

Another slate tablet, excavated from a well of a private house in the foreground of the Royal Palace of Buda, turned out to bear an inscription in Hebrew letters, and revealed the name of its owner, Chajjim Katz (Fig. 10). This proved, together with other datable materials, that the property was in Jewish ownership at the end of the fourteenth century – a conclusion that was con-

[32] K. SZENDE, "Spitalbesitz und Konfessionalisierung: Drei Inventare des Ödenburger (Soproner) Spitals aus den Jahren 1574, 1577 und 1585", in: *Stadt, Handwerk, Armut: Eine Quellensammlung zur Geschichte der Frühen Neuzeit: Festschrift für Helmut Bräuer*, ed. K. KELLER, G. DIESENER and G. VIERTEL (Leipzig, 2008), pp. 70-88.

[33] J. ŠEDIVÝ, *Mittelalterliche Schriftkultur im Pressburger Kollegiatkapitel* (Bratislava, 2007).

[34] ŠEDIVÝ, *Mittelalterliche Schriftkultur*, pp. 47, 79-81, 134-135, 176-177, 205-209, 225-227.

[35] J. BENDA, "A középkori karmelita kolostor feltárása Budán – The Excavation of the medieval Carmelite friary in Buda", in: *Régészeti kutatások Magyarországon 2002 – Archaeological Investigations in Hungary 2002*, ed. J. KISFALUDI (Budapest, 2004), pp. 117-130.

Fig. 10 Slate tablet with the name of Chajjim Katz, an inhabitant of the fourteenth-century *Platea Iudaeorum*, Buda, Szt. György tér. Excavation of András Végh, Budapest History Museum. Reproduced with the permission of the Budapest History Museum.

firmed a year later by finding the mikveh and the foundations of the synagogue in the same street.[36]

Sources and Scholarship

Most scholarly works that can be helpful for the present analysis were not conceived under the label of 'urban literacy', which is still a relatively new field of investigation in Hungary, but created as contributions to more tradi-

[36] A. Végh, "The remains of the first Jewish quarter of Buda in the light of recent excavations", in: *Régészeti kutatások Magyarországon 2005 – Archaeological Investigations in Hungary 2005*, ed. J. Kisfaludi (Budapest, 2006), pp. 125-148. On the literacy of the Jewish community, see Chapters 4 and 5 below.

tional fields of study, such as diplomatics, palaeography, or epigraphy. Nevertheless, the knowledge amassed in them can be put to very good use also in questions on literacy and on attitudes towards the written word.

The most extensively treated component of urban literacy in Hungary is undoubtedly the archival material. Until very recently, for a full overview of the available documents one had to rely on the registers of archival fonds provided by the archives themselves, which were often only available on the spot. In the last few years, however, this situation changed favourably, since the entire medieval holdings of the National Archives of Hungary up to 1526 have been made available on high-resolution digital photos partly with more or less detailed abstracts on the *Hungaricana* website. The site also includes photos of documents relating to medieval Hungary kept in the archives of the neighbouring countries. This collection was originally compiled as the result of a series of photographing campaigns in the 1970s and 1980s, coordinated by the late Iván Borsa (1917-2006). The current continuation of this research promises to offer high-resolution digital images of these documents instead of the old poor-quality black and white images. The extension of the systematic collection of materials related to medieval and early modern Hungary in Italy and Austria, among other countries, will no doubt increase the amount of available materials.[37] Another extremely useful digitising enterprise, the collaborative portal monasterium.net deserves a mention here, too. Started out, as its name indicates, as an on-line platform for documents kept in monastic collections, primarily in Austria, by now it has grown into a combined resource of more than 100 archives, collections and universities in Central Europe.[38]

Research conditions for the post-1526 period are improved by the (unfortunately only paper-based) publication of the volumes of Hungarian historical bibliography, initiated and for a long time edited by the late Domokos Kosáry (1913-2007). This project, which surveys all relevant materials and institutions in the Carpathian Basin, provides in its recently published Volume 4 a concise

[37] See https://archives.hungaricana.hu/en/charters/. The digitisation project was initiated and coordinated by Senior Archivist György Rácz, for which the entire research community owes him gratitude. A serious shortcoming of the original (DF) photography campaigns that is still to be corrected is the substandard-quality rendering of the municipal books, where even the order of the folios is often mixed up on the photos. Some medieval archival materials from Transylvania have recently been made available on the website www.arhivamedievala.ro. See the report on the presentation of this ongoing project by GY. RÁCZ in *Turul* 89 (2016), pp. 154-156.

[38] http://icar-us.eu/cooperation/online-portals/monasterium-net/ and http://monasterium.net/mom/home.

description of the holdings of all municipal archives.[39] The third volume deals with the county archives in a similar way, which, due to the close connections of some towns to the county administration, can also yield useful data.[40] Another useful regional overview is a lexicon surveying forty-seven towns of medieval origin in modern-day Slovakia. The volume pays special attention to the municipal seal, the writing offices (their personnel and output, including the municipal books) data which fall in the scope of the present volume.[41]

A further commendable feature of current scholarly output has been a revival of source publications – not only in the urban sphere. Both volumes of the Kosáry-series mentioned above include bibliographical data on the available source publications, which makes it unnecessary to give detailed references here. Instead, let me present a brief overview of the main tendencies. Although it may sound rather surprising, this seemingly neutral branch of historiography has been strongly influenced by the political situation of our region.

Taking stock of the written legacy of medieval towns goes back a long way; arranging the archival materials in a set order was already on the agenda in the medieval or the early modern period (Chapter 6 will enumerate the most instructive examples of this activity). In fact, urban administration showed a remarkable continuity between the late Middle Ages and the nineteenth century. Therefore, when the bourgeoisie asserted itself as the most potent political player on the European scene, they could easily use these documents to boast of a past that matched their (then) glorious present. Consequently, the first golden age of transcribing and editing materials from town archives were the three or four decades before World War I. This coincided with the flourishing of positivism and its sensitivity towards data and detail. Interestingly, Hungarian nationalism did not play much of a role in this movement, due to the lack of Hungarian as a written language of medieval documents (see Chapter 4).[42]

[39] D. Kosáry, K. Kulcsár, O. Szakály, *Bevezetés Magyarország történetének forrásaiba és irodalmába*, 1, *Általános rész.*, 4, *Városi levéltárak és forrásközlések.* [Introduction to the sources and literature of the history of Hungary, 1, General part, 4, Municipal archives and source publications] (Budapest, 2015).

[40] D. Kosáry, *Bevezetés Magyarország történetének forrásaiba és irodalmába*, 1, *Általános rész*, 3, *Megyei levéltárak és forrásközlések.* [Introduction to the sources and literature of the history of Hungary, 1, General part, 3, County archives and source publications] (Budapest, 2008).

[41] *Lexikon stredovekých miest na Slovensku* [Lexicon of medieval towns in Slovakia], ed. M. Štefánik and J. Lukačka (Bratislava, 2010).

[42] See, e.g. L. Fejérpataky, *Magyarországi városok régi számadáskönyvei* [Old account

Compared to this, the interwar period was clearly one of decline, when only isolated local initiatives survived, and even those with the ideological agenda of backing up modern claims for the political control of a territory. It is explicitly stated, for instance, in the introduction of Jenő Házi's otherwise excellent thirteen-volume publication of Sopron's medieval archival material, the first volume of which was published in 1921, that his purpose was to "deepen the unbroken fidelity in the souls of the contemporary inhabitants of the town towards Hungarian statehood".[43] Béla Iványi followed up his extensive pre-1920 work in the archives of Prešov and Bardejov with editing the registers of their medieval stock, and partially publishing the texts.[44] These publications served as the basis for sporadic studies on various aspects of urban literacy such as the use of heraldic symbols and the setting up of archives.[45] An early German example, not entirely void of contemporary biases, is the edition of the town book of Spisškà Nová Ves (Igló).[46]

After 1945, source-publication as a genre was regarded as of secondary importance compared to more conceptual monographs and studies. Initiatives, if any, came from abroad. The revival of the series *Urkundenbuch zur Geschichte der Deutschen in Siebenbürgen*, the edition of documents concerning the Saxons of Transylvania, who also populated most of the medieval towns in that region, was due to scholars who had emigrated from Romania to Germany.[47] The edition of several town books and mining laws from towns in

books of Hungarian towns] (Budapest, 1885); *Quellen zur Geschichte Siebenbürgens aus sächsischen Archiven*, 1, *Rechnungen aus dem Archiv der Stadt Hermannstadt und der Sächsischen Nation, 1380-1516*, (Hermannstadt, 1880); *Quellen zur Geschichte der Stadt Kronstadt*, 1, *Rechnungen, 1503-1526* (Kronstadt, 1886); *Quellen zur Geschichte der Stadt Kronstadt*, 2, *Rechnungen, 1526-1540* (Kronstadt, 1889); *Quellen zur Geschichte der Stadt Kronstadt*, 3, *Rechnungen, 1541-1550* (Kronstadt, 1886).

[43] *Sopron szabad királyi város története* [The history of the free royal town of Sopron], ed. J. Házi, 1.1-7, 2.1-6 (Sopron, 1921-1943). Quotation from 1.8 (Sopron, 1921). The referendum that decided Sopron's allegiance to the Hungarian state took place on 14-16 December 1921.

[44] Iványi, *Bártfa*; Iványi, *Eperjes*.

[45] M. Darvasy, *Középkori városaink címereinek eredete és fejlődése* [The origin and development of the coats of arms of medieval Hungarian towns] (Budapest, 1942); I. Pálffy, "Városi levéltáraink kezdetei" [The beginnings of municipal archives in Hungary], *Levéltári Közlemények* 18-19 (1940-1941), pp. 351-379.

[46] H. Weinelt, *Das Stadtbuch von Zipser Neudorf und seine Sprache: Forschungen zum Volkstum einer ostdeutschen Volksinselstadt* (München, 1940: *Veröffentlichungen des Südostinstituts* 20).

[47] *Urkundenbuch zur Geschichte der deutschen in Siebenbürgen*, ed. G. Gündisch, C. Werner, and F. Zimmermann, 9 vols. (Sibiu, Köln, Wien, and Bucharest, 1892-1991), henceforth: UGDS. The University of Trier offers online database-access to this material: http://

present-day Slovakia was initiated by the Finnish-born Germanist Ilpo Tapani Piirainen (1941-2012), from a strictly linguistic point of view (i.e. without historical apparatus), who regularly added the subtitle "*ein Beitrag zum Frühneuhochdeutschen in der Slowakei*" to his publications.[48] Unfortunately the neglect of the historical background sometimes resulted in misconceptions about the nature and purpose of some of these materials.[49] Parallel to this, Darina Lehotská (1922-1990) published thorough accounts of the development of urban chanceries and their personnel, laying the foundations of a fertile research tradition in diplomatics and archival studies in Slovakia.[50] An edition of charters of privilege granted to towns and market towns on the territory of modern-day Slovakia makes the sources available up to 1350. This is indeed the region where the largest number of such sources have survived. The edition carries the number I, but it has not been followed by further volumes.[51]

Some of the best-qualified scholars in Hungary for working on the edition of archival materials were historians who were dismissed from their teaching positions because they had been members of religious orders. An example is the rich collection of sources on the history of Buda and Pest in the Sigismund-period, compiled by Lajos Bernát Kumorovitz (1900-1992), a former Premonstratensian monk. Kumorovitz had already published important studies in

siebenbuergen-institut.de/special-menu/e-transylvanica/urkundenbuch-zur-geschichte-der-deutschen-in-siebenbuergen-online/.

48 The main editions of medieval manuscripts: *Das Stadtrechtsbuch von Sillein*, ed. I.T. PIIRAINEN (Berlin, 1972); *Das Iglauer Bergrecht nach einer Handschrift aus Schemnitz,* ed. I.T. PIIRAINEN (Heidelberg, 1980); *Das Stadt- und Bergrecht von Kremnitz*, ed. I.T. PIIRAINEN (Heidelberg, 1983); *Das Stadt- und Bergrecht von Schemnitz*, ed. I.T. PIIRAINEN (Oulu, 1986). The recently published register of German-language manuscripts, *Deutschsprachige Handschriften in slowakischen Archiven: Vom Mittelalter bis zur frühen Neuzeit*, ed. J. MEIER, K-P. WEGERA, and I.T. PIIRAINEN, 3 vols. (Berlin, 2009), takes the modern border of Slovakia as the framework of data collection, just as his overview "Městské knihy, právní knihy a soudní knihy: rukopisy ve slovenský archivech" [Town books, law books, court protocols: manuscripts in Slovak archives], in: *Stav a perspektivy*, pp. 125-136.

49 Some of these are pointed out and corrected by ŠEDIVÝ, "Deutschsprachige Beurkundung" p. 249, n. 10. Piirainen's disciples A. Ziegler and J. Meier continue their work following the same principles.

50 D. LEHOTSKÁ, "Vývoj Bratislavskej mestskej kancelárie do roku 1526" [The development of the municipal chancery of Pressburg up to 1526], *Historické Štúdie* 4 (1958), pp. 222-274; EAD., "K počatkom vedenia mestských kníh na Slovensku: Najstaršia bratislavská mestská kniha 1364-1538" [The beginnings of keeping municipal books in Slovakia: The oldest town book of Pressburg, 1364-1538], *Historické štúdie* 5 (1959), pp. 25-347.

51 *Výsady miest a mestečiek na Slovensku*, ed. Ľ. JUCK [Privileges of towns and market towns in Slovakia], 1, *(1238-1350)* (Bratislava, 1984, henceforth VMMS).

the interwar period on the use of authentic seals.[52] Beside him, Zsigmond Jakó (1916-2008), the most dedicated researcher of medieval Transylvanian written culture, must be mentioned.[53]

The year 1989 proved to be a turning point for source editions, too. New series were launched in several countries and international cooperation was strengthened.[54] A chronologically wide-ranging initiative is the already mentioned series *Quellen zur Geschichte der Stadt Ödenburg*, which publishes materials on Sopron from the fifteenth to the eighteenth century, with bilingual (German and Hungarian) introductions and critical apparatus.[55] Similarly bilingual editions have made available the guild regulations and statutes of Sibiu and Braşov in this case the German and Latin texts are complemented by Romanian translations.[56] Recent Slovak scholarship put special emphasis on editing town books from Trnava, has also published a modern edition of the earliest town book of Smolník, and has published studies on several others, too.[57]

The ambitious long-term plans of publishing abstracts of the entire archival material pertaining to Hungary in the Angevin- and Sigismund-periods (*Anjou-*

[52] *Budapest történetének okleveles emlékei – Monumenta diplomatica civitatis Budapest*, 3, *1382-1439*, ed. L.B. Kumorovitz (Budapest, 1987).

[53] See *infra*, p. 53, n. 70; Chapter 3, n. 65; and Chapter 6, n. 7.

[54] See, e.g. the edition project of town charters initiated by the International Commission for the History of Towns: EFHU 3.2 and EFHU 3.3.

[55] Since 1993, altogether 11 volumes have been published by the Sopron Archives of the National Archives of Hungary (formerly of Győr-Moson-Sopron county), including *Gerichtsbuch – Bírósági könyv, 1423-1531*, ed. J. Házi and J. Németh (Sopron, 2005: QGSÖ, *Reihe* A, 2); *Gedenkbuch – Feljegyzési könyv, 1492-1543*, ed. K. Mollay and K. Goda (Sopron, 2006: QGSÖ, *Reihe* A, 3).

[56] *Quellen zur Geschichte der Stadt Kronstadt*, 9, *Zunfturkunden*, ed. G. Nussbächer and E. Marin (Braşov, 1999); *Quellen zur Geschichte der Stadt Hermannstadt*, 2, *Handel und Gewerbe in Hermannstadt und in den Sieben Stühlen*, ed. M. Vlaicu *et al.* (Sibiu, 2003). The register book of the goldsmiths' guild of Cluj (Klausenburg, Kolozsvár), written in Hungarian, is published by Á. Flóra, "Kolozsvári ötvösregesztrum 1549-1790", *Lymbus* 2003, pp. 25-74.

[57] V. Rábik, *Mestská kniha Trnavy (1392/93) 1394-1530* [The town book of Trnava, (1392/1393) 1394-1530] (Trnava, 2008); R. Marsina, "Mestské knihy na Slovensku v stredoveku" [Town books in Slovakia in the Middle Ages], in: *Stav a perspektívy*, pp. 107-116; V. Rábik, "Libri beneficiorum farnosti sv. Mikuláša v Trnave z rokov 1481-1495" [Book of church benefices of the St. Nicholas parish in Trnava 1481-1495], *ibid.* pp. 327-336. V. Rábik, *Trnavas – Tyrnaus mittelalterliche Stadtbücher* (Kraków, 2013); H. Lisková, "Mesto Banská Bystrica a jeho obyvatelia na základe záznamov v najstaršej mestskej knihe" [The town of Banská Bystrica and its inhabitants in the first preserved town book from 1386-1399], in: *Minulosť a prítomnosť Banskej Bystrice pri príležitosti 750. výročia mesta* [The past and present of Banská Bystrica on the occasion of the 750th anniversary of the town], ed. I. Nagy, 2 vols. (Banská Bystrica, 2005), pp. 53-69.

kori oklevéltár and *Zsigmondkori oklevéltár*, respectively) also have a strong relevance for urban documents, but only address a Hungarian-speaking audience, as does the publication of sources from Transylvania, the *Erdélyi okmánytár*. The leading personalities in these enterprises are Ferenc Piti, Norbert C. Tóth, András W. Kovács, and Géza Hegyi, with László Veszprémy as the director of the project.[58] At the same time, international co-operation also promoted the publication of documents related to civic literacy, especially municipal books.[59]

At present, we are experiencing the 'digital turn', just like anywhere else in the world. Beside the electronic availability of substantial corpora of original archival materials, the most recent source editions often contain a digital appendix, or are exclusively in that form. A good example for the former is the publication of the guild book and charters of the Buda butchers; for the latter the customs registers of Sibiu attached to Mária Pakucs-Willcocks's monograph on Levantine trade.[60] Most of these editions are complemented by introductory studies that present the manuscripts in the context of local administrative literacy. In the future one can expect a growing number of exclusively digital source editions, especially since some source corpora, particularly the voluminous series of account books, do not lend themselves easily to printed editions. Similar trends can be observed in other countries of East Central Europe, including the dilemma of publishing either according to the modern political boundaries or with respect to historic regions or polities.

The question of linguistic, ethnic, and political boundaries is made even more complex by the geographically uneven survival of the sources. Due to the Ottoman occupation and the following re-conquest campaign, most collections of urban records in the territory of present-day Hungary were destroyed, apart from those of Sopron and the smaller Kőszeg, both by the western border. Towns in the northern and eastern parts of the kingdom, in modern Slovakia and Romania, as well as certain parts of Croatia, on the other hand, got away with relatively small losses. This means that anyone doing research on the Carpathian Basin must generalise from these surviving pieces of evidence. This is indeed not an easy task: whereas the Middle Ages had its own *lingua franca*,

[58] These publication series are available online under https://library.hungaricana.hu/en/.

[59] See, e.g. *Acta iudiciaria civitatis Cassoviensis 1393-1405*, ed. O.R. Halaga (München, 1994, *Buchreihe der Südostdeutschen Historischen Kommission* 34); PT 1-2.

[60] M. Pakucs-Willcocks, *Sibiu-Hermannstadt: Oriental Trade in Sixteenth Century Transylvania* (Köln, Weimar, and Wien, 2007: *Städteforschung* A 73), with the customs registers as an appendix on CD-ROM.

Latin, and in the urban context German functioned in a similar way, the modern researcher would need to master almost a dozen languages to follow the current results. Paradoxically, it often seems easier to return to the roots and read the sources themselves than to make use of our colleagues' contributions. Nevertheless, it makes little sense to use the present borders as boundaries of research areas; instead, cooperation is the only viable path to proceed.

From other fields of textual studies, codicology has had relatively little to offer for the research on urban administrative literacy, or even for the study of other sorts of texts. The catalogues of modern collections contain only scant material of urban origin, and even those volumes are usually removed from their original context. One of the notable exceptions is the 75-volume library of the parish church of Bardejov, which was moved, together with its monumental lime-wood cabinet, to the National Museum in Budapest in 1915.[61] Another possibility can be the reconstitution of the former stocks of medieval urban libraries, a task that Juraj Šedivý undertook for the Collegiate Chapter of Pressburg, uniting in his work the volumes dispersed nowadays in several different collections.[62] A third direction of research, painstaking but rewarding, can be to collect fragments of codices later used for bookbinding, a work that has been done for several decades by the project *Fragmenta et codices in bibliothecis Hungariae* of the *Res libraria research group* of the National Széchényi Library in Budapest.[63] Finally, studying the bindings themselves can reveal much information on the provenance and later use of the manuscripts.[64]

Another field of traditional textual scholarship with ample urban connotations is epigraphy. As briefly noted above regarding the forms and materials of literacy, inscriptions preserved on stone or metal objects have a rich research potential, although less directly pertaining to municipal literacy. So far, several specialised collections of material have been assembled or are under way. Zoltán Váradi and Pál Lővei have collected the inscriptions of gravestones,

[61] J. ÁBEL, *A bártfai Sz. Egyed templom könyvtárának története* [The history of the library of St. Giles church at Bardejov] (Budapest, 1885); J. KOVALOVSZKI, *Gothic and Renaissance Furniture* (Budapest, 1980), pp. 6-13.

[62] ŠEDIVÝ, *Mittelalterliche Schriftkultur*, pp. 39-43, 54-57, 140-162, 181-201, 212-217, with edition of the inventory of the chapter treasury, including its 83 manuscripts in 1425-1432, pp. 278-280.

[63] E. MADAS, "Fragmenta codicum in bibliothecis Hungariae (Egy középkori forrásterület rendszeres feltárásáról)" [The systematic exploration of a group of medieval sources], *Aetas* 23 (2008), pp. 101-115.

[64] The binding has been described in several publications of municipal books by Marianne Rozsondai, and she often identified the watermarks of the paper used for these books, too.

also surveying their art historical qualities and the social status of the persons that they commemorate.[65] Juraj Šedivý has initiated the collection of the epigraphic material from present-day Slovakia (*Corpus inscriptionum Slovaciae*), and has published a comprehensive methodological guide as well.[66]

Research on bells and their inscriptions can be regarded a special sub-field of epigraphic research as well as campanology, pursued in Slovakia by Juraj Gembický and Juraj Šedivý.[67] For Transylvania, bells and baptismal fonts have been collected and published by Elek Benkő.[68] When dealing with inscriptions on metal objects, the publications of coins can also be relevant, especially with regards to those towns which were sites of minting for longer or shorter periods. The work of Lajos Huszár on minting in Buda is the most comprehensive study in this field.[69] Sphragistics can yield data both on the municipal seals and their inscriptions, and on their use on various kinds of documents. This question will be discussed in detail in the next chapter.

Finally, a branch of scholarship dealing with scripts that can also contribute to the study of medieval civic literacy is palaeography and diplomatics. In the last few decades, several general overviews of palaeographical research in the Carpathian Basin have been compiled, which provide guidance for the analysis of urban documents as well.[70] A regional research project in Transylvania

[65] Z. Váradi, *Románkori, korai gótikus és gótikus feliratok a Dunántúlon* [Romanesque, early Gothic and Gothic inscriptions in Transdanubia], 2 vols (Szekszárd, 1999-2000); L. Varga and P. Lővei, "Funerary art in medieval Hungary", *Acta Historiae Artium* 35 (1992), pp. 115-167.

[66] *Latinská epigrafia: Dejiny a metodika výskumu historických nápisov zo Slovenska* [Latin epigraphy: The history and methodology of research on historical inscriptions in Slovakia], ed. J Šedivý *et al.* (Bratislava, 2014; *Corpus Inscriptionum Slovaciae – Súpis nápisov zo Slovenska* 1.1). The collection is organised on the basis of counties; one volume (Šariš county) is already available, another one (Nitra county) is in press.

[67] J. Gembický, "Research of the bells in Slovakia – Source for epigraphy", in: *The History of Written Culture*, pp. 106-112; J. Šedivý, "Písmo na stredovekých zvonoch z územia Slovenska" [Inscriptions on medieval bells of the territory of Slovakia], *Monument revue* 4.2 (2015), pp. 26-34.

[68] E. Benkő, *Erdély középkori harangjai és bronz keresztelőmedencéi* [Medieval bronze bells and baptismal fonts from Transylvania] (Budapest and Kolozsvár, 2002).

[69] L. Huszár, *A budai pénzverés története a középkorban* [The history of minting in medieval Buda] (Budapest, 1958); on further mints and their administration in the late Middle Ages, see M. Gyöngyössy, *Pénzgazdálkodás és monetáris politika a késő középkori Magyarországon* [Money economy and monetary policy in late medieval Hungary] (Budapest, 2003).

[70] S. Jakó and R. Manolescu, *Scrierea latină în evul mediu* [Latin script in the Middle Ages] (București, 1971); Zs. Jakó and R. Manolescu, *A latin írás története* [The history of Latin script] (Budapest, 1987); J. Šedivý, "Forschungen der mittelalterlichen lateinischen Schrift

has concentrated on the social uses of writing across all strata of society, from bishops to peasants, with special regard to the scribes as promoters of pragmatic literacy. The studies traverse the traditional boundaries between the Middle Ages and the early modern period – in fact, most of the material that allows in-depth investigation dates to the sixteenth and seventeenth centuries.[71]

The best case studies highlight the development in Sopron and Pressburg, by Jenő Házi and Károly Mollay, and by Darina Lehotská and Juraj Šedivý respectively.[72] These studies testify that the identification of hands with documents and scribes can shed light on the professionalisation of writing and the way work was distributed between a growing and more differentiated chancery personnel. The organisation of town chanceries can also be highlighted on the basis of the documents issued by them. This process has been traced in several towns of present-day Slovakia and has also been discussed as a parallel development with regard to Sopron and Pressburg.[73] The same question has been taken up from a social historical point of view by older and more recent archontological studies, which collect data on notaries, scribes and other personnel. Such information is available for Banská Bystrica, Bratislava, Cluj, Koši-

in der Slowakischen Republik", in: *The History of Written Culture*, pp. 19-32; L. VESZPRÉMY, "Zum Stand der paläographischen Forschungen in Ungarn", *ibid.*, pp. 33-51.

[71] *Scris i societate în Transilvania secolelor XIII-XVII* [Writing and society in Transylvania, thirteenth-seventeenth centuries], ed. S. ANDEA (Cluj-Napoca, [2015]), with contributions by A. ANDEA, A. DINCĂ and L. MAGINA.

[72] J. HÁZI, "A városi kancellária kialakulása Sopronban" [The emergence of the town chancery in Sopron], *Soproni Szemle* 10 (1956), pp. 202-215. K. MOLLAY, "Többnyelvűség a középkori Sopronban – a latin nyelv" [Multilingualism in medieval Sopron – the Latin language] *Soproni Szemle* 21 (1967), pp. 155-171, 205-223, 317-333 and *Soproni Szemle* 22 (1968), pp. 37-58, 130-150. K. GODA, "A városi igazgatás szerkezete Sopronban a középkor végén" [The structure of municipal government in Sopron in the late Middle Ages], *Soproni Szemle* 61 (2007), pp. 255-271. LEHOTSKÁ, Vývoj Bratislavskej mestskej kancelárie; J. ŠEDIVÝ, "Die Anfänge der Beurkundung im mittelalterlichen Pressburg (Bratislava)", in: *Wege zur Urkunde, Wege der Urkunde, Wege der Forschung: Beiträge zur europäischen Diplomatik des Mittelalters*, ed. K. HRUZA and P. HEROLD (Wien, Köln, and Weimar, 2005), pp. 81-115.

[73] J. ROHÁČ, "Entstehung der Amtsbücher in der Slowakei", in: *La diplomatique urbaine en Europe au moyen âge*, ed. TH. DE HEMPTINE and W. PREVENIER (Louvain and Apeldoorn 2000), pp. 407-417. *Diplomatická produkcia v stredovekom meste* [Production of documents in medieval towns], ed. J. RAGAČOVÁ (Bratislava, 2005), with studies on Zvolen, Kežmarok, Spišská Sobota, Poprad, Rožňava, Banská Bystrica, etc.; K. GODA and J. MAJOROSSY, "Städtische Selbstverwaltung und Schriftproduktion im spätmittelalterlichen Königreich Ungarn – Eine Quellenkunde für Ödenburg und Preßburg", *Pro civitate Austriae* 13 (2008), pp. 60-98.

ce, Kőszeg, Sibiu and Sopron, but the lists before the sixteenth century are rather incomplete.[74]

A connection to be investigated with the toolkit of palaeography is the link between scriptoria and chanceries, that is, between book culture and pragmatic literacy. This means that even if book hands and charter hands were distinct from each other in palaeographical terms, the same persons or the same workshops could stand behind them. This was nicely proven by Juraj Šedivý in the case of the Pressburg chapter by surveying the entire written legacy of this ecclesiastical body. That the 'audience', that is the users of both forms of literacy often overlapped, can be proven by those instances when townspeople ordered in their last wills (committed to writing by the town notary) to produce liturgical books for the use of the local chapter, parishes or altars.[75]

[74] See the overview by I.H. Németh, "Az archontológia és a várostörténet: Karrierek és hatalmi csoportok a kora újkori városokban (XVI-XVIII. század)" [Archontology and urban history: Careers and power groups in early medieval towns (sixteenth-seventeenth centuries)], *Fons: Forráskutatás és történeti segédtudományok* 11 (2004), pp. 197-218.

[75] Šedivý, *Mittelalterliche Schriftkultur*, pp. 140-162, 181-201, 212-217; M.-M. De Cevins, *L'Église dans les villes hongroises à la fin du moyen-âge (vers 1320 - vers 1490)* (Budapest, Paris, and Szeged, 2003: *Publications de l'Institut Hongrois de Paris, Dissertationes* 1), pp. 234-241.

Chapter 2

In the First-Person Plural: Civic Literacy and Communal Identity[1]

"*Nos Iakmynus maior ville ceterique cives de vico Strigoniensi tenore presentium significamus universis* ...". These are the opening words of the first arguably authentic document issued by an urban community in Hungary, dated 1255 at Esztergom.[2] This document was then followed by further products of civic literacy, first sporadically and then more and more frequently, up to our times. This chapter sets out to investigate how trust in writing and the need for using written documents appeared in the towns of medieval Hungary, and how documents issued by municipal authorities gained probative value and became 'trustworthy'. This also leads to the question how early written documents connected to or issued by towns contributed to creating and strengthening the sense of local autonomy in the towns of Hungary from the mid-thirteenth century onwards. Autonomy, in its turn, provided the basis for identity, a concept more difficult to define with the help of contemporary sources.

Pragmatic literacy was not the only, and certainly not the most conspicuous form of identity-building. Urban space and its various uses, as recent research has amply shown, had a much stronger visual impact and broader reach: it suffices to think of town walls, town halls and the – literally – prominent par-

[1] A shorter version of this chapter was published in Hungarian as K. Szende, "A magyar városi írasbeliség kezdetei" [The beginnings of urban literacy in Hungary], in: *Arcana tabularii: Tanulmányok Solymosi László tiszteletére* [*Arcana tabularii*: Studies in honor of László Solymosi], ed. A. Bárány, G. Dreska and K. Szovák (Budapest and Debrecen, 2014), pp. 435-458.

[2] EFHU 3.2, No. 40.

ish churches as landmarks and as nodal points of community life.[3] Nevertheless, no other genre of visual or verbal communication uses so plainly and explicitly the prime expression of community: the first person plural, the communal 'we', as the charters issued by the towns.[4] This is why the discussion of civic literacy needs to take them as its point of departure.

Royal Charters and Urban Identity

A fundamental instrument in the process of acquiring autonomy was the town charter or charter of privilege. As shown in the previous chapter, liberties were granted to towns in a written form by the kings of Hungary from the beginning of the thirteenth century onwards (the confirmation of privileges to Dalmatian cities are not discussed here).[5] Town charters addressed the inhabitants of an already existing or newly created settlement as emerging communities, and endowed them with rights and duties. At the outset, in the thirteenth century these documents were issued almost exclusively by the kings or by members of the royal family. For example, the dukes of Slavonia, the issuers of several early charters of privilege on their territory, were often sons or younger brothers of the ruling monarch. Noblemen or ecclesiastical bodies had only very limited rights to grant liberties to their private towns, but when they did so, they also used first person plural in their charters.[6]

[3] *Bild und Wahrnehmung der Stadt,* ed. F. OPLL (Linz, 2004: *Beiträge zur Geschichte der Städte Mitteleuropas* 18); *Bild und Wahrnehmung der Stadt*, ed. P. JOHANEK (Köln, Weimar, and Wien, 2012: *Städteforschung* A 63); DE CEVINS, *L'Église*, pp. 23-48.

[4] A note on terminology: 'charter' (*oklevél*) in the traditional usage of Hungarian historiography refers to any document – or even more generally, any piece of writing issued or produced before the Battle of Mohács, 29 August 1526 (!). In cases when it is difficult to specify the character of a document according to the English usage, I shall also use the word 'charter' in this general sense.

[5] E. FÜGEDI, "Középkori magyar városprivilégiumok" [Medieval Hungarian town privileges], *Tanulmányok Budapest Múltjából* 14 (1961), pp. 17-107, reprinted in ID., *Kolduló barátok, polgárok, nemesek* (Budapest 1981), pp. 238-311, 493-509 (notes below will refer to the page numbers of this edition). On charters for *hospites*: L. SOLYMOSI, *A földesúri járadékok új rendszere a 13. századi Magyarországon* [The new system of seigniorial revenues in thirteenth-century Hungary] (Budapest, 1998), pp. 7-18; K. SZENDE, "Power and identity: Royal privileges to the towns of medieval Hungary in the thirteenth century", in: *Urban Liberties and Civic Participation from the Middle Ages to Modern Times,* ed. M. PAULY and A. LEE (Trier, 2015: *Beiträge zur Landes- und Kulturgeschichte* 9), pp. 27-67.

[6] SOLYMOSI, *Földesúri járadékok*, pp. 10-11; 214-256, *passim*.

Hungarian towns and their inhabitants in the thirteenth century enjoyed rights comparable to those of West European towns from the late eleventh century onwards: the right to elect their own representatives and to be judged by them; to enjoy exemption from the compulsory provisioning of the main dignitaries; and to be able to move freely from one settlement to another. In exchange, they were obliged to pay taxes to the king and to perform military service.[7] The principal distinguishing feature of town privileges, namely the connection between rights and the ownership of a well-defined piece of land, the burgage plot as part of the town's territory – and not birth, as in case of the nobility, or special vows, as in the case of the clergy – found its way into legal regulations and practice alike. These ideas, alongside with issues of autonomy and self-governance, were most likely transmitted by new settlers (*hospites*), without any single group providing a definitive model for the entire realm or large parts of it.

Some ten charters of privilege have survived from before 1241, and there are references to at least a further five; between 1242 and 1270 at least twenty-seven, and until 1300 a further fourteen settlements or settler communities were given royal charters. The process continued by chartering further towns in the fourteenth and fifteenth centuries, although at a slower pace. Furthermore, the contents of these documents became more extensive and systematic. The town charters included commercial prerogatives, allowing for holding weekly markets and waiving customs duties for the burghers in a well-defined region of the kingdom; ecclesiastical privileges, that is the right to elect their own parish priest; but first and foremost an extensive set of justiciary measures. The immunity from the county leader's (*comes, ispán*) authority, and the right to be tried in their own court with the involvement of witnesses of the same standing, had been corner-stones of urban autonomy for centuries in towns of Western Europe. These were now, for the first time, introduced in connection with Hungarian towns as well. The right to elect a local leader (termed *villicus, maior villae,* or *iudex* in the various documents), a council, and especially the community's own parish priest were particular elements that developed locally as a result of negotiations between the monarchs and the people settling on their lands. In other words, civic communities as such were

[7] G. DILCHER, "Stadtherrschaft oder kommunale Freiheit – Das 11. Jahrhundert ein Kreuzweg?", in: ID., *Bürgerrecht und Stadtverfassung*, pp. 39-64; B. DIESTELKAMP, "Freiheit der Bürger – Freiheit der Stadt", in: *Die Abendländische Feiheit vom 10. zum 14. Jahrhundert*, ed. J. FRIED (Sigmaringen, 1991: *Vorträge und Forschungen* 39), pp. 485-510.

formed already in the process of being chartered. In the context of municipal literacy, the issuing of these charters is important not only for their legal significance, but because they introduced 'literate' thinking into a formally 'pre-literate' social milieu.

In these charters of privilege, the first person plural was used by way of the so-called *pluralis maiestatis* by the issuers, the monarchs themselves. The kings often referred to the beneficiaries of the privileges in the first person plural of the possessive pronoun, as *hospites nostri* or *cives nostri*. This was, again, a usual phenomenon under the conditions of medieval rulership. Kings and princes considered their subjects personally 'theirs' – especially when the given persons were close to the seat of power, addressing them as *fideles barones nostri* or the like, even if *fidelitas* was often more in the realm of wishful thinking, as in case of the late Árpádian rulers or in the first decades of Charles I's reign. In the rest of the text, the persons enjoying the prerogatives or charged with the duties inferred by the town charters were mentioned in the third person plural – *ipsi* ('they') – implying that the king promulgated his regulations in very general terms – 'to whom it may concern' – or to a third party, whose responsibility it was to respect the king's intentions towards the *cives et hospites*. Several authorities had to be ordered as 'third parties' to respect the rights of the emerging communities. Most frequently mentioned were the leaders of administrative units, the royal counties (*comitatus*, *Gespanschaft*) in which the given town was situated. These officials' authority was seriously curtailed by immunities granted to different groups of society, including the *hospites*, in the thirteenth century.[8]

Ecclesiastical and secular landowners also had to obey the king's command concerning his settlers when, for instance, exemption from customs and tolls or the freedom from offering compulsory hospitality (*descensus*) to the major dignitaries of the realm was on the agenda.[9] The king's own officials were no exception either: their judicial authority and use of the resources of the privileged communities was severely restricted. The addressees of the charters also included foreigners, especially foreign merchants who also had to follow the market regulations and incidental trade restrictions. Town charters defined *cives et hospites* as distinct from all these groups; before the new settlers could find out who they were as a community, it was already made clear who they were *not*.

8 On the transformation of the royal counties: SZENDE, "Von der Gespanschaftsburg".
9 SOLYMOSI, *Földesúri járadékok*, pp. 55-73.

Royal will certainly dominated the scope and formulation of the charters, but it was not the only power at work. Recent research tends to interpret these documents not as one-sided declarations of royal grace, but as the results of negotiations between the settlers and the ruler, with rights and obligations for both parties.[10] The concessions granted by the king represented an ultimate compromise between the expectations of the townsfolk and the endeavours of the seignior to improve the profitability of his domain and to ensure efficient governance. With careful analysis, it is possible to trace the influence that the community played in the shaping of town charters: their trading preferences, their aim to extend the land belonging to the settlement, their struggle to find the most favourable way of collecting tithes, and not least their detailed and not at all identical considerations for the election, rotation and eventual deposition of their leaders. These signs show that by the time they received the privileges, some of the future burghers already acted together as a group with distinct interests.

One further point worth a brief mention here with respect to identity-building is the custom of borrowing or requesting the liberties of another settlement. Such a move meant aligning the new communities with an older and more powerful urban centre, the standing of which appeared to be desirable to another community. This often reflected the desire for a point of reference rather than ambitions to emulate the model. Peculiarly for East Central Europe, no reference was made in charters of privilege in thirteenth-century Hungary to any foreign city, neither in the vicinity nor further away. Such references were extremely rare even in the fourteenth century, and were justified only if they were connected to the transfer of technology, as in case of Kutná Hora to Kremnica: "*in ceteris autem omnibus eisdem libertatibus, quibus de Kutunbana regni Bohemie existunt, iidem hospites nostri perpetuo perfruuntur*" ("otherwise our *hospites* should benefit from all those liberties that Kutná Hora in the kingdom of Bohemia has").[11]

[10] Fügedi, "Városprivilégiumok", pp. 258-280; Solymosi, *Földesúri járadékok*, pp. 7-18; in general: G. Dilcher, *Bürgerrecht und Stadtverfassung im europäischen Mittelalter* (Köln, Weimar, and Wien, 1996); E. Isenmann, *Die deutsche Stadt im Mittelalter 1150-1550* (Wien, Köln, and Weimar, 2012), pp. 173-181.

[11] VMMS p. 115; M. Štefanik, "Die Pivilegierung der Kremnitzer Bevölkerung unter besonderer Berücksichtigung der Münzer-Privilegien und ihre sozioökonomischen Zusammenhänge (1328-1526)", in: *Montanregion als Sozialregion*, ed. A. Westermann (Husum, 2012), pp. 437-456.

The small town of Žilina on the north-western edge of the kingdom, which was founded following the laws of nearby Teschen (just across the border), was ordered by king Louis I in 1369 to abandon this legal link and find a mother-town inside Hungary instead: "*quia ipsa civitas Tessen est in alio regno constituta, et ob hoc indecens exstitit eis ad illud regnum in requisitionem justitiae transcurrere*" ("because the city of Teschen is in another realm, and it is inappropriate to run over to them to that realm to seek justice").[12] On this demand, their choice fell on Krupina, a community whose privileges from 1244 provided favourable conditions for non-Hungarian groups, stating that only testimonies with the participation of Germans have full validity.[13] Krupina was consulted in cases of appeal both by Žilina and Martin in Turóc County and Varín in Trencsén County;[14] but no evidence of the same has survived from the settlements around it, which previously followed Žilina in appealing to Teschen.

As already mentioned in the previous chapter, the absence of explicit references to the city of Magdeburg and Magdeburg law in the major royal towns of Hungary is particularly conspicuous, although the concept of Magdeburg law was known and copies of its manuscript were available in several town chanceries. Notably, the term *iure teutonico* was only used for settling villages. Only a narrow strip of the northernmost region, including Krupina and consequently Žilina, took over elements of Magdeburg law, but without referring to Magdeburg as court of appeal. Instead, the most frequently mentioned liberties were those of Fehérvár, the traditional coronation city of the Hungarian kings, and from the end of the thirteenth century Buda, the newly emerging capital. The law of Buda itself developed from the South-German legal idioms.[15]

[12] CDH 11, pp. 528-532; FÜGEDI, "Városprivilégiumok", pp. 293-295

[13] *Codex diplomaticus et epistolaris Slovaciae*, 2, ed. R. MARSINA (Bratislava, 1987), No. 168; FÜGEDI, "Városprivilégiumok", pp. 294-295. The town of Korpona – apparently at the request of Žilina – sent them a detailed description of their rights and prerogatives in 1370, CDH 11, pp. 522-524.

[14] I owe special thanks to Bálint Lakatos for calling my attention to these references. Martin: DF 283574-283575, LAKATOS, *Adattár*, s.v. Martin, Nos. 3 and 4; Varín: DL 73150. M. MAREK, *Archivum familiae Majténi: Stredoveké dejiny rodiny Majténiovcov a listiny z jej archívu* [The medieval history of the Majtényi family and documents from their archive] (Trnava and Kraków, 2013; *Fontes rerum Slovacarum* 3), LAKATOS, *Adattár*, s.v. Varin, No. 3.

[15] A rare exception is the renewal of the charter of Sopron in 1317, when both models (Buda and Fehérvár) were mentioned in parallel: 1317, November 12: CDH 8.2, pp. 73-76. See also the map in MAGOCSI, *Historical Atlas*, p. 40.

Urban communities, however, were not the only ones to receive privileges in increasing number from the thirteenth century onwards. A detailed study of thirteenth-century privileges revealed that the subjects tackled by the privileges and the regulations prescribed fitted well into the series of charters issued in favour of other social groups of the time: the nobility and the clergy. The most important such liberties were the immunity from the jurisdiction of the *ispán*s in charge of the counties as local administrative units; the exemption from the *descensus* mentioned above; testamentary freedom; and the duty to send soldiers to the king's army, but only within the borders of the realm, for defensive purposes.[16] Thus the towns did not represent a fundamentally different 'foreign body' in contemporary society, but fitted into its administrative framework. The main difference was in the way of access to the prerogatives. Members of the nobility enjoyed privileges as individuals, either by birth into a noble family or by royal grace elevating them to noble rank. Clerics owed their special standing in society to their vows, by which they associated themselves to the Church. Burghers, in their turn, became beneficiaries of privileges as members of a community of ownership: rights were connected to the possession of a well-delimited piece of land, the burgage plot as part of the town's territory.[17] These special features of community-building discussed here had a strong impact on the way civic literacy emerged and spread to more and more spheres of urban life.

The Beginnings of Civic Literacy

In order to make full use of the rights obtained through the charters and to comply with the duties listed, urban communities had to familiarise themselves with the use of writing. Exercising urban autonomy and setting up town chanceries and archives closely hung together, as András Kubinyi has already shown using the example of Buda over fifty years ago.[18] As will be discussed

[16] SZENDE, "Power and identity", pp. 50-61.

[17] See Chapter 3 on the administration of the right of citizenship and the admission of new burghers.

[18] A. KUBINYI, "Buda város pecséthasználatának kialakulása" [The emergence of the use of seals in the town of Buda], *Tanulmányok Budapest Múltjából* 14 (1961), pp. 109-146. Reprinted in: ID., *Tanulmányok Budapest középkori történetéről* [Studies on the medieval history of Budapest], pp. 271-298 (references are given to page numbers of the reprint edition, also available online: https://library.hungaricana.hu/hu/view/BFLV_Vt_2009_TanBudKozepkorTort_1/?pg=272

in this and the following chapters, this does not imply a rapid and simultaneous development, but rather a gradual one. On the one hand, without autonomy there would not have been need and incentive to establish such institutions as writing offices and, later, municipal archives. On the other hand, without appropriate record management, the framework provided by the town charter and further documents could not have been fully utilised. In the following, I will present an overview of the emergence of active municipal literacy, from the mid-thirteenth century onwards. In other words, I will examine the process how written administration, including the possibility of retrieving and reproducing information whenever needed developed, and how the notion of 'we', that is, a community, grammatically expressed by the first person plural, acquired prominence and deeper meaning.

The operation and structure of both main institutions of civic literacy, the chancery and the archives, can be investigated primarily through indirect evidence, namely the documents issued by and kept in them respectively. As has been discussed in the Introduction, the uneven survival of the documents poses limitations to our work. The material at our disposal now is only a fraction of what was produced in the past. Even so, it can be instructive to start with a look at the chronological and geographical distribution of the earliest documents issued by the town authorities (see Appendix 3).

As for the time-factor, after the first sporadic traces from the 1250s to the 1280s, the written output of towns took off from the 1290s. The first document supposedly issued by the *hospites* of Dubica in 1244 is in my view not authentic, and therefore needs to be subjected to stronger criticism than has been done so far.[19] In the first decades of the fourteenth century the number of documents steadily increased, and by setting up town books and protocols in the second half of the fourteenth century it reached a different qualitative phase. The first wave of royal deeds granting *hospes*- and town charters was followed by a period of growth: not counting the ones reissued for the same settlement, forty-eight such charters of privilege are known to have been issued by 1290.[20] This

&layout=s.

[19] Dubica 1244: DL 35139; 35141-35143. One of the suspicious elements is, that the text refers to properties given to the local Pauline monastery that could not have been founded before the 1270s-1290s. See B.F. ROMHÁNYI, *Kolostorok és társaskáptalanok a középkori Magyarországon* [Monasteries and collegiate chapters in medieval Hungary] (Budapest, 1999), p. 22. B. Lakatos shares my doubt concerning the authenticity of this document.

[20] See the *Appendix* to SZENDE, "Power and identity", pp. 63-66.

connection is understandable, since an important function of the royal deeds was to invest the civic governments with judicial rights and legal immunity.

As to the geographic distribution, an interesting duality can be observed (Fig. 11). The leading position of the cities in the centre of the realm, termed the *medium regni*, Esztergom, Fehérvár and Buda, which were all royal seats as well, is unquestionable. Even if the archives of all three towns were destroyed in the period of Ottoman occupation from the mid-sixteenth to the late seventeenth century, documents surviving in other collections, most significantly that of the Esztergom cathedral chapter, testify to the early and regular work of their civic authorities. The conclusions based on these documents and their seals to be examined briefly below further underline the leading position of the *medium regni* in this respect.

Besides these three towns, however, there were communities far away from the centre which appeared as issuers early on. Instead of the political borders which followed the uninhabited ranges of the high Carpathians, these communities lay close to the borders of the areas that were populated by the mid-thirteenth century. To this group belongs Dubica in Slavonia (if the document in question was issued or forged before the end of the thirteenth century); the mining towns of Rodna and Dej, and Sibiu, the leading town of the Saxons in Transylvania; Bihač (*Biheg* in the document) in the southern parts, and Banská Štiavnica in the northern mountainous area. This corresponds with the geographical distribution of early chartered settlements explained above: thirteenth-century royal urban policy understandably aimed at settling and developing these peripheral regions, all the more since they turned out to be rich in mineral resources: precious metals and salt. Indeed, many of the settlements joining the ranks of charter-issuing communities were mining towns.[21]

After the turn of the thirteenth century, further merchant towns close to the borders joined in: Košice and Kežmarok in the north-east, Satu Mare and Beregovo in the east, Sopron, Trnava, Trenčín and Pressburg in the north-west, Zagreb in the south-west, Braşov in the south-east, and further mining towns such as Banská Bystrica, Krupina, and Kremnica. The distribution of early civic documents on the whole mirrors the urban network of the country. By the mid-fourteenth century, practically all significant towns began to issue authentic documents, with the notable exception of episcopal seats (only Esztergom and Zagreb feature in Appendix 3, but those included a royal town as well, just like Győr, where seven documents issued by "burghers of the royal town" ("*ci-*

[21] WEISZ, "Mining town privileges".

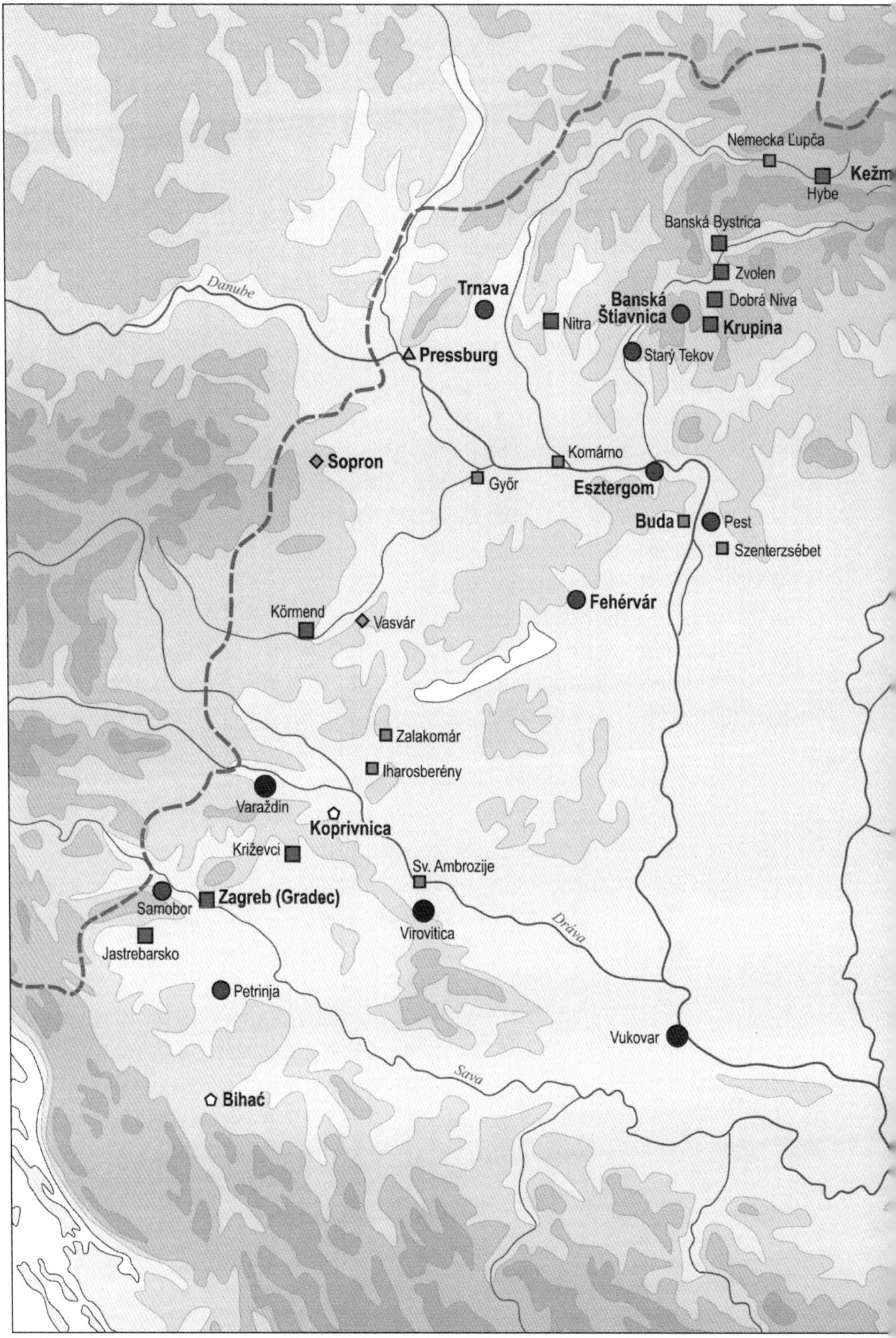

Fig. 11 Charters of privilege received and early municipal documents issued by settlements in medieval Hungary, up to 1320.

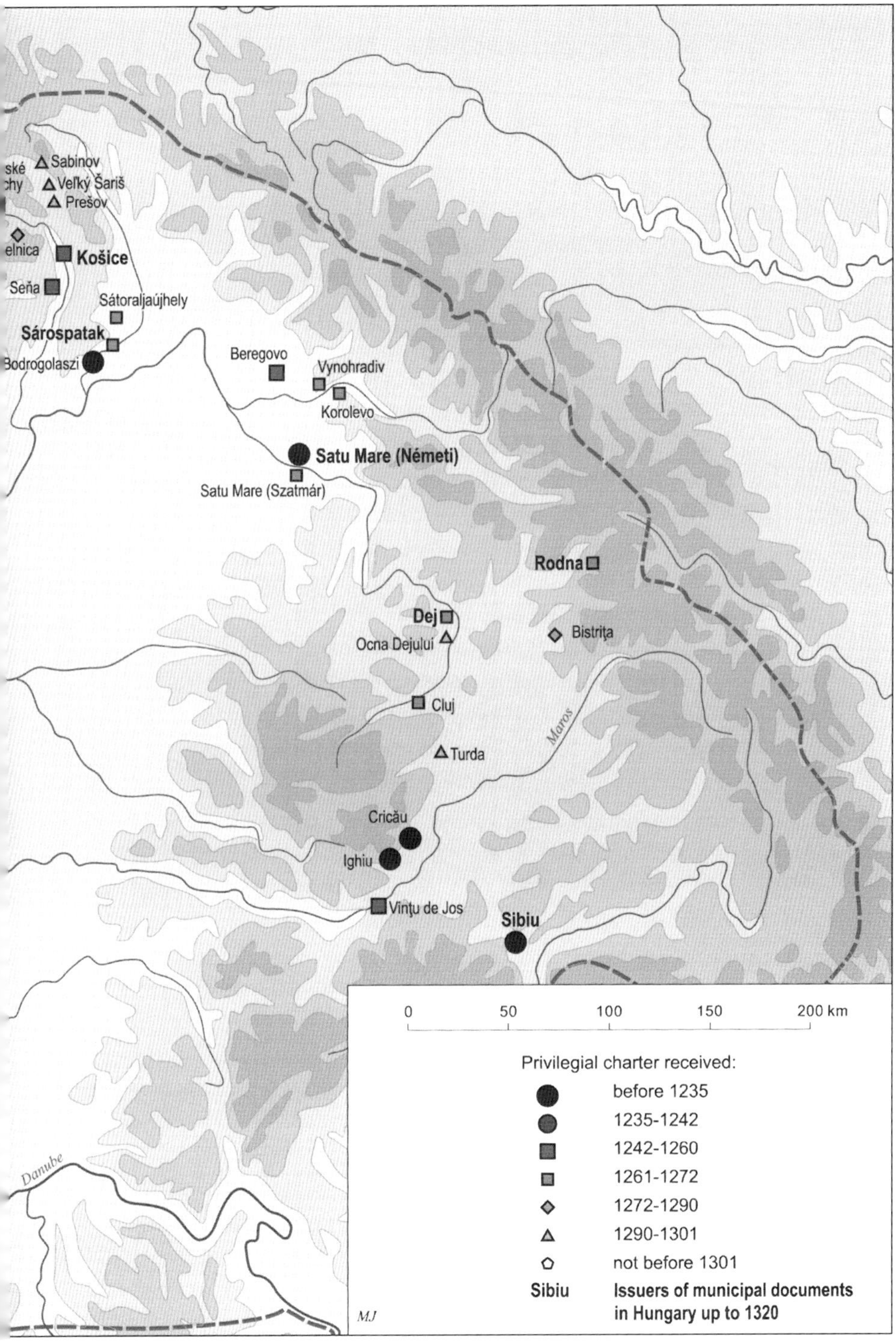

ské
chy
Sabinov
Veľký Šariš
Prešov
elnica
Košice
Seňa
Sátoraljaújhely
Sárospatak
Bodrogolaszi
Beregovo
Vynohradiv
Korolevo
Satu Mare (Németi)
Satu Mare (Szatmár)
Rodna
Dej
Ocna Dejului
Bistrița
Cluj
Maros
Turda
Cricău
Ighiu
Vințu de Jos
Sibiu
Danube
0
50
100
150
200 km
Privilegial charter received:
before 1235
1235-1242
1242-1260
1261-1272
1272-1290
1290-1301
not before 1301
Sibiu
Issuers of municipal documents in Hungary up to 1320
MJ

ves regales") between 1348 and 1394 have been preserved (see Appendix 5). This hiatus can be explained with legal rather than social factors. The participation of bishops' towns in administrative literacy was hampered by the prevalence of cathedral chapters operating as places of authentication, that is, as issuers of authentic documents. Before proceeding further, the operation of these particular institutions and their interference with civic literacy needs to be explained.

Civic Literacy and Places of Authentication

From the turn of the twelfth century, ecclesiastical institutions of higher or middle rank gained importance beyond their primary field of service by meeting an increasing demand for writing in the secular world, a need that could not have been covered otherwise because of the absence of secular *litterati*. The notaries public, as will be discussed later, remained few and far between, and never gained wide recognition in Hungary. One possible reason for this may have been that they did not have authentic seals. Instead, cathedral and collegiate chapters, as well as some monasteries, were entrusted with functions fulfilled by notaries public in other European polities. Due to their almost exclusive experience in the uses of the written word, from the late twelfth century onwards monasteries of Benedictine and Premonstratensian convents, and those of the Knights of St. Stephen and the Knights of St. John (also known as the Hospitallers) became centres of written administration and document production.[22] The contemporary name of this institution in Latin, *locus credibilis,* makes a detour to discuss it especially relevant for the central argument of the present volume. The German scholarly translation, *glaubwürdiger Ort*, captures more of the essence related to 'trust' than the English one.

The first two institutions that are attested to have performed this task were the cathedral chapter of Veszprém (1181) and the collegiate chapter of Fehér-

[22] The most important general study on the *loca credibilia* is still F. ECKHART, "Die glaubwürdigen Orte Ungarns im Mittelalter", *Mitteilungen des Instituts für österreichische Geschichtsforschung* 1914, *Ergänzungsband* 9.2, pp. 395-558. See also ZS. HUNYADI, "The Knights of St. John and the Hungarian private legal literacy up to the mid-fourteenth century", in: *"The Man of Many Devices..."*, pp. 507-519; ID., "Administering the law: Hungary's *loca credibilia*", in: *Custom and Law in Central Europe*, ed. M. RADY (Cambridge, 2003: *Faculty of Law, Occasional Papers* 6), pp. 25-35; M. RADY, *Custom and Law in Hungary* (Oxford, 2015), pp. 37-43.

vár (1184). The former institution was attached to one of the oldest bishoprics in Hungary, the bishop of which was responsible for the coronation of queens. The latter body had country-wide authority by being attached to the basilica where the kings of medieval Hungary were crowned, and most of them buried as well. The graves of two canonised members of the Árpádian dynasty, St. Stephen and St. Emeric, amplified the sacred aura of the place.[23] Most other chapters began to issue documents in the early thirteenth century, in a period when the canons of the cathedrals increasingly asserted themselves as authoritative bodies. The middling clergy's growing participation in the administration of their own matters can be observed all over Europe, but issuing documents outside their own business is a particular feature for medieval Hungary.[24]

The relevance and expertise of church authorities in the administration of legal cases was strengthened by the fact that they were in charge of registering ordeals up to the 1230s.[25] With the change of the judicial procedure in the early thirteenth century from a system of personal summonses and testimonies to one based on the involvement of ecclesiastical bodies, they continued to function as centres for issuing written documents.[26] Their activities were manifold, connected to all phases of the administration of justice, either on the initiative of private persons, recording recognizances in *litterae fassionales*, or by royal commission, answering the mandates in *litterae relationales*. They served as witnesses for the actions of the local *ispán* (whose office transformed by the second half of the thirteenth century to represent the nobility of the counties),

[23] L. Solymosi, "A székesfehérvári káptalan hiteleshelyi működésének főbb sajátosságai az Árpád-korban" [The main characteristics of the Chapter of Székesfehérvár as a place of authentication in the Árpádian period], in: *A székesfehérvári Boldogasszony bazilika történeti jelentősége* [The historical significance of the basilica of the Blessed Virgin in Székesfehérvár], ed. G. Farkas (Székesfehérvár, 1996), pp. 178-201.

[24] Koszta emphasises the common European roots of the literacy of the cathedral chapters: L. Koszta, "A magyar székeskáptalanok kanonokjai és a hiteleshelyi tevékenység 1200-1350 között" [The canons of the cathedral chapters in Hungary and the activity of the places of authentication between 1200 and 1350] in: *Loca credibilia: Hiteleshelyek a középkori Magyarországon* [*Loca credibilia*: Places of authentication in medieval Hungary], ed. I. Bilkei and T. Fedeles (Pécs, 2009), pp. 65-85.

[25] The most significant example of written records of ordeals is the Regestrum Varadiense, which contains the minutes of 389 cases by the chapter of Oradea between 1208 and 1235. See M. Lupescu Makó, "Between sacred and profane: The trial by hot iron ceremony based on the 'Regestrum Varadiense'", *Mediævalia Transilvanica* 3 (1999), pp. 5-26.

[26] See Par. 10. of the law of 1231: DRMH, 1, pp. 37-38; comments on p. 103. For suggestions for English and French patterns or comparisons, see L. Mezey, "Anfänge der Privaturkunde in Ungarn und der glaubwürdigen Orte", *Archiv für Diplomatik* 18 (1972), pp. 290-302.

and as trustworthy witnesses for other legal cases. They issued or transcribed and authenticated documents about private legal transactions. At the outset, chirographs were the only instrument of authentication (keeping one copy of the text in the chapter's or convent's archives for later reference), but they soon also appended their own seals to the documents.

By the second half of the thirteenth century, trust in the places of authentication was firmly established and the probative value of charters issued by them was fully acknowledged. In theory, the personnel of all these bodies were trained to deal with requests for different documents: in the chapters, the *lector* was commissioned with the work of writing, or, if the need was greater, a *notarius*, and eventually a *subnotarius*, was employed too.[27] It was partly because of the lack of sufficient and reliable personnel that in 1351 the rights of some twenty smaller convents to authenticate property transactions were cancelled: "*Minuti etiam conventus ab emanatione litterarum suarum super perpetuatione possessionum conficiendarum cessent et eorum sigilla omni careant firmitate*" ("Small convents must cease from issuing letters of confirmation on inheritance of property, and their seals shall be without any authority").[28] This shows the crucial importance of the authentic seal for the operation of these institutions. Until the Ottoman occupation some forty-seven chapters and convents retained their status as *loca credibilia*.[29]

The places of authentication impacted upon the formation of municipal literacy in many different ways. Understandably, their influence was the strongest in episcopal seats, where the presence of the chapters was combined with the seigniorial power of the bishop or of the chapter itself as the lord of the given city. Royal control over the bishops' cities gradually decreased in the late

[27] I. SZENTPÉTERY, *Magyar oklevéltan* [Hungarian diplomatics] (Budapest, 1930), pp. 121-130, 219-220; and E. CSUKOVITS, "A középkori írástudók 'munkaideje'" [The 'working hours' of medieval scribes], *Levéltári Közlemények* 63 (1992), pp. 3-14, esp. p. 9. Two excellent case studies on the complex activities of a place of authentication are the monograph on the collegiate chapter of Pressburg by ŠEDIVÝ, *Mittelalterliche Schriftkultur*, and the detailed discussion of the Benedictine abbey of Szekszárd by F. SZAKÁLY, "A szekszárdi konvent hiteleshelyi és oklevéladó működése 1526-ig" [The work of the Szekszárd convent as place of authentication and issuer of charters up to 1526], *Tanulmányok Tolna megye történetéből* 1 (1968), pp. 9-60.

[28] DRH, p. 131. English translation from DRMH, 2, p. 10.

[29] ECKHART, "Die glaubwürdigen Orte", pp. 420-422; HUNYADI, "The Knights of St. John", p. 508. L. SOLYMOSI, "Die glaubwürdigen Orte (*loca credibilia*) Ungarns im 14.-15. Jahrhundert", *Archiv für Dipomatik* 62 (2011), pp. 175-190. The places of authentication carried on their activity until 1848. L. PAPP, *A hiteleshelyek története és működése az újkorban* [The history and activity of the places of authentication in modern times] (Budapest, 1936) remains the only monograph on their modern development.

Árpádian and Angevin periods, and the urban community was subject to the seigniorial power of the bishops and archbishops. It must be emphasised that several sources testify to *hospites* having settled at bishops' seats from the eleventh century onwards, and some of them, such as the *Latini,* consciously preferred such cities. At Pécs a *maior hospitum*, that is, a leader of their community, was mentioned as early as 1181.[30] It also transpires from the sources of the thirteenth and fourteenth centuries that these cities did have a certain degree of autonomy and were entitled to issue authentic documents, but their activity in this respect seems to have been quite reduced.

Appendix 5 shows the earliest surviving original documents from each bishop's seat. Even if one reckons with a significant loss of sources, the material reveals some trends. Apart from those two localities where a separate royal town existed besides the parts owned by the (arch)bishop and the chapter, that is, Esztergom and Zagreb, and where municipal literacy dates back to the thirteenth century, there are only three sees, Oradea, Győr, and Pécs, which have surviving municipal charters from the fourteenth century. Five more cities (Eger, Bač, Nitra, Vác,[31] and Alba Iulia) join this circle with documents from the fifteenth century, whereas three sees (Cenad, Kalocsa, and Veszprém) do not have any surviving documents at all that would attest their municipal literacy.

This situation can best be explained – besides a presumably high number of oral transactions and agreements – by the activity of the local chapters that were able to cater for the need for written documents, since notaries public did not perform any services in secular matters. For instance, in the case of Pécs, beside the municipal authorities, the cathedral chapter and the convent of the nearby Benedictine monastery of Pécsvárad also issued charters on real estate transactions concerning urban plots, houses, mills and vineyards.[32] At the same time, Pécs is a good example to show the attraction of the place of authentica-

[30] EFHU 3.2, No. 12; I. PETROVICS, "A középkori Pécs polgárai" [The burghers of medieval Pécs], in: *Pécs szerepe a Mohács előtti Magyarországon* [The role of Pécs in Hungary before the Battle of Mohács], ed. M. FONT (Pécs 2001), pp. 163-196, esp. pp. 165-166.

[31] In Vác, the municipality of the Hungarian and the German part of the town issued documents separately, both in Latin. The earliest surviving document issued by the German town dates from 25.01.1503, DL 75491.

[32] I. PETROVICS, "A város története a 14. század közepétől 1526-ig", in: *Pécs története*, 2, *A püspökség alapításától a török hódításig* [The history of Pécs, 2, From the foundation of the bishopric to the Ottoman conquest], ed. M. FONT (Pécs, 2015), pp. 173-288, esp. pp. 197-212; T. FEDELES, *"Eztán Pécs tűnik szemünkbe": A város középkori históriája 1009-1526* ["Then we behold Pécs": The medieval history of the city] (Pécs, 2011), pp. 47-50.

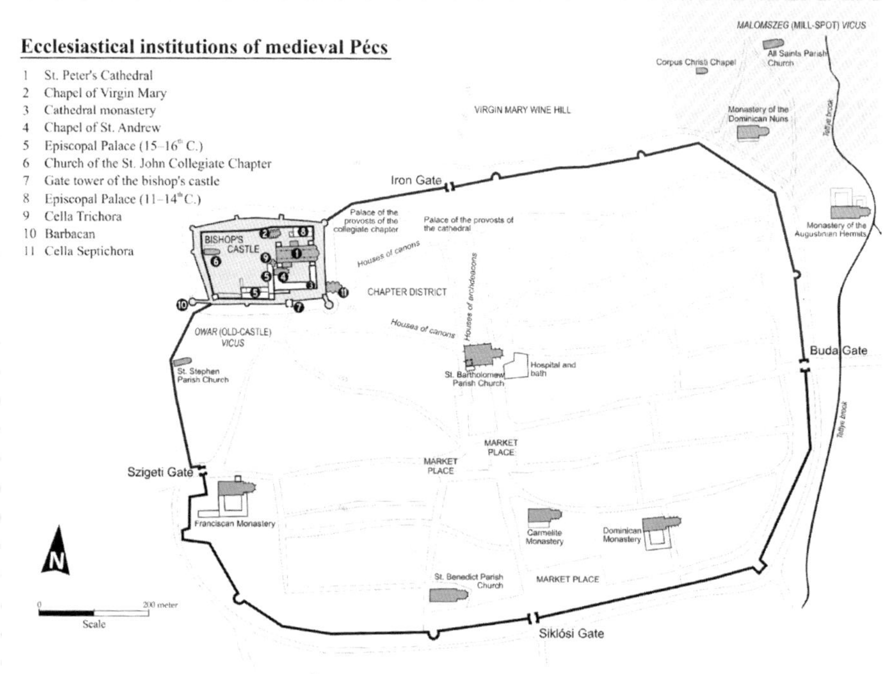

Fig. 12 Town plan of Pécs, showing the cathedral, the Chapter district and the civic part of the town. Designed by Tamás Fedeles, drawn by András Kikindai. The Hungarian version was published in FEDELES, "*Eztán Pécs tűnik szemünkbe*", p. 49. Reproduced with the permission of Tamás Fedeles.

tion for the wider neighbourhood and the strengthening of the central functions of the city. The increased openness of the chapter towards secular society is shown by the canons' leaving the closed area of the cathedral precinct after the dissolution of the *vita communis*, and settling in a street connecting the cathedral to the civic centre, the market place and the main parish church of the civic settlement (Fig. 12). This development was not unique to bishops' seats in the kingdom of Hungary, but effectively reinforced the role that this ecclesiastical body played in the extension of administrative literacy.[33]

Bálint Lakatos, in his analysis of literacy in settlements below the level of royal towns, also asserts that the cathedral or collegiate chapters frequently

[33] KOSZTA, "A magyar székeskáptalanok", pp. 74-78; DE CEVINS, *L'Église*, pp. 77-83.

issued documents concerning real estate in bishops' seats or in towns and market towns under ecclesiastical dominion.[34] He points out, very relevantly for the context here, that the local chapter or convent as seignior was considered a higher authority, and thus documents issued by them enjoyed stronger trust than those provided by the towns under their lordship. In the eyes of the recipients, the documents of their seignior provided a stronger security for their claims than those of their own community.[35]

The impact of the places of authentication can be observed in a different, although equally decisive way in some royal towns as well. Here, *loca credibilia* exerted a strong influence on the formation of urban chanceries. The chapters and convents in these places were able to offer their experience and services to the newly emerging town authorities. The two best researched examples are Sopron and Pressburg.

In Sopron, the municipal administration cooperated with the Knights Hospitaller, who were settled in 1247 by king Béla IV in the northern suburb of the fortified county seat and who played a role in issuing the town's charters for two generations, from the late 1260s up to the early fourteenth century.[36] As Jenő Házi, the chief archivist of Sopron in the interwar years has demonstrated, the first municipal documents (1276, 1278, 1292, 1303) were issued jointly by the prior of the Hospitaller convent and the *iudex* of the town. The transactions noted in these documents had nothing to do with the convent; they acted in their usual role as *locus credibilis*, but not by themselves.[37] These early docu-

[34] Lakatos, *Hivatali írásbeliség*, PhD thesis, p. 140; B. Lakatos, "Ingatlanforgalmi ügyek a késő középkori magyarországi mezővárosokban és falvakban" [Sales contracts of real estates in late medieval Hungarian market towns and villages], in: *Acta Universitatis Szegediensis: Acta Historica* 135 (2013), pp. 139-164, esp. pp. 161-162.

[35] E.g. in 1358, when a local burgher sold his house in the part of Győr owned by the chapter, this transaction was documented by the chapter as seignior See AO, 7, ed. Gy. Tasnádi Nagy (Budapest, 1920), p. 151, quoted by L. Gecsényi, "Győr középkori helyrajzáról" [The medieval topography of Győr], in: id., *Gazdaság, társadalom, igazgatás: Tanulmányok a korai újkor történetéről* [Economy, society, administration: Studies on early modern history] (Győr, 2008), p. 121. The same attitude continued in early modern times. See A. Csizmadia, *Az egyházi mezővárosok jogi helyzete és küzdelmük a felszabadulásért a XVIII. században* [The legal situation of market towns under ecclesiastical overlordship and their fight for emancipation in the eighteenth century] (Budapest, 1962), p. 31.

[36] Zs. Hunyadi, "*Extra et intra muros*: Military-religious orders and medieval Hungarian towns (c. 1150-1350)", in: *Les ordres religieux militaires dans la ville médiévale (1100-1350)*, ed. D. Carraz (Clermont-Ferrand, 2014), pp. 139-158.

[37] Házi, "A városi kancellária"; Zs. Hunyadi, "Uses of literacy by the Templars and Hospitallers in the medieval kingdom of Hungary", in: *Die Rolle der Schriftlichkeit in den geistlichen Ritterorden des Mittelalters: Innere Organisation, Sozialstruktur, Politik*, ed. R.

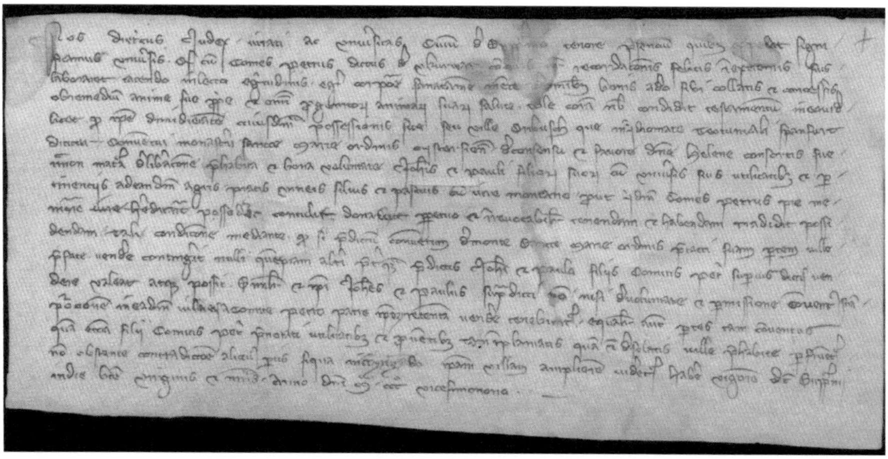

Fig. 13 An official document issued by the community of Sopron, probably written by Stephen of Harka, 5 February 1329 (MNL OL DL 2523). Reproduced with the permission of the National Archives of Hungary.

ments were often transcribed by other administrative bodies, the chapters of Győr, Vasvár, or Pressburg. When the transaction involved noblemen from the neighbouring countryside, the services of these ecclesiastical bodies were preferred. This, however, does not show lack of trust, but reflects the contemporary practice of seeking multiple security measures.

It is impossible to tell exactly when this cooperation between the town magistrates and the order came to an end – it presumably happened before the convent of the Hospitallers lost its status as *locus credibilis* because of the 1351 law quoted above. There are original documents issued by Sopron from 1329 and 1351 which do not show any sign of contribution by the Hospitallers. The deed of the Győr chapter issued concerning a property in Sopron also mentions a letter proving the credentials of the person representing the town: "*cum litteris procuratoriis iudicis, iuratorum ac universorum civium de eadem*" ("with credentials from the judge, the councillors, and all the burghers of the same place") and a similar case is known from 1336, too.[38] The town al-

CZAJA and J. SARNOWSKY (Toruń, 2009: *Ordines Militares – Colloquia Torunensia Historica* 15), pp. 39-51.

[38] DL 2523 (05.02.1329), DF 201778 (1351). For documents concerning Sopron issued by various places of authentication, see HÁZI, *Sopron*, 1.1. The mentioning of credentials: *ibid*., p. 41.

ready possessed an authentic seal, which was changed for a new one in 1340, as will be discussed below. Although until 1354 there is no evidence for a notary employed by the town, two of the leading burghers of the period, Stephen of Harka – also occasionally an envoy of king Charles I – and later his son performed the duties of the scribe. The document from 1329 may have been written by Stephen (Fig. 13).[39]

In Pressburg, according to the astute observations of Juraj Šedivý, the first important issuers of documents were the *ispáns* ('counts') of the royal castle built on a prominent hilltop by the Danube. Their charters were partly connected with their offices as palatine, judge royal, or other offices, and partly to local affairs in the county. With thirty-eight charters issued by the *ispáns* against eleven issued by the collegiate chapter of St. Saviour, one of the most important royal foundations of its kind, it seems that up to 1260 the *ispán*'s office (especially of Roland *de genere* Rátót) enjoyed the trust of most people who needed written testimony of their transactions. After 1280, however, the chapter became the leading place of authentication in the north-western border zone of Hungary.[40]

The chapter provided its document-issuing services for the urban community of Pressburg, which gradually grew out of these smaller suburban settlements in the second half of the thirteenth century. Until 1300, however, only three such instances have come down to us (1287, 1288, 1296).[41] The town and the chapter shared its main parish church, and the canons lived in a street by this building. This geographical proximity as well as the close spiritual and personal contacts resulted in an improved trust-relationship between the chapter and the town, whose royal charter from 1291 confirmed its immunity from the *ispán*. For another twenty years it sufficed for the locals to use the chapter as their prime resource for writing, and the town only added its seal to a single surviving document in 1302.[42]

[39] On the process as a whole: HÁZI, "A városi kancellária", pp. 203-206.

[40] ŠEDIVÝ, "Die Anfänge der Beurkundung", pp. 84-86. He also supports his point with palaeographic arguments. ID., *Mittelalterliche Schriftkultur* pp. 116-120; GODA and MAJOROSSY, "Städtische Selbstverwaltung", p. 80.

[41] ŠEDIVÝ, "Die Anfänge der Beurkundung", p. 88. The documents are AMB 7, 16, 9 (*Inventár* pp. 9-10). On the early history of Pressburg, see *Dejiny Bratislavy*, 1, *Brezalauspurc – Na križovatke kultúr* [History of Bratislava, 1, Brezalauspurc – At the crossroads of cultures] ed. J. ŠEDIVÝ and T. ŠTEFANOVIČOVÁ (Bratislava, 2012).

[42] This is an agreement between the chapter and the town concerning the election of the parish priest, AMB 23, DF 238647; the municipal seal indicates the consent of the magistrates.

In 1311 a seemingly new era began when the town itself appeared as issuer in the *intitulatio* of documents. This was, however, very sporadic. Until 1340 only four such items have come down to us (1311, 1314, 1323, 1336), and by comparing the scribal hands Šedivý proved that all were written by notaries of the chapter. Three concerned property transactions between them and the town, and can thus be considered as an *Empfängerausfertigung* (a document prepared by the beneficiary). Only the last one was written in an independent case, the restitution of a house in Pressburg to a nobleman called Foko in opposition to a Jew named Yezzel. The chapter was entrusted with keeping the text in its archive as place of authentication. The town magistrates also had all the important charters granted by the kings of Hungary or others transcribed by the chapter. In these decades, the chapter provided for the administrative and intellectual needs of the town in every respect: not only the manpower for issuing its documents, but also the parish priests and the schoolmasters.[43]

The situation changed radically after 1344, when suddenly several diplomatic hands appeared in documents issued by the town which cannot be traced among the scripts used in the chapter. The 'emancipation' of the civic authorities from the chapter was accompanied by a similar trend among the individual townspeople (men and women alike), who had their deeds written by the canons less and less regularly. This was also the time when, after earlier isolated examples, vernacular (German) literacy truly took root in local soil (see Chapter 4). In 1364 the name of the first notary, Siegfried, appears in the first municipal book. Since his handwriting can be traced back to 1348 or 1350 (and followed up to 1379), he must have been employed on a long-term basis and was instrumental in introducing important administrative innovations. After the town set up its own chancery, the chapter reduced its involvement in communal literacy, but did not discontinue it completely.[44]

Similar interaction can be assumed in the case of the town and the collegiate chapter of Fehérvár, a body with country-wide authority. The city was involved in royal coronations and provided the vice chancellor of the realm, who was the person effectively in charge of royal administration.[45] Unfortu-

[43] Šedivý, "Die Anfänge der Beurkundung", pp. 91-96. The 1336 document: Slovenský národný archív, Archív hodnoverného miesta, Bratislavská kapitula 14-15-5, DF 226762. See Chapter 5 for further contextualisation.

[44] Šedivý, "Die Anfänge der Beurkundung", pp. 97-101.

[45] A. Kubinyi, "Székesfehérvár középkori oklevéladása és pecsétei", in: *Székesfehérvár évszázadai* 2, ed. A. Kralovánszky (Székesfehérvár, 1972), pp. 151-168, at 151-152; Solymosi, "A székesfehérvári káptalan".

nately charters of the chapter as a place of authentication have not survived in sufficient numbers to decide whether the notaries of the chapter contributed to writing the text. However, a document issued in a court case concerning an inheritance issue between elite families from Fehérvár and Esztergom from 1325 mentions among the evidence produced "*litteras patentes capituli Albensis ecclesie ac judicis juratorum et civium de eadem civitate*", that is, a charter of the chapter and the city magistrates.[46] On a different note, Jews of Fehérvár (*judei Albenses*) also had Béla IV's 1251 *Judenprivileg* transcribed by the chapter of Fehérvár in 1256 (more on this in Chapter 5). Their trust in this Christian institution, however, was presumably due to its country-wide authority rather than its urban presence.[47] Beside the city authorities, the inhabitants of Fehérvár could also turn as individuals to the chapter or to the Hospitaller convent for written testimony, or for sealing the text composed in their names. For instance, Henc, one of the most prominent burghers of Fehérvár in the 1260s, and his two companions did so as occasional jurors in the issue of a village mill in 1264.[48]

The next phase in the development came about when town chanceries themselves were regarded as places of authentication, invested with the same authority and credibility as the original *loca credibilia*, not only in drawing up and preserving charters, but also undertaking the judicial tasks associated with the institution.[49] Their activity comprised two main fields. First, they documented legal transactions at the behest of the parties, primarily in issues that involved their own inhabitants. The second entailed legal duties on the mandate of various authorities: making inquiries, introducing new owners into their property (*statutio*), conducting perambulations, and so on. There were some notable procedural differences in their co-operation with the authorities: no royal representative (*homo regius*) was present, in accordance with the privi-

[46] DL 86972. The case is analysed in detail by A. ZSOLDOS, "Városlakók a királyi család szolgálatában" [Urban burghers in the service of the royal family], *Történelmi Szemle* 47 (2005), pp. 193-206. Unfortunately, the plural form *litteras* does not make it fully possible to distinguish whether the phrase referred to a single document of several items.

[47] 16 March 1256: MHJ 1, p. 31. The text survives in a transcription by king Sigismund from 1396, kept in the City Archives of Bratislava (AMB 817, DF 23944).

[48] A. ZSOLDOS, *Székesfehérvár története az Árpád-korban* [History of Székesfehérvár in the Árpádian period] (Székesfehérvár, 2016), pp. 179-180; the document: DF 200663.

[49] M. RADY, *Medieval Buda: A Study of Municipal Government and Jurisdiction in the Kingdom of Hungary* (Boulder, 1985: *East European Monographs* 182), pp. 54-68.

Fig. 14 A pair of chirographed documents issued by the municipality of Buda, 29 November 1392 (MNL OL DL 39270 and DL 100250). Reproduced with the permission of the National Archives of Hungary.

leges of the towns which invested the local magistrates with full jurisdiction over their own territories and inhabitants.[50] The main point for us, however, is that the functioning of town chanceries as places of authentication increased their judiciary authority as well as their reputation outside the borders of the town and the trust in the actions that they performed.

It would require philological and diplomatic investigations beyond the scope of this volume to analyse how various terms and formulaic elements were adopted by urban writing offices from the practice of *loca credibilia*. Let me just point here to a probably unexpected formal element also inspired by the practice of the places of authentication: the use of chirographs in the practice of Buda's municipal chancery. The model may have been the chancery of

[50] KUBINYI, "Buda város pecséthasználata", p. 288.

Fig. 15 Images showing the dorse. The fragments of the seals show that both halves were sealed with the smaller municipal seal before cutting the copies apart. The notes on the dorse show the customary marks of the collections where the documents ended up. Reproduced with the permission of the National Archives of Hungary.

the Buda chapter – a collegiate chapter operating at Óbuda –, the closest place of authentication, which still occasionally used chirographs in the fourteenth century. The tariffs of scribes for preparing various sorts of documents recorded in the *Ofner Stadtrecht* (see Chapter 3 for further detail) also lists "*priefen mit dem Alphabeth*" ("letters with the alphabet"), in the second highest category of tariffs, 64 denars. There are indeed several chirographs preserved among the documents issued by the magistrate of Buda in the second half of the fourteenth century (Fig. 14).[51] Drawing up a chirograph imposed extra costs

[51] Examples of chirographed documents issued by the judge and council of Buda: DL 4265

due to preparing a double document, and it may have been the wish of the parties involved in the transaction to invest in this extra element of security. These charters were also sealed with the municipal seal on the back of the parchment (Fig. 15). In the fifteenth century, registering the issued documents in a municipal book made the archaic method of chirographs unnecessary for authentication, although it still appeared sporadically.

Formulae *and Community*

After this longish detour, let us return to the earliest documents (see Appendix 3) and examine their text: how were they structured, what subjects did they take up, and how was the town community involved? Is it right to assume that the explicit or implicit use of the first person plural was an instrument for expressing common interests – or at least the interest of those who belonged to this imaginary 'we'? If so, how much trust was vested in this community? According to the terminology of diplomatics, two formal elements have special importance: the *intitulatio* and the *corroboratio*. The most detailed formal analysis of these features in the Hungarian urban context so far is that by András Kubinyi, who concentrated on the cases of Buda and Fehérvár, but also used a wide range of comparative material.[52] My account here follows in his footsteps, with the additional aim of discussing the contents of the charters.

As Kubinyi points out, all three main types of documents can be found among the early products of town chanceries: letters with hanging seal (*litterae privilegiales*); letters patent (*litterae patentes*) with the seal stamped on the parchment (later also paper) on the dorse or on the front below the text, and letters close (*litterae clausae*) sealed after having been folded. This fact in itself shows that the urban administration – the nascent chanceries – were familiar with the full range of practices in contemporary pragmatic literacy from the outset. It is the *litterae privilegiales* that have survived in the highest number, first and foremost because they recorded more important issues with a longer impact than the other document types. This was also the type that was

(22 March 1352); DL 77360 (15 March 1366); DL 74836 (6 December 1377), DF 238066 (8 September 1392); DL 39270 and DL 100250 (29 November 1392) – both parts of the same document (!) DF 286049 (BFL, DL 2, 4 October 1465. The Buda regulation: *Ofner Stadtrecht* cap. 50, p. 79.

[52] KUBINYI, "Buda város pecséthasználata"; ID., "Székesfehérvár középkori oklevéladása".

most bound to use strictly defined formulaic elements, whereas *litterae patentes* and especially *litterae clausae* were more informal and less uniform.[53]

Nevertheless, all three types contained – with very few exceptions – at the beginning of the charter or very rarely in the second place (after the *inscriptio / addresse*) the *intitulatio* in first person plural, the most common forms being "*nos iudex, iurati et cives / et omnes hospites*", "*nos rector et iurati* ..." and so forth. A wide variety of terms was used for the elected leader of the community: *villicus, maior ville, iudex*, or *rector*. This variety is present in the privileges as well; in both instances the changing terminology may reflect chronological as well as regional differences. Various influences from abroad may have played a role here: in the 1201 charter granted to the *hospites* of *Potok*, for instance, the term *prepositus* corresponds to the French *prevôt*, the *rihtardus* in Varaždin (1220/1242) to the German *Richter*, the *scabinus* in Trenčín to the *Schöffen* in German-speaking areas, but all of these terms referred to the judge. *Villicus* or *maior villae* tends to appear more frequently in early examples, often connected with *Latini*, whereas later *iudex* prevails. *Rector* was only used in Buda in exceptional circumstances, when between 1264 and 1347 the kings appointed their own representatives to lead the town instead of a judge elected by the community.[54] Furthermore, *rector* was the title of royal officials appointed to control the revenues from the mining towns, but these persons complemented, but did not replace the judges' authority.[55] In two Transylvanian cases, Rodna and Sibiu, *iudices* (judges) are mentioned in plural (names are not given), which probably refers to the *iudex regius* appointed by the king (a special arrangement for Transylvania) and the local judge elected by the community. The same practice can be observed from the early fourteenth century in Cluj as well.[56]

The *iurati* or councillors ('jurors' is a somewhat misleading translation), were usually six or twelve in number. The term implies taking an oath, as it was mentioned in the Introduction. Their election is first mentioned in the charter of Virovitica issued by prince Coloman in 1234, but the custom appar-

[53] Kubinyi, "Buda város pecséthasználata", pp. 284-287.

[54] The rector of Buda had both judicial and military authority, and was also termed *iudex pro domino rege in Buda*, or *rector capitaneusque*. See Spekner, *Hogyan lett Buda*, p. 68; Rady, *Medieval Buda*, pp. 304-309.

[55] Weisz, "Mining town privileges", pp. 296-297.

[56] Á. Flóra, *The Matter of Honour: The Leading Urban Elite in Sixteenth-Century Cluj and Sibiu* (unpublished PhD dissertation, CEU, Budapest, 2014); to be published in the series *Studies in European Urban History* (Turnhout, 2018).

ently goes back to earlier times.[57] They are frequently listed by name in charters issued as *litterae privilegiales*, but not in the patent ones. Their names often sound distinctly foreign, a trait that corresponds to their origin as we know it from other evidence. For instance, among the *Latini* of Esztergom, who were involved with more than half a dozen charters in the second half of the thirteenth century, French or Walloon-sounding names (Gean, Rubynus, Iakmynus, Godynus, etc.) were typical, but German-sounding ones (Hermannus, Cunc, etc.) also appear.[58] There are also cases, especially in the earliest examples, when the councillors are not mentioned at all.

The judge was usually elected by common consent, variously worded in the formulation of the charters of privilege as *communiter*; *ex communi consilio*; *quem voluerint*; *quem communis populus elegerit*, and so on. However, there is very little to indicate who was eligible for the position, apart from the fact that the elected person had to be part of the community (*unus ex ipsis*). The circle of those who were expected to participate in the election was also only very vaguely defined, if at all: the term *maior et sanior pars* (Trnava, 1238) probably refers to the early formation of a local elite, whose will dominated the community, as Erik Fügedi notes, on the principle of *non numerantur sed ponderantur*. The expression *maior et sanior pars* is otherwise a borrowing from medieval canon law (in relation to 'scrutiny'), where it denoted the principle of the election of abbots and provosts.[59] According to legal historians, applying the principle of the majority in counting the votes (be it a numerical majority of the majority of those whose opinion carried weight) instead of full unanimity was a sign that a community became a body corporate and assumed a legal personality, whereas the notion of *sanior pars* points to the increased authority of some of its members.[60]

The rest of the town population, at least those who possessed full civic rights, were also added in general terms to the *intitulatio*. Even if presumably not all burghers were present at the issuing of the document, this gesture indi-

[57] CDCr 3, pp. 422-423; SOLYMOSI, *Földesúri járadékok*, pp. 207-208.

[58] GY. SZÉKELY, "Wallons et italiens en Europe Centrale aux XIe-XVIe siècles", *Annales Universitatis Scientiarum Budapestinensis de Rolando Eötvös Nominatae: Sectio Historica* 6 (1964), pp. 3-71; ZSOLDOS "Városlakók", pp. 193-206.

[59] FÜGEDI, "Városprivilégiumok", pp. 282-283. On the term *maior et sanior pars* in canon law, see R.H. HELMHOLZ, *The Spirit of Classical Canon Law* (Athens, GA, and London, 2010), p. 54.

[60] H. MITTEIS and H. LIEBERICH, *Deutsche Rechtsgeschichte,* thirteenth edn. (München, 1974), p. 208.

cates that they were members of the urban body politic through their right to elect the leaders and through their general participation in communal matters. Likewise, the consequences of the recorded legal transactions were binding for each member of the community. The terminology shows strong fluctuation concerning this group, too: *omnes hospites*, *ceterique cives*, and *tota communitas* alternate; eventually *universi cives* becomes the most widespread.[61] One may argue that the first person plural of the *intitulatio* directly copies the formulas of royal charters which served as models for the issuing activity of the emerging town chanceries, just as royal seals and coins provided the patterns for the seals of towns. There is, however, an important difference: in the *intitulatio* of urban charters, the *nos* is not a *pluralis maiestatis*, but a real plural. If 'the judge, the jurors and the burghers' as issuers are taken literally, one can even speak of *pluralis pluralitatis*.

The other part of the documents where the notion of community frequently finds expression is at the end of the text, in the *corroboratio*, that is the part where the means of authentication is specified. This is almost without exception, a reference to the seal, with the addition of the possessive pronoun *nostri* or even *communitatis* or *universitatis nostri*. Only very rarely were seals of private persons or other bodies used; I will return to the question of adding the seal of an ecclesiastic community below.

The Municipal Seal: The Matrix of Identity

As discussed in the Introduction, trust in writing developed gradually and relied on specific features that ostentatiously declared the special status of the documents. The most characteristic visual signs were the seals, "the only three-dimensional element of corroboration".[62] An especially significant step was

[61] See, in general, Reynolds, *Kingdoms and Communities*, Chapter 6: "Urban Communities", pp. 155-218; B. Kümin, *The Communal Age in Western Europe, c. 1100-1800* (Basingstoke, and New York, 2013), Chapter 4: "Communal cultures", pp. 55-77. In Hungarian historical scholarship, E. Ladányi, *Az önkormányzat intézményei és elméleti alapvetése az európai és hazai városfejlődés korai szakaszában* [The institutions of self-governance and their theoretical basis in the early period of Hungarian urban development] (Budapest, 1996) pp. 121-140, points out the connection between the terminology of these documents and canon law.

[62] P. Worm, "From subscription to seal: The growing importance of seals as signs of authenticity in early medieval royal charters", in: *Strategies of Writing*, pp. 63-83, quotation from p. 71; *Das Siegel: Gebrauch und Bedeutung im Mittelalter*, ed. G. Signori (Darmstadt, 2007); B.M. Bedos-Rezak, "In search of a semiotic paradigm: The matter of sealing in medieval thought

taken when the towns themselves acquired the authority to mould and use their own seals, the most widespread media carrying early representations of urban coats of arms. The use of seals as symbolic as well as practical means of authentication deserves special attention within the broader question of the formation of communal authority and trust in writing.[63]

The limits and the focus of this work do not allow me to consider either the general framework of sphragistics or the complexity of the seals' visual symbolism in general. Mentioning some of the earliest Hungarian urban examples, however, is highly relevant – all the more since the existence of seals presents the earliest indirect proof of civic literacy. As was discussed above, the first surviving charters issued by towns date from the middle of the thirteenth century, whereas the shape and imagery of some seals show clear features referring to a few decades earlier. This is of great importance, since the existence of municipal seals presupposes a community that was identified by a visual symbol. By having a seal urban communities or specific parts thereof acquired a legal personality that had the potential of issuing authentic documents, and was authorised to do so.

Cases in point are first and foremost the double seals of Esztergom and Buda. For the former, its matrix (*typarium*) is preserved, now in the collection of the Hungarian National Museum (Figs. 16 and 17);[64] the latter is only known from its imprints (Fig. 18).[65] The obverse of both seals bears the royal coat of arms of the Árpádians, the ruling dynasty of Hungary from 1000 to 1301. It was a widespread custom in Europe that early municipal seals adopted the coats of arms of their lord, thus paying homage to him and emphasising his protection against any power that might threaten the town's autonomy.[66] Let me just refer here to the great seal of Vienna, which was made approximately

and practice", in: *Good Impressions: Image and Authority in Medieval Seals*, ed. N. ADAMS, J. CHERRY, and J. ROBINSON (London, 2008), pp. 1-8; E. NEW, "Seals and status in medieval English towns", *ibid.*, pp. 35-42.

63 The first comprehensive discussion of urban coats of arms in Hungary relies heavily on the surviving seals: DARVASY, *Középkori városaink*; revisions in KUBINYI, "Buda város pecséthasználata"; ID., "Székesfehérvár középkori oklevéladása".

64 E.F. VATTAI, "Az esztergomi latinok kettős pecsétje" [The double seal of the Latins of Esztergom], *Archaeologiai Értesítő* 90 (1963), pp. 39-45; its earliest imprint survived on DL 76145.

65 KUBINYI, "Buda város pecséthasználata", pp. 272-276.

66 I. BERTÉNYI, "A vörös-ezüst sávozat funkciója néhány városunk címerében" [The function of barry of argent and gules in the coats of arms of some Hungarian cities], in: *Eszmetörténeti tanulmányok a magyar középkorról*, ed. GY. SZÉKELY (Budapest, 1984), pp. 425-448, at pp. 427-428.

Fig. 16. a-b Both sides of the matrix of the double seal of the *Latini* of Esztergom. The original design presumably dates from the 1220s-1230s; the extant piece was restored to the community in the 1240s or 1250s, after the Mongol invasion. Reproduced with the permission of the Hungarian National Museum. See front cover for colour image.

at the same time as the seals of Esztergom and Pest, in the 1220s or the 1230s, and which bears the image of a one-headed eagle, the coat of arms of the Babenberg dynasty.[67] Furthermore, as Iván Bertényi points out, the image on the municipal seals bears a likeness to that on the royal banner. He explains this by assuming a connection to the burghers' military duties, which they had to perform under banners bearing the same symbols.[68]

The image of the Árpádian coat of arms may be helpful in dating as well: according to Kubinyi the nine cuts in Esztergom's seal were used by king Emeric and Andrew II in the first half of his reign; the seven cuts as presented in Buda's seal were customary in the last years of Andrew's reign († 1235), but not after that. Conversely, Iván Bertényi does not attribute dating value to the

[67] A. Niederstätter, "Das Stadtsiegel: Medium kommunaler Selbstdarstellung: Eine Annäherung anhand von Beispielen aus dem habsburgisch-österreichischen Alpen- und Donauraum" in: *Bild und Wahrnehmung der Stadt*, ed. Opll, pp. 143-156, at pp. 144, 148.

[68] Bertényi, "A vörös-ezüst sávozat", pp. 429-431. For the use of the same symbol by some noble families, see Gy. Rácz, "Az Árpádok sávozott címere egyes főúri pecséteken a XIII-XIV. században" [The use of the Árpádian coat of arms in some seals of noble families in the thirteenth-fourteenth centuries], *Levéltári Közlemények* 63 (1992), pp. 123-135.

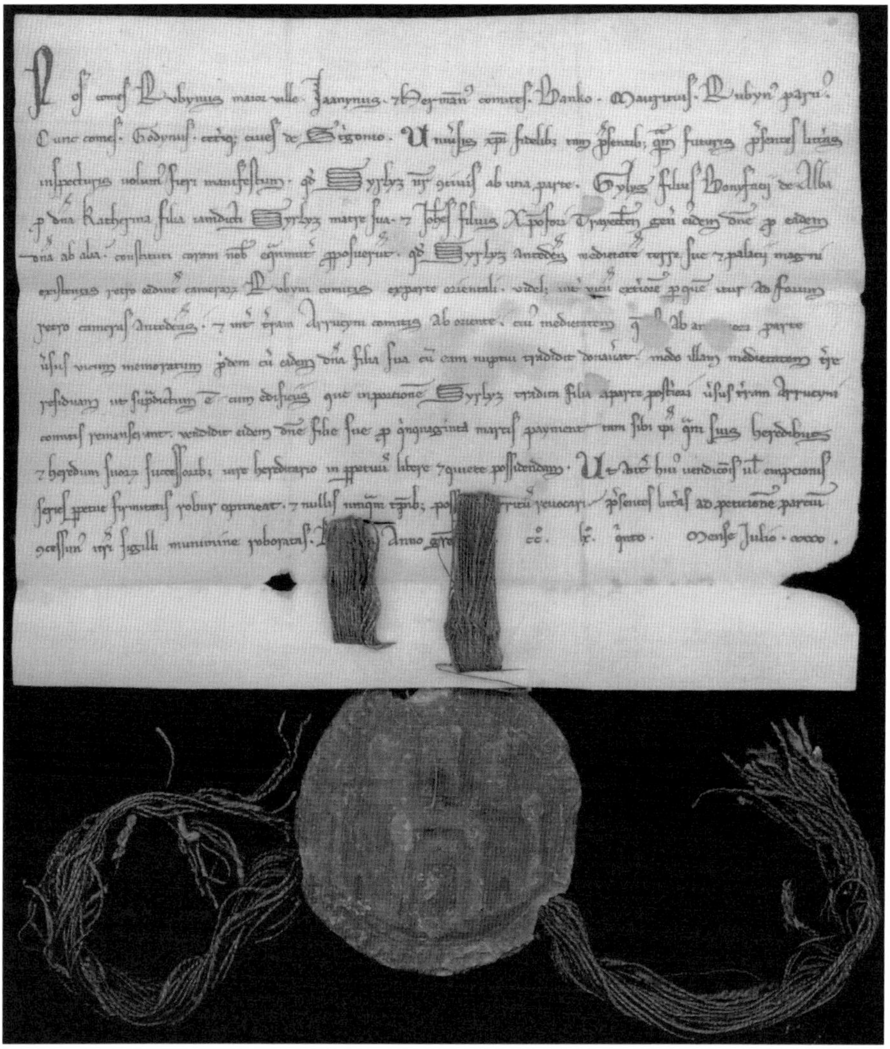

Fig. 17 Charter issued by the mayor and council of Esztergom with a perfectly preserved imprint of the double seal, July 1265 (MNL OL DL 76145). Reproduced with the permission of the National Archives of Hungary.

Fig. 18 The imprint of the double seal of Buda. The insignia were originally given to Pest in the 1230s and taken over by Buda on royal order together with the charter of Pest in the late 1240s. This imprint was preserved on a document issued in 1292. MNL, Veszprém County Archives XVI.1 T191 (DF 229 963). Reproduced with the permission of the Veszprém County Archives.

two different images. According to him "the point was to have several bars in the escutcheon, but their exact number was not definitive".[69] Recently, the art historian Etele Kiss has expressed an opinion – although without detailed explanation – that the surviving matrix of the *Latini* of Esztergom was prepared after the Mongol invasion (1241/1242) as the replacement of an original that was presumably made during the reign of king Andrew II.[70] Whichever argument one accepts, it is almost certain that the original matrix of both the Esztergom and the Pest seals (the latter became the seal of Buda in the later 1240s) as well as that of the *Latini* of Fehérvár was originally made before 1235, that is, before king Béla IV ascended the throne.[71] All this renders it likely that the first seals of Esztergom, Pest, and probably also Fehérvár (Fig. 19)[72] were

[69] KUBINYI, "Buda város pecséthasználata", pp. 276-278; BERTÉNYI, "A vörös-ezüst sávozat", pp. 427-429.

[70] E. KISS, "Ötvösség és fémművesség Magyarországon a tatárjárás idején" [Goldsmithing and metalworking in Hungary at the time of the Mongol invasion], in: *A tatárjárás (1241-42): Kiállítás a Magyar Nemzeti Múzeumban*, ed. Á. RITOÓK and É. GARAM (Budapest, 2007), pp. 60-68, at p. 65.

[71] KUBINYI, "Székesfehérvár középkori oklevéladása", pp. 151-153; A. ZSOLDOS and T. NEUMANN, *Székesfehérvár középkori kiváltságai* [The medieval privileges of Székesfehérvár] (Székesfehérvár, 2010), pp. 35-36.

[72] The image was published in KUBINYI, "Székesfehérvár középkori oklevéladása", p. 152.

Fig. 19 The seal of the *Latini* of Fehérvár, imprint from a document issued on 16 March 1270 (MNL OL DL 83 130). Reproduced with the permission of the National Archives of Hungary.

Fig. 20 The seal of the town of Vasvár on a document issued on 14 February 1414 (MNL OL DL 92434). Vasvár was protected by earthwork fortification in the eleventh to thirteenth centuries, but was never encircled by stone walls. Reproduced with the permission of the National Archives of Hungary.

made as early as the mid-1230s, or even before. The Árpádian coat of arms also appears on seals that are only attested from the fourteenth century but belonged to towns that had existed and received their charters in the thirteenth, such as Banská Bystrica.[73]

The reverse side of Esztergom's seal shows an elaborate town wall with several bastions and a palace-like building inside, Buda's as well as a few other single seals from medieval Hungary including Fehérvár, Visegrád, Zagreb, Pressburg, Sopron, Komárno, Vasvár (Fig. 20), Varaždin, Krapina and Cluj show a schematic image of a castle or fortification with three towers. This image belongs to the so-called topographical type, going back perhaps to antique roots. It was widely used on seals of different European towns as the

[73] DF 280660 (1326, with hammer and curling chisel on top of the shield, and stars and moon beside it).

Fig. 21 The seal of Kremnica on a document issued on 17 July 1331 (MNL OL DF 250 152). Drawing by Anna Grüll. Reproduced with permission.

Fig. 22 The seal of Nová Baňa. The matrix is kept in the Hungarian National Museum; its earliest extant imprint is on a charter issued on 29 January 1348 (DF 237 060). Reproduced with the permission of the Hungarian National Museum.

general symbol of urban settlements.[74] Earlier research closely connected the use of town walls on seals and coats of arms of towns with the autonomy of the given settlement. This type was particularly widespread in Hungary in the thirteenth and fourteenth centuries. András Kubinyi even advanced the hypothesis that the gate with three towers may have been a generic image given by the kings to towns that were elevated from former county seats. At the same time, he quotes examples that coats of arms of some other towns as well as noble families also displayed the same image.[75] However, communities using other images than these may have enjoyed the same level of autonomy. In any case,

[74] Darvasy, "Középkori városaink" pp. 17-21; Kubinyi, "Buda város pecséthasználata", p. 277; I. Bertényi, "Címerpajzson szereplő és pajzson kívüli ábrázolások: Buda város címerpajzsa és annak külső díszei" [Charges and other elements on and around the escutcheon: The Buda coat of arms and its surrounding elements], in: *Változatok a történelemre: Tanulmányok Székely György 80. születésnapjára*, ed. Gy. Erdei, B. Nagy (Budapest, 2004), pp. 203-208; D. Mihelić, "Siegel erzählen: Fallbeispiel: Mittelalterliche Städte auf slowenischem Gebiet", in: *Bild und Wahrnehmung der Stadt*, ed. Opll, pp. 97-117.

[75] Kubinyi, "Székesfehérvár középkori oklevéladása", pp. 163-166.

the representation of town walls as the symbol of the physical strength and unity of the towns was a most appropriate image for an object that symbolised the unity of the burghers. Nevertheless even this imagery could accommodate the symbolic presence of the seignior, as the most elaborate specimen of this type, the seal of Óbuda shows. This matrix, probably sculpted after the town had been donated by the young Louis I in 1343 to his mother, the dowager queen Elizabeth, shows the Hungarian Angevin and the Polish coats of arms on both sides of the palace tower.[76]

A further type, gradually appearing in the Hungarian material, is the depiction of the patron saint of a community on the seal. Parallel to the physical protection offered by the town walls, such images show the spiritual guardians of the towns, for instance St. Elizabeth on Košice's oldest seal,[77] St. John the Baptist on Trnava's, the Virgin Mary on that of Vác, and so on. The appearance of the image of kings as earthly founders or protectors of a town – as a human figure and not only through his family coat of arms – was the next step in the fourteenth century. The most prominent examples of the latter type appeared on the seals of some of the mining towns, Charles I on that of Kremnica[78] and his son, Louis I together with the Virgin Mary and Christ as a child, on that of Nová Baňa (Figs. 21-22).

The German name of the latter town, Königsberg, as well as the inscription of its seal, +SIGILLVM·CIVITATIS·DE·MONTE·REGIS, clearly shows the king's role as its founder, just as the inscription of Kremnica's seal: +S(IGILLVM)·CIVITATIS·REGIS·KAROLI·DE·CREMNICIA. In terms of composition the seals of the mining towns are also notable for their rather liberal arrangement and the frequent depiction of tools or processes of work, particularly on the seals of Baia Mare, Pukanec and even on those of such smaller places as Rudabánya and Telkibánya.[79]

76 Chapter by J. KOLBA in *Magyarországi művészet 1300-1470 körül*, ed. E. MAROSI, 2 vols. (Budapest, 1987), 1, p. 378, and 2, Plate 314.2.

77 D. MAGDOŠKO, *Samospráva mesta Košice v stredoveku* [The local government of Košice in the Middle Ages] (Košice, 2017), pp. 155-156.

78 D. UHRIN, "Szent Katalin és Borbála, a felvidéki bányavárosok védőszentjei" [St. Catherine and Barbara, patron saints of the Upper Hungarian mining towns], in: *Hatalom, adó, jog: Gazdaságtörténeti tanulmányok a magyar középkorról* [Power, tax, law: Studies on the economic history of medieval Hungary], ed. B. WEISZ and I. KÁDAS (Budapest, 2017), pp. 369-386, is of the opinion that the seal represents St. Catherine and not king Charles. Tamás Körmendi is currently working on a new study on the coats of arms and seals of the mining towns.

79 J. KOLBA in *Magyarországi művészet 1300-1470 körül*, 1, p. 378 and 2, Plates 315 and 763.

The main issue for us here, however, is not so much the image itself, but the interdependence of possessing authentic seals and issuing charters which follow each other over time, and indicate autonomous legal and administrative activity by the emerging urban communities. This was, however, the result of a lengthy development. The earliest municipal seals that appeared in the Rhine valley from the second half of the twelfth century became an instrument of authentication following the example of the seals of their lords. Their validity was first restricted to internal issues of the given town, and was extended only gradually to issues involving outside parties as well.[80] Seals could likewise be used for authenticating other actions and objects besides legal documents. They may have been presented by authorised representatives of the community, and were attached to special products, first and foremost textiles in the form of lead seals, to certify their origin and quality.[81]

The communities as owners of the respective seals are named in the legend. In Esztergom for example it reads SIGILLVM·LATINORVM·CIVITATIS·STRIGONIENSIS; in Fehérvár S(IGILLVM)·LATINORVM·CIVIVM·ALBENSIVM, in Buda + SIGILLVM NOUI·CASTRI·PESTIENSIS, since the town took over the privileges of Pest, being founded on the opposite side of the Danube. These examples, which could be complemented with several more from other towns, show the main varieties in naming the owner either as a community of burghers (*civium*) or as the settlement (*castrum* or *civitas*) itself. The difference is clearly reflected on two seals of Pressburg, appended within twelve years: the seal added to the charter issued by the Pressburg chapter in 1302 reads: SIGILLVM CIVIVM IN PRESPVRCH, whereas its successor in 1314 bears the inscription SIGILLVM CIVITATIS POSONIENSIS.[82] According to legal historians the latter is a conceptually more mature form, since it involves a higher degree of abstraction, shifting from the inhabitants to the place that they inhabited, or in other words from a group of natural persons to a legal personality or body corpor-

[80] M. GROTEN, "Studien zur Frühgeschichte deutscher Stadtsiegel: Trier, Köln, Mainz, Aachen, Soest", *Archiv für Diplomatik, Schriftgeschichte und Wappenkunde* 31 (1985), pp. 433-478.

[81] N.W. POSTHUMUS, *De geschiedenis van de Leidsche lakenindustrie*, 1, *De Middeleeuwen (veertiende tot zestiende eeuw)* ('s Gravenhage, 1908), pp. 157-176, quoted by N.M. RODENBURG, *Seal and Deal: Cloth Production and Trade between the Netherlands and Scania during the Late Middle Ages and Early Modern Times* (MA Thesis, Lund University, 2011), pp. 28-34; M. MORDOVIN, "Late medieval and early modern cloth seals in the collection of the Hungarian National Museum", *Archeologiai Értesítő* 139 (2014), pp. 193-237, at pp. 197-198.

[82] ŠEDIVÝ, "Die Anfänge der Beurkundung", p. 103.

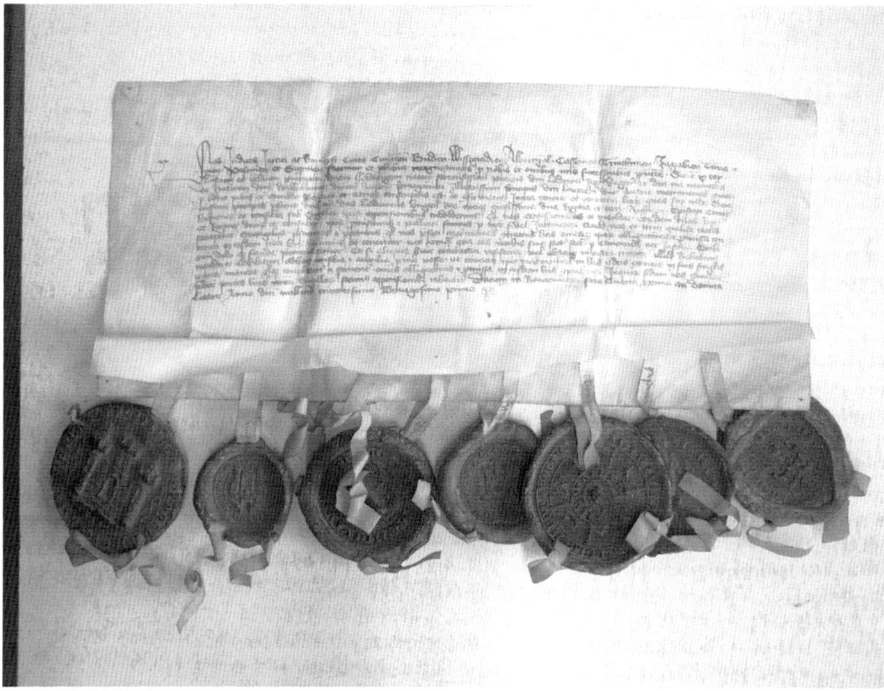

Fig. 23 Charter sealed by eight Hungarian towns endorsing the marriage contract between princess Hedwig and William, duke of Austria, 20 March 1381 (Österreichisches Staatsarchiv, Wien, Haus-, Hof- und Staatsarchiv, Urkundenabteilung, Familienurkunden, 242.1). Reproduced with the permission of the Österreichisches Staatsarchiv.

ate.[83] Practical examples do not always follow this rule consistently because of the continuing use of earlier matrices, but the general trends correspond to the sequence of identity-building. Likewise, the first surviving document of Sibiu was issued under the seal of the *universitas Saxonum*, the community of the Saxons of Transylvania, just as it was prescribed by their communal charter, the Andreanum of 1224: "*Insuper eisdem concessimus, quod unicum sigillum habeant, quod apud nos et magnates nostros evidenter cognoscatur*" ("Furthermore, we allow them to have a specific seal that is acknowledged by us and our magnates").[84]

[83] KUBINYI, "Székesfehérvár középkori oklevéladása", pp. 154-155, notes 17 a-b; LADÁNYI, *Az önkormányzat intézményei*, pp. 121-166; NIEDERSTÄTTER, "Das Stadtsiegel", pp. 152-153.
[84] UGDS 1, No. 260, DF 244566.

Appending a town's seal to a charter or a deed may predate or complement the independent issuing of documents. It can be understood as a sign of consent, adding the town's authority to the confirmation. For instance, in addition to the king's seal, Béla IV's charter issued to Fehérvár in 1249 also carried that of the chapter and the town, which attests the separation of the burghers' properties from those belonging to the Church and the royal domain at the time when the burghers were moved to the fortified town: "*magistri Achilli prepositi et capituli ecclesie Albensis ac universorum civium eiusdem loci alfabeto intercisam sub quatuor sigillis eorum*" ("under their four seals, of master Achilles the provost, and of the chapter of the church of Fehérvár, and of all burghers of that place, carved in the alphabet (*alphabeti intercisam*)).[85] The previously mentioned agreement between the town and the chapter of Pressburg was similarly authenticated by both seals. Both instances predate the earliest surviving own documents of these urban communities.

A rare example of the municipal seals authorising a legal act outside their conventional area of competence is the testimony issued by the representatives of eight Hungarian towns in Wiener Neustadt, on 20 March 1381 (Fig. 23). The towns of Buda, Visegrád, Fehérvár, Košice, Trenčín, Zagreb, Trnava, Pressburg, and Sopron authenticated the marriage contract between princess Hedwig, king Louis I's daughter, and William, duke of Austria, with their oath.[86] Eventually, it was irrespective of the towns' involvement that the contract was annulled and the role of William was taken over by Władysław Jagiełło, a marriage with long-term consequences for the history of Europe.

The use of seals on the documents issued by the municipal authorities developed in parallel with the growing complexity of tasks to be handled by the town governments. One can observe a process of differentiation in the use of seals: from the early fourteenth century onwards the charters of privilege were as a rule corroborated with the big or double seal, and the patent and closed charters with the smaller or secret seal, if the community had one, or sometimes several in different sizes. Fehérvár apparently did not have a secret seal, so its *litterae patentes* in the fourteenth century were corroborated with several signet seals. This was probably a pattern taken over from the practice of the

[85] RA p. 275, No. 919. The fourth seal, not listed in the quotation, must have belonged to the king. Another fragment of presumably the same charter is edited from a transcription of 1426 in CDH 7.5, pp. 279-280.

[86] Österreichisches Staatsarchiv, Wien. Haus-, Hof- und Staatsarchiv, Urkundenabteilung. Familienurkunden 242.1 (DF 258369), published by O. MÉSZÁROS in: *The Medieval Royal Town at Visegrád*, Charter collection, No. 39, p. 212.

Fig. 24 Imprint of the of the municipal seal of Sopron, endorsed by king Charles I in 1340 on a document issued on 15 March 1389 (MNL Sopron Archives of Győr-Moson-Sopron County DL 276). Photo: József Kücsán. Reproduced with the permission of the Sopron Archives.

counties where the private seals of the judges (*iudices nobilium*) were used instead of a non-existent common seal.[87] Whatever practical directions the development took, the fact that the community had an object with a symbolic image that impersonated and authenticated its legal actions was one of the most significant manifestations of its corporate existence and the trust in its corporate decisions.

Royal authority was indispensable for authorising the use of seals. This principle is concisely summarised in the *Tripartitum,* the summa of Hungarian customary law compiled by Stephen Werbőczy upon the request of the Diet in 1514 and printed in 1517:

> *Habent praeterea civitates et oppida sigilla authentica, per reges et principes ipsis concessa, quae in factis et rebus coram eis et in medio eorum vertentibus ac emergendis, robur sortiuntur firmitatis.*

> In addition, cities and towns have authentic seals which kings and princes have granted them, and which confirm facts and matters which are moved and come to pass before them and in their midst.[88]

[87] KUBINYI, "Buda város pecséthasználata", pp. 285-286. 14 November 1329 (three seals): AO 2, p. 446; 18 November 1329: DL 49243 (traces of four seals on the dorse).

[88] *The Customary Law of the Renowned Kingdom of Hungary: A Work in Three Parts*

The earliest royal grants to use seals were probably not put into writing, but some fourteenth-century charters to use, renew, or authenticate seals have indeed come down to us. Sopron received Charles I's approval in 1340 for sculpting a new matrix (although without describing the image on the seal granted): "*destructo et abolito sigillo ipsorum veteri et publico novum sigillum autenticum sculpendo faciant preparari*" ("having destroyed and abolished their old seal let them prepare a new authentic seal by publicly carving it").[89] Fortunately and exceptionally, the matrix mentioned in the text has survived and is still kept in the town archives of Sopron (Fig. 24).

Another similar example is king Louis I's charter attesting to the authority of the municipal seal of Cluj in 1377. His grant was issued in response to a complaint by the envoys of the town, stating that the major courts and dignitaries of the realm refused to accept documents issued under their seal. Thereupon the king confirmed that

> *Iidem cives et hospites nostri de dicta Clusuar a modo et deinceps sub sigillo communitatis eorum in quo imago trium turrium sculpta fore perhibetur, in quibuslibet factis et causis eorum propriis duntaxat in litibus et iudiciis exercendis coram quovis iudice et iustitiario regni nostri ecclesiastico sive seculari movendis et emergendis litteras procuratorias iuxta regni nostri consuetudinem instar aliarum civitatum nostrarum regalium emanari facere valeant atque possint. Quibus quidem litteris procuratoriis in toto regno nostro* plenam fidem adhiberi volumus *et committimus harum nostrarum testimonio literarum mediante.*
>
> Our burghers of the said *Clusuar* are allowed and authorised from now on, following the custom of our kingdom, like our other royal towns, to issue letters of advocacy under the seal of their community, on which the image of three towers is said to be sculpted, in whatever issues and causes pertaining to them, namely in court cases and lawsuits to be brought up and handled in front of any secular or ecclesiastical court of our kingdom. And we wish to *attribute full authority* to such letters of advocacy in our entire kingdom through the testimony of our present charter.[90]

It needs to be added that in 1377 Cluj had not reached the highest level of autonomy yet (it was granted to the town in 1405), and the *littere procuratorie*

Rendered by Stephen Werbőczy (The "Tripartitum"), ed. J.M. BAK, P. BANYÓ, and M. RADY (Budapest and Idyllwild, 2005: DRMH 5), pp. 242-243 (Part II, title 13, 3§); the translation is also taken from this volume.

[89] HÁZI, *Sopron*, 1.1, pp. 77-78.

[90] 18 May 1377, edited in UGDS 2, No. 1071.

Fig. 25 Illuminated grant of arms featuring the coat of arms of the town of Košice depicted on the charter issued by king Sigismund, 31 January 1423 (Archív Mesta Košíce, Archivum secretum C2, MNL OL DF 269 164). Reproduced with the permission of Archív Mesta Košíce.

('letters of advocacy') were only interim documents in a court case. However, the king's intention to increase the trust in the probative value of the municipal seal added significantly to the authority of the urban community. As Ágnes Flóra states:

> This was not only an important step in the development of urban literacy and the establishment of a local chancery, but it also represented one step forward towards the free status of the town, i.e. direct subordination to the king.[91]

Exercising his authority in a similar vein, in 1369 Louis granted Košice the use of a new coat of arms based on the royal insignia. The grant letter gives a

[91] FLÓRA, *The Matter of Honour*, p. 39.

detailed description – although no depiction – of the image, which evokes the seals of Buda and Esztergom discussed above:

> *Formam clipei de signo nostro regio extortam desuper, videlicet unum tractum seu lineam flavei coloris tribus ymaginibus liliorum conpaginatum, et de subtus quatuor lineas rufas et totidem albas lateraliter habentis inperpetuum gestare valeant atque possint.*
>
> They should be allowed forever to carry the shape of a shield taken from our royal emblem, namely on top a blue-coloured band or chief decorated with the images of three lilies, and below four red and the same number of white bars placed side by side.

The king also added that the town was allowed to use this image "*in sigillo ipsius civitatis secreto et missivo ac vexillo*" ("on the secret or missive seal of the town and on its banner"). This grant is one of the earliest of its kind in Europe addressed to an urban community and not to an individual. It was renewed by king Sigismund in 1423 in an illuminated grant of arms (Fig. 25), to remunerate (or ensure) the fidelity of this wealthy and strategically important merchant town.[92]

Sigismund's other urban grant of arms was addressed to Pressburg. Being the westernmost town under Hungarian rule along the Danube, it was well suited for diplomatic meetings for Sigismund, wearing the crowns of Hungary and Bohemia as well as that of the Holy Roman Empire. In his old age the emperor was even considering moving his primary residence here. This can be concluded from several topographical changes that may be explained by the presence of the royal court, and above all the large-scale building operations carried out in the early 1430s on the castle, from which the detailed accounts of the summer building season of 1434 have survived.[93] The town was pressured to contribute to the costs well beyond its means. Probably both parties

[92] 7 May 1369: DF 269163; 31 January 1423: DF 269164. Both charters are still kept in the secret archives of the town of Košice: Archív mesta Košíc Archivum secretum C1 and C2. See J. Kirst, "The oldest coat of arms in Europe awarded to a city", in: *Košice in the Coordinates of European History*, ed. M. Hajduová and M. Bartoš (Košice, 2013), pp. 66-73.

[93] Sz. Papp, "Die neue Residenz Sigismunds in Preßburg", in: *Sigismundus Rex et Imperator: Kunst und Kultur zur Zeit Sigismund von Luxemburg, 1387-1437: Ausstellungskatalog*, ed. I. Takács (Mainz, 2006), pp. 239-245; J. Majorossy, "A foglalkozás topográfiája: A társadalmi tértől a személyes térig: A társadalmi mobilitás térbeli elemei a 15. századi Pozsonyban" [The topography of profession: From social space to personal space: Spatial elements of spatial mobility in fifteenth-century Bratislava], *Korall* 45 (2011), pp. 102-135.

Fig. 26 Grant of arms to Pressburg issued by king Sigismund on 9 July 1436 (Archív Mesta Bratislavy, Nr. 1436, MNL OL DF 274 282). Photo: Judit Majorossy. Reproduced with the permission of Archív Mesta Bratislavy.

were relieved when, partly as an act of reconciliation close to the end of the great work and partly to mark the end of the Hussite wars, on 8 and 9 July 1436 Sigismund issued a pair of solemn charters granting and further promoting the use of the town's coat of arms – the most spectacular of this kind ever given to any town in medieval Hungary. Alongside these, the magistrate of Pressburg managed to get the town's old privileges confirmed.[94]

From the fifteenth century, the practice of using the community's authentic seal also spread to the market towns. In their case it was their seignior who had to allow the use of this symbol and specify its validity, which usually extended to issues of property transfer within the boundaries of the settlement.[95]

[94] SZENDE, "Between hatred and affection", p. 206.
[95] GULYÁS *Mezővárosi önkormányzat,* pp. 210-212.

The seal as an object and as a source of communal authority needed and deserved special protection. The regulations of the *Ofner Stadtrecht* offer a good insight in how this should happen:

cap. 53. Wer das Statsigil uber iarr pehalten sol

Es sol auch ein deutscherr des Rats der stat sigil paÿde, das klain und das gros, inne haben, ydoch gesundert, das gros do man anders nicht mit sigilt, dan hantfesten, das sol verslossen sein und zum minsten mit zwayrr deütscherr purger petschaft versigilt sein. Aber das klain petschaft sol ein deutscherr geschwornerr purgerr haben verslossen in seiner lad und dar zu sol der statschreiberr den schlussel haben.

cap. 62. Von der stat insigel inhaltung so uns man ein ander richter und rat erwelt und pestëtiget

Alle zeit zu Sand Iörgen tag [...] sol man das gemain insigel zu dem Rathaus pringen, verslossen in der lad, do sol man es aus nemmen und sol es zaigen der gemain, darnach sol man es wider ein legen und versliessen und versigellen mit zwayr oder dryer deutschen herren sigil, dy des rats gewesen sein, und also verslossen und versiglt sol man es antwurtten dem pfarrerr zu unserr hauppharkirchen zu unserr lieben frawn zu pehalten, untz das derr richterr und der rat pestet warden, sunderr den slussel sol der statschreiberr pey ym haldenn.

cap. 53. Who should keep the municipal seal over the year

A German councillor has to keep both municipal seals, the small and the large, but separately; the large that one does not use for anything else than for sealing letters of privilege has to be locked up and sealed with the signet rings of at least two German burghers. The small seal has to be kept by a German councillor, locked in his chest, and the town notary should have the key to that chest.

cap. 62. The keeping of the municipal seals when one elects and confirms a new judge and council

Always on St. George's day [...] one has to take the seals of the community to the town hall, locked in the chest, and then one has to take it out and show it to the community, and thereafter one has to return it and lock it and seal it with the seals of two or three German gentlemen who had been members of the council, and once the chest is closed and sealed, one has to hand it over to the parish priest of our main parish of Our Lady until the [new] judge and council are confirmed; otherwise the town notary has to keep the key.[96]

These arrangements extend to several aspects that go beyond the practicalities of preparing and issuing documents. Some points, such as the ethnic division and participation in municipal governance and literacy, will be discussed in a later chapter of this book, but others merit special attention here. The first article, placed in the context of the regulation of the town chancery, indicates that the great seal of the town used for sealing charters of privilege (*hantfeste*), similarly to the use of the royal majesty seal in its own contexts, was in very infrequent use.[97] Most of the documents, as the surviving items also testify, were issued under the smaller seal of the town, to which the town's notary had regular access. But even if he was a trusted and respectful employee of the town, he had to cooperate with one of the councillors when using the seal, in whose chest the precious object was held. According to the statutes of Košice from 1404, the sealing of documents had to happen in the presence of the majority of the councillors.[98] It is also important to note the role that the private seals of the Buda councillors played in the custody of the municipal seal: the former ones were in themselves not authorised to authenticate documents of the community, but they authenticated the preservation of an object with higher authority.

The sources of Pressburg reveal a similar practice of differentiation between the two seals, and in 1439 both were cut anew by a local goldsmith.[99] The practice of keeping the small seal with one of the councillors must have been like that in Buda, judging from the fact that in 1455 the councillor Niklas Flins lost it and had to have it replaced.[100] However, he obviously did not lose

[96] *Ofner Stadtrecht*, cap. 53 and 62, pp. 81 and 84 respectively.

[97] This may have related to the custom of so-called sealing days that Bálint Lakatos observed in his analysis of the pragmatic literacy of market towns. LAKATOS, *Hivatali írásbeliség*, pp. 78-86.

[98] *Corpus statutorum municipalium*, ed. S. KOLOSVÁRI and K. ÓVÁRI (Budapest, 1885), 2.2, p. 87; MAGDOŠKO, *Samospráva mesta Košice*, p. 159, n. 730.

[99] AMB *Kammerrechnungen* 1439: "*Item am erichtag nach heiligen drey kunig tag hab wir gebn den Jost golschmid nach des purgermeister gescheft von den zwen stat insigln dy er gegrabn hat. – awsgenomen das silber nicht 2 fl. auri*", quoted by J. KIRÁLY, *Pozsony város joga a középkorban*. [The law of the town of Pressburg in the Middle Ages] (Budapest, 1894), p. 80, n. 1.

[100] AMB *Kammerrechnungen* 1455: "*hab ich gebn Hansen Feyertag den goltschmid umb das stat insigl, so der Flins verloren hat und wider ein neus hat begrabn lassn*", quoted by KIRÁLY, *Pozsony város joga*, p. 80, n. 4.

his compatriots' trust after this accident, since he was subsequently elected as the vice judge of the town.[101]

The second article (cap. 62) was entered in the *Stadtrechtsbuch* in the context of the yearly renewal and election of the magistrates on St. George's day, and describes events with a strong ritual character. First, the seal had to be taken out of its chest and presented to the community (*ostentatio*) which was part of the old magistrate's stepping down. Afterwards, the members of the old council had to seal the chest. Secondly, for the period of the election procedure, that is, during the time when the authority of the old council ceased and the new one was not elected yet, the chest holding the seal was entrusted to the leading priest of the main parish church of the town. This was a liminal time, without any council in force, and thus special arrangements had to be found to fill the power vacuum. The need for an interim solution was more symbolic than practical, otherwise the chest could have been kept simply at the town hall. However, with the involvement of the priest, the shift from one council's authority to the next acquired a spiritual dimension. Thirdly, to show that the Church nonetheless did not have a saying in the town's governance, it was noted that the key to the chest had to be kept as a rule by the town notary. To sum up, the handling of the municipal seals shows an intricate balance of trust relationships and their limits, as well as an intricate balance between public and private, church and secular, the elected leadership and the broader community.

That caution and vigilance surrounding the municipal seals could indeed be justified is shown by a gruesome case from Gradec, the royal town of Zagreb, where a falsifier of seals and documents was sentenced to death by burning in 1383:

> *Item, quod quia circa Paulum litteratum, filium Clementis, tria falsa sigilla invenimus et cum ipsis sigillis multas falsitates idem fecisse est repertus, ideo ipsum cremari facimus et comburi, ne ab eo forent exemplati.*
>
> Item, since we have found three false seals at Paul litteratus, son of Clement, and it was revealed that he committed much fraud with those seals, therefore we have him burnt, so that no one should follow his example.[102]

[101] GODA and MAJOROSSY, "Städtische Selbstverwaltung", p. 76, n. 75.

[102] I.K. TKALČIĆ, *Monumenta historiae liberae regiae civitatis Zagrabiae metropolis regni Dalmatiae, Croatiae et Slavoniae* 1 (Zagreb, 1889), No. 408, pp. 393-394.

This scandal compelled the town council to have a new seal cut and to order all previously issued documents to be presented for authentication and re-sealing within two years. This was a practice employed by the royal chancery when the king's majesty seal got lost during military campaigns, for instance in the ill-fated Wallachian campaign of Charles I in 1330, and later Louis I's venture in Bosnia in 1363. Recipients of documents all over the kingdom were affected by the requirement of verification, so it must have been known to the citizens of Zagreb as well.[103] Copying the documents into a municipal book was another remedy proposed, as will be discussed below.

The vicissitudes around the seals of Gradec, however, did not end with this. As an intriguing entry in the town's book of judgements describes, thirteen years later the castellans of Medvedgrad (a castle near Gradec that belonged to the king until 1398) invited the judge of Gradec and some other townspeople to the castle for lunch, assuring them of their good will ("*assecurando eosdem fide ipsorum*"). There, after the meal, the castellans robbed the judge of the town's seal as well as of his own, and imprisoned their 'guests' for a week, while they hid the seal somewhere. It is not explained in the description, though, why the judge carried the seals to the meeting – maybe there were some plans for drawing up a deal ... If one thinks of the strict rules of how Buda's seals had to be kept, the careless attitude of the judge of Gradec makes it likely that the town book only tells part of the story. In any case, the council declared the seal invalid ("*prefatum sigillum commisimus fore suis viribus cariturum*") and the documents issued under it, both before and after the robbery, null and void.[104]

Interestingly, there is no reference to appealing to the king or invoking his help in either of these cases. The town acted fully within its own authority, probably because of the turbulent times when royal authority was challenged. The first instance happened shortly after Louis I's death, when his daughter

[103] See A. GRÜNN [GÁRDONYI], "I. Lajos király megerősítő záradéka" [The confirmation clause of king Louis I], *Turul* 19 (1901), pp. 27-37. The charter of privilege of Debrecen, issued in 1361 and confirmed in 1364, is a good example from the urban context that carried this royal verification document: L. SOLYMOSI, "Debrecen 1361. évi kiváltságlevele" [The charter of privilege of Debrecen from 1361], in: *Debrecen város 650 éves: Várostörténeti tanulmányok* [650 years of Debrecen as a town], ed. A. BÁRÁNY, K. PAPP, and T. SZÁLKAI (Debrecen, 2011), pp. 9-22, at pp. 11-12.

[104] This is edited, together with the previous incident, in TKALČIĆ, *Monumenta Zagrabiae* 1 (Zagreb, 1889) No. 408, pp. 393-394; K.-D. GROTHUSEN, *Entstehung und Geschichte Zagrebs bis zum Ausgang des 14. Jahrhunderts* (Wiesbaden, 1967: *Osteuropastudien der Hochschulen des Landes Hessen, Reihe* 1, 37), pp. 147 and 232-233.

Mary inherited the throne, and the second one in 1397, when Ladislaus of Naples as a pretender tried to subvert Sigismund after the lost battle at Nicopolis. High politics and urban self-assertion met in a peculiar way in these crimes of abuse.

Communal Concerns: The Contents of Early Municipal Documents

After the survey of some formal elements and indispensable accessories of the charters issued by towns, let us return to the question whether this activity meant a common involvement. Naturally, the elected leaders were supposed to represent the town community as such. One can also assume that in many cases the councillors were present as witnesses at the transactions, or witnesses and jurors at court decisions described in the charters. This question can also be approached by looking at the contents of the texts and examining the issues they took up, and at the ways in which they reflected the interests of the community.

As to early urban documents, a significant proportion was connected to property transactions, one of the prime issues that required the testimony of writing from early on. This could apply to any kind of property, but it is even more understandable in the light of the significance of real estate ownership in towns. Owning a plot with a house was the entrance ticket to participation in the life of the community as a full-right burgher. Therefore it was crucial and legally binding for the civic administration to keep track of what happened to each plot within the town and its boundaries.[105] Some of the thirteenth-century charters also contain stipulations for controlling the change of ownership. The charter of Pest (1244) that was in a few years taken over by Buda, explicitly states that property can only be sold to outside persons if they are willing to move to the town and live there: "*Nullus hospes ex ipsis possessiones suas vel domos vendere valeat alicui extraneo, nisi in eadem villa volenti amodo habitare*" ("None of those guests may sell his possessions or houses to another outsider, unless to someone who wishes to reside in the same town from now on"). Such regulations had to be enforced by active municipal control. Another point in the same charter of Pest states that whatever properties a burgher buys he should enjoy without legal impediment if no one raises any objections with-

[105] See, e.g. *Power, Profit, and Urban Land: Landownership in Medieval and Early Modern Northern European Towns*, ed. F.-E. ELIASSEN and G.A. ERSLAND (Aldershot, 1996).

in a year and a day. It was the task of the civic authorities to control the observance of this rule, including the appropriate registration of the transaction date.[106]

The surviving texts of early municipal documents provide good examples for all these issues. The first certainly authentic document issued in Esztergom, for instance, not only testifies to the sale of a piece of property, in this case outside the town, but gives the exact measurements for it as well. This work of surveying and registering surely needed expertise that the civic authorities had to be able to provide. They also added the legally irrelevant piece of insider information that the lady selling the land needed the money in order to get medical treatment.[107] Most other documents from Esztergom, as well as the oldest pieces from Rodna, Fehérvár, Sopron, and Zagreb, also fall into the category of property transactions. In a couple of instances (Esztergom 1299, Patak 1305) the sale was the consequence of a previous pledging, when the debtor was not able to redeem his former property.[108] Countless other examples could be cited *ad libitum* from further fourteenth- and fifteenth-century documents. For instance, the earliest surviving municipal records from bishops' seats (see Appendix 4) also deal almost exclusively with real estate. Managing such transactions needed legal expertise to avoid any further claims and insecurity. The recurrent appearance of property transactions in front of the urban magistrates points to the expansion of municipal authority. The same was summarised and proclaimed, about 150 years after the first examples of such cases, in the *Ofner Stadtrecht* in the following way:

> *Keÿn kauffen nach verkauffen nach verphendung sol nicht mugen geschen dan nürt mit der stat prif allein. Vnnd was mit andern priefen geschicht, das wider bindet nach nicht kraft hat.*
>
> No buying or selling or pledging can happen without a deed issued by the town. And what is done with other deeds is neither binding nor has any force.[109]

In 1451 the council of Pressburg arrived at a similar resolution, namely that

[106] Pest 1244: EFHU 3.2, No. 34, p. 40.
[107] Esztergom 1255: EFHU, 3.2, No. 40, DF 236285.
[108] Esztergom 1299: DF 236351; Patak 1305: DL 57733.
[109] *Ofner Stadtrecht*, cap. 201.

> *khainlay brief die auf wern gebn worden ins der Stat Grundt, erb, weingartn oder hewser under des Capitl Sigl oder under frommder herschaft Sigl nit Kraft soln habn, ob die auch wern aufgangn, so sind dy chraftlos gesprochen word(en).*
>
> no deeds issued under the seal of any other authority, particularly not by the chapter of Pressburg, should carry any authority.[110]

What a difference compared to the close cooperation of the two authorities 150 years earlier! This principle also became part of the *Tripartitum*:

> *Item Fassio coram iudice aut duobus iuratis civibus ratione & pretextu quarumcunque rerum sive mobilium, sive immobilium in eorum medio vel territorio existentium & adiacentium facta semper rata permanet; [§1] nec valet alia Fassio inter ipsos cives super huiusmodi rebus coram aliis iudicibus regni vel in locis testimonialibus iure perennali facta.*
>
> Then, any recognisance regarding any movable or immovable goods whatsoever made among them or on their territory before a judge or two sworn burghers is always valid. Any other recognisance with perpetual right on such matters made by burghers before other judges of the realm or at places of authentication is not valid.[111]

When discussing property transactions, a particular clause is worthy of note, the so-called *evictio* ('warranty') specifying that the seller is obliged to protect the buyer from any future legal claims at his own expense. This was a typical element of Hungarian legal culture, also stipulated by royal legislation.[112] It was put into practice by the Fehérvár collegiate chapter already before the date when the civic authorities adopted it.[113] The presumably forged 1258 charter of Trnava also contains this element; a charter issued by the town of Buda in 1318 already terms it *antiqua consuetudo*.[114]

The second main issue, partly overlapping with property transactions, was inheritance. Testamentary freedom, a right of both legal and economic signifi-

[110] KIRÁLY, *Pozsony város joga*, p. 134, n. 1.

[111] *Tripartitum* Pars III. titulus 13; DRMH 5, pp. 392-393.

[112] DRMH 1, 1298: 69§. On the significance of this item of customary law see A. KUBINYI, "A budai jogkönyvről: Ismertetés Mollay Károly monográfiájáról" [On the Ofner Stadtrecht: Review of Károly Mollay's monograph], *Tanulmányok Budapest Múltjából* 14 (1961), pp. 643-645, see further RADY, *Medieval Buda*, pp. 60-61; LAKATOS, *Hivatali írásbeliség*, pp. 109-110.

[113] Fehérvár 1270: DL 83130.

[114] Trnava 1258: CDES 2, No. 625 (probably a forgery); Buda 1318: MNL OL, DF 229964.

cance, was one of the basic prerogatives included already in the earliest charters granted to *hospites*. This meant that for most urban families their acquired property, including all movables and an increasing amount of immovable assets, could be disposed of at their owners' free will. This was yet another issue stated in the charters of privilege which needed written administration in order to ensure the rights of the beneficiary and exclude any claims by the testator's relatives. To quote the royal charter of Pest (1244) again: "*item quicumque ex ipsis sine herede decesserit, possessiones suas dimittendi facultatem habeat, cui volet*" ("whoever from among them dies without an heir should have the right to leave his goods to whomever he wishes"). Smooth, peaceful, and reliable inheritance procedures were indispensable for the operation of any urban community.[115]

In one of the earliest urban documents the magistrates of Sopron, together with the local Knights Hospitaller, testify to the testamentary donation of Pero, burgher and former judge of the town, of his village Klingenbach (Kelénpatak) to the abbey of Klostermarienberg (Borsmonostor).[116] This example shows that the town had authority in the matter even if the donated land was outside its borders and the beneficiary was a religious community. Foreign business partners (from Utrecht: Esztergom, 1265; from Ghent: Esztergom, 1272 from Venice: Esztergom, 1299) were also subject to civic administrative authority in case the other party or the property involved was under the town's jurisdiction.

A small, but still significant group of early town charters is connected to the relationship of civic authorities and ecclesiastical institutions, especially as far as church revenues were concerned. Such an instance was the 1268 agreement between the ferrymen of Pest and the Buda chapter on the duties on salt. The transaction was mediated by the magistrates of Buda as a third party.[117] Among the ecclesiastical revenues, tithe collection was a crucial issue among a community's prerogatives. As early as 1238 the charter granted to Trnava specified the particular way of collection: "*more Teutonico*" ("according to German custom"), meaning that the one-tenth of the crop owed to the Church was taken from the fields and not from the people's barns. A closer involvement (and perhaps a preceding conflict) can be assumed in 1282, when the burghers of Esztergom obliged themselves in writing that they would pay their

[115] FÜGEDI, "Városprivilégiumok", pp. 270-273. The administration of last wills will be discussed in detail in Chapter 3.

[116] Sopron, 1276: UBB 2, pp. 91-92.

[117] Buda 1268: *Budapest történetének okleveles emlékei – Monumenta diplomatica civitatis Budapest*, 1, *1148-1301*, ed. A. GÁRDONYI (Budapest, 1936), pp.100-101; DL 106084.

tithes to the chapter without any delay or reluctance. They even promised the chapter to send one of their councillors to assist the tithe-collectors' work.[118]

A different kind of involvement between town and gown can be observed in the case of the agreement between the town of Bihač and the Cistercian abbey of Topusko about not seducing each other's tenant peasants.[119] Securing the stability of workforce for both parties on the one hand, and providing the right of free movement for the settlers on the other, were two, often hardly compatible, intentions. The use of written rules and agreements was one way of preempting conflicts arising from this contradiction.

Two further early charters regulate the coexistence of towns and religious orders within the confines of the towns. In 1275 the magistrates of Banská Štiavnica joined their parish priest in transferring the local St. Nicholas chapel to the use of the friars. The text even describes briefly the ritual how the parish priest performed the transfer: "*ablato almacio de capite et tradendo ad manus fratrum et dicendo: Investio vos ex nunc capella beati Nicolai, quam vobis dono et confero perpetuo possidendam*" ("after having taken off the *almacium* from his head and handing it over to the brothers, saying: I invest you from now on with the Chapel of St. Nicholas that I donate and assign to you for possessing it forever").[120] Another charter, issued by the civic administration of Sibiu in 1292, records the transfer of the local hospital from the town authorities to the Order of the Holy Spirit under the condition that the monks celebrate masses for the spiritual benefit of the inmates. This issue is remarkable for at least two reasons. First, it reports about the very first hospital managed by civic authorities in Hungary, and secondly, the town gives up this institution in favour of a religious order. The general trend was exactly the opposite: towns usually took over monastic hospital foundations from the previous ecclesiastical management. Unfortunately, no further documents are at our disposal which would explain the reason for this course of events.[121] It is clear, however, that in all these cases between church and town authorities, the outcome of the negotiations was binding and definitive for the whole town

[118] Esztergom 1282: EFHU 3.2. No. 75; DF 237567.

[119] Bihač 1271: CDCr 5, 613; DF 283328.

[120] Banská Štiavnica 1275: CDH 5.2, pp. 308-309; DL 923.

[121] Sibiu 1292: UGDS 1, No. 260; DF 244566. See J. MAJOROSSY and K. SZENDE, "Hospitals in medieval and early modern Hungary", in: *Europäisches Spitalwesen: Institutionelle Fürsorge in Mittelalter und Früher Neuzeit*, ed. M. SCHEUTZ, A. SOMMERLECHNER, H. WEIGL and A.S. WEIß (Wien and München, 2008: *MIÖG Ergänzungsband* 51), pp. 409-454.

community, and writing was the means to confirm and stabilise such decisions that dissented from customary arrangements.

A third kind of town document was connected to carrying out orders from the central administration, such as conducting investigations or introducing a new owner into a property. An example of such a task is the report sent to king Andrew III by the magistrates of Németi (as its name shows, a town of German settlers, now part of Satu Mare) about the result of their investigation concerning the expulsion of a nobleman from his estates.[122] Such orders implied trust between the king and his town, and they show that the king used royal towns to perform tasks in order to assist the central administration in such duties similar to the *loca credibilia* discussed above.

Finally, there is a group of documents that reflected another form of extending written communication as well as taking care of communal concerns: the missives. Towns sent letters of inquiry, information, or warning to each other often on a daily basis in later medieval Europe.[123] Inter-urban correspondence did not have a legally binding character but rather followed the pattern of interpersonal exchange. Missives adhered to a different format, that of personal letters, with an invocation at the beginning and a signature at the end, written, as a rule, on paper. This signature, however, did not contain the name, but only the title of the sender: "*richter und rat zu Prespurg*" or similar. This was also an expression of the first person plural, the 'communal we' of the town authority. This feature was strengthened by sealing the letter in the format of *litterae clausae* with the municipal seal, and not with the personal seal of the judge or mayor in whose name the letter was sent.

Naturally, inter-urban contacts worked most intensively between communities close to each other and sharing the same concerns, for instance the towns forming the Pentapolis alliance in the north-east, or the group of royal towns close to the western border: Sopron, Pressburg, and Trnava.[124] Another typical pattern was that smaller towns (market towns) turned to bigger urban centres in their neighbourhood for help, advice, or information. This custom spread gradually to all levels of the settlement network. Bálint Lakatos, studying the late medieval pragmatic literacy of market towns, observed that on the level of Hungary as a whole, about one third of all surviving documents are missives,

[122] Németi 1299: HO 7, p. 277; DL 56570.

[123] M. JUCKER, "Trust and mistrust in letters: Late medieval diplomacy and its communication practices", in: *Strategies of writing*, pp. 213-236.

[124] K. SZENDE, "Beziehungen zwischen Preßburg und Ödenburg im späten Mittelalter", in; *Städte im Donauraum*, ed. R. MARSINA (Bratislava, 1993), pp. 135-148., at pp. 138-140.

although with strong regional variation: in the northern counties (present-day Slovakia) it was almost 50 per cent, reflecting the dense network of bigger and smaller towns there. However, this proportion is calculated for the entire medieval period, and most of the missives were written in the late fifteenth and early sixteenth centuries. At the same time in Slavonia, the region between the Dráva and Sava rivers, a much lower percentage of the surviving documents belong to the group of missives.[125]

Lakatos also points out the strong correlation between the range of town-market town correspondences and the market areas of major towns. Even if the surviving material is largely one-sided (mostly the letters written by smaller places have been preserved in the archives of their bigger counterparts), the spatial distribution of these letters nicely circumscribes the contacts cultivated by the towns in their hinterlands.[126]

Procuring information and sustaining broad-ranging and trustworthy information networks was vital for every town; the further investigation of this issue, which would warrant a modern, quantitative analysis of urban correspondence with the methods of network studies, would go beyond the scope of the present volume. But even such an advanced analysis would capture only a fraction of real-life contacts, and even less or their contents. For one can observe a frequent practice, used both in communication between towns and by envoys of kings or noblemen, which shows the limits of trust in writing – or rather the mistrust in those who may seize the letters. It often happened in Hungary, just as elsewhere in Europe, that the envoys presented only a letter asking the recipient to trust what the carrier of the letter would say – and the rest was left to oral communication. The standard phrase in these letters of reference evoked, once again, trust: "*fidem creditivam adhibeatis*" or in German "*wellet im daz gelawben*".[127]

[125] LAKATOS, *Hivatali írásbeliség*, pp. 39-40.

[126] LAKATOS, *Mezővárosi oklevelek*, forthcoming, Chapter 3.4.2. I am grateful for the opportunity of reading the text of this chapter before publication.

[127] Royal towns were both senders and recipients of such letters, see e.g. HÁZI, *Sopron*, 1.2, p. 40 (the town of Sopron sends its *subiudex* – a rarely used title – to the castellans of Sárvár, 1411); *ibid.*, p. 69 (the town of Sopron sends an envoy to János Kanizsai, archbishop of Esztergom, 1413); HÁZI, *Sopron*, 2.6, p. 15 (István Kanizsai, former master of the doorkeepers, sends an envoy to Sopron, 1402-1408); *ibid.*, p. 33 (the former judge of Szombathely sends his son to the judge of Sopron, undated, early fifteenth century); *ibid.*, p. 45 (István, son of János Kanizsai, *comes* of Sopron County, sends an envoy to Sopron, 1413); *ibid.*, p. 104 (Laurentius de Swr, castellan of Landsee, sends an envoy to Sopron to seize the properties of his debtor, *c.* 1430); IVÁNYI, *Bártfa*, p. 278 (king Matthias Corvinus sends an envoy to Bardejov, 1473).

Let me finish this section with quoting the full text of a letter sent by the council of Pressburg to Sopron, presumably in 1433. This case may be considered a late and asymmetrical parallel of the trick of the Mongols quoted in the Introduction. The letter describes the physical features of an impostor who pretended to be the king's messenger carrying his letter, and warns the magistrates of Sopron against him, advising them to capture the man to please the king:

Vnsern freuntlichen dinst zuuor! Erbern, Weisen, libn freunde! Wir tun ewch zu wissen, das nulichen zu vns ein pot mit vnsers gnedigen herrn des kuniges brief kumen ist. Derselbe brief nicht recht gewest ist mitsambt dem poten vnd hat gelt von vns gefordert. Darumb liben freund merkt eigentlich wie der pot ein gestalt hab: er ist einawket an dem tenken awg vnd er hat ein grosse schrammen vbr das rechte wang hyncz in kynpakken, vnd ab derselb zu ewch qwäm vnd ichts an ewch fordern ader eyschen würde, so sehet euch fur vnd haldet in, wann wir wol derfarn haben von vnsers gnedigen hern des kunig gnad, das er falsch ist. Habt auch dorinne ewern fleiss pey ewern vmbsessen, das er derfarn vnd aufgehalden werden möchte, dorinne derczeigt ir vnserm gnedigen herrn dem kunig vnd auch vns ein sunderlich gut gefallen. Gegeben zu Prespurg, am freitag vor dem suntag Cantate.

Richter vnd rat der stat Prespurg.

We offer our friendly service! Our honourable, wise and dear friends! We inform you, that recently a messenger came to us with a letter of our gracious lord the king. This letter was not real, and nor was the messenger, and he demanded money from us. Therefore, our dear friends, remember what the messenger looks like: he is blind in the left eye and he has a large cut above his right cheek back to his temple. Should the same person come to you and should he demand or claim something, watch out and stop him, because we have learned it for sure from our gracious lord the king that he is an impostor. So, watch out carefully in your neighbourhood that he be caught and retained, and do our gracious lord the king and us a great favour. Given at Pressburg, on the Friday before Cantate Sunday.

The judge and the council of the town of Pressburg.[128]

[128] HÁZI, *Sopron,* 2.6, pp. 105-106.

Conclusions: Trust in Charters

This chapter traced the process how Hungarian royal towns started issuing their own authentic documents from the middle of the thirteenth century onwards. This breakthrough was dependent on the convergence of two major processes. One of these was the establishment of trust in writing within the urban communities, and, in broader terms, the institutionalisation of urban governance. The judge and the members of the council were subject to election and could change yearly (although it was not always the case),[129] but the documents issued by them kept their validity beyond their office, thanks to the possession of an authentic seal by the civic community. The examples presented above also showed that familiarity with the written word, at least in the upper strata of urban society, preceded the issuing of documents by the towns themselves. Towns were recipients of royal charters and mandates from the king and other dignitaries of the realm. Townspeople could also turn to royal officials and to places of authentication to obtain documents. Finally, some of the settlers in cities in the *medium regni*, especially with Walloon or Venetian background, but some of the Germans, may have been familiar with pragmatic literacy from their previous homelands or home towns.

The second process was the acceptance of the legal significance and probative value of the documents in the legal practice of medieval Hungary. The recognition of charters as reliable evidence was a long process. Up to the end of the twelfth century, old charters were seldom mentioned, because they did not provide strong enough proof in themselves without the support of witnesses' testimonies. From the thirteenth century, the situation changed radically, and charters were generally accepted in all fields of administration and justice.[130] In the administration of the right of landownership, the possession of a piece of land was satisfactorily proven by the possession of the relevant documents: letters of donation or purchase, seisin (*statutio*, *introductio*), and perambulation of the boundaries. On the other hand, anyone holding such charters

[129] Data are too scanty for generalisation, but as a trend one can assume that long office-holding was more frequent in the thirteenth-fourteenth century than later. Rectors of Buda, subject to royal appointment, changed rarely: between 1307 and 1347 there were only three persons serving in this capacity, and a few judges of Pressburg elected by the community also held their office for decades.

[130] SZENTPÉTERY, *Magyar oklevéltan*, pp. 79-80. See also K. GUOTH, *Az okleveles bizonyítás kifejlődése Magyarországon* [The development of using documentary evidence in Hungary] (Budapest, 1936).

concerning a certain landed property could claim rights to that piece of land. In other fields of life, the certification of the line of descent, cases of inheritance, and division of property between the descendants all needed the presentation of written evidence. Trials and subsequent phases of litigation were also preceded and followed by documents.

Latin usage expressed this feature very clearly: the word *iura*, which originally meant 'rights of possession', sometimes also denoted charters providing these rights. For example, in a letter of donation from 1438, king Albert referred to some lost charters as "*iura seu literalia instrumenta*". In a will from 1488 the testator simply said that his *iura* were to be found in his chest.[131] This also meant that when an estate was sold or alienated in other ways, the charters had to be transferred to the new owner of the property. If this did not happen peacefully, it could involve a long series of litigation or violent actions, and if the former owner still retained something from the documents, they lost their validity.[132] A telling example of the validity of written evidence crossing the boundaries of human life is that, according to cap. 248 of the *Ofner Stadtrecht*, if someone died while being involved in a court case, a sealed charter would suffice to prove his case.[133]

Comparative diplomatic analysis of early charters issued by town authorities can disclose characteristic elements of the charter-issuing practice in the Carpathian Basin. While this type of analysis is not the focus of the present study, it is instructive to quote some of the results summarised by András Kubinyi in his work on the usage in Buda and Fehérvár. He pointed out that, apart from some general features, the documents issued by the magistrates of Hungarian towns divert in many formal and formulaic elements from the practice of the neighbouring countries. For instance, besides the general type of charters presented above, where the *intitulatio* starting with *nos* is the first element of the *protocollum* part, elsewhere (in the Austrian provinces, Regensburg, Magdeburg, etc.) charters starting with an *invocatio* or *addresse*, or even with an *arenga*, are not infrequent. This feature can be observed in royal charters as well.[134] Equally striking is the difference that everywhere in the region

[131] A. CZOBOR, "A családi levéltárak a középkorban" [Family archives in the Middle Ages], *Levéltári Közlemények* 18-19 (1940-1941), pp. 380-440, at pp. 381-382.

[132] CZOBOR, "A családi levéltárak", pp. 417-420.

[133] *Ofner Stadtrecht,* cap. 55 and 248, pp. 82 and 143.

[134] KUBINYI, "Buda város pecséthasználata", pp. 286-287. An example of a charter starting

apart from the Carpathian Basin, thirteenth-century charters contain a separate list of witnesses of the recorded legal transaction, while in Hungary this element is missing or was amalgamated with the *intitulatio*, listing the members of the council who performed the role of witnesses as well. Another difference is that in many other regions municipal seals are used to authenticate documents issued by private persons. In these instances, the *intitulatio* mentions the issuer in first person singular, and only the *corroboratio* reveals the fact that the town's seal was used for this purpose. This practice seems to have been extremely rare in Hungarian towns, the few surviving examples all coming from the western border region.[135]

Conversely, there is a great degree of similarity between the usage of formal elements in civic documents within the Carpathian Basin. Furthermore, this practice shows several common traits, on the level of the use of identical formulas, with documents issued by other authorities: the kings, the main magistrates of the realm (palatine, judge royal, etc.), and the places of authentication. Since the chancery activity of these other bodies started earlier than that of the towns, the former obviously exerted a strong influence on the latter. It is especially evident in case of property transaction documents that these took charters issued by places of authentication as their models. An important element is the common use of the warranty clause (*formula evictionis*) which, as we saw above, became widespread in the thirteenth century with identical formulation in charters of various issuers.

Although it was not discussed in detail in this chapter, at the time when the value of charters increased due to the special respect attributed to authentic documents, the production of forgeries is evident as well.[136] At least two of the allegedly thirteenth-century municipal documents (Dubica, 1244 and Trnava, 1258) are strongly suspected of being forgeries. Detecting and identifying fakes was of primary importance for administering justice on a country-wide

with an arenga is DF 201647 (UBB 2, pp. 91-92) issued in Sopron in 1276. In this case the unusual arrangement was probably because the document was issued together with the local Hospitaller convent.

[135] KUBINYI, "Buda város pecséthasználata", pp. 287-288. A good example for private charters corroborated by the town's seal is the letter of debt issued in 1461 by the Eisenstadt burgher Christoff Stockhaimer and his wife under the town's hanging seal. See its edition and analysis in B. LAKATOS, "Kismarton város két oklevele (1461, 1502): Városi szervezet és oklevéladás" [Two charters of the town of Eisenstadt (1461, 1502): Urban governance and charter-issuing], *Soproni Szemle* 71 (2017), pp. 286-306. The same practice was followed in some credit contracts issued on behalf of Jewish creditors. See Chapter 5 for further details.

[136] MOSTERT, "Forgery and trust".

level as well as for the individual issuers, to maintain their own credibility and the stability of administering justice. When exposed, producers of fake charters were to be branded with a burning seal on their forehead and face, and their chapter or convent was punished by losing their seals, that is, the right of issuing documents.[137] The crime and punishment of the above-mentioned *Paulus litteratus* from Zagreb for using falsified seals is the most severe that we know about from the period, but certainly not the only one of its kind.

How did these processes connect to the formation of trust and authority, the central question of this volume? First, in all these issues, towns acted as communities not only in name, but also concerning the range and relevance of subjects tackled in the documents. Decisions taken and promulgated in writing were binding on all members of the community. At the same time, fitting into the overall legal system of the kingdom, and using the models provided by the pragmatic literacy of other social groups (the ruling dynasty, the chief dignitaries, and, most importantly, the places of authentication) offered urban communities important points of reference and interconnectedness. This observation confirms a similar conclusion drawn on the basis of the analysis of town charters, namely that the form and content of these documents was informed by practices created by and for other social groups: the nobility and the Church in the land, rather than by towns in other European regions.

By adopting the practice from already established bodies, and in some towns even co-operating with these in the issuing of the earliest municipal documents, town magistrates established their authority and reinforced the trust in their documents. This trust enabled civic authorities to extend their document-producing activity to matters beyond property transactions, and becoming non-negligible partners in communication with the king and the nobility. In towns with well-preserved archives, such as Pressburg and Sopron, one can also observe a shift of trust from one model institution to another. Research by Jenő Házi and particularly Juraj Šedivý has shown this shift from reliance on the local *comes* to the local chapter or convent as place of authentication, and then from this body to the independent chancery of the town.

Co-operation with ecclesiastical bodies or with seigniorial *scriptoria* in writing up charters was a common phenomenon in many European towns, even in the highly urbanised Low Countries, where the first writing office with its

[137] There is evidence to prove that at least the second part of the punishment was imposed on the chapter of Pressburg in 1373, and on the chapter of Eger under king Matthias, although later both places regained their right to issue charters. SZENTPÉTERY, *Magyar oklevéltan*, p. 216.

own notary was documented in 1277. In the most important cities of the Holy Roman Empire, the first data on professional notaries appear somewhat earlier: Cologne (1227), Braunschweig (1231), Strasbourg (1233), and Lübeck (1243) were the protagonists.[138] The eastern border regions were fully in accordance with this pace, particularly in Villach and in Wiener Neustadt, where the first civic notaries were mentioned in 1227 and 1232 respectively. The corresponding dates for Vienna (1260) and Linz (1262) are closer to those of the Moravian and Bohemian towns: Most (Brüx) seems the earliest (1264), followed during the next couple of decades by Litoměřice, Jihlava and Kolín. Heinrich, notarius civitatis of the Old Town of Prague appears by name 1288, but on stylistic grounds his activity can be traced back to 1282. Demand for administrative documents in the Bohemian capital increased at such a pace, that under the next notary, the council decided to have a town hall built, not only with an office, but also a 'service apartment' for the notary.[139] The list of these dates indicates that the western half of Central Europe was clearly among the trend setters, followed by the Polish lands and Hungary with a few decades' delay.

The date of the first document issued by the council of Pressburg independently from the scriptorium of the chapter, 1344, coincides with the royal grant to hold an annual fair in the town.[140] This was one of the very first grants of its kind in the Angevin period, followed by similar ones to all important border towns within a couple of decades. This coincidence, in my view, cannot be by chance:[141] the fair grant acknowledged the commercialisation of towns which gradually transformed from military and agricultural communities to merchant towns linked in a Europe-wide trade network. The autonomy and self-esteem of towns increased accordingly. It is telling that the revenues from

[138] W. PREVENIER, "Urban chanceries in the Low Countries from the twelfth to the fourteenth century: The European context", in: *Stadt, Kanzlei und Kultur im Übergang zur Frühen Neuzeit: City Culture and Urban Chanceries in an Era of Change*, ed. R. SUNTRUP and J.R. VEENSTRA (Frankfurt am Main, 2004), pp. 3-13; J. KEJŘ, *Die mittelalterlichen Städte in den böhmischen Ländern: Gründung – Verfassung – Entwicklung* (Köln, Weimar, and Wien, 2010: *Städteforschung* A, 78), pp. 328-329.

[139] R. ZEHETMAYER, "Notare und Schreibpersonal in steirischen Städten im 13. Jahrhundert", in: *Rutengänge: Studien zur geschichtlichen Landeskunde: Festgabe für Walter Brunner zum 70. Geburtstag* (Graz, 2010), pp. 47-59; L. VODRÁŽKOVÁ and V. BOK, "Prag", in: *Schreiborte des deutschen Mittelalters: Skriptorien – Werke – Mäzene*, ed. M. SCHUBERT (Berlin, 2013), pp. 425-459, at p. 454; KEJŘ, *Die mittelalterlichen Städte*, pp. 330-337.

[140] VMMS p. 138.

[141] There were significant chronological differences in this process. The wave of commercialisation reached Buda earlier; it had the right to hold annual fairs already in the thirteenth century. Cluj, e.g. obtained the right at a later date, and the small market towns even later.

the fairs were in several cases directed towards the building of town walls or other defensive structures, key features of urban security and prestige.[142] All these changes were bound to leave their imprint on administrative literacy, too: the establishment of regular chanceries with their appropriate municipal books, to be examined in the next chapter, may be regarded as a direct consequence.

The image presented here, however, may seem too idealistic, and to show only one side of the coin. There were certainly cases where the discrepancy between the 'official we' and the 'real we', in other words, the administrative elite in power and other groups within the town population, led to dissent, factions, and revolts. Investigating what role the written word in general, and official documents in particular, played in the emergence and escalation, as well as the later settlement of conflicts would form another chapter in the history of civic literacy, and indeed, social history.[143] It will be the task of future studies to follow how, through royal intervention or other forms of compromise, urban communities managed or were forced to find viable solutions for communal life. As we have learned from studies by Franz-Josef Arlinghaus and others, "establishing certain texts as independent points of reference in the discourses of the time may have helped to alleviate the problem".[144] An important element in settling conflicts was to have a written protocol of the investigation and the steps to be taken. Having a reliable point of reference such as a document of this kind may be one of the many examples to show how trust (in writing) was indeed, in the sense as Luhmann explained it for modern times, a tool for overcoming social complexities.

[142] K. SZENDE, "*Nundinae seu forum annuale*: Sokadalomtartási engedélyek Nagy Lajos várospolitikájában" [*Nundinae seu forum annuale*: Grants to hold annual fairs in the urban policy of Louis the Great], in: *Hatalom, adó, jog*, pp. 231-262.

[143] For an exemplary study of these issues in regions of Europe with much more copious source material, see P. LANTSCHNER, *The Logic of Political Conflict in Medieval Cities: Italy and the Southern Low Countries, 1370-1440* (Oxford, 2015), esp. pp. 40-59.

[144] ARLINGHAUS, "Point of reference", p. 299.

Chapter 3

From Charters to Books and Back

The Institutionalisation of Writing Offices

The emergence of urban literacy was a gradual process: its legal framework and authority had appeared before a fully-fledged infrastructure was in place. As Ágnes Flóra has recently summarised,

> one cannot speak of established urban chanceries before the notaries appear as permanently employed in town services, since the simple issuing of individual documents concerning urban matters did not necessarily entail the presence of an established chancery.[1]

In fact, it may have taken several decades, even up to a century from receiving the first charters of privilege and the right to have an authentic seal to reach the level when a *litteratus* was permanently employed for keeping the municipal records. The transitional period could be managed in several different ways. Documents issued in the town's name and under the town's seal could be written by a literate member of the urban elite, the parish priest, by officials of the royal administration, or various ecclesiastic institutions as places of authentication. In other cases, town magistrates requested documents to be issued or authenticated by these bodies. It could also happen that the recipients themselves took care of the preparation of the document in the name of the town

[1] Flóra, "*Laborem circumspecti*", p. 314.

(following the practice of *Empfängerausfertigung*), and just had it sealed by the municipal authorities.[2]

There is very little information at our disposal concerning the social background and provenance of the notaries – even less than in case of the town judges and councillors. Only the frequency of the German-sounding names among them may give some indication. The pattern of the first appearance of this office in each town, however – even if there is an element of chance in the survival of the data – can reveal interesting trends (see Appendix 4).

The earliest civic notary from Hungary known by name is "*magister Johannes filius Cantus prothonotarius [...] castri novi montis Pesthientis*", that is, of Buda, founded as a 'relocation' and taking over the privileges of Pest after the Mongol invasion. *Magister Johannes* is mentioned in 1315 as a witness, invited *ad maiorem cautelam*, that is, for the sake of surety, to the last will of Peter, *medicus et confector medicinarum* at Buda.[3] The testator must have been one of Buda's first secular intellectuals. His trust in the notary who appeared besides two Dominican friars and seven (!) priests of the Holy Virgin parish church testifies to his high esteem for the literate profession. Even if the document in question was not issued by the town, the mention of a *prothonotarius* indicates that Buda as the foremost commercial centre and soon-to-be capital of Hungary had several scribes, headed by Johannes and his successors. Arguably, a chancery had been set up by that time; this is also supported by the relatively high number of surviving fourteenth-century documents with a provenance from Buda, despite the destruction of the town's medieval archives.[4]

The 'silver medalist', as far as the surviving sources allow us to tell, is "*magister Thomas, principalis notarius civitatis Grecensis*", that is from Gradec, the royal town of Zagreb. He represented his town in 1321 in front of the

[2] This is proven in detail based on palaeography by J. Šedivý for the Pressburg chapter and Pressburg. The deed issued by the town of Krupina on 24 February 1316 on the donation of a mill to the Premonstratensian convent of Bzovík can also considered as the beneficiary's copy (*Empfängerausfertigung*) based on its appearance, particularly the decorated initials (DL 1865). Likewise, the earliest charter of Nová Baňa, from 1347 (DF 237050), on the donation of a mill, and the charter of Stary Tekov of 1358 (DF 237074) in favour of the monastery of St. Benedict (Hronsky Benadík), both written in bookhand, fall presumably in this category.

[3] DF 262657, 30.12.1315. The document was issued by the seven priests and sealed by two of them, but it may have been written by the notary. Edited in *Monumenta Ecclesiae Strigoniensis*, ed. F. KNAUZ, 2 (Esztergom, 1882), pp. 716-717; summary in *Anjou-oklt.* 4, pp. 79-80.

[4] RADY, *Medieval Buda*, pp. 54-56; I. KENYERES, "The fate of the medieval archives of Buda and Pest", in: *Medieval Buda in Context*, pp. 52-68.

ban of Slavonia (the king's local governor) in a court case concerning the introduction of new sorts of customs against their next-door neighbours and rivals, the cathedral chapter of Zagreb. He was still in office three years later, when he had the charter of Gradec granted in 1242 by Béla IV transcribed under Charles I's new seal.[5] Zagreb, the main link in the communication network between the Adriatic (or more broadly speaking, the Mediterranean world) and the inland area of the Carpathian Basin, was understandably in the forefront of the development of civic literacy. Its contacts with the Dalmatian cities as well as with the German lands provided valuable models. At the same time, any cooperation with the cathedral chapter of Zagreb, and using its place of authentication for the purposes of the civic community, was jeopardised by the constant enmity between the two parts of modern-day Zagreb, Kaptol and Gradec; therefore Gradec had to set up its own chancery at a relatively early date. Incidentally, Gradec and Buda were the first two towns to receive written royal endorsement to hold annual fairs, in 1256 and 1287 respectively.

"*Magister Jacobus notarius ... civitatis Pestiensis*", representing his town in a court case against the chapter of Buda over the salt tax in 1326, is the third in the row. His employment by the magistrate of Pest is remarkable, since after the 1240s Pest had formally lost its autonomy to Buda.[6] Nevertheless, the two towns on opposite banks of the Danube formed an agglomeration with strong central functions and busy commercial life early on, which presupposed the use of pragmatic literacy on both sides.

The next piece of evidence relates, somewhat surprisingly, to the mining towns of Upper Hungary (present-day Slovakia), some of which had been founded just a decade or two earlier. Colinus, notary from Gelnica, is mentioned in 1327; "*magister Nycolaus notarius ... de Smulnychbana*" (Smolník) appeared in 1340 and again in 1344, whereas in 1353 the town had a notary called Johannes. Sifridus from Kremnica figures in the record in 1342, Johannes from Nova Baňa in 1346, "*magister Petrus notarius*" from Baia Mare (in Transylvania) in 1347. Notaries from the earlier established centres of silver and copper mining are detectable with a slight delay: Wilhelm from Banská

[5] TKALČIĆ, *Monumenta Zagrabiae*, 1 (Zagreb, 1889), No. 115, pp. 98-99; No. 128, pp. 108-109; K.-D. GROTHUSEN, *Entstehung und Geschichte Zagrebs*, pp. 146-147; N. KLAIĆ, *Zagreb u srednjem vijeku. Povijest Zagreba*, 1 [Zagreb in the Middle Ages: History of Zagreb, 1] (Zagreb, 1982), pp. 529-536.

[6] DL 106092, dated to 09.06.1326. N. KNAUZ, "A budai káptalan regesztái 1148-1649" [Abstracts of the records of the Buda chapter], *Magyar Történelmi Tár* 12 (1863), pp. 113-116, dates it to 02.06.1326.

Štiavnica from 1365 (following an unnamed "*antiquus notarius*" on the town's payroll),[7] Nicolaus from Banská Bystrica in 1379 (followed by "*Henricus staetshreybir*" in 1395), as well as "*Nicolaus filius Nicolai civis et notarius*" from small Ľubietová in 1382.[8] The early development of professional chanceries in the mining towns follows from the importance of these places and their products for the royal treasury. These *litterati* were most likely involved in the smooth operation of the mines as well as the running of the settlement and providing them with manpower. In fact, there are several examples attesting that officials of the royal financial administration and the magistrates of a mining town issued official records together.[9]

The first evidence for professional notaries from Sopron and Pressburg, two towns that developed from early administrative centres into royal towns, also dates to the mid-fourteenth century. "*Magister Sewfridus notarius civitatis Supruniensis*" approached the cathedral chapter of Győr as place of authentication in 1354 to have an important document received by the town transcribed "*ad uberiorem rei cautelam*". Apparently, his name was preserved not through a document written by him, but through his mediation between the products of two other writing offices. He was followed in his office by "*Wylhelmus notarius et scolasticus*", mentioned in 1358, who combined his office with that of a schoolmaster, a career path that could be occasionally found elsewhere, for instance in Cluj and Gradec, as well.[10] In Pressburg, the name of the first municipal notary, also Siegfried, was noted down in the town book that he was in charge of. He was definitely not identical with his namesake from Sopron, since his handwriting could be identified already on documents from 1348 and 1350.[11]

[7] From the context it transpires that the entry in the town book of Banská Štiavnica in 1365, "*dedit notario de Puckans*", cannot be taken as proof of a notary of Pukanec, as stated by M. ŠTEFÁNIK, "Pukanec", in: *Lexikon stredovekých miest*, p. 365. This and several similar entries from the same year denote expenses paid by Banská Štiavnica to their own notary and messengers to procure official documents. See the edition in FEJÉRPATAKY, pp. 7-8.

[8] Some of these data, such as those from Gelnica and Kremnica, were only preserved in the form of eighteenth-century transcriptions of the medieval charters, but since they fit a pattern supported by original documents, their content may be accepted as authentic.

[9] Lupoldus / Leopoldus *magister machinarum* and the council of Kremnica, 14 July 1331 (DF 250152); 10 November 1342 (DF 249505 and 249507); Nicolaus Bohemicus *comes urburarius* and the magistrates of Ľubietová, 18 December 1382 (DF 261423).

[10] HÁZI, *Sopron*, 1.1, pp. 104 and 115; HÁZI, "A városi kancellária", pp. 207-209. Similar examples from Bohemian towns: KEJŘ, *Die mittelalterlichen Städte*, p. 336.

[11] ŠEDIVÝ, "Die Anfänge der Beurkundung", pp. 97-99; AMB No. 109; LEHOTSKÁ, "K počiatkom", 326. Documents written by him are, according to Lehotská: AMB Nos. 188, 196, 197,

At the same time, the custom of employing a professional notary spread to other merchant towns in the northern border areas. The earliest example here is Kežmarok in 1348, at that time still under royal dominion,[12] followed by Žilina in 1357, and with some delay by Bardejov (1376 by title, 1385 by name). Košice also invested in attracting skilled personnel; direct evidence for this is only preserved from 1395.[13] In Transylvania, pride of place is given to Cluj, where the municipal notary, Reymarus, figures as legal representative and envoy in two cases in 1352 and 1353 respectively; the notary of Brașov was mentioned accidentally as a witness in 1388.[14] One may wonder why the third and perhaps in the fourteenth century the richest urban community, Sibiu is not represented among the examples. One explanation may be that, being the centre of the *universitas Saxonum*, the management of its administration was tied to this larger community, just as the town used the seal of *provincia Cibiniensis* on their earliest preserved charter in 1292 (No. 19 in App. 3). "*Magister Johannes de Cluswar procurator communitatis civium de Cybinio*", acting on behalf of the town and its parish priest in 1321, seems to have been only an advocate, with no administrative duties.[15] The first notary of Sibiu, Johannes Goldner, acting as an envoy to acquire a transcription of the Andreanum, is attested from 1423.[16]

The author of the late fourteenth-century *Ars notarialis* already takes the presence of municipal notaries in towns for granted.[17] Several of these earliest names of notaries appeared for the first time in the town accounts drawn up by themselves, one of the items among the expenses being their regular salaries. In free royal towns and mining towns, the notaries would be recruited from among lay intellectuals; it was only in market towns that the scribal services of local priests were requested in the fourteenth century. For instance, two re-

232, 234, 235, 248, 249, 288, 290, 313, 315, 359; see LEHOTSKÁ, "Vývoj bratislavskej", p. 234.

[12] DF 288969. LAKATOS, *Hivatali írásbeliség*, p. 88, n. 533, quotes it as 1348, and likewise *Anjou-oklt.* 32, *1348*, ed. F. SEBŐK (Budapest and Szeged, 2015) pp. 449-450, No. 932. The database DL/DF mistakenly has 1368. On the town: K. FÁBROVÁ, "Kežmarok", in: *Lexikon stredovekých miest*, pp. 171-182.

[13] MAGDOŠKO, *Samospráva mesta Košice*, pp.158-159.

[14] See the data in Appendix 4.

[15] UGDS 1, No. 380, pp. 350-352; *Anjou-oklt.* 6, Nos. 189, 191.

[16] UGDS 4, No. 1932, pp. 190-191.

[17] "*Ars notarialis formularia sub Ludovico I rege Hungariae conscripta*", in: M.G. KOVACHICH, *Formulae sollennes styli in cancellaria ... regni Hungariae olim usitati* (Pest, 1799), p. 23. On the formulary book, see GY. BÓNIS, "Uzsai János Ars notariája" [The *Ars notaria* by János of Uzsa], *Filológiai Közlöny* 7 (1961), pp. 229-260.

markably early charters concerning properties at Sátoraljaújhely (at that time simply Újhely) from 1307 and 1310 respectively, when the town was still in royal ownership, were issued by Achilles, the parish priest of Patak, under his own seal. From the fifteenth century, laypersons, usually the schoolmaster, took over this task.[18]

As the first paid employees of municipal authorities, notaries provided a previously unseen level of professionalism and continuity in administration, laying the foundations of the regular handling of cases in writing. Already the earliest representatives of this profession were often entitled *magister*, and from the early fifteenth century the richest towns routinely employed notaries who had studied abroad, completed their degrees at the *facultas artium*, and acquired some basic legal education, if not a degree in law. They were fairly mobile and often crossed borders: the fifteenth-century notaries of Sopron came from nearby Vienna, and Žilina in the northern border zone recruited its chancery personnel from Moravia.[19] From the fourteen notaries known by name from medieval Bardejov, one came from Sabinov, one from Zvolen, and one from as far as Uničov in Moravia. From among the notaries of Prešov, three proudly used the title of *baccalaureus*, which they obtained at the conveniently close university of Cracow.[20]

The earliest description of the election of a town notary by the local community has been preserved in the municipal register of Gradec for 1397. It shows an already consolidated routine concerning the procedure and the payment, but does not mention the required qualifications:

> *Item nos communitas fecimus et creavimus nostrum in notarium Thomam filium Isip in nostro generali consilio promittentes sibi plenarie dare suos proventus prout aliis notariis administrabantur.*

[18] DL 1709 and DL 1759, presented in L.Sz. Gulyás, "From Latin to Hungarian: Transforming of official written practice in the market-towns of Hegyalja from the 14th to the 17th Century", *Studia Historica Nitriensia* 21.1 (2017), pp. 67-86, at p. 73; for the later practice: Gulyás *Mezővárosi önkormányzat,* pp. 208-209.

[19] J. Sopko, "Pisári a vzník Žilinskej knihy" [The scribes and the genesis of the Žilina book], in: *Národnostný vývoj miest na Slovensku do roku 1918* [Ethnic development in the towns of Slovakia until 1918], ed. R. Marsina (Martin, 1984), pp. 41-71, at p. 70. S. Andea, "Scriere i societate: de la *magister* la *litteratus*" [From magister to litteratus in Transyvanian medieval writing], in: *Scris i societate*, pp. 29-46, 281-286, discusses the uses of the term *magister* in all possible social contexts.

[20] On Bardejov: *Lexikon stredovekých miest*, pp.89 and 95, nn. 210-232; on Prešov: *ibid.*, p. 342.

> Item, we as a community have appointed Thomas son of Isip as our notary in our general meeting, promising publicly to give him his revenues as it has been administered to other notaries.

The *Ofner Stadtrecht* stipulates the yearly appointment of the notary by the judge and the council, and includes models for an oath at his entry and for a resignation speech after his year in office.[21] However, in towns where sources survive in greater density than in Buda, one can find plenty of notaries who remained in office for several years, even decades. It was indeed in the town's best interest to keep these skilled people, who became intimately familiar with the internal affairs as long as possible, to ensure continuity and confidentiality. From the early fifteenth century onwards one finds an increasing number of cases when small biographies of long-serving notaries can be reconstructed, mainly from the documents composed by themselves. For instance, Niklas Kromer, hailing from Nová Baňa, was the notary of Trnava between 1394 and 1447 and organised the municipal records into archives.[22] His counterpart in Sopron was Konrad Ernst, a distinguished burgher of Vienna, who had to flee from his debts and the wrath of Albert V, duke of Austria (1404-1439). He found a safe haven in Sopron as the leader of the local writing office between 1419 and 1450. His erudition is indicated by his ownership of a copy of Alexander de Villa Dei's famous Latin grammar, the *Doctrinale puerorum*.[23]

Finally, let me mention Liebhart Egkenfelder, one of the most notable intellectuals working in the urban administration in fifteenth-century Hungary. He served first as a scribe beside Konrad Ernst in Sopron, between 1437 and 1441, from where he moved to Pressburg to take on the task of the town's notary until his death in 1457. As testified by his last will, he owned one of the most outstanding secular private libraries of his time, 38 hand-written volumes, partly copied or compiled by himself. These included, besides the Old and New Testament, several liturgical books and theological treatises, novels about King Arthur and Alexander the Great, and various books pertaining to his profession

[21] *Ofner Stadtrecht*, cap. 44 and 61; RADY, *Medieval Buda*, pp. 54-55.

[22] V. RÁBIK, "Pôsobnosť pisárov a notárov v Trnave v stredoveku" [The activity of scribes and notaries in Trnava], in: *Mestská kniha príjmov trnavskej farnosti sv. Mikuláša z roku 1495* [The book of benefices of the St. Nicholas parish in Trnava from 1495], ed. V. RÁBIK (Trnava, 2006), pp. 79-89; *Lexikon stredovekých miest*, pp. 540, 548.

[23] HÁZI, "A városi kancellária", pp. 213-214; MOLLAY, "Többnyelvűség", *Soproni Szemle* 21 (1967), pp. 317-333.

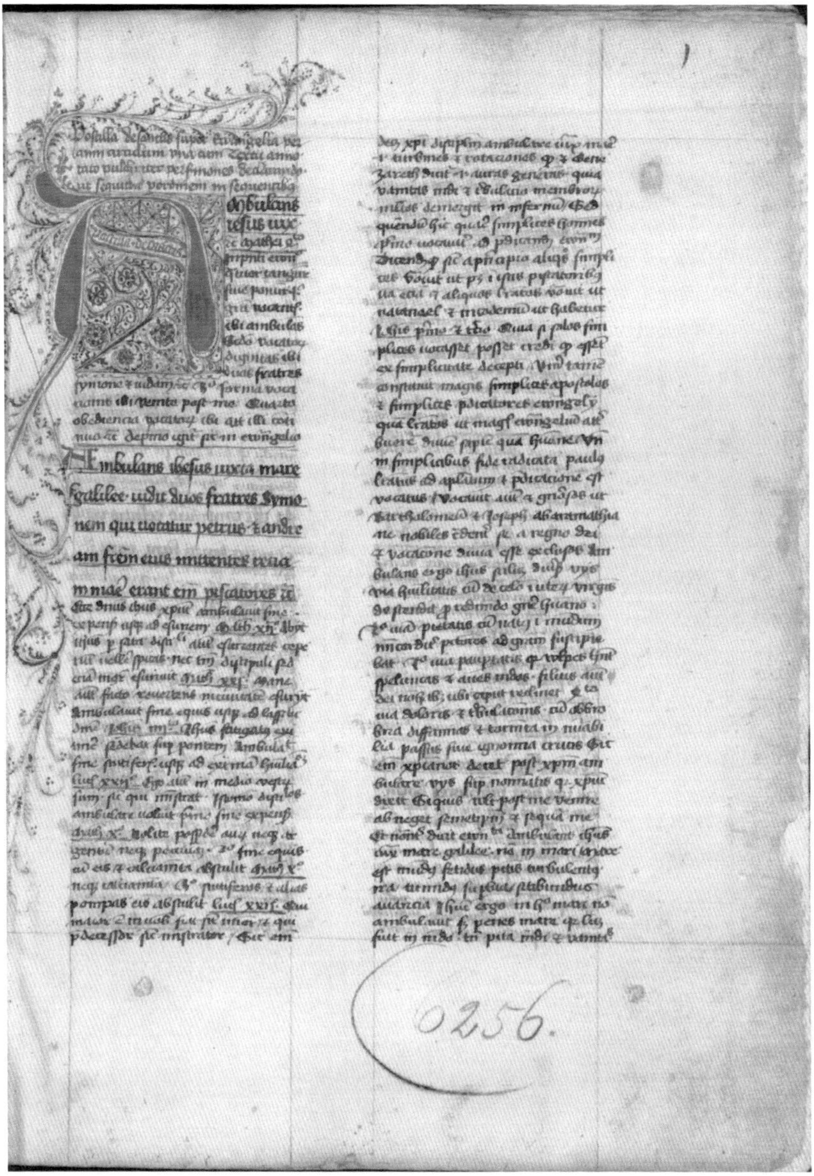

Fig. 27 First page of a book of sermons copied by Liebhart Egkenfelder, vice notary of Sopron, notary of Pressburg, *c.*1425-1450 (Budapest, Library of the Hungarian Franciscan Province, Múz.1, Esztergom bequest). Photo: Zoltán Fáy. Reproduced with permission.

as a notary.[24] Two of the volumes mentioned in his last will are still extant and testify to his intellectual as well as scribal capacities (Fig. 27).[25]

With the increasing expansion of administration, town chanceries became diversified and usually employed more persons than a single notary. In Gradec, a *vicenotarius* is mentioned already in 1355, and by the early sixteenth century even smaller towns such as Krupina employed auxiliary personnel, occasionally from abroad, in their writing offices.[26] Studies of larger bodies of fourteenth- and fifteenth-century archival material, for instance in Sopron and Pressburg, enable the identification of hands with documents and scribes, and this can shed light on the professionalisation of writing and the way work was distributed between the personnel of increasingly differentiated writing offices.[27]

Often additional scribes were enlisted to help the notaries, or occasionally the services of the local schoolmaster, or even of some of the pupils, were requested. For instance, in Sopron, in 1459-1460, students helped with collecting the thirtieth tax (customs on foreign trade) that was farmed by the town.[28] In Bardejov during the building operations of the town walls, they were responsible for keeping account of the stones. The accounts of 1439 of the same town name both "*Nicolaus scriptor*" and "*Franciscus notarius*". The former received small sums (50-150 den.) on a weekly or fortnightly basis, so he was probably charged with specific tasks. Previously, in 1437 a certain Georgius "*scripsit in absentia notarii bibales*"; in 1440 another person, "*Laurentius iuvenis*", "*fuit*

[24] Egkenfelder's last will is published in PT 1, No. 183, pp. 241-248; quotations from pp. 242-243. On his book list, see J. SPIRITZA, "Testament Liebharda Egkenfeldera, bratislavského mestského notára v rokoch 1441-1456" [The last will of Liebhart Egkenfelder, town notary of Pressburg], *Zborník Slovenskeho Narodneho Múzea História* 7 (1967), pp. 165-182.

[25] One of the volumes is in the library of the Hungarian Franciscan Province (Múz. 1); see L. SZELESTEI NAGY, "Liebhard Eghenvelder egy kódexe az Esztergomi Ferences Könyvtárban" [One of Liebhard Eghenvelder's codices in the Franciscan library of Esztergom], *Magyar Könyvszemle* 93 (1977), pp. 271-274; *Kódexek a középkori Magyarországon* [Codices in medieval Hungary]. Exhibition catalogue, ed. A. VIZKELETY (Budapest, 1986), No. 112; the other one is in Brussels, Bibliothèque Royale Albert I., Ms. 8879-80; see *Kódexek* No. 112a. See also ŠEDIVÝ, *Mittelalterliche Schriftkultur*, pp. 141, 143, 163; SZENDE, *Otthon a városban*, pp. 223-231.

[26] TKALČIĆ, *Monumenta Zagrabiae* 4, pp. 11, 14. Thomas *prothonotarius* appears in 1365 (*ibid.*, p. 350), but since all of them were named Thomas it is impossible to tell if he is identical with the notary mentioned in 1321 and 1324, or with the *vicenotarius* from 1355. For Krupina, see LAKATOS, *Mezővárosi oklevelek*, forthcoming.

[27] LEHOTSKÁ, "Vývoj bratislavske mestske kancelárie"; ŠEDIVÝ, "Die Anfänge der Beurkundung", pp. 101-109.

[28] HÁZI, *Sopron*, 2.4, pp. 78-79, 97-98.

notarius in absentia notarii": he took over the tasks on a temporary basis.[29] At the same time, most market towns had no professional notaries until the second half of the sixteenth century; before that, they relied on similar interim solutions as the royal towns had done two centuries earlier.[30]

Notaries regularly appeared in roles other than scribes: as delegates sent to the king or other authorities, usually accompanying the town judge, petitioning for the donation or renewal of some earlier prerogatives granted to the town. In fact, most of the first appearances of civic notaries in the written record can be found in preambles of renewed charters of privilege. The first notaries known from Gelnica, Kremnica, Ľubietová, Smolník, and Baia Mare, as well as Gradec, Sopron, and Žilina from among the non-mining towns, all appeared in their capacities of diplomats and mediators, that is, trusted representatives of their respective towns.[31] This role is fully understandable, since the deputations had to present the appropriate documents to the royal chancery and make sure that they received what they expected. Educated literacy and legal expertise were indispensable for this activity. For instance, "*magister Johannes*", representing Smolník, pleading for the control over some newly discovered gold deposits in 1344, presented to the Master of the Treasury two charters by king Charles I, one by Louis I, one by Queen Elizabeth, two more by the chapter of Spiš, and his own letter of reference – convincingly, since the town won the case against the archbishop of Esztergom.[32]

Notaries were paid quite handsomely, as an entry of the earliest town book in Pressburg in 1364 concerning the notary Siegfried under the heading of communal expenses ("*pro civitate et pro necessitate civitatis*") testifies: "*Item cives dederunt notario civitatis pro precio huius anni XX libras*" ("Item the burghers gave the municipal notary twenty pounds as this year's salary").[33] From the same year, the wages of the notary in Banská Štiavnica were entered (most likely, by himself) into the earliest surviving town book of this important mining town: "*Item notario 18 flor*".[34] Other items due for the notary in several

[29] Entry in the town account book: "*Item scolaribus qui conscripserunt lapides 12 den.*", FEJÉRPATAKY, p. 487. Further data: *ibid.*, pp. 372, 469, 485, 509.

[30] LAKATOS, *Hivatali írásbeliség*, pp. 86-87.

[31] The latter one asked for the grant of an annual fair, see SZENDE, "Nundinae", pp. 238-239.

[32] *Csáky* 1.1 (Budapest, 1919), pp. 93-97.

[33] The manuscript is kept as Archív mesta Bratislavy 3.a.1; edited: FEJÉRPATAKY, pp. 40-41; described in GODA and MAJOROSSY, "Städtische Selbstverwaltung", pp. 89-90. On the notary: ŠEDIVÝ, "Die Anfänge der Beurkundung", p. 109.

[34] FEJÉRPATAKY, p. 1; further data on his wages and reimbursements: *ibid.*, pp. 2-23, *passim*.

towns were reimbursements for travel expenses for diplomatic missions and other errands on behalf of the town, as indicated above. In Pressburg in 1410 and 1411 the "*Ratio notarii civitatis*", the pay of notary Johannes, was a separate heading in the town accounts, and each time he received yearly wages (*jar lewn*). Some entries indicate that notaries were also entitled to official attire (*hoffgewant*), which testifies to their representative role.[35] The accounts show that it was in the towns' best interest to settle their debts and to keep their notaries in their service as long as possible.[36]

The notaries were welcome to participate in other urban businesses, too. In Zagreb, the statutes of the cathedral chapter from 1334 prescribed that one percent of the wine- and grain-tithes of Gradec had to be given "*pro notario communitatis pro suis laboribus in exigendo*" ("to the municipal notary for his labours in claiming") – an effective incentive to increase the chapter's revenues, too.[37] In Bardejov, where linen-bleaching was a communal enterprise supported by royal charters, the notaries also took their share in the accounting of the bleaching plant. Their involvement in trade was even more common. For instance, the notary's house in Bardejov had a cellar with wine barrels. This town lies far north of the wine-growing districts, but transit trade in wine towards Cracow was an excellent source of income, and such facilities allowed notaries to benefit from this opportunity. The notaries were also involved in transporting commodities on behalf of the town, and were recorded for this reason in the customs registers.[38]

Besides receiving regular salary from the town, the notaries were also entitled to fees for fulfilling commissions for single documents for private persons. The *Ofner Stadtrecht* includes under the heading *Von des Statschreibers schreib lonn* ('Of the municipal clerk's writing salary') the most complete list of notary's tariffs for drawing up different sorts of legal documents, with altogether thirty-one types of letters listed (Fig. 28).[39]

[35] FEJÉRPATAKY, p. 309, Bardejov 1432: "*statschribers hoffgewant Philipp Cromern flor. auri 6*"; Banská Štiavnica, 1364: *Lexikon stredovekých miest*, p. 66.

[36] FEJÉRPATAKY, pp. 64, 67. similar data from Trnava: *ibid.*, pp. 121, 127. In 1419 the notary's yearly wages were 40 florins, a respectable sum. In Bardejov in 1432 the notary recived 200 florins. This sum probably included some reimbursement, too, plus a special allowance "*pro adductione sue uxoris huc*", a sort of relocation allowance. This shows how eager the town was to employ him (*ibid.*, p. 314). Further information on the wages and revenues of notaries from Transylvanian towns: FLÓRA, "*In laborem*", pp. 320-321.

[37] TKALČIĆ, *Monumenta Zagrabiae* 1 (Zagreb, 1889), Appendix to No. 166, p. 146.

[38] FEJÉRPATAKY, pp. 254-286, *passim*; pp. 308, 372, 376, 378.

[39] *Ofner Stadtrecht*, cap. 50.

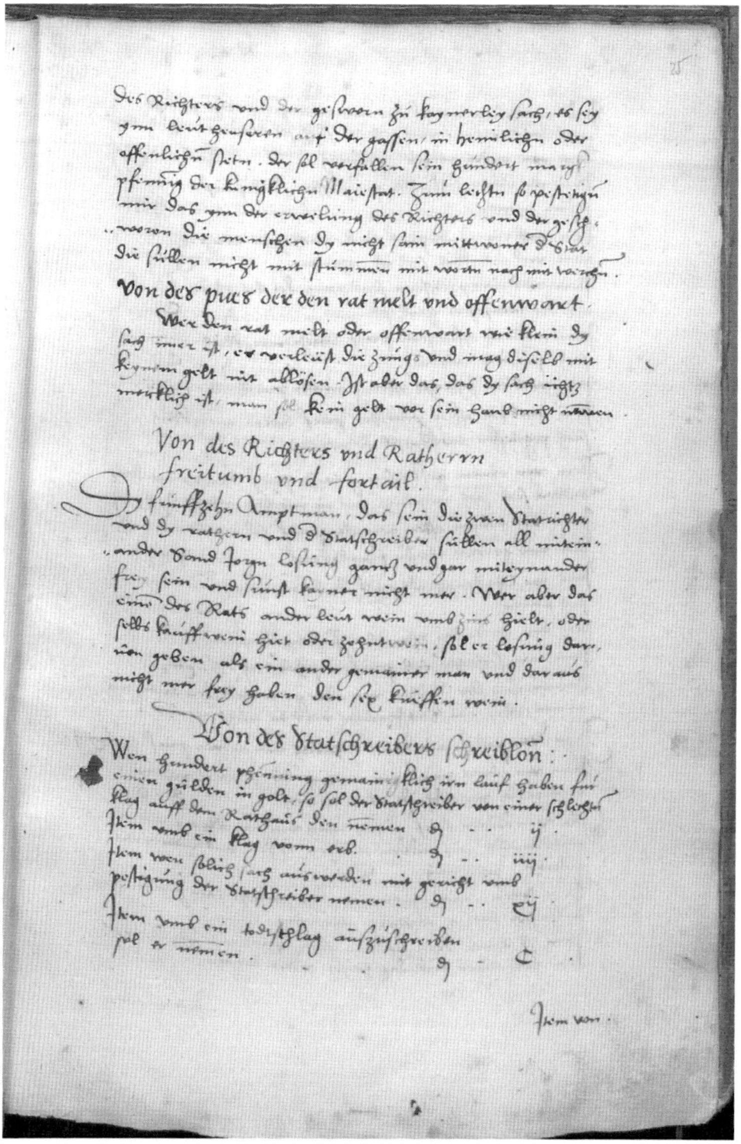

Fig. 28 Sixteenth-century copy of the *Ofner Stadtrecht*, so-called Cromer-Handschrift, formerly owned by Leonhard Cromer, notary of Košice († 1582). On the lower part of this page, under the heading "*Von des Stadtschreiber schreiblon*" begins a detailed list of the notarial tariffs for preparing various documents (ELTE University Library, Collection of Manuscripts and Rare Books, No. B 31). Reproduced with the permission of the ELTE University Library.

This was the highest level of professionalisation that writing in towns reached in Hungary. No scribes' guilds, like the one in Vienna that had its 'headquarters' in Mary Magdalene's chapel beside the Stephansdom,[40] are mentioned in connection with any of the towns. Neither do notaries public make a frequent appearance, because the places of authentication served the needs of secular parties; furthermore, in his so-called urban decrees of 1405, king Sigismund expressly forbade their involvement in court cases between laypeople in towns:

> *Decrevimus insuper quod nullus publicus notarius in causis, quae inter duos laicos vertentur, sive coram iudice ecclesiastico sive saeculari procurare audeat vel ullatenus advocare*
>
> We have decreed, furthermore, that no notary public dare to intervene in any way or act as an advocate in cases between two laymen, either before an ecclesiastical or a lay judge.[41]

Only clerics having issues to be settled at canon law courts needed their services; therefore, they mostly settled in bishop's seats with a high proportion of clergy, or took on other jobs as parish priests or prebendaries.[42]

A growing professionalisation of town administration, possibly following the model of the royal chancery practised from the early fourteenth century,[43] is attested by the addition of notes on the documents referring to chancery procedures: the council's order to the writing office to issue the document (*commissio*), or the report on this given by one of the councillors (*relatio*). Understandably, most examples of this procedure have been preserved on charters from Buda, but Pest, Fehérvár, and Košice also followed this path. It was partly a practical arrangement, partly an issue of prestige.[44] Other marks on

[40] R. KOHN, "Versuch einer Nutzungs- und Ausstattungsgeschichte des Kapellenkomplexes aus historischer Sicht", in: *Die Virgilkapelle in Wien: Baugeschichte und Nutzung*, ed. M. KRONBERGER (Wien, 2016), pp. 167-171.

[41] 15 April 1405; art. III. DRMH 2, p. 36.

[42] E. CSUKOVITS, "Közjegyzők a középkori Magyarországon" [Notaries public in medieval Hungary], in: *700 éves a közjegyzőség Magyarországon* [700 years of notaries public in Hungary], ed. G. ROKOLYA (Budapest, 2008), pp. 54-73.

[43] Charters with such notes by the royal chancery reached the towns in ample numbers. The earliest specimen, e.g. in the Sopron archives dates to 1333, see HÁZI, *Sopron* 1.1, pp. 62-63.

[44] See the examples of documents issued by the councils of Buda, Fehérvár, Pest and Košice in: B. IVÁNYI, *Debrecen és a budai jog* [Debrecen and the law of Buda] (Debrecen, 1924), pp.

the dorse of the documents indicate that they were registered in the relevant municipal books. This was the next step in the growing professionalisation of the town chanceries.

Municipal Books as Instruments of Civic Governance

Municipal books or *libri civitatum* indicate fundamental changes in the concept and practice of written administration and authenticity. The reasons and sequence of their appearance shed light on broader issues of governance, authority – and trust. Historians of administration have long been interested in this process, especially on the level of taking stock of the material and describing the archival collections and the individual examples of town books at our disposal. Many of the volumes were edited recently in modern editions, and there have also been numerous attempts at their classification.[45] In the Hungarian context, so far local case studies concentrating on one or two books or municipalities have dominated the research agenda; general overviews are relatively rare.[46]

In this survey, I shall use a broad definition of municipal books, considering all collections of documents in book format that were kept and regularly used at town chanceries for administrative purposes. Town books can clearly be distinguished from individual documents by their multiple entries, structured content, and the lack of sealing as means of authentication. A contemporary definition can be found in the *Ofner Stadtrecht,* summarising the custom-

20-21, n. 42-44; e.g. Fehérvár, 1471: "*Relatio Emerici parvi et Francisci carnificis iuratorum*", DL 17267.

[45] E. PITZ, *Schrift- und Aktenwesen der städtischen Verwaltung im Spätmittelalter: Köln – Nürnberg – Lübeck* (Köln, 1959), pp. 17-23; D. GEUENICH, "Was sind eigentlich 'Stadtbücher'? Versuch einer Definition", in: *Stadtbücher als namenkundliche Quelle,* ed. F. DEBUS (Mainz and Stuttgart, 2000), pp. 17-29. On the editions of town books from medieval Hungary, see Appendix 6.

[46] L. BLAZOVICH, "Die Stadtbücher und das Ödenburger Gerichtsbuch", in: *Gerichtsbuch – Bírósági könyv*, pp. 17-32; J. MAJOROSSY and K. SZENDE, "*Libri civitatum*: Városkönyvek a középkori Magyar Királyság közigazgatásában" [*Libri civitatum*: Town books in the administration of the medieval kingdom of Hungary], in: *Tiszteletkör: Történeti tanulmányok Draskóczy István egyetemi tanár 60. születésnapjára,* ed. G. MIKÓ, B. PÉTERFI, and A. VADAS (Budapest, 2012), pp. 319-330; in Czech: J. MAJOROSSY and K. SZENDE, "Městské knihy ve středověkých uherských městech se zvláštním zřetelem na bratislavskou knihu Protocollum Testamentorum", in: *Stav a perspektivy*, pp. 199-212; ROHÁČ, "Entstehung der Amtsbücher", pp. 407-416.

ary law used in Buda. It includes the following statements on the use and value of municipal books:

> *cap. 52. Dy stat sol haben ein pesunderr mergklich puech, das sol alle iarr in anfang und in gang des gerichtes vermergkt und vernewt warden under des richter und der ratherren namen, als das statgrundtpuech, do sol der statschreiberr dÿ maÿnung und inhaltung aller prief, dy uber erb und gescheft und ander namhaftige trefliche sach geschriben und under der stat sigil gesigelt werden, gar ordenlich und gruntlich vermergken. [...] Auf das, ob einem menschen sein prief verloren oder verprandt oder sunst under christen oder juden entpfrömbt worden, so sol man dem selbigen menschen ob er des pegert, des rechten helfen mit andern statbriefen [...].*
>
> *cap. 55. [...] wan dem stat puech zu glauben ist als den statpriefen versigilt mit dem stat sigil.*
>
> cap. 52. The town needs to have a special particular book that has to be marked and renewed when the court starts to operate under the names of the judge and the councillors, as the basic municipal book (*statgrundtpuech*), where the municipal notary has to enter and write up properly and thoroughly the essence and contents of all letters that had been written about inheritance and wills and other notable relevant issues and had been sealed under the municipal seal. [...] So that, if a document gets lost, or it is burnt, or alienated otherwise by Christians or by Jews, one should be able to help legally the person to whom it belonged with other charters [...].
>
> cap. 55. [...] since one has to entrust the town book just as much as the municipal documents sealed with the town's seal.

This regulation clearly proves that by the early fifteenth century, municipal books were considered as the approved instruments of urban pragmatic literacy in Hungary; the practice of using them must have been established long before they were codified.[47]

Since Buda as the most important royal city played a model role in the legal life of other cities and towns in the realm, it is reasonable to assume that this applied to the use of municipal books as well. The *Ofner Stadtrecht* – a town book itself – has come down to us in three manuscripts, from three differ-

[47] Kenyeres, "The fate of the medieval archives", pp. 57-59.

ent towns: Pressburg, Košice, and probably Cluj.[48] This fact indicates that the leaders of local administration were positively interested in copying and applying the regulations of the Buda law, including the above-quoted chapters on town books. Before the fifteenth century, however, there must have been other sources for the dissemination of the idea.

During the process of adapting the use of town books, urban authorities got into contact with at least four different tiers of administration, each representing different levels of literacy. The first of these was the royal chancery; the second the local authorities executing the king's commands at county level;[49] the third were the chapters and convents operating as places of authentication. The fourth were the writing offices of other cities and towns both in Hungary and abroad, first and foremost as previous residences of some of the burghers and the domiciles of their commercial partners. Contacts across borders were the strongest with municipalities in the southern part of the Holy Roman Empire and in Lower Austria (Regensburg, Cologne, Nuremberg, Vienna, Hainburg), as well as with Moravia, Silesia, and Lesser Poland (Olomouc, Wrocław, Cracow). These towns provided models for the legal acceptance and probative value of town books.

Many of the authorities listed above, notably the royal chancery, the places of authentication, and the writing offices of cities abroad used some sort of books in their administrative practice, which served as potential models for Hungarian royal towns. These books can be classified in broad terms concerning the origin of their contents as follows:

– Cartularies (copies or abstracts of charters received);
– Register books (texts or abstracts of charters issued);
– Books of 'original content'.

It is impossible to estimate how many cartularies existed in medieval Hungary, but only a handful of them have survived. The oldest and best-researched volume is the so-called *Liber Ruber* of the Benedictine Abbey of Pannonhal-

[48] GÖNCZI, *Ungarisches Stadtrecht*, pp. 82-83.

[49] G. ISTVÁNYI, "A megyei írásbeliség első korszaka" [The first period of county literacy], *Századok* 71 (1937), pp. 517-552; I. TRINGLI, "Megyék a középkori Magyarországon" [Counties in medieval Hungary], in: *Honoris causa: Tanulmányok Engel Pál tiszteletére* [*Honoris causa*: Studies in honour of Pál Engel], ed. T. NEUMANN and GY. RÁCZ (Budapest and Piliscsaba, 2009), pp. 487-518.

ma.[50] The *Liber privilegiorum episcopatus Zagrabiensis* consists of copies of charters related to the bishopric of Zagreb up to the middle of the fourteenth century. Places of authentication in a few exceptional cases compiled cartularies of their own charters of privilege from the first half of the thirteenth century, to have them always at their disposal. This practice represented an important conceptual change of cartularies all over Europe. As pointed out by Paul Bertrand, the early books under this name had a memorial function, the later ones had a pragmatic purpose.[51]

Register books containing documents issued by places of authentication themselves appeared later. The model for these religious communities may have been the central church administration, the registers kept at the Papal Curia, the busiest hub of European written communication, and the most developed overarching bureaucracy. Here the registering of outgoing bulls and the introduction of the book format as the most suitable technical solution for the easy retrieval of information were put into practice already from the eleventh century, and were renewed and extended by Pope Innocent III (1198-1216).[52] However, a more direct model for Hungarian towns was offered by other municipalities. In several cities and towns of Europe, including Vienna as the closest example, or Cologne, which was a regular business partner of Hungarian merchants in the decades before and after 1400, town books started to be compiled already in the thirteenth century.[53] Likewise in Prague, the first municipal books were drawn up from the turn of the thirteenth century onwards.[54]

Since the entries in the town books were considered legally authentic, they were in regular use for information retrieval. Routines were developed both for entering the contents of charters into town books, and for preparing charters

[50] Compiled around 1240, it contains copies of sixty charters from the period between 1002 and 1240, some of which have not been preserved in any other form. See G. SARBAK, "A pannonhalmi *Liber Ruber*" [The *Liber Ruber* of Pannonhalma], in: *Mons Sacer 996-1996: Pannonhalma 1000 éve* [*Mons sacer*: Thousand years of Pannonhalma], ed. I. TAKÁCS, 3 vols. (Pannonhalma, 1996), 1, pp. 401-421.

[51] BERTRAND, *Les écritures ordinaires*, p. 388.

[52] A. MEYER, "The Curia: The apostolic chancery", in: *A Companion to the Medieval Papacy: Growth of an Ideology and Institution*, ed. K. SISSON and A.L. LARSON (Leiden, 2016), pp. 249-258. The incoming supplications were only registered from the mid-fourteenth century onwards. See L.E. BOYLE, *A Survey of the Vatican Archives and of its Medieval Holdings*, 2nd rev. edn. (Toronto, 2001: *Subsidia Mediaevalia* 1), pp. 51, 103-113, 132-148.

[53] G. HIRSCHFELDER, *Die Kölner Handelsbeziehungen im Spätmittelalter* (Köln, 1994), pp. 122-148.

[54] VODRÁŽKOVÁ and BOK, "Prag", p. 455; *Liber vetustissimus Antiquae Civitatis Pragensis 1310-1518*, ed. H. PÁTKOVÁ *et al.* (Praha, 2011).

based on data extracted from the volumes. In fact, the emergence of the concept of 'data' in the pragmatic sense of the word owes much to the systematic use of municipal books, particularly those of financial or fiscal content. The requirement of capable and authorised personnel ties this issue even more strongly to the development of local chanceries – and, as we shall see in more detail Chapter 6, to that of the local archives.

Information retrieval was also facilitated by an increased orderliness of the layout of municipal books, the division of the text into paragraphs and columns. The systematic use of auxiliary tools extended beyond the traditional marginal notes: tables of contents and indices of names show the process of institutionalisation of the local and municipal writing offices. This phenomenon has been studied in detail for the northern regions of France by Paul Bertrand, and many of his observations are helpful in understanding the dynamics of the changes in layout of the Hungarian municipal books as well.[55]

One of the relevant examples among the sources discussed here is the index of the first testamentary protocol of Pressburg (Fig. 29). These are seldom complete – they do break down at some point due to changes in the personnel of the writing office or miscalculation of the number of pages needed to cover the full contents of the given book. These shortcomings, however, do not detract from the intention to make the books handier and their use more efficient.

Municipal books were indeed consulted as repositories of documents. As is described by the *Ofner Stadtrecht* quoted above, documents that had been entered in the town book but were later damaged or consumed by fire, were reissued in charter form, with their text copied from the register. For example, the statutes of the German butchers' guild in Buda were reissued from the book by the town authorities of Buda first on 2 May 1481 as *litterae patentes*, then on 22 March 1482 with a hanging seal, which was in turn reconfirmed two years later by king Matthias Corvinus as a royal charter.[56] Another example, crossing several administrative boundaries, is a charter issued in Latin by the imperial notary public, "*Michael natus Conradi lapicide*", authenticating a German-language paper excerpt which the notary of Pressburg had made from the town book of Vienna ("*quoddam rescriptum in papiro scriptum de libro*

[55] BERTRAND, *Les écritures ordinaires*, pp. 151-197; on the indices: pp. 193-197.

[56] *Zunftbuch und Privilegien der Fleischer zu Ofen aus dem Mittelalter / A budai német mészárosok középkori céhkönyve és kiváltságlevelei*, ed. I. KENYERES (Budapest, 2008), pp. 352-366 (Nos. 10-11), edited by Péter KIS and Iván PETRIK.

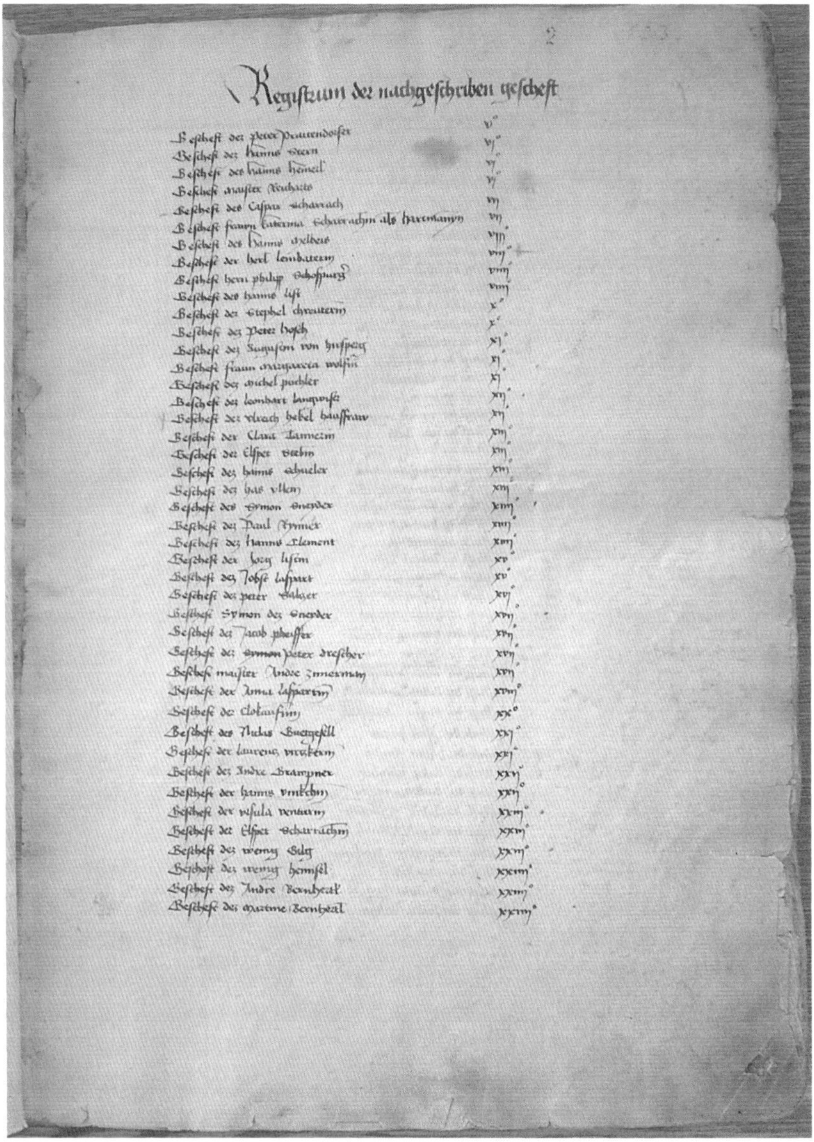

Fig. 29 Index of entries in the first *Protocollum testamentorum* of Pressburg, indicating the name of each testator and the page number where their last will begins (AMB, Nr. 4.n.1, f. 2r). Photo: Judit Majorossy. Reproduced with the permission of Archív Mesta Bratislavy.

civili civitatis Wyennensis") concerning a huge donation to the two hospitals of Pressburg.[57]

Town books could be subject to critical examination, just as sealed charters were. If a charter and the contents of a town book contradicted each other, it was the court's (and ultimately the king's) task to compare them and decide which one should be accepted. As it transpires from a court case at Kremnica in 1424, if an entry in the town book was proven to be "*minus iuste et fraudulenter conscriptum*" ("incorrectly and fraudulently written"), the notary who wrote it could be sentenced to capital punishment. The same sentence applied to the town book itself, in the form of burning.[58]

The Material Basis of Town Books: The Use of Paper in Administration

The introduction of town books was also dependent on a technical issue: the availability of sufficient amounts of paper as a relatively cheap writing material.[59] The first cartularies of monasteries as well as town books abroad, such as the *Eisenbuch* in Vienna, were written on parchment,[60] but it was their precious content, namely various royal charters and title deeds, that justified the expenses involved. Once town books started to register regular practical issues, they were written on paper.

The use of paper in administration was, perhaps surprisingly, initially not a question of supply, but of demand. And it was also a question of trust. Paper was produced in Muslim-ruled al-Andalus, and marketed throughout the Mediterranean from the eleventh century onwards, with little success in Europe until the thirteenth century. Even such an open-minded monarch as Roger II of Sicily, found paper "flimsy and untrustworthy". In 1145, he ordered that all documents pertaining to governmental bureaucracy that happened to be on paper be copied onto parchment. As the statutes of the kingdom prescribe: "Of instru-

[57] DF 239549, 1430.09.19.

[58] HÁZI, *Sopron* 1.2 (Sopron, 1923), pp. 288-291. More on this case below, under 'account books'.

[59] In general terms, see the research project Materielle Textkulturen: http://www.materiale-textkulturen.de/teilprojekt.php?tp=A06&up= (last accessed: 20.05.2018) and their edited volume *Papier im mittelalterlichen Europa Herstellung und Gebrauch*, ed. C. MEYER, S. SCHULTZ and B. SCHNEIDMÜLLER (Berlin, 2015), particularly the "Einleitung" by B. SCHNEIDMÜLLER and F.-J. ARLINGHAUS, "Materialität und Differenzierung der Kommunikation: Zu Funktionen des Pergament- und Papiergebrauchs in der spätmittelalterlichen Ständegesellschaft", *ibid.*, pp. 179-190.

[60] F. OPLL, *Das große Wiener Stadtbuch, genannt 'Eisenbuch'* (Wien, 1999).

ments written on sheets of paper, none is to have any authority".[61] This attitude only changed gradually in the course of the thirteenth century with the expansion of local administration, especially in the Italian communes, and with the increasing correspondence and written output of the papal legates. Both of these groups purchased much of their writing material from the newly established Italian papermill of Fabriano.[62]

Paper appeared in the Carpathian Basin at the beginning of the fourteenth century, through the activity of the papal legate Gentile da Montefiore (†1312), entrusted by the papacy to help the Angevin dynasty to the Hungarian throne. According to its watermark, the paper used for his letter, issued on 2 May 1310, was produced in Fabriano, and taken to Hungary by the legate himself.[63] There are no sources testifying to the early trade in paper, but the advantages of this light, easily transportable and relatively cheap material must have become known soon, since within a few decades evidence of its use can be found all over the country. In the 1310s some chapters and convents as places of authentication started issuing testimonials on paper. By the 1320s paper as a writing material reached the county authorities, that is, the regional authorities of the local nobility, as issuers. After a decade or so of parallel use of parchment and paper, from 1337 the latter became the general and customary writing material in the counties. This means that trust in the new fabric was established relatively fast.[64] As Zsigmond Jakó noticed in his research on Transylvania, the previously lesser-developed administrative literacy of the counties could adopt the new writing material more easily, because they were not bound by their own traditions. Furthermore, the rather ephemeral character of the cases that

[61] Quoted by M. Kurlansky, *Paper: Paging through History* (London and New York, 2016), p. 78; see also the chapter on "Administration" in H. Houben, *Roger II of Sicily: A Ruler between East and West* (Cambridge, 2002), pp. 147-158.

[62] G. Corinaldesi, *Fabriano Paper and Paper Mills from its Origins to Modern Day* (Fabriano, 1948; reprinted 2010).

[63] Gy. Rácz, "Gentilis és Károly: Levélírás Pozsonyban – Koronázás Fehérvárott: A papír megjelenése Magyarországon" [Gentilis and Charles: Letter from Pressburg – Coronation at Fehérvár: the appearance of paper in Hungary], in: *Károly Róbert és Székesfehérvár*, ed. T. Kerny and A. Smohay (Székesfehérvár, 2011), pp. 32-43. The letter is kept in the National Archives of Hungary, DL 40326 (issued in 1310; in the Hungaricana database mistakenly dated to 1311.05.02.)

[64] Gy. Rácz, "Az első megyei papíroklevelek" [The first paper documents in the counties], in: *Erősségénél fogva várépítésre való: Tanulmányok a 70 éves Németh Péter tiszteletére* [Due to its strength it is apt for building castles: Studies in honour of Péter Németh's seventieth birthday], ed. J. Cabello and N.C. Tóth (Nyíregyháza, 2011), pp. 307-313; Szentpétery, *Magyar oklevéltan*, pp. 191, 230.

they had to engage with (receipts, imposition of fines, prorogation of court cases, etc.) reduced the risk caused by the lesser durability of the material.[65]

From the 1340s (or probably even earlier) the Hungarian royal chancery, and from the mid-fourteenth century the offices of the 'major judges' of the realm (the palatine and the judge royal) also opted for the regular use of the new writing material.[66] These issuers: the places of authentication, the counties, the royal chancery, and the main office-holders, were the channels through which the emerging town chanceries became familiar with the use of paper in administrative literacy. Indeed, if one browses through the holdings of those town archives that managed to withstand the test of time, paper documents from all these bodies appear slowly but steadily from the mid-fourteenth century. Considering that items that lost their relevance may have been removed,[67] the surviving items probably represent the tip of the iceberg. It is conspicuous, for instance, that even in well-preserved civic archives, such as the one in Bardejov, the earliest holdings consist almost exclusively of charters of privilege written on parchment; until 1400, only four paper documents were preserved, whereas from the next decade the majority of the documents was already written on paper.

The use of paper for documents issued by the town chanceries in the kingdom of Hungary followed suit with some decades of delay.[68] Those documents, however, that were compiled to adjust the internal administration of the towns, especially in financial matters, were regularly written on paper, often earlier than the sealed charters were. This applies both to the earliest municipal

[65] Zs. Jakó, "Az oklevélírások fejlődése Erdélyben a xiv-xvi. században" [The development of diplomatic scripts in Transylvania in the fourteenth and fifteenth centuries], *Levéltári Híradó* 8 (1958), pp. 123-162, at p. 127. Quoted by Rácz, "Az első megyei papíroklevelek", p. 308.

[66] Unfortunately, the dl/df database of the National Archives of Hungary does not indicate the material of the documents, and therefore the range of data used here depends on those document editions that have this information (e.g. Házi, *Sopron*; *Inventár stredovekých listín, listov a iných príbuzných písomností*, ed. D. Lehotská, V. Horváth *et al.* [Inventory of medieval charters, documents and related written materials], 2 vols. (Praha, 1956 and 1966); Iványi, *Bártfa*; Iványi, *Eperjes*), or on autopsy. See Rácz, "Az első megyei papíroklevelek", pp. 307-308.

[67] Iványi, *Bártfa*, pp. 1-14.

[68] Some examples: Buda, 20 February 1404, edited in Házi, *Sopron*, 1.1, pp. 278-279; Sopron, 27 January1406, Paul, parish priest of Sopron, ed. *ibid.*, pp. 286-287 (under the priest's own seal).

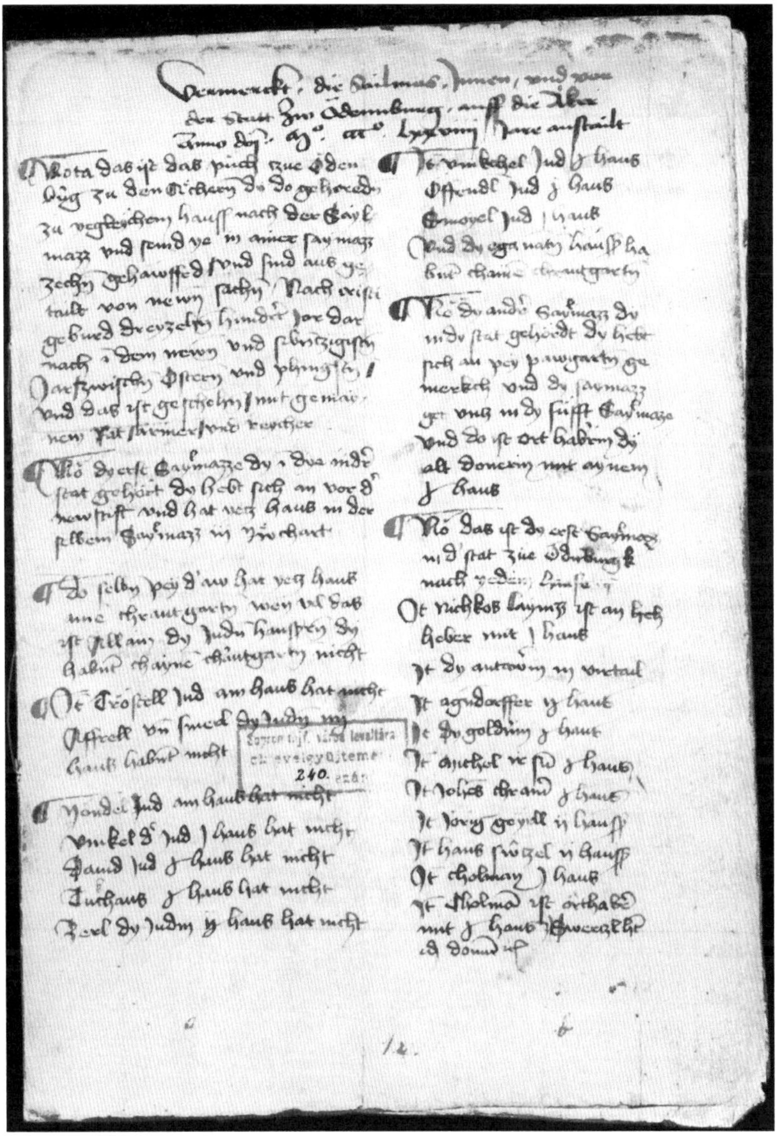

Fig. 30 List of house owners in Sopron, compiled in German in a paper booklet in 1379. The names are listed together with the sizes of the plots owned by them. The list begins with the Jewish house owners in column 'a' and proceeds afterwards in topographic order from the lower half of column 'b'. (SVL DL 240; MNL OL DF 201 873). Reproduced with the permission of the Sopron Archives.

books[69] and to the documents written on separate sheets or in smaller, unbound booklets. For example, the oldest surviving list of taxpayers in Pressburg's suburbs as well as the list of house owners of Sopron recorded in order to regulate the division of land pertaining to their plots date from 1379. Both documents were prepared on paper, the latter in the form of a ten-page paper booklet, with two columns on each page (Fig. 30).[70]

The sequence described above seems to indicate that the spread of paper as writing material was dependent on adopting certain administrative models. On the contrary, Franz Irsigler and other economic historians claim that the rapid takeover of paper as writing material depended on the merchants.[71] The apparent contradiction can be resolved by pointing out that the models in administration helped establish trust in paper, and the merchants secured the regular availability of the new material. Paper was indeed an ideal commodity for long-distance trade: with excellent weight / value ratio, transport was convenient, and production swiftly spread from Italy to the rest of the continent, where the use of water power offered favourable energy resources to operate paper mills.

The most flourishing paper-producing enterprise north of the Alps was established in 1390 by the Stromair (Stromer) family, a lineage of Nuremberg-based patricians (Fig. 31).[72] This family had business representatives also in Buda, who were related through marriage and business partnerships to several major commercial hubs of the country, whereas other branches worked on marketing their paper and diverse products in a broad area between the Low Countries and Livonia and Geneva to the Black Sea.[73] There are even some references proving that paper was being manufactured in Buda in the second

[69] Although occasionally some sheets of parchment were bound together with the paper, for instance in the town book of Kremnica from 1426, the first 14 folios are made of parchment, MMKR, *Stadtbuch*, DF 274522.

[70] AMB No. 405; HÁZI, *Sopron,* 1.1, pp. 183-190. The statutes of Bardejov from 1404, folded in a stand-alone booklet, were also written on paper. IVÁNYI, *Bártfa,* No. 51. Edited in: KOLOSVÁRI and ÓVÁRI, *Corpus Statutorum* 2.2. p. 71.

[71] F. IRSIGLER, "Papierhandel in Mitteleuropa, 14.-16. Jahrhundert", in: *Miscellanea Franz Irsigler: Festgabe zum 65. Geburtstag,* ed. V. HENN and M. PAULY (Trier, 2006), pp. 309-348, quotation from p. 315.

[72] W. VON STROMER, "Die erste Papiermühle in Mitteleuropa: Ulman Stromeirs 'Hadermühle' Nürnberg 1390-1453, an der Wiege der Massenmedien", in: *Produzione e commercio della carta e del libro secc. XIII-XVIII,* ed. S. CAVACIOCCHI (Firenze, 1992), pp. 297-311; W. VON STROMER, "Große Innovation der Papierfabrikation in Spätmittelalter und Frühneuzeit", *Technikgeschichte* 6 (1993), pp. 1-6.

[73] IRSIGLER, "Papierhandel", pp. 310-314.

half of the fifteenth century. In the industrial district of Felhévíz *(Aquae calidae superiores)* north of the Watertown *(Víziváros)* suburb, all-year watermills built on the local hot springs serving various crafts (fulling mill, sawmill, gunpowder mill) may have included a paper mill as well.[74]

It would go beyond the scope of the current work to conduct detailed investigations concerning the watermarks of the paper used in the Hungarian towns, and to trace the exact routes and markets by which the material reached its destination. The main suppliers were Italy (through Venice or through the Dalmatian cities) and the South-German industrial centres, primarily Nuremberg, directly or through the mediation of Viennese merchants. In any case, by the second half of the fourteenth century the material preconditions of expanding urban administration through town books were already in place. From the late fourteenth century onwards, when town accounts are available, expenses connected to the purchase of paper also regularly occur.[75] We know, for instance, that the western part of Hungary was supplied with paper from Vienna or Wiener Neustadt, but not necessarily with local products.

Another related issue, the full exploration of which would go far beyond the limits of the present volume, is the change in script towards the prevalence of cursive. This shift can be observed in the single-sheet documents, particularly the missives and the *litterae clausae*, and to some extent the *litterae patentes* as well in the fourteenth and fifteenth centuries. But the 'hotbeds' of cursive script were the municipal books, where the amount of material to be entered necessitated economising on scribal effort, especially by increasing the speed of writing. The fact that most of the books were meant for the internal use of civic administration, for trained eyes, familiar with daily routines, made it easier to accept the use of this kind of less representative script.[76]

[74] A. KUBINYI, "Budafelhévíz topográfiája és gazdasági fejlődése" [Topography and economic development of Budafelhévíz], *Tanulmányok Budapest Múltjából* 16 (1964), pp. 85-180. Reprinted in ID., *Tanulmányok Budapest középkori történetéről*, pp. 115-182, at pp. 159-160. In Upper Hungary paper production started in the first quarter of the sixteenth century: V. DECKER, *Dejiny ručnej výroby papiera na Slovensku* [The history of manual paper production in Slovakia] (Martin, 1982). I owe this reference to Juraj Šedivý.

[75] Some examples: Trnava, 1394: "*Item dedi 40 den. vmb eyn puch papir, quod recepit notarius civitatis* (FEJÉRPATAKY, p. 109). Bardejov, 1419: "*Dedimus pro papiro 18 den.*" (*ibid.*, p. 180.); "*Dedimus pro papiro Martino pellifici 28 1/2 den.*" (*ibid.*, p. 181); "*Item dedimus pro papiro medium flor.*" (*ibid.*, p. 190); and later years. In the last two cases expenses connected to travels to Vienna are also recorded, although it was not explicitely stated that the paper was purchased there.

[76] BERTRAND, *Les écritures ordinaires*, pp. 221-242, 386. Further research on Hungarian material would be needed to compare the local developments to Bertrand's observations.

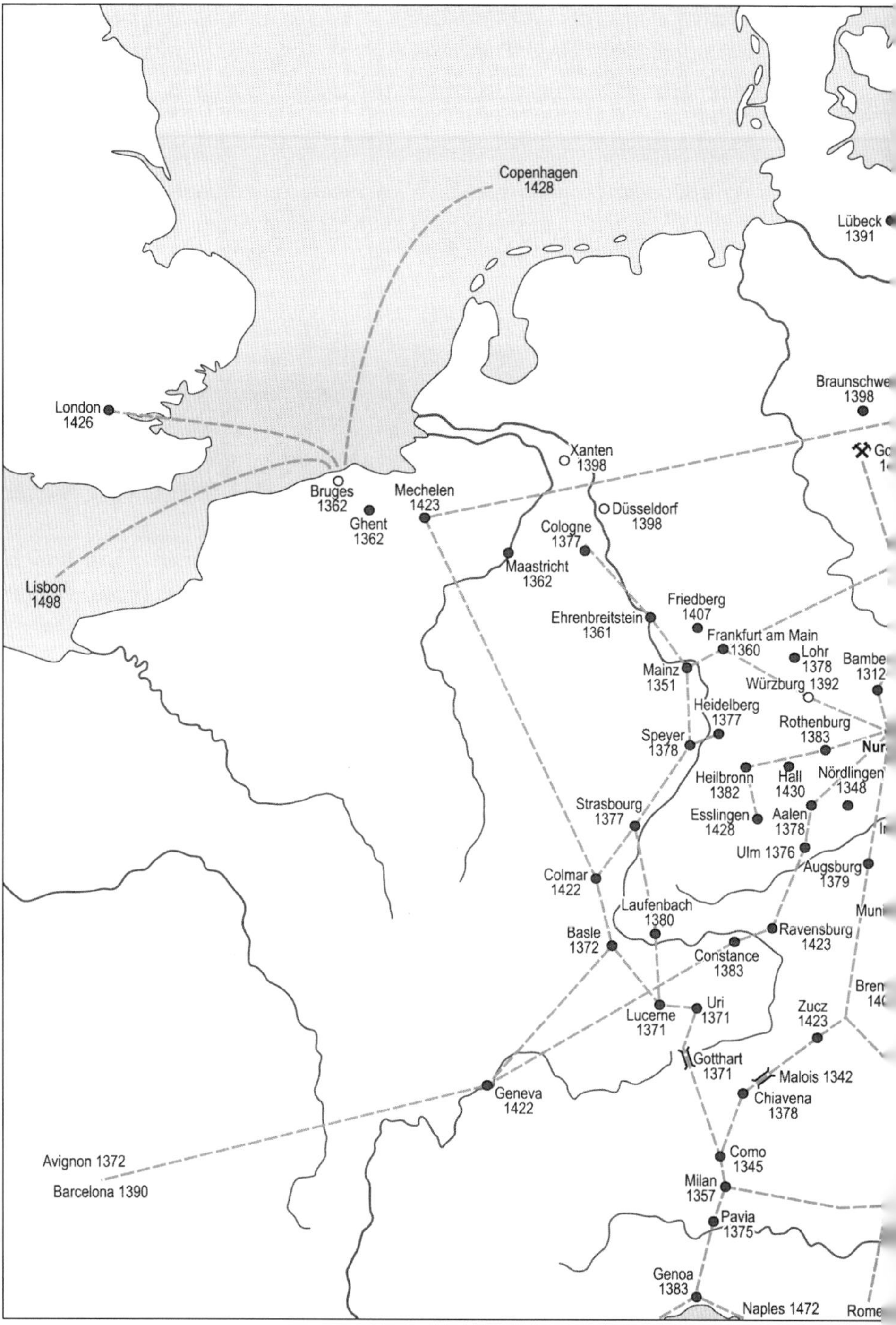

Fig. 31 Distribution of the products of the Hader paper mill in Nuremberg, an enterprise founded by the Stromer family. Map prepared by Lore Sporhan-Krempel, reproduced in IRSIGLER, "Papierhandel", p. 311.

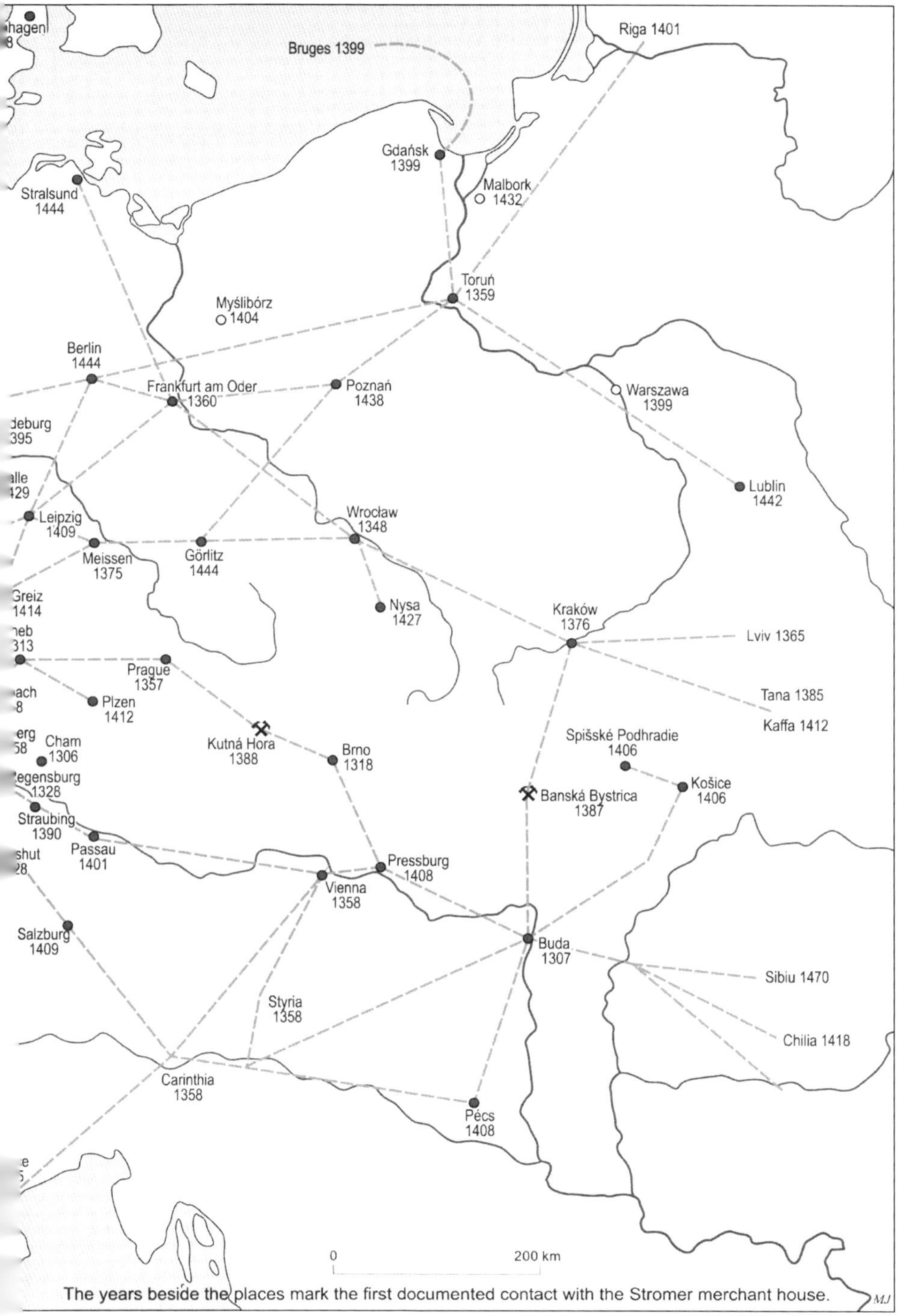

The years beside the places mark the first documented contact with the Stromer merchant house.

The Contents of the Municipal Books: Thematic Differentiation

The categorisation of municipal books, or the creation of a typology, has been a long-standing challenge to scholarship. Diplomatic studies as well as current international projects run by archivists, legal historians, linguists, and social historians provide detailed overviews of the thematic varieties of town books. For instance, the ambitious Wittenberg-based *Index librorum civitatum* (henceforth: ILC) project uses the following categories (quoting the German terms is relevant because of the language of most municipal books in medieval Hungary was German):

1. *Stadtbücher mit vermischtem Inhalt* (town books of mixed content);
2. *Kopiare*, *Register* (copial books and registers);
3. *Statuten*, *Willküren*, *Ordnungen*, *Rezesse* (statutes, legal regulations, ordinances);
4. *Bücher des Rates* (books of the council);
5. *Bürgerbücher*, *Erbhuldigungen* (registers of new burghers, hereditary agreements);
6. *Gerichtsbücher* (court protocols);
7. *Zinsregister* (registers of loans and interests);
8. *Steuerbücher* (tax protocols);
9. *Zollregister* (customs registers);
10. *Rechnungsbücher* (account books);
11. Sonstige Stadtbücher (other municipal books).[77]

Dieter Geuenich, in his turn, suggests using only three categories: (1) books of the town council (*Bücher des Rates*: council minutes, pledge, cadastral, testamentary etc. books), (2) town court books (*Bücher des Stadtgerichts*) and (3) municipal account books (*Bücher des Rechnungsamtes*).[78] This contrast demonstrates the controversial nature of the question and the difficulties of creating clear-cut categories. Instead of establishing a failsafe system of classification as a scholarly exercise, used as a research tool these categories may help understand changes in the competence and authority of local administration. It is in this sense that I present an overview of the first period of keeping municipal books in the kingdom of Hungary, from the beginnings until the

[77] http://www.stadtbuecher.de/ (last accessed: 20.05.2018).
[78] GEUENICH, "Was sind eigentlich Stadtbücher?", p. 26.

mid-fifteenth century. Concerning their availability,[79] however, a methodological proviso needs to be added. Whereas the charters and missives of town chanceries were sent to various addressees and thus have a greater statistical chance of at least partial survival (this is how the operation of Buda's chancery can be partially reconstructed), the municipal books were always kept locally.[80] Therefore, any major disaster such as fires, floods, or wartime events could lead to the destruction of an entire archival assemblage, like the fires at Bistrița (Transylvania) in 1457, Banská Bystrica in 1500, or Levoča in 1550. Consequently, one must be aware of the gaps in the material before drawing conclusions about chronology and geographical distribution.

Miscellaneous Books

The earliest volumes of town books, which appeared in the cities and towns of the kingdom in the last few decades of the fourteenth century, served basically as 'notepads' for the local administration (see Appendix 6 for their list).[81] As in most other towns of Europe, their content was structured only occasionally, and comprised any issues dealt with in front of the city council, be it matters of the town as a community or cases of individual citizens. This mixed character is pointed out in the introductory heading of the first town book of Pressburg, started in 1364:

[79] Most of the municipal books of medieval Hungarian towns have been preserved in present-day Slovakia, see LEHOTSKÁ, " počatkom vedenia mestských kníh", pp.25-347; J. SOPKÓ, "Kódexy stredoslovenských banských miest" [The codices of mining towns in central Slovakia], *Historické štúdie* 19 (1974), pp. 149-179; A. ŠVECOVÁ, "Die Stadtrechtsbücher in der mittelalterlichen Slowakei und Ungarn als Beispiel des eigenen selbstbewusstseins im Rahmen der europäischen Rechtskultur", *Krakowskie Studia z Historii Państwa i Prawa* 9 (2016), pp. 327-343.

[80] The few exceptions, such as the town book becoming part of another collection during its later history, include the book of Smolník that is kept in the manuscript collection of the National Széchényi Library, two municipal books of Banská Štiavnica in the medieval collection of the Hungarian National Museum, and the book of Žilina that was found in 1928 at Opava, now in the Moravian-Silesian Museum.

[81] Since the aim of the present work is to reconstruct the formation of the practice of using municipal books, only volumes drawn up before 1500 will be considered. The list only includes those documents of book format that consist of multiple entries entered over a time span of more than one year. Single-purpose documents set up for a specific occasion, e.g. tax records of a single year, are not considered as municipal books here.

Daz ist der stat register, darynne all sache und gewanheit der stat zu Prespurgk geschriben schol werden, alzo waz dy stat gelt hat und waz dy stat schuldig ist, vnd auch all reyttung inn geschriben schol werden von jar zu jare, und auch waz dy stat hantfest und freytumb hat.

This is a register book where all the issues and customs of the town of Pressburg should be entered, and also what money the town has and what it owes, and all the accounts have to be entered each year, and also what liberties and prerogatives the town has.[82]

The dates and circumstances of the appearance of the first town books as *libri mixti* varied from town to town, as did their thematic coverage (see Appendix 6). The two earliest extant volumes were both drawn up in 1364. The volume from Pressburg mentioned above covers the period between 1364 and 1538, but earlier texts were also retrospectively copied there. It may even be possible that it consists of fascicles that were originally separate and bound together later.[83] This might apply to some other volumes that are now bound together as well, and can explain the illogical sequence of their contents. It is conspicuous that half of the entries of the volume concern the Corpus Christi confraternity, one of the most prestigious religious brotherhoods in Pressburg; the earliest item copied is their foundation charter from 1349.[84] Furthermore, the volume contains accounts on the expenditure of the town, inventories of the St. Martin parish church (the most important church under the town's patronage), the earliest regulations of the most basic crafts (the butchers, the bakers, and the cobblers, 1376), the list of new year's gifts that the town owed to the king and the queen, accounts of the costs incurred during the visit of king

[82] FEJÉRPATAKY, p. 38. Arne Ziegler's claim that the Procollum Actionale be "*das älteste Stadtbuch*" in Pressburg (see the title of the edition and pp. 15-17 of his introduction in: *Actionale Protocollum: Das älteste Stadtbuch von Bratislava – Preßburg aus den Jahren 1402-1506*, ed. A. ZIEGLER (Bratislava, 1999: *Acta Carpatho-Germanica* 4) is therefore mistaken. See also: GODA and MAJOROSSY, "Städtische Selbstverwaltung", pp. 89, 91.

[83] This opinion was expressed by Judit Majorossy in GODA and MAJOROSSY, "Städtische Selbstverwaltung", p. 89.

[84] J. MAJOROSSY, "A Krisztus Teste konfraternitás helye a középkori pozsonyi polgárok életében" [The role of the Corpus Christi confraternity in the life of the Pressburg burghers], in: *Bártfától Pozsonyig: Városok a 13-17. században.* [From Bardejov to Pressburg: Towns in the thirteenth-seventeenth centuries], ed. E. CSUKOVITS and T. LENGYEL (Budapest, 2005: *Társadalom- és Művelődéstörténeti Tanulmányok* 35), pp. 253-291; J. MAJOROSSY, "Late medieval confraternities in Pressburg", in: *Pfarreien im Mittelalter: Deutschland, Polen, Tschechien und Ungarn im Vergleich*, ed. N. KRUPPA (Göttingen, 2008), pp. 339-362.

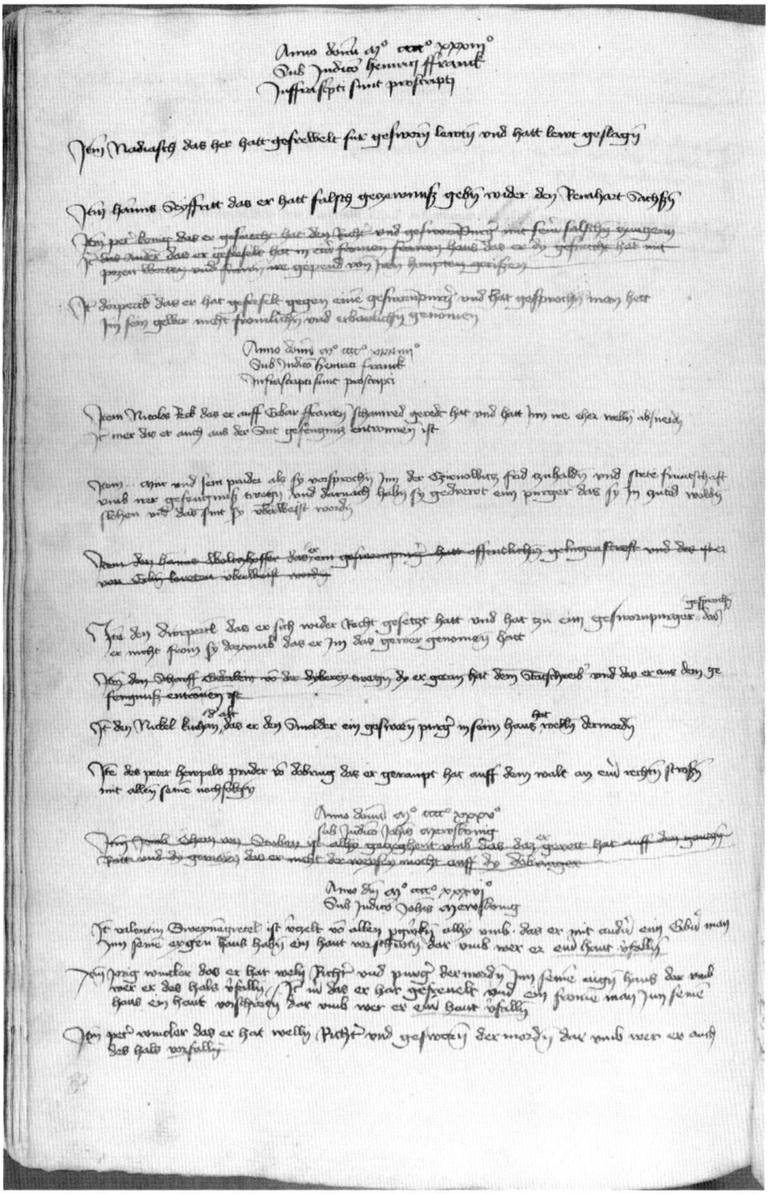

Fig. 32 Entries on proscribed persons in the second municipal book of Banská Štiavnica, inscribed in 1434-1436. The names of those persons who were forgiven for their crime were crossed out (MNM 61.54.C, f. 188v). Reproduced with the permission of the Hungarian National Museum.

Sigismund and duke Ernest of Habsburg in 1410, shortly before Sigismund's election to the German throne, and many more issues.[85]

Banská Štiavnica's first municipal book was also drawn up in 1364, initially mainly for recording the tax collected from the burghers, as well as other accounts, for instance expenditure of visiting the royal court at Visegrád.[86] As Enikő Csukovits demonstrated in her detailed analysis, court records were added first in the free spaces between the tax lists and on the last folios, but from the 1380s these became the dominant type of content in the book.[87] The entries on criminal cases were so-called *proscriptiones*, when the criminals' names and their crimes were noted. This act, a sort of secular 'excommunication' (which was also practiced in the county courts, where separate charters were issued with the list of criminals after each session) disqualified the culprits from the urban community and exposed them to public punishment.

Being inscribed in the town book served as a written reinforcement and reminder of the decision made by communal authority; but the same book also contained absolutions, when the criminals were pardoned, for instance after completing a penitentiary pilgrimage. Such persons were offered full grace, including 'writing them out' (*ausschreiben*) of the town book, a practice also known from elsewhere. This usually happened by crossing out the case, similarly to the way in which paid debts were indicated (Fig. 32). However, this also came at a price: according to the *Ofner Stadtrecht*, if someone was pardoned by royal grace or through the intervention of guarantors and was let out of jail, he had to pay one florin to the notary and half a florin to the judge's scribe to have the relevant entry deleted.[88]

The language of the Banská Štiavnica book shifted from Latin to German during the sixty years of its use. In the late fourteenth century, macaronic entries such as "*Jorge Suerossel proscriptus propter causam efficientem quod dicitur um eyn orhabe in causa unius jurati*" appeared;[89] from the early fifteenth century, the entries were almost exclusively in German. It seems from

[85] The volume is kept under AMB, 3.a.1; its financial accounts were edited in FEJÉRPATAKY, pp. 39-78.

[86] DF 235721. The entries on fiscal issues were published in FEJÉRPATAKY, pp. 1-38.

[87] E. CSUKOVITS, "Bűn és büntetés a középkori városi gyakorlatban: A selmecbányai 14-15. századi városkönyv bűnesetei" [Crime and Punishment in the medieval urban practice: Criminal cases in the fourteenth-fifteenth-century municipal book of Banská Štiavnica], in: *Bártfától Pozsonyig*, pp. 199-222, at pp. 205-207.

[88] *Ofner Stadtrecht*, cap. 56.

[89] DF 235721, p. 23 (photo 59).

the entries of the volume that the society of this mining town was particularly prone to violent crimes, as a kind of 'wild west' of its time, with high mobility and strong temptation to make an easy fortune; however, town books of judgements from other towns of the period (Zagreb and Košice, see below) also recorded many cases of bloodshed. The practice – both the crimes and their recording – was similar on the other side of the border, in Cracow, too. The first municipal book of Banská Bystrica, a close neighbour of Banská Štiavnica, from which only a fragment from between 1386 and 1399 survived the fire of 1500, showed a similar structure, a medley of financial and criminal records.[90]

It seems reasonable to assume that the first town book of the third and perhaps richest of the leading mining towns, that of Kremnica, had a similar content and structure; however, it was burnt during a court case. The case was the result of enmity between the town and Matthias Ebner of Nuremberg. The royal *comes urburarum*, Peter Raychel wanted to appoint (!) Ebner as town judge, but the townspeople refused to accept him due to an embezzlement case testified by the town book. Ebner produced a written receipt (*littere*) to prove his innocence. First, the court of the vice-master of the Treasury accepted this, declared the entry in the town book a fraud, and ordered the book to be burned. After the appeal, king Sigismund changed the verdict: "*tamen eedem littere librum civitatis reprobare nequaquam potuissent et ideo eundem librum civitatis nullatenus igne comburi debere [...] cognovimus*" ("but these documents could not condemn the municipal book by any means, and therefore we acknowledge that the said municipal book must not be burnt"). Nevertheless, in spite of the royal pardon, the old book had meanwhile been burned and a new one was drawn up (see below).[91]

Let us return to the western border zone. In Sopron, the first two miscellaneous town books were drawn up almost simultaneously, and were in use between 1390-1517 and 1393-1472 respectively. The entries in both books are in

[90] CSUKOVITS, "Bűn és büntetés", p. 215, n. 65; edition in FEJÉRPATAKY, pp. 76-101.

[91] The original writ issued by Sigismund (DF 249964) and its copies and transcriptions are listed in ZsO 13 (1426), ed. N.C. TÓTH, G. MIKÓ and B. LAKATOS (Budapest, 2017), No. 59. The full text is edited in HÁZI, *Sopron*, 1.2, pp. 288-291, quotation from p. 290, from the copy of the charter kept in the Sopron municipal archives (Sopron and several other towns were involved as jurors in the appeal). The case is also discussed by M. ŠTEFÁNIK, "The Kremnica town book of accounts: The economy of a mining and mint town in the kingdom of Hungary", in: *Money and Finance in Central Europe*, pp. 42-56, at pp. 51-53.

German.[92] In spite of keeping two books side by side, there did not seem to be any clear thematic distinction between them: both books contained statutes of the town council (at random, probably following the agenda of the council meetings) and last wills. The first book also contains some criminal cases (mainly roadside robberies), declarations of guarantee and of guardianship; agreements over property division, and promissory notes of priests who received chantries from the town. The notary also entered the customs tariffs to be levied at the western gate, on the road to Vienna (1394).

The second book has more entries of financial content: credit contracts and various accounts. It also contains the narrative description of the uprising of the townsfolk against the council in 1426, composed by the notary, Konrad Ernst, presented at the beginning of this chapter. The council, listed in full number by name, ordered entering the description "in their (!) town book" with the following instructive justification: "*zü einer ewigen gedechtnüss in dicz ir gegenburtig statbuch haissen schreiben der wart, das sich reich vnd arm hinfür von sölichen vnpillichen sachen desterbas süllen huetten*" ("had these events written in their present town book for eternal memory, so that in the future rich and poor should refrain from doing such indecent things").[93]

There would be no point in describing the contents of each town book. The earliest examples should suffice to show that practically all issues within the council's authority found their written expression in the volumes: the administrative, the judicial, as well as the financial agendas. By the beginning of the fifteenth century, presumably most royal merchant and mining towns, including small, but financially significant settlements, such as the smaller mining towns, had set up their own *liber civitatis*. Let me just add two examples where the original book of mixed contents saw the community through until the seventeenth or eighteenth century. The copper-mining centre of Smolník had a volume of *c.* 140 folios that was used regularly between 1410 and 1527, and had occasional entries from as late as the seventeenth century.[94] Further examples include Gelnica (1434-1728), where the lists of the town magistrates were

[92] Both books are edited in HÁZI, *Sopron*, 2.1, pp. 1-139 and 140-177, respectively. See also GODA and MAJOROSSY, "Städtische Selbstverwaltung", p. 82.

[93] The entries on the uprising are on pp. 164-170.

[94] OSZK Manuscript Collection, Cod. Lat. 385 *(Liber Civitatis Szomolnok)*. Edition: M. LACKO and E. MAYEROVÁ, *Das älteste Stadtbuch von Schmöllnitz 1410-1735: Eine Quelle zu den mitteleuropäischen wirtschaftlichen Verflechtungen* (Limbach, 2016). See also S. GÁRDONYI, "Das Stadtbuch von Schmöllnitz: Beiträge zur Geschichte der deutschen Kanzleisprache in der Slowakei", *Német Filológiai Tanulmányok* 2 (1966), pp. 109-138.

Fig. 33 Image of the Calvary from the second town book of Banská Štiavnica, 1432, attributed to the illuminator Valentin Gobil. The image faces the oath of the town judge and the first verses of the Gospel of St. John (HNM, Medieval Department, 61.54.C) Reproduced with the permission of the Hungarian National Museum.

entered year after year, together with mining ordinances of the Upper-Hungarian mining towns and a description of the campaign led by king John Albert of Poland to Hungary in 1494.[95]

In significant towns with a reasonably sophisticated administration, however, thematic differentiation of the town books became necessary, with several decades' difference, from the mid-fourteenth century onwards. The time and ways of specialisation of town books followed different paths from town to town (see Appendix 6). Court protocols, collections of last wills, registers of real estate (mainly houses and vineyards), account books, tax rolls, and lists of new burghers were kept in separate volumes. Besides their advantages for daily use, these books preserved many documents for posterity that would otherwise have been discarded due to their short-term validity.

The most plausible grouping on the basis of contents was to distinguish between books related to accounting, and those with legal relevance. This corresponds to the distinction made by contemporaries. When Hans Scheutzlich, the notary of Košice, organised the holdings of the municipal archives between 1503 and 1512, he made a distinction between 'registers' and 'books'. 'Registers' denoted the accounts and other financial records, including those pertaining to the minting chamber (*registra et libri cussionis camerae*); 'books' contained materials from the courts (*judicialia aut libri civitatis*). This corresponds to the difference in the legal relevance of these volumes: registers were valid depending on the operational rules of the office that produced them, whereas court decisions and other books of legal content were kept for 'eternity'. An even more sophisticated tripartite classification into honour-related books (*per honestum*), utility-related books (*per utile*) and justice-related books (*per iustum*) was devised by Procopius, the erudite scribe of the New Town of Prague in the mid-fifteenth century.[96]

The significance of justice-related books for the prestige of the towns is often shown by an elaborate binding (although these bindings may have been

[95] H. PROTZE, *Das älteste Stadtbuch der Königlich freien Bergstadt Göllnitz / Gelnica in der Unterzips und seine Sprache* (Frankfurt am Main, 2002); KOSÁRY, KULCSÁR, and SZAKÁLY, *Bevezetés* 4.1, p. 409.

[96] O. HALAGA, "A kassai városi könyvek, 1394-1797" [The town books of Košice], *Levéltári Híradó* 7 (1957), pp. 518-549. It is a translation of his *Košické mestské knihy (1394-1737)* (Košice, 1956). I used the Hungarian version. See also MAGDOŠKO, *Samospráva mesta Košice*, p. 159; S. PAVLICOVÁ, and J. TŘIKAČ, "The documentary clerical agenda of Prague's municipal offices during the Middle Ages", in: *The Development of Literate Mentalities*, pp. 183-197, at p. 186.

added later), and in some cases, the artful illumination added to their contents. In the case of both Kremnica and Banská Štiavnica, the position of the image on the verso of f. 2, opposite an oath formula for new town judges entering their office, connected it to the solemn rites of avowal (Fig. 33). In any case, the image of the Calvary, otherwise a standard element of illuminated missals, imbued these profane books with sacred authority.[97]

Financial Registers

The most frequent and often earliest form of differentiation is when accounts or notes of financial significance were detached from the books holding court decisions and other legal matters. Financial registers were indeed varied; categories 7-10 of the ILC quoted above, for instance, include account books, registers of loans and interests, tax registers, and customs registers, but even these cannot always be set apart. For instance, account books may incorporate tax registers, as one of the sources of income, and there can be other registers resulting from specialised activities, such as linen-bleaching (see below), which do not fit into any of these groups. The comprehensive definition of account books proposed by Mark Mersiowsky: "*schriftlich fixierte Aufstellung von Einnahmen und / oder Ausgaben, die aus dem der Abrechnung zugrundeliegenden Verhältnis zwischen Rechnungsleger und Rechnungsempfänger resultieren*" ("a statement fixed in writing of payments and / or expenses, which results from the relationship between the accountant and the receiver underlying the settlement"), emphasises that these texts were compiled as the result of the interdependence between the accountants and the recipients of the accounts.[98] Indeed, when one seeks to understand the way how the account books worked, how the information to be included was selected, and why they were preserved for posterity, both sides need to be considered.

[97] Kremnica, 1426: *Gotika: Dejiny slovenského výtvarného umenia* [Gothic style: The history of fine arts in Slovakia], ed. D. BURAN (Bratislava, 2003), n. 6.1.15, pp. 785-786; Banská Štiavnica, 1432, signed by the illuminator, Valentin Gobil: Hungarian National Museum, Medieval Department, 61.54.C, in this book the page facing the Calvary also contains the first fourteen verses of the Gospel According to John. See: GY. TÖRÖK, "Középkori magyarországi könyvfestészet" [Book illumination in medieval Hungary], in: *Kódexek*, pp. 35-46 and No. 96; CSUKOVITS, "Bűn és büntetés", p. 204, n. 6.

[98] M. MERSIOWSKY, *Die Anfänge territorialer Rechnungslegung im deutschen Nordwesten: Spätmittelalterliche Rechnungen, Verwaltungspraxis, Hof und Territorium* (Stuttgart, 2000: *Residenzenforschung* 9), pp. 308-314.

The need to keep financial registers separately from the rest of the administrative books followed from the different time span of their relevance, but this also diminished the chances of their survival. Therefore the few items at our disposal deserve special attention. The earliest town accounts survived in the already discussed *libri mixti*, or occasionally on separate sheets, for instance the one from Zagreb for the year 1368.[99]

The first extant separate book of financial records is the *Conscriptum perceptorum et debitorum ac distributorum civitatis Tyrnaviensis*, containing information on Trnava's urban household between 1394 and 1530.[100] The entries across such a long period were, understandably, not coherent and uniform. According to Vladimír Rábik, the editor of the book, it seems to have been originally set up by Johannes Talkner, the councillor responsible for the town finances, as his private aide-memoire before presenting his yearly accounts, which were gradually also included as approved by the rest of the magistrate. A similar *Gabbuch* for summarising the yearly accounts is known from nearby Pressburg, which probably served as a model for Trnava. It took about seven years until the public character of the book as a standard tool for the accounting of town incomes and expenditure was established. Most items were subsequently entered as a list, but exceptionally, for the year 1403, a text discharging the councillor in charge from any debts, was copied in charter format; this format returned after 1478.

This was not the only interference between text and charter: the records for 1437 include a detailed account of what it cost to have Trnava's municipal charter confirmed by king Albrecht after the tribulations of Hussite rule over the town (1435-1436). The procedure started with redeeming Béla IV's golden bull (1238) from the Hussites, then the judge and two burghers visiting the king after his coronation, staying in Buda for five weeks, paid the royal chancery for the preparation of the charter confirming the 1238 original and gave the king gifts in kind as *captatio benevolentiae*. The sum of the expenses at the court exceeded 200 florins, from which the charter itself cost 84.[101]

The magistrate of Sopron followed a different procedure, keeping the yearly accounts by the officials in separate booklets of 2-8 paper sheets, folded and

[99] TKALČIĆ, *Monumenta Zagrabiae* 11 (Zagreb, 1905), pp. 221-226.

[100] RÁBIK, *Mestská kniha Trnavy*.

[101] RÁBIK, *Tyrnaus mittelalterliche Stadtbücher*, pp. 16-38, esp. pp. 32-34. The expenditure is noted on f. 60r. Paradoxically, while the 1238 charter is still extant, king Albert's confirmation charter has not come down to us, the only proof of its existence being the entries in the account book.

sometimes tied together with a hemp cord, but not bound as a book. From the 1410s separate booklets of tax and tithe revenues were drawn up, which were not copied in either of the two miscellaneous municipal books. The tax lists often only comprised one quarter of the town, following the official division according to how different burghers handled the tax collection of each part.[102] Yearly accounts and tax records in separate booklets were the practice for most towns throughout the fifteenth century.[103] It is tempting to speculate why these apparently ephemeral loose accounts were kept in the town archives. Most likely this happened because beyond the daily needs of the local officials they responded to queries from various authorities outside the town: the bishop of Győr concerning the tithes, and the king regarding the taxes. Their occasional requests to present the accounts established the practice of preserving them in the long run, and some of them were eventually bound together under a common cover.

A receipt by the Master of the Treasury from 1422 proves the case in point nicely. It testifies that Sopron's magistrates (including the notary, Konrad Ernst) handed over fifteen tax registers from the past twelve years: "*quindecim quaternos in vulgo scriptos totam racionem eiusdem civitatis a duodecim annis elapsis regestris et quaternis in eisdem contineri referentes nostro conspectui presentarunt*" ("they presented to us fifteen volumes written in the vernacular rendering the full accounts registered in the past twelve years"). The issue was presumably connected to the compensation inflicted on the town after the execution of a nobleman back in 1420. This is not the place to explain the details of this gruesome story.[104] It pertains more to our argument that the receipt provides data on the format (*quaterni*) as well as the language (*in vulgo*, that is in German) of the accounts. In its preamble, it also gives a comprehensive list of all possible documents that the townspeople were expected to have, clearly showing that written accounting and record-keeping by the town authorities was by that time taken for granted: "*omniaque regestra, cauciones, quittancias, libros et annales eorum super collectis eiusdem civitatis perceptis et dispensatis factas, confectas et emanate*" ("all their registers, schedules of debts, receipts, books and yearbooks on the income and expenses made, agreed, and

[102] All such extant lists are edited in HÁZI, *Sopron*, 2.2-2.6, *passim*.

[103] These individual yearly accounts are not included in Appendix 6, as they cannot be termed as 'books'.

[104] See the contemporary description in the so-called 'Second Town Book', HÁZI, *Sopron*, 2.1, pp. 186-187.

issuing from the same municipality").[105] This also explains why accounts specifying the 'hospitality costs' connected to royal visits to towns (holding precious details on everyday life and eating habits) feature so prominently in the surviving material: the towns wished to have their expenses subtracted from their yearly tax obligations. More detailed data and the exceptionally surviving royal account books from the late fifteenth century contain explicit evidence for this practice.[106]

Likewise, the survival of the earliest accounts of Kremnica from 1423/1424 can also be tied to an inspection by the Master of the Treasury, which then led to the burning of the first town book, as described above. As Martin Štefánik describes, the contents of this book

> include closed and current income and expenses, debts that the town owed to other entities and debts owed by other entities or persons to the town, as well as loans to the king and specific taxes listed on the occasion of his visit.[107]

Without this scandal, our knowledge of the internal economy of Hungary's leading mining town and its contribution to the king's budget would have been much poorer, since no other similar accounts from more peaceful times have come down to us.

The best and most complete series of Town Chamber Accounts (*Kammerrechnungen*) have been preserved at Pressburg. After the first volume in 1434, their uninterrupted flow from 1439 is unique among the Hungarian urban source material and can be regarded as exceptional in Central Europe. Pressburg's finances were managed from that time by the *Kammerer* ('chamberlain'), a burgher who swore an oath of loyalty to his office, and whose name as the ultimate responsible person figures at the beginning of each year's registers. He was helped by two *ladherren* and a scribe, the *kammerschreiber* who was employed specially to take care of the registers. The accounts also excel in

[105] HÁZI, *Sopron*, 1.2, pp. 213-214.

[106] Examples of accounts connected to royal visits: Pressburg, 1410 and 1419: FEJÉRPARAKY, *Magyarországi városok*, pp. 41-59; Kremnica, 1424: *ibid.*, pp. 623-624; Sopron, 1425: HÁZI, *Sopron*, 2.2, pp. 337-339. On the late fifteenth century: T. NEUMANN, "'Minden időkben kegyelmes uratok kívánunk lenni': A királyi városok adóztatása a 15. század végén" ['We always wish to be your gracious lord'. Taxation of royal towns at the end of the fifteenth century], in: *Hatalom, adó, jog*, pp. 13-106. I am grateful for Tibor Neumann's personal communication on this question.

[107] ŠTEFÁNIK, "The Kremnica town book of accounts", p. 43. The text is edited in FEJÉRPATAKY, pp. 618-625.

comparison to any other similar lists by their clearly structured contents that appear under the same headings year after year. The incomes were collected, besides the yearly taxes of the burghers, from the Danube ferry, the customs tolls, the duties on wine, beer, salt, and firewood, the rents of town property such as the bath and the brothel, the duty after using the town scales at the market, and the fees of the new burghers.

Recurrent expenses included the regular and extraordinary taxes due to the royal treasury, the new year's gifts to the main dignitaries, the hospitality costs of royal and other visits, the costs of messengers and envoys, the wages of paid officials (first and foremost the notary and his scribes) and craftsmen (carpenters, blacksmiths, locksmiths, etc.) employed by the town and the labourers cultivating the lands and vineyards of the town, the cost of provisions for the town hall (wood, candles) and many other miscellaneous costs. The disciplined character of the volume presupposes the existence of several sub-accounts for each of the main subjects, from which fair copies would be entered in the main account.[108] The closest and most influential model for this structured and orderly accounting was beyond doubt the city chancery of Vienna, just as the *Satzbuch* installed in Pressburg in 1439 follows to some extent its Viennese counterpart.[109]

The royal towns were owners of seigniorial villages and other kinds of real estate, and operated several enterprises, which all figure in some form in their accounts. In the bigger towns, such as Košice, references to various specialised officials appointed by the town council indicate a sophisticated system of financial administration, even if the accounts of these officers have been preserved only sporadically. This organisation and accounting served the best interest of the town. According to the calculations of Drahoslav Magdoško, in 1487, a year from which exceptionally detailed accounts have survived, as much as 80% of the municipal incomes derived from the town's properties and enterprises.[110]

[108] The AMB *Kammerrechnungen* series contains from 1434 to 1550 altogether 103 volumes. On their structure, see F. KOVÁTS, "Pozsony városának háztartása a XVI. században" [The accounts of the city of Pressburg in the fifteenth century], *Magyar Gazdaságtörténeti Szemle* 9 (1902), pp. 433-466; GODA and MAJOROSSY, "Städtische Selbstverwaltung", pp. 78, 96-97.

[109] Wiener Stadt- und Landesarchiv (WSTLA) *Oberkammeramt* B 1/1. Band 1-15. (1424-1529); O. BRUNNER, *Die Finanzen der Stadt Wien von den Anfängen bis ins 16. Jahrhundert* (Wien, 1929), pp. 66-70; F. OPLL, "Preßburg und Wien im Mittelalter – Unterschiede, Parallelen und Begegnungen", in: *Städte im Donauraum*, pp. 97-120, esp. 108.

[110] MAGDOŠKO, *Samospráva mesta Košice*, pp. 168-201, p. 232 (English summary).

The most widespread of the municipal enterprises were the hospitals, an intricate mix of piety, social care, and business. With the increase of their wealth and literacy, hospitals also drew up their own accounts and inventories. These records were ultimately subject to municipal control, but had their own internal logic.[111] They were rarely preserved after they had lost their relevance, but were kept if they relied on a special bequest or long-term endowment, although their scope and complexity never reached the level of, for instance, the Viennese Bürgerspital.[112] Other religious brotherhoods under civic control also drew up their own register volumes, such as the Corpus Christi confraternity of Pressburg, containing lists of members and their joint properties.[113]

Records of a very special urban enterprise, the linen-bleaching plant of Bardejov, offer an insight in the management of a co-operative industry. Termed, with a degree of exaggeration, 'pre-capitalistic' by some historians, the town indeed "established a centralized network of textile producers, and managed the market distribution of the final product" by investing real estate and, above all, administrative capital. The latter was developed through the keeping of a series of diverse accounts from the early fifteenth century onwards. By providing facilities for the final phase of the work, when the woven linen obtained its attractive white colour, the town co-ordinated the efforts of many local producers and profited from the added value when selling the ready textiles at the distant markets of Oradea, Buda and Fehérvár. In their regulation, written down in 1450 but definitely formulated earlier, the town magistrates expressly forbade anyone from trading in bleached linen on his or her own.[114]

[111] See the introduction and some examples edited in K. SZENDE and J. MAJOROSSY, "Sources for the hospitals in medieval and early modern Hungary", in: *Quellen zur Geschichte des Spitals und der institutionellen Fürsorge in Mittelalter und Neuzeit,* ed. M. SCHEUTZ, A. SOMMERLECHNER, H. WEIGL and A.S. WEIß (Wien, 2010: QIÖG 3), pp. 323-368, at pp. 324, 341-346.

[112] B. POHL-RESL, *Rechnen mit der Ewigkeit: Das Wiener Bürgerspital im Mittelalter* (München, 1996).

[113] AMB, E.L.3, GODA and MAJOROSSY, "Städtische Selbstverwaltung", p. 91.

[114] S. GYARMATI, "The great linen register of Bardejov", *Annual of Medieval Studies at CEU* 14 (2014), pp. 117-132, quotations from pp. 117-118; previously: J. SZŰCS, *Városok és kézművesség a XVI. századi Magyarországon* [Towns and craftsmanship in fifteenth-century Hungary] (Budapest, 1955), pp. 220-240. On other accounts and financial records kept in the archives of Bardejov, see KOSÁRY, KULCSÁR, and SZAKÁLY, *Bevezetés*, pp. 143-144. The 1450 regulations are edited in FEJÉRPATAKY, pp. 193-194.

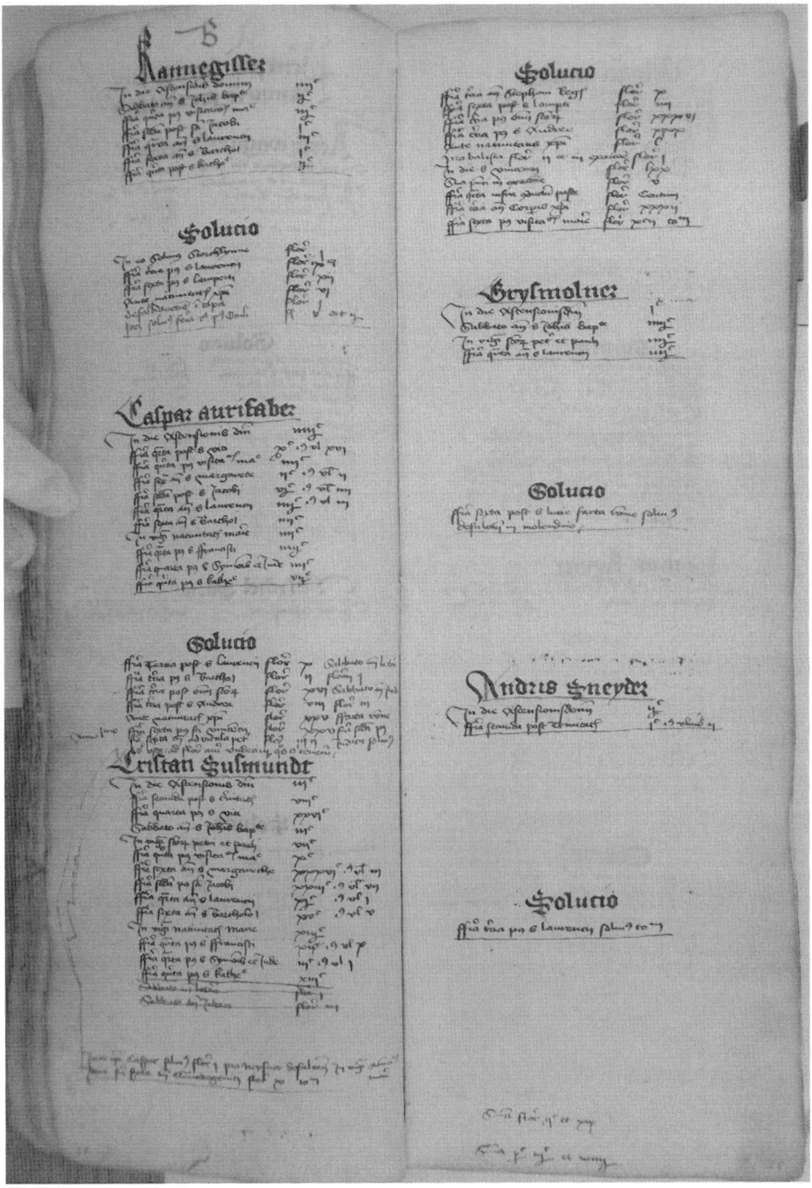

Fig. 34 A page from the 'Great Linen Register' of Bardejov. The pages show the deliveries of unbleached linen by various persons and the payments by the town to them. Note the finger pointing to an addition on the left margin (MMB Kníhy 1510, pp. 67-68) Photo: Sándor Gyarmati. Reproduced with permission.

This work required written records (*registra sindonum*) that kept track of "primarily production-related, that is, intra-organisation data regarding ... the linen sector". Sándor Gyarmati's comparison of the registers from the 1420s and the 1450s demonstrates how the layout developed by the municipal notaries became more and more suitable and sophisticated for recording the flow of the semi-finished material on the one hand and the cash payments to the producers on the other. The key to a good overview was the parallel recording of these two features under the names of the producers (in alphabetical order!) and the word *solutio*, respectively (Fig. 34). The alphabetical registration method was applied to the annual municipal accounts of Bardejov as well, where the initial of the subject of each item (e.g. *avena, argilla, aqua*, etc. under 'a') or the name of the person receiving the sum served as the registering principle. This method allowed the items to be arranged and for pieces of information to be retrieved in a systematic manner, but was less advantageous for getting an overview of the financial balance during the year. Probably this is why later town accounts turned to recording the expenses in chronological order.[115]

Similarly to the town accounts mentioned above, the most extensive 'Great Linen Register', used between 1447 and 1457, also owed its preservation to litigation. The challenge posed to Bardejov's monopoly in linen-bleaching by neighbouring Prešov compelled the town to present neat and orderly records in the ensuing litigation, even provided with rubrics in red, to prove their long tradition and competence in the industry.[116] Bardejov's rich linen accounts, covering much of the fifteenth century, are unparalleled in the Hungarian material, and may be further investigated in the context of business literacy in other regions of Central Europe.[117]

Court Books and Judicial Administration

After an overview of financial records in urban administration, let us turn our attention to the more 'durable' municipal books stemming from and contributing to the judicial authority of the towns. The right to adjudicate crimes and legal transactions was indeed a cornerstone of urban authority that needed

[115] See FEJÉRPATAKY, pp. 233-253, 263-280, 287-300.

[116] GYARMATI, "The great linen register", p. 121.

[117] E.g. H.C. PEYER, *Leinwandgewerbe und Fernhandel der Stadt St. Gallen von den Anfängen bis 1520*, 2 vols. (St. Gallen, 1959-1960).

to rely on accurate record-keeping. Records of legal significance were entered in book form in many different ways. At the outset, they were probably kept as personal notes taken at court sessions, as a formulary from the time of king Louis I suggests:

> *quod prudens notarius in locis talibus acta partium in sede judiciaria solummodo debeat registrare, et tandem de sede judiciaria recedens si cum suis judicibus et juratis sic tacite potest convenire, postmodum in hospitio suo formabit literas sana mente.*

> that the prudent notary just takes note of the actions of the parties at court in these places, and then returning from the court, if he can meet quietly his judges and councillors, and later he will formulate the documents at his lodging with a clear mind.[118]

This means that the notes taken by the notary at court sufficed for writing out the authentic documents later, but these drafts were not authentic legal instruments: only the charters prepared from them were. The term *registrare*, used in the formulary, suggests that they may have been kept in a book, but not yet a town book. The notaries also possessed formulary books that helped them compose authentic documents. Such volumes were in the possession of Liebhart Egkenfelder, who was introduced briefly at the beginning of this chapter. He owned "*ain deutscher formulary in ainer roten losch hawt verpunden, guete dictamina und ist meiner hanntgeschrifft*"("a German formulary bound in a loose red parchment, a good *dictamina* in my handwriting"), and he also bequeathed two lawbooks ("*ain teutsch rechtpuch*" – "a German law book" and "*ain chlains alts rechtpüch in pergamen von alten stat und lanndesrechten*" – "a small, old law book in parchment dealing with old town and land laws") in his will to the town of Pressburg.[119] The archives of Košice offer an insight to the 'reference library' of legal handbooks at the disposal of the magistrates: The town had a copy of the *Schwabenspiegel*, the Laws of the tavernical court, the *Ofner Stadtrecht*, and the laws of the kingdom copied into four volumes, probably from earlier separate manuscripts, in the sixteenth century.[120]

[118] KOVACHICH, *Formulae sollennes styli*, pp. 22-23. See also RADY, *Medieval Buda*, pp. 56-57.

[119] PT 1, No. 183, pp. 241-248, quotations from pp. 242-243.

[120] These volumes are still kept in the town archives of Košice, among the town book collection (*supplementum Halaganum*), with photos in the National Archives of Hungary, DF 271710 (*Schwabenspiegel*), 271715 (*Articuli sedis tavernicalis*), 271711-271714 (laws of the

The above-mentioned 'interim' registers of the notaries gained stronger legal significance in the procedure advocated by the *Ofner Stadtrecht*:

> *darumb sol derr stadtschreiberr ein pesunderr register haben, das sol er al tag zu richt tragen, dar ein sol der statschreiberr al sach schreiben und vermergken, wie sich al sach verlauffen und vollenden in dem rechten nach klag und antwurtt*
>
> therefore the town notary has to have a special register that he takes to court, and he has to enter and note all issues in that book how the cases proceed and are decided at court after plaint and defense.

The *Ofner Stadtrecht* also mentions "*zedeln, registeren und quateren*" ("sheets, registers, and quires") of court notes which had to be immediately seized by two councillors upon the death of a notary, in case he passed away during his term in office. As Martyn Rady points out, "in no other parts of the customary are the practices to be followed upon the death of a town official given such treatment".[121] These terms are similar to the expressions used in the above-mentioned letter of the Master of the Treasury in 1422, and may have referred to financial registers as well as legal records. Drafts and final copies were, however, seldom kept side by side; the case of Košice where both series (*maculatorium* and *pura*) were preserved, albeit only from the 1460s onwards, is rather the exception that corroborates the rule.[122]

Registering the issued charters required yet another book, the use of which was bound by strict rules. As the *Ofner Stadtrecht* specifies, no one other than the sworn notary of the town was allowed to write in this book, with the approval of the town judge, and under he supervision of two council members. This *grunt puech* was the 'main municipal book' (not the same as the property registers to be discussed later): a special repository, it had the same evidential value as sealed charters and could be used for issuing those anew.[123] It is often difficult to trace procedural matters, but evidence from Košice suggests that these rules were meticulously observed there – as indicated above, the town had a copy of the *Ofner Stadtrecht*. Notes such as "*In absentia notarii Acta*

kingdom). The so-called Cromer-Handschrift of the *Ofner Stadtrecht*, now kept in the University Library in Budapest, was also kept (and perhaps prepared) in / for Košice, see MOLLAY's Introduction, p. 26.

[121] *Ofner Stadtrecht*, cap. 54-55, pp. 81-82; RADY, *Medieval Buda*, p. 55.

[122] HALAGA, "A kassai városi könyvek", pp. 525-526; MAGDOŠKO, *Samospráva mesta Košice*, p. 14, 160-167.

[123] *Ofner Stadtrecht,* cap. 54, p. 81.

Iudiciaria per dominum Oswaldum collecta et post reversionem de Buda inscripta" ("in the absence of the notary the acts of justice were collected by mister Oswald and entered in the book after [the notary's] return from Buda"), or "*Sequuntur arestationes ... in absentia notarii per dominum iudicem Mathiam Greff interim consignate*" ("follow the arrests ... in the absence of the notary meanwhile entered by Mathias Greff, town judge") refer to the authoritative role of the sworn notary when it came to writing in the municipal book.[124]

The earliest extant examples of thematically arranged town books from the kingdom of Hungary are attested in Zagreb (Gradec), just as one of the first mentioning of a professional notary has come down to us from there. In 1355 *Notae sententiarum* were set up with the names of plaintiffs and defendants who were summoned to court. The entries start without any special introduction, by simply entering the date and the name of the judge in the heading, which probably implies that the earliest extant quires added up to volumes were not the first ones drawn up. In fact, in 1376, an entry refers to a "*statutum antiquum ut in katerna antiqua plenius continetur*" ("an old statute that is covered in more detail in an old town book"), which is no longer available.

From 1375 onwards the protocols also included the verdict, and could thus be used for issuing charters based on their text.[125] Remarkably, the word *quaterna* (that is 'quire', in the form *katerna*) became a common noun for 'municipal books' in the local usage. The early appearance of specialised registers of judgements went hand in hand with frequent court sessions (twice a week); they registered a large number of cases per session. However, on average more than half of these were cancelled because of the failed attendance (contumacy) of one of the parties. But entries about contumacy in the town book carried much weight, because according to customary law, after three instances the party who did turn up in court automatically won the case. This was a similar procedure to summons being read aloud at three markets in the countryside.[126]

The second oldest court book takes us to the northernmost part of the kingdom, to Žilina. As was mentioned before, this small town was compelled by royal order to change its legal model. The *Protocollum fassionum et transactionum,* used between 1378 and 1561, also owes its existence, or at least its

[124] HALAGA, "A kassai városi könyvek", pp. 526 and 545, n. 51-56.

[125] The *Libri citacionum* are edited in five subsequent volumes by TKALČIĆ, *Monumenta Zagrabiae* 4, *1355-1365* (Zagreb, 1897); 5, *1375-1391* (Zagreb, 1898); 6, *1412-1448* (Zagreb, 1900), 7, *1450-1480* (Zagreb, 1902); and 8, *1481-1526* (Zabreb, 1902). Quotation from 5, p. 59.

[126] On the administration of justice in Zagreb, see GROTHUSEN, *Die Entstehung*, pp. 149-162; on the three summonses: RADY, *Custom and Law*, pp. 123-125.

early starting date, to this unprecedented change of legal system from the law of Teschen to the law of Krupina. To mark the event, the burghers not only issued a charter on this matter, in fact the earliest extant charter issued by the municipality in 1379, but also requested Niklas of Litovel (a locality near Olomouc) to prepare a copy of the law of Krupina – in practice, the Magdeburg law – for the town, in German. This marks the beginning of the book, which from this point onwards served as a kind of 'all-in-one' legal hand- and notebook for the council.[127] In 1473, they even had the text of the law translated into Slavic, to which the translator added the following closing lines in Latin, the first line in hexameter:

> *Finis adest operis, mercedem possco laboris.*
>
> *Sub anno Domini* MCCCCLXXIII *tunc temporis existente advocato magnifico domino domino Wenceslao Pangracz in urbe Zylina, ad cuius instanciam et rei publice utilitatem presens opus est translatum per manus Wenceslai de Kromierzyz.*
>
> Work has come to an end, I ask for due compensation.
>
> In the year of the Lord 1473, when the gracious lord Wenceslas Pangratz was the Vogt of the town of Žilina, upon whose request and for the common good the present work was translated by the hand of Wenceslas of Kroměříž.[128]

This book is the earlier of the two medieval town books in the Carpathian Basin that have entries on court cases in three languages: Latin, German and Slavic (a dialect of Czech used by the notaries, who came from Moravia). The other one, from Trenčín, drawn up in 1476, is not discussed here in detail.

The entries of the Žilina court protocol show the takeover of the local vernaculars, but also the strong dependence on the mother tongue of the notary: they begin in 1386 in Latin; from 1403, German entries also appear, and the date of the first Slavic entry is 1417; between the 1430s and 1450 Latin entries return, but after that Slavic is used continuously, and from 1462 exclusively.[129]

[127] DF 266966; M. BADA, "A zsolnai városkönyv" [The Žilina town book], in: *Bártfától Pozsonyig*, pp. 187-197; ID., *Život v Žiline v zrkadle jej mestskej knihy: každodennosť Žilinčanov na základe analýzy zápisov Žilinskej mestskej knihy* [Life in Žilina in the mirror of the town book] (Bratislava, 2011). The 1379 charter is now kept in Budapest, DL 42119.

[128] DF 266966, f. 87r. See also the editions cited in the next footnote.

[129] The town book and the municipal literacy of Žilina have generated extensive scholarly literature, mainly because of its languages. Earlier editions: V. CHALOUPECKÝ, *Kniha žilinská*

Whereas the Žilina book was the first and only of its kind in the town, in Košice the single municipal book prior to 1460 (used between 1393 and 1405) is the only extant part of a longer series of court protocols that summarised the legal cases negotiated in front of the council. It also includes further agreements made out of court (*note extra judicium*), usually described in some detail. Besides criminal cases, a high number of civil ones, mainly commercial disputes are recorded, particularly with the inhabitants of Cracow, the main destination of Košice's merchants at the time. The intensity of court activity is shown by the number of entries, reaching more than 5500 within 12 years. During the early sixteenth-century organisation of the material, there were three more such protocols in the town archives, starting with 1404, 1406, and 1424, which prove the continuity of the practice as well as the losses that decimated the surviving material.[130]

After the first examples in the late 1300s, the first decades of the fifteenth century heralded the keeping of specialised books of judgements in merchant towns. Especially in cases involving external parties, it was crucial to have easily accessible notes that were not mixed up with the internal financial management of the town. Foreign plaintiffs frequently appear already in the Košice protocol. The *Protocollum actionale* of Pressburg (1402-1506) represents an interim phase in the process of specialisation: from 1402 to 1451, the municipal notaries continuously recorded legal cases in the volume; afterwards they only used it occasionally for guild-related entries, inventories, and miscellaneous cases. It contains mostly civil cases: sales contracts of real estate (houses, vineyards, land), pledges, credit contracts, letters of warrant, bans on sale, last wills, and even a marriage contract. All these issues were recorded because of the financial obligations taken on by the parties. Occasionally, cases or accusations of murder and theft were also noted. The entries follow the

[The book of Žilina] (Bratislava, 1934); PIIRAINEN, *Das Stadtrechtsbuch von Sillein*. The latest critical edition is *Žilinská právna kniha, magdeburské právo* [The Žilina code book of the Magdeburg law], ed. R. KUCHAR (Bratislava, 1993). From the rich literature: SOPKÓ, "Pisári a vznik", p. 70; M. PAPSONOVÁ, "Das Silleiner Rechtsbuch (1378-1524) im Spiegel der Forschung", *Brücken N.F.* 5 (Berlin, Prag, and Prešov, 1997), pp. 255-267; L. SOLYMOSI, "Muttersprache und rechtliche Schriftlichkeit im mittelalterlichen Königreich Ungarn", *Archiv für Diplomatik* 59 (2013), pp. 133-163, esp. pp. 153-156; LAKATOS, *Hivatali írásbeliség*, pp. 37-38.

[130] Edition: HALAGA, *Acta iudiciaria*; description: HALAGA, "A kassai városi könyvek", pp. 520-524. See also ZS. TEKE, "Kassa külkereskedelme az 1393-1405. évi bírói könyv bejegyzései alapján" [The foreign trade of Košice as reflected in the entries of the court protocol, 1393-1405], *Századok* 137 (2003), pp. 381-404.

chronological order of the court sessions and are based on the oral testimony of the parties or the witnesses.[131]

The mixed character of the contents derives mainly from the variety of cases handled at the Pressburg town court. From the 1420s further town books were drawn up additionally for the most frequent types of cases: the *Protocollum testamentorum* for last wills (1410/1427-1529, see below), the *Ächtpuch* for the proscription of criminals (1435-1519), and a *Rechtsbuch* that holds besides laws and statutes also guild regulations and council decisions.[132] This sudden upswing in the 1430s, including also the previously mentioned account books and the *Grund- und Satzbücher* to be discussed below, owes much to the interaction between the royal administration and the town chancery. It is no simple coincidence that this expansion of town books took place exactly in those years, between 1429 and 1436, when king Sigismund set up and extended his new secondary residence in the castle beside Pressburg. In the early 1430s there was even a minting chamber operated jointly by the court and the town council. The royal chancery did not interfere directly with the work of the civic administration, but through its presence and frequent (although not always amiable) contacts with the town magistrates, it provided a model for more sophisticated record-keeping.[133] Unfortunately, the archives of the other two royal seats of the period, Buda and Visegrád, have not come down to us, so it is hard to tell if the royal chancery played a similar model role in the municipal literacy of those towns as well. The example of Pressburg, even if it is fitting and plausible, cannot be projected onto other towns without due caution.

In Sopron, the first entry in the earliest specialised volume, the *Gerichtsbuch*, is from 1423.[134] It was drawn up by the previously introduced notary, Konrad Ernst, a 'refugee' from Vienna. From 1437, when the note "*Das puech ist das gerichtpüch*" was entered (No. 15) and thus the character of the book was determined, the contents of the volume are fairly uniform. It lists mainly civil and a smaller number of criminal cases. The entries of agreements out of

[131] *Actionale Protocollum*, marriage contract: f. 280 (ed. p. 267), murder accusations: f. 59 (ed. p. 82), f. 71 (ed. p. 90).

[132] The individual books are described in GODA and MAJOROSSY, "Städtische Selbstverwaltung", pp. 92-97. On the *Ächtbuch*, see M. ŠTEFÁNIK, "Kriminalität im mittelalterlichen Preßburg, Aechtbuch: Das erste mittelalterliche Gerichtsbuch der Stadt Bratislava – Preßburg aus den Jahren 1435-1519", *Wiener Geschichtsblätter* 65.1 (2010), pp. 47-60.

[133] SZENDE, "Between hatred and affection", pp. 205-206.

[134] SVL DL 3796 (DF 205047). Edition: *Gerichtsbuch – Bírósági könyv*; see also the introduction by L. BLAZOVICH there.

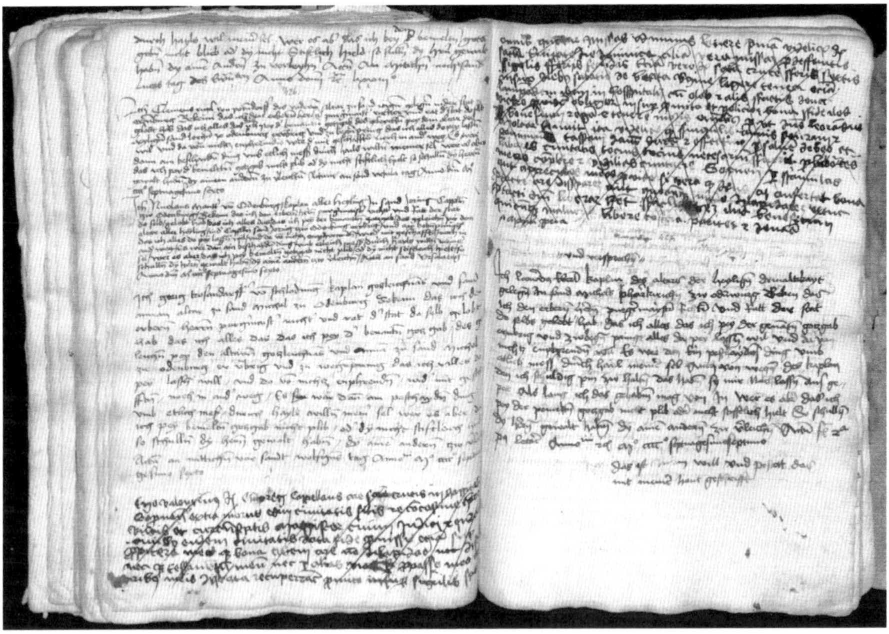

Fig. 35 Promissory letters in the *Gerichtsbuch* of Sopron by priests serving in the town. The entry crossed out was written by Valentinus de Chepreg, chaplain of the hospital chapel, in faulty Latin. (SVL DL 3796, pp. 426-427). Reproduced with the permission of the Sopron Archives.

court are due to the general acceptance of the town chancery as place of authentication, which greatly simplified the written administration of local affairs such as sales and inheritance. Occasionally, the list of the town magistrates and guild regulations were added. The last folios of the book were used, somewhat incidentally, for promissory letters of priests and chaplains, entered in their own hands, 15 in Latin and 28 in German. These notes date from between 1452 and 1506, and they are worth mentioning as precious testimony of late medieval literacy, since they preserve a great variety of personal handwriting of the urban lower clergy and testify to their diverse levels of education (Fig. 35).[135]

By the mid-fifteenth century Sopron clearly lagged behind Pressburg in economic importance, and further thematic specialisation of the municipal books can only be observed from the late fifteenth century.[136] At that time the

[135] J. NÉMETH, "Die Sprache des Ödenburger Gerichtsbuches", *ibid.*, pp. 47-67.
[136] The *Erstes Grundbuch – Első telekkönyv, 1480-1553*, ed. K. MOLLAY (Sopron, 1993:

introduction of the thematically specialised town books went hand in hand with the centralisation of civic governance. As Károly Goda's research has recently demonstrated, town leadership was concentrated in the hands of much fewer burghers than before, and these persons used the increased professionalisation of town governance as a tool for a more efficient control over public matters. Investigations that examine the introduction of administrative innovations in parallel with changes in the circle of persons in power can much better explain the course of development than looking at these phenomena in isolation.[137]

Sometimes the process of differentiation can only be followed from references of one town book to the other, especially if a case was relevant for more than one book, or if by mistake or coincidence it first ended up in the 'wrong' place. For instance, the account book of Trnava briefly mentions a court session that took place on 2 August 1417 concerning the custody of Peter Junkherr's children and summarises the sums involved. Then the notary added that for the sake of testimony the case was entered into their town book: "*zw-spruche zw geczewginisse haben wir dise sache in unser statbuch schreiben lassen*" ("[in] approval of this testimony we have had this case written in our municipal book"). From this note one can conclude that the third royal town in northwestern Hungary also had a town books of judgements like Košice, Pressburg, and Sopron.[138]

In the north-eastern part, Bardejov has an extant book of *Judicium bannitum,* a protocol of criminal cases between 1416 and 1443, a book of court depositions (*Libri fassionales*, 1436-1498), as well as the fragment of a *Verbotbuch* (book of bans imposed because of debts) from 1429.[139] Its southern neighbour (and sometimes rival), Prešov drew up its court protocol under the title *Nota liber secretarii civitatis Eppries* in 1424; this volume served its purpose until 1509. This book contains a wide variety of civic cases brought up in the presence of the councillors, including sales and marriage contracts, bequests

QGSÖ, Reihe A, 1), the *Gedenkbuch,* a volume of mixed, mainly judicial entries (1492-1543), and the *Priesterbuch*, a volume on loans taken from church benefices and further promissory letters by priests. For short descriptions see HÁZI, *Sopron*, 2.6, pp. IV-V; GODA and MAJOROSSY, "Städtische Selbstverwaltung", pp. 82-87.

[137] K. GODA, "Die Rolle des Gedenkbuches in der Geschichte der Ödenburger Stadtverwaltung", in: *Gedenkbuch – Feljegyzési könyv*, pp. 11-22.

[138] FEJÉRPATAKY, p. 126.

[139] No full-text edition of any of these volumes has been published. *Judicium bannitum*: MMB 77 6, DF 250507; IVÁNYI, *Bártfa,* No. 78. *Liber arrestationum*: MMB 202, DF 212882. *Libri fassionales*: MMB 305, DF 218492. See also *Lexikon stredovekých miest*, pp. 89-95; KOSÁRY, KULCSÁR, and SZAKÁLY, *Bevezetés*, p. 141.

(including real estate given to the Church as *donatio post obitum*) and property divisions between various family members. There may have been a separate volume for criminal cases that has not come down to us.[140]

In the biggest mining towns, Kremnica and Banská Štiavnica,[141] after the establishment of separate registers for the financial accounts, books containing a combination of law code and legal cases dominated the administrative scene. Similarly to Žilina, these were 'all in one' manuals of varied contents for the local law courts. In Kremnica, to continue the comparison, the origin of the new book in 1426 likewise goes back to a big 'shock'. The magistrates had to face the hard task of restoring trust in the community, and to start over with a *tabula rasa* after the enmities that upset the internal peace of the town. To this end, the book begins with the already mentioned illuminations, the Last Judgment and the Calvary. Then it continues with the detailed description of the gruesome events leading to the destruction of the previous book; after that it contains the German translation of the mining law of Kremnica.[142]

The second municipal book of Banská Štiavnica, used between 1432 and 1508, also begins with an image of the Calvary, and the entire book is sometimes called the Gobil-Codex after the illuminator. Besides individual criminal and civil cases, sales contracts and pious bequests, it also contains a perambulation of the town's boundary from 1444 and the text of the local mining law from 1466. The fact that the entries in the book commenced in the 1430s simultaneously in the first and the last quire, with court cases and short entries of proscription respectively, shows that the notary of that time had a vision of structured record keeping. His successors, however, only partially followed this principle, the entries becoming increasingly irregular over time, and much of the mighty volume (from f. 34v to f. 183r and some pages before and after as well) remaining unused.[143]

The surviving town books represent only part of all the documents in use in the municipal writing offices in the Middle Ages. Entries in the town books

[140] MMP K 2677 (old signature 133), DF 282529. See IVÁNYI, *Eperjes*, No. 194, and SZENDE, *Otthon a városban*, p. 78. The testamentary bequests to churches were entered in a separate booklet from 1472.

[141] In the third most important mining town, Banská Bystrica, the archives were burned in 1500.

[142] DF 274522; R. LACKO, "Kremnická mestská kniha z rokov 1426-1700" [The town book of Kremnica from 1426-1700], *Slovenská archivistika* 19.2 (1984), pp. 96-114.

[143] The manuscript is kept in the National Museum of Hungary, MNM 61.54.C; SOPKO, "Kódexy stredoslovenských banských miest", pp. 152-153; *Lexikon stredovekých miest*, p. 66 (M. ŠTEFÁNIK). I thank Gábor Tomka for the possibility of inspecting the manuscript.

often refer to volumes that no longer exist, and these references also indicate the parallel use and complementary character of these books. For instance in Bardejov in 1439 the *Registrum expositionum civitatis*, an account book of tax incomes and communal expenses mentions "*conventionem et rationem notarii require in libro memoriali*" ("look for the consultation and account of the notary in the record book"), referring to a by now lost *liber memorialis* (*Gedenkbuch*).[144] Guild statutes frequently demand that the newly accepted guild members be inscribed "*in librum civitatis*", in the register of new burghers.[145] Unfortunately, hardly any such books survive from medieval Hungary; the only one under this name, the *Burgerbuechl und Ächt buchl* from Sopron (see Fig. 50) contains very diverse pieces of information.[146]

The destruction of the archives of Buda, the medieval capital of the kingdom and the main model for urban governance and justice, leaves a gap that cannot be properly filled with indirect evidence, and there are other significant losses as well. However, it is conspicuous even from the surviving fragmentary material, that the so-called free royal towns, which had the tavernical court as their court of appeal, were way ahead of the other towns of Hungary as far as the specialisation of administration and particularly the keeping of municipal books was concerned. Much like the proverbial chicken and the egg, the question remains whether these towns qualified for the special status of 'tavernical cities' because they had a more sophisticated judicial and administrative system, or conversely, that the special status triggered a more efficient system of keeping the court records. The two aspects most likely developed hand in hand and made these towns the most stable elements of the urban network. As a notable exception, the royal free town of Gradec (Zagreb) had a well-developed written administration even if it was outside the group of tavernical cities because of the special jurisdiction of the *ban* of Slavonia in that part of the country.

The late appearance of municipal books in the Transylvanian towns raises questions that cannot be answered in the framework of the present study. Apart from some fragments of council protocols and accounts, no municipal books before the mid-fifteenth century can be found in any of the significant towns of

[144] FEJÉRPATAKY p. 469.

[145] KOVACHICH, *Formulae*, p. 434.

[146] SVL DL 3830 (DF 283614). On its description and contents: K. SZENDE, "Polgárnak lenni: A polgárjog megszerzésének elvei és gyakorlata a késő-középkori Sopronban" [To be a burgher: Principles and practice of acquiring burghers' right in late medieval Sopron], in: *Urbs: Magyar Várostörténeti Évkönyv* 1 (2006), pp. 85-107, at pp. 92-94.

Transylvania such as Bistrița, Brașov, Cluj, and Sibiu.[147] Account books appear from the 1460s and 1480s onwards, but other kinds of books can only be traced back to the early sixteenth century. A random reference to a *statpuch* in Sibiu in a marriage contract from 1419 cannot be verified and connected with any existing volume.[148] Apparently, when the first extant judicial protocol of Sibiu was drawn up in 1522, it was considered a novelty, and the notary Georg Reichersdorffer felt obliged to start the volume with a detailed justification. After a lengthy exposition of the commonplace opposition between *memoria* and *oblivio*, he states that

> *clarissimus inclite civitatis huius Cibiniensis senatus [...] statuit [...] ut hunc in codicem seu prothocollon omnes he in pretorio sentencie [...] per notarium civitatis diligenter et accurate inseri et inscribi debeant.*

> the most illustrious senate of this famous city of Sibiu has decided that the civic notary must enter diligently and exactly all the decisions of the court in this codex or protocol.[149]

The judicial protocol (*Liber Actuarius*) of the other great Transylvanian trading hub, Brașov, and the surrounding Burzenland was set up even later, in 1558. According to its editor, the creation of this municipal book was a consequence of the activity of the town chancery as a place of authentication.[150]

It is impossible to tell whether this chronological difference was due to the separate legal status of these towns in the Saxon University (*universitas Saxonum*) of Transylvania (except for Cluj), or the governance of Transylvania within the kingdom of Hungary. The lack of stimuli or models arriving from the areas that these towns were in regular contact with may also have played a role, just as in the case of the belated introduction of written administration in vernacular (i.e. German), which will be discussed in the next chapter. Such a

[147] The edition of the earliest protocol fragments: *Hermannstadt und Siebenbürgen: Die Protokolle des Hermannstädter Rates und der Sächsischen Nationsuniversität, 1391-1705*, ed. K. Hientz, B. Heigl, and T. Șindilariu (Sibiu, 2007).

[148] UGDS 4, No. 1874, p. 116, mentioned in the Introduction by the editor of the volume, M. Pakucs-Willcocks, *"zu urkundt in das Stadbuch lassen einschreiben": Die ältesten Protokolle von Hermannstadt und der Sächsischen Nationsuniversität (1522-1565)* (Hermannstadt and Bonn, 2016), in the context of the late appearance of town books in Transylvania, p. 9.

[149] Pakucs-Willcocks, *"zu urkundt"*, p. 17.

[150] *Das Gerichtsbuch des Kronstädter Rates (1558-1580)*, ed. J. Derzsi (Kronstadt [Brașov], 2016: *Quellen zur Geschichte der Stadt Kronstadt* 10), at p. vi.

significant difference cannot be seen in the use of seals, the employment of notaries and the issuing of authentic documents, and therefore the explanation may have to be sought elsewhere.

Municipal Books for Property Administration

Among the legal cases with long-term economic relevance, sales or pledgings of landed property (houses, vineyards, mills, arable lands, shambles, etc.) deserve special mention. The authority of the municipal councils to register transactions of real estate and issue deeds about them, as the most fundamental way of controlling the territory of the town, a crucial resource for residence, production and taxation alike, has been discussed above. Towns asserted their authority explicitly in this field. The statutes of Pressburg of 1451 rendered null and void all testimonies concerning immovables within their boundaries that had been issued under the seal of the local chapter or any other authority.[151] By the late Middle Ages, the customary law of the entire kingdom acknowledged that municipal authorities (the judge or two councillors) were the only right instance for recognisances regarding any movable or immovable goods in the territory of towns.[152] This exerted a strong pressure on the municipal administration. Besides issuing individual title deeds to the parties, the complex structure and the high number of houses, plots, vineyards, and other properties under municipal control in the biggest towns warranted special administrative arrangements for these transactions in the form of specialised registers.

After the previous chapters, it will not come as a surprise that the earliest example of these arrangements has, again, come down to us from Gradec (Zagreb), starting with 1384. How it came about is, however, highly unusual. Let me quote the introduction of the book itself, which is in fact the copy of a charter issued by the council:

> *Nos Miklinus filius Johannis judex, jurati, consiliarii et universi cives montis Grechensis notificamus omnibus presentem katernam inspecturis, quum malicia maxime gubernabat et ne per ipsius malicie gubernacionem in conservacione jurium possessionariorum in nostra civitate et eius territorio existencium aliquod*

[151] KIRÁLY, *Pozsony város joga*, p. 134.
[152] S. WERBŐCZY, *The Customary Law,* Pars III, tit.13, pp. 392-393.

nephas seu scandallum generetur, tum eciam pro tuciori conservatione ipsorum jurium possessionariorum in generali nostro consilio unanimi et pari voluntate hanc presentem nostrum katernam fecisse et sigillum nostre communitatis in quibusdam locis renovasse decrevimus et statuimus eo modo, ut universe littere factum possessionarium contingentes [...] ipso sigillo renovato consignari et in ipsam katernam inscribi debeant; quemcumque vero litere dicto sigillo renovato a data presencium per duos annos integros non consignerentur et in presentem katernam non inscriberentur, has litteras volumus esse viribus eorum karituras et inanes ac eorum exhibitoribus nocituras.

We, Miklinus, son of John, judge, jurors, councillors and all burghers of the Grec Hill notify all who inspect the present book, that since falsehood was reigning and lest this reign of falsehood lead to any abomination or scandal concerning the preservation of property rights in our city and its territory, and for the safer preservation of these property rights, we have unanimously and with equal will decided in our general council to set up our present volume, and we decided to have the seal of our community renewed, and decreed that all deeds concerning property issues have to be sealed with the renewed seal and entered into the book; whoever fail to have their deeds consigned with the renewed seal and entered in the book within two years from the issuing on the present document, we declare their deeds invalid and futile and harmful to those who present them.

The text refers to the incident of the three false seals, discovered with *Paulus litteratus* the preceding year, 1383. Therefore, the protocols were drawn up as a safety precaution, to preserve the property rights of the townspeople against any eventual fraud. The quires later named *Libri fassionum seu funduales* were kept and used in a continuous sequence up to 1526 and beyond.[153] In the first few years only the seller, the buyer, and the type of property were recorded, without any closer reference to their location, neighbours, or let alone the price. The person of the judge in the given year, however, is always carefully noted. In later years, the entries become more detailed and show more similarity with the charter on which they are based.

The other town where evidence of sophisticated property management can be found, albeit only indirectly, is Buda. Due to the destruction of the archival material, the registers are not available, but from the text of the deeds on sales or exchange of real estate it transpires that depositions concerning property

[153] The *Libri fassionum seu funduales* are edited in three subsequent volumes by TKALČIĆ, *Monumenta Zagrabiae* 9, *1384-1440* (Zagreb, 1903); 10, *1441-1470* (Zagreb, 1904); and 11, *1471-1526* (Zagreb, 1905). Quotation from 9, p. 1.

were entered in the town book. The first such reference dates from 1423: "*quam fassionem ad tabulam seu librum civitatis conscribere fecisset* ... *quam fassionem* ... *in libro civitatis predicte asserentur esse facta et conscripta*" ("which confession he had made written down in the table or town book ... in the town book the matters aforesaid are asserted to have been done and written down").[154] A mandate by Matthias Corvinus from 1459 to issue a letter of record on a property transaction that had been previously entered in the *registrum* of the city, proves that even the king acknowledged the probative value of Buda's property registers.[155]

It is impossible to tell whether the structure of the Buda property registers was similar to those of Zagreb; but the *Grundbuch* and the *Satzbuch* of Pressburg were definitely different from those of the Slavonian town. Drawn up in 1439, the *Grundbuch* is presented by the town magistrate in the introduction of the gigantic 667-folio manuscript as:

> *Vermerckt das bey tzeyten der erbern weysen und fürsichtigen Stephan Ränes statrichter, Stefan List pürgermaister, und all gesworen purger des ratts der stat zu Presspurg ist angevangen und vernewt worden ditz grüntpüch darinn aygentlich und grüntleich verschrieben sind alle hewser inner und aüsserhalb der vorgenanten stat und all weingarten die auf derselben stat gepiet ligend sind wer der selben hewser und weingarten in nüttz und gewer syttzt und welich frey oder diennschafft sind und wem oder wye sy dient es sey clösteren kirichen gottzhewseren spitalen priesteren oder layen.*
>
> Note that this *Grundbuch* was drawn up and renewed during the office of the wise and circumspect Stephan Ränes, town judge, Stefan List, mayor, and all the sworn burghers in the council of Pressburg, in which all houses inside and outside the said town and all vineyards on the territory of the same town are properly and thoroughly listed, and those who have property rights over these houses and vineyards, and which are free or encumbered, and to whom and how they are encumbered, be it monasteries, churches, chapels, almshouses, priests, or laypersons.[156]

[154] DF 238 091, quoted in KENYERES, "The fate of the medieval archives", pp. 59-60, n. 36; edited in: BTOE 3.2, p. 73. (No. 821). All the extant documents pertaining to property transactions in medieval Buda are collected and analysed by A. VÉGH, *Buda város középkori helyrajza* [The topography of medieval Buda], 2 vols. (Budapest, 2006-2008: *Monumenta Historica Budapestinensia* 15-16).

[155] DL 38 821. Discussed in RADY, *Medieval Buda*, p. 57; KENYERES, "The fate of the medieval archives", p. 60.

[156] AMB 4.1.2, f. 6r (p. 1). Quoted by Judit Majorossy in GODA and MAJOROSSY, "Städtische Selbstverwaltung", pp. 95-96.

As the text states, the volume was already a replacement of a previous one (presumably from 1379), the main purpose being not so much the registering and safekeeping of property transfers, as in Gradec, but controlling the mortgages, pledges and credits that the properties were encumbered with. The need for such a list clearly arose from the frequent use of real estate to obtain liquid capital for mercantile enterprises. Another recurrent reason for mortgages was the fulfilment of pious legacies (eternal masses, yearly commemorations, contributions to building funds, etc.) to the churches in Pressburg or its vicinity. The *Grundbuch* consists of two main parts: the houses, ordered by streets and quarters, and the vineyards in the surrounding countryside. The basic units of the register were the properties, each on a separate page, with space left for adding information on the eventual encumbrances.

The *Satzbuch*, with its 742 folios, is even more voluminous. This book was set up to register changes in property ownership, always adding the name of the new owner and the data on the transaction, and crossing out (often to the degree of illegibility) the name of the previous holder of the property rights (Fig. 36). The book was in use for about seventy years, the last entries referring to 1509/1511.[157] The plot-based structure of *Realfolien*, i.e. using one register folio per property, was the most advanced cadastral system in the late Middle Ages, and clearly fitted the book as a format different from the individual sales or credit contracts. It offered an easier overview than the rather complex Viennese property administration, which operated with four parallel series of property-related municipal books from the mid-fourteenth century onwards.[158]

Finally, let me refer to the *Grundbuch* of Sopron, a latecomer to this group of sources. After the occasionally prepared register of 1379 (see above, Fig. 30), it took the town one century to erect a purpose-oriented book for registering the property transactions in 1480. The notaries of Sopron opted for the 'conservative' method of entering transfers directly in a continuous list, regardless of the location and the kind of property. Each entry has a very similar basic structure, naming the buyer, his wife (just by her first name), the property, its location (street or field), its neighbours, previous owner, the way of transfer (sale, exchange, pledge), and any eventual encumbrance. Each entry ends with

[157] The descriptions are adapted from: GODA and MAJOROSSY, "Städtische Selbstverwaltung", pp. 95-96. See also F. KOVÁTS, *Preßburger Grundbuchführung und Liegenschaftsrecht im Spätmittelalter (1439-1517)* (Weimar, 1918).

[158] These were: the *Kaufbuch*, the *Gewerbuch*, the *Satzbuch* and the *Verbotbuch*. Currently Thomas Haffner is conducting research on these in the framework of his dissertation project at the University of Vienna.

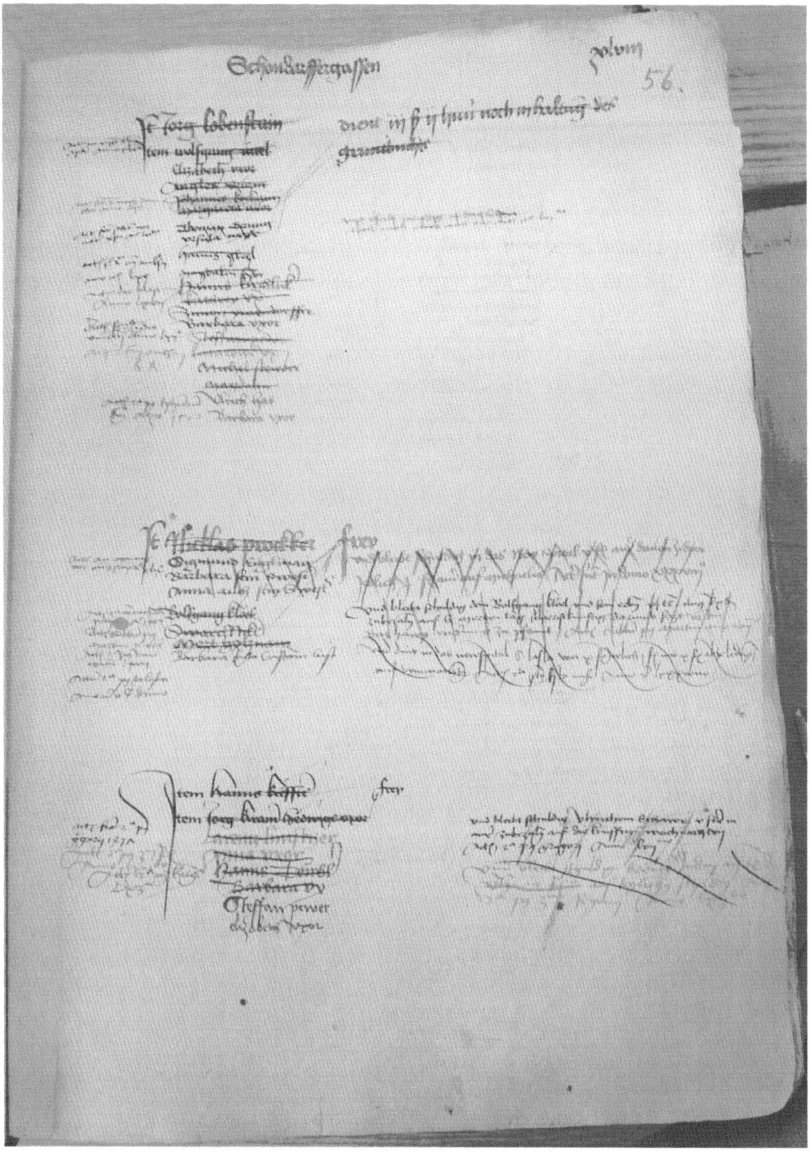

Fig. 36 A page from the Pressburger Satzbuch, showing house owners and the encumbrances on their properties in the Schöndorfergasse, one of the suburban streets of Pressburg. Repaid charges as well as former owners were crossed out (AMB, Nr. 413, f. 56r). Photo: Judit Majorossy. Reproduced with the permission of Archív Mesta Bratislavy.

a date and the names of the mayor and judge in office.[159] This shows that the registration was highly institutionalised and fully replaced separate contracts. In other towns of the Carpathian Basin, however, the administration did not reach the level of sophistication that would have necessitated specialised property registers. Mixed town books, individual charters, or even oral agreements catered for any arising needs.

Town Books and Testamentary Practice

The analysis of the contents of every type of specialised town books would require a special study and would reach well beyond the scope and intentions of the present volume. I shall therefore use just one example, that of the administration of last wills, to show the innovative potential of using the book format in civic administration. Last wills were important elements of medieval everyday life – and death –, and play a comparably important role in the archival material of many European towns. Therefore, the points presented here may be compared to practices observed by other scholars in various parts of Europe.[160] This is not the place to discuss the legal and religious issues, let alone the contents and human dramas behind these versatile sources. The only question that will be elaborated here is how written documents were used to record last wills, and how the introduction of town books as novelties in the administrative toolkit influenced the creation and survival of last wills.

Late medieval testamentary practice was the result of the gradual development of several legal systems that were made to fit the needs and interests of various social groups. From a very early phase, orality and literacy were both present in making wills, but even if the role of literacy increased, it never became exclusive. Elements of oral communication, including dialogues between the testator and people standing by his or her deathbed found their way into the documents. Therefore testaments provide a good example for investigating the coexistence and combined use of oral and written communication in a situation

[159] *Erstes Grundbuch*, ed. MOLLAY.

[160] See, e.g. P. BAUR, *Testament und Bürgerschaft: Alltagsleben und Sachkultur in spätmittelalterliche Konstanz* (Sigmaringen, 1989), pp. 14-35; G. JARITZ, "Österreichische Bürgertestamente als Quellen zur Erforschung städtischer Lebensformen des Spätmittelalters", *Jahrbuch für Geschichte des Feudalismus* 8 (1984), pp. 249-264. On Hungary: SZENDE, *Otthon a városban*, pp. 58-79; MAJOROSSY, "Church in town".

which was extreme and inevitable for the individual – the testator – and crucial for the community – the survivors.[161]

In the first decades of urban communal life townspeople could turn to an ecclesiastical body – in the case of Pressburg, the collegiate chapter – to have their last will issued as an authentic charter. However, since the bequests often concerned several pieces of real estate, representatives of the civic community from the late fourteenth century onwards started to demand that they also be present at the sealing of the will, and added the seal of the town to the document as the sign of approval. This was the case with five out of the eight fourteenth-century last wills that have been preserved in the municipal archives of Pressburg.[162] The next phase in this development occurred when the civic authorities started issuing authenticated last wills without the contribution of the collegiate chapter.

Due to the growing number of such documents and the need to retrieve information from them at various phases of their execution, it became necessary to keep 'backup copies' of them with the town authorities in the form of a town book. First, in the early fifteenth century the above-presented *Protocollum actionale*, otherwise used for registering legal cases of economic relevance, was chosen for this purpose.[163] A couple of decades later, from 1427 onwards, the town chancery decided to centralise the process of registering last wills by setting up a special book for this purpose, the first *Protocollum testamentorum*, a book that was then followed by an uninterrupted series of similar volumes up to 1872 (!).

This change in administrative practice led to a sharp increase in the number of surviving last wills. This can be observed already from the 1430s, when

[161] K. SZENDE, "Testaments and testimonies: Orality and literacy in composing last wills in late medieval Hungary", in: *Oral History of the Middle Ages*, pp. 49-66; LUPESCU MAKÓ, "Spoken and written words". Committing last wills to writing based on oral testimonies became part of the administrative practice in market towns as well: GULYÁS, *Mezővárosi önkormányzat*, pp. 177-178.

[162] See more in the Introduction to PT 1, pp. 17-18. The documents where the chapter or one of the canons sealed the testament together with the civic authorities are the following: AMB 108 (13 January1350) – priest; AMB 133 (06 March1356); AMB 327 (21 January1375); AMB 429 (18 October 1381); AMB 448 (03 July 1382); AMB 227 (1390); AMB 539 (12 May1390); DF 248984 (26 June 1343) – priest. On the process: ŠEDIVÝ, *Mittelalerliche Schriftkultur*, pp. 123-124; ID., "Anfänge der Beurkundung", pp. 99-100; J. MAJOROSSY, "Archives of the dead: Administration of last wills in medieval Hungarian towns", *Medium Aevum Quotidianum* 48 (2003), pp. 13-28, at pp. 22-23.

[163] The *Protocullum Actionale* includes the text of ten wills; see *Actionale Protocollum*, ed. ZIEGLER, *passim*.

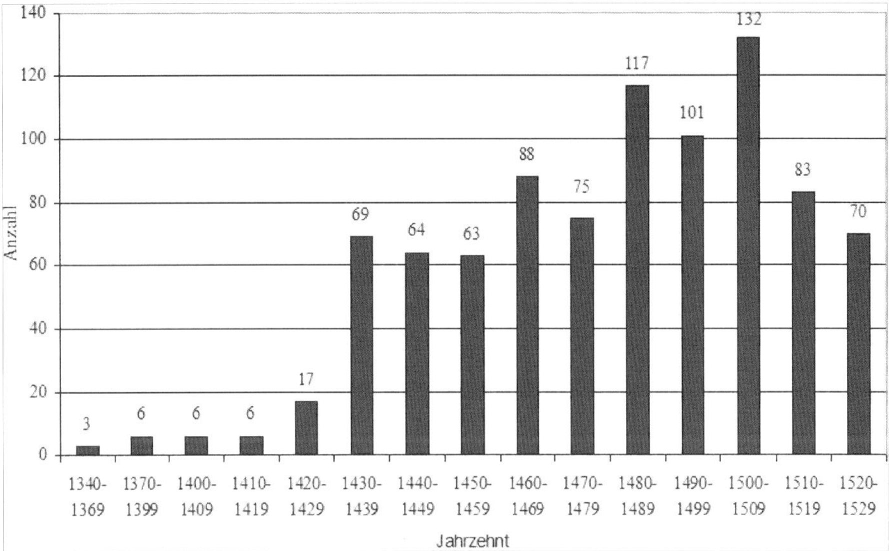

Fig. 37 Distribution of last wills per decade in Pressburg. Designed by Judit Majorossy, in: PT, 1, p. 20.

more than 60 testaments per decade were entered in the *Protocollum* (Fig. 37). The number of entries peak in the first decade of the sixteenth century, when no less than 132 last wills were registered. The increase was largely due to the plague epidemic that raged in Pressburg between 1501 and 1504. Besides the actual number of the deceased carried off by the disaster itself, the fear of death may also have increased the willingness to make a written bequest.[164] In the entire town 901 last wills have been preserved from the mid-fourteenth century up to 1529, and out of these, 844 documents, that is, 94 per cent, are to be found in the *Protocollum testamentorum*. This testifies to the overwhelming importance of this administrative innovation in the preservation of the evidence.[165]

The Book of Wills, as its outward appearance (large folio size, 456 paper folios, leather binding on cardboard) suggests, was intended for long-term use and preservation. The same notion is expressed by the introductory note of its

[164] MAJOROSSY, "Church in town" [Manuscript], pp. 43-46. Similar conclusions are reached by S.K. COHN, *The Black Death Transformed: Disease and Culture in Early Renaissance Europe* (London 2002).

[165] AMB 4.n.1; DF 277506; edition: PT in two volumes.

first notary: "*Hie in disem puech sint verschriben alle geschaft, die erber lewt an iren leczten czeiten getan und geordent haben, und die unczebrochen und stet beleiben schullen in der stat zu Prespurg*" ("This book contains all those deeds that honest people made and ordered at the end of their lives, which should stay undisturbed and constantly in the town of Pressburg").[166] Many of the documents have a double dating: a *datum* and an *actum* (*inscriptionis*). The discrepancy between the two proves that the wills were only entered in the book following the testator's death, but the relatively short intervals indicate that most people drew up their last will immediately before their death, annulling any previous versions of their testament.

The *Ofner Stadtrecht* clearly describes the procedure for recording one's last will:

> *Der zu eynem gescheft wirt gepeten, das er das furen sulle, der sal dor zu gehen geczeugen. Unnd so der mensch, der das gescheft gethon hat, stirbt, so sullen dÿ gescheft hern unnd dÿ geczeugen mit schrift ader mit priefen vor den rat chomen, ap das seÿ geschriben worden. Ist aver des nicht, so ist iß genug mit den czeugen, unnd school melden alle stuck, dÿ der mensch hat geschaft. Dan alles ordenlich sol peschriben warden ÿn das stat puech ...*
>
> If someone is asked to attend making of one's last will, he must go there as a witness. And once the person who made the last will dies, the executors of the will and the witnesses have to go to the council, with [their own] writing or existing documents, if it had been put into writing. If that was not the case, it suffices to go there with the witnesses, and they should report all the items that had been bequeathed. Then all that must be entered in the town book in due course.[167]

Entering the texts of the wills in this book did not preclude issuing them as separate documents, but the existence of a specialised volume rendered it more likely that wills made in oral form in the first place would also be committed to writing based on the testimony of the witnesses. During this process there was ample room for the control by the civic authorities over the recording as well as the execution of the wills. The latter role is testified by a high number of marginal notes as well as by interpolated passages and remarks in the volume. Most of these remarks concern the payment of monetary bequests, and they may have been added (when dated at all) months or even years later than the

[166] PT 1, p. 52.
[167] *Ofner Stadtrecht*, cap. 309.

wills in question. These remarks show that the *Protocollum* was continuously used as a source of information, and was updated if necessary.[168]

With more than 900 preserved last wills Pressburg clearly takes the lead among all cities and towns of medieval Hungary.[169] The second highest number of such documents, 314 in number, have come down to us from Sopron. The preservation of wills, despite the physical proximity of the two towns, took an entirely different course there: the earliest wills were entered into two miscellaneous town books. After the 1470s, however, the local chancery gave up this practice, whereas other issues started to be entered in specialised town books. After this time last wills from Sopron were only preserved as separate single documents.[170]

In Prešov, where the town archives also hold some 120 testaments, the usual practice was likewise to have them drawn up as individual pieces, whereas the so-called *Liber testamentorum* only recorded extracts of pious bequests.[171] The local chancery also had a book of judgements at its disposal (see above), but they only entered agreements on property divisions between living persons, typically married couples, and not last wills. In Cluj, one of the major towns of Transylvania, the locals still mainly turned to the closest place of authentication, the convent of Cluj-Manaştur, when they wanted to commit their wills to writing.[172] These examples that could be complemented with data from other towns, clearly testify to the manifold testamentary practices, as well as to the crucial role of the town books in the long-term preservation of these sources.

Outlook 1: The Beginnings of Pragmatic Literacy in Craft Guilds

An important step in the expansion of civic literacy occurred when civic authorities started issuing statutes describing the modus operandi of guilds and confraternities as legal bodies, 'semi-autonomous social fields' – or, in Wim Blockmans's terminology quoted in the Introduction, trust networks. The con-

[168] See the "*am Rande*" remarks in the PT Nos. 79, 100, 118, 121, 159, 206, etc.

[169] MAJOROSSY, "Archives of the dead", p. 21.

[170] GODA and MAJOROSSY, "Städtische Selbstverwaltung", pp. 82-83, n. 104.

[171] B. IVÁNYI, "Eperjes város végrendeleti könyve, 1474-1513" [The testamentary book of Prešov], *Történelmi Tár* 10 (1909), pp. 438-449; MAJOROSSY, "Archives of the dead", p. 27.

[172] M. LUPESCU MAKÓ, "'*Item lego ...*': Gifts for the soul in late medieval Transylvania", *Annual of Medieval Studies at CEU* 7 (2001), pp. 161-185; EAD., "Spoken and written words".

firmation of guild statutes as a legal act generally practised by town chanceries is often mentioned in the scholarly literature, but its implications as 'multiplication of trust' have not been pointed out so far.

The collaboration between towns and guilds was conveniently supported by personal connections. The elected leaders of the guilds were usually members of the urban elite: councillors, chamberlains, or other dignitaries who were interested in the smooth operation of professional or religious associations, eliminating conflicts between the representatives of the various crafts and ensuring their commemorative activities.[173] Models for guild statutes as typical documents to be put into writing by civic authorities were included in the formulary book of János Magyi, a notary public active between 1476 and 1493, using the example of the guild of blacksmiths and swordsmiths of Pest.[174]

Guild literacy in Hungary for a long time suffered the birth pangs of a nascent system. The spheres of authority were not clearly demarcated until the absolutist regimes of the early modern period: guild statues could be confirmed by several different authorities such as the king, the Palatine, the Master of the Treasury, by places of authentication, or by the civic magistrates as a governing body; and in case of seigniorial towns evidently by the *dominus*. Kings could act both as rulers and as seigniors of the town where the guild in question operated. For example, the extant set of documents by the butchers of Buda testifies that the masters had their statutes confirmed by the magistrates of Buda as well as king Matthias Corvinus.[175] The seemingly earliest guild statutes issued by urban authorities are those of the furriers' guild from Košice, dated to 1307, but it is apparently a forgery written in German, reflecting conditions of the fifteenth century.[176] From this time there is indeed a collection of guild statutes preserved in the town archives, although it does not contain reference to furriers.[177]

[173] R. SKORKA, "The formation of the guild system", in: *The History of Handicraft in Hungary*, ed. J. SZULOVSZKY (Budapest, 2012), pp. 109-150; DE CEVINS, *L'Église*, pp. 194-195.

[174] KOVACHICH, *Formulae sollennes styli*, pp. 433-437.

[175] *Zunftbuch und Privilegien*, ed. KENYERES, pp. 352-366 (Nos. 10-11), edited by Péter KIS and Iván PETRIK.

[176] DF 271754. *Anjou-oklt.* 2, No.189, p. 88. *RegSlov* 1, 225, presumes a Latin 'original', but the early date makes this highly unlikely. Further proofs for the fact that this document is a forgery are provided by A. KUBINYI, "Die Anfänge des städtischen Handwerks in Ungarn", in: *La formation et le développement des métiers au moyen âge*, ed. L. GEREVICH (Budapest, 1977), pp. 139-153, at p. 144.

[177] DF 271722 (AMK Suppl. H. 1043/3), statutes of millers, shoemakers, butchers, merchants, poachmakers and swordsmiths.

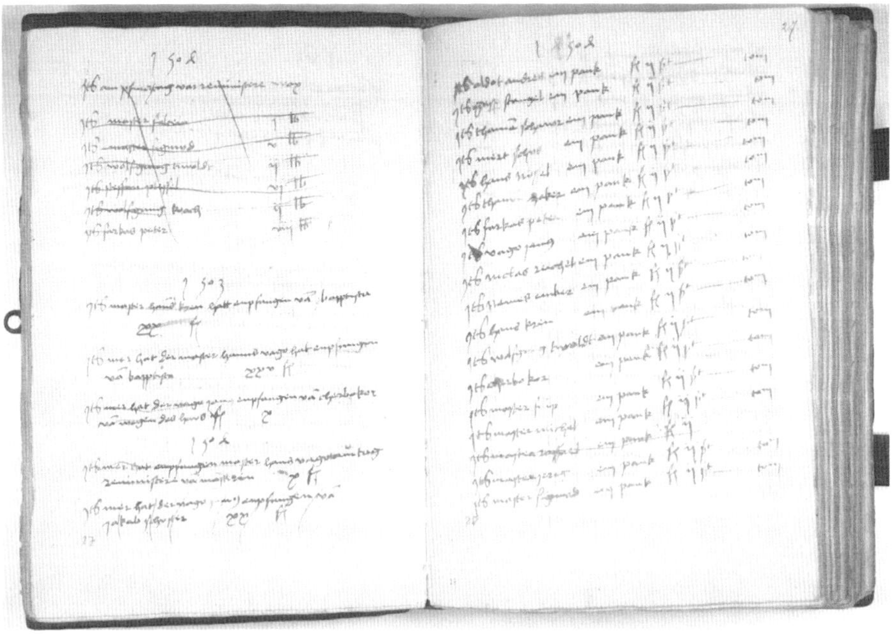

Fig. 38 Two pages from the guild book of the German butchers' guild of Buda. The left page contains contributions in wax and some monetary transactions, the right page shows rental payments for meat stalls (*pank*) in the common meat hall (BFL XV. 5. No. 8, ff. 26v-27r). Reproduced with the permission of the Budapest City Archives.

Guild statutes are often not preserved as single documents, but they were entered in various municipal books, such as the first *liber mixtus* (with the regulations of the butchers, the bakers, and the cobblers in 1376), the *Protocollum actionale* or the *Rechtsbuch* of Pressburg and the *Gerichtsbuch* or the *Gedenkbuch* of Sopron.[178] The fact that the procedures to follow were far from obvious shows that administrative literacy entered a new phase, similarly to the birth of civic literacy itself, a couple of hundred years earlier.

To take a closer look at just one example: the *Protocollum actionale* includes the regulations of three craft guilds: the baker journeymen (*pekenchnecht*, 1444), the furriers (*kursner*, 1467) and the shearers (*tuechscherer*, 1470), which were approved by the Pressburg council. Whether the approval

[178] GODA and MAJOROSSY, "Städtische Selbstverwaltung", p. 90.

was based on written documents submitted to the magistrates cannot be answered with full certainty – or rather, it differed from case to case. The bakers referred to the Vienna model, which may imply having a written copy of their statutes at hand; in the other two instances, it seems that the entry in the *Protocollum* was based on the oral testimony of the masters. In both cases the notary mentioned the issuing of a copy of the text to the guilds under the secret seal of the town, which supports the assumption that they had not had any written statutes prior to coming to court.[179]

The written word gained increasing importance in the lives of craftsmen when the guilds demanded to receive, and eventually issued themselves, letters and testimonials on the legitimate birth and orderly behaviour of apprentices and journeymen. The furriers' guild of Pressburg prescribed in 1467 that the journeymen "*sol gnuegsam briefflich urkund bringen eelichen geporen ze sein sich frunklich und erlich gehalten zu haben*" ("must bring proper written testimony of their legitimate birth and their honourable conduct"); the above-mentioned statutes of the swordsmiths of Pest formulated the same request in the 1490s in Latin "*volumus litteras a genealogia et conversatione experiri*" ("we want to inspect the documents about their descent and behaviour").[180]

As a next step, guild books as documents with probative value within the craft's own circles were introduced following the models of town books. Just as drawing up municipal books was guided by outer influences, so did these in their turn promote the appearance of further instruments of pragmatic literacy in their own environment. For instance, the guild of German butchers at Buda, one of the richest craft associations in medieval Hungary due to their involvement in the burgeoning cattle trade, developed a very sophisticated system of administration by the late fifteenth century. Their only guild book survived the period of the Ottoman occupation because the masters saved their guild chest when they fled from the endangered capital in 1529. It is a relatively late one: it includes entries from 1500 to 1529. This book is a *liber mixtus* in its own way, containing guild regulations, records of loans and other financial issues, and entries on the yearly rental fees of the shambles (Fig. 38). However, it was

[179] *Actionale Protocollum*, ed. ZIEGLER: Baker journeymen: ff. 284-285 (ed. pp. 270-271); furriers: ff. 335-337 (ed. pp. 308-310); shearers: f. 343 (ed. p. 312). The mistakes (words crossed out) in the bakers' statutes may also suggest that the notary had a text in front of him and missed a line. This is in stark contrast with Vienna, where a special municipal book of guild-related issues was drawn up in 1430, in which documents reaching back until 1364 were also copied.

[180] Furriers: *ibid.*, p. 309; swordsmiths: KOVACHICH, *Formulae sollennes styli*, pp. 433-437.

not the only one, as it refers to at least three other sorts of account books and registers kept by the same guild.[181]

Since these guilds also functioned as religious confraternities, the towns got very close to interfering in church matters through their control. This, however, did not create tension between the towns and the clergy, since guild leadership tightly overlapped with the urban elite, that is, several master craftsmen were members of the town councils. Furthermore, the towns had the right of patronage over the parish churches, where most of the guilds' altars were founded.

Outlook 2: Town Chronicles and Municipal Literacy

All over medieval Europe, the municipal administration (the council, the various specialised offices, as well as the chancery or writing office) assembled the secular intellectual elites of urban communities. Notaries in particular, the professional and paid keepers of urban memory, have produced an abundance of historical accounts and chronicles in many cities and towns.[182] However, as noted in the introductory chapter, very few works of this kind have come down to us from medieval Hungary, and little indirect evidence allows us to assume that such works have existed in the medieval period and have simply perished through the vicissitudes of time. From Agnieszka Bartoszewicz's account it seems that town notaries in the Carpathian Basin shared their 'historiographic inertia' with their Polish colleagues:

> There is no doubt that the urban clerks working in the chanceries of Polish towns possessed the skills needed to produce historical accounts; and yet they did not leave behind works comparable to those of their colleagues from neighbouring countries.[183]

The latter statement refers mainly to German and Bohemian towns.[184]

[181] BFL 16.5, No. 8, edited by I. BARACZKA, I. KENYERES, E. SPEKNER, and K. SZENDE in: *Zunftbuch und Privilegien*, ed. KENYERES, pp. 175-326, with introductory studies on the guild by A. KUBINYI and A. VÉGH. Besides the book, the assemblage preserved in the guild chest consists of eight charters transcribed and confirmed by a series of subsequent kings.

[182] P. JOHANEK, "Das Gedächtnis der Stadt – Stadtchronistik im Mittelalter", in: *Handbuch Chroniken des Mittelalters*, ed. G. WOLF and N.H. OTT (Berlin, 2016), pp. 337-398.

[183] BARTOSZEWICZ, *Urban literacy*, p. 164.

[184] P. JOHANEK, "Geschichtsschreibung und Geschichtsüberlieferung in Augsburg am Aus-

This short outlook has a twofold aim: first, taking stock of those exceptions that still show a reflection and interest in this genre of urban literacy in Hungary; and secondly, offering some suggestions on why so few such writings were compiled. To be sure, records of a historical character were not completely absent from manuscripts kept in urban collections. Occasional notes on catastrophes, on floods, earthquakes, and fires can be found in prayer books and liturgical manuscripts. The same volumes carry sporadic entries on the deaths of parish priests or other important persons, presumably to solicit prayers for the salvation of their soul.[185] The calendar parts or Easter tables of missals lent themselves easily to noting extraordinary phenomena.

The municipal books discussed above also contain occasional references to events that were important in the life of the community. The most typical occurrences that found their way to works of administrative literacy were the yearly elections of judges (or mayors) and councillors. The names of these office-holders feature in the books of judgements – even more since the elected council was responsible for the decisions noted in the books. Good examples for this practice are the town books of judgements of Gradec, and that of Košice kept from 1460,[186] as well as the *Gerichtsbuch* and *Gedenkbuch* of Sopron (see Appendix 6). Similar practices of entering scattered notes in an irregular fashion can be observed in Polish towns as well.[187]

Important events that justified the drawing up a new book, or at least coincided with its inception, were also likely to be registered. As mentioned above, in Gradec the introduction of the first book of judgements describes the scandal of forged seals in 1383; whereas the first folio of the Sopron *Grundbuch* reports on the inauguration the new town hall in 1497 and the solemn entry of the council into the building.[188] Likewise in Sopron, the Second Town Book of

gang des Mittelalters", in: *Literarisches Leben in Augsburg während des 15. Jahrhunderts*, ed. J. Janota and W. Williams-Krapp (Tübingen, 1996), pp. 160-182; M. Blahová, "Stadt, Bürgertum und Städtewesen im Spiegel der Geschichtsschreibung. Wege zur städtischen Historiographie in den böhmischen Ländern im Spätmittelalter und in der frühen Neuzeit", in: *Städtische Geschichtsschreibung im Spätmittelalter und in der frühen Neuzeit*, ed. P. Johanek (Köln, Weimar, and Wien, 2000), pp. 233-246.

185 J. Šedivý, "Stredoveká písomná kultúra na Spiši" [Medieval written culture in Spiš], in: *Historia Scepusii*, ed. M. Homza and S. Sroka, 1 (Bratislava and Kraków, 2009), pp. 483-520, at p. 507. He quotes as an example the description in a breviary, by a parish priest, of the fire of Levoča in 1462.

186 Magdoško, *Samospráva mesta Košice,* p. 14.

187 Bartoszewicz, *Urban literacy,* pp. 165-167.

188 *Erstes Grundbuch*, ed. Mollay, p.1.

miscellaneous contents offers a detailed description of the conflict between the council and the rest of the community in 1420.[189] These and similar events were considered noteworthy of commemorating in one of the municipal books, but they did not form part of a continuous narrative, nor were they used subsequently as sources by later chroniclers.[190]

Instead of looking for historical data, consulting earlier documents, either as single sheets or in municipal books, usually had legal significance. While compiling a survey of the laws of a community, just like during court cases, old documents were looked up to prove ancient rights, customs, or competences in various issues. Here we may refer again to the *Ofner Stadtrecht*, whose author gives a clear 'programme' for using charters in the first chapter of his work. As we can see from his quotations throughout the text, he indeed extensively used the town archives of Buda.[191]

The connection with legal sources and legitimacy can be observed likewise in case of manuscripts of historiographic character. The earliest example that goes beyond the fragmented notation of individual events has been discovered and still is preserved in Spišská Sobota, one of the small towns of Spiš (it is also termed *Georgenberger Chronik* after the German name of Spišská Sobota). This region in north-eastern Hungary, including its towns, received its charter in 1271, and remained royal property until it was pledged by king Sigismund to Poland in 1412, a transaction that did not change the allegiances and the daily life in its settlements. The centre of the region's rich historiographic tradition was Levoča, its biggest town, and this chronicle was also probably compiled here.[192] The manuscript of the chronicle is a small paper codex – practically a town book – of 25 folia, divided into three parts: first comes a

[189] Házi, *Sopron*, 2.1, pp. 186-187.

[190] Exceptionally, individuals also entered notes of historical events, including urban issues, in their privately owned books, like János Budai Kakas, the son of a burgher from Buda around 1513 (with a hindsight to 1504), but by that time he was a canon of Pécs, so his notes are not formally part of an urban historical tradition. See A. Kubinyi, "Budai Kakas János és történeti feljegyzései" [János Kakas of Buda and his historical notes], *Tanulmányok Budapest Múltjából* 18 (1971), pp. 59-79.

[191] "*Hye hebet sich an das Rechtpuch nach Ofner stat rechten, [...] vnd ist geschriben nach allen ausgesprochen vrtaillen vnd nach gueterr löblicher gewonhait, vnd allermaisten nach sag hantfestlicher prieff, damit dy selbe Ofenstat gestifft, gefreyet vnd pegabet wardenn ...*", *Ofner Stadtrecht*, p. 58. See also Rady, *Medieval Buda*, p. 46.

[192] A.P. Szabó, "Caspar Hain lőcsei krónikája – egy kompiláció forrásai" [The chronicle of Caspar Hain at Levoča: The sources of a compilation], in: *Clio inter arma: Tanulmányok a 16-18. századi magyarországi történetírásról* [*Clio inter arma*: Studies on Hungarian historiography in the sixteenth-eighteenth centuries], ed. G. Tóth (Budapest, 2014), pp. 169-202, at p. 191.

copy of the law code of the Spiš region (the *Zipser Willkür*); secondly, a copy of king Sigismund's 1433 confirmation of the privileges given to the Saxons of Spiš; and thirdly, on folios 18v to 24v, the text of the Chronicle in the local German dialect.[193] The narrative runs from 997, the start of the reign of St. Stephen, to 1457, the time of the compilation of the text (although the end of the manuscript is damaged). It is ordered by years in the way of annals. From the references in the text it transpires that the author, a layman of local extraction, had access to a copy of the Hungarian chronicle ("*dy ungarische cronica*", preserved in the text of the Hungarian Illuminated Chronicle) for the events preceding 1330.[194] He admitted the scarcity of evidence for the period until *c.* 1400, but had an abundance of sources including his own memory and oral tradition for the last half century. It is no coincidence that the historical events were entered in the same volume as the law code and the charter of privilege, since the chronicle also served the purpose of proving the special status of the local Germans. The author explains this intention in the first few lines: "*Sint dem mole das dy Czipser Saxen genant seyn und geste, so ist es not zu wissen von wan sy bekomen seyn und durch wilchen konig und wenne sy in den Czips komen seyn*" ("Since it is noteworthy that the Saxons of Spiš have a special standing as guests, it is necessary to know how they came about, and under which king and when they have come to Spiš").[195] Its material became part of the local tradition and its data reappear in later regional historiography.[196]

The *Georgenberger Chronik* was followed by a rich corpus of local chronicles that are already known under the names of their compilers. The earliest and most relevant for the present inquiry on the interconnection between mu-

[193] "*Chronicon quod conservatur in monte S. Georgii*", ed. B. PUKÁNSZKY, in: *Scriptores rerum Hungaricarum tempore ducum regumque stirpis Arpadianae gestarum* ed. I. SZENTPÉTERY, 2 (Budapest, 1938), pp. 273-288; GY. KRISTÓ, *Magyar historiográfia*, 1, *Történetírás a középkori Magyarországon* [Hungarian historiography, 1, Historical writing in medieval Hungary] (Budapest, 2002), p. 101; I.T. PIIRAINEN and S. POLLÁKOVÁ, *Die Chroniken der frühen Neuzeit aus der Zips* (Levoča, 2013), pp. 35-52. The manuscript is kept in the Poprad (Spišská Sobota) filial of the Levoča State Archives; photocopy at DF 266946.

[194] J. SOPKO, *Kroniky stredovekého Slovenska* [Chronicles of medieval Slovakia] (Budmerice, 1995), pp. 224-226, is of the opinion that the author may refer here to the *Ungerische Chronik* of Heinrich von Mügeln.

[195] "*Chronicon quod conservatur in monte S. Georgii*", p. 279. On the general trend of using historical data as a reinforcement and 'legitimation' of legal evidence, see G. MIKÓ, "A középkori magyar királyok ismeretlen lajstroma Monoszlóy András könyvtárából" [An unknown list of medieval kings from András Monoszlóy's library], *Acta Universitatis Szegedinensis: Acta Historica* 135 (2013), pp. 125-138, at pp. 126-127.

[196] SZABÓ, "Caspar Hain lőcsei krónikája", pp. 190-191.

Fig. 39 Wall chronicle on the southern wall of the porch in the parish church of Levoča, *c.*1500. Photo: Juraj Šedivý. Reproduced with permission.

nicipal books and historiography is the 758-page *Diarium* by Konrad Sperfogel (as the manuscript was named by one of his successors). This volume, comprising twenty-three years between 1515 and 1537, contains the most detailed historical records on Levoča and Spiš. It was originally drawn up as an account book of Sperfogel's activity as *provisor hospitalis* and was turned into a municipal *Gedenkbuch* under his tenure as town judge ("*Aliqua acta sub judicatu meo anno 1516*"). In the later part of the volume accounts of local events dominate, and the language turns to Latin instead of German. Sperfogel lived in Levoča but hailed from Konstanz, uniting in his writing the annalistic convention of Spiš with the better-established historiographical traditions of the South German territories.

There is a reference to a lost manuscript entitled the *Mirabilia urbis Kesmarkiensis*, from Kežmarok, a neighbour (and sometimes rival) of Levoča, which was allegedly written in two instalments between 1433 and 1547. If this is correct, it reinforces the existence of a regional historiographic tradition.[197] The later chronicles of the sixteenth and seventeenth centuries continued the agenda of legal justification of the special standing of Spiš already observed in the *Georgenberger Chronik*, and added the defence of a religious cause, that of the Lutheran Reformation.[198]

The local tradition of historiography was not limited to ink and paper. The southern wall of the porch of the St. James parish church of Levoča, an open space visible to everyone entering the church, carries inscriptions commemorating events from the history of the town between 1431 and 1494 in annalistic brevity, starting with a devastating fire that is also mentioned in the *Georgenberger Chronik*. There is considerable overlap with the entries of 1433, 1440, and 1454, but the *Chronik* does not mention the earthquake of 1453 that is noted on the church wall, so there must have been a third source from which the other two selected their information. The text was written on the wall in Latin, in late Gothic epigraphic minuscule around 1500 (Fig. 39). Another 'wall chronicle' is to be found in the library of the same church, listing events from between 1241 and 1516, whereas by the window of the library the election of parish priests of Levoča between 1410 and 1513 is recorded.[199]

[197] *Bibliotheca Hungarica*, 3. Data on lost volumes, p. 168.

[198] The Sperfogel Chronicle has not been published; its original is kept in the archives of the Lutheran community of Levoča (Archív evanjelického cirkevného zboru A.V. Levoča), V/A/2. See SZABÓ, "Caspar Hain lőcsei krónikája", pp. 180-181.

[199] ŠEDIVÝ, "Stredoveká písomná kultúra na Spiši", pp. 508 and 517, Fig. 196. I thank Juraj Šedivý for this reference. The text of both 'wall chronicles' and the list of priests is edited in C.

Similar 'wall chronicles' were prepared (although not preserved in their original form, survive as later copies in books) in the choir of the parish church of Braşov, in the south-eastern part of the Transylvanian Saxon region. Their texts were compiled in the late sixteenth century, starting with the presumed year of the Saxon settlement (1141) and listing a series of notable events up to the time of compilation. Indirect references point to the existence of similar inscriptions in the other important Transylvanian Saxon towns, including Sibiu, but none of these substantiate the existence of municipal chronicles predating the fall of the medieval kingdom in 1526.[200]

The relative abundance of evidence from Levoča does not overshadow the fact that similar writings are lacking from other royal towns. The small number and limited scope of municipal chronicles as independent volumes, in municipal books, or in other media is even more conspicuous, since on the level of 'national' historiography there is a strong and mutual interconnectedness between pragmatic literacy, particularly title deeds, and historiography. From the references of the late medieval chronicles of Hungary it is clear that the authors had access to the royal archives, and used particularly the lengthy *narrationes* of the royal charters registered there; in other cases, the texts of the chronicles were used for composing – or even forging – the description of the beneficiary's merits in the charters.[201]

However, all this remained limited to the royal chancery and the royal court. The chronicles of the realm reflect the governance of the kingdom, the agenda being set by a traditionally strong royal authority. Chronicles concentrated on events involving the king and the state; the presentation (or self-representation) of other social groups or communities was negligible. Besides the towns, narratives describing the history of religious orders, dioceses, or noble kindreds were equally scarce.[202] The examples described above are just exceptions that corroborate this general statement: a distinct local agenda can be pointed out precisely in those regions, in Spiš and the Saxon seats of Tran-

WAGNER, *Analecta Scepusii sacri et profani*, 2, *Scriptores rerum Scepusiacarum, quibus accedunt inscriptiones templorum Scepusiensium* (Wien, 1774), pp. 346-349.

[200] E. SZEGEDI, "A városi történetírás kezdetei Brassóban" [The beginnings of urban historiography in Braşov], in: *Erdélyi várostörténeti tanulmányok* [Studies on the urban history of Transylvania], ed. J. PÁL and J. FLEISZ (Csíkszereda, 2001), pp. 98-118; KRISTÓ, *Magyar historiográfia*, p. 126.

[201] K. SZENDE, "The uses of archives in medieval Hungary", in: *The Development of Literate Mentalities in East Cental Europe*, pp. 107-142, at pp. 135-140.

[202] KRISTÓ, *Magyar historiográfia*, pp. 126-127.

sylvania, that received collective regional privileges, the validity of which had to be inscribed in the collective memory generation after generation.

In the urban context the lack of municipal chronicles is paralleled by the absence of praises or detailed descriptions of towns. The local elite, the usual commissioners of these genres of writing in other parts of Europe, did not have an incentive to initiate the writing of such works, and the local audience did not demand them either.[203] Establishing a civic historiographic tradition was not only dependent on the general level of literacy and education. Several mayors and notaries mentioned books in their last wills, such as the legend of King Arthur or the story of Troy, which testify to the presence of historical interest among the urban elites.[204] The decisive difference was, in my view, the strong dependence of the towns on royal favour and on the general state of the realm. This subordination conditioned the political identity of the towns, and limited the active participation by the civic governance of medieval Hungarian towns in shaping the memory of decisive events or even merely closely observing them. Engaging with public political debate, as for instance their counterparts in York did, was missing from most Hungarian towns, or at least it did not leave behind any written evidence.[205]

In this context, it is not a coincidence that the late sixteenth- and seventeenth-century chronicle compilations in Sopron do not reach back beyond the year 1526, the fall of the medieval kingdom of Hungary.[206] Likewise in Braşov, the first contemporary chronicle, the *Scheda memorialis* of Lucas Grüngrass kept in a brass sphere decorating the town hall tower, records the tumultuous events taking place between 1526 and 1528.[207] The main difference compared to Sopron is that, as noted above, in the Transylvanian town the later compilations reach back to the mid-twelfth century, the beginnings of Saxon settlement according to local tradition. However, once the flow of urban chronicles

[203] K. SZENDE, "'Innen-' und 'Außensicht': Das Bild der ungarischen Städte vom Spätmittelalter bis zur Mitte des 16. Jahrhunderts" in: *Bild und Wahrnehmung*, ed. OPLL, pp. 241-264. Similar trends could be observed in medieval Czech towns: L. DOLEŽALOVÁ, "Lack of self-praise: A search for *Laudes Urbium* in medieval Czech lands", *Medium Aevum Quotidianum* 47 (2003), pp. 33-43.

[204] SZENDE, *Otthon a városban*, pp. 223-231.

[205] S. REES JONES, "Emotions, speech, and the art of politics in fifteenth-century York: House Books, mystery plays and Richard duke of Gloucester", *Urban History* 44 (2017), pp. 586-603.

[206] *Die Chronik des Marx Faut und Melchior Klein – Faut Márk és Klein Menyhért krónikája, 1526-1616,* ed. J.L. KOVÁCS (Sopron, 1995: *QGSÖ Reihe* C, 1). A systematic critical analysis of the local chronicle tradition of Sopron has not been undertaken.

[207] SZEGEDI, "A városi történetírás", pp. 99-100.

started, from the mid-sixteenth century onwards, they showed remarkable openness towards events affecting the whole country and even beyond. Paradoxically, the loss of the prominent position of the Hungarian state in the wake of the Ottoman advance triggered the historic consciousness of the local urban elites.

Conclusions: Trust in Municipal Books

This chapter pursued a long path of development over two centuries. It departed from the appearance of civic chanceries following various models and arrived at a stage when the towns themselves became models for the literacy of other institutions. The institutionalisation of chanceries was a good indicator of the growing importance of towns, and at the same time it allowed the handling of increasingly complex tasks.[208] The notaries employed by the towns were not only responsible for writing up single documents; they held the entire town administration – literally speaking – in their hands. Chanceries had to meet growing demands of the royal administration and the town's inhabitants as well. Civic authorities took over the management of a number of issues such as sales contracts, inheritance cases, preparing and executing last wills, and more, which previously had been domains of the places of authentication. The increasing amount of tasks could only be met by an increasing level of professionalisation, which inevitably led to the use of town books, registers of accounts, and documents issued by the town or protocols of litigation brought before the local court.

The fourteenth century brought along the establishment and increasing authority of municipal books. Two innovations went hand in hand. One was the introduction of the book format into the chanceries, which was the most practical way of keeping large amounts of information accessible in whatever order was needed (as opposed to rolls). This was facilitated by the extensive use of paper as writing material, although establishing trust in paper was far from obvious initially.[209] The format and size of the extant volumes is also indicative of the process of 'book formation'. If the quires were folded lengthwise to create stand-alone booklets, these may have only been added up and bound together as a book later. The examples of the first judicial protocols and property

[208] PREVENIER, "Urban chanceries", pp. 3-13.
[209] ARLINGHAUS, "Materialität und Differenzierung", pp. 181-182.

registers from Gradec illustrate this practice very well. However, in case full-width paper folios were bound together, such as the account books and other registers in Pressburg, the book format was consciously chosen from the outset. The other innovation was vesting the administrative books with the same probative power as sealed charters. Given the strong position of seals as visually and physically expressed imprints of the issuers' identity, the act of sealing can be considered a breakthrough in legal procedure as well as in mentality.

The town chanceries of Europe did not have to invent the wheel themselves but had good models to follow: the practices of the Papal Curia and the royal chanceries. The latter were by far the more accessible, especially with the frequent summoning of urban representatives to the royal court in financial and legal matters. In Hungary, the most immediate models were the registers of the places of authentication. These bodies with notarial authority were obliged to have a copy or a register of the documents that they issued, so they were able to issue authentic replacements upon request. Finally, an equally important model was provided by the writing offices of other towns.

The earliest municipal books appeared in the late thirteenth century in the Italian cities, and in the northern part of the Holy Roman Empire and the Low Countries. From these regions, the innovation spread across Europe through commercial contacts and through the movement of skilled chancery personnel. In Central Europe, municipal books appeared from the late thirteenth century onwards: first in Vienna and the lands of the Bohemian crown, and soon afterwards in Poland, starting with Cracow, and then Hungary. Understandably, more populous cities with a dense administrative agenda introduced registration earlier than small towns, which took decades to embrace this innovation. Very often the employment of a new and better educated notary triggered the practice in these places.

The acceptance of municipal books as evidence in litigation was already established in urban legal practice both in the Magdeburg law and in the more loosely-knit legal family of South German towns. The former had a limited impact in Hungary, almost exclusively in the northernmost region, which was in contact with Silesia and Lesser Poland. Buda took over much of its legal framework from the latter, adapted it to the already existing customary law, and created its own standards that soon became known in and were adopted by the major towns of the kingdom.

However decisive it may have been, the legal framework that supported the trust in municipal books as a new format of municipal administration was only known and appreciated by a small educated elite at the royal court and in the towns. The majority of those who had their charters registered, replacement charters reissued, or had the sealed documents replaced by the books, needed other features to increase the trustworthiness of the entries. This was provided by an appropriate level of detail. To be sure, the notaries seldom copied entire charters into the books, economising on space and scribal effort – with some initial difference in this respect between the Magdeburg law and the South-German legal tradition. However, there were a few pieces of essential information that were practically always included, and the entries showed a high level of conformity, even from one notary to another.

The first such piece of information was the exact dating and the regular mention of the judge's name, which also defined the year, due to the system of annual elections. When relevant, the location where the court session or the agreement took place was also added. For instance, in Trnava, when recording the yearly control and approval of the municipal accounts, not only the building but also the room, for instance "*im unteren Saal des Richterhauses*" ("in the ground floor hall of the judge's house")[210] was noted. The persons present also werw relevant to trust in the written word. When the recorded event took place in court, the phrase "*actum coram domino iudice et toto consilio*" ("done in front of the judge and the entire council") was often added, just as it would have appeared in the *intitulatio* of a document issued by the town. When actions or agreements took place out of court ("*note extra judicium*"), the names of the witnesses were added – an interesting throwback to living memory. Finally, the fixed and orderly structure of information, signs of consolidation and professionalism, contributed significantly to the establishment of trust. The thematic specialisation of the books was an important step in this direction.

The development described above enabled the town magistrates to authorise the operation of other legal bodies (or trust networks, in Blockmans's words), most notably the craft guilds. A further significant step in the expansion of trust and authority in municipal books was recording an increasing number and variety of private affairs of townspeople, taking up the function of a place of authentication. The administration of last wills may be one of the most fitting examples to explain this process. The registration could be based on a written document produced by a scribe, by one of the parties, or by any

[210] Rábik, *Tyrnaus mittelalterliche Stadtbücher*, p. 30.

other literate person – or by the oral testimony of the parties or trustworthy witnesses.

But before painting an idyllic image of civic governance and autonomy reaching unprecedented hights with the help of improved administrative literacy, let us remember the strong pressure that royal control exerted on the leadership and administration of towns. For instance, accounting was subject to the permanent need of contributing to royal finances – no wonder that the court of appeal of the most significant towns of the realm was headed by the Master of the Treasury. This control was particularly tight in mining towns. The king appointed local officials, the *exactores urburarum*, who clearly had the upper hand over the local magistrates, whose 'election' was more like an 'appointment' in many cases.[211] Due to this royal attention, several administrative innovations appeared in mining towns much more swiftly than in other towns, almost immediately after their foundation. This statement applies to municipal seals (often with reference to the ruler's person), as well as to notaries who contributed to the administration of the mines and to the royal revenues coming from them. Municipal books were also present there, often among the earliest ones. To take a step further: even on the level of small or seigniorial towns, the earliest evidence for the operation of professional notaries can be attested in mining settlements.[212]

The introduction of town books was interrelated with other important aspects of municipal literacy. Their language shows significant variety and a much stronger presence of vernacular, mostly German, literacy. The parallel (or mixed) use of various languages will be further explored in Chapter 4. The interaction of setting up town archives and using the book format in civic administration will be discussed in Chapter 6. The next qualitative leap in the development of civic literacy in Hungary took place in the second half of the sixteenth century, when the authorities of market towns on the Hungarian Plain and elsewhere also embarked on setting up town books, particularly protocols of their council meetings. To name a few examples: in Debrecen the earliest town book was set up in 1547, in Miskolc in 1569, in Kecskemét in 1591, and Szombathely and Győr followed suit in the early 1600s. In all these cases the language of the books was primarily Hungarian, a development already con-

[211] WEISZ, "Mining town privileges", p. 297.

[212] LAKATOS, *Hivatali írásbeliség*, p. 88, notes that a notary appears in 1411 at Turda (a salt mining town), and in 1428 at Telkibánya.

nected with the spread of Protestantism, which is beyond the boundaries of the present study.[213]

[213] GULYÁS, "From Latin to Hungarian", pp. 79-85; GULYÁS, *Mezővárosi önkormányzat*. See also, on the general development: V. BÁCSKAI, "A mezővárosi önkormányzat a 15. században és a 16. század elején" [Self-government in market towns in the fifteenth and the beginning of the sixteenth century], in: *Tanulmányok a magyar helyi önkormányzat múltjából* [Studies on the history of Hungarian local self-government], ed. GY. BÓNIS and A. DEGRÉ (Budapest, 1971), pp. 9-34; G. NÉMETH, "Mezővárosi önkormányzat és társadalmi meghatározói a 16-17. századi Abaúj és Zemplén megyében" [Self-government and its social determinants in Abaúj and Zemplén counties in the sixteenth and seventeenth centuries], *Agrártörténeti Szemle* 32 (1988), pp. 306-338. Two further examples for the use of Hungarian town books: *Misztótfalu mezőváros jegyzőkönyve 1596-1803* [The protocol of the market town Tăuţii de Jos, 1596-1803], ed. L. KIRÁLY, postface by I. DANKÓ, notes by I. BARACZKA (Debrecen, 1985); *Gyöngyös város becsületes tanácsa elhatározta ... 1659-1848: Válogatás két évszázad városi határozataiból* [It was decided by the honest council of Gyöngyös ... 1659-1848: Selection of two centuries of municipal resolutions], ed. B. KOVÁCS (Eger, 1984).

Chapter 4

Language and Literacy[1]

Language on the Research Agenda

Social relationships, with trust taking pride of place, are "fundamentally mediated through language".[2] This statement applies to all historic periods, but gains particular emphasis in situations where members of society had a choice of different languages. Looking at this question from a different angle, language as a mediator could easily become a source of trust or distrust, depending on the social environment.

The ethnic and linguistic plurality of towns, past and present, stands high on the international research agenda.[3] It is encouraging to see that the old national master narratives of linear processes are gradually replaced by more dynamic approaches. It is no longer customary to describe the relationship of

[1] The bulk of this chapter is based on my article K. SZENDE, "Integration through language: The multilingual character of late medieval Hungarian towns", in: *Segregation – Integration – Assimilation*, pp. 205-234. It is reproduced here with the publisher's consent, with updates and minor adjustments to fit the context of the present volume. Some parts of the argument were further developed in a more recent article, K. SZENDE, "*Alter alterius lingua loquatur?* Mehrsprachigkeit zwischen Konsens und Konflikt – Zum Sprachgebrauch in den mittelalterlichen Städten Ungarns", in: *Mittelalterliche Stadtsprachen*, ed. S. EHRICH and M. SELIG (Regensburg, 2016: *Forum Mittelalter, Studien* 11), pp. 77-91.

[2] JOHNSTONE, "*Pistis* and citizens", p. 383.

[3] A. ADAMSKA, "Latin and three vernaculars in East Central Europe from the point of view of the history of social communication", in: *Spoken and Written Language: Relations between Latin and the Vernacular Languages in the Earlier Middle Ages*, ed. M. GARRISON *et al.* (Turnhout, 2013: USML 24), pp. 325-364; I. HLAVÁČEK, "Dreisprachigkeit im Bereich der Böhmischen Krone: Zum Phänomen der Sprachbenutzung im böhmischen diplomatischen Material bis zur Hussitischen Revolution", in: *The Development of Literate Mentalities*, pp. 289-310.

Latin and the respective vernacular languages as a contest, with the 'advancement, breakthrough and final victory' of the latter. Instead, concepts of cultural transfer and mutual influences have permeated the field, both historians and linguists pay closer attention to the contexts of the use, retention, and shift of various languages in towns and countryside alike. Nevertheless, from among all issues connected to urban literacy, language use seems to be the politically most sensitive one. Some of the main trends in historiography have been outlined in the Introduction; here I would like to point out a few further points pertaining to the research on language use within urban literacy.

The question of ethnic minorities and their languages was not on the research agenda of medievalists in the multi-national Habsburg monarchy – following its dissolution after World War I, however, it quickly gained a foothold as the newly established 'nation states' set out to discover (or create) their ethnic past.[4] Parallel to this, in the 1930s and early 1940s, ethnically biased German researches, using concepts of historical geography such as *Volksboden* or *Kulturboden*, embraced traces of German presence in the past as a justification for territorial claims in their own times. Consequently, all related research was strongly discredited after the end of World War II. After decades of silence, linguists interested in language contacts took up the issue again. The most prominent representative of this direction in Hungary was Károly Mollay, who did pioneering work by analysing the medieval sources of his birthplace, Sopron, as evidence for the coexistence of several languages.[5] He was among the first to use the term 'multilingualism' in the context of urban life in medieval Hungary. Historians tackled the issue of linguistic, ethnic, and religious communities on a European scale in the 1980s, and particularly after the political changes in 1989. This time the guiding principles were 'cohabitation', 'tolerance', and 'integration'. From among the Hungarian medievalists working on this theme, András Kubinyi's research is the most important. He devoted several studies to various ethnic groups, particularly the Germans, who settled in medieval Hungary.[6] In the last couple of decades, literary historians and archi

[4] See, e.g. E. MÁLYUSZ, *A középkori magyarság település- és nemzetiségpolitikája* [Settlement- and ethnic policy of the Hungarians in the Middle Ages], ed. I. SOÓS (Budapest, 2002), with a postscript; originally published in 1939-1941.

[5] MOLLAY, "Többnyelvűség". Unfortunately, these important studies were only published in Hungarian, in a local history review.

[6] A. KUBINYI, "Zur Frage der Toleranz im mittelalterlichen Königreich Ungarn", in: *Toleranz*, ed. A. PATSCHOVSKY and H. ZIMMERMANN (Sigmaringen, 1998: *Vorträge und Forschungen* 45), pp. 187-206; A. KUBINYI, "Deutsche und Nicht-Deutsche in den Städten des mittelalterlichen

vists also took up the issues of multilingualism. Among others, historian László Solymosi,[7] Germanist András Vizkelety[8] and codicologist Edit Madas[9] have enriched the field with new results. With all this being said, offering evidence-based explanations remains of prime importance for keeping to the historical context and avoiding the pitfalls of projecting modern-day concepts of 'multiculturalism' or nationalistic agendas onto past times.

As this short overview suggests, the ethnically heterogeneous nature of the urban population in the medieval kingdom of Hungary has been a subject of research and discussions for about a century. The roles of the indigenous (Hungarian, Slovak, Croatian, and so forth) and immigrant (German, Italian, Walloon, and other), Christian and non-Christian elements in the process of urbanisation have been investigated both on a country-wide basis and on the level of individual towns. It became clear that the diverse ethnic groups were not occasional elements, but fundamental constituents that played a crucial role in creating and shaping urban form and identity in the towns of the Carpathian Basin.[10] The main directions of immigration and the contribution of settlers to the emergence of towns have been discussed in Chapter 1; here the impact of these processes on language use and literacy in the major towns of the kingdom will be explored.

There seems to be a general agreement that the basic analytical criterion to define both the ethnic constitution of a settlement and the allegiances of individual town-dwellers is whether the person or the segment of the population in question spoke the language of a given ethnic group. In studies of urban social development, however, further questions concerning the use of language or languages have not been given much attention.[11] For instance, is it true that a

ungarischen Königreichs", in: *Internationales kulturhistorisches Symposion Mogersdorf* (Eisenstadt, 1996), pp. 145-177.

[7] SOLYMOSI, "Muttersprache und rechtliche Schriftlichkeit".

[8] A. VIZKELETY, "Die deutsche Sprache und das deutsche Schrifttum im ungarischen Mittelalter", in: *The Development of Literate Mentalities*, pp. 277-287; A. VIZKELETY, *Beschreibendes Verzeichnis der altdeutschen Handschriften in ungarischen Bibliotheken*, 2 vols. (Wiesbaden, 1969-1973).

[9] E. MADAS, "La naissance du Hongrois ècrit", in: *The Development of Literate Mentalities*, pp. 311-319.

[10] See Chapter 1 above, and the chapter on "Trade and towns" in: ENGEL, *The Realm of St. Stephen*, pp. 244-66; FÜGEDI, "Das mittelalterliche Königreich Ungarn als Gastland", pp. 471-507; I. PETROVICS, "Foreign ethnic groups in the towns of southern Hungary in the Middle Ages", in: *Segregation, Integration, Assimilation*, pp. 67-88.

[11] The most important exception is the work of András Kubinyi who in his articles on ethnic groups often included references to their languages. See, e.g. A. KUBINYI, "Ethnische Minder-

language was used only by people who belonged to the ethnic group defined by the given language? The short answer to this question, it seems, is 'not necessarily'. A somewhat longer and more nuanced answer will be given in the pages that follow.

Why Not Monolingual?

That the Hungarian towns were not monolingual was noted already by contemporaries. As the humanist court historian of Matthias Corvinus, Pietro Ransano, remarked around 1490,

> *... nam propter propinquitatem regionum innumeri e Germania mortales (transmisso Danubio) in Hungaria propter soli eius feracitatem habitandi sibi locum iam pridem elegerunt, quo fit, ut Germanus cum Hungaro mixtim vitam degens habitu moribusque magna ex parte conveniat, utque alter alterius lingua loquatur.*
>
> Due to the proximity of their territories, a great number of people from Germany (crossing the Danube), had chosen Hungary as their place of habitation because of the fertility of its soil, from which it follows that Germans who live their lives together with Hungarians come to resemble them to a great extent in their appearance and customs, and that they speak each other's language.[12]

A couple of generations earlier, in 1414 king Sigismund also emphasised this linguistic plurality when he characterised his kingdom in front of the representatives of the Holy Roman Empire as "*delectabilem indigenis et advenis sub diversitate linguarum et nacionum exhibet incolatum*" ("it provides a pleasant

heiten in den ungarischen Städten des Mittelalters", in: *Städtische Randgruppen und Minderheiten,* ed. B. Kirchgässner and F. Reuter (Sigmaringen, 1986), pp. 183-199. On Hungary, see J.M. Bak, "'Linguistic pluralism' in medieval Hungary", in: *The Culture of Christendom: Essays in Medieval History in Commemoration of Denis L.T. Bethell*, ed. M.A. Meyer (London and Rio Grande, 1993), pp. 269-279; id., "A kingdom of many languages", in: *Multilingualism in the Middle Ages and Early Modern Age: Communication and Miscommunication in the Premodern World*, ed. A. Classen (Berlin, 2016), pp. 165-176.

[12] P. Ransanus, *Epithoma rerum Hungararum*, ed. P. Kulcsár (Budapest, 1977), p. 60.

abode both for natives and newcomers with its diversity of languages and peoples").[13]

These excerpts can serve as a starting point for discussion of some of the factors that contributed to the situation described – which was apparently a reason for pride to the polyglot king but something unusual to the Italian bishop. The importance of constant immigration due to regular demographic deficit in towns has already been pointed out in Chapter 1. From the varied sources that furnish data about numbers of children – charters, last wills, the lists of Hungarian members of the Holy Spirit Confraternity in Rome – it turns out that urban families on the average had less than two surviving offspring.[14] For instance, charters related to 80 families in late medieval Buda contain references to 115 children;[15] last wills from Pressburg up to 1529, briefly summarised in the previous chapter, allow us to reconstruct 804 families with altogether 839 children at the death of one of the parents;[16] while the above-mentioned confraternity list contains data on 834 lay families with 3187 members, yielding an average family size of 3.82 persons, but with the urban families being significantly smaller than the average.[17] Therefore, without any input from the outside, the population of the towns in question would have drastically decreased, which was apparently not the case.

Compared to the 'old stock' of the respective urban populations, the ethnic composition of the newcomers showed considerable variation and often involved ethnic groups or individuals that were different from the resident major-

[13] *Deutsche Reichstagsakten*, ed. J. WEIZSÄCKER *et al.*, 14 vols. (München and Gotha, 1867-1935), 7, p. 240; D. WALLACE, "Constance", in: *Europe, 1348-1418: A Literary History*, ed. D. WALLACE (Oxford, 2016), pp. 655-682, at p. 669.

[14] One needs to work with sources that were not meant for demographic record keeping, because neither parish registers nor census lists are available for the period investigated.

[15] A. KUBINYI, "A budai és pesti polgárok családi összeköttetései a Jagelló korban" [Family connections of the burghers of Buda and Pest in the Jagellonian period (1490-1526)], *Levéltári Közlemények* 37 (1966), pp. 227-291, at p. 233, reprinted in ID., *Tanulmányok Budapest középkori történetéről*, pp. 513-570.

[16] SZENDE, *Otthon a városban*, pp. 101-103 and Table 9.

[17] E. CSUKOVITS, "Családi viszonyok a középkor végi Magyarországon" [Family relations in late medieval Hungary], in: *"Magyaroknak eleiről": Ünnepi tanulmányok a hatvanesztendős Makk Ferenc tiszteletére* ["On the forebears of the Hungarians": Studies in honour of the sexagenarian Ferenc Makk], ed. Ferenc PITI (Szeged, 2000), pp. 107-125. The most detailed research on the family structure and demography of late medieval and early modern Hungarian towns has been carried out by György Granasztói. See, e.g. GY. GRANASZTÓI, "The Hungarian bourgeois family in the late Middle Ages: Presumptions and additions to the nature of a welfare society", *Acta Historica Academiae Scientiarum Hungaricae* 30 (1984), pp. 257-320.

ity. A full survey of this process is beyond the aims of this volume; however, three cases can be presented to exemplify some of the patterns that may be encountered.[18]

At one end of the scale, the Transylvanian town of Sibiu, founded by German settlers around 1150, was one of the few places in medieval Hungary where the acceptance of the new inhabitants was limited on an ethnic basis. Non-Germans had difficulties even in acquiring burgher's rights and were almost totally excluded from the elite (apart from a few assimilated Italians).[19] This rule, which can be deduced from the sources from the middle of the fourteenth century onwards, was established to keep away not only Hungarians, but especially Romanians and 'Greeks' who appeared in increasing numbers around the town due to the Ottoman advance on the Balkans. The ethnic policy of Sibiu was applied with considerable success, which for the newcomers at least meant that they did not have to cope with new language(s), only the special Saxon dialect of the first settlers, which became somewhat petrified over the centuries.[20]

At the other end of the Carpathian Basin, the western border town of Sopron followed a different path. As was presented in more detail in the earlier chapters, Sopron became a royal town during the great social transformations of the thirteenth century. From this time onwards, royal policy consciously fostered the immigration of new settlers – be they "*Christiani sive Judei*" ("Christians or Jews"; 1324), "*de Austria seu Bohemia vel de aliis quibuscunque partibus extraneis*" ("from Austria or Bohemia or from whichever other foreign parts"; 1360).[21] Among them Germans from the nearby Austrian villages and market towns seem to have formed a majority over the Hungarian population by the 1370s, even if Hungarian newcomers did not cease to appear in the town. Although we have no sources to establish the exact numerical relation of Germans, Hungarians, and other ethnic groups, it seems at any rate

[18] In more general terms see FÜGEDI, "Das mittelalterliche Königreich Ungarn als Gastland".

[19] G. GÜNDISCH, "Die Oberschicht Hermannstadts im Mittelalter", in: ID., *Aus Geschichte und Kultur der Siebenbürger Sachsen: Ausgewählte Aufsätze und Berichte* (Köln and Wien, 1987: *Schriften zur Landeskunde Siebenbürgens* 14), pp. 182-200; FLÓRA, "The matter of honour", pp. 49-62.

[20] T. NÄGLER, *Die Ansiedlung der Siebenbürger Sachsen* (Bucharest, 1979), pp. 195-196. The similarity of the Transylvanian German dialects to the German spoken in Luxembourg is still noticeable; see K.K. KLEIN, "Luxemburg und Siebenbürgen: Aus den Vorarbeiten zum Siebenbürgisch-Deutschen Sprachatlas", in: *Luxemburg und Siebenbürgen,* ed. K.K. KLEIN (Köln and Graz, 1966), pp. 1-111.

[21] HÁZI, *Sopron,* 1.1, pp. 41, 123-124.

that from the middle of the fifteenth century their relative proportions stabilised. The influx of new settlers spontaneously maintained an equilibrium between the German majority, a smaller but still significant Hungarian presence, a Jewish community, and a few occasional other elements. This resulted in a similar balance concerning the use of languages.[22]

Buda, the capital and the most populous town was subject to ethnic transformations on an even larger scale. After the Mongol invasion, the newly founded town had very little remaining local population to build on, but attracted a high number of German settlers who by the second half of the fourteenth century clearly had gained the upper hand in controlling the affairs of the town.[23] During the following decades, however, beside the appearance of Italian merchants and the continuous existence of a Jewish community, the proportion of Hungarian inhabitants increased significantly. The growing number of Hungarians can be connected to the almost continuous presence of the royal court and the members of the noble families attached to it, and even more to the reproductive potential of the surrounding closer and further countryside, whose inhabitants were overwhelmingly Hungarians. Altogether this led to both the contraction of the urban area inhabited by Germans and the increasing role of Hungarians in the local administration.[24]

Another crucial expression found in the above-quoted text by Ransano that applies practically to the entire kingdom is "*mixtim vitam degens*" ("living their lives together"). This refers not only (and perhaps not primarily) to the topographical aspects of mixed populations but also to the need for communication with political and business partners alike. This need called for practical solutions both inside and outside urban communities, preferably through the medium of languages familiar to all parties involved.

What Ransano did not specifically mention – perhaps because it was as natural for him as the air that he breathed – was the wide discrepancy between the oral and written forms of communication. In particular circles and for particular functions the use of a given language might be appropriate, while in other situations the same idiom would have sounded or looked completely odd.

[22] MOLLAY, "Többnyelvűség".

[23] A. KUBINYI, *Die Anfänge Ofens* (Wiesbaden, 1972: *Osteuropastudien der Hochschulen des Landes Hessen*, Reihe 1, 60); VÉGH, "Buda: The multi-ethnic capital", pp. 89-100; VÉGH, *Buda Atlas*, p. 17, Maps B.1.1 and B.1.2.

[24] A. KUBINYI, "Buda, medieval capital of Hungary", in: *Medieval Buda in Context*, pp. 366-383, and VÉGH, "Buda: The multi-ethnic capital".

The several languages enjoyed varying levels of prestige which affected their parallel use. Which languages were these?

Latin was the 'official' language in which the majority of documents were formulated – a usage which conveyed high (and due to its use in the Church, sacred) prestige from the earliest period of urban life in medieval Hungary. András Vizkelety's apt statement that "anyone who was able to read and write was by definition bilingual" applies to most of the medieval literate population.[25] Latin's position was strengthened by the strong correlation between the language itself and the script used to render it: no wonder that our characters are still called the Latin alphabet.

From the turn of the fourteenth century, however, the use of written vernaculars had begun to challenge the primacy of Latin in many areas of urban life. This happened especially in towns with a significant population whose vernacular had a tradition of being put into writing elsewhere on the continent (mainly German, but to a smaller extent also the various dialects of Italian). Besides crafts and commerce, in several towns local administration and justice did not have a conscious policy of using Latin in internal affairs. In Hungary and its western and northern neighbours, the Latin alphabet was adapted for rendering sounds in various vernaculars, initially without solid conventions, let alone orthography. In regions south and east, other scripts derived from the Cyrillic were chosen and developed for the Croatian, Ruthenian and Romanian languages that will be briefly mentioned below.

Through the influence of Humanism, which reached the towns of the kingdom of Hungary mainly through university graduates who had studied in Vienna and Cracow or, in smaller numbers, at Italian universities, this tendency was eventually reversed. The re-latinised administration of the Upper Hungarian town Prešov under its ambitious notary Christan Czibner (*Cristanus baccalaureus*) in the early sixteenth century is the best example.[26] Even the various town offices might be renamed following classical patterns: in the second *Grundbuch* (1554-1580) of Sopron, for instance, the town hall is called *praetorium*, the town judge *consul*, the mayor *praetor*, the chamberlain (*Stadtkammerer*) *praefectus aerarii*, and the council members *senatores*.[27]

[25] VIZKELETY, "Die deutsche Sprache", p. 278; ADAMSKA, "Latin and three vernaculars", pp. 331-335.

[26] On his activity, see B. IVÁNYI, "Das Deutschtum der Stadt Eperies im Mittelalter", *Südost-Forschungen* 5 (1940), pp. 361-402, at p. 378.

[27] *Második telekkönyv – Zweytes Grundbuch 1554-1580*, ed. P. DOMINKOVITS (Sopron, 2015), *passim* in the edited text and pp. 10-11 of the Introduction.

Similar terms were used in the above-mentioned sixteenth-century books of judgement of Transylvanian Sibiu and Braşov. These developments should make one cautious about considering the takeover of the vernaculars as a straightforward and linear process. A stronger adherence to Latin in the administration could also have been due to its official recognition and its preferred use by the seigniors of the towns as well as by other nobles, and by the county administration who generally did not understand German.[28] As a mediatory language, Latin maintained its role even in oral communication well into the early modern period.[29]

German was used for internal communication ever since the first arrival of settlers from various German-speaking territories (termed in the sources *Teutonici* and *Saxones*, probably according to their respective regions of origin). Written German first appeared in Hungary in an urban context in the early fourteenth century. For this, as Juraj Šedivy revealed, beside the century-long presence of the speakers of German, an impetus from a community cherishing its use in administrative literacy was needed. In Pressburg, this was the Cistercian abbey of Heiligenkreuz in Lower Austria, which received several vineyards as pious donation from the inhabitants. The earliest German charters issued on Hungarian soil, dated 14 September 1319 and 4 July 1320 in Pressburg, testify to such donations. Similarly to two earlier German charters issued in the name of Pressburgers, it was written in the *scriptorium* of the abbey, and can thus be identified as *Empfängerausfertigungen*. Seven years later the same abbey, realising how unusual German charters in Hungary were, presented another of their donation charters concerning a vineyard to the chapter of Pressburg for transcription: "*scriptas ydiomate teutonicali, petentes cum instantia, quod nos tenorem et seriem earumdem in latinum commutando nostris litteris transscribi faceremur*" ("written in the German language, asking steadfastly that we transcribed it by translating its contents and wording into

[28] E.g. in his letter to the council of Sopron in 1577, the royal captain of the town, János Devecseri Csóron, returned a German letter with the following comment: "*Litteras ipsas Germanicas in specie remisimus, rogamusque vestras prudentes ac circumspectas dominationes, velint nobis de ista re et alias semper Latine scribere, nam alioquin nos voluntatem vestrarum dominacionum intelligere non possumus*", in: *XVI. századi magyarnyelvű levelek Sopron sz. kir. város levéltárából* [Sixteenth-century Hungarian letters in the town archives of Sopron], ed. J. HÁZI (Sopron, 1928), pp. X-XI.

[29] I.GY. TÓTH, *Literacy and Written Culture in Early Modern Central Europe* (Budapest, 2000), pp. 130-145.

Latin").[30] The first German charter issued in Pressburg without any connection to Heiligenkreuz, on the pledging of a house, written by a local scribe, dates from 1 May 1346, and the first German charter written in Sopron from 1361.[31] Both towns adopted a dialect resembling the Bavarian-Austrian dialect of Middle High German. This was half a century earlier than in the case of official documents of the state chancery,[32] which issued the earliest known German charter in 1397 – significantly, in a case concerning townspeople, in this instance from Trnava. In this respect, German literacy in Hungary shows a similarly strong role played by urban initiatives as in the case of Czech literacy in Bohemia, where the writing offices in towns were the pioneers of putting vernacular texts (first legal and administrative ones) into writing.[33]

In many royal towns of the Hungarian kingdom German became dominant, especially in crafts and commerce, that is, in those fields of life where oral communication, which played a much greater role in everyday life than written communication, was also mostly conducted in this language. The urban population produced not only documents of pragmatic (mainly administrative) literacy, but was also familiar with the achievements of the vernacular lay and religious literary activity in other German-speaking areas of Europe. Furthermore, they asserted themselves as authors of a modest number of historiographic works as well as of smaller pieces of epic and poetry.[34]

New research by Bálint Lakatos has shown that German as a written language also spread remarkably fast among the small private towns and market towns. Places like Levél (1381), Kőszeg (1382), or Csepreg (1391) issued German documents under their civic seal at particularly early dates.[35] This is to

[30] Šedivý, "Deutschsprachige Beurkundung", pp. 253-254. The text quoted by Šedivý comes from Heiligenkreuz, Stiftsarchiv, 21 April 1327.

[31] Šedivý, "Deutschsprachige Beurkundung", pp. 258-259. K. Mollay, *Német-magyar nyelvi érintkezések a XVI. század végéig* [German-Hungarian language contacts until the end of the sixteenth century] (Budapest, 1982), pp. 120-128; K. Mollay, "Ungarisch – Deutsch", in: *Sprachgeschichte: Ein Handbuch zur Geschichte der deutschen Sprache und ihrer Erforschung*, ed. W. Besch, O. Reichmann, and S. Sonderegger (Berlin nd New York, 1984), pp. 893-897.

[32] There is an earlier state agreement between Louis I and the dukes of Austria from 1371 (CDH IX/7 309-312), but according to Šedivý, "Deutschsprachige Beurkundung", p. 262, this was also an *Empfängerausfertigung*.

[33] Hlaváček, "Dreisprachigkeit", pp. 289-310.

[34] A. Vizkelety, "Die deutsche Sprache"; id., *Beschreibendes Verzeichnis der altdeutschen Handschriften*.

[35] Levél (1381): DF 238361. Kőszeg (1382): DF 201877, edited in Házi, *Sopron*, 1.1, pp. 195-196. Csepreg (1391): the charter is known from a Latin translation of a German original, copied into the cartulary of the Cistercian abbey of Klostermarienberg. This text was transcribed

be explained by a general 'orientation towards prestige', and by the strong contacts of these localities with Sopron, where by the 1380s German became the dominant language in local administration.[36] Sopron played the role of mother-town and court of appeal in juridical matters for these small towns, and missives reporting or inquiring about political events in the western border-zone were also written in German.[37] The fact that many of the town books were kept in German further strengthened the model role of this language in local administration.

It is remarkable and hard to explain, however, that among the Saxons of Transylvania, the area that had perhaps the most homogeneous German-speaking community in the entire Carpathian Basin, Latin remained for so long the exclusive written language, and the usage of German in local administration developed so much later than elsewhere in the country, at the turn of the fifteenth century. Before this time, only a single indirect reference to "*litteris [...] sedis Cibiniensis [...] nativa eorum lingua emanatis*" ("the document of Szeben seat, issued in their native language") can be found, although not concerning urban issues.[38] Perhaps the late appearance of municipal books in this region, that was discussed in the previous chapter, need also to be considered here. Even these books used Latin until the mid-sixteenth century: in case of the town book of judgements of Sibiu, the shift to German occurred in 1556, with the employment of a new notary, Johannes Rhyssus.[39] The lack of regular and direct contacts between Transylvania and major German-speaking towns in Western Europe may have played a role in the belated appearance of both phenomena.[40]

by the Vasvár chapter on 10 May 1393: DL 7672. In the transcription, it is mentioned that the abbot "*exhibuit nobis quasdam literas privilegiales civitatis Chepreg idiomate Teutonicali scriptas offerens quoddam registrum cum eisdem, asserens tenorem eorundem contineri in eodem*". Edited in CDH 10.1, p. 730, the transcription: CDH 10.2, p. 146; summary: ZsO 1, Nos. 1889 and 2926. See on this LAKATOS, *Adattár*, s.v. Csepreg, No. 2.

36 LAKATOS, *Hivatali írásbeliség*, pp. 36-37.

37 I. BARISKA, "Sopron a kőszegi források tükrében a 14-17. században" [Sopron in the mirror of sources from Kőszeg], *Soproni Szemle* 52 (1998), pp. 4-14. See also, on the mediatory role of German: ADAMSKA, "Latin and three vernaculars", pp. 336-342.

38 MOLLAY, *Német-magyar*, pp. 124-127; SOLYMOSI, "Muttersprache", p. 150. On the archival material of the Transylvanian Saxons, see the UGDS series. The reference to a vernacular document: *ibid*., 1, No. 527, p. 479 (24 August 1336).

39 PAKUCS, *Die ältesten Protokolle von Hermannstadt*, pp. 12-13.

40 There were contacts on personal level, e.g. the number of Transylvanian Saxon students at foreign universities was remarkably high: S. TONK, *Erdélyiek egyetemjárása a középkorban* [University attendance of Transylvanians in the Middle Ages] (Bucharest, 1979), table on p. 68

Hungarian, although used in oral communication by a large number of urban dwellers, was limited to those areas of life which did not require the use of writing. This primarily oral character of the Hungarian language makes it difficult to give a realistic assessment of its role and spread. Interest in communicating with those using Hungarian is testified by the compilation of glossaries. The three earliest extant examples of this genre, denoted by their place of modern discovery, are the Königsberg glossary (*c.*1380), the Beszterce glossary (*c.*1395), and the Schlägl glosses (*c.*1405). These consist of thematic groupings of Latin and Hungarian words and phrases suitable for using at school and in chanceries alike. Glossaries survive from, among other places, towns with a clear German majority such as Bistriţa and Sopron, in the latter case from the bequest of Konrad Ernst, a town notary of Austrian origin. A short practical phrasebook of Hungarian expressions (including some rather obscene ones) compiled in Buda by Hans von Rotenburg, a *litteratus* of German-Czech descent, from 1419-1422, contains Latin and German explanations of vernacular phrases which had evidently been recorded from hearing.[41]

Further sporadic data, for instance that in 1469 the daughter of the mayor of Sibiu was sent to Cluj, the other Transylvanian centre, where she made good progress in learning Hungarian, point in the same direction.[42] However, it was not until the second half of the sixteenth century that Hungarian became an equal counterpart to Latin or German for use in municipal and guild administration, for instance in Cluj or in Miskolc, a market town in north-eastern Hungary.[43] Such examples show well the explosion of vernacular literacy, and can shed a sharper light on a previous period of fundamental changes in the fourteenth and fifteenth centuries, when the expansion of German literacy was a

and his Appendix, indicates the following numbers of enrolled students for the period between 1401 and 1520: Sibiu: 285, Braşov: 267, Cluj: 122 (Hungarians and Germans together), Sighişoara: 95. Artistic production also reached Braşov, Sibiu, and Sighişoara from Vienna and other cities: E. SARKADI NAGY, *Local Workshops – Foreign Cconnections: Late Medieval Altarpieces from Transylvania* (Ostfildern, 2012). However, this does not make up for the lack of administrative contacts.

41 MADAS, "La naissance", pp. 311-319. On the word-lists and phrase-collections, see *Régi Magyar Glosszárium* [Old Hungarian glossary], ed. J. BERRÁR and S. KÁROLY (Budapest, 1984), especially the Introduction, pp. 36-47, with a list of editions and further literature.

42 M. AUNER, "Két adalék a magyar nyelv tanulására a XV. századból" [Two examples of learning Hungarian in the fifteenth century], *Magyar Nyelv* 10 (1914), pp. 419-420.

43 On the growing role of Hungarian in municipal literacy in Cluj, see A. KISS, "A kolozsvári városi levéltár első levéltári segédlete" [The first finding aid of the municipal archives of Cluj], *Levéltári Közlemények* 66 (1995), pp. 197-219, at pp. 203-205.

similarly efficient motor of the 'administrative boom' of town books in the Carpathian Basin.[44]

Other vernaculars, such as various dialects of *western and southern Slavic* languages (different Czech, Moravian, Slovak, or Croatian dialects), followed much the same path, but with a longer time lag and in a more limited territory and urban presence (apart from Dalmatia). Western Slavonic was used in the northern-northwestern corner (Nyitra and Trencsén counties) and further east in Sáros County. Southern Slavic was used in the southwest, in parts of Zagreb County south of the River Sava. In the latter case, the script was also different: the Glagolitic script which testifies to the influence from the maritime regions of medieval Croatia.[45]

Further languages such as *Cuman, Ruthenian*,[46] and *Romanian* were extremely marginal in most royal towns, since they were not used by the basic constituent elements of any towns, only by smaller groups without manifest ambitions to literacy – although individual members of these groups could exceptionally reach positions of prestige.[47] Certain Romanian idioms gradually appeared as loanwords in charters and missives from the late fifteenth century onwards, but this did not lead to the appearance of entire documents in that language – similarly to the occasional Hungarian expressions in documents between the eleventh and the fifteenth century.[48]

[44] G. ISTVÁNYI, *A magyarnyelvű írásbeliség kialakulása* [The formation of Hungarian literacy] (Budapest, 1934); B. BAK, "A XVI-XVIII. századi magyar nyelvű források kiadásának kérdései" [The edition of Hungarian sources from the sixteenth-eighteenth centuries], *Fons* 7 (2000), pp. 91-137.

[45] LAKATOS, *Hivatali írásbeliség*, p. 38.

[46] Ruthenian as a vernacular language was spoken mainly in the territory of Red Rus', in the late Middle Ages incorporated into Poland as 'Rus' Palatinate', nowadays part of Ukraine. However, *Rutheni* were also living in villages and some market towns in north-eastern Hungary, neighbouring the 'core' Ruthenian territories. No medieval written document of their language has come down to us.

[47] On these groups in general, see GY. KRISTÓ, *Nem magyar népek a középkori Magyarországon* [Non-Hungarian peoples in medieval Hungary] (Budapest, 2003), pp. 191-244. A good example of individual social advance is Johannes Myser, who was mayor of the royal town of Szeged in the 1460s and whose surname clearly indicates his Cuman origin. See L. BLAZOVICH, "A kiskunsági kunok és Szeged a XV. században és a XVI. század első felében" [The Cumans of the Kiskunság district and Szeged in the fifteenth and the first half of the sixteenth century], *Jászkunság* 35.1 (1989), 85-88. Perhaps the most spectacular example is Nicholas Oláh (1493-1568), a burgher's son of Romanian descent in Sibiu and Orăştie (his surname can be translated as 'Wallachian' or 'Romanian'), who later became archbishop of Esztergom.

[48] LAKATOS, *Hivatali írásbeliség*, p. 92, quotes examples from Caransebeş from the 1450s.

The various dialects of *Italian* and other Romance languages were apparently used in oral communication by some settlers (the *Latini*) already during the first centuries of Hungarian urban development, but at that time no other language than Latin is attested in written usage; later, these people were probably absorbed into the Hungarian- or German-speaking population. However, new waves of immigrants could from time to time revive these languages, especially in the spoken context. For instance, the French traveller Bertrandon de la Broquière, who visited Buda in 1433, remarked that

> *Et est ceste ville gouvernée par Allemans en tous estas, tant au faict de la justice et de la merchandise que aussi au faict des mestierz [...] Il y a en ceste ville beaucoup de Juifz qui parlent tresbon françoys, et en y a de ceulx qui furent chaciés hors du royaulme de France.*

> the town is governed by Germans, as well in respect to police and commerce and what regards the different professions as well. [...] Many Jews live there who speak French well, several of them being descendants of those driven formerly from France.

Their forefathers had been forced to leave France by the order of Charles VI, king of France, in 1394.[49] In the late Middle Ages, Italian played a prominent role mainly in the Dalmatian coastal towns, which were formally under Hungarian rule until the 1410s, and especially in Dubrovnik (Ragusa), which acknowledged the Hungarian kings as its sovereigns until 1526.

The dialect used in Dalmatian cities was mostly Venetian; in Ragusa, due to its strong trading links to southern Italy, besides Venetian there are also traces of the Apulian dialect and even some sporadic Tuscan words can be found.[50] However, due to the distance of these towns from the centre of the kingdom, the Dalmatians' otherwise well-developed Italian literacy had no effect on the use of this language elsewhere in the kingdom. In Zagreb, where

[49] *Le Voyage d'Outremer de Bertrandon de la Broquière*, ed. Ch. SCHEFER (Paris, 1892), p. 235; translation: B. DE LA BROQUIÉRE, *Travels to Palestine and his Return from Jerusalem Overland to France*, trans. T. JONES (Hafod, 1807), pp. 309-311. See B. NAGY, "The towns of medieval Hungary in the reports of contemporary travellers", in: *Segregation – Integration – Assimilation*, pp. 169-178, at p. 177.

[50] I owe the information on the dialects to Lovro Kunčević (Dubrovnik). See also B. KREKIĆ, "On the Latino-Slavic cultural symbiosis in late medieval and renaissance Dalmatia and Dubrovnik", *Viator: Medieval and Renaissance Studies* 26 (1995), pp. 321-333. For Zagreb, see N. BUDAK, "I fiorentini nella Slavonia e nella Croazia", *Archivio Storico Italiano* 153 (1995), pp. 681-695.

according to the ethnic division of the council from 1377 one quarter of the councillors were chosen from among the 'Italians' (see below), no dialect of Italian played any role whatsoever in the town's administrative literacy. In Buda, which had a small but economically important Italian population of mostly Florentine origin, especially strong in the first half of the fifteenth century,[51] no traces of Italian literacy – neither in Tuscan nor in other dialects – are to be found either. The only small trace is a late-fifteenth-century Italian-Hungarian phrase-list which may originate from the capital. Its forms show a preponderance of southern dialects, which can point to Italians arriving to Buda from 1476 onwards in the entourage of Beatrix of Aragon, the second wife of king Matthias Corvinus.[52] The private account books of Italian merchants connected to their commercial and money-lending activity were probably kept in their vernacular, following the customs of their respective home towns. For maintaining contacts with their local partners (burghers, noblemen, and the royal court), however, they had to use Latin, and probably had to acquire some knowledge of Hungarian and German too.

The *Hebrew* language was perhaps in the most ambiguous situation of all: even though it was a sacred language, its connection to the Jewish population and religion lead to its lack of acceptance by the Christian majorities of every town. Nevertheless, its use within the Jewish communities, which could draw on age-old traditions of literacy, was not restricted. Passages of text written in Hebrew script occur from time to time inserted into town books or added to charters issued by the municipalities.[53] This question will be further explored in Chapter 5.

[51] Zs. Teke, "Operatori economici fiorentini in Ungheria nel tardo Trecento e primo Quattrocento", *Archivio Storico Italiano* 153 (1995), pp. 697-707; K. Arany, "Generations abroad: Florentine merchant families in Hungary in the first half of the fifteenth century", in: *Generations in Towns: Succession and Success in Pre-Industrial Urban Societies*, ed. F.-E. Eliassen and K. Szende (Newcastle-on-Tyne, 2009), pp. 129-152; Végh, "Buda, the multi-ethnic capital".

[52] Published in Zs. Simonyi, "Az Ábel-féle szójegyzék" [The word list found by Ábel], *Nyelvtudományi Közlemények* 31 (1901), pp. 225-227. I owe the identification of dialectal forms to Krisztina Arany, who also pointed out that there are some Venetian forms in the text as well, which might be due to contacts of Italians of various origins in the Hungarian capital. Concerning the use of this phrase-list, similarly to the one by Hans von Rotenburg mentioned above, one notes the high proportion of expressions connected to sexual life. This may indicate the visitors' need to communicate with prostitutes, many of whom probably originated from neighbouring Hungarian villages.

[53] See the series *Magyar Zsidó oklevéltár – Monumenta Hungariae Judaica*, ed. Á. Friss, F. Grünvald, F. Kováts, J. Házi, *et al., 18 vols.* (Budapest, 1903-1980).

Areas of Urban Life where Language Became an Issue

The various languages listed above permeated all aspects of urban life. From our point of view, the fields of the greatest interest are those where the use of language was not only reflected in daily practice, but became itself a point of special concern.

Administration and Justice

The first and most public such field was the election of the leading bodies of each town. Here the language used by the council members was connected to the ethnic composition of the council. By the time this issue surfaces in the sources, there was already a customary arrangement or tradition established, which could be centred on three main options. The first was to disregard any ethnic differences and elect the most suitable or influential persons for the leading roles. This was the case in towns like Szeged and Sopron, where the ethnic composition of the towns, although not homogeneous, was fairly stable.[54] The second possibility was to reserve access to the ranks of the administrative elite to one ethnic group only. This was the practice in the Saxon towns of Transylvania: Braşov, Sibiu, Sighişoara, Bistriţa,[55] as well as in Buda and Cluj before the changes in the middle of the fifteenth century which will be discussed below. The third and most sophisticated arrangement was to elect the council on a parity basis from among the representatives of the main ethnic groups. The first such instance was recorded in Zagreb in 1377, when the council members divided the eligible places between themselves according to no less than four 'nationes': the Slavs (= Croats), the Hungarians, the Latins (= Italians) and the Germans.[56] There is an assumption that these groups them-

[54] PETROVICS, "Foreign ethnic groups", pp. 70-82; K. GODA, "A város élén: Sopron polgármesterei a 15-16. század fordulóján" [At the helm of the town: The mayors of Sopron at the turn of the fifteenth century], *Soproni Szemle* 58 (2004), pp. 308-328.

[55] K. GÜNDISCH, *Das Patriziat Siebenbürger Städte im Mittelalter* (Köln, Weimar, and Wien, 1993), pp. 68-100.

[56] GROTHUSEN, *Entstehung und Geschichte Zagrebs*, pp. 143-146; B. ŠKREBLIN, "Ethnic groups in Zagreb's Gradec in the late Middle Ages", *Review of Croatian History* 9 (2013), pp. 25-59.

selves had their respective councils and even their own notary, but this is difficult to prove.[57]

Four years later, during the reign of the same king, similar measures became necessary in Žilina, where the Slavs (*Sclavi*), that is Slovaks, and the Germans were entitled to provide the councillors. In this town Germans and Slavs (Slovaks) lived together from the time of its foundation in the early fourteenth century. The switch from the legal filiation of Teschen to Krupina, and the town book that was drawn up as a consequence in 1378, were discussed in the previous chapters. According to the royal charter of 1381, in which the parity arrangement was confirmed, the equal participation of Germans and Slavs in the council had been an "old custom" ("*antiqua consuetudo*"); however, at the time of the petition, the Germans refused to admit the Slavs among the jurors. The petitioners also emphasised that they were more numerous among the inhabitants than the Germans, and that they contributed equally to the taxes and other revenues due to the king. Based on these arguments, king Louis confirmed in writing the parity arrangement. Keeping up the balance must have needed continuous attention, as sixty years, that is two generations later the representatives of the Slavic community approached the Convent of Turóc (Turiec) as place of authentication to transcribe the text of Louis's charter; that is how it has come down to us.[58] The administrative literacy of Žilina also follows the pattern described above, this town being the only one within the Carpathian Basin which issued authentic documents both in German and Slavic, and its town book (presented in Chapter 3) also used both languages.[59]

In the capital, Buda, the solution developed more gradually – or at least the sources have more to tell about the events that preceded the parity arrangement which was eventually settled on. Until the turn of the fourteenth century, ten places out of twelve in the council were taken up by the old land-owning German elite, the two remaining being given to Hungarians. After the revolt of a new commercial elite against the old leading families in 1402/1403 a new group of cloth merchants acquired access to the council, which now included three or four Hungarians each year instead of two as before. However, the

[57] The idea of separate notarial offices for each 'language' was proposed by J.V.A. FINE, *When Ethnicity Did Not Matter in the Balkans: A Study of Identity in Pre-Nationalist Croatia, Dalmatia, and Slavonia in the Medieval and Early-Modern Periods* (Ann Arbor, 2006), p. 75.

[58] R. MARSINA, "Výsady pre žilinských Slovákov z roku 1381" [Privileges for the Slovaks of Žilina in 1381], in: *Národnostný vývoj*, pp. 13-40, esp. pp. 37-38; FÜGEDI, "Das mittelalterliche Ungarn als Gastland", pp. 500-501; ID., "Városprivilégiumok", pp. 292-295.

[59] LAKATOS, *Hivatali írásbeliség*, pp. 37-38 and *Appendix*, pp. 273-275.

urban middle classes were not content with this situation. After a series of bloody events in 1436-1439, when a self-conscious Hungarian elite tried to assert itself as full-right members of the town leadership, king Albert (1437-1439) had to come up with a more balanced arrangement. From then onwards, the leaders of the town were chosen by a 100-member electoral body (*centumviri*) of 50 German and 50 Hungarian burghers. These elected, in turn, the judge each year alternately from among the German and the Hungarian burghers of the town, while the vice-judge (*iudex minor* or *iudex pecuniarum*) always belonged to the opposite community. The council of twelve also consisted now of an equal number of Germans and Hungarians.[60]

The reforms not only stabilised the situation in Buda until the end of the Middle Ages, they were also implemented in 1458 in Cluj, a town where the ethnic development followed very similar lines to that of Buda.[61] What the parity system meant with regard to the use of languages was most clearly recorded in the correspondence of these two towns. In obedience to a royal edict of 1488, the council of Buda sent Cluj a detailed description (in Latin!) of their own practice of German-Hungarian parity arrangement in order to help settle the debate concerning the election of the magistrates in the latter town. This contains, among other things, the following regulation for the *centumviri*:

> *... ibidem ordinatim consedere debeant, ita ut semper inter duos Hungaros Alemannus medium locum teneat ... Quibus ita consedentibus notarius civitatis nomina Centum Hominibus ordinatim pronunciabit, incipiendo a pocioribus, quorum singulus suo lingwagio respondebit "assum".*

> ... they have to take their seats in a row so that there is always a German sitting between two Hungarians ... After they have sat down this way, the town notary calls the names of the Hundred Men in order, starting with the mightier, whereupon each of them should answer in their own language, "I am here".[62]

[60] A. KUBINYI, "Die Zusammensetzung des städtischen Rates im mittelalterlichen Königreich Ungarn", *Südostdeutsches Archiv* 34-35 (1991-1992), pp. 23-42, at pp. 27-38; RADY, *Medieval Buda,* pp. 35-38.

[61] M. LUPESCU MAKÓ, "Der Ausgleich von Klausenburg 1458", in: *Klausenburg: Wege einer Stadt und ihrer Menschen in Europa*, ed. U. BURGER and R. GRÄF (Cluj-Napoca, 2007), pp. 39-50; FLÓRA, "The matter of honour", pp. 46-48.

[62] *Oklevéltár Kolozsvár története I. kötetéhez* [Cartulary to Volume 1 of the History of Cluj], ed. E. JAKAB (Buda, 1870), pp. 280-285, at p. 282.

Uttering this short expression in one's own language was not a test of linguistic proficiency; it counted much more as a declaration of one's ethnic identity, and the basic condition for representing the given ethnic group. It was also easy to control in this way whether the required number and proportion of councillors was present in order to make the decisions valid and legitimate for both main groups. Thereafter the discussion must have gone on in a common language that everyone could understand, but this is not specified in the sources, apparently because it was self-evident. Notably, the protocols of the council meetings were recorded in Hungarian.[63]

The parallel use of the languages of the main urban communities had important practical as well as symbolic connotations. This is revealed by a series of articles in the German-language *Ofner Stadtrecht*, a compilation otherwise heavily biased towards the German elite, to the extent of stating that only those could be elected as judges and councillors whose four grandparents were all Germans.[64] Nevertheless, when it came to the town officials' speeches on leaving their office, the titles of the articles specify the following requirements:

> cap. 59: *Der Richterr sol also sprechen des ersten in deütscher zung vnd darnach in vngerischerr Zung*
>
> The judge has to give a speech, first in German and then in Hungarian.
>
> cap. 60: *Dy Ratsherren sullen also sprechen, der erste in deütscherr zungen, darnach in Vngerischer*
>
> The councillors have to give a speech, first in German and then in Hungarian.
>
> cap. 61: *Der statschreiber spricht von erst in deütsch, darnach in Vngerisch*
>
> The town notary speaks, first in German and then in Hungarian.[65]

These procedures show, on the one hand, that the main officials were expected to speak the language of the political minority as well; on the other, they imply

[63] FLÓRA, "The matter of honour", pp. 86-87.

[64] *Ofner Stadtrecht*, article on German ancestors c. 32 (p. 70). The examination of the names preserved in the lists of dignitaries shows, however, that this condition was not followed exclusively.

[65] *Ofner Stadtrecht*, pp. 83-84.

that the minority was supposed to feel honoured and be supportive towards the administration because of this symbolic gesture.

The administration of justice must have been carried out in a language understandable to all parties involved, but again the concrete arrangements are not discussed in the sources. In local statutes and accounts special technical terms appear, expressed in another than the main language, referring to types of documents. For instance, the compiler of the *Ofner Stadtrecht*, when stating that outsiders' testimonies are not to be accepted against the burghers of Buda, used the following formulation:

> *Fremde gezeugnuß mit priefen ader mit leuthen schol nicht ap genomen werden wider sÿ. So aber ir eyner an gesprochen werd, Alle prieff, dÿ man nennet zu Latein* Inquisitor, *das ist zu Teutsch* eyn irfoerscher, *In Vngerischer sprach* Tudo: *Man schol keÿne craft wider sÿ nit haben zu keynen zeiten.*
>
> Outsiders' testimonies by charters or by witnesses are not to be accepted against them. However, if one of them is accused, all letters that are called *inquisitor* in Latin, that is *ein erförscher* in German and *tudó* in the Hungarian language, must always be considered valid.[66]

Terms for persons or concepts involved in the judicial process also needed the precision of the vernacular terms. In the accounts of Prešov, to be quoted in more detail below, the following legal terms occur in Hungarian: *solgabyro* (*szolgabíró*: 'county district administrator'), *utwarbiro* (*udvarbíró*: 'court administrator'), *tudeman* (*tudomány*: 'letter of inquest'), *potwarey* (*patvar*: 'court case' – a Hungarian noun with a German suffix added), and so on. In urban matters vernacular words found their way into country-wide legislation as well. In king Sigismund's so-called urban code from 15 April 1405, one finds the following expressions in Ch. I on the unification of measures: "*demptis tantummodo mensuris decimarum et montium tributis vulgo* heguam, *in teutonico* pergreht" (*hegyvám*, *Bergrecht*); in Ch. XV: "*currus in quibus balle et pondera deferuntur magni onerati, in vulgo* masa *dicti*" (*masa* refers to a large capacity cart used in long-distance trade; in current usage the word *mázsa* means 'hundredweight').[67]

The laws themselves were mainly in Latin, even the so-called *Codex Tavernicalis*, the common codebook of the free royal towns – although at the time

[66] *Ofner Stadtrecht*, cap. 203, p. 129.
[67] DRMH, 2, pp. 36, 41.

of its redaction in the middle of the fifteenth century all the towns that fell into this category had a German majority, and indeed one of its main sources, the *Ofner Stadtrecht*, was written in German. As this text exemplifies, however, local statutes were often formulated in German, similarly to guild regulations. Local notaries procured special German legal codices for the purpose, among others copies of the *Sachsenspiegel* and the Magdeburg law.[68] Considering that Slavs also sat on the council, as described above, it is understandable that the town of Žilina even possessed a Czech translation of the Magdeburg law, in which some dialect words point towards the development of the Slovak language. This indicates the local composition of the work and suggests the increasing usage of this vernacular in juridical practice.[69]

External Relations

Keeping up relations with the surrounding world added to the linguistic plurality of towns in late medieval Hungary. The towns had to employ scribes or other officials who were able to communicate not only in the languages of the given town, but also in the languages of the neighbouring territories. These included Czech and Polish in the case of Upper Hungary, and in the southern Transylvanian towns of Braşov and Sibiu, Old Slavonic (written in Cyrillic script), one of the languages used in correspondence with the principalities of Moldavia and Wallachia.[70] Which languages were used in which contexts depended partly on the haphazard availability of competent scribes in the princely courts, and partly on the relationship between the sender and the recipient of the letter or charter in question. The town of Braşov handled the case with the help of the Orthodox inhabitants of the suburb called *Bolgárszeg* ('settlement of Bulgarians'). Their clerics in the service of civic administration are men-

[68] L. BLAZOVICH, "Der Sachsenspiegel und das Recht der Zips", in: *Eike von Repgow, A Szász tükör* [The Sachsenspiegel], ed. L. BLAZOVICH and J. SCHMIDT (Szeged, 2005), pp. 83-91.

[69] See Chapter 3, nn. 127-129.

[70] See, e.g. *Documente slavo-române din Sibiu (1470-1653)* [Slavonic-Romanian documents from Sibiu, 1470-1653], ed. P.P. PANAITESCU (Bucharest, 1938); *534 documente istorice slavo-române din Ţara Românească şi Moldova privitoare la legăturile cu Ardealul, 1346-1603* [534 Slavonic-Romanian historical documents from Wallachia and Moldavia concerning the connections with Transylvania, 1346-1603], ed. G.G. TOCILESCU (Bucharest, 1931); GOINA, *The Uses of Pragmatic Literacy*.

tioned in the sources as *scriba Wallachicus*, or even *Stadtloguffet*, from the Byzantine title *logothetes*.[71]

Furthermore, it was an efficient way of seeking the recipients' good will to use their favoured language. Therefore the early and frequent use of German in the letters addressed to Sopron and Pressburg by the market towns and even villages around them often indicates a *captatio benevolentiae* on behalf of the senders rather than their ethnic background. The same tendency is less visible in missives addressed to Košice and Bardejov from their respective neighbourhoods: the market towns in the Spiš region and Gömör County tend to use German whereas those of the Hegyalja region (except for Gönc) preferred Latin. Long-distance correspondence tended to favour Latin.[72] From the fifteenth century onwards this can be examined on a country-wide level in the king's correspondence with his towns. Here it is notable that if he wanted something from them, for instance the payment of extraordinary taxes or their participation in a military enterprise, he tended to use German, while in case of orders and declarations of royal favour or disfavour, Latin documents were dispatched.[73]

The local administration might have to make special arrangements in case one of their key officials did not possess a necessary knowledge of languages. For instance, between 1419 and 1450 Sopron had a notary of Viennese origin, Konrad Ernst. As was discussed at the beginning of Chapter 3, he was a leading figure in local diplomacy and provided continuity in the town's external relations with his services beside the yearly elected mayors. But since he never acquired the necessary level of proficiency in Hungarian, the town employed a Hungarian vice-notary, Tamás Sörös, to travel with Ernst and help him as an interpreter.[74] Likewise, the notaries of Cluj were also allowed to have an assistant to complement their missing language competence.[75]

In spite of such efforts at flexibility, there were cases when the linguistic gaps were not bridged. Such an instance occurred in connection with the participation of the representatives of Pressburg at the national assembly in Pest. In their report (in German) to the town council dated 6 June 1446, they tell about

[71] SZEGEDI, "A városi történetírás", p. 110.

[72] This question is discused in detail in LAKATOS, *Mezővárosi oklevelek*, Chapter 3.4.2.

[73] See the royal charters edited in IVÁNYI, *Bártfa*, ID., *Eperjes*, and particularly in HÁZI, *Sopron*, I.2-6; on addressing towns concerning taxation, see NEUMANN, "Minden időben kegyelmes uratok", pp. 29-30.

[74] MOLLAY, "Többnyelvűség", p. 332.

[75] FLÓRA, "The matter of honour", pp. 101-110.

their hard and thorough negotiations with other towns and a series of leading aristocrats; then they quote the pre-formulated decisions of the assembly (in Latin) on which the towns declined to swear; finally, one of them added: "*Der ander ist ungrisch den chan ich euer weishait nit zuschreiben*" ("The rest is in Hungarian, about that I cannot inform Your Wisdom" – that is, the council).[76] This may further suggest that the half-hearted participation of the towns at the diets[77] could have been due, apart from the financial burdens, to a decline in interest arising from difficulties in communication.

Trade and Accounting

Business connections were an area where the parties involved could not afford to fail in their communication, and where pride or representation had to give way to practical considerations. This must have been the case above all with the spoken language. A faint reflection of this can be observed in late medieval account books – one of the most widespread types of town books – which, due to their ephemeral character captured more of the everyday linguistic plurality than the official documents. As discussed in Chapter 3, the accounts of Banská Bystrica already used German extensively in the late fourteenth century, just as those of Pressburg and Sopron.[78] For instance, the accounts of Kremnica in the 1420s reflect the changes from a purely Latin accounting to a mixed usage of Latin and German.[79] In Prešov, which had a mixed German, Hungarian and Slavic (Slovak) population, German expressions were often inserted into the town's Latin accounts for clarity's sake:[80]

[76] Published in *A Hunyadiak kora Magyarországon* [The age of the Hunyadis in Hungary] 10, ed. J. Teleki (Pest, 1853), p. 185.

[77] A. Kubinyi, "A városok az országos politikában, különös tekintettel Sopronra" [The towns in national politics, with special regard to Sopron], in: *A város térben és időben: Sopron kapcsolatrendszerének változásai* [The town in space and time: Changes in the relational network of Sopron], ed. É. Turbuly (Sopron, 2002), pp. 29-53.

[78] M. Štefánik, "Die Anfänge der slowakischen Bergstädte: Das Beispiel Neusohl", in: *Stadt und Bergbau*, ed. K.-H. Kaufhold and P. Johanek (Köln, Weimar, and Wien, 2004: *Städteforschung*, A 64), pp. 295-312.

[79] Štefánik, "The Kremnica town book of accounts", p. 44; Fejérpataky, pp. 618-625.

[80] B. Iványi, "A középkori Eperjes magyarsága" [Hungarians in medieval Prešov], *Szegedi Füzetek* 1 (1934), pp. 85-97, 169-175, 263-274, and Iványi, "Das Deutschtum der Stadt Eperies", pp. 361-402.

Item pro laminibus wlgo blech ... [for metal sheets]
Item pro ferro ad ducillos wlgo czappin ... [for taps]
Item pro sagittis ignium wlgo fewerpfeyl ... [for fire-arrows]
Item pro una sporta wlgo flechte ... [for a wicker basket]
Item pro una liga equo wlgo gurt *pro sella* ... [for a strap to a saddle] ...[81]

A more 'organically' mixed use of German and Latin can be observed, for instance, in the early cadastral notes of Sopron, where switching from one language to the other and back can occur several times within the same sentence:

Jorg Engelmar inquilinus in Sopronio vendidit I saffrangarten in der Aiczeil *in suburbio* zenachst ausserhalb des Kuncz Schidan hausung vmb *XV ½ tal(leris) den(ariis) honorabili viro Domino Johanni plebano Sancti Michaelis in eadem Sopronio* ledig vnd frey. Sigel *Eylinsgrab et ego.*

Jorg Engelmar, lodger in Sopron, sold a saffron garden in the Aiczeil in the suburb next to the house of Kuncz Schidan on the other side for 15 and a half taler denarius to the honourable John, the parish priest of St. Michael's in the same Sopron, free and unencumbered. Sealed by Eylinsgrab and me.[82]

One can even find examples in the Prešov account books when three languages were mixed within the same text:

Item dem Solgabyro *den. XVI; Item dem* Solgabiro *zcu uortrinckenn den. IIII; Item dem* Solgabiro *pro calciis den. XV; Item* Solgabironac *pro expensis den. LV; Item dem* Solgabiro *vor eyn bryff den. XXIII; Item vor steffelen dem* vtwarbiro *den. LII; Item vor eyn Bryff off Kapy Janus* tudoman *den. 100; Item dem* Solgabiro *vor eyn bryff* tudeman *den. XII; Item auf dy stat gegangen auff* potwarey *fl. ½*

Item, to the *solgabiro* [district administrator] 16 pennies; Item, to the *solgabiro* for drinks 4 pennies; Item, to the *solgabiro* for shoes 15 pennies; Item to the *solgabiro* for his expenses 55 pennies, Item to the *solgabiro* for a document 24 pennies; Item for boots for the *vtwarbiro* [court administrator] 52 pennies; Item for a *tudoman* [letter of inquest] concerning Kapy Janus 100 pennies; Item to the *solgabiro* for a *tudeman* 12 pennies; Item for going to town for a *potwarey* [court case] half a florin.[83]

[81] MMP, Account books No. 210a and No. 349, *passim*; IVÁNYI, *Eperjes*, pp. 127, 190.
[82] HÁZI, *Sopron*, 2.6, p. 204. The text was written by Hans Ziegler, town notary.
[83] See above, n. 81.

A peculiarity of the text is that while the Hungarian words are declined mostly in the German way (*dem* Solgabiro, *dem* vtwarbiro), the Hungarian form of declension with a suffix (solgabiro*nac*) also occurs. This shows that the writer was competent in Hungarian and did not necessarily follow the rules of German when he noted down a Hungarian expression. Further analysis of fifteenth-century urban accounts would not only add to the number of examples but also help define more exactly the role of alternating languages in this type of text.[84] Similar examples can be found in the municipal books of Košice, both concerning the accounts and the books of judgements.[85]

The only extant private account book from a medieval Hungarian urban context, that of the Sopron retailer Paul Moritz, is another example of the mixing of two languages.[86] The main language of the volume used between 1520 and 1529 is German, but a good number of Latin words and phrases appear often within the same sentence. The syntactic and semantic role of this book has been analysed by the linguist János Németh. The main conclusions of his investigation show that the use of Latin was subject to strong semantic and syntactic restrictions. Apart from the strictly formulaic parts like the dating (in keeping with practices widely used in the local administration as well), it is especially verbs connected with commercial activity and names of some traded commodities that appear in Latin. Even these words were, however, restricted in their syntax, so that for any forms outside the most usual ones German is commonly substituted. For instance, first person singular and plural or subjunctive forms of Latin verbs hardly ever come up even for those where the third person singular forms (for instance *tenetur*, *dedit*) are frequently used.[87] These findings are in reassuring conformity with the analysis of account books from other parts of medieval Europe, in which the appearance of such macaronic sentences is almost a defining mark of the genre.[88] Tax lists can also mix dif

[84] FEJÉRPATAKY, *passim*, already contains ample material for the analysis of alternating German and Latin texts, and unpublished material would no doubt furnish more examples.

[85] HALAGA, "A kassai városi könyvek", p. 534.

[86] *Das Geschäftsbuch des Krämers Paul Moritz, 1520-1529*, ed. K. MOLLAY (Sopron, 1994: QGSÖ, Reihe B, 1), with an introduction on the owner of this account book and his experience in the town administration.

[87] J. NÉMETH, "Lateinische Relikte und Graphemverwendung im Geschäftsbuch des Krämers Paul Moritz: Ein Beitrag zum Frühneuhochdeutschen in Ungarn", *Neuphilologische Mitteilungen* 104 (2003), pp. 437-454.

[88] L. WRIGHT, "Bills, accounts, inventories: Everyday trilingual activities in the business world of later medieval England", in: *Multilingualism in Later Medieval Britain*, ed. D.A TROTTER (Cambridge, 2000), pp. 149-156; L.C. WRIGHT, "The records of Hanseatic merchants:

ferent languages: for instance those from the Transylvanian Bistriţa from 1461 onwards have the names of the taxpayers and streets in German and the rest of the text in Latin.[89]

The careful linguistic analysis of the guild book of the German butchers in Buda (already introduced in Chapter 3) by János Németh pointed out another kind of ethnic interference in language use. The survey of the guild members' names by András Kubinyi already showed that 'German' in the guild's name has to be understood in a legal and not an ethnic sense, because the association had several Hungarian members. Likewise, Németh demonstrated through the use of graphemes by the various scribal hands who compiled the German-language guild book that one of them (the so-called 'scribe C') had Hungarian as his mother tongue. In his way of spelling German words and names he employed different graphemes as equivalents for certain phonemes than his German fellow scribes did, and whenever he came across a 'speaking name', he translated it to Hungarian. Table 1 shows a few selected examples of this practice.[90]

Table 1 Some characteristics of the various scribal hands in the guild book of the German butchers of Buda (based on J. NÉMETH, "Lateinische Relikte").

Features	**Rendered by 'scribe C'** (mother tongue: Hungarian)	**Rendered by the other scribes** (mother tongue: German)
Simple vowel instead of diphthong	m**a**ster, r**a**tung	m**ai**ster, r**ai**ttung

Ignorant, sleepy or degenerate?", *Multilingua* 16.4 (Berlin, 1997), pp. 337-349. The only important difference compared to the tendencies observed in the English material is that neither German nor Hungarian has etymological similarities to Latin, so the process of the amalgamation of Latin and the vernaculars – through common abbreviations and suspensions that may refer to either a Latin or a vernacular word – cannot be established.

[89] The transcription of the account books of Bistriţa (1461-1521) was a project of the Ungarisches Institut in Regensburg, prepared by Zsolt Simon and Péter András Szabó. It is available at http://www.ungarisches-institut.de/forschungen/projekte/laufende-projekte/251-die-mittelalterlichen-rechnungsb%C3%BCcher-der-stadt-bistritz-in-siebenb%C3%BCrgen-2.html (last accessed: 20.05.2018).

[90] J. NÉMETH, "Die Sprache des Zunftbuches und der Zunfturkunden der Fleischer zu Ofen", in: *Zunftbuch und Privilegien*, pp. 159-168.

Stressed vowel instead of schwa	Hak**a**r	Hak**e**r
Unrounded vowel instead of rounded one [o]	Th**a**man, Jak**a**b	Th**o**man, Jak**o**b
Unstable rendering of [ʃ]	Fark**a**s / Farka**chs**, Janu**s**	Varka**sch**, Janu**sch**
Hypercorrection when rendering [ʃ]	Fi**chsch**er, fa**chsch**ang	Fi**sch**er, fa**sch**ang
Unstable rendering of fricative sounds	**Pf**ilip, **F**ilip	**Ph**ilip
Translation to Hungarian	Nemes ember	Edelman
Keeping the original Hungarian form (with a different rendering of the fricative sound)	Koa**ch**	Koa**cz**, Schmidt

Pastoral Care and Preaching

Even more than the prestigious and pragmatic worlds of administration and trade, ecclesiastical life showed perhaps the strongest concern about the use of languages. With its twin policy of preserving Latin as the language of the liturgy and promoting the practice of preaching in the vernacular,[91] the Church became a protagonist in the parallel use of different languages. This practise was established already at the synod of Tours (813), long before the Christianisation of Hungarians started at the turn of the tenth century. By the time urban development had speeded up in the thirteenth century, vernacular preaching was an established phenomenon in the country. Listening to parishioners' confessions also presupposed some knowledge of the local vernacular(s). The regulations of the Fourth Lateran Council (1215), particularly its constitution

[91] S.v. "Predigt" in: *Lexikon des Mittelalters* 7, CD-ROM (Stuttgart, 2000), pp. 171-183. Examples from Britain suggest that sermons and other religious prose texts also tended to be written there in a mixture of Latin and vernacular. See H. SCHENDL, "Linguistic aspects of code-switching in medieval English texts", in: *Multilingualism in Later Medieval Britain*, ed. D.A. TROTTER (Cambridge, 2000), pp. 80-88.

21 entitled *Omnis utriusque sexus*, which prescribed all Christians had to confess their sins at least once a year to their local parish priest, reinforced the same requirement.[92]

Religion in general and preaching and confession in particular must have been fields where the issues related to the use of various languages became most pressing, especially as far as orality was concerned. In written sources reflecting daily practice, however, the use of the vernaculars did not find a strong reflection until the turn of the fourteenth century and even later, similarly to the other fields discussed above. One must also keep in mind that the free election of parish priests was a much more widespread element in Hungarian urban liberties than in those of western European cities.[93] This probably indicates that in the first centuries of town life, oral arrangements, the right of the local communities to use their own language in church, and the right to elect their own parish priests sufficed to attract clerics with the necessary language skills.

The earliest known conflict which arose in connection with vernacular preaching is recorded in Buda in 1390. It seems that the main issue was not the use of languages per se, but the subordination of the Hungarians' church of St. Mary Magdalene to the parish of the Assumption of Our Lady. The latter was, due to its royal foundation, the main parish church of the town, but was in practice under complete control of the German majority during the fourteenth century. Parallel to this, the Hungarian community had established the Mary Magdalene church in the northern part of the town over which, as its founders, they exercised the right of patronage. The independence of this church was subsequently questioned by the parish priest of Our Lady's, who claimed that Mary Magdalene's was only a filial chapel within his parish. In his accusation addressed to the Holy See, however, the plaintiff's argument centred on the question of languages, a point which was likely to be respected by an ecclesiastical court. He claimed that the priest of Mary Magdalene's (and of St. Peter the Martyr's in the suburb) were entitled to administer the sacraments

[92] The argument for the connection between the Fourth Lateran Council and the advance of vernacular pastoral care was first advanced by L.E. BOYLE, "The Fourth Lateran Council and elements of popular theology", in: *The Popular Literature in Medieval England*, ed. T.J. HEFFERNAN (Knoxville, 1985), pp. 30-43.

[93] A. KUBINYI, "Stadt und Kirche in Ungarn im Mittelalter", in: *Stadt und Kirche*, ed. F.-H. HYE (Linz, 1995: *Beiträge zur Geschichte der Städte Mitteleuropas* 13), pp. 179-197.

> *Ungaris seu advenis et peregrinis ac aliis hominibus ad dictum castrum pro suis negotiis ibidem expediendis pro tempore confluentibus, qui ydioma Theutonicum, quod parochiani predicti communiter loquuntur, non intelligunt.*[94]
>
> only to the Hungarians or visitors, pilgrims and other people who come to that castle temporarily to look after their business, and who do not understand the German language which is generally spoken by the aforementioned parishioners.

In the end, in spite of the plausible argument, the court of Pope Boniface IX must have realised that the main point in the debate was not the vernacular church services, but the autonomy of a church founded by a community. Thus the defendant won the case and the boundaries between the two parishes were codified.[95] Besides the language aspect, the way how the issue was settled through a series of written documents also makes this case relevant for the present discussion.

Another case of discord reported from Cluj, a town that has already been mentioned in connection with its adoption of the Buda parity system in its local administration, shows the intricacies in the co-existence of the Saxon and Hungarian parish communities. In 1568, already after the local victory of the Reformation, a court case broke out over the election of parish priests and town officials. In the course of this, the Saxons emphasised that, although during the time of the 'Papist religion' Hungarians used the town's main parish church for masses, baptisms, weddings, and funerals on equal terms with the Saxons, "*numquam in eodem templo lingua Hungarica concionatum fuisset, neque plebanus unquam Hungarus in eadem civitate Coloswar extitisset ...*" ("preaching had never taken place in that church in Hungarian, and there had never been a Hungarian parish priest in the city of Cluj")[96] – which was true only in

[94] The text is quoted in a letter written by Pope Boniface IX to the abbot of the Schottenstift in Vienna, whose task was to investigate the case. Published in BTOE 3.1, pp. 52-53.

[95] A. VÉGH, "A budai plébániák határjárásainak helyrajzi elemzése" [Topographical analysis of the perambulations of the Buda parishes], in: *Quasi liber et pictura: Tanulmányok Kubinyi András hetvenedik születésnapjára – Studies in Honour of András Kubinyi on his Seventieth Birthday*, ed. GY. KOVÁCS (Budapest, 2004), pp. 641-654; The change of the boundaries is visualised also on Maps B.1.1 and B.1.2 of the atlas: A. VÉGH, *Buda*, 1.

[96] *Oklevéltár Kolozsvár története 2. és 3. kötetéhez* [Cartulary to vols. 2 and 3 of the History of Cluj], ed. E. JAKAB (Budapest, 1888), pp. 80-88, at p. 81.

the sense that the parish church of the Hungarians, St. Peter and Paul's, was situated in the suburb.[97]

In most other cases the appointment of a separate preacher did not infringe any parish rights and therefore was accepted without any complaint. It was even made the duty of the priests of ethnically mixed parishes to employ preachers in the major languages of the community. Thus in 1454 it was laid down that Andrew, the parish priest of Prešov "*debeat et teneatur servare duos predicatores, qui verbum Dei populo predicent, unum Tewtonicorum, alium vero Hungarorum*" ("is obliged to keep two preachers who should preach God's word to the people, one to the Germans and one to the Hungarians").[98] Similarly, priors of mendicant friaries appointed preachers who were able to address all the relevant ethnic groups. For example, the basically German-speaking friaries of Sighişoara and Sibiu had at least one Hungarian preacher each in the 1520s.[99] In many places references to a preacher of a given ethnic group serve as the first indication of the existence of a more or less organised community in the settlement in question. From the second half of the fifteenth century one can find separate 'ethnic' chapels even in small towns such as Sabinov, where in 1481 "*erectum est Sclavorum templum*" ("a church for the Slovaks was built").[100] In major towns such as Košice Hungarians and Slovaks all had separate preachers, in others, including Banská Bystrica, Levoča, and Trnava, only the Germans and Slovaks are mentioned expressly in this regard. The trend to employ vernacular pastors was further strengthened during the Reformation.[101]

The discussion of the role of languages in ecclesiastical life cannot be separated from their role in teaching, which was for most of the Middle Ages a monopoly of the Church and therefore mainly carried out in Latin. Many

97 E. BENKŐ, *Kolozsvár magyar külvárosa a középkorban* [The Hungarian suburb of Cluj in the Middle Ages] (Kolozsvár, 2004).

98 Town Archives of Prešov, No. 278. The source does not tell to which group the parish priest himself belonged.

99 B.F. ROMHÁNYI, "Egy régi-új forrás az erdélyi domonkosok történetéhez" [A rediscovered source on the history of the Dominicans in Transylvania], *Communicationes Archaeologicae Hungariae* 2004, pp. 235-247, esp. p. 239; F.G. KISS, "Latin és népnyelv a késő-középkori magyarországi domonkos kolostorokban: Leonhard Huntpichler: Directio pedagogorum" [Latin and vernacular in late medieval Dominican friaries in Hungary], *Irodalomtörténeti Közlemények* 120 (2016), pp. 225-247.

100 F. ULIČNÝ, "K výskumu národnostnej štruktúry stredovekých miest na Slovensku" [Data on the ethnic structure of medieval towns in Slovakia], in: *Národnostný vývoj*, pp. 153-162; for Sabinov, see p. 159, with further examples.

101 ULIČNÝ, "K výskumu národnostnej štruktúry", pp. 154-161.

school statutes from all over Europe emphasise that students had to converse in Latin even outside the lessons, and schools in Hungary were no exception to this rule. However, during their studies at parish or chapter schools, future clerics had to prepare for their duties of vernacular preaching as well. It is hardly by chance that the first surviving extensive and continuous text in Hungarian is a model sermon to be delivered at a funeral.[102]

Doubtlessly most of such knowledge was transmitted orally, but during the fifteenth century a growing number of vernacular marginal glosses in preaching manuals or collections of sermons indicate that written reminders in vernacular languages were starting to play a role in the educational process.[103] This led to the stage when the use of vernaculars in education was reflected in literacy as well, especially at lower levels as mediator languages in the acquisition of Latin. A good example of this development is presented by the first two printed schoolbooks with Hungarian text. The earliest one was Melanchthon's *Elementa Latinae grammatices*,[104] followed by a quadrilingual (Latin, German, Polish, and Hungarian) edition of Sebald Heyden's *Formulae puerilium colloquiorum*,[105] for the use of parish and town schools printed in Cracow in 1526 and 1527 respectively. The practical choice of languages ensured a wide market for these volumes in and around the Polish capital.

[102] MADAS, 'La naissance', p. 315; K. KOROMPAY, "Naissance des premiers textes hongrois", in: *Les hongrois et l'Europe: Conquête et integration*, ed. S. CSERNUS and K. KOROMPAY (Szeged and Paris, 1999), pp. 368-371. On the funerary sermon and its originality, see I. HORVÁTH, *Ómagyar szövegemlékek mint textológiai tárgyak* [Old Hungarian texts as objects of textology] (Budapest, 2015: Információtörténeti Műhely) pp. 78-116, 126-127; http://renaissance.elte.hu/wp-content/uploads/2016/01/Omagyar_szo%CC%88vegemle%CC%81kek_d-ed-150bb.pdf (last accessed: 20.05.2018).

[103] See the examples in *Régi Magyar Glosszárium*, e.g. Laskai-glosszák (Osvaldus de Lasko), Temesvári-glosszák (Pelbartus de Temesvár), pp. 41, 46. For a case study on the role of vernacular glosses in educational practice, see A. NÉMETH, "Learning and preaching in Central Europe: The evidence of a late medieval rhyming Decalogue", *Annual of Medieval Studies at CEU* 11 (2005), pp. 77-96, at pp. 80-83.

[104] F.G. KISS, "Az első, részben magyar nyelvű nyomtatvány (Melanchthon: Elementa Latinae grammatices, Krakkó, Vietor, 1526)" [The first, partially Hungarian printed volume], in: *MONOKgraphia: Tanulmányok Monok István 60. születésnapjára* [Studies for István Monok's sixtieth birthday], ed. J. NYERGES, A. VERÓK, E. ZVARA (Budapest, 2016), pp. 375-379.

[105] A contemporary best-seller, it was reprinted several times. The only extant copy of the 1527 edition, preserved in the Municipal Library of Gdańsk (CB 5775), has been published in facsimile with an index in: *A két legrégibb magyar nyelvű nyomtatvány* [The two oldest Hungarian prints], ed. J. MELICH (Budapest, 1912), pp. 1-76.

Medieval Urban Language Use in the Light of Sociolinguistic Research

Modern sociolinguistics has developed a detailed and sophisticated system of categories for investigating the simultaneous use of two or more languages by individuals or communities. Most of these investigations are based, naturally, on observations of live situations and on tests conducted on contemporary speakers. As such they can measure language attitudes and motivations to a depth that can never be achieved on historical material. Nevertheless, the examples enumerated above invite analysis according to some of the categories established by modern linguistic research. The advantages in doing so can be mutual. On the one hand, sociolinguistic studies can reach a new chronological depth by considering historical examples which shed light on the characteristics that the respective languages developed due to their various roles. On the other, researchers investigating the development of social and ethnic structure in towns can gain a deeper insight into the accompanying communicative, intellectual, and behavioural processes. International historical research and literary studies have embraced this methodology extensively in the past couple of decades.[106] In Hungarian scholarship, such an approach has not been applied extensively so far, other than in the context of local history or linguistic case studies.[107] As Anna Adamska's studies have demonstrated, a more extensive overarching treatment of this subject, focusing on Central Europe as a prime territory for multilingual courtly, urban, and rural societies, would be highly desirable.[108]

Bi- or multilingualism is the most general category where two languages are used in parallel, both of which serve as mother tongue to some members of a speech community.[109] It is directly induced by the coexistence of various

[106] See, e.g. the edited volumes, *Multilingualism in the Middle Ages*, ed. A. CLASSEN; *Medieval Multilingualism: The Francophone World and its Neighbours*, ed. C. KLEINHENZ and K. BUSBY (Turnhout, 2011); *Multilingualism in Medieval Britain (c. 1066-1520) Sources and Analysis*, ed. J. JEFFERSON and A. PUTTER (Turnhout, 2013).

[107] MOLLAY, *Német-magyar nyelvi érintkezések*, and ID., "Többnyelvűség". Recently the linguistic introductions by J. NÉMETH to several source publications tackle the issue of multilingualism. The most comprehensive historical overview is SOLYMOSI, "Muttersprache".

[108] ADAMSKA, "Latin and three vernaculars"; EAD., "Latin and vernacular – Reading and meditation: Two Polish queens and their books", in: *Cultures of Religious Reading in the Late Middle Ages*, ed. S. CORBELLINI (Turnhout, 2013: USML 25), pp. 219-246; EAD., "Away with the Germans". The same volume also includes several further articles (A. JANECZEK, J. NIEDZWIEDZ) on aspects of multilingualism in the towns of the region.

[109] S. ROMAINE, *Bilingualism* (Oxford, 1989: *Language in Society* 13), pp. 1-75.

ethnic and language groups. This category of language use was the most widespread in late medieval Hungarian towns, and it is the phenomenon that can be observed in most of the examples quoted above. Our sources do not permit us to apply the fine categorisation developed by modern scholars to measure degrees of bilingualism, but some distinctions may be made.

The first question is whether this bilingualism had an active or a passive character. The picture is somewhat distorted because written sources tend to reflect written rather than oral usage. Still, most of the references point in the direction of the active use of both (or all) languages involved, though not to the same degree in each situation. The abundant occurrence of words for numerals, commodities, dignitaries, and other administrative categories in phrase lists, charters, and accounts points to an intention to acquire active bilingualism in fields of daily usage. At the same time, the emphasis of the Church on vernacular sermons and confessions indicates that in the elevated sphere of spiritual life it was more convenient to address everyone in one's 'own' tongue than to use a mediator language. Trying to determine the level of knowledge of the various languages is all the more important since, as Suzanne Romaine formulates it,

> the speaker's knowledge of a language will to some extent determine the functions to which it is put; and vice versa, the contexts in which an individual has the opportunity to use a particular language will affect his competence in it.[110]

Therefore, for any subsequent and more advanced analysis not simply the choice, but the qualitative characteristics of the chosen languages have to be taken into consideration, to the extent that the sources permit.

As to whether the acquisition of bilingualism was a spontaneous or learned / cultural process, one can find examples of both, but on balance it seems that the spontaneous acquisition of both (or all) languages predominated. In the absence of a local bilingual environment, young people moved or were sent to a different community in order to learn a language, as in the case of the daughter of the mayor of Sibiu mentioned above, as well as in that of the university students who went to study in Vienna and Cracow, where they probably learned some German and Polish beside the obligatory Latin. Such and similar questions would merit a thorough discussion in the light of more widely and more specifically collected source material.

[110] ROMAINE, *Bilingualism*, p. 11.

Another relevant category, *societal bilingualism*, should also be mentioned. This refers to the socially and situationally differentiated choice of languages, as for instance in the examples of external relations.[111] But before discussing the consequences of such choices, a special variety of bilingualism needs to be taken into consideration.

Diglossia is a more restrictive term that denotes the parallel use of two languages whereby not the ethnic origin of the users, but the social character of the situation is the determining factor. The definition of the term is based on an opposition between a vernacular language (or variety) learned in the home – the 'low' version – and a superposed language (or variety) acquired after childhood due to special, often institutional learning – the 'high' version.[112]

In late medieval terms, in the whole territory of Western Christianity Latin was the most universal 'high' code. Its preponderant role in diplomacy, administration, liturgy, science, medicine, and education is undisputed. This does not mean that Latin might not also be used as a spoken language, for instance at diplomatic or church council meetings, or in any sort of education above the elementary level. The occurrence of code-switching both between and within sentences, especially in texts for practical use, however, does not strictly fit the traditional definitions of diglossia.[113] Furthermore, as the number of references to the situations where Latin was used in everyday communication increases, its exclusive character seems to diminish. There were situations when it was not due to the social context, but to sheer practical needs that conversation turned to what we would now call a dead language.[114] Still, although Latin

[111] The situational variation of language choice would merit closer attention, with a systematic collection of what language various speakers / writers used towards which interlocutors. For a modern study that can be stimulating in this respect, see S. GAL, *Language Shift: Social Determinants of Linguistic Change in Bilingual Austria* (New York, 1979). One of her observations that may be relevant to our present study is that 31 out of 32 interviewed members of a Hungarian / German bilingual, formerly Hungarian-speaking rural community used Hungarian when speaking to God.

[112] A. HUDSON, "Outline of a theory of diglossia", in: *Focus on Diglossia*, ed. J.A. FISHMAN (Berlin and New York, 2002: *International Journal of the Sociology of Language,* Special Issue 157), pp. 1-43, with a comprehensive bibliography on pp. 43-48.

[113] On code-switching, see ROMAINE, *Bilingualism,* pp. 110-164. Contemporary sociolinguistic research suggests that code-switching in general is "an honoured practice and that speakers use it with great pride" (S.G. THOMASON, *Language Contact* (Washington, 2001), p. 54). In a historical context, see SCHENDL, "Linguistic aspects of code-switching", pp. 77-92.

[114] TÓTH, *Literacy and Written Culture*, pp. 130-138. For a Europe-wide overview of the use of Latin around and after 1500, see P. BURKE, "*Heu domine, adsunt Turcae*: A sketch for a social history of post-medieval Latin", in: ID., *The Art of Conversation* (Cambridge, 1993); ID.,

could play a mediatory role to some extent, its clearly 'high register' character and the need of formal education to gain proficiency in it made Latin insufficient to be used in every communicative situation. The isolated, formulaic, and more and more petrified use of Latin expressions in texts for practical everyday use shows a growing distance to the classical idioms.[115] This had the consequence that the various ethnic groups that lived together were practically compelled to learn and use each other's vernaculars as well, leading again to various degrees of bilingualism.

For a more marginal community, that of the Jews, the 'high register' language was Hebrew, the religious connotation of which was bound up with its own particular script, an important feature in shaping identity. At the same time, this script was used for recording other languages than Hebrew, too, in our case German. This phenomenon was characteristic of the whole East Central European region, and it gave birth to a separate variety of German, the Yiddish language.[116] 'Transliteration' of German words with Hebrew letters can be observed, for instance, in charters issued on business matters connected to the Jews of Sopron which sometimes contain a summary of the charter written in Hebrew characters but essentially German in language.[117] More discussion on this matter, from the viewpoint of trust in writing, will follow in Chapter 5. This phenomenon is part of a broader conceptual framework, that of biscriptality, that exists in different cultures and sociolinguistic contexts. Concepts such as digraphia and graphic code-switching offer valuable tools for a deeper understanding of the parallel use of scripts; however, a detailed analysis of these issues would go beyond the level of civic literacy, into the realm of analytical linguistics.[118]

"Diglossia in early modern Europe", in: *European Francophonie: The Social, Political and Cultural History of an International Prestige Language*, ed. V.S. Rževckij, G. Argent, and D. Offord (Oxford, 2014), pp. 33-50.

[115] Hudson, "Outline of a theory of diglossia", pp. 20-22, also quotes several instances of the petrified use of a high register language.

[116] See in general E. Wenzel, "Alt-Jiddisch oder Mittelhochdeutsch?" in: *Grenzen und Grenzüberschreitungen: Kulturelle Kontakte zwischen Juden und Christen im Mittelalter* ed. E. Wenzel (= *Aschkenas* 14.1 (2004)), pp. 31-49.

[117] For an example of Hebrew script in a town book, see an agreement between a burgher and the Jew Kassariel, in Sopron, 1497, edited in: MHJ 5.2 (Budapest, 1960), pp. 317-318, also published in: *Gedenkbuch*, pp. 64-65. As a possible model for the use of Hebrew in official urban documents, including town books, the example of the town chancery of Vienna can be quoted, where even the most prestigious town book, the *Eisenbuch*, contains a Hebrew text. See Opll, *Das große Wiener Stadtbuch*, p. 21.

[118] *Biscriptality: A Sociolinguistic Typology*, ed. D. Bunčić *et al.* (Heidelberg, 2016), offers

The Jewish communities in medieval Hungary maintained their well-developed Hebrew literacy and possessed a notable amount of religious manuscripts.[119] This was the case all over Europe: when it came to writing commentaries on Scripture, scientific treatises, or simply corresponding between each other, "medieval Jews relied on a Hebrew superstrate, rather than a Latin one".[120] The relation between the two 'high' status languages is also revealing: Latin was accepted and used extensively by Jews in their external relations, in documents which may exhibit a mastery of the most elaborate humanist style,[121] whereas Hebrew was valued mainly within their own community – although its tradition of literacy was granted some respect or at least tolerance in official administration as well.

The present discussion of diglossia has stressed that the languages involved were not of equal rank, but this also applies to the parallel use of different vernaculars. There was a noticeable hierarchy between the languages. To make the situation more complex, this hierarchy could change both in time, in space, and according to the context of communication.[122] Let us recapitulate our observations in this respect by surveying again the main vernaculars and the changes in their use in late medieval Hungarian towns.

German enjoyed an increasing prestige between the thirteenth and the sixteenth centuries. It found its way into local administration and justice, although even in urban legislation and judicial practice it was not accepted as an official language on a country-wide basis. This is clearly shown by the fact that the highest-ranking legal documents issued in German were local or guild

and excellent introduction and several case studies from different historic periods. I thank Marco Mostert for calling my attention to this work.

[119] A catalogue of fragments of medieval Hebrew maanuscripts from Hungary: S. SCHEIBER, *Héber kódexmaradványok magyarországi kötéstáblákon – Hebräische Kodexüberreste in ungarländischen Einbandstafeln: die Buchkultur der ungarischen Juden im Mittelalter* (Budapest, 1969).

[120] C. ASLANOV, "From Latin into Hebrew through the Romance vernaculars: The creation of an interlanguage written in Hebrew characters", in: *Latin-into-Hebrew: Texts and Studies* 1, *Studies*, ed. R. FONTAINE and G. FREUDENTHAL (Leiden, 2013), pp. 69-84, at p. 74.

[121] See, e.g. the florid Latin letters, in flawless Humanist style, composed by the Jews of Sopron in protest against their expulsion from the town in September 1526 (HÁZI, *Sopron*, 1.7, pp. 282-284).

[122] The same phenomenon was observed and discussed extensively for Britain by M. RICHTER, *Sprache und Gesellschaft im Mittelalter: Untersuchungen zur mündlichen Kommunikation in England von der Mitte des elften bis zum Beginn des vierzehnten Jahrhunderts* (Stuttgart, 1979).

statutes (discussed at the end of the previous chapter),[123] whereas other charters and royal decrees were formulated in Latin. German also contributed to the end of Latin's monopoly as the language of education, which was challenged by the opening of the first German municipal primary schools in the first decades of the sixteenth century, although these institutions were clearly less prestigious, since they only played a role in what we would today call vocational training. Within ecclesiastical circles, German ranked simply as one of the many languages of preaching, though this situation was to change fundamentally with the Reformation and the publication of Luther's Bible translation, which gradually set the literary norms for the whole German-speaking population of the continent.

Hungarian was used as a spoken language by a growing proportion of the urban population towards the end of the Middle Ages – perhaps by more town-dwellers on the whole than any of the other vernaculars, especially if one takes into account also the population of the market towns. Its presence is also attested by the sporadic occurrence of Hungarian terms in legal documents and by the above-mentioned phrase collections compiled by persons of various mother tongues. In spite of this, Hungarian can be classified as a generally low-prestige language in the urban context. This was neither due to the small number nor to the low status of its speakers – a great part of the nobility and even the royal court used it – but because it lacked a tradition in literacy. This meant that for a long time Hungarian did not appear in contexts related to administration, diplomacy, or even account-keeping. In ecclesiastical life, however, it was not ranked behind German. The appointment of Hungarian preachers could lead to a stronger coherence of local communities and to the acknowledged use of the language outside the private sphere.

The same can be said of the *Slovak* (*'Slavonic'*) preachers who appeared in the towns of Upper Hungary from the second half of the fifteenth century. The esteem given to this language and its partial acceptance in administration were connected to the stronger literary traditions of Czech, which was closely related to it, even though Slovak was showing more and more the characteristics of a separate language in the fifteenth-century sources.[124] Notaries arriving to many of the merchant and mining towns in the northern part of the kingdom

[123] Some examples: *Zunftbuch und Privilegien der Fleischer*; *Handel und Gewerbe in Hermannstadt und in den Sieben Stühlen (1224-1579)*, ed. M. VLAICU *et al.* (Sibiu, 2003), and several other publications of guild regulations.

[124] Editorial practice between the two World Wars also favoured solutions that brought these texts closer to the Czech language.

from Moravia (and to a lesser extent from Silesia) both reinforced the use of Slavic languages in writing and had an influence on the dialect used for it.[125]

The advance of the *Croatian* language can also be observed in the same period, but the spread of its official and written use in towns using Latin script can rather be dated from the sixteenth century, and its use in correspondence in Glagolitic script does not go back beyond the mid-fifteenth century either.[126]

As mentioned above, *other vernaculars* (Cuman, Ruthenian, and Romanian) were extremely marginal because of the limited role their speakers as a group played in urban life. If individuals belonging to these groups wanted to get on in towns, they inevitably had to master one of the major local tongues. The use of these languages in pastoral care in towns was probably also more limited, at least no mention of ethnic preachers in connection with these languages has come down to us, and particularly not Orthodox ones. Nevertheless, in ecclesiastical life they must have played some role, as a surviving Cuman text of the *Paternoster* testifies.[127]

The only exception among the 'marginal' languages in Hungary were the various dialects of *Italian*, regarding which the minority position of its users limited its spread, but this did not infer low prestige. The presence of graduates from Italian universities, court humanists, and influential businessmen in the capital contributed to Italian's acknowledgement as a language of culture. Its close relation to Latin also helped its speakers to get along in Hungary and elsewhere north of the Alps without mastering much of the local vernaculars.

Observing the hierarchy of languages is not only interesting per se, but has a potential for answering the question raised at the end of the Introduction about the correlation of language use and ethnicity. The general principle seems to be that the higher prestige a language enjoyed, the greater the variety

[125] *Slovenské listiny a listy z XV. a XVI. storočia* [Slovak charters and letters from the fifteenth and sixteenth century], ed. B. VARSÍK (Bratislava, 1956). For the use of Czech in the Hungarian central administration, see J. MACŮREK, "K otázce české listiny a české kanceláře na dvoře uherském v 2. pol. 15 století" [On the question of Czech charters and Czech chancellors in the Hungarian court in the second half of the fifteenth century], *Historický Časopis* 6 (1958), pp. 560-569. I thank Antonín Kalous for calling my attention to this article and translating its relevant parts.

[126] For Croatian glosses from the first half of the sixteenth century see, e.g., J. MELICH, "Magyar-horvát glosszák" [Hungarian-Croatian glosses], *Nyelvtudományi Közlemények* 28 (1898), p. 33; LAKATOS, *Hivatali írásbeliség*, p. 38 and Appendix p. 41 (Bović), and pp. 225-226 (Steničnjak); and *Acta Croatica – Listine hrvatske,* ed. I. KUKULJEVIĆ SAKCINSKI (Zagreb, 1863: *Monumenta historica slavorum meridionalium – Povjestni spomenici južnih Slavenah* 1).

[127] I.K. MÁNDOKY, "A kun miatyánk" [The Cuman *pater noster*], *Szolnok Megyei Múzeumi Évkönyv* 1973, pp. 117-125.

of people of different ethnic origin who used it. This does not necessarily mean the highest absolute number of users, but it implies that high prestige languages could be used in communicative situations when none of the speakers had it as their mother tongue. Latin, the highest prestige language within our context, was mainly used by the educated upper stratum of urban society, but among those by everyone, irrespective of ethnic affiliation. German was broadly understood and used by most of the other ethnic groups that lived in towns with significant German communities. The same attraction did not apply to Hungarian to a similar extent, although one can find records of attempts by people of various mother tongues to learn it. The use of other vernaculars was even more restricted: Slovak or Croatian were only considered to be worthwhile learning in a close regional context, not to speak of the Ruthenian or Cuman languages.

The hierarchy of languages can explain several features of language maintenance and shift as well, which is another crucial concept of linguistic analysis.[128] This is a field where perhaps the most detailed primary work needs to be done in co-operation between linguists and social historians. One of the fields that could well yield promising results is research on loanwords: which items were borrowed from the various languages in which context? It has been emphasised that the bi- or trilingual urban population was an ideal mediator of loanwords.[129] To quote just one example, key expressions on urbanisation in Romanian were borrowed from Hungarian: *oraş <város* ('city', 'town'); *pirgar < polgár* ('citizen'); *bălciu < búcsú, vásár* ('fair', 'market'); *vama < vám* ('customs', 'toll').[130] Among interferences syntactic, stylistic, graphematic, and palaeographic features have to be taken into account. For instance, in case of the Italian-Hungarian phrase list quoted above, it is not only clear that its writer denoted the Hungarian expressions with Italian graphemes, but it is also likely because of some mistakes in the grammar that he heard them from another Italian – probably one speaking a different dialect than him – and not from a native speaker of Hungarian.

As to the possible broader results of inquiries on language maintenance, the limits of the present work allow me to list only a few main points. In the

[128] ROMAINE, *Bilingualism*, pp. 38-50. See also THOMASON, *Language Contact*, esp. chapters 4 and 9, and the special issue of the *International Journal of the Sociology of Language*: *Language Change and Social Networks*, ed. K. DE BOT and S. STOESSEL (Berlin and New York, 2002: *International Journal of the Sociology of Language* 153).

[129] MOLLAY, *Német-magyar nyelvi érintkezések*, pp. 53-54.

[130] L. MAKKAI, *Magyar-román közös múlt* [Hungarian-Romanian common past] (Budapest, 1948; reprinted Budapest, 1989), p. 52.

first place, the investigated material confirms how great a role writing played in keeping up and strengthening the prestige of a language. As examples of its positive impact, one can recall the case of German, users of which could strongly rely on the traditions of literacy laid down earlier outside the borders of Hungary; the beneficial influence of Czech literacy on the development of the Slovak language; and even the awe which Hebrew literacy had for the non-Jewish population. On the negative side, the lack of a literary tradition held back Hungarian, Croatian, and Romanian, at least for a time; while in the case, for instance, of the Cuman language, it led to its complete extinction.

Generally, low-prestige languages were more threatened by marginalisation in towns: subsequent generations of individuals belonging to these ethnic groups may have abandoned their mother tongue altogether in an urban environment. However, the extinction of these languages could be avoided in a wider context by strong and lively use in rural communities (as was, for instance, the case with Romanian and Ruthenian, and to some extent even Hungarian); at the same time, the acquisition of a more prestigious language or even a shift to such a language was necessary to maintain or improve one's social position.

At the present state of research, three factors can be singled out as strongly influential in determining the prestige enjoyed by the various languages in the context of late medieval Hungarian towns. In the order of importance they are:

1. literate traditions;
2. the number of individuals who used the language; and
3. the social status and gender of the individuals using it.

However, to warn of the dangers of generalisation, let me end this section with two examples which seem to call for a refinement of the above-formulated principles.

The first one concerns a group of Romance-speaking immigrants who settled at an early date in Hungary, lived largely in isolation, and did not have their own written traditions. According to the text of a fifteenth-century chronicle, a handful of pilgrims from the Eger diocese who were on their way to Aachen discovered on their journey that their language was identical with the one spoken in and around Liège. They attributed this to the fact that their ancestors several centuries ago had migrated to Hungary from that region and to the role that their mothers had played in maintaining the old language:

Licet viri propter sua commercia exercenda per diversas et vicinas regiones se transferant et Hungarorum linguam idcirco omnes addiscant, tamen quia semper et continuo feminae in suis domiciliis residentes filiorum educationibus intentae nusquam vadunt aut evagantur, nativum propterea conservantes idioma et in eodem soboles suas instruentes...

Although the men have to go to various neighbouring regions in order to deal with their business and therefore all learn the Hungarian language, the women always and continuously stay at home, dedicating themselves to the upbringing of their children, and do not go anywhere, therefore they preserve their native tongue and instruct their offspring in it.[131]

The excerpt shows both the role of the female line of families in transmitting the knowledge of the old vernacular in an isolated rural community, and the role of commercial settlements (probably market towns) in the men's acquiring the language of the majority. However, it also makes clear that in this case writing played no role whatsoever as far as language maintenance (of the 'mother' tongue) was concerned.

The second instance comes from the multilingual environment of Sopron. Here the town's notary, Hans Gugelweit (who died around 1495), who had a German name and a German ethnic background, noted down two lines of a Hungarian love song on the soft parchment cover of a town book. This is the second of the *libri mixti* from Sopron, discussed in Chapter 3, with entries from 1393 to 1472. It was a volume into which Gugelweit and his predecessors had recorded various documents, some of which were in Latin but most in German. The song on the cover runs as follows:

Wÿrag th[u]dÿad, theuled el kel mennem
es the ÿrethed kel gÿazba ewlteznem.[132]

[131] *Chronicon Cornelii Zantfliet Sancti Jacobi Leodiensis monachi*, ed. E. MARTÈNE, in: *Veterum scriptorum et monumentorum historicorum dogmaticorum et moralium amplissima collectio*, ed. E. MARTÈNE and U. DURAND, 9 vols. (Paris, 1724-1733), 5, p. 455.

[132] Town Archives of Sopron, No. 2989. The outer appearance of the volume is described in HÁZI, *Sopron*, 2.1, p. 140, and the poem was first edited as J. HÁZI, "A soproni virágének" [The flower-song of Sopron], *Magyar Nyelv* 25 (1929), pp. 88-90; latest edition: J. MOLNÁR and GY. SIMON, *Magyar nyelvemlékek* [Vestiges of the Hungarian language] (Budapest, 1976), p. 107. The song is the earliest preserved example of the so-called flower songs, a typical genre of Hungarian renaissance love-poetry. On the notary: K. MOLLAY, "Gugelweit János, a Soproni virágének lejegyzője" [Hans Gugelweit, the man who wrote down the 'flower song of Sopron'], *Soproni Szemle* 3 (1939), pp. 78-80.

Flower, you know, I have to leave you
and I have to dress in mourning for you.

A few decades later another German notary, Hans Kreusl of Kremnica, also put a Hungarian poem into writing in an account book of the town.[133] As professionals in the official administration, these German literates were probably required to have some knowledge of Hungarian, the main vernacular of the country. But why they chose to express emotions in Hungarian will probably remain their secret forever. At any rate, their choice from among the three languages they knew was evidently not influenced by the hierarchy set out above.

Conclusions: Trust in Language

For the understanding of the use of various languages in the Hungarian urban milieu, we need to extend the temporal scope of the investigation to the first few decades of the sixteenth century. This broadening itself attests that the inclusion of further languages beyond Latin in the sphere of pragmatic (administrative) literacy constitutes a further step in expanding the scope of trust in the use and usefulness of writing. Although it does not seem to be a huge leap at first sight to accept that a short note in a paper book in German or a Slavic language can be just as valid a proof of the sale of a house, a piece of land, or a vineyard as a sealed charter on parchment, was indeed a move crossing many intellectual and legal boundaries. Authorities authenticating earlier documents did remark even in the fifteenth century if the piece of writing was *in vulgo*, and therefore implied that a Latin authentication meant, at the same time, translation – an aspect that may have had an impact on the trust vested in the given document.

Not all authorities shared this move. Places of authentication, for one, only issued documents in Latin throughout their period of activity, well beyond the Middle Ages. In this way, they retained their character as clerical institutions, even if they worked on secular commission. This applied also to bodies that worked in a community with a strong German literacy, such as the collegiate

[133] R. GERÉZDI, *A magyar világi líra kezdetei* [The beginnings of Hungarian lay poetry], (Budapest, 1962: *Irodalomtörténeti Könyvtár* 7), pp. 298-299.

chapter of Pressburg.[134] Some scholars assume that it was partly because of the reluctance of the *loca credibilia* to embrace the vernaculars that their importance diminished in the urban milieu. This niche gave room for the town chanceries to expand, cut the apron strings of their previous suppliers of written documents, and assume many of the tasks that the places of authentication used to perform previously.[135] However, this argument may also be turned around: the spread of the vernaculars in civic literacy and their appearance both in the town books and the charters made it unnecessary for the chapters and convents to change their routines. Furthermore, German and other vernaculars did not reach the top of the hierarchy of languages, and did not assume full legal authority throughout the period under investigation, which may have been one more reason why the *loca credibilia* stuck to Latin. Latin remained the official language of the kingdom, used at diets and in country-wide legal literacy up to 1844.

One may notice, both in this chapter and in other parts of the volume, the importance of contacts and models in adopting – and placing trust in – innovations. This applies to the use of various vernaculars in writing, too. The quick spread of German in the western border zone, first from abroad to the major towns and then from those towns to the market towns and villages around them, is in stark contrast with the late appearance of German literacy in the ethnically almost homogenous land of the Transylvanian Saxons. German literacy reached Buda and the mining towns also through personal contacts with regions where written German had a longer tradition. The same process can be observed on a smaller scale concerning Slavic literacy in the northern border areas of Hungary. The fact that the magistrate of Žilina invested in borrowing the law code of Krupina and having it translated into their vernacular,[136] similarly to other translations in the Czech lands before, shows that these models enhanced the trust in the written language as an efficient tool of advancing "the common good" – "*ad ... rei publice utilitatem*", as the translator wrote.

[134] The single German document issued by this body on 3 August 1348 (DL 7544) was argued by J. Šedivý to have been prepared by the abbey of Heiligenkreuz, and was only sealed by the Pressburg chapter; as a beneficiary's copy (*Empfängerausfertigung*), this is an exception that corroborates the rule. See Šedivý, "Deutschprachige Beurkundung", p. 256-257 and id., *Mittelalterliche Schriftkultur*, pp. 132-133, with a photograph of the document.

[135] Solymosi, "Die glaubwürdigen Orte", pp. 177-180.

[136] See Chapter 2, n. 13, and Chapter 3, nn. 127-128.

In the same vein, it remains an intriguing question if the late appearance of Slavic secular literacy in Slavonia (and even then, tied to a different script, the Glagolitic) may be explained by the lack of prestigious models close by. It is perhaps less likely that the lack of vernaculars in the official administration of Gradec was due to the coexistence of many ethnic groups which needed a *lingua franca* instead of the preferred use of one of the languages. In general, Slavonia, in spite of its Slavic population, closely followed the model of the central, Hungarian-speaking parts of the kingdom, and the administrative practice of their market towns preserved many archaic traits. They even called the judge *villicus* instead of *iudex* until the late fifteenth century.[137]

Finally, beyond the realm of administration, the examples quoted above show both the integrative role of language and its limits. To quote Susan Reynolds, "though language had not yet been made such a sensitive marker of collective identity as it would be from the eighteenth century, it could still be an occasion for distrust as well as frustrated communication".[138] On the one hand, by understanding and in some contexts using the languages of the 'others', both orally and in writing, the various ethnic groups could avoid segregation. On the other hand, by maintaining situations in which the use of their mother tongue was not only permitted but indeed required, they consciously counteracted assimilation. Only in very few and isolated instances was the use of a single language made compulsory.

The analysis of the available data with the help of certain tools borrowed from historical sociolingusitics helps us gain a deeper insight into the multilingual character of late medieval Hungarian towns. I have pointed out various elements of bilingualism and diglossia, and emphasised the different and changing level of prestige that Latin and the various vernaculars had. This helps explain language choices on the individual and community level, and understand how social and cultural development, as well as changes in the ethnic structure of urban populations, affected and were reflected in language use. It has also become clear that – contrary to the nationalistic tendencies of the nineteenth century and beyond –, in the Middle Ages and the early modern period language was not first and foremost an expression of ethnic identity. It was much more an object and an instrument of trust, a tool that could be used

[137] T. PÁLOSFALVI, *The Noble Elite in the County of Körös (Križevci), 1400-1526* (Budapest, 2014), pp. 13-23; A. MOLNÁR, *A zágrábi püspökség és a magyarországi katolikus egyház a 17. században* [The bishopric of Zagreb and the Hungarian Catholic Church in the seventeenth century] (Budapest, 2012: *METEM Könyvek* 77), Introduction and p. 115.

[138] REYNOLDS, "Trust in medieval society", pp. 7-8.

for a wide variety of purposes from information exchange to self-promotion, from communication with God to the display of secular power.

Chapter 5

"*in cartula scribere faciat*": The Uses of Writing between Christians and Jews[1]

In the preceding chapter, a variety of languages and the communities using them were discussed; now let us turn to an example that combines elements from several previous parts of this study. This chapter addresses, within the broad spectrum of Jewish-Christian contacts in medieval Hungarian towns, the issues of legal status and literacy in economic contacts, especially money-lending activities. Besides the legal and factual content of the various kinds of available evidence such as laws, statutes, charters, deeds, entries in town protocols, and the like, the role and limitations of the written word in sorting out practical problems of coexistence will be discussed. In this latter context questions of language use, script, authentication, accessibility, and the safekeeping of the documents deserve attention. The ultimate question that this chapter attempts to answer – in accordance with the main questions guiding this volume – is whether and to what extent the use of writing inspired trust between the parties involved, or in what ways it became the source of further conflicts.

[1] This chapter is based on my article "Laws, loans, literates: Trust in writing in the context of Jewish-Christian contacts in medieval Hungary", in: *Religious Cohabitation in Medieval Towns*, ed. S. Boissellier and J. Tolan (Turnhout, 2014), pp. 243-271, with updates and additions.

Legislation on Jews and Literacy – A Chronological Overview

Jews have been present in Hungary in varying numbers and roles from the time of the foundation of the state in the tenth century to our own times.[2] The Jewish presence, although it never completely ceased, was not uniformly continuous: it can be understood as consisting of several distinct phases, with the transitions often connected to new groups of immigrants. These periods partly overlapped, but had their own specific characteristics.[3] The first part of the chapter will briefly examine these phases up to the late fifteenth century, in order to establish the changing roles of royal and local legislation, and of the various forms of literacy.

From the late tenth to the late twelfth centuries, Jews were present in the Carpathian Basin mainly as long-distance traders. These traders were few in number and quite mobile. Some families probably lived under the protection of counts and bishops already at the turn of the eleventh century, but most Jewish traders operating in the Carpathian Basin were not permanently settled in Hungary. This feature is in stark contrast with the other major non-Christian minority in the kingdom of Hungary, the Muslims, who, according to both written and archaeological evidence, had been settled and had their stable residence in villages.[4] It is difficult to tell from the sporadic evidence whether the Jewish traders of this early period were of eastern or western origin, but judging from their strong contacts with Mainz and Regensburg,[5] the latter seems to be the

[2] For the Árpádian period, the most detailed modern synthesis can be found in N. Berend, *At the Gate of Christendom: Jews, Muslims and 'Pagans' in Medieval Hungary, c.1000-c.1300.* (Cambridge, 2001). G. Komoróczy, *A zsidók története Magyarországon* [The history of Jews in Hungary], 2 vols. (Pozsony, 2012) covers the period to the present, but has several shortcomings and is not accessible to a non-Hungarian audience; see its review by T. Visi, "Sok adat, kevés állítás" [Tons of data, few statements], *Budapesti Könyvszemle* 25.1 (2013), pp. 16-26.

[3] The issue of periodisation and the discontinuities are discussed in more detail in Szende, "Traders, 'court Jews', town Jews".

[4] Berend, *At the Gate,* pp. 237-244; on the growing number of archaeological sites connected to Moslems, especially from the Great Hungarian Plain, see Z. Rózsa and B. Tugya, "Kik voltak az első Orosháza lakói?" [Who were the inhabitants of the first Orosháza?], *Mozaikok Orosháza és vidéke múltjából* 6 (2012), pp. 17-31.

[5] *Urban Civilization in Pre-Crusade Europe*, ed. I.A. Agus, 2 vols. (New York and Leiden, 1965), 1, pp. 232-238; *Héber kútforrások Magyarország és a magyarországi zsidóság történetéhez a kezdetektől 1686-ig* [Hebrew sources on the history of Hungary and its Jewry from the beginnings up to 1686], ed. S.J. Spitzer and G. Komoróczy (Budapest, 2003: *Hungaria Judaica* 16), pp. 116-119.

more likely. This means that one cannot label these Jews as members of an 'oriental diaspora group'.

The royal legislation of this period survives in written form in medieval (but not contemporary) codices and deals with the Jews from the last third of the eleventh century onwards.[6] The appearance of this new ethnic dimension in the laws of Hungary may be connected to a new wave of immigration of Jews to Hungary following the atrocities of the First Crusade, but it is impossible to tell how many persons could have been involved. The main concern of these early laws was to impose restrictions on Jews in various respects, especially on marriage and on keeping Christian slaves, but it did not prescribe or advocate their conversion to Christianity. This was again completely different from royal policy towards the Muslims, who were prime targets for forced conversion and resettling among Christians.[7] It is hard to decide whether this difference was due to the higher population of Muslims in Hungary, to their different economic or military roles from those of the Jews, or to some other factors.

The legislation on Jews issued by king Coloman (also known as 'the Learned') was intended to regulate various aspects of trade and money-lending. Among other articles, it included an intriguing item on contracts and their testimonies, namely that

> *Si Christianus Iudeo aut Iudeus Christiano duarum vel trium pensarum pretium accommodare voluerit, mutuator a mutuante vadimonium recipiat et testes Christianos ac Iudeos in testimonium assumant ...*
>
> If a Christian wants to lend the value of two or three *pensae* to a Jew, or a Jew to a Christian, the lender shall receive a pawn from the borrower and they shall enlist the testimony of Jewish and Christian witnesses ...[8]

Another article makes an explicit reference to pragmatic literacy:

> *Si Iudeus a Christiano aut Christianus a Iudeo aliquid emere voluerit, coram ydoneis testibus Christianis et Iudeis rem venalem emat, eandemque rem et nomina testium in cartula scribere faciat ...*

[6] See the edition and introduction in DRMH 1, pp. 125-131.

[7] Coloman I: §§ 46-49, 74-79; Ladislas I (Synod of Szabolcs): §§ 9, 10, 15, 16; edited in DRMH 1, pp. 28, 30-31, 55-56. See also BEREND, *At the Gate*, pp. 74-87.

[8] Coloman, *Statuta de Iudeis*, § 2, ed. DRMH 1, p. 66.

> If a Jew wants to buy anything from a Christian or a Christian from a Jew, he shall buy the merchandise in front of suitable Jewish and Christian witnesses, and have the same item and the names of witnesses written down in a charter (*cartula*).[9]

The most notable feature of this legislation is its reciprocity: the roles of the two parties were considered equal and so were their obligations. Moreover, there is evidence that this rule was indeed followed in practice.[10] Jews were also allowed to own real estate (landed property) in the country, even if they were in theory restricted by law to residing within episcopal sees: "*Possessiones quidem Iudei, qui possunt emere, habeant; sed ipsi nusquam, nisi ubi sedes episcopalis est, manere sinantur*" ("Let the Jews possess the properties that they are able to buy; but they are not allowed to stay anywhere else than in episcopal seats").[11]

The insistence on written evidence, later termed *cartula sigillata* was a notable innovation in a period when pragmatic literacy was far from being common daily practice in most parts of Europe, let alone in the newly founded kingdom of Hungary. This requirement may reflect a certain degree of mistrust towards the parties concerned, but it may equally well be connected to the mobile nature of traders, which called for methods of record beyond orality. Furthermore, it supposed familiarity with a common language, Latin, and with the techniques of writing – an aspect where they perhaps relied on the services of the clergy.

As to the level of literacy among the Jewish communities themselves, our sources of information are very limited. It seems reasonable to assume that the financial management of long-distance trade necessitated written notes and accounts, but no such documents have come down to us. The closest insight one can get into business practices are descriptions of litigations in a couple of

9 Coloman, *Statuta de Iudeis*, § 4, ed. DRMH 1, p. 66.

10 Kumorovitz offers a careful analysis of the last will of a rich Christian landowner from the early 1140s who had purchased slaves from the "people of Bodrog", apparently a group of Jews, and had the business testified by a document that was transcribed in his will. See L.B. KUMOROVITZ, "Szent László király vásár-törvénye és Kálmán király pecsétes cartulája" [St. Ladislas's law on fairs and king Coloman's sealed *cartula*], in: *Athleta Patriae: Tanulmányok Szent László történetéhez* [*Athleta patriae*: Studies on St. Ladislas's history], ed. L. MEZEY (Budapest, 1980), pp. 85-109.

11 Coloman I, § 75, ed. DRMH 1, p. 31. Notably, a *mons Iudeorum* as placename is known from Nitra, a bishopric particularly supported by Coloman: CDES 1, p. 67.

rabbinic *responsa*, when the parties refer to agreements between each other.[12] In this period Hungary was a well-known region of transit, but was not yet a prime destination for major groups of Jewish immigrants.

The next distinct phase of Jewish presence extends over much of the thirteenth century, and may be characterised with the anachronistic-sounding term 'court Jews'. It refers to a few select persons in high positions who played similar roles as court Jews in the early modern period: managing the state finances and providing loans to the ruling family. Such tasks were performed by Jewish financiers in many countries all over Europe from the ninth to the early thirteenth centuries.[13] In Hungary the most typical title they held was *comes camerae* ('count of the chamber'), a position involving responsibility for salt distribution, toll collection, and the mint. These were the most lucrative offices in the whole realm: a list compiled by king Béla III of his incomes in the late 1180s or early 1190s attributed to minting 36 per cent, to the salt monopoly 10 per cent, and to tolls, ferries, and markets 18 per cent of total royal revenues.[14] By that time several individuals are already known by name, and the most prominent of them have family connections to moneylenders active in the Austrian provinces.[15]

Royal legislation in this period was mainly concerned with placing restrictions on the office-holding of Muslims and Jews (*Ismaelite et Iudei*). In such cases the two ethnic groups are always treated together and are mentioned side by side, although no Muslim counts of chamber or other financial officials are known as individuals. The phrasing of these laws and statutes, in this and other respects alike, shows the strong impact of the Fourth Lateran Council. In fact, the practice in Hungary of granting offices to non-Christians may go back to even earlier times, as a result of a growing demand for skills in managing an increasingly coinage-based economy; however, it may have been these synodal

[12] The complicated transmission of the *responsa* in later copies makes the dating of the pieces of information contained in them sometimes problematic.

[13] M.J. WENNINGER, "Juden als Münzmeister, Zollpächter und fürstliche Finanzbeamte im mittelalterlichen Aschkenas", in: *Wirtschaftsgeschichte der mittelalterlichen Juden*, pp. 121-138.

[14] G. BARTA and J. BARTA, "Royal finance in medieval Hungary: The revenues of king Béla III", in: *Crises, Revolutions and Self-sustained Growth: Essays in European Fiscal History, c. 1130-1830*, ed. M.W. ORMROD and M. BONNEY (Stamford, 1999), pp. 24-40.

[15] See the individual biographies in B. WEISZ, "Zsidó kamaraispánok az Árpád-korban" [Jewish Counts of Chamber in the Árpádian period], in: *Tanulmányok a középkori magyar történelemről* [Studies on medieval Hungarian history], ed. S. HOMONNAI, F. PITI, and I. TÓTH (Szeged, 1999), pp. 151-161; BEREND, *At the Gate*, pp. 118, 126-131; K. LOHRMANN, *Die Wiener Juden im Mittelalter* (Berlin and Wien, 2000), pp. 32-34.

resolutions that prompted direct legal engagement with this issue. Judging from the Hungarian kings' other actions, it may well be that the legislation did not particularly reflect their own views or interests. It seems that the members of the ruling Árpádian dynasty took a rather pragmatic stance on such matters. At any rate, the kings of Hungary continued to employ Jews in spite of the prohibitions in their own laws – alongside with a good number of Christians – until the 1280s.[16]

The issue of pragmatic literacy in thirteenth-century Jewish-Christian interaction mainly revolves around loans provided by Jewish financiers and land donations that they received in pawn or in exchange for these services. It is understandable that these are the types of documents that survive, since generally the same properties later passed into the hands of Christian private landowners who needed to preserve all written proofs connected to the acquisition and ownership of their estates.[17] Besides these charters, there is another, more curious sort of epigraphic evidence which scholars often connect to 'court Jews': the Hebrew mint-marks on coins (silver *denarii*) minted in the mid-thirteenth century. There have been several attempts to connect these Hebrew letters as supposed initials of the few known names of *comites camerae*, but it is just as likely that they refer to persons whose names have not otherwise been preserved.[18] For the present inquiry on trust and the use of writing, what is significant is that Jewish officials employed in the mint – similarly to their Christian counterparts – left their signs on the coins that they were responsible for. It seems that the use of Hebrew script was considered just as appropriate for this purpose as the Latin one was in the case of Christian mint masters.[19]

The third and most significant period for the Jewish presence in medieval Hungary can be associated with the 'town Jews'. It lasted from the mid-thirteenth century (including a few decades' overlap with the 'court Jews') until the expulsion of the Jews from the towns of Hungary in the 1520s and 1530s.

[16] BEREND, *At the Gate*, pp. 116-129.

[17] Most of such charters have been collected and published in the MHJ series.

[18] GY. RÁDÓCZY, "Héber betűjeles Árpád-kori pénzek" [Árpádian-age coins marked with Hebrew letters], *Numizmatikai Közlöny* 70-71 (1971-1972), pp. 33-37; most recently: J.G. KISS and R. ÚJSZÁSZI, "Megjegyzések a késő Árpád-kori pénzek jegyrendszereinek kérdéseivel kapcsolatban" [Remarks on the marking-system of the late Árpád age coins], *Numizmatikai Közlöny* 112-113 (2013-2014), pp. 43-60, with a detailed catalogue.

[19] See, in general: E. HAVERKAMP, "Jewish images on Christian coins: Economy and symbolism in medieval Germany", in: *Jews and Christians in Medieval Europe: The Historiographical Legacy of Bernhard Blumenkranz,* ed. Ph. BUC, M. KEIL, and J. TOLAN (Turnhout, 2016), pp. 189-226.

Of course, most of the 'traders' and 'court Jews' also lived in towns; but they were subject to special restrictions, whereas this third group had much closer relations in their activities and everyday life to their fellow townsmen in the urban communities that emerged from the first third of the thirteenth century onwards.

In this period Jews found their way into Hungarian towns in significantly higher numbers than before, although their total number, estimated as at most 4000 for the whole kingdom, was still small in absolute terms (about 0.2 per cent of the total population of the country).[20] Also more numerous were the settlements where they can be attested: up to the end of the thirteenth century these were mainly towns west of the Danube, but in the following two centuries Jews appeared in small numbers in other parts of Hungary as well (except, for some unknown reason, in Transylvania).[21] Their choice of settlements was based on the good economic and especially commercial potential these offered, to the extent that a Jewish presence might almost be considered as an indicator of prosperity; while the withdrawal of Jews from a place, as happened for instance in Körmend and Vasvár in the western border region, signalled the decline and loss of importance of a locality.[22] Predictably, they soon settled in Buda, the most significant new royal foundation in the late 1240s, by the last decades of the thirteenth century, and later in other towns further east as well.[23]

The basis of royal legislation concerning 'town Jews' was the charter of 1251 granted by king Béla IV on the model of a similar document issued in 1244 by duke Frederick II the Quarrelsome (1230-1246) to the duchies of Austria and Styria. This document shows a completely new attitude to Jews. Whereas the laws mentioned above restricted Jewish presence and office-holding, Frederick's and Béla's charters encouraged them to settle and rewarded their loyalty by special ducal or royal protection. A very similar charter was issued in 1254 by king Ottokar II Přemysl (1253-1278) to the Jews in the lands of the Bohemian Crown.[24]

[20] A. KUBINYI, "A magyarországi zsidóság története a középkorban" [The history of Jews in Hungary in the Middle Ages], *Soproni Szemle* 48 (1995), pp. 2-27, at pp. 20-21.

[21] See and compare the maps in BEREND, *At the Gate,* p. 59 and KUBINYI, "A magyarországi zsidóság", p. 27.

[22] KUBINYI, "A magyarországi zsidóság", pp. 6, 18; B. IVÁNYI, *A középkori Vasvár* [Vasvár in the Midle Ages] (Vasvár, 1992), pp. 21, 28, 38; ZS. BÁNDI, *Körmend a középkorban* [Körmend in the Middle Ages] (Körmend, 1987), pp. 29-31.

[23] VÉGH, "The remains of the first Jewish quarter of Buda".

[24] MHJ 1, No. 22, pp. 23-31. BEREND, *At the Gate,* pp. 76-77, 118 connects the issuing of this charter to the "elite of the Hungarian Jewish communities", whereas in my opinion their

To be sure, it was in the king's material interest to increase the number and financial prospects of new settlers into his realm, and such privileges were one of the means towards achieving that. The 1251 charter deals mainly with the protection of business interests, with pawns and loans, as well as with other areas involving possible legal or physical conflict between Christians and Jews, just as its model from 1244 did. The following two points can serve as examples:

> *Item si Christianus obligaverit pignus Iudeo, affirmans, quod Iudeo pro minori pecunia obligavit, quam Iudeus dicat, iurabit Iudeus super pignore sibi obligato, et quod iurando probaverit, Christianus ei solvere non recuset.*
>
> Item, if a Christian owes a Jew money on a pawn, which he claims to have pawned for a smaller sum than the Jew states, the Jew should take an oath on the pawn and if he proves it by the oath, the Christian should not be reluctant to repay it.
>
> *Item quicunque Christianus Iudeo per vim abstulerit pignus suum, et violenciam in domo sua exercuerit, ut dissipator camere nostre graviter puniatur.*
>
> Item, if a Christian takes away the pawn by force from the Jew and if he commits this violence in the Jew's home, he [the Christian] has to be punished severely as a squanderer of the royal treasury.[25]

The main difference between the documents issued by Frederick II and Béla IV comes in their last article, a special clause on justice. This obliges the town judges, under the penalty of being removed from office, to observe the "statutes, customs and liberties that they [the Jews] have observed" and "to judge them according to the contents of our [Béla's] present privilege". This measure was intended to uphold their special status as settlers (*hospites*), who were allowed to keep many of their customs as well as the language that they brought with them from their place of origin.[26] This general principle continued to be affirmed by Béla's successors, as testified by a charter issued by king Charles I in 1324, inviting new settlers to the town of Sopron:

contents were more relevant for the everyday business of average town Jews: SZENDE, "Traders, 'court Jews', town Jews", pp. 130-134.

[25] MHJ 1, pp. 28, 30.

[26] I have dealt in detail with these issues in relation to Christians in SZENDE, "Power and identity". On the *hospes* status of Jews, see BEREND, *At the Gate*, pp. 76, 107, n. 122.

> *universos homines libere condicionis, qui sive sint Christiani sive Iudei, assecuramus tenore presencium, quod ad ipsam civitatem nostram Supruniensem causa commorandi libere veniant et secure commorentur sub nostra proteccione speciali*
>
> we assure with our present charter all persons of free standing, be they Christians or Jews, that they are free to come to our town of Sopron and stay there safely under our special protection.[27]

To number the Jews among the other *hospites* strengthened their position as inhabitants of the kingdom, within which they were regarded as servants of the royal chamber, a status similarly accorded to them in many other parts of Europe.[28] This bound the Jewish population closely to the monarch and afforded them his protection, but at the same time exposed them to direct royal taxation and other financial demands by the sovereign.

The privilege of Béla IV remained the cornerstone of legislation on Jews throughout the Middle Ages. This is why the leaders of the Hungarian Jewry had it transcribed and confirmed so many times. Remarkably, the earliest transcription was issued in 1256 by the Fehérvár chapter, a place of authentication invested with country-wide authority of issuing authentic charters or copies of such, apparently also to non-Christians.[29] Thereafter it was not necessary to have the charter reissued during the next 140 years, but it was then transcribed four times under the reign of king Sigismund, and it was confirmed and extended by him in 1436. The extension defines, among other things, the interest on loans given by Jews to Christians as two *denar*s per week for every hundred *denar*s, which adds up to a yearly interest of 104 per cent.[30] After Sigismund, each ruler was asked by the representatives of the Jewish community upon ascending to the throne to confirm these privileges.[31]

27 29 January 1324, published in UBB 3, No. 319, p. 169.

28 B. WIEDL, "Jews and the city: Parameters of Jewish urban life in late medieval Austria", in: *Urban Space in the Middle Ages and Early Modern Times*, ed. A. CLASSEN (Berlin, 2009), pp. 273-307, at pp. 278-280.

29 See more on this in Chapter 2 above.

30 The first transcription by the Fehérvár chapter: 16 March 1256: MHJ 1, p. 31. Later transcriptions by the same body: 24 February 1396: MHJ 1, pp. 108-109; 7 September 1406: MHJ 1, pp. 124-125; by king Sigismund: 10 August 1422: MHJ 1, p. 165; 18 October 1431: MHJ 1, p. 168. The extended confirmation: 4 November 1436: MHJ 1, pp. 168-172.

31 King Albert, 26 May 1438: MHJ 1, pp. 174-176; Ladislas V, 9 February 1453: MHJ 1, pp. 190-192; Matthias Corvinus, 19 June 1458: MHJ 1, 198-200; Matthias Corvinus after his coron-

The main activity of the Jewish population that was promoted and regulated through the above-mentioned royal privilege was moneylending; unlike in the early period, trading was not encouraged. There is, however, surviving evidence of an attempt to secure trading privileges for Jews through a forged charter. The matter came to light when a clerk, a certain Gabriel *literatus* de Zömlen, was revealed as a forger of charters and sentenced to death in 1448. In order to prevent any later misuse of his forgeries or copies of them, his confession containing a list of 48 (!) forgeries was inserted into Werbőczy's collection of the customary laws of Hungary, the already mentioned *Tripartitum*. (This was compiled in 1514, which means that the legislators calculated with the damaging effect of this scandal even two generations after the event.) This list contains, among other items,

> *una litera gratiosa Judaeis facta sub sigillo quondam domini Sigismundi Regis cum medio capite aquilae privilegialiter facta ut ipsi mercantias facere valeant*

> a letter of grant to the Jews under the seal of the late king Sigismund, issued with a hanging seal with an eagle head in the middle, allowing them to engage in trading.[32]

Although Gabriel stated before his execution that "the recipients of his forgeries had nothing to do with the crime", it is very hard to believe that he produced such a charter on his own initiative. It is more likely that the leaders of the Jewish community had sought to prevent any possible curtailment of their trading rights by town authorities through whatever means they could find. This instance, in its own paradoxical way, again testifies to trust placed in the written word, and the primacy of (presumed) royal charters over urban statutes.[33]

ation, 4 June 1464: MHJ 1, pp. 202-204; Wladislas II, 26 July 1493: MHJ 1, pp. 234-36; 10 January 1494: MHJ 1, pp. 238-239; Louis II, *c.* 1516, mentioned in a letter of the bishop of Vác: MHJ 1, p. 301.

32 WERBŐCZY, *The Customary Law,* Pars II. Tit. 14. § 74. edited as Appendix II, p. 439.

33 KUBINYI, "A magyarországi zsidóság", p. 15; B. WEISZ, "Zsidók a budai jogkönyvben" [Jews in the *Ofner Stadtrecht*], in: *"Magyaroknak eleiről"*, pp. 681-694, at p. 689.

Records of Urban Administration as Sources on Jewish-Christian Coexistence

Normative Legislation – Local Statutes

In the period of 'town Jews', most information that has come down to us was produced by the administration of the towns where they lived. This statement applies both to normative sources, that is, legislation, and pragmatic ones, including charters, deeds, municipal books and registers, and the like. The coverage is, unfortunately, uneven: not all towns where a Jewish presence is attested have equally well-preserved archives. The destruction of the Buda municipal archives during the town's Ottoman occupation (1541-1686) is the greatest loss, especially since Buda as Hungary's late medieval capital was home to the most numerous and influential Jewish community.[34]

The earliest local statutes relating to Jews have come down to us from Pressburg. This may not be so surprising: Jews must have had a prominent presence there, as – exceptionally for Hungary – they even appeared in the 'regular' town privilege. The charter issued in 1291 expressly states that "*Iudei in ipsa civitate constituti habeant eandem libertatem quam et ipsi cives*" ("Jews living in this town should enjoy the same liberties as the burghers themselves").[35] The statutes on the Jews comprise three articles from 1371 and a fourth one added five years later. These articles regulate the record-keeping in the *Judenpuech*, the interest on loans (stipulating the same percentage as Sigismund recorded later in 1436), and the forum of appeal. And they explain the procedure in case the pledged objects are stolen. The additional article lays down prescriptions on the slaughtering and sale of meat by the Jews. These are all issues connected to practical problems of everyday life and do not aim at a comprehensive regulation.[36] The information in these statutes is complemented by copious charters and books, mainly on financial activities, to which we shall return later.

A wider variety of normative regulations has been preserved in the *Ofner Stadtrecht*, which provides an overview of the main contexts of interaction and

[34] KUBINYI, "A magyarországi zsidóság", pp. 16-19.
[35] VMMS pp. 74-76.
[36] Editions: KIRÁLY, *Pozsony város joga*, pp. 371-372; MHJ 1, pp. 82-84.

possible conflict between Jews and Christians. The main articles of interest here are the following:[37]

50. On the fees of the town scribe (see Chapter 2) [Jews always have to pay double for their credit contracts];
191.What kind of clothes the Jews have to wear and what taxes do they have to pay for their wine;
192. On the attitudes of the Jews; and that they should not charge interest;
193. On the clothes that they have to wear;
194. On the Jews' market;
195. On the Jews' oath when they want to prove their claims against a Christian;
196. On the credit contracts of the Jews;
197. That they must not take church accessories as pawns;
258. On homicide [it is not allowed to kill a heretic, a pagan, or a Jew];
331. On sorcerers and witches [mentions the wearing of the *Judenhut*];
425. No one is allowed to trade with Jews [this refers to foreigners and guests, i.e. those who are not burghers of Buda].

Of the many issues worthy of discussion in this source, the references to the uses of writing deserve the closest attention in the present context. Article 196 is the most relevant from this point of view:

Dÿe Juden sullen alle ire phant prieff ainsten yn dem Jar auff pieten vor gerichte auff dem Rathauß unnd der richter sol den mensschen das lossen wissen, uber welchen dÿe prieff sagent, auf das dÿ posen Juden mit arger list icht dÿe Christen ummb ir erb pringen. Unnd dÿ vor halten prieff sullen fur paß nichten craft habenn.

The Jews shall present all their credit contracts once a year in the town hall, and the town judge shall inform those people who are mentioned in these letters, so that the wicked Jews do not with their greed deprive the Christians of their properties. And the letters that are not presented shall not be valid any more in the future.[38]

One can immediately notice the involvement of the main site and the role of the main person in charge of urban justice: the town hall and the town judge. The unequal weight of the written and spoken word also merits attention: debt-

[37] *Ofner Stadtrecht*, pp. 79, 126-28, 146, 169, 197. Analysis: WEISZ, "Zsidók a budai jogkönyvben", pp. 681-694.

[38] *Ofner Stadtrecht*, cap. 196, p. 127.

ors have to be orally informed of the presentation of the written contracts, and failing to present the documents would threaten their validity.

In Sopron the magistrates did not prepare any special legal code; we just find individual statutes or decisions of council meetings noted down in a rather haphazard manner in different town books. The issues were usually put on the agenda because of some previous problematic cases, and were noted in one of the municipal books currently at hand. A note from 1497, entered in the towns's *Gedenkbuch*, deals with the precautions to be taken when one borrows money from a Jew:

> *Auch soll der Jüdenrichter khainem khain eerbphanndt einschreiben, ausgenomen derselb bring dann von seinen nachberen oder Richter genügsame khundtschafft das es seinn vnd nit eins anderen sey.*

> The *Judenrichter* is not allowed to inscribe any real estate as collateral, unless he [the debtor] brings sufficient testimony from his neighbours or the judge that it [the property] belongs to him and no one else.

Remarkably, the legislation is meant to protect the interest of the moneylenders by asking for the (oral!) testimonies of the debtor's neighbours on his credentials and ascertaining the ownership of the property offered by him as collateral. It also mentions the *Judenrichter*, the member of the city council dealing with affairs concerning the Jews (see more on this official below), as the person responsible for making a written note of the encumbrances on landed properties ("*eerbphanndt einschreiben*"). This suggests the existence of a special register that has not come down to us.[39]

To my knowledge these are the only instances from Hungarian towns where local statutes have been preserved that are specifically concerned with the presence of Jews and their relationship to Christians. It is impossible to tell whether similar regulations may have been enacted in other towns as well. The existence of a general royal privilege for Jews may have meant that is was not necessary to formulate legal norms on a local level; but this absence of legal prescriptions may also have been due to the relatively small number of Jews in most places. But what little we have points to an ambiguity concerning the use of administrative literacy: written documents were often required in Jewish-Christian contacts, but their validity could easily be overruled by circumstances

[39] *Gedenkbuch*, No. 75, p. 66.

outside the realm of writing, such as failure to present the credit contracts on the day specified by the town magistrates.

Administering Justice

How was central or local normative legislation reflected in daily practice? There are three main and closely connected fields that most records cover: property ownership, justice, and financial issues. Let us take these in turn, paying attention to Jewish participation in the documentary practice. The examples will be taken from the two best preserved archival assemblages, both of them at the western border of the country: Pressburg and Sopron.[40] Due to the relatively late development of town chanceries in Hungary (as was discussed in Chapter 3, in the two towns in question there was a significant time-lag of about 50-70 years between the first surviving charters of privilege issued by the rulers and the real take-off of urban administration and record keeping) the records pertain to the period from the second half of the fourteenth century onwards. Obviously, not every single document can be studied here.

It followed from the autonomous character of royal towns that they had the right to administer justice over their own inhabitants. This was performed in much the same way between Jews and Christians as between any other locals, that is, by the town judge and in special cases by the councillors. The main difference was that, as the last paragraph of the 1251 privilege emphasises, the judge had to respect the special customs and liberties of the Jewish population. In order to ensure this, special officers, so-called *iudices Iudeorum* (*Judenrichter*) were appointed, centrally as well as at the local level. These were always Christians, and they were put in charge of administering justice in issues between Jews and Christians with the help of Christian and Jewish assessors.[41] They had a duty – at least in theory – to protect the Jews and assist them in collecting what they were owed. In the local context members of the elite –

[40] The materials pertaining to Jewish inhabitants are published *in extenso* in the following publications: M. POLLÁK, *A zsidók története Sopronban a legrégibb időktől a mai napig* [The history of Jews in Sopron from the oldest times to the present] (Budapest, 1896), Appendix of 75 documents, pp. 251-386. Those documents that contained several misreadings were republished in HÁZI, *Sopron,* vols. 1.1-7 and 2.1-6, *passim.* The documents pertaining to Pressburg are collected in MHJ 4. The outward appearance of the documents can be inspected with the help of the https://archives.hungaricana.hu/en/charters/ database.

[41] GODA and MAJOROSSY, "Städtische Selbstverwaltung", p. 80, esp. nn. 92-93.

mayors, town judges, or councillors – were charged with this task, either having been appointed by the *iudex Iudeorum* of the entire realm, or elected by the town magistrates – the procedures are unclear.

The earliest charter issued by the town judge of Pressburg in 1336, in a case outside the realm of property transactions with the local collegiate chapter, also involved as a mediator "*Ruedlinus dictus Waldner*", burgher of Pressburg and *iudex Iudeorum*. This text already mentions (and renders invalid) "all the documents" ("*universas litteras*") that the Jew Yezzel had concerning a house in Pressburg, presuming a more advanced level of literacy on the side of the Jewish party than the town had.[42] *Judenrichter* were part of the local administration in all towns were Jews lived in significant numbers, and their language use reflected local customs. For instance, the market town of Vrbové sent a letter in a Slavic dialect, addressed to "*Mudremu a opatrnemu panu Jacubowy Ssaflarowy v Trnawie, richtary zidovzkemu*" ("the wise and prudent gentleman Jacob Schaflar of Trnava, judge of the Jews") on the seizure of some commercial goods.[43]

There were also Jewish bodies adjudicating internal affairs, the so-called *beth-din*, the judge of which was called *magister Iudeorum*.[44] The system of Christian judges operated similarly in Vienna, where the *iudex Iudeorum* was appointed from among the town councillors by the duke of Austria.[45] This is, however, still very far from the practice on the Iberian Peninsula, where the major cities were obliged to employ Jewish and Muslim legal experts in order to ensure administering justice correctly to all groups in common affairs.[46]

[42] The 1336 document: Slovenský národný archív, Archív hodnoverného miesta – Bratislavská kapitula (SNA AHM-BK) 14-15-5, MNL OL DF 226762, ŠEDIVÝ, "Die Anfänge der Beurkundung", pp. 95-96. See Chapter 2 above on the preparation and keeping of the text by the chapter.

[43] 6 June 1522, DF 279916, edited by B. VARSÍK, *Slovenské listy*, pp. 115-116.

[44] On the regulation of jurisdiction concerning the Jews, the most detailed work is still SZ. BALOG, *A magyarországi zsidók kamaraszolgasága és igazságszolgáltatása a középkorban* [The status of Jews in Hungary as servants of the chamber and their jurisdiction in the Middle Ages] (Budapest, 1907), especially pp. 58-67. A shorter summary is provided in KUBINYI, "A magyarországi zsidóság", pp. 11-13.

[45] R. PERGER, *Die Wiener Ratsbürger: Ein Handbuch* (Wien, 1988), pp. 24, 30-52. The same institution was known in other towns as well in the eastern part of present-day Austria, but in the light of the Hungarian examples it was not completely unique to that territory, as assumed by WIEDL, "Jews and the city", pp. 290-291.

[46] A. ECHEVARRIA, *The City of the Three Mosques: Ávila and its Muslims in the Middle Ages* (Wiesbaden, 2011).

An interesting example concerning procedural issues is provided by a letter of the town council of Kőszeg, at that time under the lordship of the Garai family, one of the mightiest aristocrats of the time. On 30 January 1413 the council approached Sopron as their standard court of appeal in civil and criminal cases to settle a dispute between Baruch the Jew and Niclas von Marichprag. Baruch had been commissioned to sell Niclas's paternal inheritance and was then called to give an account. He was only ready to do this if the case was taken up by the court of the place where he as the defendant was settled, whereas Niclas claimed that the matter should be examined in the place where the property in question was situated (probably Kőszeg). The local council was of the same opinion as Niclas, but asked Sopron for a final verdict.[47] This apparently routine case is interesting for at least two reasons: the councils treated the sale of real estate between Christians and Jews as a matter of course, and in the system of appeal the same rules applied as with any other dispute. From the late fourteenth century Sopron was regarded as the 'mother town' in the judicial practice of five market towns within a semicircle of *c.* 60 km to the south-east.[48] This relationship made it unnecessary to involve the *iudex Iudeorum* of the country, palatine Miklós Garai – who was by coincidence the lord of Kőszeg at the same time.

Although it is usually impossible to follow up a single court case from its beginning to its conclusion, there are documents preserved from various stages of different litigations which taken together allow us to understand the course of the procedures. As a rule, the Jewish party appeared in front of the local court in person (*fur uns in recht chomen ist* is the standard expression) and presented the case orally or replied to it in the same way. Jews are also regularly recorded in the *Gerichtsbuch* of Sopron as claimants who summoned to court other townspeople, presumably their debtors, and the same rule applied of winning the case after three summonses if the defendant did not show up. Jews having taken the oath in front of the town council are also mentioned.[49]

Sometimes a decision was reached through the involvement of elected judges or mediators, as a case between Sigismund the Jew and the wife of Niklas Juding, councillor of Sopron, testifies. Sigismund appeared in the court as the representative of his baptised mother Sara, who had lent money to the councillor's wife. The document was apparently written by the town notary

47 HÁZI, *Sopron* 1.2, pp. 65-66.
48 See Chapter 4 on this legal filiation, and BARISKA, "Sopron a kőszegi források tükrében", p. 7.
49 E.g. *Gerichtsbuch*, No. 48. p. 122.

(who was one of the elected judges himself) who put the following words into Sigismund's mouth: "*ich egenanter Sigmund an stat Sara der jüdin und von den genaden gotes diczmals ein kristnÿn, meiner rechten muter*" ("I, the said Sigmund, on behalf of the Jewess Sara, *by God's grace* now a Christian woman, my own mother").[50] Another entry in the *Gedenkbuch* likewise involved a baptised Jewish woman and her daughter. To enforce their claim with the Jew Isaac, town and clergy joined forces: the parish priest, the mayor, and one more councillor were parties to the contract with Isaac when he settled his debt towards the women.[51]

The various phases of litigation might on occasion be documented by individual charters or entered in books kept by the town chancery from the late fourteenth century onwards (see Chapter 3). There was no particular book used for cases involving a Jewish counterparty (apart from registers of credit; see below). An official municipal book could be used, depending on the kind of case, or even on the availability of the book. In Pressburg in the early period of town book use, the previously introduced *Protocollum actionale* was the book especially frequently taken for entering court cases connected to Jewish moneylending. According to the examples contained in the books, the Jewish creditors did not hesitate to appear in person in front of the town court, and in a respectable number of cases managed to enforce repayment of the loans; in other cases, the entries recorded already settled business.[52]

In critical times, however, the procedures of justice could easily be turned upside down. Let me mention just one example for this.[53] In April 1490, the gruesome events following king Matthias Corvinus's unexpected death in Vienna and the unsettled issue of succession led to atrocities against the Jews both in Trnava and Sopron, and even in smaller towns such as Tata.[54] The town council of Sopron arrested a Jewish couple who only managed to avoid the death penalty (for a crime unspecified in the document) by offering as a 'gift'

[50] HÁZI, *Sopron*, 1.2, pp. 209-210.

[51] *Gedenkbuch*, No. 265, p. 149 (22 April 1517). The baptised woman, Anna *neuchristin* appears even in 1531 as moneylender in Sopron (ibid. No. 397, p. 217).

[52] The entries in the *Protocollum actionale* referring to Jewish money-lending are published in MHJ 4, pp. 47-48, 50, 55-56, 60-61, 69, 75-76, 80-81. See also *Actionale Protocollum*, ed. ZIEGLER, and GODA and MAJOROSSY, "Städtische Selbstverwaltung", pp. 91-94.

[53] On the broader context, see K. SZENDE, "Scapegoats or competitors? The expulsion of Jews from Hungarian towns on the aftermath of the battle of Mohács (1526)", in: *Expulsion and Diaspora Formation: Religious and Ethnic Identities in Flux from Antiquity to the Seventeenth Century*, ed. J. TOLAN (Turnhout, 2015), pp. 51-83.

[54] MHJ 1, pp. 225-226. (DL 19678)

("*geben und geschenckht haben*") 800 golden florins to the town to cover their great needs after king Matthias's death. Besides the huge sum – more than the ordinary yearly tax paid to the royal treasury by the entire town – the seriousness of the case is testified by the Hebrew signatures on the testimony of five other Jewish witnesses from the same town.[55] Hebrew literacy had been almost completely absent from Sopron's administrative practice in times of peace, but it gained significance under circumstances of pressure and dissent, as being considered more binding on the Jewish party than the German or Latin text. Three days later the whole Jewish community of Sopron, with nine Jewish signatories listed, offered to relieve the interest on all loans given by them to the inhabitants of Sopron on condition that the capital was repaid within half a year, and they also contributed one hundred guilders to the cost of hiring mercenaries to defend the town in the insecure situation following the king's death. The document states that all these special allowances were made by the Jews "by [their] free will, without any force, stress, or pressure" ("*willigklichenn, ungenött, ungescháczt unnd unbetwüngen*"), but this was obviously not true, for two days later the widowed queen and the dignitaries of the realm ordered the council of Sopron to release unconditionally all the imprisoned Jews.[56]

Real Estate and Moneylending

Property administration was a field where the involvement of local authorities was perhaps the most necessary – and rewarding – for reasons explained in detail in Chapter 3.[57] Since burghers' rights and obligations were tied to the ownership of a house plot in town, it was essential for the town magistrates to keep track of the owners of city properties. As there was a relatively high degree of mobility of the population and a high turnover of real estate, since

[55] MHJ 1, pp. 218-221; 2, 530-534. The declaration of the queen and the royal council: *ibid.*, pp. 217-218.

[56] The offers of the Sopron Jews, 19 April 1490: HÁZI, *Sopron,* 1.6, pp. 59-63. The document contains both the testimony of five witnesses in Hebrew and a note in German language but Hebrew script by the issuers. The order of release: 21 April 1490: S. KOHN, *A zsidók története Magyarországon: A legrégibb időktől a mohácsi vészig. 68 kiadatlan okirattal* [The history of Jews in Hungary from the oldest times to the battle of Mohács, with 68 unpublished documents], (Budapest, 1884), pp. 432-433.

[57] K. SZENDE, "Some aspects of urban landownership in western Hungary", in: *Power, Profit, and Urban Land*, pp. 141-166.

urban property could be sold and brought with fewer restrictions than the estates of the nobility, accurate record-keeping had to be ensured by the local chanceries. However, town properties served as a basis of taxation, and keeping the number of taxpayers high was essential; so too was limiting the number of owners who would be exempt from this obligation. This applied especially to limiting donations of real estate to the Church, a problem outside our present scope. *Mutatis mutandis*, the same concerns applied to properties owned by Jews, since their status also differed from the norm: Jews were not entitled to burghers' rights (citizenship) simply by virtue of their property ownership.[58] Neither were they part of the regular local tax collection, since Jews owed their taxes directly to the royal chamber, unless the king leased this revenue to the locals as a repayment of some loans.

These principles are reflected in the earliest preserved record of property administration comprising a whole town, the list of plots and their owners in Sopron, compiled in 1379 (see Fig. 30). This list, which remained a one-off undertaking, was intended to facilitate the division of outfields pertaining to each plot. It includes the names of ten Jews, presumably family heads, who owned altogether eleven houses, including the property where the *mikhwe* (*tukchaus*, 'ritual bath') connected to the synagogue was situated. The list also mentions that each plot-owner is also entitled to a cabbage garden on the outskirts of the town, except for the Jews ("*allain dy Juden hausseren dy habent chaynen chrautgarten nicht*"). The Jewish properties are listed twice: first in a summary way at the beginning because of the regulation on the gardens, and then in topographical order, together with the Christians' properties.[59] Due to fortunate circumstances, the synagogue and its outbuildings and even the plot sizes have been identified through building archaeological research and thus the accuracy of the 1379 list could be verified (Fig. 40).[60]

Unfortunately, for the later period no such comprehensive lists have come down to us. The Sopron *Grundbuch*, set up in 1480, records brief accounts of

[58] The situation was similar in the Austrian towns as well: WIEDL, "Jews and the city", pp. 292-293. The explanation offered by Birgit Wiedl, namely that the princely authority overwhelmed that of the towns, is perhaps even more appropriate for the Hungarian context.

[59] HÁZI, *Sopron*, 1.1, pp. 183-88. The list is presented in SZENDE, "Urban landownership", p. 149.

[60] F. DÁVID, *A soproni ó-zsinagóga* [The old synagogue in Sopron] (Budapest, 1978), pp. 11-35; F. DÁVID, K. GODA, and G. THIRRING, *Sopron belvárosának házai és háztulajdonosai 1488-1939* [Houses and house-owners in the central part of Sopron, 1488-1939] (Sopron, 2008), pp. 247-289.

Fig. 40 Reconstructed view of the Jews' Street (*Judengasse,* present-day Új utca) of Sopron with its two synagogues. Drawing by János Sedlmayr. Reproduced with permission.

occasional sales and purchases of property, with no regard to what religion the owners followed.[61] There are a few cases where title deeds have been preserved in the form of original documents; here again Jews are recorded among the owners in the same way as Christians. Property transactions involving only Jewish persons were likewise entered in the municipal documents: it was the town's control over the real estate that mattered, not the ethnic affiliation of the parties. Jewish ownership extended occasionally to vineyards and arable lands as well; these properties were usually acquired as collaterals in lieu of payment of debts. This happened, for instance, with the oft-mentioned notary Konrad Ernst, who apparently did no better with his finances in Sopron than before his flight from Vienna. After his death, Köphel the Jew from Wiener Neustadt appeared in court to recover the debts secured by two sealed credit contracts ("*czwen pergamenen brief, yder mit czwain anhangunden insigeln*"). Since there was no cash available in Ernst's bequest, the town court awarded Köphel one of his vineyards, with the obligation to pay off all other debts of the deceased notary.[62] It is only in tax lists that Jewish residents remain unrecorded, due to their being taxed directly by the royal treasury. This fact at times causes difficulties in the reconstruction of continuous ownership lists.

In Pressburg, as was already discussed in Chapter 3, property administration relied on a combination of individual deeds and a central cadastral register kept by the town from 1439 onwards. In this *Grundbuch*, the houses on the Jews' steet (*Judengasse*) were entered separately at the end of the volume; otherwise the system of recording did not differ from the rest of the town. Jewish property ownership is also attested in the other town book kept by the Pressburg chancery, the *Satzbuch*, a register of mortgages on individual properties.[63]

Financial transactions, first and foremost moneylending, were the most frequent reasons for producing documents in the Jewish-Christian context. Some of these issues have already been discussed in the context of justice and property administration. In late fourteenth- and fifteenth-century Hungary, just as in countries further west, towns as corporate bodies as well as private persons frequently took up loans from Jewish creditors. The town archives of Pressburg have preserved several such contracts – altogether more than 40

[61] *Erstes Grundbuch, passim.*

[62] *Gerichtsbuch*, No. 91, pp. 136-137 (31 March 1451).

[63] KOVÁTS, *Preßburger Grundbuchführung*; the edition of the relevant parts: MHJ 4, pp. 325-349. A new reconstruction of Pressburg's topography and house-owners (including the houses of Jewish inhabitants) is forthcoming by Judit Majorossy.

cases – from the period between 1371 and 1426.[64] This material, much of which may have come to Pressburg as a consequence of the *Wiener Gesera*, the tragic destruction of the Jewish community in Vienna in 1420/1421 under duke Albert V, later king of Hungary,[65] is certainly remarkable and in many respects exemplary in the Hungarian urban context. The economic significance of Jewish moneylending to the town of Pressburg and its changing importance over time has already been analysed in detail by the editor of these sources, the prominent economic historian Ferenc Kováts. He examined the aggregate sums of loans taken out by the town from Jewish and Christian creditors over twenty-year periods between 1360 and 1500. According to his results, although Jewish loans remained on the same level or even showed some increase in the decades between 1381 and 1440, they were overtaken and then greatly exceeded by the sums provided by Christian creditors (Table 2).[66]

Table 2 Loans taken out by the town of Pressburg from Jewish and Christian creditors, 1360-1500 (compiled by F. KOVÁTS).[67]

Years	loans from Christians (*f*)	loans from Jews (*f*)
1361-1380	0	1782
1381-1400	3564	2137
1401-1420	10777	2488
1421-1440	20847	2513
1441-1460	17296	235
1461-1480	9905	248
1481-1500	1300	0

64 MHJ 4, pp. 3-81, including 12 entries from the *Protocollum actionale* and 5 other charters that cannot be classified as credit contracts.

65 S. KRAUSS, *Die Wiener Geserah vom Jahre 1421* (Wien, 1920); LOHRMANN, *Die Wiener Juden*, pp. 155-167.

66 F. KOVÁTS, "Bevezetés" [Introduction], in: MHJ 1, pp. XXIX-CVIII, esp. pp. LVI-CVI.

67 F. KOVÁTS, "Bevezetés", p. LXXII.

This is a tendency characteristic for most Central European towns over the same period, and it has been extensively discussed by economic historians.[68] For our present purposes, the implications of these data for the use of legal frameworks and literacy bear more relevance. In order to better understand this important aspect of Jewish-Christian relations and to define the particularities of credit contracts concluded with Jewish business partners, a sample of contemporary Christian credit contracts needs to be taken into account as well.[69]

Not surprisingly, the contracts with the two main groups of moneylenders show more similarities than differences as far as their structure and validity are concerned. The principal common point is that in case of cash loans, the credit contract was the main proof of the whole transaction. As the standard clauses of such documents stated, whoever produced the contract had the right to reclaim in the creditor's name the sum indicated therein. Therefore the loss or physical damage of the document risked the annulment of its contents unless it was reported to the issuing authority.[70] By the same reasoning, after repayment, the parchment of the charter (for even in a period when paper was available, credit contracts were as a rule issued on this more prestigious and durable material) was cut through in a 'V'-shape, probably with a pair of scissors, in two or three places in the middle of the sheet, to show the cancellation of the debt (Fig. 41).

A further common point is that the contracts were issued by the debtor party, who had to take responsibility for repaying the debt and offer some sort of collateral. As a rule, full liability was assumed, with ultimately all the goods and properties of the debtor being made available to repay the credit, if necessary. In more concrete terms, private persons usually offered some real estate, a house or a vineyard, whereas if the town as a community took up the loan, the so-called *arrestatio* (or its German equivalent, *Gefangnus*) applied. This allowed the creditor to seize any member of the debtor community on his way, together with his merchandise, and take wares to the value of the debt or else

[68] M. TOCH, "Economic activities of German Jews in the Middle Ages", in: *Wirtschaftsgeschichte der mittelalterlichen Juden,* ed. M. TOCH (München, 2008), pp. 181-210.

[69] Digital photos of the majority of the medieval archival material from Archív Mesta Bratislavy are available in the database of the National Archives of Hungary. Unfortunately, at the time of research, the Bratislava City Archives were being relocated and the original material was not available for consultation. The Christian credit contracts were not examined in their entirety, only a sample from the 1390s to the 1410s was surveyed for the sake of comparison.

[70] Such an instance was recorded in the Pressburg town book in 1386 (MHJ 4, pp. 15-16), when the town judge testified to the Jewish creditors reporting the loss of an otherwise already repaid credit contract.

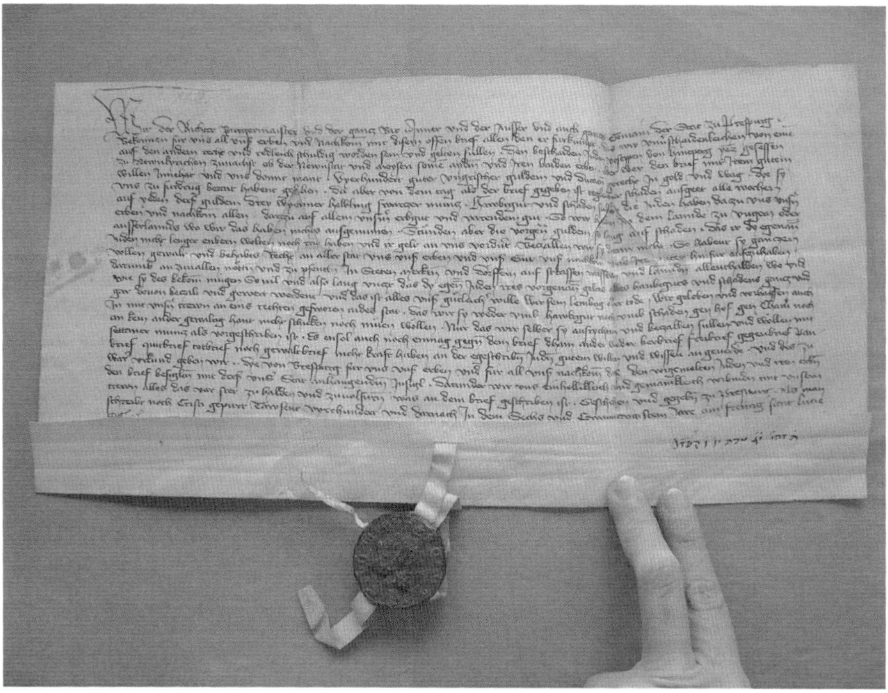

Fig. 41 Credit contract between the town of Pressburg and Yosepp von Himberg and his son-in-law Moyse, 13 December 1426, with cuts indicating repayment (AMB Listine Nr. 1000) Photo: Judit Majorossy. Reproduced with the permission of Archív Mesta Bratislavy.

keep the person as hostage until the debt was repaid. *Arrestatio* was an element of Hungarian, and indeed European, customary law, applied in various cases of financial disputes, and it seems that debts to Jews were no exception to this rule.[71]

Credit contracts were issued in the form of charters of privilege, with hanging seals. If the town was the debtor, obviously it was the town seal that corroborated the document; but this was usually the case also when private persons took out the loan. In such cases the text mentioned the party upon whose request the community seal was appended – commonly the debtor, but it could also be the Jewish creditor, presumably because the town seal offered stronger

[71] I. Tringli, "Vásártér és vásári jog a középkori Magyarországon" [Marketplace and market law in medieval Hungary], *Századok* 144 (2010), pp. 1291-1344, at pp. 1325-1330; H. Planitz, *Grundlagen des deutschen Arrestprozesses* (Leipzig, 1922).

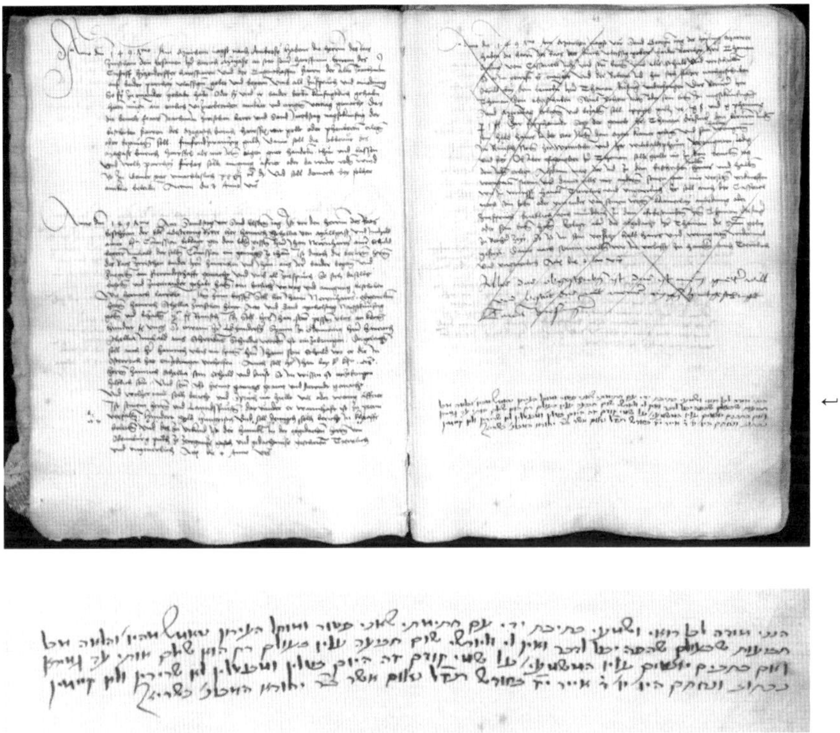

Fig. 42 Sopron, *Gedenkbuch*, agreement between Thaman Dreissinger, councillor, and the Jewish moneylender Kassariel concerning a loan, 19 April 1497. The creditor acknowledges the fulfilment of the conditions in Hebrew script on the bottom of the page on the right side (SVL DL 3797, f. 43r). Reproduced with the permission of the Sopron Archives.

security.[72] This arrangement applied not only in the case of Pressburg as a free royal town, but also in the case of Devín, a market town west of it, on the border with Lower Austria, from where eight credit contracts from the period between 1402 and 1420 have survived in the Pressburg archives, all of them bearing "*Markt Theben anhangendes insigel*".[73]

[72] An example for the Jewish creditor asking for the town seal: MHJ 4, p. 63 (1 September 1416). An exception where a private credit contract was corroborated with the debtors' and the witnesses' seals: MHJ 4, pp. 12-13. (6 May 1383)

[73] MHJ 4, pp. 45-47, 49-50, 64-65, 69-70, 71-72, 72-73, 74-75, 77-78.

The *Gedenkbuch* of Sopron has preserved a peculiar case concerning the use of private seals. One of the burghers, Hans Zirkendorffer, had, quite imprudently, mortgaged his own seal (perhaps a signet ring) to the Jew Isaac. When Zirkendorffer was absolved of his debt, Isaac had to declare that any eventual credit contract that may have been issued meanwhile under that seal and would be produced by any Jew in court should be null and void; furthermore, the presenter of such a letter should be justly punished. When this declaration was entered in the municipal book, the old Merhell rabbi and one more Jew were present, and Isaac had to sign the book in Hebrew. If we recall the above-quoted example of a Hebrew clause, we can understand how serious this issue was. Likewise, the Jewish moneylender Kassariel had to testify in his own handwriting that the councillor Thomas Dresinger is not indebted to him any longer (Fig. 42).[74]

Returning to the credit contracts from Pressburg, there is another special clause that appears in a great number of them. This clause secures for the creditor that the debtor cannot get out of repaying the debt by obtaining any special liberties or letters of grace:

> There must not be any other document, neither charter, privilege, receipt, annulling or prohibitory letter, nor any mandate (*verbrief, freibrief, gegenbrief, panbrief, quitbrief, totbrief noch gewaltbrief*) which would have validity against the present contract without the will and knowledge of the above-mentioned Jews.[75]

One would imagine, considering these circumstances, that such a 'no-escape'-clause would commonly be included in contracts with Jewish creditors, but in fact, it is equally present from the 1390s onwards in documents on loans taken from Christians.[76] The only difference is, that in the contracts with Jewish creditors these clauses are more elaborate and provide a longer list of such documents that should not influence the validity of the original contract.

The practice of 'killing the charters', that is cancelling the interest on loan, was a real danger to creditors. Charters which liberate the debtors in some degree have indeed come down to us. For instance, on 25 October 1426, Albert V, duke of Austria (the same person who initiated the *Wiener Gesera* in 1420/1421) cancelled half of the debts of the Pressburgers to Jews expelled

[74] *Gedenkbuch,* Nos. 153, pp. 98-99 and 73, p. 65.

[75] DF 241482 = MHJ 4, pp. 78-80 (13 December 1426). A similarly detailed list: DF 239195 = MHJ 4, pp. 39-41 (14 December 1400).

[76] E.g. 239112 (13 October 1392); DF 239135 (12 March 1395), DF 239405 (8 April 1419).

from Hainburg and Bruck an der Leitha as a reward for the town hosting king Sigismund, Albert's father-in-law.[77] Apparently it was his authority over the creditors that gave Albert the authority to dispose of their loans, even if the debtors were subject to a different political entity:

> *Nu haben wir angesehen ir fleissige gepete und haben dadurch und von sundern gnaden unsern willen und gunst darczu gegeben und geben auch wissentleich mit dem brief in solicher mass was derselben geltschuld seÿ, es seÿ auf brieuen, juden-pühern, oder kuntscheften, oder wie die geweist und ungeuërleichmag eingeuorert oder inpracht warden, daz wir denselben bürgern gleich halben tail derselben geltschuld geben.*
>
> Now, considering their diligent request and because of our special grace, we have agreed and announce with this letter in the following way that whatever debts there may be, be it on contracts, in Jewish loan books or letters of inquest, or in whatever way they might be demanded to be regained, we give half of these debts to the burghers.[78]

As the quotations testify, written words competed with written words, but the final settlement of the issues depended on the power relations of the parties that stood behind the documents in question. This is an issue that bears a crucial significance for the entire volume. But before returning to that point, let us consider those features of the credit contracts that were specific for Jewish moneylending.

One element is certainly the accurate recording of the interest rate and due date of the loan. The conditions varied a great deal, depending on the debtor's credentials and social standing, the sum of the loan, and the urgency of the transaction. It was common knowledge, however, that the terms of Jewish loans were generally stricter and financially more demanding. Interest rates were particularly high in East Central Europe compared to other parts of the continent.[79] In one of the clauses of the contract that the town of Pressburg concluded with a Christian creditor, Hans der Rokk, burgher of Vienna, the town authorised him that, in case they were not able to repay an instalment on time, he could take up a loan from others, including Jews, at their expense.[80] In other words, a Jewish loan would be the last resort in case of financial need.

[77] See Chapter 3 on the reimbursement of the hospitality expenses.

[78] DF 239465 (25 October1426). This document has not been included in MHJ 4.

[79] Toch, "Economic activities", pp. 199-200.

[80] DF 239124 (10 September 1393).

In the case of married Jewish creditors, the wife's name as a rule was also included in the contract, showing the equal entitlement of both spouses to reclaim the debt.[81] A further specific clause in letters of debt to Jews was the *Einlager* ('depositing'), expressed in Hebrew as 'eating on someone' (that is, at someone's expense) as warranty'. This was a relatively archaic custom known in the High Middle Ages in German-speaking lands; it was meant to speed up the process of repayment by having a party housed and fed at the debtor's expense in an inn specified by the creditor.[82] In the sample of credit contracts examined here, the stipulation of *Einlager* was mainly connected to Jewish creditors from Hainburg, a small town about half-way between Pressburg and Vienna, but it was known and practised in Pressburg as well.[83]

The most particular feature of the contracts with Jewish creditors examined here was, however, the frequent presence of notes in Hebrew script added after the completion of the text on the dorse, on the *plica* ('fold'), or even on the thin parchment band holding the seal.[84] The layout of these remarks suggests that the documents were stored hanging, perhaps nailed or clipped to a board, with their seals or their side margins closest to the viewer's eyes. (Similar arrangements can be seen on some fifteenth-sixteenth-century panel paintings depicting studies or offices.) The notes were thus meant to summarise the most relevant pieces of information contained by the text, and consisted of one or more of the following items:

- Name of the debtor. The names are phonetic transcriptions of the German names, even if these represented an unusual occupation (e.g. *Nachrichter* = 'hangman'). The only exception is when the town as a corporate body took up the loan: in this case the Hebrew word *adonim*

[81] M. Keil, "Mobilität und Sittsamkeit: Jüdische Frauen im Wirtschaftsleben des spätmittelalterlichen Aschkenas", in: *Wirtschaftsgeschichte der mittelalterlichen Juden*, pp. 153-180.

[82] Toch, "Economic activities", pp. 193, 198.

[83] Hainburg: MHJ 4, pp. 4-6 (DL 41965); *ibid.* pp. 25-27 (DF 239123); *ibid.* pp 36-38 (DF 239160); *ibid.* pp. 44-45 (DF 239234). Pressburg: *ibid.* pp. 6-8 (DF 238933); MHJ 1, pp. 86-88 (the editor in his summary of the transaction misunderstood the situation, writing that "a servant was offered as security").

[84] These remarks in Hebrew script are not mentioned, let alone reproduced, in the edition of the texts in MHJ 4. I owe special thanks to my colleague, Carsten Wilke, for deciphering these often hardly legible texts. Unfortunately, in some cases the digital copies of the credit contracts do not include a photo of the verso, which may have contained such texts in Hebrew script. The inspection of the originals, once they become available for research, will probably reveal further information. The main patterns are, however, visible already in the present sample.

('lords') was used, as the equivalent of *Herren* [*des Rats*]. The practice of recording the debtor's name implies that each creditor had a number of debtors among his clients.

- Name of the creditor. The Jewish creditors' names are usually given in the same form as in the German text of the charter (although without the German diminutive: *Hosia* instead of *Hoschlein*). Only in one case is it added that the creditor (Musch / Moses) was the son of Rabbi Sabbatai of blessed memory.[85] In some cases, when the German text refers to three or four creditors, the Hebrew text only mentions one of them. Mentioning the creditors' names may refer to the fact that certain contracts were transferred to other creditors than the original ones, for otherwise the mention of one's own name might be seen as superfluous.
- The sum on loan. This is the most frequently mentioned information, although the numbers are sometimes very hard to decipher. The word *libra* ('pound') is usually rendered as *litrin*, the Hungarian golden florins as *Hagari*.[86] The sums are as a rule identical to the sums mentioned in the German text. In one exceptional case a series of sums including sums of interest were added in different hands to the Hebrew text on the dorse.[87]
- The due date. This was the most crucial information that allowed the creditor to act swiftly and with effect when repayment was due. There were different possible arrangements: interest sometimes started to accumulate from the date of the contract, but more frequently there was a specified grace period of a few months, and if the debtor repaid the loan within that time, no interest was due.[88] The date indicated in the Hebrew texts was usually that of the taking out of the contract, but sometimes it could be the end of the grace period, from which the in-

[85] DF 241349 (MHJ 4, p. 3, edited without the Hebrew text).

[86] Hungary was commonly denoted in Hebrew as the Country of Hagar. The most detailed discussion of this term is still by S. KOHN, *Héber kútforrások és adatok Magyarország történetéhez* [Hebrew sources and data on the history of Hungary] (Budapest, 1881; reprinted Budapest, 1990), pp. 144-159.

[87] DF 239123 (MHJ 4, pp. 25-27, edited without the Hebrew text).

[88] In a few cases the sums repaid by the creditors, mostly the town of Pressburg, are also indicated (in German), together with the date of payment, on the dorse of the charters. With the help of this information, F. KOVÁTS asserts in his introduction to MHJ 4, pp. LXIV-LXXII, that the creditors often gave a discount from the interest, which would have been higher if calculated according to the rate indicated in the contract.

terest was calculated. The dates in the German text are always given in relation to Christian feast days, but are regularly expressed in terms of the Hebrew calendar in the remarks. This act of translation could have been guided by convenience as much as by resentment against the Christian calendar and its saints. In the rare cases when the Christian calendar was used, the adjective 'saint' was never added (e.g. *am Micheltag*).[89]

Besides the credit contracts, the classical types of documents connected to moneylending were the debt registers – the *Judenbücher*.[90] These were in the form of books or booklets, arranged usually by creditors. In the Pressburg statutes from 1371 mentioned above we read:

> *dy Juden sullen haben ein puech und dasselb soll ein kristen ein geschworn man inne haben, [...] die kristen und juden darzu erwellent und dieselbe zwen gesworn [...] sullen dass puech versiegeln mit ihren insigeln*
>
> the Jews should have a book and that should be kept by a Christian councillor [...] who is entrusted with this by Christians and Jews, and two councillors [...] should seal the book with their seals.[91]

The ownership of and authority over the debt registers that recorded legally binding financial transactions was of crucial significance in Jewish-Christian relations. The issue of contention was often not the amount of the loan, but the interest rate that in a couple of years could multiply the debt to as much as three times the original capital.[92] Some of the debts were repaid in kind, for example with agricultural produce such as grain and wine, or with commercial wares like cloth and spices of contested value, the resale of which may have been held against the Jews as offering unjust competition against the local

[89] E. CARLEBACH, *Palaces of Time: Jewish Calendar and Culture in Early Modern Europe* (Cambridge MA, 2011), Chapter 5, "Keeping Christian time in Jewish calendars", pp. 115-140.

[90] On the genre, see TH. PETER, "Judenbücher als Quellengattung und die Znaimer Judenbücher", in: *Räume und Wege: Jüdische Geschichte im Alten Reich 1300-1800,* ed. R. KIEßLING *et al.* (Berlin, 2007), pp. 307-334; on the Austrian practice: WIEDL, "Jews and the city", pp. 291-293.

[91] MHJ 1, pp. 82-83.

[92] After the invention of printing, broadsheets warning against taking up loans from the Jews were published. The pamphlet kept at the Deutsches Historisches Museum, Inv.-Nr. Gr 92/1, is bilingual: the top part has a Latin text demanding the authorities to take measures, the bottom features a model calculation of interest in German.

merchants.[93] Keeping the accounts as precise and safe as possible was the only way of coming to terms with these transactions. It is no wonder that the archives of the Jews were seized and destroyed during the atrocities connected with the expulsion of the Jews from the major towns of Hungary in the first decades of the sixteenth century.[94]

One may assume a continuous practice of keeping such books until the expulsion of Jews from Sopron and Pressburg in 1526; however, only a few fragmented pages from the period between 1498 and 1503 have come down to us. The entries have preserved precious information on Jewish creditors and their debtors, but they also testify to the strikingly reduced scale of business compared to the loans provided a century earlier.[95] Loans to private debtors were also occasionally mentioned in the last wills of some of the people recorded in another town book from Pressburg, the *Protocollum testamentorum*. These also refer to small-scale businesses, with pawns as security.[96]

Conclusions: Trust in Writing between Christians and Jews

The examples discussed above – although a broader study on a larger body of comparative material would undoubtedly give a more precise and perhaps a somewhat different picture – allow us to draw some conclusions on the uses (and misuses) of writing in legal and business contacts between Jews and Christians in medieval Hungary.

First of all, one can observe that trust in writing was a major factor in facilitating and regulating Jewish-Christian relationships in everyday matters. The Jewish population was aware of and integrated into these practices in many ways, and in some cases, because of their mobility and long-distance connections, they were even pioneers in the use of writing. Let us just consider again the use of the *cartula sigillata* back in the twelfth century, or the regulation

[93] This was one of the accusations after the expulsion of the Jews from Sopron in September 1526. HÁZI, *Sopron*, 1.7, pp. 208-213.

[94] SZENDE, "Scapegoats or competitors", pp. 65-66.

[95] F. KOVÁTS, "A pozsonyi zsidókönyvtöredék, 1498-1503" [The fragment of a *Judenbuch* from Pressburg, 1498-1503], in: *Emlékkönyv Dr. Gróf Klebelsberg Kunó negyedszázados kultúrpolitikai működésének emlékére* [Festschrift for Count Dr. Kunó Klebelsberg on the twenty-fifth anniversary of his activity in the field of cultural policy], ed. I. LUKINICH (Budapest, 1925), pp. 331-343, with edition at pp. 344-346, and in MHJ 4, pp. 412-428.

[96] PT, *passim*.

that there should be a special book set up for the registering of Jewish loans in Pressburg in 1371, at a time when the use of town books had barely began.

Of the many different aspects of pragmatic literacy, there are in my view three that are especially suitable to highlight the integrative process of the Jewish minority, but also its limits and the obstacles to it: the use of language and script; the means of assuring authenticity; and the problem of the safekeeping of documents. First, as has been explained in the previous chapter, Jewish communities were by necessity at least bilingual, using Hebrew as their sacred language side by side with the local vernacular, meaning in our urban context, mainly German. In their literacy Latin had to be understood, too, for even if the urban chanceries of the western Hungarian towns and to some extent Buda were increasingly embracing German as their language of administration from the mid-fourteenth century, the royal chancery and the nobility retained Latin in their written practice. The variety of spoken languages was even greater. Some Jews moved to Hungary from the Bohemian-Moravian lands, and Bertrandon de la Broquiére in 1433 encountered French-speaking Jews in Buda.[97] After 1492, a small but influential group of Spanisch-speaking Sephardi immigrants arrived from Spain in the Hungarian capital[98] – where one can assume some comprehension of spoken Hungarian, too.

The role of the Hebrew language and script was highly controversial throughout the Middle Ages. To the majority it was alien and incomprehensible, but in the internal communication and in contacts between Jewish communities it represented the high register, drawing on age-old traditions of the written word. As we saw above, Hebrew letters were accepted as visual symbols to identify mint masters in the thirteenth century. The widespread quotidian use of Hebrew literacy is also testified by some archaeological finds. A clay beaker and a slate tablet with scratched Hebrew inscriptions, the latter most probably featuring the name 'Chajjim Katz' came to light from a well on a house-plot in what had been in the fourteenth-century the Jewish street in Buda (see Fig. 10).[99] More important and frequent are tombstones carrying

[97] See above, Chapter 4, n. 49.

[98] A. Kubinyi, "Les Cotta de Tolède et la colonie espagnole à Bude aux 15e et 16e siècles", in: *Mélanges offerts à Szabolcs de Vajay,* ed. Gh. Vaernewyck, X. d'Adhémar de Panat, and P. d'Brière (Braga, 1971), pp. 381-390; Y.T. Assis, "Shlomo Seneor from Segovia to Buda", in: *Jewish Studies at the CEU* 7 (2009-2011), ed. A. Kovács and M.L. Miller (Budapest, 2013), pp. 7-18.

[99] D.B. Nyékhelyi, *Középkori kútlelet a budavári Szent György téren* [Finds from a medieval well on St. George Square at Buda] (Budapest, 2003: *Monumenta Historica Budapestinensia*

Hebrew inscriptions, with early specimens from Buda and fragments of later ones from several other towns, usually having been reused as building materials.[100]

At the intersection of pragmatic, legal, and liturgical literacy were the rabbinical *responsa*, a genre already briefly referred to above. The number of such texts that have come down to us is higher from the fourteenth and fifteenth centuries than from the earlier periods. Some of them, preserved, for instance, in the works of the famous rabbis of Wiener Neustadt, Shalom and Isserlein, deal with issues connected to Jews living in the Carpathian Basin, first and foremost in the western border regions. Overall, the *responsa* of presumably local origin show a general respect for observing the rules of religion, but do not testify to outstanding scholarship among the Jews or their leaders in medieval Hungary.[101] At the same time, the communities maintained their Hebrew literacy and possessed a notable amount of religious manuscripts.[102]

In official records kept by the town chanceries, passages of texts written in Hebrew script occur from time to time inserted into town books or added to charters issued by the municipalities. The appearance of an 'alien' script in an environment where writing in the municipal books or on the sheets of authentic documents was strictly controlled, reveals the gravity of the given situation. The closest possible involvement of the Jewish party enforced their obligation, visually, mentally, and legally alike. Authorities recurred to this solution when it was in the interest of the Christian party; no cases are known when such an addition to the official record would have happened at the request of the Jews. The analysis of the credit contracts from Pressburg has revealed a more pragmatic use of Hebrew script: there it was a 'shorthand' for personal notes on business documents. Notably, some of the contents (such as the dates) were translated into Hebrew terms, but most words were simply transcribed from German. Charters issued on business matters connected to the Jews of Sopron

12), pp. 33-34, 40-41; VÉGH, "The remains", pp. 137, 148: Fig.14.

[100] S. SCHEIBER, *Jewish Inscriptions in Hungary from the 3rd Century to 1686* (Budapest, 1983). None of the Jewish cemeteries from the modern period in Hungary show continuity with medieval Jewish burial grounds.

[101] *Héber kútforrások*, pp. 172-320; M. KEIL, "Juden in Grenzgemeinden: Wiener Neustadt und Ödenburg im Spätmittelalter", in: *Studien zur Geschichte der Juden in Österreich* 2, ed. M. KEIL and E. LAPPIN (Berlin, Bodenheim / Mainz, 1998), pp. 9-33, esp. nn. 64 and 68.

[102] SCHEIBER, *Hebräische Kodexüberreste*. A re-evaluation of the material is in progress by a research group directed by Tamás Turán (Hungarian Academy of Sciences).

sometimes also carry a summary written in Hebrew script, but essentially German in language.

To sum up, the language use of the Jewish minority in Hungary, similar to other parts of Central Europe, shows a strong imbalance. Latin and German were accepted and used extensively by the Jews of the Hungarian towns in their external relations, whereas Hebrew was valued basically within their own community, although its tradition of writing was granted some respect or at least tolerance in official administration. This limited toleration, however, only applied to financial matters; its linguistically complementary role did not extend to justice outside the Jewish communities or to public administration. It remains an open question to what extent – if at all – the growing respect for Hebrew as a sacred language among humanist theologians contributed to its partial acceptance in late medieval pragmatic literacy in local contexts.[103]

Secondly, issues of authentication as means of enforcing trust deserve attention. The most frequent document in everyday practice until the late Middle Ages was the charter or deed claimable in court, for which the most important authenticating instrument was, besides several internal and external formal criteria, the seal (see Chapter 2). As has been indicated above, credit contracts entered by municipal authorities naturally enough carried the seal of the issuing town (that is, as debtor), but so too did contracts on loans taken up by burghers of the same municipality. In some cases, the local *iudex Iudeorum* and the witnesses of the transaction also added their personal seals beside that of the debtor.[104] Matters of broader significance, or those involving a nobleman as one of the parties, were committed to writing by the *iudex Iudeorum* under his seal.[105]

Jews apparently also possessed seals, most probably in the form of signet rings, but these carried limited public authority in Hungarian judicial practice,

[103] The best-known protagonist of the Hebrew language was Johannes Reuchlin; see D.H. PRICE, *Johannes Reuchlin and the Campaign to Destroy Jewish Books* (Oxford, 2010). In the Hungarian context, Petrus Niger, one of the professors at the Dominican *studium generale* at Buda between 1480 and 1483, can be connected to this movement, although his relationship to the Jews was more controversial. See B. LAKATOS, "Petrus Niger", in: *Magyar Művelődéstörténeti Lexikon* [Lexicon of Hungarian cultural history], ed. P. KŐSZEGHY, 9 (Budapest, 2009), pp. 223-224; H. SCHRECKENBERG, *Die christlichen Adversus-Judaeos-Texte und ihr literarisches und historisches Umfeld (13-20. Jh.)* (Frankfurt am Main, 1994), pp. 544-547.

[104] As a rule, the seal used on a document is mentioned in its *corroboratio*, and therefore it is possible to determine it even when the actual object is lost. Examples for the seal of the *iudex Iudeorum*: MHJ 4, pp. 4-6 (DL 41965) and pp. 6-8 (DF 238933).

[105] E.g. MHJ 1, pp. 89-90.

just as seals of other private persons. According to the 1371 regulations on how to keep the *Judenpuech* in Pressburg, "*ein kristen und ein jud sullen dass puech versiegeln mit ihren insigeln*" ("a Christian [= a councillor] and a Jew had to seal the book with their seals").[106] In case of the so-called *praefectus Iudeorum* ('Jewish prefect') of Buda, royal appointment to this special position warranted his right to use his own seal on authentic documents. The person holding this office from the 1470s – customarily a member of the Mendel family – was, in fact, the administrative leader of all the Jews in Hungary.[107] But cases when Jews acted as witnesses, or used their seals in issues among Christians, which occasionally happened in Austria and further west, have not been recorded from medieval Hungary. The use of the so-called Hebrew signature was not widespread either, and confirmatory signatures of rabbis were confined to very precarious cases.[108]

Further ways to claim legal authority for a transaction or a court decision was to have them entered into the town book, the authority of which, as the formulation of the *Ofner Stadtrecht* demonstrates, was equal to that of a sealed charter (see Chapter 3). In Pressburg and Sopron, where the town archives have survived fairly intact, practically all the town books, general and special ones alike, contain entries connected to Jews. These entries are typically mixed with those involving Christians alone, according to the internal (chronological, topographical, or thematic) logic of the given books.

Apart from having access to the town authorities, Jews could also turn to the so-called places of authentication, which, as mentioned above, had much the same function as notaries public in other parts of medieval Europe. Besides the Fehérvár chapter, noted for confirming Béla IV's Jewish privilege in 1256 and again in 1396 and 1406, other such bodies, namely the Buda, Pressburg, Győr, and Esztergom chapters, also issued charters connected to business transactions involving Jews. Their services were especially needed in the fourteenth century, before the fully-fledged development of town chanceries. These documents were all composed in Latin.[109] In many cases it was the Jewish party who

[106] MHJ 1, p. 83.

[107] KUBINYI, "A magyarországi zsidóság", pp. 16-19; BALOG, "A magyarországi zsidók kamaraszolgasága", pp. 68-72. The seal of Jacob Mendel, *praefectus Iudeorum*, has been preserved impressed on documents.

[108] WIEDL, "Jews and the city", pp. 289-290. An example of a Hebrew signature: MHJ 1, p. 245; for confirmatory signatures of rabbis: MHJ 1, pp. 220-221. Most other Hebrew signatures date to the first decades of the sixteenth century.

[109] Fehérvár chapter: MHJ 1, pp. 31, 107-108 (1396), 124 (1406); Buda chapter: MHJ 1, pp.

approached the given chapter or convent with the request that they issue an original document or an authentic copy. Apparently, in most such cases the chapters followed their usual practices in spite of the petitioner's different religious affiliation. The adjective *perfidus* ('treacherous') starts to appear beside the Jewish parties' names only from the beginning of the sixteenth century.[110]

Taken together, these examples testify that Jews in medieval Hungary had access to a variety of ways of authenticating texts as well as to bodies producing them, but on unequal terms. As the *Ofner Stadtrecht* quoted above stipulated, Jews had to pay more for such services than their Christian counterparts; furthermore, the terms and conditions according to which documents had to be accepted as authentic were also set by the Christian authorities. Testimonies given or documents produced by Jews were accepted in Christian courts, but had to be accompanied by the seal of an official magistrate or entered in a book or register which was commonly accredited.

Finally, let us turn to the question of safekeeping written documents as material proofs of proprietary status or transactions. As will be discussed further in the next chapter, ownership and custody of authentic documents was also regulated in conformity with the rules of the majority society. This implies – and it was often spelled out – that anyone who produced a particular charter could demand the fulfilment of the actions therein. The name of the 'original' creditor mentioned in the Hebrew summary of some credit contracts may indicate that the charter was indeed taken over by someone else. The above-mentioned stipulation of the *Ofner Stadtrecht*, that Jews should present their credit contracts once a year in the town hall on pain of losing their validity, also shows the desire of the Christian authorities to exercise regular control.

The accidental loss or wilful destruction of a document annulled the validity of the act to which it testified, and so did any physical damage to it. The best illustrations of this are the cuts on the credit contracts of debts to Christians and Jews alike. In these cases, the cuts meant that the issue was settled and the loan was repaid. However, in other instances (some of which ended up in court), the debtors unjustly obtained, violently confiscated, or seized the charters or account books from a third party.[111] As direct rulers of the Jews, the

66 (1349), 67 (1350); Pressburg chapter: MHJ 1, pp. 69 (1353), 73-75 (1367), 81 (1371), 100-104 (1387); Győr chapter: MHJ 1, pp. 94-95 (1378); pp. 112-114 (1400).

[110] Esztergom chapter: MHJ 1, pp. 271-272 (1509).

[111] See, e.g. king Sigismund's charter of 4 October 1421 in favour of three Pressburg Jews who had been expelled from the duchy of Austria following the *Wiener Gesera* of 1420/1421, and

kings had the prerogative to order the 'killing of the charters', which meant cancelling the interest on the loans they recorded, or even, in extreme cases, cancelling the debts themselves.

The *Judenbücher*, the cumulative registers of Jewish loans, served the practical purpose of keeping track of these financial transactions. Since they were deposited as a rule with the Christian authorities, they were instruments of control over Jews even at the best of times. In times of peace they could provide security for Jewish creditors, because the debtors could not claim that the contracts presented by the Jews were forgeries; in times of conflict, however, the documents could very easily become targets of misuse. In case of persecutions and expulsions, these were the first items to be seized and destroyed in order to get rid of the debts. Overall, the vulnerable nature of the documents that were supposed to secure different transactions posed a great threat to Christians and Jews alike. This is why the majority society developed institutional frameworks for their storing and safekeeping, increasingly denoted as 'archives'. But these frameworks were not shaped or controlled, only passively used, by the Jewish population.

To conclude, trust in writing was a strong factor in Christian-Jewish coexistence, but it could only function if trust was in place on all fronts. Writing in this context appeared on the Hungarian territories from almost the earliest times after the state foundation, and its role there, as elsewhere in Europe, became stronger – and more asymmetrical in favour of the Christian population – with the passage of time. As Michael Toch formulated it concerning the German territories,

> The increasing use of written contracts claimable in court [...] argues for the integration of credit arrangements into the legal machinery of the period. Even so, this was risky business, and things could go very wrong.[112]

Indeed, the strong reliance on writing could easily be turned against the Jews. In my view this reflects on structural contradictions in their legal position. As far as everyday judiciary and administrative practice was concerned, the Jews were subject to the court of the place where they lived. The real estate

whose debtors got hold of their credit contracts illegally. The king ordered the town of Pressburg to issue receipts of the repaid sums under their seal. MHJ 1, pp. 157-160 (the date was corrected to 4 October (from 30 September) in MHJ) in: ZsO 8, ed. I. BORSA and N.C. TÓTH, (Budapest, 2003), No. 1033, pp. 79-82, 265-266).

[112] TOCH, "Economic activities", p. 193.

that they owned was also subject to the civic administration. The overall legal and economic situation of the Jewish population, however, was determined by the king, who held general sovereignty over them and considered them almost as his personal property. This corresponded to the claims of the emperor in the Holy Roman Empire.[113] But in practice the kings of Hungary had a much stronger grip and authority in this matter, which reduced the influence of the town magistrates and the variation in local practices. In times of tension and crisis, for instance at the change of reigns, Jews could easily get caught between a rock and a hard place. During conflicts of interest, when trust was no longer present, writing could not offer security, but exposed the weaker party to illegal interventions.

[113] WIEDL, "Jews and the city", p. 279.

Chapter 6

From Charters to Archives

The emergence of archives of different social groups in medieval Hungary – similarly to the rest of Western and Central Europe – followed the establishment of lay and ecclesiastical administration, and was closely linked to the development of the legal system and literacy in subsequent centuries. This chapter concentrates primarily on the archives of cities and towns, placed in the context of the overall development.[1]

The modern term 'archive' had two main equivalents in medieval usage. The archival material itself, that is, a collection of documents in the possession of a person or a legal body, was most frequently denoted by the expression *litterae* or *litteralia instrumenta*. In contrast, the place where these documents were kept was usually called *conservatorium* – a word used for royal, ecclesiastical, and family archives alike. Less frequently the word *archivum*, primarily denoting the repository or treasury of human mind and memory, also occurs in this sense, and sometimes the pieces of furniture or other containers (*scrinium, armarium*, etc.) used for storing the documents are named with reference to their contents.[2]

Lacking direct evidence, indirect references such as employing notaries, making registers or inventories of charters, or looking up documents that were

[1] The origins of this chapter go back to K. SZENDE, "The uses of archives in medieval Hungary", in: *The Development of Literate Mentalities in East Cental Europe*, pp. 107-142, but the material presented has been thoroughly revised and re-focused here.

[2] For the various meanings and usages of the term see the relevant entries in *Lexicon latinitatis medii aevi Hungarie*, vols. 1-6 (at present published up to the letter 'M'), ed. I. BORONKAI, K. SZOVÁK *et al.* (Budapest, 1987-). For some examples of usage see CZOBOR, "A családi levéltárak", pp. 382-389.

previously issued by the body in question can also imply the existence of a collection of documents at a certain place. Besides the physical environment and holdings, the human element was also constitutive of the archives as 'institutions' in the sociological sense of the word.[3] This entailed the employment of persons especially *entrusted* with taking care, safeguarding, and regulating access to the collections of administrative documents, be they clerics or clerks.

Variations on Archives

Civic archives were latecomers both with regard to the beginnings of issuing authentic documents by cities and towns, and as compared to the archives of other authorities. Their time lag compared to the former can be calculated in decades; to the latter in centuries. This means that by the time civic authorities reached the level of establishing purposefully organised collections of their written records, there had been age-old models at their disposal, as well as some recent innovations to consider.

The establishment of town archives was preceded by and in many ways connected to the existence and the repositories of the *loca credibilia*. One of the preconditions of the reliable administrative activity of these bodies was precisely to set up their own archives, usually under the care of a *custos*, and to keep track of the issued charters.[4] At first, they simply stored the original mandates received to perform a duty, as well as the chirographed copies of the documents they issued. Apart from the protocols of ordeals, registers became common from the end of the thirteenth century, beginning with the recognizances made in front of the chapters or convents (*litterae fassionales*), and only seldom the reports (*litterae relatoriae*), which were in a few cases recorded on the dorse of the mandates (*litterae mandatoriae*). The convent of Leles was among the first to introduce this practice. Other ecclesiastical bodies also set up registers of the most important documents that they received and possessed

[3] ARLINGHAUS, "Point of reference", with reference to J. ASSMANN, *Das kulturelle Gedächtnis: Schrift, Erinnerung und politische Identität in frühen Hochkulturen* (München, 1992), pp. 91-94.

[4] See notes Chapter 2, nn. 23-27 above, and GY. BÓNIS, "Les autorités de foi publique et les archives des '*loci credibiles*' en Hongrie", *Archivum* 12 (Paris, 1961), pp. 87-104; L.B. KUMOROVITZ, "A leleszi konvent országos levéltárának története" [The history of the public archives of the convent of Leles], *Levéltári Közlemények* 10 (1932), pp. 223-255, on the medieval archives: pp. 223-227.

in their private archives. The earliest preserved register is the inventory of the archives of the Veszprém bishopric from 1352,[5] and the most detailed one is probably that of the Esztergom archbishopric from the beginning of the fifteenth century.[6] Both of them contained selected lists of charters concerning the privileges and possessions of these bodies.

In the fifteenth century, the places of authentication started to set up protocols that gradually replaced storing the original documents. The earliest extant example is the protocol of the convent of Cluj-Mănăştur, the continuous notes of which start in 1438.[7] In addition to all these, private families often entrusted their archives to the *loca credibilia* for safekeeping, either because they considered it safer than their own home, or because the family did not want to divide the charters that concerned the estates of various family members. These private documents were stored in boxes sealed by the owner(s) and were returned to them only if they could produce the same seal.[8]

The already existing archives offered models for spatial arrangements. The collections of documents at the chapters and convents in question were most likely to be placed in their sacristies. Some clues in charters suggest that much of the actual work took place in the sacristies, namely that the charters were formulated, put into writing, and sealed in these rooms.[9] The sacristy was generally the place where the liturgy-related valuables of the church (chalices, chasubles, books, and similar artifacts) were deposited, so it was natural to find a place for the documents here, too. There are occasional references to this practice in contemporary documents. For example, the royal mandates addressed to the convent of Leles to look up a certain charter in their archives referred to the "*sacristia seu conservatorium*". A 1328 charter issued by the Convent of St. John at Fehérvár, itself a transcription of an earlier document from 1277, reports that the original was "*in registro ecclesie nostre olym depo-*

[5] I. BORSA, "A veszprémi püspökség levéltárának első jegyzéke 1352-ből" [The first inventory of the archives of the Veszprém bishopric from 1352], *Levéltári Közlemények* 20-23 (1942-45), pp. 384-388.

[6] GY. PROKOPP, "Az esztergomi prímási levéltár 15. századi leltára" [The fifteenth-century inventory of the archbishop's archives in Esztergom], *Levéltári Közlemények* 37 (1966), pp. 113-137, with the publication of the source and comments on the still extant documents in the list.

[7] See on the registers in general: ECKHART, "Glaubwürdigen Orte", pp. 474-483; in particular: ZS. JAKÓ (ed.), *A kolozsmonostori konvent jegyzőkönyvei 1289-1556* [The protocols of the convent of Cluj-Mănăştur, 1289-1556], 2 vols. (Budapest, 1990: *A Magyar Országos Levéltár kiadványai* 2.17), pp. 133-136.

[8] E.g. CZOBOR, "A családi levéltárak", pp. 390-391, 436.

[9] CSUKOVITS, "A középkori írástudók", p. 11.

situm et conservatum".[10] The visitation of the Esztergom chapter in 1397 also mentioned the sacristy as the place where documents were deposited.[11] In churches lacking sacristies the towers could fulfil similar functions.

Adding a new sacristy to an earlier church or rebuilding the existing one in the late Middle Ages was relatively frequent in Hungary. Usually it related to the growing wealth of a settlement or its landowners – or a rivalry with its neighbours. As a new aspect of research, it would be worthwhile to collect the archaeological and architectural evidence on these building activities. Comparing these with references to the role of the sacristy as a storage space for written and other treasures of the community as well as a place for other activities, may shed new light on its role in the connections between churches or monasteries and the lay society surrounding them.

The royal court and the institutions of central administration began the systematic collection of their documents in the last quarter of the twelfth century.[12] The initiative came from king Béla III, who also played an instrumental role in the introduction of written petitions into the royal administration of justice. Still, until the beginning of the fourteenth century only documents connected to royal possessions were kept under the king's control, while the most important charters of donations and privileges that did not directly affect the royal estates were deposited at the collegiate chapter of Fehérvár (see Chapter 2).

New measures in the arrangement of the royal archives were undertaken during the reigns of king Charles I and his son, Louis I. The most important of these was the introduction of the so-called *libri regii*, the central register books of charters issued by the royal chancery.[13] Registering of documents had been a well-known practice in the Papal Curia, and was adopted from there by several other lay and ecclesiastical courts during the thirteenth and fourteenth

[10] Hunyadi, "The Knights of St. John", p. 514.

[11] F. Kollányi, "Visitatio capituli e. m. Strigoniensis anno 1397", *Történelmi Tár* 24 (1901), pp. 71-106, 239-272 ; N.C. Tóth, "Az esztergom-szentistváni prépostság második vizitációja" [The second visitation of the provostry of Esztergom-Szentistván], *Egyháztörténeti Szemle* 15.1 (2014), pp. 3-23, at p. 16.

[12] A. Kubinyi, "A királyi kancellária és udvari kápolna Magyarországon a XII. század közepén" [The royal chancery and the court chapel in Hungary in the mid-twelfth century], *Levéltári Közlemények* 46 (1975), pp. 59-121; I. Hajnal, "Die Kanzlei König Bélas IV", Hungarian version: *Turul* 32 (1914), pp. 1-42.

[13] The most detailed, old, but still reliable study on the *libri regii* is I. Hajnik, *A királyi könyvek a vegyes házakbeli királyok korszakában* [The 'royal books' in the period between 1301 and 1526] (Budapest, 1879: *Értekezések a történelmi tudományok köréből*).

centuries. In Naples, the homeland of the subsequent Hungarian branch of the Angevins, the royal chancery registered the issued charters from 1265 onwards. As to fourteenth-century Hungarian practice, the current register books were kept at the royal chancery by specially appointed clerks named *conservatores*. The full volumes were stored in the treasury (the *domus tavernicalis*) of the Buda palace. It was also towards the end of Louis's reign that the *capella regia*, another place where archives were kept, first appeared in the sources.[14]

The noble counties also embraced administrative literacy, both as recipients and as issuers of charters, soon after the establishment of their self-government as the forum of the local landed nobility, around the mid-thirteenth century. Their early acquaintance with paper as a writing material and its regular use, as was discussed at the outset of Chapter 3, shows the rapid take-off of their written administration. However, the fact that the earliest extant documents issued by the county authorities go back to the late thirteenth or early fourteenth century (with great regional variation) does not mean that a systematic collection and arrangement of documents also started at that early date. The administrative structure of the counties was built up gradually, and the real development of the county archives did not begin before the late fourteenth century. Before this time the jurisdiction of the county had not extended to cases that made the long-term safekeeping of records necessary. Likewise, this explains why drawing up register books or protocols was not on the agenda of the county administration until the end of the Middle Ages.

Private archives of the leading noble families were also established around the turn of the twelfth century. They emerged as recipients' archives par excellence, and remained such until the end of the Middle Ages. Documents issued by private persons, even if they possessed a personal seal or signet ring, did not have any legal validity outside the scope of their private affairs. Thus, apart from charters connected to the possession of landed property, only documents like ledgers or missives concerning the administration of larger estates entered the family collections. For keeping accounts of the estates, the richest families relied on the help of learned men (*litterati*) who were employed as their *familiares* or servants to take care of the administration. Otherwise the storage and use of the documents, as part of the family treasures, had to be arranged either within the family (often in one of their castles) or in cooperation with an ecclesiastical body.

[14] I. Takács, "Königshof und Hofkunst in Ungarn in der späten Anjouzeit", in: *Sigismundus rex et imperator*, pp. 68-86, at p. 71.

The Advent and Advantage of Civic Archives: Storage and Safekeeping

It is impossible to put an exact date to the appearance of archives in each town in the way one can find the date of the first mention of a notary or the earliest extant charter. The development of the archives was a more piecemeal process. In the first decades of their existence, civic archives were primarily recipients' archives, their main concern being the safekeeping of the royal charters that granted the town's privileges. This was the basis of the later 'secret archives', the most valuable part of the civic collections. In fact, in this early period, "documents were a treasure to be guarded, and not a working administrative collection".[15] This situation changed during the next couple of centuries. In the following paragraphs, I shall survey what records were collected and kept, where and how. Since the placement and physical conditions greatly determined what kind of material could be stored, I shall start with the location.

It is uncertain whether the emerging urban communities initially kept their collected documents with their elected judges, in their parish church, or at a close-by place of authentication. All options had pros and cons.

Judges were vested with authority by the community, but their person frequently changed, and their house was not necessarily safe and fireproof. Nevertheless, as the example of market towns that copied the practice of royal towns shows, this was the most obvious option. The judge was in charge of the seal and the money chest of the community, and the meetings of the town council also took place in his house, where consulting or depositing certain documents may have become necessary.

Urban parish churches were by the late thirteenth century usually built in stone and had a suitable tower or sacristy, and the priests, usually elected by the burghers, represented continuity between the council elections. However, they had to obey the bishops just as much as the townspeople, the patrons of the parish.

The places of authentication had the necessary storage place and the best-skilled personnel to handle the records, but were not under civic patronage and often were not present in the town either. In any case, until the advent of paper

[15] This fitting description was applied to the documents kept in the Wasserturm of Lucerne by R. HEAD, "Knowing like a State: The transformation of political knowledge in Swiss archives, 1450-1770", *The Journal of Modern History* 75 (2003), pp. 745-782, at p. 757, quoted by M. JUCKER, "Urban literacy and urban Ssecrecy? Some new approaches to an old problem", in: *Writing and the Administration of Medieval Towns*, pp. 231-241.

documents, the collections only comprised a few dozen items per town, which could easily fit into a small chest.[16]

The preferred solutions indeed varied from one town to the other. In Bardejov, for example, the municipal archives were stored in the Chapel of St. Barbara on the upper floor of the sacristy in the local St. Giles parish church until the early sixteenth century.[17] Keeping the documents in custody of a church was a plausible solution elsewhere, too, since most towns did not have a town hall until quite late. The example of the town hall and its 'notarial apartment' in the Old Town of Prague built in the 1290s did not become a viable model for Hungary (with the possible exception of Esztergom) for quite a few decades. In Pressburg, the collegiate chapter took care of the town's few charters until the 1350s, and the Hospitallers of Sopron probably offered the same service. The judge's house appeared as a place for council meetings and document storage, for instance at Zagreb and Trnava. For many incipient civic archives, no information is preserved as to where exactly they were kept. However, the best and most reasonable long-term solution was to use the town hall for this purpose – once the town could afford to have one and, more importantly, the social need for such a building emerged. In most urban centres of the kingdom of Hungary town halls were not set up or built until as late as the fifteenth or early sixteenth century. Once established, "the town hall also grew already in medieval times as an office-building", providing space for administering justice, operating the chancery, and organising and controlling trade (which is not our focus here).[18]

In a few fortunate cases the combination of architectural and archival research sheds light on the process how the town halls took shape and how the archival function was accommodated in them. The buildings in question originated as elite dwellings of the middling or lower nobility, who moved to the

[16] LAKATOS, *Hivatali írásbeliség*, pp. 84-85; PÉTER, "Az egyszerű ember", pp. 345-347 on the town chest.

[17] *A magyar levéltártörténet kronológiája* [The choronology of Hungarian archival history], ed. K. DÓKA, V. MÜLLER, and M. RÉFI OSZKÓ (Budapest, 2000), pp. 27-39; IVÁNYI, *Bártfa*, p. V-VI, quotes the parish accounts from 1487: "*Item exposita super labore et edificatione reservatorii privilegiorum in capella Sancte Barbare*". The new *almarium* for keeping the records in the town hall was ordered by the town in 1511.

[18] J. MAJOROSSY, "From the judge's house to the town's house: Town halls in medieval Hungary", in: *Rathäuser als multifunktionale Räume der Repräsentation, der Parteiungen und des Geheimnisses*, ed. S.C. PILS, M. SCHEUTZ, CH. SONNLECHNER, and S. SPEVAK (Innsbruck, 2012: *Forschungen und Beiträge zur Wiener Stadtgeschichte* 55), pp. 155-210, table 1 at pp. 193-194; quotation from p. 191.

Fig. 43 Architectural changes of the town hall complex in Pressburg from the late thirteenth to the seventeenth century. Reproduced from: HOLČÍK, *Bratislavská radnica*.

emerging towns (often previous centres of royal counties) during the great social transformations of the thirteenth century. These families constituted the earliest urban leadership; their members were often elected as judges and used the *comes* title.[19] Their houses were built on plots in the town centres and consisted of a one-storey wooden building facing the street or square, and a vertically structured, multi-storey tower-like stone building at the back of the plot.[20]

[19] J. ŠEDIVÝ, "Najstarší patriciát v stredovekej Bratislave: šľachtici alebo mešťania?" [The oldest patriciate of medieval Pressburg: nobles or burghers?], *Forum Historiae* online journal 1 (2008), at http://forumhistoriae.sk/-/najstarsi-patriciat-v-stredovekej-bratislave-slachtici-alebo-mestania (last accessed: 20.05.2018); SZENDE, "Von der Gespanschaftsburg", pp. 400-405.

[20] J. PIEKALSKI, "Die Rolle der Wohntürme bei der Entwicklung städtischen Wohnens im 12. und 13. Jahrhundert im Mitteleuropa", *Offa* 63-64 (2006-2007), pp. 173-196; P. MITCHELL, "Early stone houses in Vienna", *Fontes Urbis Medii Aevi* 3 (2006), pp. 18-25; G. ENTZ, "Városi

In the late fourteenth or early fifteenth century some of these 'private towers' were transferred to the communal sphere by becoming town hall towers. Although the evidence is somewhat conjectural, this was presumably the case of Vienna's *Altes Rathaus* at Salvatorgasse 7.[21] It is more certifiable, however, that the same happened in two Hungarian towns by the western border. First, in 1387 the town of Pressburg purchased a house with a tower ("*domus cum turri*") in the middle of the town, that is, the corner building on the Main Square "*pro pretorio seu domo consilii*". The house originally belonged to the descendants of one of the old elite families, the sons of *comes* Jacob, a former judge of the town, but the seller in 1387 was Ysaak, a Jew from Marchegg, to whom the house had been pledged. From that time onwards up to the present, the tower on the corner was used, eventually extended and embellished, as a town hall tower, and included storage facilities for the town's collected documents (Fig. 43).[22]

The second example (or rather examples) of Sopron are architecturally less spectacular, but equally instructive. The town hall moved three times during the fifteenth century, and all three buildings had towers from before. The first building (Kolostor utca 11) was donated to the town by king Sigismund in 1422 "*pro domo iudiciali seu pretorio*". The ruler acquired the house by escheat from a Jew called Wolf, who probably fell victim to the pogrom in Vienna (the *Wiener Gesera*) in 1421. In full accordance with what had been said before, the petitioners approaching the king were the mayor of Sopron and our old acquaintance, the notary Konrad Ernst. The pompous words that justified the king's donation reflect Sigismund's spirit, but may also reveal some of the arguments that the town's deputies brought forward:

> *pro bono commodo et utilitate eiusdem, ut eadem nostra civitas regalis nostris regiis favoribus prosecuta gaudeat plena populo, ampliorisque profectus optata suscipiat incrementa ...*

lakótornyok a középkori Magyarországon" [Urban dwelling towers in medieval Hungary] *Soproni Szemle* 40 (1986), pp. 339-342.

21 R. Perger, "Wohntürme im mittelalterlichen Wien", *Beiträge zur Mittelalterarchäologie in Österreich* 8 (1992), pp. 103-115; F. Opll, "Das älteste Wiener Rathaus", *Jahrbuch des Vereins für Geschichte der Stadt Wien* 46 (1990), pp. 107-122.

22 S.P. Holčík, *Bratislavská radnica* [The Town Hall of Pressburg] (Bratislava, 1990); J. Majorossy, "From the judge's house", pp. 164-165.

for its good, convenience and benefit, so that, supported by royal generosity, this royal town of ours enjoys the growth of its population and receives the desired increase of greater success.[23]

With such a prelude, the town had presumably no word in the choice of the building, but quickly discovered further uses for the tower. In the accounts preserved from 1426 onwards, there are regular entries concerning repair works on the tower: for covering its roof with tiles, installing a new iron door, re-plastering its basement room, and so on. The lower part of the tower was used as a prison, the upper level(s) probably as archives, as in the case of Vienna. The expenses of the transformation of this dwelling house into a town hall included an advertisement board for the meeting room of the council (*tauel*; *täffl die in der ratstuben hangt*), a specific form of literacy for which we seldom have evidence. For the subsequent two town halls of Sopron, Fő tér 7, and later Fő tér 1, taken over in 1459 and 1496 respectively, it is reasonable to assume that the town magistrates already kept in mind the need for a strong and safe tower when purchasing the buildings (Fig. 44).[24]

Account books of other towns may also occasionally contain evidence for measures taken to improve the storage facilities of the documents at the town hall. In Prešov, where a *stuba pretorii* had existed by 1429, a room designated for storing the town privileges is mentioned in 1510, when its windows were reinforced with an iron grid made by a blacksmith. The grid was then painted by a local craftsman, who on another occasion executed a painting for the court room: "*Antonio fabro pro cratere ad fenestram conservationis privilegiorum den. 250; Petro pictori ex eo quod craterem fenestre coloravit den 50*" ("to Anthony the carpenter, for the window bars for the conservation of the charters of privilege, 250 den.; to Peter the painter, for having painted the window bars, 50 den."). This shows how the town magistrates intended to prevent the corrosion of the iron bars and improve both the safety and the physical appearance

[23] HÁZI, *Sopron*, 1.2, pp. 233-234. It is to be noted that this was a period of internal turmoil in Sopron, when the community revolted against the council, as it was later entered in the 'Second Town Book'; see above, Chapter 3, n. 104.

[24] K. MOLLAY, "A három középkori városháza" [The three medieval town halls], *Soproni Szemle* 31 (1977), pp. 234-247. Mollay identifies the building as Kolostor utca 9, but recent research by I. HOLL and F. DÁVID point at the neighbouring Kolostor utca 11 instead. I thank Ferenc Dávid for his personal communication. The accounts of the main refurbishment in 1426-27 are edited in HÁZI, *Sopron*, 2.2, pp. 347, 375-398; for further expenses see *ibid.*, 2.3, *passim*.

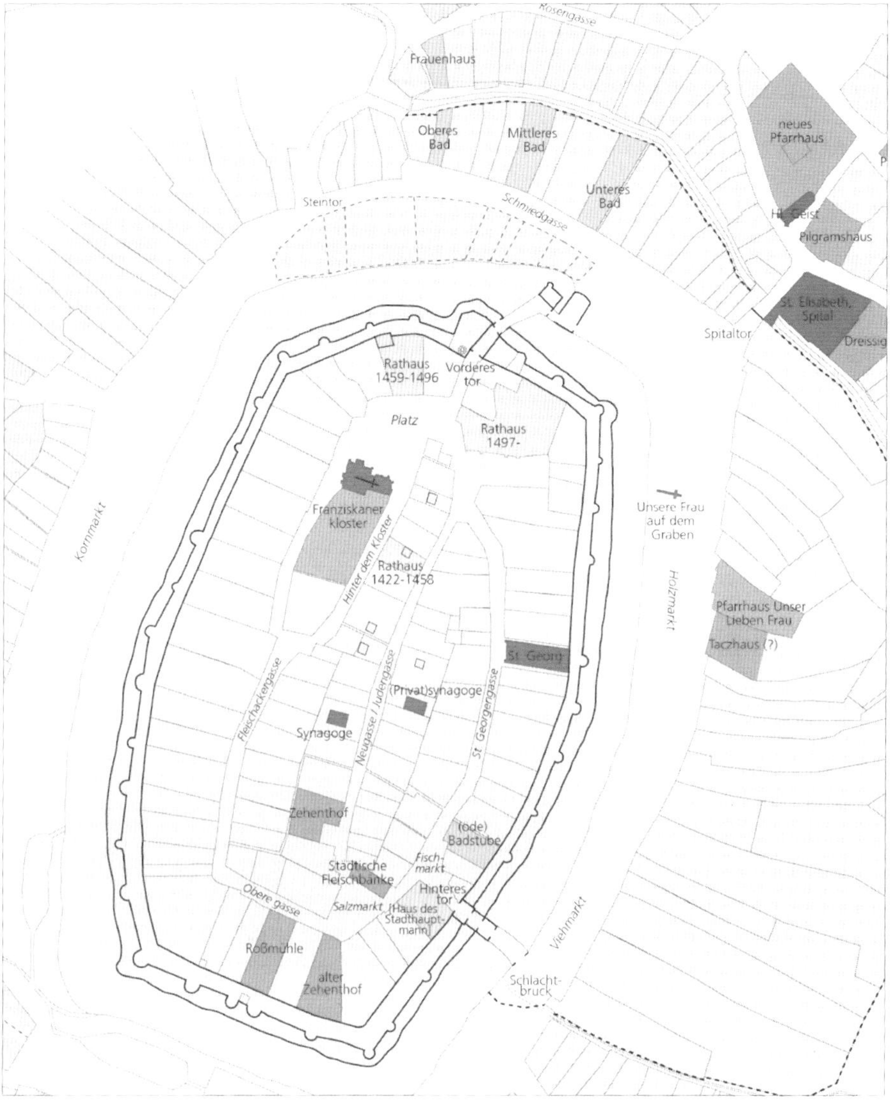

Fig. 44 The three subsequent medieval town halls in Sopron. Map A.3.3, in: JANKÓ *et al.*, *Sopron*. Cartography: Péter Banyó. Reproduced with permission.

Fig. 45 The town hall of Bardejov seen from the west. Photo: Béla Zsolt Szakács. Reproduced with permission.

of the room at the same time.[25] In the case of Bardejov, the entire set of accounts for the building and decoration of the town hall between 1505 and 1511 have been preserved (Fig. 45).[26]

Considering the uncertainties around the placement of the civic archives, it is even more significant that the collections were kept together, and kept continuously growing. Once the towns' written activities became independent from the church or the places of authentication, the charters concerning the community must have been handed over to the council. This is suggested by the fact that the earliest documents of the best-preserved town archives date from the middle of the thirteenth century. The other way in which the old stock was increased was through acquiring property for communal ownership and incorporating the charters assuring their provenance and property rights. This

[25] B. Iványi, "Eperjes középkori festői" [Medieval painters at Eperjes], *Muzeumi és Könyvtári Értesítő* 11 (1917), pp. 88-116, at pp. 100-101.

[26] Á. Mikó, "A bártfai városháza. Adalékok a Jagelló-kori reneszánsz történetéhez Felső-Magyarországon" [The town hall of Bardejov: Data on the history of Renaissance in the Jagellonian era in Upper Hungary], *Művészettörténeti Értesítő* 53 (2004), pp. 19-52.

process can be observed in Sopron, where the town systematically extended its territory by the acquisition of seigneurial rights to the neighbouring villages, building a kind of *contado*. The royal title deeds of these lands, given to their former owners, constitute much of the pre-1350 material of the civic archives.[27]

The bulk of the material, and with it the urge to find a long-term solution for its storage, exponentially increased after the advent of paper documents. Parallel to the introduction of town books, the management of the original charters in the municipal archives also became more professional. In towns that have maintained well preserved archives from the Middle Ages up to the present, e.g. Bardejov, Buda, Pressburg, Košice, Prešov, or Sopron, this process is traceable by the analysis of the short summaries on the dorses of the charters. These contemporary notes were written by notaries to facilitate retrieving the relevant charters in case they were needed as evidence, and indicate that the largest municipal archives were thematically arranged from the mid-fifteenth century onwards.

Targeted investigation of the material between the mid-thirteenth and the mid-fifteenth century in four town archives, Sopron and Pressburg in the west and Prešov and Bardejov in the north-eastern part of Hungary, indicates that there are discernible similarities between the main tendencies in the composition of the material as far as the issuers are concerned and the changes it underwent over time (Fig. 46.a-d). Royal charters prevail in the stock everywhere up to 1387, and continue to represent a significant proportion even after that date. Royal dignitaries took over part of the correspondence with towns after 1387, which was a sign of increasing professionalisation and departmentalisation in the central administration. The places of authentication made their strongest contribution in the fourteenth century. However, they retained their presence even in the later decades, especially in the context of the towns' relations to noblemen, but also in carrying out orders from the central administration such as conducting investigations or introducing a new owner into a landed property, for instance as neighbours of the town. As was discussed in Chapters 2 and 3, the administrative literacy of the towns themselves took off, depending on the locality, in the second half of the fourteenth or the first decades of the fifteenth century. This was reflected in the archival stock both through charters

[27] These documents are edited in HÁZI, *Sopron*, 1.1. The process of territorial expansion through the acquisition of seigniorial villages was typical for other Hungarian towns as well (Pressburg, Košice, Baia Mare, Cluj, etc.) and should be considered when analysing the constitution of their civic archives.

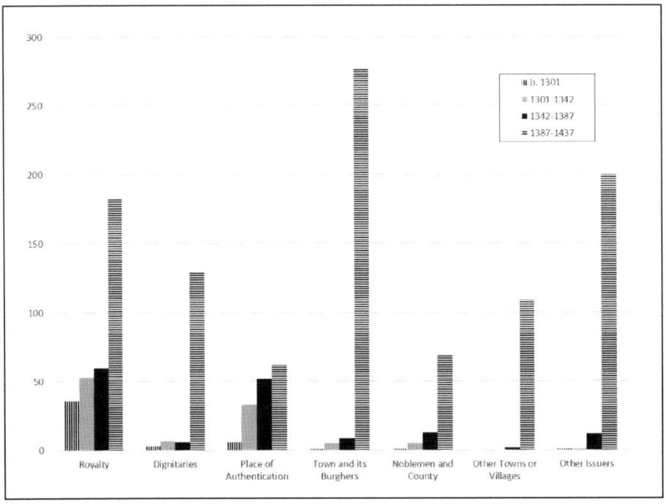

Sopron

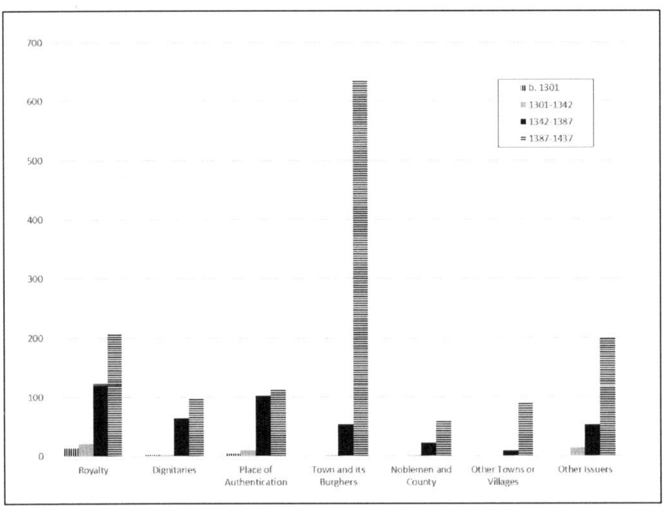

Pressburg

Fig. 46.a-d The distribution of documents by different issuers in the town archives of Sopron, Pressburg, Prešov, and Bardejov up to 1437. The white bar in the 'Town and its Burghers' column shows the proportion of municipal books in the preservation of documents. Graphs prepared by the author on the basis of the respective editions or inventories of archival holdings.

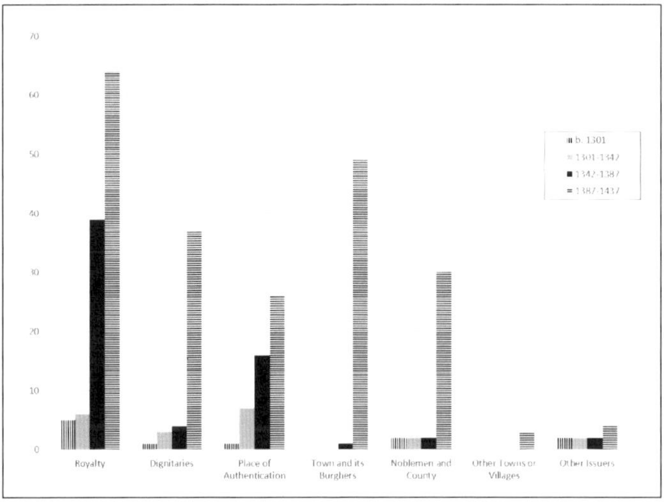

Prešov

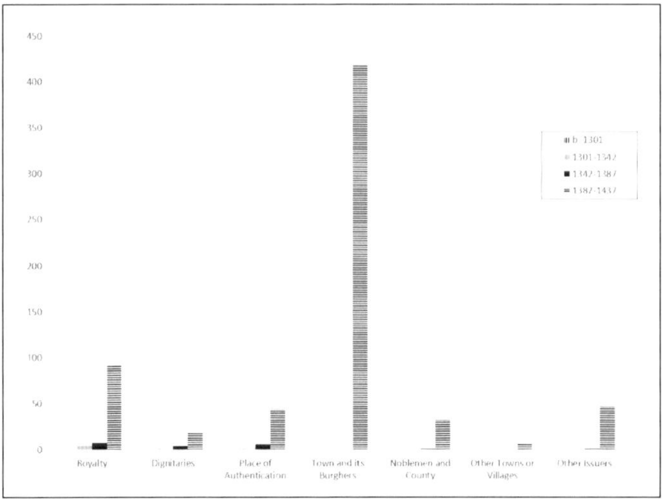

Bardejov

and correspondence received from other towns, and through keeping records (drafts and books) of their own production. Receiving deeds and missives written by private persons followed suit in western Hungary simultaneously, while in the north-eastern towns it started only after the middle of the fifteenth century.

Inside the archive rooms, the charters were kept in containers that were either made especially for this purpose, or sometimes (re)purposed for storing documents. Presumably the same arrangements applied for towns as for archives of other authorities. The names for some of these containers indicate a smaller size (*ladula, cistula, vasculum, scatularium*), others were bigger versions of the same shape (*cista*, *vas*, *retentorium*) or even larger *scrinia*. The latter term, which denoted a piece of furniture similar to a chest (*scrinium seu cista*) rather than a modern cabinet, was the most frequent name for furniture in the medieval archives. The most precious charters had their own individual containers (*theca*, *pixis*) or linen bags. The chests (*cistae*) were often strengthened with iron bands and with a lock (*cista serata*).[28] A remarkable reference concerning the storage of documents in Sibiu can be found in a letter of a burgher from Braşov. *Magister Paulus* was charged with representing his town in a court case concerning the payment of tolls at Oradea. After admitting that he had problems with finding the necessary documents, he proposed that "*nos literas et privilegia certa in ladula nostra repositis desuper habeamus, quem admodum ipse Cibinienses triplicia sua privilegia adduxerunt*" ("we should have our charters and certain letters of privilege stored in our chest, in the way as those of Sibiu keep the third / threefold examples / copies of their privileges").[29] This instance shows how best practices were followed as models in a regional context.

The only surviving medieval pieces of furniture certainly used for storing the stock of civic archives are the bookcase and chest of Bardejov. The former is now kept in the National Museum of Hungary in Budapest. This monumental, 430 cm long and 238 cm high construction consists of three pairs of double

[28] CZOBOR, "A családi levéltárak", pp. 385-386; IVÁNYI, *Eperjes*, pp. 4-5.

[29] DF 246380, edited in UGDS 7, No. 4128, pp. 101-102. Quoted by A. DINCĂ, "Preserving charters in late medieval Sibiu", *Transylvanian Review* 24.4 (2015), pp. 69-76. The editor of the text identifies Paul as town notary, but the script of the letter gives a rather casual impression. On the court case, see A. KUBINYI, "A városi rend kialakulásának gazdasági feltételei és a főváros kereskedelme a XV. század végén" [The economic conditions of the formation of towns as an estate and the trade of the capital at the end of the fifteenth century], *Tanulmányok Budapest Múltjából* 15 (1963), pp. 189-226.

Fig. 47 Archives cabinet in the town hall of Bardejov. This is the only purpose-made furniture for any civic archives surviving in its original place in the medieval kingdom of Hungary. Photo: Béla Zsolt Szakács. Reproduced with permission.

chests with double front doors on each. It is a transitional type before the cabinets emerging later. It was designed around 1480 for the parish church of the town, primarily to contain the library, but the archives of the town were also deposited here until a special chest was ordered for the town hall in 1511: "*Anno 1511. Item magistro Johanni de almario pro conservatione literarum privilegiarum facto fl. 9½*". The latter piece of furniture, an ash cabinet with four doors can still be seen on the first floor of the town hall of Bardejov (Fig. 47).[30] The documents were stored conveniently next door to the hall where the judicial procedures took place, under the auspices of the depiction of the Last Judgment.[31]

Besides these solid pieces of furniture, bags (*capsae*) were also hung from the ceiling to protect the parchment from rodents. The disadvantage of these bags, as that of some other small containers, was that the charters had to be folded up to fit into them, and unfolded each time the keepers of the collection were searching for a particular document. As this type of handling potentially damaged the originals, from the fourteenth century onwards an abstract of the contents was written on the dorse to facilitate the search. Apparently, the most significant or most frequently used documents were provided with such summaries first, and it took several decades if not a century before this practice became common.[32] From the middle of the fifteenth century, some Latin charters were provided with summaries in the vernacular.

Organising the documents was introduced gradually, as the number of items and the need for looking them up increased. Since even those archives that have survived in a fairly intact state have been rearranged several times since the Middle Ages, the one-time order of the documents can only be reconstructed on the basis of the special signs found on the charters and the few contemporary inventories that make reference to the arrangement of the material. The most common practice was to create a system based on the subjects and genres of the documents: charters of privileges were usually separated from the rest of the archives, and so were other documents connected to privi-

[30] KOVALOVSZKI, *Gothic and Renaissance Furniture*, pp. 10-13, tables II-III; IVÁNYI, *Bártfa*, p. VI.

[31] B. SZEGHYOVÁ, "The topography of justice: Symbols, rituals, and the representation of urban justice in early modern Hungary", in: *Faces of Community: Images, Symbols and Performances in East Central European Towns (1400-1700)*, ed. K. HORNÍČKOVÁ (Lanham, MD, 2018), pp. 65-90.

[32] KUMOROVITZ, "A leleszi konvent", p. 225. Bálint Lakatos has come to this conclusion based on his editorial work on the ZsO series.

leges. A further important section was formed by charters concerning landed properties (donations, *seisins*, perambulations, etc.), grouped according to the estates they referred to. Documents of judicial processes (letters of summons, advocacy, complaints, sentences, and so on) and economic administration (accounts, receipts, contracts, tax lists) were also kept separately, and, to the great detriment of historical research, were culled from time to time. The signs of identification, which appeared in urban municipal archives as well, were the forerunners of modern reference or classification numbers.[33] As by-products of organising these archives, lists or inventories of the documents were compiled, sometimes including short thematic abstracts as well.[34] On the basis of these summaries, many items can be identified that still form part of the original collection, or were transferred to other archives in the meantime, but it is also apparent that there are big lacunae in the extant stock.

The keepers of the documents can seldom be identified by name. The practical tasks were certainly performed by the notary and his scribes, while the moral responsibility was taken by the mayor or the judge. We are better provided with personal data on municipal archivists from the sixteenth century. The most notable early organisation campaigns were undertaken by Hans Scheutzlich in Košice (1503-1512), Christian Baumgartner (Pomarius) in Sibiu (1546) and in Braşov (1552), Georgius Seraphin in Bistriţa (1562), and Gergely Diósy in Cluj (1592).[35] As the dates suggest, these were projects with a humanist agenda, but references to the earlier stock of the archives make the lists compiled by these sixteenth-century notaries relevant for medievalists as well.

Other private persons, especially burghers, also possessed collections of documents (in most cases it would be an exaggeration to call them archives), but these were almost exclusively recipients' holdings. Most references to such collections are known from last wills. Townspeople produced written material

[33] See, e.g. their description in the introductions to IVÁNYI, *Eperjes*, pp. 4-5; IVÁNYI, *Bártfa*, pp. IV-V; PÁLFFY, "Városi levéltáraink", pp. 355-370.

[34] The earliest inventories were published as appendices to the studies analysing them. A thorough comparative study of early archival notes and inventories would be highly desirable.

[35] HALAGA, "A kassai városi könyvek", pp. 533-534; FLÓRA, "*Laborem circumspecti domini notarii*", pp. 323-326; G. NUSSBÄCHER, "Din activitatea arhivistică a lui Christian Pomarius" [The activity of Christian Pomarius as archivist], *Revista Arhivelor* 1965, No. 2, pp. 169-180; G. GÜNDISCH, "Zur Geschichte des Archivs der Stadt Hermannstadt und der sächsischen Nation", in: *120 Jahre öffentliches Archiv in Siebenbürgen* (Sibiu, 1996). KOSÁRY, KULCSÁR, and SZAKÁLY, *Bevezetés*, summarises the information available on the early ordering of the archives under each locality, wherever available.

themselves (accounts, receipts, private letters, and so on), but these had such limited legal value that they were not considered worth keeping for very long.[36]

Binding Records: The Example of Sopron[37]

The storage and preservation of documents, as it was discussed above, mirrored the consciousness and inner organisation of urban society. The case study of the archival material in Sopron demonstrates that the turning points in its pragmatic literacy can be determined and explained by following the history of the town, parallel with the development of its archives and the forms and bindings of documents therein. The results also highlight the way in which the acquisition of town halls influenced the storage and even the binding of the archival stock (see Table 3). In Sopron, more than 40 Hebrew and 325 Latin codex folios, mainly from medieval liturgical (and to a smaller extent, legal, theological, philosophical, and medical) manuscripts were used for binding local archival material, first and foremost various town books and accounts. Based on the dates of the documents found in the bindings and other archival material, it was possible to define the period in which the reuse took place, trace the spread of this practice, and compare it with other preferred binding methods.[38]

[36] The validity of private documents was limited even in internal cases. E.g., Chapter 376 of the *Ofner Stadtrecht* stated that merchants' accounts could be accepted as proof of payment only up to the value of one *marca*, and even so only if a merchant referred to his own accounts. See *Ofner Stadtrecht*, p. 182.

[37] The observations summarised here were made during my work on a project to determine the archival origins of medieval codex fragments in Sopron: K. SZENDE, "Einleitung: Zur Geschichte der Sammlungen", in: *Mittelalterliche lateinische Handschriftenfragmente in Sopron*, ed. E. MADAS (Budapest, 2006: *Fragmenta et Codices in Bibliothecis Hungariae* 5), pp. 7-16; a more detailed study on the same subject in Hungarian: K. SZENDE, "'*In geschribn pergament einbunden*': A könyvkötéshez felhasznált kódextöredékek társadalom- és kultúrtörténeti összefüggései Sopronban [Fragments of codices used for bookbinding in Sopron in social and cultural context], *Magyar Könyvszemle* 123 (2007), pp. 278-310.

[38] Although the codex folios are all medieval, much of the archival material bound in them dates to the sixteenth and seventeenth centuries; this material is not discussed here.

Table 3 Correlation of town history, archival bindings and chancery development in Sopron

Town history	**History of archives**	**Bindings**
1250-1300 transformation from military-administrative centre into royal town	first documents received, first preserved privileges (1277)	–
1300-1350 – economic development, market privileges – building of threefold wall system	own seal; charters issued in cooperation with the local place of authentication; new seal in 1340	–
1350-1400 – extension of suburbs – export / import customs collection – acquisition of neighbouring villages	– establishment of separate town chancery, with town notary as paid employee – acquisition of family archives pertaining to properties bought from noble families	First documents in booklet format (1370); first town books of mixed contents; parchment binding, paper as main writing material
1400-1450 – staple right (1402) – acquisition of town hall by royal donation (1422) – ranked among the most important towns of Hungary	– notary Konrad Ernst, exile from Vienna (1417-1451) – further scribes beside him – first specialised town book (*Gerichtsbuch*)	– parchment with Hebrew text reused as binder of tax list (1424) – town book in red parchment binding
1450-1500 – town pledged to Frederick III Habsburg (1441-1463) – further privileges for annual fairs – court of appeal for neighbouring towns – new town halls bought by the town (1459, 1496)	– further differentiation of chancery, various seals – first attempts to compile a register of documents (1469) – further specialised town books – public library beside parish church	– various leather bindings for town books – occasional use of parchment with Latin or Hebrew text as binders (1460s, 1496)

1500-1550 – trial against followers of the Reformation (1524) – expulsion of the Jews (1526) – steady supporter of Habsburg rule	– special furniture and bags ordered in third town hall for archival material – regular series of town books, chamber accounts – registers of new burghers (from 1535) – document collections of guilds and private persons	– regular binding of certain series (esp. chamber accounts, tax and tithe list) in reused parchment – mainly Hebrew codex leaves reused between 1528 and 1541

In the first century of its existence, there was no need to employ a professional bookbinder at the Sopron municipal writing office. The routine jobs connected to the technical preparation of documents, including the binding of the first couple of town books with soft parchment covers in the late fourteenth century, were executed either by the notaries or scribes themselves, or by the schoolmasters (Fig. 48). The first person known by name who bound books in Sopron was precisely that, "*herr Hans, diezeit schulmaister*". He bound some books for a local priest who mentioned this in his last will in 1400.[39]

The next pieces of evidence about binding, this time already from the civic archives, follow immediately on the acquisition of the town hall. One of these is the first thematically arranged town book, the previously discussed *Gerichtsbuch* (1423-1531) in purple parchment binding; the second is the tax register for the year 1424, bound in a sheet from a Hebrew codex (H. 18).[40] This volume is the first extant tax list that covers the entire town – the earlier ones were, as noted in Chapter 3, handed over to the Master of the Treasury in 1422. This Hebrew fragment is a folio from a liturgical codex – the only one of its kind known from Sopron.[41] Its demotion to bookbinding material may be connected to the *Wiener Gesera* of 1420-1421, just as the death of Wolf, the former owner of the building that became the town hall. The new owners of the

[39] Last will of Urban von Weyten, chaplain of the Corpus Christi altar of the Sopron parish church, 21 April 1400, ed. in: HÁZI, *Sopron*, 2.1, pp. 178-183.

[40] HÁZI, *Sopron*, 2.2, pp. 316-337. The numbering of the codex fragments refers to the shelf marks in the Sopron Archives.

[41] On the Jewish ban on selling liturgical manuscripts to Christians, see M. KEIL, "Heilige Worte – Schriften des Abscheus: Der Umgang mit Büchern als Paradigma des jüdisch-christlichen Spannungsverhältnisses", in: *Text als Realie* (Wien, 2003: *Sitzungsberichte der ÖAW, Phil.-Hist. Kl.* 704), pp. 49-61.

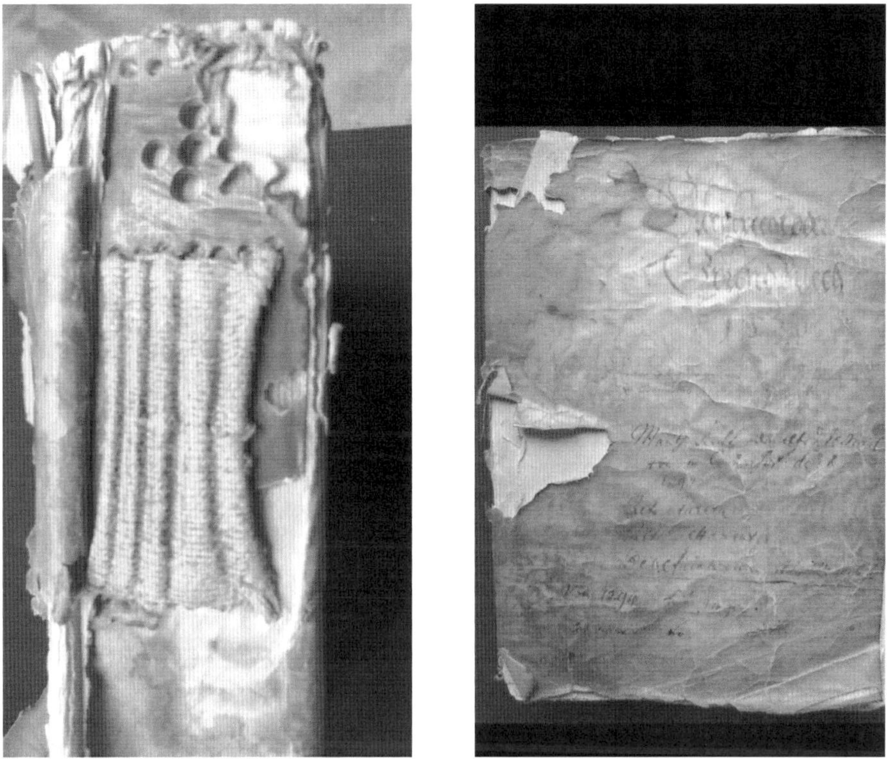

Fig. 48 Spine and binding of the first municipal book of Sopron, started in 1390 (SVL DL 2988). Photos by the author. Reproduced with the permission of the Sopron Archives.

building may have found the manuscript on the spot, or it may have reached Sopron via the Viennese second-hand trade of parchment. In any case, it is reasonable to assume that there was a connection between the acquisition of the new town hall and the appearance of new sorts of bound documents.

Not all archival materials needed binding. The single-sheet documents were of course kept by themselves, folded or unfolded, as has been mentioned above, in leather or linen bags. For smaller booklet formats, consisting of 8-12 folios, tying them with a hemp cord sufficed. For instance, the tax and tithe lists after 1424 were only tied together with a cord, and reinforced at the fold with small (4-5 cm long) pieces of cut parchment with some writing. Protective covers were only needed for thicker booklets of several sheets, particularly if

Fig. 49 The Main Square of Sopron, with the possible image of the buildings on its northern side. The building in the middle, with a tower in the back yard by the town wall, was the second town hall. Drawing by János Sedlmayr. Reproduced with permission.

they were frequently consulted or in continuous use. Such documents included the tax registers and the accounts, first emerging with the professionalisation of municipal financial administration, as well as the municipal books. Contemporary bindings can thus provide information about the frequency of use and the demand for information retrieval from archival documents.

In 1459 the second town hall at Fő tér 7 was taken into use (Fig. 49). This was the middle building on the northern side of the main square, clearly a more prestigious location than its predecessor, with a still extant massive stone tower in its north-eastern corner. The move coincided with the earliest surviving reference to the reorganisation of the archival material. Hans Ziegler, the notary at the time, divided the records into two groups, separating the still valid charters from the outdated ones. He also compiled a list of the first group, from which only the cover has been preserved, with the inscription:

> *Registrum super universis libertatibus civitatis Sopronienisis per Johannem notarium eiusdem collectum tempore circumspecti domini Philippi Zawkan magistri civium, anno domini etc 60 nono [i.e. 1469] in profesto beate Katherine.*
>
> The register of all the privileges of the town of Sopron, collected by John, civic notary, in the time of the honorable mayor Philipp Zawkan, in 1469.[42]

(A similar list, likewise concentrating on the privileges of the town and their authentic copies kept in the municipal archives, has come down to us from Sibiu.[43]) The reorganisation of the archival material in Sopron may have resulted in an increased consciousness of the physical protection of the documents: from the 1450s and 1460s a further five codex folios were used for bookbinding (Fragm. 30, 65, 212, 213, 250), but there were also other makeshift solutions, such as using rough pieces of parchment or paper sheets with letter drafts.

Documents exceeding one sheet (16 pages) were either covered in the same paper or in earlier parchment charters, which were apparently no longer valid or relevant. Paper with writing was also occasionally recycled as binding mater-

[42] This cover is itself a reused sheet of parchment: Ziegler wrote his text on the back side of Louis I's 1346 confirmation of Charles I's privilegial charter for Sopron. See Házi, *Sopron*, 1.1, p. 89. Perhaps the charter lost its validity because it was not reconfirmed with Louis I's new seal after 1363 (see above, Chapter 2, n. 103).

[43] Dincă, "Preserving charters", p. 73 and n. 15.

Fig. 50 Binding of the *Burgerbuechl und Ächtbuchl* (SVL DL 3830). Photo: Zsolt Kálócz. Reproduced with the permission of the Sopron Archives.

ial: the wine-tithe list from 1447 was bound in a folio from a paper copy of the rhyming grammar by Alexander de Villa Dei (Fragm. 56);[44] the property register of 1459 contained the above-mentioned Hungarian-Latin glossary,[45] in later years the accounts of 1502-1510 were covered in a German broadsheet calendar for 1509 printed in Nuremberg by Wolfgang Huber,[46] to quote a few examples.

These bindings did not require more sophisticated skills than those of an average notary. For more complicated tasks, however, including the binding of further town books, better-trained masters were commissioned on an ad hoc

[44] HÁZI, *Sopron*, 2.3, pp. 378-385. The manuscript was identified by MOLLAY, "Többnyelvűség", pp. 327-332.

[45] J. HÁZI, "A soproni magyar-latin szójegyzék" [The Hungarian-Latin glossary from Sopron], *Magyar Nyelv* 20 (1923), pp. 149-168. The property register: HÁZI, *Sopron*, 2.4, pp. 113-128.

[46] HÁZI, *Sopron*, 2.5, pp. 96-118.

basis. A good example for this is the most artistic bookbinding of the archival collection, the cover of the *Burgerbuechl und Ächtbuchl*, drawn up in 1476 and used until 1548, a cover made of skillfully engraved thick leather (Fig. 50). However, leather engraving was more conventionally used for decorative leatherworking of furniture or dress accessories than bookbinding. There is also a discrepancy between the elaborate cover and the mixed notebook character of the contents of the volume. All this may indicate an incidental acquisition for the chancery. The binding of the *Grundbuch*, drawn up in 1480, is entirely different – Gothic leather binding on wooden plates, decorated with roller stamp and brass fittings –, whereas the *Gedenkbuch* (started in 1492) had a soft purple parchment cover.[47]

The third move of the town hall – as well as the archives – took place in 1497, after the municipal administration acquired an even more spacious block in 1496. The new town hall was on the eastern side of the main square, where it has been located up to the present. The move was commemorated in a festive entry on the first page of the *Grundbuch*.[48] The move to the new building coincides with the binding of the accounts of 1495/1496 in a codex folio (Fragm. 254); this is the first municipal account book bound this way, and it is the reintroduction of this binding method after an interval of 30 years. In 1514 another Hebrew manuscript was reused (H. 19), on which paper was glued on the outside.[49] In this municipal building the charters (*briefe*) were stored in the council room (*ratstuben*) in black linen bags. The accounts of 1523 also mention iron grids for six windows, and the painting of the iron bars, just as had happened in Prešov.[50]

Binding archival volumes in reused codex folios spiked in the late 1520s, when, after the expulsion of the town's Jewish population in 1526, a large amount of parchment became available for secondary use.[51] When this source

[47] É.B. KOROKNAY, "A soproni metszett kötéstábla" [The engraved bookcover from Sopron], *Soproni Szemle* 16 (1962), pp. 164-167; *Erstes Grundbuch*, p. IX, description by Marianne Rozsondai.

[48] *Erstes Grundbuch*, p.1 (f.1r). This entry dates from 1496, although the book was already in use since 1480. Most probably the first folio was deliberately left blank at the outset.

[49] HÁZI, *Sopron*, 2.5, pp. 205-241. Does this mean that the contemporaries intended to cover the Hebrew script?

[50] HÁZI, *Sopron*, 2.5, pp. 420-422; MOLLAY, "A három középkori városháza", p. 245.

[51] Over 40 Hebrew codex fragments were used for binding Sopron's archival material; see SCHEIBER, *Hebräische Kodexüberreste*. See also the letter of complaint by the Sopron Jews of 24 March 1528: "*Item sinagogam nostram devastavere, libros hebraicos exportavere ...*" HÁZI, *Sopron*, 1.7, p. 284.

dried up, discarded liturgical manuscripts were taken over by the bookbinders. The fate of these parchment leaves, turning from mediators of spiritual culture to material protecting more down-to-earth pieces of pragmatic writing, tells two stories at once. The story of the 'life and death' of some liturgical manuscripts also reminds us about a growing need to produce, bind, and safeguard documents in the local archives.

Using Civic Archives

Providing a safe, fire-proof, and orderly storage place for documents was only part of the functions performed by medieval civic archives. These institutions also had to enable – under well-defined and limited circumstances – the retrieval of information contained in the chests and bags. It is hard to make a precise distinction between using the individual charters and using the archives which held them. It may not be necessary to do so either, since, as we have shown above, most documents were in fact incorporated into some kind of archives. Reference to specific written records, decades or centuries after they had been issued, meant looking them up at a place where they could be found and read. Therefore it is reasonable to consider references to using earlier charters as at least indirect evidence of using the relevant archives as well.

The most obvious users of the civic archives were the town magistrates themselves, who were 'the closest to the fire'. The main instances when the *archivum secretum* part of the assemblage was accessed were the renewals of the privileges by the subsequent monarchs. On those occasions the charters had to be taken out, presented to the king by a deputation, and solemnly returned, together with the new acquisition, to their chest. Chapter 3 describes some examples of these 'diplomatic' enterprises, and the notaries' involvement in them *ex officio* (since they were the most knowledgeable about the chancery and legal procedures), as well as the costs that it entailed to get a charter of privilege confirmed.[52]

Transporting the valuable and unique documents carried great risks: it was a privilege in itself to be allowed to present a less precious copy of a charter instead of a golden bull, and to accord full trust to that substitute. The earliest

[52] See the reference to the accounts of Trnava concerning the costs of redeeming and renewing their golden bull after the Hussite attacks, Chapter 3, n. 101 above.

such grace in the urban context was granted to Pest in 1244, in a clause to the privileges that were soon to be taken over by Buda:

> *Verum quia exhibitio privilegii ipsorum existentis sub aurea bulla propter viarum discrimina esse periculosa videbatur, transcriptum eiusdem de verbo ad verbum sub munimine dupplicis sigilli nostri consessimus, tantam presentibus* fidem volentes adhiberi, *ut ad exhibitionem illius nullatenus compellantur.*

> But since it seemed to be risky for them to present their golden bull, due to the dangers of the roads, we granted them our word-for-word transcription under our double seal, willing to *entrust it with such an authority* that they never be compelled to present the original.[53]

Viarum pericula was indeed the most frequently mentioned risk that threatened the documents, but other chances of damage had to be averted likewise. Archives were set up exactly for this purpose.

To act swiftly when a privilege needed to be renewed or when it had to be presented to counteract the violation of a right (for instance when burghers were compelled to pay tolls at a place where they formerly used to enjoy exemption), the validity of the documents was a paramount issue. In principle, privileges were augmented, rather than deleted, and the most recent and updated versions had to be at hand exactly because of this practice. Failing to have a charter resealed by the royal chancery if this was required could also jeopardise its validity. Separating valid from outdated charters, as notary Hans Ziegler did in Sopron when he organised the archival collection in 1469, was essential for efficiently representing the town's interests. Besides the charters of privilege, royal mandates reminding officials or other noblemen to observe the town's prerogatives were also carefully preserved.

In addition to codifying the laws and statutes of a community, old documents were looked up to prove ancient rights, customs, or competence in various issues. Here we may refer again to the *Ofner Stadtrecht*, in which the first chapter contains a clear rationale for using charters. As we see from the author's quotations throughout the text, he indeed heavily relied on the town archives of Buda:

[53] EFHU, 3.2, p. 41 ; republished with small corrections in *Medieval Buda in Context*, pp. 557-558.

> *Hye hebet sich an das Rechtpuch nach Ofner stat rechten, [...] und ist geschriben nach allen ausgesprochen urtaillen vnd nach gueterr löblicher gewonhait, vnd allermaisten nach sag hantfestlicher prieff, damit dy selbe Ofenstat gestifft, gefreyet vnd pegabet wardenn ...*
>
> Here begins the Lawbook according to the town laws of Buda, [...] written on the basis of all pronounced judgments and according to good and laudable customs, and above all following the wording of charters of privilege granted, endowed, and donated to the said town of Buda.[54]

In fact, as Martyn Rady points out, this source base is responsible for the limitations of the work, too, since some of the most complex cases were tackled in the outgoing, and not the incoming charters.[55]

Most users of the archives were involved with the 'present tense' operation of municipal document collections, but there was an acute mental awareness of the potential of the earlier materials. Very few citizens of Buda ever saw Béla IV's Golden Bull or even its transcription, yet when the town needed to prove its exemption from paying tolls at certain toll stations, the magistrates knew that this text had to be exhibited. Likewise, very few Jews ever saw Béla IV's Jewish privileges of 1251, but their prefects knew exactly what they had to have confirmed by kings ascending to the throne.[56]

In the great majority of cases, however, archival material was used for the immediate needs of financial administration or administering justice, meaning that it was produced as evidence in court cases. The evidence could go back to decades or even centuries, because customary law gave priority to earlier rights, for instance when it came to collecting tolls, or to building a watermill by a stream. Economic transactions often necessitated looking up receipts, trade contracts, and records of the purchase of properties.

Full authority was attributed to the town books, which often served as a basis for consulting or reissuing some of the documents entered in them. Marginal notes next to accounts from years back, or recording the execution of a will (for instance, adding *dedit* or *solvit* – often in Latin, even beside German texts) clearly show that the executors revisited the text, not simply as aide memoire, but also using it as a proof of discharging their duties. By the middle

[54] *Ofner Stadtrecht*, cap. 1, p. 58.

[55] RADY, *Medieval Buda*, p. 46; RADY, "The government of medieval Buda", in: *Medieval Buda in Context*, pp. 303-321, at pp. 316-320.

[56] See Chapter 5.

of the fifteenth century, the system of entering transactions into and deleting data from town books was well established. The latter feature deserves special attention. We have already encountered the special term for this act, *ausschreiben*, about pardoning criminals and removing their names from among the outlawed. The same phrase was used for deleting someone's name and obligation from other town books. Of course, it came at a price. For instance, the first *Grundbuch* (property register book) of the town of Sopron included the following remark, glued to the inside cover:

> *Item vermerck das mein herren von wegenn dicz kegenwurtigen grund puchs solhe ordnung gemacht habenn, das ein jeder verkauffer, es sei hewser, weingarten ader wisenn, was er vermaint in das gruntpuch zu fertigen, sol er von einem jeden post gebenn* XXXII *den. vnd von dem selbigen gelde sol der statschreiber nemen* XVI *den. vnd gemaine stat* XVI *den. Item welher sich ausschreiben last, der sol gebenn von ausschreiben* VIII *den. vnd sol der statschreiber von dem selbigen gelde nemen* IIII *den. vnd gemaine stat* IIII *den. vnd das ausschreib gelt sol geben der kawffer.*

> Item note that my lords made the following regulation concerning the present property register, that every seller of a property, be it a house, a vineyard, or meadow that he intends to have included in the Grundbuch, has to give after each item 32 denars, and from this fee the town notary should get 16 denars and the town community 16 denars. Item, if someone wants to have himself deleted from the register, that person has to give 8 denars, and from this sum the town notary receives 4 denars and the town community 4 denars, and the fee for the deletion [of the previous owner] has to be paid by the buyer.[57]

Finally, the consolidation of civic archives is attested by the fact that by the fifteenth century the practice of preserving missives of ephemeral significance developed. Inquiring about the moves of the Hussite troops or reporting about the king's ill health, let alone announcing the arrival of a messenger, were matters that did not have lasting significance but were still deposited and kept until our own times. This respect for the written word, especially when it also carried a seal, could not have developed without establishing a stable place for the town's documents, usually at the town hall, where these missives were delivered. In the early, 'itinerant' phase of some archives, when they were carried over from one judge's house to the next, or when the documents had to

[57] *Erstes Grundbuch*, p. 1. On the ritual element of this practice see ZUPKA, "Communication", p. 360.

be taken to church towers or sacristies, such pieces of paper would have been easily lost.

Conclusions: Trust in Archives

"It could be very fruitful to investigate the use of urban archives. We should take inventories as mirrors of political organisation", as Peter Rück put it. In Michael Jucker's words,

> The chancery with its boxes, registers, collections and drawers in some way represented political organisation. The inventories displayed homologies with the larger system they served. Thus, the archives mirror the understanding of literacy and its use in an urban context.[58]

In this statement, Jucker aptly summarises the general relevance of the topic discussed in the last chapter of this book, even if the complexity of the political organisation of Hungarian towns was never near that of the Swiss Confederation, let alone Florence or Venice.

As explained in Chapter 2, exercising urban autonomy and preserving the charters granting it hung closely together. The establishment of archives was a direct consequence of this connection. On the one hand, the framework provided by the town charter and by further privileges could not have been fully utilised without appropriate record management. On the other hand, without a certain degree of autonomy and authority, there would not have been any need and incentive to erect such institutions as the town archives. Therefore, the remit and operation of the archives reflect the practical implementation of autonomy. In ideal cases, when the material has not been affected by large-scale physical damage or modern selection, the history of its town archives can be instructive on the extent (or limitations) of the autonomy of any given town.

The history of town archives can be approached from two angles. The first is considering the external circumstances of record keeping in historical perspective: the material aspects of record management and placement, as well as the system of registering and the organisation of the documents. The second approach is tracing the internal history of the archival collections, namely the constitution of the material according to its issuers and contents, which in ideal

[58] JUCKER, "Urban literacy and urban secrecy", p. 237; quotation from Rück *ibidem*.

cases (that is, with preferably intact assemblages) may reflect the processes that affected its accumulation.

In well-preserved town archives there seems to be a correlation between the stack of archival material and the overall development of the town. The external history of the archives shows that attempts at organising and registering the stock were made from the mid-fifteenth century onwards, when the growth of the material necessitated it. On the one hand, this went hand in hand with the acquisition of town halls and the differentiation of the records issued by the town magistrates. On the other hand, it impacted on their outer appearance, namely by the introduction of the book or booklet format. The personnel employed, the space used, the number and types of documents issued, and the registers prepared by the notaries seem to have evolved in parallel with the growing complexity of tasks faced by municipal authorities. Adopting new techniques in the physical form, layout, material, and binding contributed to meeting the increased demands for the preservation and retrieval of information. This complex and intertwined history of governance, administration, and record-keeping makes the history of archives and archiving an intriguing part of urban history.[59]

And how about trust? It may have occurred to the attentive reader that the question of archives seems to be surrounded by the least controversy among the topics discussed in this volume, and rightly so. Trust was at the very foundation of establishing archives. As Marco Mostert explains in his essay on the reinterpretation of forgeries in the light of the "thirteenth-century explosion in charter production":

> Charters were considered as valid evidence when they could be criticised. This became possible when two conditions were met: their forms had to be stable and they had to be preserved in credible places, in registers and in archives.[60]

These criteria were met by the Hungarian *loca credibilia*, par excellence the 'credible places' in the kingdom, and, in their turn, by the civic archives as

[59] A distant example, the archival history of the hanseatic Kontor at Bergen, Norway, offers many parallels: the separate treatment of royal charters and documents connected to property ownership; the change in the range of surviving materials depending on new administrative practices; the acquisition of a separate administration building boosting the development of practice as well as survival are the most relevant points. See in detail: G.A. Ersland, "The archive of the kontor in Bergen", in: *Neue Studien zum Archiv und zur Sprache der Hanseaten*, ed. G.A. Ersland and M. Trebbi (Bergen, 2008), pp. 11-46.

[60] Mostert, "Forgery and trust", p. 56.

well. Mostert, however, adds a critical qualifier to 'credible places': they had to be "acknowledged by those in power", in this case the lords of the town, namely the kings of Hungary. This, as seen in the previous chapters, adds reservations to the autonomy argument. The material kept in the archives could just as much be used for controlling or exploiting the towns as the towns found the archival stock instrumental in reinforcing the settlement's special standing.

Ideally, the two interests coincided in the kings' intention to keep their towns operational. But it was not only these high-minded considerations that reinforced trust in civic archives; there were equally important grass-roots processes going on. These were the increase in the population's literacy resulting from schooling[61] and a growing exposure to writing among those who were in contact with civic administration in a local context, at least as semi-litterates. For instance, the proportion of persons whose last wills have been preserved in writing in late medieval Pressburg reached about 10 per cent – even if they did not write their wills themselves, and only relatively few of them mentioned books or other written materials.[62] This percentage would count as high even in the eighteenth or nineteenth centuries.

To be sure, plenty of conflicts arose from town-dwellers' mistrust in the statements of others, oral or written, but there seem to have been hardly any cases when burghers or persons belonging to other strata of society expressed mistrust in civic archives. Even during the uprising of the Sopron burghers in 1422, mentioned a few times above, the complaint against the council was not directed at their failure to keep the accounts of the town, but at failing to present them to the entire community.[63]

Trust in notaries as keepers of the civic archives was hardly ever challenged, according to the surviving record. Even when controversies about ethnic participation in the council or the employment of ethnic chaplains arose (see Chapter 4), the person of the notary was not subjected to these,[64] and there

[61] This issue is elaborated in due detail by BARTOSZEWICZ, *Urban literacy*, pp. 57-68, 82-86, 322-326. For Hungary, the most detailed work is still R. BÉKEFI, *A népoktatás története Magyarországon 1540-ig* [The history of primary education in Hungary until 1540] (Budapest, 1906); see also the exhibition catalogue: *A magyar iskola első évszázadai, 996-1526* [The first centuries of schooling in Hungary, 996-1526], ed. K. SZENDE and P. SZABÓ (Győr, 1996).

[62] Introduction to PT, 1, p. 29.

[63] HÁZI, *Sopron*, 2.1, pp. 164-169.

[64] With the exception of the claim in the *Ofner Stadtrecht* that the notary had to have four German grandparents, which was probably the author's wishful thinking. M. RADY, *Medieval Buda*, p. 61, observes that from the four notaries known from Buda by name before 1450, only one may have fulfilled this criterion, but even he was not born in Buda.

was no duplication of this office. This may have been partly due to the notary's being a paid job and the town not being able to afford to pay more than one person, but the main reason must have been the notaries' expected professionalism and the well-circumscribed nature of their office. The same trust was manifest in the notaries' involvement in the representation of their home towns as envoys and diplomats. The notary's oath in the *Ofner Stadtrecht* covers the keeping of the secrets of the town ("*des rats haimlichkait verswigenn haltenn*"), but contains no remarks about handling the documents apart from the already-mentioned control on the entries to the *Stadtgrundbuch*. The only punishable crime seems to have been if the notary demanded higher payment for his services than allowed.[65] Forgeries or fraudulent misuse of municipal documents also appear remarkably seldom in the sources surveyed here, and even these frauds concerned seals misappropriated or counterfeited by 'outsiders', rather than falsifying or damaging documents in other ways.[66] What one may notice, particularly in the town books of smaller towns, is the uneven quality of the entries and the often sloppy handling of duties. This attitude of some notaries may have been damaging the town's interests and be annoying for modern historians, but it did not shake the foundations of trust vested in the archives.

To sum up, the gradual expansion of pragmatic literacy discussed in the previous chapters facilitated the daily use of writing, and brought written administration closer to an increasing proportion of urban dwellers. This closeness could, of course, also inspire awe. The introduction of procedures and fees for annulling documents and 'writing out' pardoned culprits from the books of judgements and debtors from the property registers, either by obliteration or strikeout, demonstrate the solidification of trust from the 'opposite direction'.

[65] *Ofner Stadtrecht* cap. 44 (oath), cap. 51 (payment), pp. 76 and 81 respectively.

[66] The question of a possible fraudulent entry in the Kremnica town book seems to have been an unfounded allegation, see Chapter 3, nn. 58 and 91 above. A. Bartoszewicz, pp. 272-291, based on a much larger and more varied body of data, shows a more controversial image of notaries in Polish towns, where a high number of unsuitable or incompetent persons seem to have been employed.

Final Conclusions

Geoffrey Hosking closes his essay on *Trust and Distrust* with the following words:

> I believe that examining the way trust has worked in different societies can provide a way towards investigating problems which are otherwise difficult to conceptualise adequately. That is a good reason for suggesting that historians should ask more systematic questions about the operations of trust.[1]

This volume has used the key terms of 'trust' and 'authority' to investigate and explain the growing complexity of (urban) society and its management, and the impact of various uses of writing on this process. Municipal documents were investigated, beyond their contents and physical appearance, as the physical manifestations of the increase in institutional authority in the sociological sense of the term. From describing the paths of urbanisation in the Carpathian Basin the line of thought led us to cases and issues that are familiar to most readers of this volume from their home grounds. My intention was indeed to show that, although towns in Hungary underwent a development of their own, questions arising in connection with their literacy are not unlike those in other towns of medieval Europe. Thus the example of this region and its towns can broaden the framework of research and at the same time benefit from more general approaches and results in Europe and beyond.

The main observation is that trust in administrative literacy needed to be built up gradually, through a series of decisive, but usually chronologically distinctive steps. Agnieszka Bartoszewicz in her monograph on pragmatic literacy in medieval Polish towns makes a strong point of the ongoing and

[1] Hosking, *Trust and Distrust*, p. 115.

unresolved discussion about the origins and earliest emergence of urban chanceries.[2] Instead of taking sides with one or another viewpoint, she answers the question by writing about the "stages of emergence of urban chanceries". The findings of this volume are in full conformity with this approach. Municipal writing offices did not spring up at once like a fountain. To use a natural metaphor for the history of their activities: they started out as an underground stream, and were joined by more and more tributaries to become a river, a network of fully-fledged branches of civic literacy. To conclude this survey, let us follow – first in very general terms – how the concepts of 'trust' and 'authority' traverse these stages.

The process started (the 'underground stream phase') with the granting of some sort of autonomy to settlements that were preferred by the rulers for the better exploitation of resources (strategic location, natural resources, manpower). This autonomy had to be managed with the help of persons who were trusted by the lord as well as the community; they appeared under various denominations such as 'aldermen', 'council', or 'the sworn'. Alternatively, if no formal privileges were granted, an emerging leading body assumed one of these titles and acted accordingly. The leadership had to be reinforced by a legal system that set limits and rules for exercising their authority.

It took several decades, often as long as a century, from the first appearance of this communal leading group to the first authentic document issued in their names. A crucial attribute of the group was constituted by their seal, a visual marker of their identity. The seal was a medium that could be multiplied innumerable times to convey the will of its owners; models for this had been wrought by numerous ecclesiastical and secular authorities long before the emergence of towns. Typically, the inscriptions of early seals refer to a group of people and not to a place. It is difficult to tell if the community had already possessed a seal before they began their regular charter-issuing activity, because in most cases the impressions survived only on documents authenticated by them. Surviving early matrices (*typaria*), like the one from Esztergom (Fig. 16), are very rare exceptions. However, seals definitely preceded the writing bodies attached to their owners. Seals expressed the authority of an urban community, and trust in their actions, but not necessarily any kind of 'innate' liter-

[2] BARTOSZEWICZ, *Urban Literacy in Late Medieval Poland*, pp. 4-9, 48-52, 89-92, 180-183; KEJŘ, *Die mittelalterlichen Städte*, pp. 329-330, also emphasises the gradual development from possessing and authentic seal and issuing documents to the employment of a notary and setting up a writing office.

acy – for one thing, because the communities did not yet have the routine for producing it. Cases of sealing other issuers' documents or co-issuing documents with other (mainly ecclesiastical) authorities support this point. The length of the interim period between acquiring an authentic seal and commencing the regular issuing of charters varied immensely; owning a seal did not in itself ensure that the process of institutionalisation would continue.

If it did, the next 'current' was the employment of a notary or town clerk. This was a position entailing trust and cooperation on many levels. It must have been a difficult decision for any community to commit themselves to employing such a person: they had to be convinced not only of his skills and competence, but also that there would be enough tasks to warrant the employment, which, in turn, would yield sufficient returns in the form of direct financial revenues or more indirect benefits, such as diplomatic service, legal advice, or the intangible gain of asserting the authority of the community more efficiently than before.

The examples taken from medieval towns all over Europe show that decisions for the employment of notaries were made on sound presumptions. There are no examples for the complete failure or discontinuity of the activity of municipal writing offices, even if strong fluctuation of their output can be presumed. The clearest evidence for the successful extension of chancery activity was setting up municipal books, often first as all-in-one notebooks and then narrowing down their scope. This was a large leap forward in the mentality and concept of authenticity: instead of the visual evidence of the seal, the regulation of routines for entering texts into the books entrusted those texts with the same probative value as that of sealed charters. Once established, the format of the books was exploited and adapted to new uses in flexible ways. They had an agency in changing attitudes too, for instance by accommodating multiple cases or by reducing the amount of required information to the bare essentials and abandoning many features of the charters that originally contributed to the corroboration of their contents (*invocatio*, *arenga*, various sanctions and clauses, etc.).

A next 'current' to join the stream was the passage to the vernacular(s). In some cases this was a consequence of introducing the book format, but it also occurred without or preceding it, keeping the traditional format of charters. This change did not necessarily mean using one's own mother-tongue, but a trusted mediatory language that was the most appropriate in the given communicative situation. Embracing the vernaculars was often a 'passage' not only in a figurative sense, but was connected with real physical movement and mobility of texts, practices, and people. The very thought that writing in the vernacular can carry the same contents and the same weight as Latin needed trustworthy models: receiving authentic documents in the vernacular but sealed with well-known seals; or meeting notaries and intellectuals (during university studies for instance) writing in the vernacular. This was not a linear process: promoting one vernacular could lead to the reduction of another, and Latin could make a comeback for reasons of prestige or practicality.[3]

Finally (or at least latest in time in most places), setting up special repositories for the stock of records of a municipality completed the process. Archives were crucial for establishing trust in documents and played an instrumental role in the possibility to control questionable charters, financial accounts, or retrieve information from one of the court protocols. Ideally, the assemblage found safe storage in town halls, close to all the functions which produced the reports. The elements outlined above all formed constitutive steps of chancery formation. They can be considered a 'bundle of criteria': the more of these are traceable in the sources, the more certain we can be that the system functioned, that the 'stream' was flowing.

In the preceding chapters, the organising principle – the 'weft' of the narrative – was the medium of communication, written or oral: charters, town books, languages, repositories. Let us now recapitulate the main findings from medieval Hungary 'along the warp threads', in chronological order, taking account of the main town types. The main categories that I shall use are: the old royal towns of Esztergom, Fehérvár, and Óbuda; the bishops' cities (except for Esztergom and Zagreb); Buda and Pest; the royal town of Zagreb (Gradec); the merchant towns of north-western and north-eastern Hungary (Pressburg, Sopron, Košice, Bardejov, Prešov); the Transylvanian merchant towns of Sibiu, Braşov, Cluj, and Bistriţa; the major mining towns (Banská Bystrica, Banská Štiavnica, and Kremnica), smaller mining towns, as well as market towns which were not subject to investigation in the present volume. These categories do not correspond to traditional legal or regional groupings and have been assembled arbitrarily, but they have shown strong similarities during the research, which is why they are listed in this form here in the conclusions.

[3] Several of these ideas have been put forward by A. ADAMSKA, "Latin and three vernaculars".

Table 4 Appearance of innovations in administrative literacy in various town types, up to the mid-fifteenth century (with approximate dates)

Town, type or group	Authentic seal	Issuing documents	Notary, chancery	Municipal books	Vernacular admin.	Archives in town hall
Old royal	before 1250	1250s	probable; many documents	no trace; archives lost	only Latin	early data on town hall
Episcopal	fourteenth-fifteenth c.	fourteenth-fifteenth c.	?	–	fifteenth c.	?
Buda	before 1250	1260s	1315	not preserved	*c.* 1350	probably
Zagreb / Gradec	?	1290s	1321	*c.* 1355	–	1371
Merchant Western Hungary	late thirteenth c.	1270s/1310s with loca credibilia	*c.* 1350	from 1360s/1390	1346/1361	1378/1422
Merchant Transylv.	late thirteenth c.	1290s/1300	*c.* 1350?	–	–	? 1420
Mining, major	early fourteenth c.	1290s-1340s	1320s-1340s	1360s-1380s	1360s	Late fifteenth c.
Mining, small	mid fourteenth c.	1350s	1380/1430s	1380s/1430s	1380s	–
Market towns	mid fourteenth c.	mid fourteenth/early fifteenth c.	occasional	–	1360-1380	–

The story starts in the first decades of the thirteenth century, when the most significant royal privileges were issued, to incipient towns as well as specific ethnic communities. The most influential of these, the *Latini* of Esztergom and Fehérvár, and also the *hospites* of Pest, presumably possessed authentic seals already before 1250, and they began issuing authentic charters in the 1250s and 1260s. Pest was succeeded by Buda, which in economic terms took over the role of a capital by the end of the thirteenth century. The high number of charters surviving from Esztergom, in spite of the destruction of its municipal archives, makes it likely that a chancery was operating there: this is where the earliest reference to a town hall (*domus iudicialis*) has come down to us.[4]

In the last decades of the thirteenth century, merchant towns in western Hungary (Sopron and, with a slight delay, Pressburg) began to use their own seals, albeit initially not on documents issued by themselves, but for several decades written by ecclesiastical bodies. Sibiu in Transylvania joins in, but uses the seal of the Saxon province, as its special status requires. Gradec, the royal town of Zagreb, also joins the trend and remains in the forefront of the development of municipal literacy throughout the examined period. Likewise, the earliest established mining towns show up as issuers of charters, both in Transylvania and in Upper Hungary before the turn of the century. They seem to have owned authentic seals instantly after their foundation, and this remains the case for those bigger and smaller mining towns that were established in the 1320s and 1330s.

In the first decades of the fourteenth century the first notaries are mentioned by name, at Buda, Gradec and Pest, and from the 1320s in the mining town of Gelnica. Thereafter, the mid-fourteenth century is a time of fundamental changes in several town groups in many regards. Permanently employed notaries and documents written by them feature in the records of merchant towns both in the north-west, the north-east, and in Transylvania; the issuing of documents takes up in several mining towns; the first thematically arranged municipal book is drawn up in Gradec; and after some earlier contacts with German literacy, the first locally written vernacular charters are issued in the western Hungarian merchant towns, and probably also in Buda. Furthermore, this is the time when, after the earlier occasional sealing of municipal charters by the clergy, documents begin to be issued under the authentic seals of market towns (seigniorial towns), especially in the wine-growing districts, in north-eastern and north-western regions of Hungary.

The 'literacy boom' continues in the 1360s to 1380s, too: municipal books (mainly *libri mixti*) are drawn up in practically all merchant and mining towns in the northern areas, and judging by references this is likely in Buda, too (if not before). These books usually start to be written in Latin, but German soon takes over in part or completely. The advent of vernacular literacy affects the market towns in the western and north-western parts of the country as well, which begin to use German in their correspondence with their bigger neighbours with remarkable ease.

[4] MAJOROSSY, "From the judge's house", p. 164.

Amidst all this bustle, it is even more conspicuous that the episcopal seats show very little activity in the field of pragmatic literacy: only three of them have issued any charters at all that have come down to us. Municipal books are not in use in these cities either, and it seems to be very unlikely that they have an operational writing office. Throughout the fourteenth and fifteenth centuries municipal books also seem to be missing from the written output of the market towns, and – more surprisingly – from that of the Transylvanian merchant towns as well.

At the turn of the fourteenth century, smaller mining towns set up their chanceries and start their town books, too, although their needs are satisfied often with a single book of mixed contents well into the early modern period. Vernacular (German) literacy also spreads in bigger and smaller mining towns as well as in all merchant towns apart from Transylvania – even the bishop's town of Pécs corresponds in German in a couple of instances. In the northern part, Slavic literacy takes root and is practised in medium-sized and small towns alike. Even this cursory chronology shows that the thirteenth century is indeed a period of profound transition from 'illiterate' to 'semi-literate', and the fourteenth century from 'semi-literate' to 'literate' urban societies.[5]

These processes are undergirded by a spectacular increase in the output of silver, gold, and copper in the mining towns as well as by the rapid integration of the kingdom of Hungary in the long-distance trade networks of Europe. In the fifteenth century, the development evolves by the sporadic acquisition or building of towns halls, but this aspect is not completed before the sixteenth century, and the smaller mining towns do not possess a town hall at all.

***

The emergence of urban literacy in the Carpathian Basin was certainly part of a broader tendency all over Europe, where towns asserted themselves as legal entities and bodies corporate, among other things by setting up their independent document production and chanceries. How do the processes described above compare with other towns? A full-range comparison with all those places that have been enumerated under the heading 'European frameworks' in the Introduction would require another book-length study. As a compromise I

[5] Šedivý, "Deutschsprachige Beurkundung", pp. 248-249. Mostert, "Medieval urban literacy", p. 11, even distinguishes between "semi-illitterati" and "semi-litterati".

have selected three examples from various parts of Europe with published data, which had varying levels of contact and relevance for medieval Hungary. The main emphasis here is, however, not on contacts, but comparisons.

The first example is Ghent, one of the leading early commercial metropolises of Flanders, from where some settlers arrived in Hungary occasionally in the twelfth and thirteenth centuries. The expansion of pragmatic literacy, as presented by Walter Prevenier, took the following steps. The first benches of Ghent aldermen (councillors) appeared in the written record in 1067, several decades before the first surviving charters; its urban statutes were compiled in 1192. This was a document formally corroborated but not written by them (1169). The first surviving charter issued by the aldermen dates from 1200, thirty years after Ypres, but preceding those from Bruges (1211), and Liége, (1212). Even these were regularly prepared with the help of clerics from nearby monasteries. Juridical acts pertaining to businesses of Ghent burghers begin to surface in the decades from 1210 onwards. The establishment of local bureaucracy owed much to the nearby abbey of St. Peter.

A municipal writing office with a permanently employed clerk was set up by the city of Ghent only at the end of the thirteenth century, with bookkeeping (accounts) preserved from 1280 and a register of outgoing documents from 1339 onwards. A fire of 1297 may have destroyed some of the earlier books. A shift from Latin to the vernaculars, two different languages even, took place in the mid-thirteenth century: the aldermen composed the first document in French in 1251 and that in Dutch two years later. The sequence of development in practices of literacy shows the increasing level of trust of the local burghers in the aldermen as issuers of documents. In addition, a significant literacy developed among the craft guilds, whose lavishly decorated member registers and cartularies crowned their regular everyday practice of written business management.[6]

The second example takes us to Augsburg, an early cathedral city which was elevated to free imperial status in 1276. The development of its administrative literacy was recently analysed in a thorough monograph by Mathias Franc Kluge. He pointed out that the later spectacular development commenced in 1234, when the community began using its authentic seal, but it was handled by the *Vogt*, together with the first documents in book format, the *Acht- und Bürgerverzeichnisse*. At the outset the king and the clergy played an

[6] PREVENIER, "Urban chanceries", pp. 3-11; M. BOONE and G. DENECKERE, *Ghent: A City of All Times* (Ghent, 2010), pp. 46-47, 60-67.

active role in promoting literacy in the city, which developed through the stages of the acquisition of the seal, then the legal privileges, and subsequently the use of town books and that of setting up a chancery. It took about 200 years until pragmatic literacy became part of the everyday life of even the ordinary craftsmen.

In the course of this development the municipal leadership used literacy for the legitimation of its rule beyond the practical needs of administration. From the early fourteenth century, the entries in the town books show increasing regularity and conformity, and the use of the vernacular also sets in. The account books were kept in German from 1340 onwards. The changes in the municipal administration after the revolt of 1368, when the craft guilds secured their access in the council, resulted in a great expansion of literacy to all aspects of daily life. The specialisation of municipal books and their numbers became difficult to keep track of, even for contemporaries. Altogether, a gradual expansion of literacy at increasing speed can be observed until it reached an overwhelming extent. This gave rise to a well-developed and self-conscious tradition of urban historiography along the lines of the *Reichsstadtchronistik*, complemented by private chronicles of the leading patrician families.[7]

Finally, as the third and last comparative example, let us look at the development of pragmatic literacy in the cities and towns of Poland, described in the already mentioned monograph by Agnieszka Bartoszewicz. As might be expected, the chronology of development here is the closest to that of Hungary. The present research revealed a similarity in the involvement of the rulers in the strengthening of the kingdom, and in using towns as instruments for increasing the revenues and strengthening the military potential of the kingdom. The prevalence of new urban growth on private estates in the fifteenth century also shows strong parallels with the Hungarian situation.

The most relevant point for us is, that the development of municipal writing offices underwent those four stages that are already familiar to us from the previous examples: the acquisition of an authentic seal; the appointment of a clerk (notary); starting a town book; and finally establishing an archive from the assemblage of collected documents. As a fifth element, the passage from Latin to vernacular can be added. However, one can observe substantial differ-

[7] M.F. Kluge, *Die Macht des Gedächtnisses: Entstehung und Wandel kommunaler Schriftkultur im spätmittelalterlichen Augsburg* (Leiden, 2014: *Studies in Medieval and Reformation Traditions*), pp. 354-366; Johanek, "Geschichtsschreibung und Geschichtsüberlieferung", pp. 169-182.

ences as well, which emerged because of the different legal background to town foundation, and the particular nature of municipal autonomy. In Polish towns, the decisive legal act was the *locatio* by the ruler or seignior, in which usually some variant of German law was granted (Magdeburg law, Kulm law, Lübeck law, etc.) Due to this, the person(s) responsible for the *locatio*, the *Vogt / advocatus* and his office, retained an important position. In judicial practice, the model of German law resulted in a large number of different books, and in the relatively smaller importance of sealed charters as evidence in court.[8]

There are apparent chronological differences between the selected examples due to events in broader history. A comparison with cities south of the Alps would show differences in an even sharper light. But the point here is not to repeat the usual laments about the belatedness of East Central Europe, as has been so frequently done in historical scholarship. It is much more revealing to show that, even if the development had its own dynamic in each town and each country, the main logic – the sequence and the elements of the development of chancery practices and trust in writing in the urban context – show remarkable similarities. Even the chronology is comparable: after the early examples of Italy and the Low Countries in the twelfth century, for much of Europe the turning point arrives in the thirteenth century.[9] Transcending the differences in timeframes or legal systems, this points to a shared dynamic of the development of trust networks.

***

Let me conclude on a general note. The cross-cultural overview entitled *Verschriftung und Verschriftlichung*, mentioned in the Introduction of this volume, was published in 1998, just before the great boom of modern electronic media, the latest wave of media change. Fundamental transformations in human communication and society, including but not restricted to academic life, have again generated a strong interest in media change and the phenomenon of mediality as a historical subject. Many studies appear year after year that explore the use and distribution of new forms of (mass) media, their im-

[8] BARTOSZEWICZ, *Urban Literacy in Late Medieval Poland*, pp. 89-97, 108-122.

[9] R. BRITNELL, "Pragmatic literacy in Latin Christendom", in: *Pragmatic Literacy East and West*, pp. 4-7.

pact on society, and the ways the individual can navigate this vast flow. The concept of literacy itself has been broadened to hitherto unexplored realms: besides textual literacy and numeracy, one writes about 'visual literacy' or even 'digital visual literacy', with their own methodology and need for source criticism.[10]

Examining trust in these forms, from broadsheets through newspapers to blogs and tweets (and their credibility, as the other side of the same coin) has been crucial for understanding our own roles in a world of constant transition. A current multinational interdisciplinary research project entitled InterPARES Trust (or ITrust in short), led by a renowned expert of archival studies, Luciana Duranti, was set up for "exploring issues concerning digital records and data entrusted to the Internet". The aim of the project is

> to generate theoretical and methodological frameworks to develop local, national and international policies, procedures, regulations, standards, and legislation in order to ensure public trust grounded on evidence of good governance, a strong digital economy, and a persistent digital memory.[11]

It is probably not by chance that the word 'trust' figures so prominently in the title as well as the mission statement of this typically twenty-first-century project.

In public discourse, the concepts in question apparently reach beyond the realm of literacy: "the research on happiness, social capital, political trust, and sustainable economic growth [...] now shapes public policies around the world", but it has also been argued that "what have been characterised as social capital and trust are in fact an epiphenomenon for, and relatively robust indicator of, paternalism and over-reliant dependence on the state".[12] I hope that my study of the development of trust and authority as the cement of both horizontal and vertical relationships in society in the more distant past has contributed to the better understanding of this complex process in a historical perspective.

[10] A. MORGAN SPALTER and A. VAN DAM, "Digital visual literacy", in: *Digital Literacies in the Age of Sight and Sound* (= *Theory into Practice* 47.2 (2008)), pp. 93-101.

[11] www.interparestrust.org, last accessed: 20.05.2018.

[12] L. KONTLER and M. SOMOS, "Introduction: Trust, happiness, and the history of European political thought", in: *Trust and Happiness in the History of European Political Thought*, pp. 2-3.

Appendices

Appendix 1	Gazetteer of Names of Towns in the Medieval Kingdom of Hungary Discussed in the Book	336
Appendix 2	Regnal Years of the Kings of Medieval Hungary	339
Appendix 3	Documents Issued by Civic Authorities in Hungary, (1244) 1255-1321	340
Appendix 4	Earliest Mentioning of Municipal Notaries (up to 1400)	352
Appendix 5	The Earliest Preserved Charters of Bishops' Towns (Issued by the Municipality)	357
Appendix 6	Municipal Books Started before 1500	359

Appendix 1: Gazetteer of Names of Towns in the Medieval Kingdom of Hungary Discussed in the Book

The name version used in the text is set in bold. For alternative names of localities outside the Kingdom of Hungary, see the Index of geographic names.

Modern name and country	**Hungarian name**	**German name**	**Latin name**
Baia Mare (RO)	Nagybánya	Frauenbach	Rivulus Dominarum
Banská Belá (SK)	Bélabánya	Dilln	–
Banská Bystrica (SK)	Besztercebánya	Neusohl	Novisolium
Banská Štiavnica (SK)	Selmecbánya	Schemnitz	–
Bardejov (SK)	Bártfa	Bartfeld	–
Beregovo (UA)	Beregszász	Lampertshaus	–
Bistrița (RO)	Beszterce	Bistritz / Nösen	–
Brașov (RO)	Brassó	Kronstadt	Corona
Bratislava (SK)	Pozsony	**Pressburg**	Posonium
Budapest (HU)	**Buda**	Ofen	Buda, Castrum Novi Montis Pestiensis
Budapest (HU)	**Pest**	(Ofen)	Pestinum
Budapest (HU)	**Óbuda**	Altofen	Buda Vetus
Cenad (RO)	Csanád	–	Chanadinum
Cluj-Napoca (RO)	Kolozsvár	Klausenburg	Claudiopolis
Debrecen (HU)	Debrecen	Debrezin	–
Dej (HU)	Dés	Burglos	–
Devín (SK)	Dévény	Theben	–
Esztergom (HU)	Esztergom	Gran	Strigonium
Gelnica (SK)	Gölnicbánya	Göllnitz	–

Győr (HU)	Győr	Raab	Jaurinum
Kežmarok (SK)	Késmárk	Käsmarkt	Forum Caseorum
Komarno (SK)	Komárom	Komorn	–
Košice (SK)	Kassa	Kaschau	Cassovia
Kőszeg (HU)	Kőszeg	Güns	–
Kremnica (SK)	Körmöcbánya	Kremnitz	Cremnicia
Krupina (SK)	Korpona	Karpfen	Corpona
Levoča (SK)	Lőcse	Leutschau	Leutsovia
Ľubietová (SK)	Libetbánya	Libethen	–
Modra (SK)	Modor	Moder	–
Nitra (SK)	Nyitra	Neutra	Nitra
Nová Baňa (SK)	Újbánya	Königsberg	Regiomontanum
Oradea (RO)	Várad, Nagyvárad	Wardein	Varadinum
Pécs (HU)	Pécs	Fünfkirchen	Quinque Ecclesiae
Prešov (SK)	Eperjes	Preschau	Eperies
Pukanec (SK)	Bakabánya	Pukkantz	–
Rodna (RO)	Radna	Rodenau	–
Sabinov (SK)	Kisszeben	Zeben	Cibinium
Satu Mare (RO)	Szatmár, Németi	Sathmar	–
Sibiu (RO)	Szeben (Nagyszeben)	Hermannstadt	Cibinium
Sighişoara (RO)	Segesvár	Schäßburg	–
Smolník (SK)	Szomolnokbánya	Schmölnitz	–
Sopron (HU)	Sopron	Ödenburg	Sopronium, Sempronium
Spišská Nová Ves (SK)	Igló	Zipser Neudorf	Villa Nova
Spišská Sobota (SK)	Szepesszombat	Georgenberg	Forum Sabathi

Stary Tekov (SK)	(Ó)bars	Altbarsch	–
Szeged (HU)	Szeged	Segedin	Segedinum
Székesfehérvár (HU)	**Fehérvár**	Stuhlweissenburg	Alba Civitas
Szombathely (HU)	Szombathely	Steinamanger	Sabaria
Trenčín (SK)	Trencsén	Trentschin	Trencinium
Trnava (SK)	Nagyszombat (Szombatély)	Tyrnau	Tirnavia
Varaždin (CR)	Varasd	Warasdin	Varasdinum
Vasvár (HU)	Vasvár	Eisenburg	Castrum Ferreum
Virovitica (CR)	Verőce	Wirowititz	–
Visegrád (HU)	Visegrád	Plindenburg	Altum Castrum
Zagreb (CR), **Kaptol** / **Gradec**	Zágráb	Agram	Zagrabia
Žilina (SK)	Zsolna	Sillein	Solna

Appendix 2: Regnal Years of the Kings of Medieval Hungary

Árpád dynasty
Stephen I (Saint) 1000-1038
Peter Orseolo 1038-1041 and 1044-1046
Samuel Aba 1041-1044
Andrew I 1046-1060
Béla I 1060-1063
Salamon 1063-1074
Géza I 1074-1077
Ladislas I (Saint) 1077-1095
Coloman (the Learned) 1095-1116
Stephen II 1116-1131
Béla II (the Blind) 1131-1141
Géza II 1141-1162
Stephen III 1162-1172
Béla III 1172-1196
Emeric 1196-1204
Ladislas III 1204-1205
Andrew II 1205-1235
Béla IV 1235-1270
Stephen V 1270-1272
Ladislas IV (the Cuman) 1272-1290
Andrew III 1290-1301

Přemysl dynasty
Wenceslas 1301-1305

Wittelsbach dynasty
Otto 1305-1307

Angevin dynasty
Charles I (Charles Robert) 1301-1342
Louis I (the Great) 1342-1382
Mary 1382-1395
Charles II (the Short) 1385-1386

Luxemburg dynasty
Sigismund 1387-1437

Habsburg dynasty
Albert 1437-1439
Ladislas V (Postumus) 1440-1457

Jagiellonian dynasty
Wladislas I (Warneńczyk) 1440-1444

Hunyadi dynasty
Matthias Corvinus 1458-1490

Jagiellonian dynasty
Wladislas II 1490-1516
Louis II 1516-1526

Appendix 3: Documents Issued by Civic Authorities in Hungary, (1244) 1255-1321

The list contains documents preserved in the original or as contemporary authentic transcriptions. Documents from the cities of Dalmatia are not included. ** indicates documents of doubtful authenticity.

Abbreviations in the 'Type' column: Pr = *litterae privilegiales;* Pa = *litterae patentes*; Cl = *litterae clausae*; Tr = *transcriptio*.

No.	Date	Town	DL / DF	Edition	Type
1	**1244	Dubica	35139, 35141, 35142, 35143	CDCr 4.264 CDH 4.1	Tr 1270; *forgery*
2	1255	Esztergom	236285	EFHU 3.2, No. 40	Pr
3	**1258	Trnava		CDES 2, No. 625	Pr *forgery* fourteenth c.
4	1265	Esztergom	76145	EFHU 3.2, No. 46	Pr?
5	18 October 1268	Buda	106084	BTOE 1, pp. 100-101	Pr?
6	20 December 1268	Rodna	73625	UGDS 1, No. 118	Pa

Intitulatio	Coram nobis	Sigillatio	Contents
Nos Erney villicus, Fridericus, Marcellus et Laztica ac omnes hospites libere ville de Dobycha	*Ad terram ... liberaliter fuissemus congregati*	*Sub sigillo communitatis nostre*	Relates that Coloman, duke of Slavonia (†1241!) asked the *hospites* to allow the hermits [Paulines] to settle on a piece of land (includes perambulation).
Nos Iakmynus maior ville ceterique cives	*Sub nostro testimonio*	*Dupplicis nostri sigilli munimine*	Sale of a piece of property because of infirmity, after measurement
Nos C., villicus de Tyrna ac cives eiusdem	*In nostra presentia*	*sigilli nostri munimine, ad petitionem partium*	A burgher of Trnava sells a piece of land to the chapter of Esztergom for the storage of tithes; *evictio*
Nos comes Rvbynus maior villae + 7 jurors	*Coram nobis*	*ad petitionem partium, nostri sigilli munimine*	Sale of half of a *palatium*
Nos comes Walterus rector castri Budensis et duodecim iurati Also transcribed by Ladislas IV, 1273, DL 105993	*Coram nobis*, dialogue style	*ad petitionem partium, sigillo communitatis nostre*	Agreement between Buda chapter (!) and the ferrymen of Pest over salt duties. Buda rector gives judgment.
[N]os iudices (!) *et iurati de Radna*	*Coram nobis et viris religiosis fratribus minoribus et domino cruciato fratre Detrico; "novimus pertinere"*	*Sub munimine sigilli communitatis civium*; Fragmented seal on dorse.	Sale of property (stone tower, wooden house, silver mines, house, fields, mill). Text on judicial authority.

No.	Date	Town	DL / DF	Edition	Type
7	1269	Esztergom	687	EFHU 3.2, p. 49	
8	16 March 1270	Fehérvár	83130	–	Pr
9	1271	Bihač (Biheg)	283328	CDCr 5, p. 613	Toplica cartu-lary
10	28 September 1272	Esztergom	812	BTOE 1, pp. 126-127	Pr
11	1275	Banská Štiavnica	923 235719	CDH 5.2, pp. 308-309	Orig., pr. copy
12	1276	Sopron	201647	UBB 2, pp. 91-92; EFHU 3.2, p. 57	Tr (1277)
13	8 November 1282	Esztergom	237575	MES 2, pp. 156-157; EFHU 3.2, No. 61	Pr

Intitulatio	Coram nobis	Sigillatio	Contents
Nos Rubynus comes + 5 jurors	*Coram nobis*	*sigilli nostri munimine*	Sale of *terra* in Cholnuc *cum fundo curie*
Nos comes Egidius iudex castri Albensis et duodecim iurati ac universi cives castri	*Constituti corum nobis personaliter*	Seal is preserved. *S. Latinorum Albensium*	Sale of a property in Somogy County to a burgher of Fehérvár; *evictio*
Jacobus maior ville et tota communitas civitatis de Bihig	*Inter nos et ipsum [abbatem de Toplica] ordinavimus composicionem*	No *corroboratio* in the transcription	Agreement not to seduce each other's tenant peasants in specified districts
Arcynus comes iudex de vico Latinorum Strigoniensi + 6 jurors *ceterique cives de Strigonio*. Also transcribed by *Gregorius prepositus et capitulum ecclesie Strigoniensis* upon Arcynus' request, DL 813 (28 November 1272) and by Philip, archbishop of Esztergom, DL 814 (7 December 1272).	*Coram nobis* (both parties).	*sigilli nostri munimine* [preserved hanging double seal]	Town testifies to the selling of a vineyard that had been set as security for a debt to a merchant from Ghent. *assignavimus secundum consuetudinem et libertatem civitatis nostrae*
Halmannus iudex et XII iurati, vniuersique cives Banenses	*ad petitionem et instantiam nostram*	*Sigillum nostrum presentibus apponendum*. Preserved, *s. civium Scheba ...*	The judge and burghers join their parish priest in donating the St. Nicholas chapel to the Dominicans
Arenga + *nos ... Stephanus iudex et frater Theodericus crucifer cum universitate civium*	*Emerat in nostra presentia*	*Sigillo universitatis et sigillo cruciferi* + *testes* (9)	Testamentary donation of previously bought Klingenbach to the abbey of Klostermarienberg by *Pero concivis noster*
Nos comes Elkynus iudex Strigoniensis + 6 *iurati* + *universi cives*	*Nos promissimus*	*Sigilli nostri munimine*	The town obliges itself to pay the tithes to the chapter, sends a juror with the collectors

No.	Date	Town	DL / DF	Edition	Type
14	4 June 1284	Esztergom	237804	MES 2, p. 181	Pr
15	1287	Dej	253362	–	Tr 1491
16	1291	Esztergom	104482	MES 2, pp. 311-312	Pr
17	11 August 1291	Zagreb	36277 104482 230277	Tkalčić, *Zagreb*, No. 73.	Pr? Fragment.
18	1292	Buda	39088 229963	BTOE 1, p. 283.	Pr
19	24 June 1292	Sibiu	244566	UGDS 1, No. 260.	

Intitulatio	Coram nobis	Sigillatio	Contents
Nos comes Elkynus iudex ceterique cives Strigoniensis civitatis	*ad nostram supplicationem*	no *corroboratio*; fragments of hanging double seal	*Locum seu terram eorum pro edificatione domus iudicialis civitatis nostre ad nostram supplicationem nobis perpetuo iure concesserunt* – in return for the town hall the citizens pay taxes to the chapter and assist them in collecting it.
Nos Ladislaus No[..] iudex et iurati et uni-		[illegible]	[illegible copy]
Comes Belgymus iudex, iurati et universi cives	Several phrases of judicial procedure	*Appensione dupplicis sigilli*	Sale of a pledged property which the original owner was not able to redeem.
Nos Katharinus maior ville, iudices et consiliarii Transcription of royal charter by town, of	*Introducentes eundem auctoritate regia nobis tradita*	*sigilli communitatis nostri munimine*	The town transcribes Andrew III's charter concerning the possession of a ruined palace and two houses in the
Vernerius rector novi castri + 12 *iurati* (listed)	*Coram nobis constitutus retulit viva voce*	*Dupplicis sigilli munimine*; preserved intact!	Agreement about the sale of half of a property.
Nos iudices, iurati ac tota communitas ville Cibiensis	Own decision; *salutatio, arenga*	*Litteras Cibiniensis provinciae sigillo sigillatas*	The town transfers the ownership of a house which used to functon as the hospital to the Order of the Holy Spirit on the condition that the monks celebrate masses for the inmates

No.	Date	Town	DL / DF	Edition	Type
20	15 June 1295	Buda	200052	BTOE 1, pp. 290-291.	Pa
21	4 May 1298	Košice	271723	–	Copy in later *Verbotbuch*
22	25 March 1299	Esztergom	236351	MES 2, pp. 458-459.	Pr
23	26 April 1299	Satu Mare (Németi)	56570	HO 7, p. 277.	Cl
24	1301	Kežmarok	281692	CDH 7.1, pp. 246-247; (1307) *Reg. Slov.* 1, 55; *Anjou-oklt* 1, No. 135, p. 99.	Pr
25	1305	(Sáros) Patak	57233	*Reg. Slov.* 1, 185; *Anjou-oklt* 1, No. 804, p. 384.	Pa
26	1305	Banská Štiavnica	243697	AO 1, No. 99, pp. 103-104; *Anjou-oklt* 1, No. 805, p. 384.	Pr
27	2 March 1307	Esztergom	269947	*Anjou-oklt* 2, No. 130, pp. 62-63.	Pr

Intitulatio	Coram nobis	Sigillatio	Contents
Nos comes Vernherius rector castri Budensis et iurati de eodem	No presence mentioned.	No seal mentioned; imprint on dorse.	The council testifies that the bishop of Veszprém pledged his tithe revenues from the outskirts of Buda to two burghers.
Comes Stephanus iudex ... iurati [listed] *ceterique cives de Strigonio*	*Nostris litteris mediantibus ... secundum libertatem nostre civitatis*	*Sigilli nostri munimine roboratas* Hanging double seal.	A Venetian merchant pledged houses and palaces in the town to the chapter but was unable to redeem them, and therefore sells them to the chapter.
iurati et universi hospites de Nemythy	On royal demand *exhibuit nobis litteras vestras ... quod nos sciscitaremur et queremus*	With closing seal on dorse. No *corroboratio*.	The authorities of the town conducted an investigation at the king's command concerning the expulsion of a nobleman from his property.
Nos Theodericus iudex ceterique iurati totaque universitas civium in Foro Caseorum	Starts with *arenga*: *apud nos*	*Sigillis comitis et terrenorum* (no civic seal!)	Sale of some ploughlands to Tylo, *iudex de Bela*, with possibility of settling people.
Nos villicus Vincencius et iurati de Potok	*Coram nobis*	*Sigillo nostro roboratas*; seal on the dorse	Sale of a vineyard that was pledged, but the owner was not able to redeem it. *Evictio*.
Nos Syfridus et [list] *iurati*	*plenarie reddidit expeditos*	*Cum sigillo maiori civitatis nostre*	Sale of a piece of land.
Comes Kunchulinus f. Raad iudex et [list]	*Personaliter ad nostrum accedendo presentiam*	*Dupplicis sigilli nostri munimine*	Sale of a piece of land (garden) between two priests.

No.	Date	Town	DL / DF	Edition	Type
28	**12 July 1307	Košice	271754	*Reg. Slov.* 1, 225; *Anjou-oklt* 2, No. 189, p. 88.	Tr 1448; German forgery
29	10 November 1308	Koprivnica	40360	AO 1, 386-387; *Anjou-oklt* 2, No. 483, p. 209.	Tr 1309, 1315. orig. Pa
30	10 August 1309	Trnava	237269	*Reg. Slov.* 1, 301; *Anjou-oklt* 2, No. 714, p. 314.	Tr 1435 orig. Pr
31	1311	Pressburg	227611 c238651	MES 2, 643-644; *Anjou-oklt* 3, No. 88, p. 46.	Pr
32	1314	Esztergom	269946	*Anjou-oklt* 3, No. 664, p. 303.	
33	6 December 1314	Pressburg	238657	AO 1, 366-367; *Anjou-oklt* 3, No. 853, p. 376.	Pr
34	26 January 1315	(Sáros) Patak	76235	*Zichy* 1, pp. 149-150; *Anjou-oklt* 4, No. 20, p. 16.	Pa
35	24 February 1316	Krupina	1865 c.25069	AO 1, 391-392; *Anjou-oklt* 4, No. 244, p. 96.	Pr

Intitulatio	Coram nobis	Sigillatio	Contents
Wir Arnold richter, die geschworne purger ud dye gancze gemeyne	'transcription'	*mit unsern ingesigil* [no distinction]	Statutes of the furriers' guild [reflects fifteenth-century conditions].
Nos Benedictus villicus Draganus Matheus Chuche et uniuersa tota communits tam maiores quam minores de Kapruncha	*de bona nostra voluntate [...] quamdiu nostra communitas duretur*	No seal mentioned in transcription.	Agreement with former villicus over collecting *iobagiones* by a mill for having built three bridges [suspect for terminology].
Comes Janslynus judex jurati ceterique cives de Tyrnavia	*coram nobis personaliter constituti*	*Sigilli mostre civitatis appensione*	Burgher rents a plot from the chapter of Esztergom, undertakes paying civic duties.
Nos Hertlo iudex, iurati et universi cives Posonienses [written by the chapter]	*nos pure et simpliciter conferemur*	*Nostre civitatis predicte munimine* [*sigilli* missing]	Exchange of territories between the chapter and the town.
Comes Rubinus filius comitis Godini [list] *iurati ceterique cives de Strigonio*	*ad nostram personaliter accedendo presenciam*	*duplicis sigilli nostri munimine*	Sale of a vineyard by *Nicolaus Gallicus institor noster concivis.*
Nos Hertlo iudex, rector civitatis Posoniensis necnon duodecim coniurati [list] *ac universitas civitatis eiusdem*	*Nos* [own decision]. Royal donation charter from 1288 to James RA 3482	*nostrum sigillum duximus apponendum* Seal extant.	Town exempts a piece of land from its jurisdiction and gives to James, former judge, who had received it *ex donatione et collatione regia.*
Nos Paulus et Andreas judices [and 4 listed] *iurati cum universis hospitibus de Pothok*	*coram nobis personaliter constitutis*	*nostro sigillo munitas* Seal on dorse.	Exchange of a piece of inherited land.
Nos Nicolaus iudex de Corpona, [and 4 listed] *iurati ac ceteri cives de eadem* [*Empfängerausfertigung*]	*ad nostram presenciam accedendo*	*cum sygillo civitatis* Remains of seal.	Sale of two parts of a mill to the Premonstratensians of Bzovík.

No.	Date	Town	DL / DF	Edition	Type
36	20 January 1318	Buda	229964	*Anjou-oklt* 5, No. 20, p. 16.	Pr
37	5 December 1318	Buda	263191	MES 2, p. 753; *Anjou-oklt* 5, No. 321, p. 130.	Pr
38	30 April 1321	Košice	60177	AO 1, pp. 608-609; *Anjou-oklt* 6, No. 104, p. 45.	Cl paper?

Intitulatio	Coram nobis	Sigillatio	Contents
Nos comes Johannes rector castri novi montis Pestiensis [and 11 listed] *iurati ipsius castri*	*coram nobis personaliter constituti*	*duplicis sigilli nostri munimine*	Sale of a house on the hilltop.
Nos comes Johannes rector castri novi montis Pestiensis [and 12 listed] *iurati ipsius castri*	*coram nobis personaliter constituti*	*dupplicis sigilli nostri munimine* Seal preserved.	Sale of a vineyard and a piece of uncultivated land at Óbuda between two burghers of Buda.
Nos Arnoldus judex et jurati de Cassa	*Constituti personaliter in nostri presentia*	No *corroboratio*; seal on dorse.	Agreement out of court on compensation for defamation of a girl.

Appendix 4: Earliest Mentioning of Municipal Notaries (up to 1400)

Town	**Date**	**Name and title of notary**	**function**	**DL/DF**	**Edition**
Buda	1315.12.30	*magister Johannes filius Cantus prothonotarius eiusdem castri*	witness of last will	262657	MES II, pp. 716-717
Zagreb (Gradec)	1321.08.21	*magister Thomas, principalis notarius civitatis Grecensis*	legal representative of town	256335	TKALČIĆ I, No. 115 pp. 98-99.
Zagreb (Gradec)	1324.03.08	*Magister Thomas notarius civitatis nostre de monte Grech*	envoy petitioning confirmation of privileges	255413	TKALČIĆ I, No. 128 p. 108.
Pest	1326.06.02	*magister Jacobus notarius ... civitatis Pestiensis*	legal representative of town	106092	KNAUZ, TT XII (1863), 113-116.
Gelnica	1327.10.17 eighteenth c. copy	*magister Colinus notarius universitats hospitum [...] de Gölnicz Banya*	envoy petitioning confirmation of privileges	71419	VMMS No. 131. *Anjou-oklt* XI, No. 496
Smolník	1340.12.06	*magister Nycolaus notarius ... de Smulnychbana*	envoy petitioning confirmation of judicial privilege	71412	*Csáky* I. p. 86.
Kremnica	1342.11.19 eighteenth c. copy	*data sunt autem her per manus Sifridi tunc temporis notarii civitatis Crembniciensis*	writer of document	249506 249507	*Anjou-oklt* XXVI, 598 p. 398

Smolník	1344.10.21	*Nicolaus notarius dicte civitatis de Smulnuchbanya*	legal representative of town	248676	*Csáky* I. p. 93.
Nova Baňa	1346.10.03	*in presencia [...] Johannis notarii* [private document issued under the town's seal]	witness of transaction writer of document?	237045	MES III. No. 806 p. 615
Baia Mare	1347.09.20 conf. 1503	*magistro Petro notario [...] ad nostrae maiestatis presentiam accedentibus*	envoy petitioning confirmation of privileges	72092	CDH XI/1. 498.
Kežmarok	1348	*datum per manus magistri Nicolai nostri notarii*	writer of document	288969	*Anjou-oklt* XXII, No. 932, pp. 449-450.
Cluj	1352.08.22	*magister Remarus notarius et civis de eadem [Cluswar]*	legal representative of town	281204	UGDS II. No. 673 pp.88-89.
Cluj	1353.03.30	*Reymarus notarius civitatis nostre de Kuluswar*	envoy petitioning confirmation of privileges		JAKAB *Oklt.* I. p. 34. UGDS II. No. 678 pp. 96-97.
Smolník	1353.12.02 1456 transc.	*magister Johannes notarius civitatis nostre Smulnuchbanya*	legal representative of town	3125	*Csáky* I. p. 113.
Sopron	1354.06.16	*magister Sewfridus notarius civitatis Supruniensis*	envoy petitioning transcription of privileges	201786	HÁZI, *Sopron* I/1, p. 104.

Zagreb (Gradec)	1355.03.27	*Item Thomas vicenotarius contra eandem dominam Katherinam ... non comparuit.*	cited to court as defendant	not in DF; HAZU 11 c 71.	TKALČIĆ IV, p. 11.
Žilina	1357.10.28	*Wolfardus notarius civitatis nostre de Sylna*	envoy petitioning for grant of annual fair	274715 274714	CDH XI. p. 514.
Sopron	1358.02.26	*Wylhelmus notarius et scolasticus ... civitatis*	legal representative of town	201797	HÁZI, *Sopron* I/1, p. 115.
Pressburg	1364	*Item cives dederunt notario pro precio huius anni XX libras. Seyfridus / Seydlinus / Siegfried.* [his script is known between 1348 and 1379]	Item in account book, on town payroll; writer of town book	277806 AMB 3 n 1 f. 31r	FEJÉRPATAKY p. 40.
Banská Štiavnica	1364	*notario 18 flor.*	on town's payroll	235721	FEJÉRPATAKY pp. 1-3.
Banská Štiavnica	1365	*mihi notario; notario Wilhelmo ... et notario moderno*	writer of account book; on payroll	235721	FEJÉRPATAKY pp. 7-8.
Sopron	1366.02.23	*Pertheramus notarius civitatis Supruniensis*	legal representative of town	201823	HÁZI, *Sopron* I/1, p. 136.

Banská Bystrica	1379.06.04	*Nicolaus predicti loci notarius ... iurati cives*	among councillors and issuers, writer of doc.?	280665	–
Ľubietová	1382.02.11	*Nicolaus filius Nicolai civis et notarius civitatis nostre de Lwbeta*	envoy petitioning confirmation of privileges	261422	–
Cluj	1384.01.25	*Hernicus notarius civitatis eiusdem [Cluswar]*	envoy petitioning transcription of privileges	281036	UGDS II. No. 1186, p. 586.
Bardejov	1385.11.29	*magister Nicolaus notarius civitatis Barthfa*	envoy petitioning transcription of privileges	212704	–
Brașov	1388.07.26	*notario 18 flor.; dedit ... notario pro Peglino; pro notario Thomel Schaller; notarius antiquus*	witness to testimony in notarial document	–	UGDS II. No. 1230, p. 628.
Banská Bystrica	1393	*Judex quando erat cum ... Henrico notario in Crempnyz*	Expense in account book	280646	FEJÉRPATAKY p. 83.
Banská Bystrica	1393.05.13	*tenetur Henrico staet schryebir*	sum due to him	280646	FEJÉRPATAKY p. 95.
Trnava	1394-1395 1396	*notarius civitatis* *Nicolaus notarius expeditus est suo salario*	writer of town book, on payroll	MNL OL Microfilm X 1864 MK Trnava I No. 43, p. 148	RABÍK, *Mestka kniha Trnavy*, p. 148.

Kosiče	1396-1399	*Petrus fidelis scriba*	writer of entries	not in DF. AMK suppl. H. III/2, pur. 1	*Acta Iudiciaria civitatis Cassoviensis*, No. 1229, p. 95; No. 2806, p. 164.

Appendix 5: The Earliest Preserved Charters of Bishops' Towns (Issued by the Municipality)

All documents up to 31 December 1405 are listed. In case no document is preserved before this date, the earliest extant charter is mentioned. For a complete list of charters extant until 1526, see LAKATOS, *Appendix*.

Name[1]	**Date**	**DL/DF**	**Contents**	**Material,**[2] **sealing**	**Lakatos, *Appendix***
Alba Iulia	1440-1480	277441	Sale of a vineyard, text fragment	nineteenth c. copy	Gyulaf.1
Alba Iulia	1489.05.01	29326	Sale of a vineyard	B on dorse	Gyulaf.2
Bač	–	–	–	–	–
Cenad	–	–	–	–	–
Eger	1410.03.17	43036	Sale of a vineyard	A on dorse	Eger 1
Esztergom, royal town[3]	1255.00.00	236285	Sale of house; see Appendix 3.	A hanging	–
Győr, *c. regales*	1348.04.14	226748	Sale of plot and *locus molendini*	A not visible	Győr 1
Győr, *c. regales*	1369.10.06	292925	Sale of suburban property	eighteenth c. copy	Győr 2
Győr, *c. regales*	1376.07.04	42014	Sale of half a plot *in castro* to neighbours	A on dorse	Győr 3
Győr, *c. regales*	1378.02.05	243825	Sale of plot *in castro*	A on dorse	Győr 4
Győr, *c. regales*	1380.06.29	226691	Sale of suburban property	A on back	Győr 5
Győr, *c. regales*	1391.10.31	278080	Sale of shambles	A on dorse	Győr 7

[1] *c.* = *cives*.

[2] A = parchment, B = paper.

[3] 10 charters from the thirteenth century, 37 charters from the fourteenth century, and 7 charters form the fifteenth century are extant.

Győr, *c. regales*	1394.04.10	278080	Decision in court case	A not visible	Győr 8
Kalocsa	–	–	–	–	–
Nitra	1461.09.08	98100	Sale of a vineyard	A hanging	Nyitra 1
Oradea	1347.11.02	285820	Student leaving host without paying.	B on dorse	Várad 1
Pécs	1375.08.23	6294	Sale of a mill	B on dorse	Pécs 1
Pécs	1379.03.22	6599	Sale of a vineyard	A on dorse	Pécs 2
Vác, *c. Teuton. et Ungaricalis*	1468.02.23	45284	Testimony of legitimate descent	B under text, green	Vác 1
Veszprém	–	–	–	–	–
Zagreb / Gradec	1291.08.11	230227	Property ownership; see Appendix 3	A hanging	–

Appendix 6: Municipal Books Started before 1500

Place	**Years**	**Name / Title / Contents**	**Arch.sign.**	**MNL OL DL / DF**	**Edition**
Banská Belá	1471-1685	miscellaneous	MMBŠ 1827	–	–
Banská Bystrica	1386-1399	miscellaneous	MMBB 370/16	280646	FEJÉRPATAKY pp. 76-101.
Banská Bystrica	1482-	account book	MMBB 915/26	280652	–
Banská Bystrica	1489-	account book	MMBB 262/2	–	–
Banská Štiavnica	1364-1426	miscellaneous / book of judgements	MMBŠ-MOL, IV-759, škat. 15, č. 1101	235721	FEJÉRPATAKY pp. 1-38. PIIRAINEN, *Das älteste Stdtb.*
Banská Štiavnica	1432-1508	miscellaneous, incl. *Stadt- und Bergrecht* (1466)	MNM 61.54.C (Gobil codex)	–	PIIRAINEN, *Das Stadt- und Bergrecht* partial
Banská Štiavnica	1486-1575	book of judgments (*Stadtbuch*)	MMBŠ-MOL IV-755, škat. 13, č. 1097	235718	–
Bardejov	1416-1443	*Iudicium bannitum*, mainly legal	MMB 77 6	250507	FEJÉRPATAKY pp. 286-287 partial
Bardejov	1424, 1427, 1428	*Registrum sindonum*	MMB 149, 150, 164, 167, 189, 190. Knihy 1504, 1505, 1506	212789 212867 212868	FEJÉRPATAKY pp. 193-233, 234-263, 280-286
Bardejov	1429-	*Liber arrestationum*	MMB 202	212882	–
Bardejov	1436-1498	*Libri fassionales*	MMB 305	218492	–

Bardejov	1432-1438	*Registrum omnium expositorum*	old. sig. MMB 249 (IVÁNYI)	–	FEJÉRPATAKY pp. 300-408.
Bardejov	1435-1444	*Registrum exposito-rum civitatis*	MMB 553	213233	FEJÉRPATAKY pp. 418-617.
Bardejov	1447-1458	Great linen register	MMB Kníhy 1510	218495, pages mixed	GYARMATI MA Appendix
Bardejov	1448-1517	parish books	MMB 524	–	–
Bardejov	1484-1525	*Registrum fraternita-tis Marie virginis mi-sericordie*	MMB 1678	–	–
Buda	1403-1516	*Stadtrechtsbuch*	3 mss: *Bp., Cr., Lyc*	See edn.p. 32	MOLLAY 1959
Gelnica	1434-1728	miscellaneous, incl. mining statutes, 1487	MMG, Misc. Prot. A. 1434 Nr. 1	267885	PROTZE 2002
Kežmarok	1434-1568	Miscellaneous, incl. tax and accounts	MMKK IB13-IB31.	–	–
Košice	1393-1405	*Acta Iudiciaria*	AMK Suppl. H III/2, pur 1	–	HALAGA 1994
Košice	1460-1643	*Liber Civitatis Maior*	AMK Suppl. H III/2, pur 2	–	–
Košice	1471-1477	*Judiciale huius famo-se civitatis Cassa* (ma-cul.)	AMK Suppl. H Libri c.m.1	271716	–
Košice	1489-(1526)	*Verbotbuch*	AMK Suppl. H III/2, pur 5	271723	–
Kremnica	1426-1700	New town book	MMKr Stadtbuch	274522	

Kremnica	1490-1543	*Protocollum curiale*	MMKr Prot, curiale	274523	
Krupina	1487-1640	miscellaneous	MMKa No. 812	–	
Krupina	1487-1525	*Excessorum*	MMKa No. 68.	282637	
Krupina	1491-1512	Appelationes	MMKa No. 18.	282636	
Krupina	1497-1525	*Testamenta*	MMKa No. 124	282638	
Modra	1464-1634	*Grundbuch*	MMM Pozemková kniha	–	
Nová Baňa	1430-1563	miscellaneous	MMNB, Mestská kniha	–	
Prešov	1412	*Liber legum civitatis Epperies*	MMP – K 113/I	282528	
Prešov	1424-1509	*Liber secretarii civitatis Epperies*	MMP – K 2677	282529	
Prešov	1441-1470	account books	MMP – LL 365/a	282533	
Prešov	1474-1513	*Liber testamentorum* (excerpts of wills)	MMP – LL 399	228890	IVÁNYI, "Eperjes város végr. könyve"
Prešov	1497-1514	account book	MMP – K 598R	282535	
Prešov	1496-1507	account book	MMP – K 577R	282534	
Prešov	1490-1491	Account book and tax register	MMP – K 510	229013	
Pressburg	(1349) 1364-1538	Miscellaneous, mainly accounts	AMB 3 a 1	277806	–

Pressburg	1402-1506	*Protocollum actionale*	AMB PA, 2 a 1.	286772	ZIEGLER 1999
Pressburg	1424-1606	*Register der Fronleichnambruder-schaft*	AMB E.L.3	277990	
Pressburg	1426-1457	Rechtbuch	AMB 4.s.1	277814	KIRÁLY 1894, pp. 373-419, with mistakes
Pressburg	1427-1529	*Protocollum testamentorum*	AMB IB 4n-1	277056	PT 1-2
Pressburg	1439-1492	*Grundbuch* (on vine-yards)	AMB 4-1-1	C489 microf.	–
Pressburg	1439-	*Grundbuch*	AMB 4-1-2	C490 microf.	–
Pressburg	1439-1509/11	*Satzbuch*	AMB 4-1-3	C491 microf.	–
Pressburg	1434, 1439-yearly	*Kammerrechnungen*	AMB K 1-77 series	277057 - 277133 series	–
Pressburg	1435-1519	*Aechtbuch*	AMB 4.g-1	277947	–
Sabinov	1446-1523	*Liber memorialis / L. annualium* (miscella-neous)	MMS, kr. 2, sign. 38	259014	–
Smolník	1410-	miscellaneous	OSZK Cod. Lat. 385	252482	LACKO – MAYEROVÁ 2016
Sopron	1390-1517	miscellaneous 1	SVL DL 2988	204421	HÁZI II/1, pp. 1-139.
Sopron	1393-1472	miscellaneous 2	SVL DL 2989 v	204422	HÁZI II/1, pp. 140-177.
Sopron	1423-1531	*Gerichtsbuch*	SVL DL 3796	205047	HÁZI – NÉMETH 2005
Sopron	1476-1548	*Bürgerbüchl und Ächtbüchl*	SVL DL 3830	283614	–

Sopron	1480-1553	*Erstes Grundbuch*	SVL DL 3798	205049	MOLLAY 1993
Sopron	1492-1543	*Gedenkbuch*	SVL DL 3797	205048	MOLLAY – GODA 2006
Sopron	1493-1580	*Priesterbuch*	SVL DL 3799	205050	–
Spišská Nová Ves	1383-1637	miscellaneous	MMSNV, kniha č. 1-K/I	Microfilm X 4671	WEINELT 2002
Trenčín	1476-1532	miscellaneous, mainly judgements	MMTr, Mestská kniha	282577	–
Trnava	1394-1530	*Registrum civitatis racionum et debitorum maius*	MMTT , *Rationes camerae* III/1.	microfilm X 1864	RÁBIK 2008
Trnava	1481-1545	Incomes of the parish of St Nicholas	MMTT, *Ecclesiastica: Acta parochialia* – FM1	279985	RÁBIK 2013, pp. 69-165.
Trnava	1495-1543	*Liber beneficiorum*	Trnava parish archives	–	
Trnava	1470-1510	*Urbarium*	MMTT *Ecclesiastica* 2 *parochialia* 2	279954	RÁBIK 2013, pp. 166-169.
Zagreb / Gradec	1355-1358	*Notae sententiarum*	HAZU II c 71, 1 quire	–	TKALČIĆ 4, pp. 1-108.
Zagreb / Gradec	1375-1391	*Notae ex cathernis civitatis Zagrabiensis* [traces of binding]	HAZU II d 233, in 11 quires	–	TKALČIĆ 5.
Zagreb / Gradec	1384-1402	*Protocollum fassionale super possessiones et fundis* [perhaps once bound]	HAZU II d 233, in 6 quires	–	TKALČIĆ 9, pp. 1-126.

Zagreb / Gradec	1412-1448	*Liber citacionum et sentenciarum* [perhaps once bound]	HAZU II d 234, in 10 quires	–	TKALČIĆ 6.
Zagreb / Gradec	1427-1508	*Libri funduales* [in quirres covering 3-17 years each, probably bound at some point]	HAZU II d 234, in 11 quires	–	TKALČIĆ 9 (until 1441), 10 (1441-1470), 11 (1471-1526).
Zagreb / Gradec	1450-1527 (1567)	*Prothocolon civitatis regiae liberae montis Grecie* [bound]	HAZU II d 235	–	TKALČIĆ 7 (1450-1480), 8 (1481-1526).
Žilina	1378-1561	Miscellaneous, with German (1378) and Slavic (1473) text of Magdeburg law	MMŽ *Protocollum civitatis*	266966	KUCHAR, *Žilinská právna kniha;* CHALOUPECKÝ

Bibliography

Sources and Catalogues of Documents

534 documente istorice slavo-române din Țara Românească și Moldova privitoare la legăturile cu Ardealul, 1346-1603 [534 Slavonic-Romanian historical documents from Wallachia and Moldavia concerning the connections with Transylvania, 1346-1603], ed. Grigore G. TOCILESCU (Bucharest, 1931).

A Hunyadiak kora Magyarországon [The age of the Hunyadis in Hungary], ed. József TELEKI, 11 vols. (Pest, 1852-1853).

A kolozsmonostori konvent jegyzőkönyvei 1289-1556 [The protocols of the convent of Cluj-Mănăștur, 1289-1556], ed. Zsigmond JAKÓ, 2 vols. (Budapest, 1990: *A Magyar Országos Levéltár kiadványai* 2.17).

A zichi és vásonkeői gróf Zichy-család idősb ágának okmánytára [Cartulary of the elder branch of the Count Zichy family], ed. Imre Nagy *et al.*, 11 vols. (Pest, then Budapest 1871-1915).

Acta Croatica – Listine hrvatske, ed. Ivan KUKULJEVIĆ SAKCINSKI (Zagreb, 1863: *Monumenta historica slavorum meridionalium– Povjestni spomenici južnih Slavenah* 1).

Acta iudiciaria civitatis Cassoviensis 1393-1405, ed. Ondrej R. HALAGA (München, 1994, *Buchreihe der Südostdeutschen Historischen Kommission* 34).

Actionale Protocollum. Das älteste Stadtbuch von Bratislava – Preßburg aus den Jahren 1402-1506, ed. Arne ZIEGLER (Bratislava, 1999: Acta *Carpatho-Germanica* 4).

Anjoukori oklevéltár [Charter collection from the Angevin period], ed. Gyula KRISTÓ, László BLAZOVICH, Ferenc PITI, Ferenc SEBŐK, *et al.*, 48 vols. (Budapest and Szeged, 1990-2017).

Anjoukori okmánytár [Cartulary of the Angevin period], ed. Iván NAGY and Gyula NAGY, 7 vols. (Budapest, 1878-1920).

Bártfa szabad királyi város levéltára, 1319-1526 [The archives of the free royal town of Bardejov], ed. Béla IVÁNYI (Budapest, 1910).

Bertrandon de la Broquière, *Le Voyage d'Outremer de Bertrandon de la Broquière*, ed. Charles SCHEFER (Paris, 1892).

Bertrandon de la Broquiére, *Travels to Palestine and his Return from Jerusalem Overland to France*, trans. T. JONES (Hafod, 1807).

Bibliotheca Hungarica: Kódexek és nyomtatott könyvek Magyarországon 1526 előtt [Codices and printed books in Hungary before 1526], 1-2, *Fönnmaradt kötetek* [surviving volumes] (Budapest, 1988, 1993), and 3, *Adatok elveszett kötetekről* [Data on lost volumes], ed. Csaba CSAPODI and Klára CSAPODINÉ GÁRDONYI (Budapest, 1994).

BOYLE, Leonard E., *A Survey of the Vatican Archives and of its Medieval Holdings*, second revised edn. (Toronto, 2001: *Subsidia Mediaevalia* 1).

Budapest történetének okleveles emlékei – Monumenta diplomatica civitatis Budapest, 1, *1148-1301*, ed. Albert GÁRDONYI (Budapest, 1936).

Budapest történetének okleveles emlékei – Monumenta diplomatica civitatis Budapest, 3, *1382-1439*, ed. Lajos Bernát KUMOROVITZ (Budapest, 1987).

"Chronicon Cornelii Zantfliet Sancti Jacobi Leodiensis monachi", ed. Edmond MARTÈNE, in: *Veterum Scriptorum et monumentorum historicorum dogmaticorum et moralium amplissima collectio*, ed. Edmond MARTÈNE and Ursinius DURAND, 9 vols. (Paris, 1724-1733), 5, pp. 67-504.

Codex diplomaticus et epistolaris Slovaciae, ed. Richard MARSINA, 2 vols. (Bratislava, 1971, 1987).

Codex diplomaticus Hungariae ecclesiasticus ac civilis, ed. Georgius FEJÉR, 11 vols. in 48 parts (Buda, 1829-1844).

Codex diplomaticus regni Croatiae, Dalmatiae et Slavoniae, ed. Tadija SMIČIKLAS *et al.*, 18 vols. (Zagreb, 1904-1990).

Corpus Inscriptionum Slovaciae – Súpis nápisov zo Slovenska, 1, ed. Juraj ŠEDIVÝ *et al.* (Bratislava, 2014).

Das Gerichtsbuch des Kronstädter Rates (1558-1580), ed. Júlia DERZSI (Kronstadt [Braşov], 2016: *Quellen zur Geschichte der Stadt Kronstadt* 10).

Das Geschäftsbuch des Krämers Paul Moritz, 1520-1529, ed. Karl MOLLAY (Sopron, 1994: *Quellen zur Geschichte der Stadt Ödenburg*, Reihe B, 1).

Das Iglauer Bergrecht nach einer Handschrift aus Schemnitz, ed. Ilpo Tapani PIIRAINEN (Heidelberg, 1980).

Das Ofner Stadtrecht: Eine deutschsprachige Rechtssammlung des 15. Jahrhunderts aus Ungarn ed. Karl MOLLAY (Budapest, 1959: *Monumenta Historica Budapestinensia* 1).

Das Preßburger Protocollum Testamentorum 1410 (1427)-1529, 1, *1410 (1427)-1487,* and 2, *1488-1529,* ed. Judit MAJOROSSY and Katalin SZENDE (Köln and Wien, 2010, 2014: *Fontes rerum Austriacarum: Fontes Iuris* 21.1-2).

Das Stadt- und Bergrecht von Kremnitz, ed. Ilpo Tapani PIIRAINEN (Heidelberg, 1983).

Das Stadt- und Bergrecht von Schemnitz, ed. Ilpo Tapani PIIRAINEN (Oulu, 1986).

Das Stadtrechtsbuch von Sillein, ed. Ilpo Tapani PIIRAINEN (Berlin, 1972).

Das Wiener Handwerksordnungsbuch (1364–1555): Edition und Kommentar, ed. Markus GNEIẞ (Wien, 2017: *Quelleneditionen des Instituts für Österreichische Geschichtsforschung* 16).

Decreta Regni Hungariae: Gesetze und Verordnungen Ungarns 1301-1457, ed. Ferenc DŐRY, György BÓNIS, and Vera BÁCSKAI (Budapest, 1976: *Magyar Országos Levéltár kiadványai, II. Forráskiadványok* 11.)

Decreta Regni Medievalis Hungariae, 1, *(1000-1301)*, trans. and ed. János M. BAK, György BÓNIS, and James Ross SWEENEY, second. edn. (Idyllwild, 1999).

Decreta Regni Medievalis Hungariae, 2, *(1301-1457)*, trans. and ed. János M. BAK, Pál ENGEL, and James Ross SWEENEY (Salt Lake City, 1992).

Deutsche Reichstagsakten, ed. Julius WEISZÄCKER *et al.*, 14 vols (München and Gotha, 1867-1935).

Deutschsprachige Handschriften in slowakischen Archiven: Vom Mittelalter bis zur frühen Neuzeit, ed. Jörg MEIER, Klaus-Peter WEGERA, and Ilpo Tapani PIIRAINEN, 3 vols. (Berlin, 2009).

Die Chronik des Marx Faut und Melchior Klein – Faut Márk és Klein Menyhért krónikája, 1526-1616, ed. József László KOVÁCS (Sopron, 1995: *Quellen zur Geschichte der Stadt Ödenburg, Reihe C* 1).

Documente slavo-române din Sibiu (1470-1653) [Slavonic-Romanian documents from Sibiu, 1470-1653], ed. Petre P. PANAITESCU (Bucharest, 1938).

Elenchus Fontium Historiae Urbanae, 3.2, ed. András KUBINYI (Budapest, 1997).

Elenchus Fontium Historiae Urbanae, 3.3, ed. Paul NIEDERMAIER (București, 2005).

Eperjes szabad királyi város levéltára (Archivum liberae regiaeque civitatis Eperjes), 1245-1526, ed. Béla IVÁNYI (Szeged, 1931).

Erstes Grundbuch – Első telekkönyv, 1480-1553, ed. Károly MOLLAY (Sopron, 1993: *Quellen zur Geschichte der Stadt Ödenburg, Reihe A* 1).

Gedenkbuch – Feljegyzési könyv, 1492-1543, ed. Károly MOLLAY and Károly GODA (Sopron, 2006: *Quellen zur Geschichte der Stadt Ödenburg, Reihe A* 3).

Gerichtsbuch – Bírósági könyv, 1423-1531, ed. Jenő HÁZI and János NÉMETH (Sopron, 2005: *Quellen zur Geschichte der Stadt Ödenburg, Reihe A* 2)

Gyöngyös város becsületes tanácsa elhatározta ... 1659-1848: Válogatás két évszázad városi határozataiból [It was decided by the honest council of Gyöngyös ... 1659-1848: Selection of two centuries of municipal resolutions], ed. Béla KOVÁCS (Eger, 1984).

Handel und Gewerbe in Hermannstadt und in den Sieben Stühlen (1224-1579), ed. Monica VLAICU *et al.* (Sibiu, 2003).

Hazai okmánytár – Codex diplomaticus patrius, ed. Arnold IPOLYI, Imre NAGY, and Dezső VÉGHELYI, 8 vols. (Győr and Budapest,1865-1891).

Héber kútforrások Magyarország és a magyarországi zsidóság történetéhez a kezdetektől 1686-ig [Hebrew sources on the history of Hungary and its Jewry from the beginnings up to 1686], ed. Shlomo J. SPITZER and Géza KOMORÓCZY (Budapest, 2003: *Hungaria Judaica* 16).

Hermannstadt und Siebenbürgen: Die Protokolle des Hermannstädter Rates und der Sächsischen Nationsuniversität, 1391-1705, ed. Käthe HIENTZ, Bernhard HEIGL, and Thomas ŞINDILARIU (Sibiu, 2007).

KNAUZ, Nándor, "A budai káptalan regesztái 1148-1649" [Abstracts of the records of the Buda chapter], *Magyar Történelmi Tár* 12 (1863).

KOHN, Sámuel, *Héber kútforrások és adatok Magyarország történetéhez* [Hebrew sources and data on the history of Hungary] (Budapest, 1881; reprinted Budapest, 1990).

KOLLÁNYI, Ferenc, "Visitatio capituli e. m. Strigoniensis anno 1397", *Történelmi Tár* 24 (1901), pp. 71-106, 239-272.

KOLOSVÁRI, Sándor, and Klemen ÓVÁRI *Corpus statutorum municipalium* (Budapest, 1885).

KOVACHICH, Martinus Georgius, *Formulae sollennes styli in cancellaria ... regni Hungariae olim usitati* (Pest, 1799).

LACKO, Miroslav, and Erika MAYEROVÁ, *Das älteste Stadtbuch von Schmöllnitz 1410-1735: Eine Quelle zu den mitteleuropäischen wirtschaftlichen Verflechtungen* (Limbach, 2016).

LEHOTSKÁ, Darina, HORVÁTH, Vladimir *et al.* (ed.), *Inventár stredovekých listín, listov a iných príbuzných písomností I-II.* [Inventory of medieval charters, documents and related written materials in the city archives of Bratislava] (Praha, 1956 and 1966).

Liber vetustissimus Antiquae Civitatis Pragensis 1310-1518, ed. Hana PÁTKOVÁ *et al.* (Praha, 2011).

Magyar Zsidó oklevéltár – Monumenta Hungariae Judaica, ed. Ármin FRISS, Ferenc KOVÁTS, Fülöp GRÜNVALD, Jenő HÁZI, *et al.*, 18 vols. (Budapest, 1903-1980).

Magyarországi városok régi számadáskönyvei [Old account books of Hungarian towns], ed. Lászlo FEJÉRPATAKY (Budapest, 1885).

Második telekkönyv – Zweytes Grundbuch 1554-1580, ed. Péter DOMINKOVITS (Sopron, 2015).

Master Roger's Epistle to the Sorrowful Lament upon the Destruction of the Kingdom of Hungary by the Tartars, trans. and annotation János M. BAK and Martyn RADY (Budapest and New York, 2010).

Misztótfalu mezőváros jegyzőkönyve 1596-1803 [The protocol of the market town Tăuţii de Jos, 1596-1803], ed. László KIRÁLY, postface by Imre DANKÓ, notes by István BARACZKA (Debrecen, 1985).

Mittelalterliche lateinische Handschriftenfragmente in Sopron, ed. Edit MADAS (Budapest, 2006: *Fragmenta et Codices in Bibliothecis Hungariae* 5).

MOLNÁR, József, and Györgyi SIMON, *Magyar nyelvemlékek* [Vestiges of the Hungarian language] (Budapest, 1976).

Monumenta Ecclesiae Strigoniensis, ed. Ferdinandus KNAUZ *et al.*, 4 vols. (Esztergom, 1874-1999).

A nagykállói Kállay-család levéltára [Archives of Kállay family of Nagykálló], ed. Imre SZENTPÉTERY, 2 vols. (Budapest, 1943).

Oklevéltár a gróf Csáky család történetéhez [Cartulary to the history of the Count Csáky family], ed. László BÁRTFAI SZABÓ, 1.1 (Budapest, 1919).

Oklevéltár Kolozsvár története 1. kötetéhez [Cartulary to vol. 1 of the History of Cluj], ed. Elek JAKAB (Buda, 1870).

Oklevéltár Kolozsvár története 2. és 3. kötetéhez [Cartulary to vols. 2 and 3 of the History of Cluj], ed. Elek JAKAB (Budapest, 1888).

PROTZE, Hans, *Das älteste Stadtbuch der Königlich freien Bergstadt Göllnitz – Gelnica in der Unterzips und seine Sprache* (Frankfurt am Main, 2002).

Quellen zur Geschichte der Stadt Hermannstadt, 2, *Handel und Gewerbe in Hermannstadt und in den Sieben Stühlen,* ed. Monica VLAICU *et al.* (Sibiu, 2003).

Quellen zur Geschichte der Stadt Kronstadt, 1, *Rechnungen, 1503-1526* (Kronstadt, 1886).

Quellen zur Geschichte der Stadt Kronstadt, 2, *Rechnungen, 1526-1540* (Kronstadt, 1889).

Quellen zur Geschichte der Stadt Kronstadt, 3, *Rechnungen, 1541-1550* (Kronstadt, 1886).

Quellen zur Geschichte der Stadt Kronstadt, 9, *Zunfturkunden,* ed. Gernot NUSSBÄCHER and Elisabeta MARIN (Braşov, 1999).

Quellen zur Geschichte Siebenbürgens aus sächsischen Archiven, 1, *Rechnungen aus dem Archiv der Stadt Hermannstadt und der Sächsischen Nation, 1380-1516* (Hermannstadt, 1880).

RÁBIK, Vladimír, *Mestská kniha Trnavy (1392-93) 1394-1530* [The town book of Trnava, (1392-93) 1394-1530] (Trnava, 2008).

RÁBIK, Vladimir, *Trnavas – Tyrnaus mittelalterliche Stadtbücher* (Kraków, 2013).

RANSANUS, Petrus, *Epithoma rerum Hungararum*, ed. P. KULCSÁR (Budapest, 1977).

Régi Magyar Glosszárium [Old Hungarian glossary], ed. Jolán BERRÁR and Sándor KÁROLY (Budapest, 1984).

SCHEIBER, Sándor, *Héber kódexmaradványok magyarországi kötéstáblákon – Hebräische Kodexüberreste in ungarländischen Einbandstafeln: die Buchkultur der ungarischen Juden im Mittelalter* (Budapest, 1969).

SCHEIBER, Sándor, *Jewish Inscriptions in Hungary from the 3rd century to 1686* (Budapest, 1983).

Scriptores rerum Hungaricarum tempore ducum regumque stirpis Arpadianae gestarum ed. I. SZENTPÉTERY, 2 vols. (Budapest, 1938; reprint Budapest, 1999).

Slovenské listiny a listy z XV. a XVI. storočia [Slovak charters and letters from the fifteenth and sixteenth century], ed. Branislav VARSÍK (Bratislava, 1956).

Sopron szabad királyi város története [The history of the free royal town of Sopron], ed. Jenő HÁZI, vols. 1.1-7, 2.1-6 (Sopron, 1921-1943).

SZENTPÉTERY, Imre, *Az Árpád-házi királyok okleveleinek kritikai jegyzéke – Regesta regum stirpis Arpadianae critico-diplomatica* (Budapest, 1927).

The Customary Law of the Renowned Kingdom of Hungary: A Work in Three Parts Rendered by Stephen Werbőczy (The "Tripartitum"), ed. János M. BAK, Péter BANYÓ, and Martyn RADY (Budapest and Idyllwild, 2005: DRMH 5).

TKALČIĆ, Ivan Krstitelj, *Monumenta historiae liberae regiae civitatis Zagrabiae metropolis regni Dalmatiae, Croatiae et Slavoniae*, 11 vols. (Zagreb, 1889).

Urban Civilization in Pre-Crusade Europe, ed. Irving A. AGUS. 2 vols. (New York and Leiden, 1965).

Urkundenbuch des Burgenlandes und der angrenzenden Gebiete der Komitate Wieselburg, Ödenburg, und Eisenburg, ed. Hans WAGNER, Irmtraut LINDECK-POZZA, Leonard PRICKLER, *et al.*, 5 vols. (Wien, Köln, and Graz, 1955-1999).

Urkundenbuch zur Geschichte der deutschen in Siebenbürgen, ed. Gustav GÜNDISCH, Carl WERNER, and Franz ZIMMERMANN, 9 vols. (Sibiu, Köln, Wien, and Bucharest, 1892-1991).

Výsady miest a mestečiek na Slovensku [Privileges of towns and market towns in Slovakia], 1, *(1238-1350)*, ed. Ľubomír JUCK (Bratislava, 1984).

VIZKELETY, András, *Beschreibendes Verzeichnis der altdeutschen Handschriften in ungarischen Bibliotheken*, 2 vols. (Wiesbaden, 1969-1973).

WAGNER, Carl, *Analecta Scepusii sacri et profani*, 2, *Scriptores rerum Scepusiacarum, quibus accedunt inscriptiones templorum Scepusiensium* (Vienna, 1774), pp. 346-349.

XVI. századi magyarnyelvű levelek Sopron sz. kir. város levéltárából [Sixteenth-century Hungarian letters in the town archives of Sopron], ed. Jenő HÁZI (Sopron, 1928).

Žilinská právna kniha, magdeburské právo [The Žilina code book of the Magdeburg law], ed. Rudolf KUCHAR (Bratislava, 1993).

Zsigmondkori oklevéltár, ed. Elemér MÁLYUSZ, Iván BORSA, Norbert C. TÓTH, *et al.*, 13 vols. (Budapest, 1951-2017).

Székesfehérvár középkori kiváltságai [The medieval privileges of Székesfehérvár], ed. Attila ZSOLDOS and Tibor NEUMANN (Székesfehérvár, 2010).

"zu urkundt in das Stadbuch lassen einschreiben": Die ältesten Protokolle von Hermannstadt und der Sächsischen Nationsuniversität (1522-1565), ed. Mária PAKUCS-WILLCOCKS (Hermannstadt and Bonn, 2016).

Zunftbuch und Privilegien der Fleischer zu Ofen aus dem Mittelalter – A budai német mészárosok középkori céhkönyve és kiváltságlevelei, ed. István KENYERES (Budapest, 2008).

Literature

A két legrégibb magyar nyelvű nyomtatvány [The two oldest Hungarian prints], ed. János MELICH (Budapest, 1912).

A magyar iskola első évszázadai, 996-1526 [The first centuries of schooling in Hungary, 996-1526], exhibition catalogue, ed. Katalin SZENDE and Péter SZABÓ (Győr, 1996).

A magyar levéltártörténet kronológiája [The chronology of Hungarian archival history], ed. Klára DÓKA, Veronika MÜLLER, and Magdolna RÉFI OSZKÓ (Budapest, 2000).

ÁBEL, Jenő, *A bártfai Sz. Egyed templom könyvtárának története* [The history of the library of the St. Giles church at Bardejov] (Budapest, 1885).

ADAMSKA, Anna, "Away with the Germans and their language? Linguistic conflict and urban records in early fourteenth-century Cracow", in: *Uses of the Written Word*, pp. 65-85.

ADAMSKA, Anna, "Intersections: Medieval East Central Europe from the perspective of literacy and communication", in: *Medieval East Central Europe in a Comparative Perspective: From Frontier Zones to Lands in Focus,* ed. Gerhard JARITZ and Katalin SZENDE (London, 2016), pp. 223-238.

ADAMSKA, Anna, "Latin and three vernaculars in East Central Europe from the point of view of the history of social communication", in: *Spoken and Written Language: Relations between Latin and the Vernacular Languages in the Earlier Middle Ages*, ed. Mary GARRISON *et al.* (Turnhout, 2013: USML 24), pp. 325-364.

ADAMSKA, Anna, "Latin and vernacular – Reading and meditation: Two Polish queens and their books", in: *Cultures of Religious Reading in the Late Middle Ages,* ed. Sabrina CORBELLINI (Turnhout, 2013: USML 25), pp. 219-246.

ADAMSKA, Anna, "Orality and literacy in medieval East Central Europe; Final prolegomena", in: *Oral Art Forms and their Passage into Writing,* ed. Else MUNDAL and Jonas WELLENDORF (Copenhagen, 2008), pp. 69-84.

ANDEA, Susana, "Scriere i societate: de la magister la litteratus" [From magister to litteratus in Transyvanian medieval writing], in: *Scris i societate*, pp. 29-46, 281-286.

ARANY, Krisztina, "Generations abroad: Florentine merchant families in Hungary in the first half of the fifteenth century", in: *Generations in Towns: Succession and Success in Pre-Industrial Urban Societies*, ed. Finn-Einar ELIASSEN and Katalin SZENDE (Newcastle-on-Tyne, 2009), pp. 129-152.

ARLINGHAUS, Franz-Josef, "Materialität und Differenzierung der Kommunikation: Zu Funktionen des Pergament- und Papiergebrauchs in der spätmittelalterlichen Ständegesellschaft", in: *Papier im mittelalterlichen Europa*, pp. 179-190.

ARLINGHAUS, Franz-Josef, "Point of reference: Trust and the function of written agreements in a late medieval town", in: *Strategies of Writing*, pp. 277-299.

ARLINGHAUS, Franz-Josef, "Rituelle und referentielle Verwendung von Schrift: Textgebrauch in der spätmittelalterlichen Stadt", *Frühmittelalterliche Studien* 38 (2004), pp. 393-413.

ASLANOV, Cyril, "From Latin into Hebrew through the Romance vernaculars: The creation of an interlanguage written in Hebrew characters", in: *Latin-into-Hebrew: Texts and Studies,* 1, *Studies,* ed. Resianne FONTAINE and Gad FREUDENTHAL (Leiden, 2013), pp. 69-84.

ASSIS, Yom Tov, "Shlomo Seneor from Segovia to Buda", in: *Jewish Studies at the CEU 7 (2009-2011)*, ed. András KOVÁCS and Michael L. MILLER (Budapest, 2013), pp. 7-18.

ASSMANN, Jan, *Das kulturelle Gedächtnis: Schrift, Erinnerung und politische Identität in frühen Hochkulturen* (München, 1992).

AUNER, Mihály, "Két adalék a magyar nyelv tanulására a XV. századból" [Two examples of learning Hungarian in the fifteenth century], *Magyar Nyelv* 10 (1914), pp. 419-420.

BÁCSKAI, Vera, "A mezővárosi önkormányzat a 15. században és a 16. század elején" [Self-government in market towns in the fifteenth and the beginning of the sixteenth century], in: *Tanulmányok a magyar helyi önkormányzat múltjából* [Studies on the history of Hungarian local self-government], ed. György BÓNIS and Alajos DEGRÉ (Budapest, 1971), pp. 9-34.

BÁCSKAI, Vera, "Small towns in Eastern Central Europe", in*: Small towns in Early Modern Europe*, ed. Peter CLARK (Cambridge, 1995), pp. 77-89.

BADA, Michal, "A zsolnai városkönyv" [The Žilina town book], in: *Bártfától Pozsonyig*, pp. 187-197.

BADA, Michal, *Život v Žiline v zrkadle jej mestskej knihy: každodennosť Žilinčanov na základe analýzy zápisov Žilinskej mestskej knihy* [Life in Žilina in the mirror of the town book] (Bratislava, 2011).

BAIER, Annette, "Trust and antitrust", *Ethics* 96.2 (1986), pp. 231-260.

BAK, Borbála, "A XVI-XVIII. századi magyar nyelvű források kiadásának kérdései" [The edition of Hungarian sources from the sixteenth-eighteenth centuries], *Fons* 7 (2000), pp. 91-137.

BAK, János M., "'Linguistic pluralism' in medieval Hungary", in: *The Culture of Christendom: Essays in Medieval History in Commemoration of Denis L.T. Bethell*, ed. Marc Anthony MEYER (London and Rio Grande, 1993), pp. 269-279.

BAK, János M., "A kingdom of many languages", in: *Multilingualism in the Middle Ages and Early Modern Age: Communication and Miscommunication in the Premodern World*, ed. Albrecht CLASSEN (Berlin, 2016), pp. 165-176.

BAK, János M., "Legitimization of rulership in three narratives from twelfth-century Central Europe", *Majestas* 12 (2004), pp. 43-60.

BALOG, Szidónia, *A magyarországi zsidók kamaraszolgasága és igazságszolgáltatása a középkorban* [The status of Jews in Hungary as servants of the chamber and their jurisdiction in the Middle Ages] (Budapest, 1907).

BÁNDI, Zsuzsanna, *Körmend a középkorban* [Körmend in the Middle Ages] (Körmend, 1987).

Banské mestá na Slovensku [Mining towns in Slovakia], ed. Richard MARSINA (Martin, 1990).

BARISKA, István, "Sopron a kőszegi források tükrében a 14-17. században" [Sopron in the mirror of sources from Kőszeg], *Soproni Szemle* 52 (1998), pp. 4-14.

BARTA, Gábor, and János BARTA, "Royal finance in medieval Hungary: The revenues of king Béla III", in: *Crises, Revolutions and Self-sustained Growth: Essays in European Fiscal History, c. 1130-1830*, ed. Wiiliam Mark ORMROD and Margaret BONNEY (Stamford, 1999), pp. 24-40.

Bártfától Pozsonyig: Városok a 13-17. században [From Bardejov to Pressburg: Towns in the thirteenth-seventeenth centuries], ed. Enikő CSUKOVITS and Tünde LENGYEL (Budapest, 2005: *Társadalom- és Művelődéstörténeti Tanulmányok* 35).

BARTLETT, Robert, *Trial by Fire and Water: The Medieval Judicial Ordeal* (Oxford, 1986).

BARTOSZEWICZ, Agnieszka, "Urban literacy in small Polish towns and the process of 'modernisation' of society in the later Middle Ages", in: *Writing and the Administration*, pp. 149-182.

BARTOSZEWICZ, Agnieszka, *Urban Literacy in Late Medieval Poland* (Turnhout, 2017: USML 39).

BAUR, Paul, *Testament und Bürgerschaft: Alltagsleben und Sachkultur in spätmittelalterlichen Konstanz* (Sigmaringen, 1989).

BEDOS-REZAK, Brigitte Miriam, "In search of a semiotic paradigm: The matter of sealing in medieval thought and practice", in: *Good Impressions*, pp. 1-8.

BEHRMANN, Thomas, "The development of pragmatic literacy in the Lombard city communes", in: *Pragmatic Literacy*, ed. BRITNELL, pp. 25-41.

BÉKEFI, Remig, *A népoktatás története Magyarországon 1540-ig* [The history of primary education in Hungary until 1540] (Budapest, 1906).

BENDA, Judit, "A középkori karmelita kolostor feltárása Budán – The excavation of the medieval Carmelite friary in Buda", in: *Régészeti kutatások Magyarországon 2002 – Archaeological Investigations in Hungary 2002*, ed. Júlia KISFALUDI (Budapest, 2004), pp. 117-130.

BENKŐ, Elek, *Erdély középkori harangjai és bronz keresztelőmedencéi* [Medieval bronze bells and baptismal fonts from Transylvania] (Budapest and Kolozsvár, 2002).

BENKŐ, Elek, *Kolozsvár magyar külvárosa a középkorban* [The Hungarian suburb of Cluj in the Middle Ages] (Kolozsvár, 2004: *Erdélyi Tudományos Füzetek* 248).

BEREND, Nora, *At the Gate of Christendom: Jews, Muslims and 'Pagans' in Medieval Hungary, c.1000-c.1300.* (Cambridge, 2001).

BERTÉNYI, Iván, "A vörös-ezüst sávozat funkciója néhány városunk címerében" [The function of barry of argent and gules in the coats of arms of some Hungarian cities], in: *Eszmetörténeti tanulmányok a magyar középkorról* [Studies on medieval Hungarian intellectual history], ed. György SZÉKELY (Budapest, 1984), pp. 425-448.

BERTÉNYI, Iván, "Címerpajzson szereplő és pajzson kívüli ábrázolások: Buda város címerpajzsa és annak külső díszei" [Charges and other elements on and around the escutcheon: The Buda coat of arms and its surrounding elements], in: *Változatok a történelemre: Tanulmányok Székely György 80. születésnapjára* [Variations on history: Studies for György Székely's eightieth birthday], ed. Gyöngyi ERDEI and Balázs NAGY (Budapest, 2004), pp. 203-208.

BERTRAND, Paul, *Les écritures ordinaires: Sociologie d'un temps de révolution documentaire (1250-1350)* (Paris, 2015).

Bild und Wahrnehmung der Stadt, ed. Ferdinand OPLL (Linz, 2004: *Beiträge zur Geschichte der Städte Mitteleuropas* 18).

Bild und Wahrnehmung der Stadt, ed. Peter JOHANEK (Köln, Weimar, and Wien, 2012: *Städteforschung A* 63).

Biscriptality: A Sociolinguistic Typology, ed. Daniel BUNČIĆ *et al.* (Heidelberg, 2016).

BLAHOVÁ, Marie, "Stadt, Bürgertum und Städtewesen im Spiegel der Geschichtsschreibung: Wege zur städtischen Historiographie in den böhmischen Ländern im Spätmittelalter und in der frühen Neuzeit", in: *Städtische Geschichtsschreibung im Spätmittelalter und in der frühen Neuzeit*, ed. Peter JOHANEK (Köln, Weimar, and Wien, 2000), pp. 233-246.

BLAZOVICH, László, "A kiskunsági kunok és Szeged a XV. században és a XVI. század első felében" [The Cumans of the Kiskunság district and Szeged in the fifteenth and the first half of the sixteenth century], *Jászkunság* 35.1 (1989), pp. 85-88.

BLAZOVICH, László, "Der Sachsenspiegel und das Recht der Zips", in: *Eike von Repgow, A Szász tükör* [The Sachsenspiegel], ed. László BLAZOVICH and József SCHMIDT (Szeged, 2005), pp. 83-91.

BLAZOVICH, László, "Die Stadtbücher und das Ödenburger Gerichtsbuch", in: *Gerichtsbuch – Bírósági könyv*, pp. 17-32.

BLOCKMANS, Wim, "Inclusiveness and exclusion: Trust networks at the origins of European cities", *Theory and Society* 39 (2010), pp. 315-326.

BÓNIS, György, "Les autorités de foi publique et les archives des 'loci credibiles' en Hongrie", *Archivum* 12 (Paris, 1961), pp. 87-104.

BÓNIS, György, "Uzsai János Ars notariája" [The *Ars notaria* by János of Uzsa], *Filológiai Közlöny* 7 (1961), pp. 229-260.

BOONE, Marc, and Ghita DENECKERE, *Ghent: A City of All Times* (Ghent, 2010).

BORSA, Iván, "A veszprémi püspökség levéltárának első jegyzéke 1352-ből" [The first inventory of the archives of the Veszprém bishopric from 1352], *Levéltári Közlemények* 20-23 (1942-1945), pp. 384-388.

BOYLE, Leonard E., "Diplomatics", in: *Medieval Studies: An Introduction*, ed. James M. POWELL (Syracuse, 1992), pp. 82-93.

BOYLE, Leonard E., "The Fourth Lateran Council and elements of popular theology", in: *The Popular Literature in Medieval England*, ed. Thomas J. HEFFERNAN (Knoxville, 1985), pp. 30-43.

BRUNNER, Otto, *Die Finanzen der Stadt Wien von den Anfängen bis ins 16. Jahrhundert* (Wien, 1929).

BUBALO, Đorđe, *Pragmatic Literacy in Medieval Serbia* (Turnhout, 2014: USML 29).

BUDAK, Neven, "I fiorentini nella Slavonia e nella Croazia", *Archivio Storico Italiano* 153 (1995), pp. 681-695.

BURKE, Peter, "Diglossia in early odern Europe", in: *European* francophonie*: The Social, Political and Cultural History of an International Prestige Language*, ed. Vladislav S. RŽEUCKIJ, Gesine ARGENT, and Derek OFFORD (Oxford, 2014), pp. 33-50.

BURKE, Peter, "*Heu domine, adsunt Turcae*: A sketch for a social history of post-medieval Latin", in: ID., *The Art of Conversation* (Cambridge, 1993), pp. 34-65.

CARLEBACH, Elisheva, *Palaces of Time: Jewish Calendar and Culture in Early Modern Europe* (Cambridge, MA, 2011).

DE CEVINS, Marie-Madeleine, *L'Église dans les villes hongroises a la fin du moyen-age (vers 1320-vers 1490)* (Budapest, Paris, and Szeged, 2003: *Publications de l'Institut Hongrois de Paris, Dissertationes* 1).

CHALOUPECKÝ, Václav, *Kniha žilinská* [The book of Žilina] (Bratislava, 1934).

CHARTIER, Roger, *Inscrire et effacer: Culture écrit et littérature (XIe-XVIIIe siècle)* (Paris, 2005).

CLANCHY, Michael, *From Memory to Written Record. England 1066-1307*, third edition (Oxford, 2012).

CLARK, Peter, "Introduction", in: *The Oxford Handbook of Cities in World History*, ed. P. CLARK (Oxford, 2013), pp. 1-29.

COHN, Samuel K., *The Black Death Transformed: Disease and Culture in Early Renaissance Europe* (London 2002).

CORINALDESI, Giuseppina, *Fabriano Paper and Paper Mills from its Origins to Modern Day.* (Fabriano, 1948; reprinted 2010).

CSIZMADIA, Andor, *Az egyházi mezővárosok jogi helyzete és küzdelmük a felszabadulásért a XVIII. században* [The legal situation of market towns under ecclesiastical overlordship and their fight for emancipation in the eighteenth century] (Budapest, 1962).

CSUKOVITS, Enikő, "A középkori írástudók 'munkaideje'" [The 'working hours' of medieval clerks], *Levéltári Közlemények* 63 (1992), pp. 3-14.

CSUKOVITS, Enikő, "Bűn és büntetés a középkori városi gyakorlatban. A selmecbányai 14-15. századi városkönyv bűnesetei" [Crime and punishment in the medieval urban practice: Criminal cases in the fourteenth-fifteenth-century municipal book of Banská Štiavnica], in: *Bártfától Pozsonyig*, pp. 199-222.

CSUKOVITS, Enikő, "Családi viszonyok a középkor végi Magyarországon" [Family relations in late medieval Hungary], in: '*Magyaroknak eleiről*', pp. 107-125.

CSUKOVITS, Enikő, "Közjegyzők a középkori Magyarországon" [Notaries public in medieval Hungary], in: *700 éves a közjegyzőség Magyarországon* [700 years of notaries public in Hungary], ed. Gábor ROKOLYA (Budapest, 2008), pp. 54-73.

CZOBOR, Albert, "A családi levéltárak a középkorban" [Family archives in the Middle Ages], *Levéltári Közlemények* 18-19 (1940-1941), pp. 380-440.

DARVASY, Mihály, *Középkori városaink címereinek eredete és fejlődése* [The origin and development of the coats of arms of medieval Hungarian towns] (Budapest, 1942).

Das Siegel: Gebrauch und Bedeutung im Mittelalter, ed. Gabriela SIGNORI (Darmstadt, 2007).

DÁVID, Ferenc, *A soproni ó-zsinagóga* [The old synagogue in Sopron] (Budapest, 1978).

DÁVID, Ferenc, Károly GODA, and Gusztáv THIRRING, *Sopron belvárosának házai és háztulajdonosai 1488-1939* [Houses and house owners in the central part of Sopron, 1488-1939] (Sopron, 2008).

DECKER, Viliam, *Dejiny ručnej výroby papiera na Slovensku* [The history of manual paper production in Slovakia] (Martin, 1982).

Dejiny Bratislavy, 1, *Brezalauspurc – na križovatke kultúr* [History of Bratislava, 1, Brezalauspurc – At the crossroads of cultures], ed. Juraj ŠEDIVÝ and Tatiana ŠTEFANOVIČOVÁ (Bratislava, 2012).

DIESTELKAMP, Bernhard, "Freiheit der Bürger – Freiheit der Stadt", in: *Die Abendländische Freiheit vom 10. zum 14. Jahrhundert*, ed. Johannes FRIED (Sigmaringen, 1991: *Vorträge und Forschungen* 39), pp. 485-510.

DILCHER, Gerhard, "Stadtherrschaft oder kommunale Freiheit – Das 11. Jahrhundert ein Kreuzweg?" in: ID., *Bürgerrecht und Stadtverfassung*, pp. 39-64.

DILCHER, Gerhard, *Bürgerrecht und Stadtverfassung im europäischen Mittelalter* (Köln, Weimar, and Wien, 1996).

DINCĂ, Adinel, "Preserving charters in late medieval Sibiu", *Transylvanian Review* 24.4 (2015), pp. 69-76.

Diplomatická produkcia v stredovekom meste [Production of documents in medieval towns], ed. Júlia RAGAČOVÁ (Bratislava, 2005).

DOLEŽALOVÁ, Lucie, "Lack of self-praise: A search for *Laudes Urbium* in medieval Czech lands", *Medium Aevum Quotidianum* 47 (2003), pp. 33-43.

ECHEVARRIA, Ana, *The City of the three Mosques: Ávila and its Muslims in the Middle Ages* (Wiesbaden, 2011).

ECKHART, Ferenc, "Die glaubwürdigen Orte Ungarns im Mittelalter", *Mitteilungen des Instituts für österreichische Geschichtsforschung* 1914, *Ergänzungsband* 9.2, pp. 395-558.

ENGEL, Pál, *The Realm of St. Stephen: A History of Medieval Hungary, 996-1526* (London, 2001).

ENTZ, Géza, "Városi lakótornyok a középkori Magyarországon" [Urban dwelling towers in medieval Hungary] *Soproni Szemle* 40 (1986), pp. 339-342.

ERSLAND, Geir Atle, "The archive of the kontor in Bergen", in: *Neue Studien zum Archiv und zur Sprache der Hanseaten*, ed. Geir Atle ERSLAND and Marco TREBBI (Bergen, 2008), pp. 11-46.

FEDELES, Tamás, *"Eztán Pécs tűnik szemünkbe": A város középkori históriája 1009-1526* ["Then we behold Pécs": The medieval history of the city] (Pécs, 2011).

FINE, John V.A., *When Ethnicity Did Not Matter in the Balkans: A Study of Identity in Pre-Nationalist Croatia, Dalmatia, and Slavonia in the Medieval and Early-Modern Periods* (Ann Arbor, 2006).

FLÓRA, Ágnes, "'Laborem circumspecti domini notarii': Town notaries in early modern Transylvania", in: *Writing and the Administration*, pp. 313-335.

FLÓRA, Ágnes, "Kolozsvári ötvösregesztrum 1549-1790" in: *Lymbus* 2003, pp. 25-74.

FLÓRA, Ágnes, *The Matter of Honour: The Leading Urban Elite in Sixteenth-Century Cluj and Sibiu* (unpublished PhD dissertation, CEU, Budapest, 2014), to be published in the series *Studies in European Urban History* (Turnhout, 2018).

FREVERT, Ute, "Vertrauen – Eine historische Spurensuche", in: *Vertrauen: Historische Annäherungen*, ed. Ute FREVERT (Göttingen, 2003), pp. 7-66.

FÜGEDI, Erik, "Das mittelalterliche Ungarn als Gastland", in: *Die deutsche Ostsiedlung des Mittelalters als Problem der europäischen Geschichte*, ed. Walter SCHLESINGER (Sigmaringen, 1975: *Vorträge und Forschungen* 18), pp. 451-490.

FÜGEDI, Erik, "Középkori magyar városprivilégiumok" [Medieval Hungarian town privileges], *Tanulmányok Budapest Múltjából* 14 (1961), pp. 17-107.

FÜGEDI, Erik, *Kings, Bishops, and Burghers in Medieval Hungary*, ed. János M. BAK (Aldershot, 1986).

FÜGEDI, Erik, *Kolduló barátok, polgárok, nemesek* (Budapest, 1981).

GAL, Susan, *Language Shift: Social Determinants of Linguistic Change in Bilingual Austria* (New York, 1979).

GÁRDONYI, Sándor, "Das Stadtbuch von Schmöllnitz Beiträge zur Geschichte der deutschen Kanzleisprache in der Slowakei", *Német Filológiai Tanulmányok* 2 (1966), pp. 109-138.

GECSÉNYI, Lajos, "Győr középkori helyrajzáról" [The medieval topography of Győr], in ID., *Gazdaság, társadalom, igazgatás: Tanulmányok a korai újkor történetéről.* [Economy, society, administration: Studies on early modern history] (Győr, 2008).

GEMBICKÝ, Juraj, "Research of the bells in Slovakia – Source for epigraphy", in: *The History of Written Culture*, pp. 106-112.

GERÉZDI, Rabán, *A magyar világi líra kezdetei* [The beginnings of Hungarian lay poetry], (Budapest, 1962: *Irodalomtörténeti Könyvtár* 7).

GEUENICH, Dieter, "Was sind eigentlich 'Stadtbücher'? Versuch einer Definition", in: *Stadtbücher als namenkundliche Quelle,* ed. Friedhelm DEBUS (Mainz and Stuttgart, 2000), pp. 17-29.

GIDDENS, Anthony, *Modernity and Self-identity: Self and Society in the Late Modern Age* (Stanford, 1991).

GODA, Károly, "A város élén: Sopron polgármesterei a 15-16. század fordulóján" [At the helm of the town: The mayors of Sopron at the turn of the fifteenth century], *Soproni Szemle* 58 (2004), pp. 308-328.

GODA, Károly, "A városi igazgatás szerkezete Sopronban a középkor végén" [The structure of municipal government in Sopron in the late Middle Ages], *Soproni Szemle* 61 (2007), pp. 255-271.

GODA, Károly, "Die Rolle des Gedenkbuches in der Geschichte der Ödenburger Stadtverwaltung", in: *Gedenkbuch – Feljegyzési könyv*, pp. 11-22.

GODA, Károly, and Judit Majorossy, "Städtische Selbstverwaltung und Schriftproduktion im spätmittelalterlichen Königreich Ungarn – Eine Quellenkunde für Ödenburg und Preßburg", *Pro civitate Austriae* 13 (2008), pp. 60-98.

GOINA, Mariana, *The Uses of Pragmatic Literacy in the Medieval Principalities of Moldavia and Wallachia* (unpublished PhD dissertation, CEU, Budapest, 2009).

GÖNCZI, Katalin, *Ungarisches Stadtrecht aus europäischer Sicht: Die Stadtrechtsentwicklung im spätmittelalterlichen Ungarn am Beispiel Ofens* (Frankfurt am Main, 1997).

Good Impressions: Image and Authority in Medieval Seals, ed. Noël ADAMS, John F. CHERRY, and James ROBINSON (London, 2008).

GOODY, Jack, and Ian WATT, "The consequences of literacy", *Comparative Studies in Society and History* 5.3 (1963), pp. 304-345.

Gotika: Dejiny slovenského výtvarného umenia [Gothic style: The history of fine arts in Slovakia], ed. Dušan BURAN (Bratislava, 2003).

GRANASZTÓI, György, "The Hungarian bourgeois family in the late Middle Ages: Presumptions and additions to the nature of a welfare society", *Acta Historica Academiae Scientiarum Hungaricae* 30 (1984), pp. 257-320.

GROTEN, Manfred, "Studien zur Frühgeschichte deutscher Stadtsiegel: Trier, Köln, Mainz, Aachen, Soest", *Archiv für Diplomatik, Schriftgeschichte und Wappenkunde* 31 (1985), pp. 433-478.

GROTHUSEN, Klaus-Detlev, *Entstehung und Geschichte Zagrebs bis zum Ausgang des 14. Jahrhunderts* (Wiesbaden, 1967: *Osteuropastudien der Hochschulen des Landes Hessen, Reihe* 1, 37).

GRÜNN [GÁRDONYI], Albert, "I. Lajos király megerősítő záradéka" [The confirmation clause of King Louis I], *Turul* 19 (1901), pp. 27-37.

GULYÁS, László Szabolcs, "From Latin to Hungarian: Transforming of official written practice in the market-towns of Hegyalja from the 14th to the 17th Century", *Studia Historica Nitriensia* 21.1 (2017), pp. 67-86.

GULYÁS, László Szabolcs, *Mezővárosi önkormányzat a középkori Hegyalján* [Self-government of market towns in the medieval Hegyalja region] (Budapest, 2017).

GÜNDISCH, Gustav, "Die Oberschicht Hermannstadts im Mittelalter", in: ID., *Aus Geschichte und Kultur der Siebenbürger Sachsen: Ausgewählte Aufsätze und Berichte* (Köln and Wien, 1987: *Schriften zur Landeskunde Siebenbürgens* 14), pp. 182-200.

GÜNDISCH, Gustav, "Zur Geschichte des Archivs der Stadt Hermannstadt und der sächsischen Nation", in: *120 Jahre öffentliches Archiv in Siebenbürgen* (Sibiu, 1996), pp. 2-6.

GÜNDISCH, Konrad, *Das Patriziat Siebenbürger Städte im Mittelalter* (Köln, Weimar, and Wien, 1993).

GUOTH, Kálmán, *Az okleveles bizonyítás kifejlődése Magyarországon* [The development of using documentary evidence in Hungary] (Budapest, 1936).

GUYOTJEANNIN, Olivier, "'*Super omnes thesauros rerum temporalium*': Les fonctions du trésor des chartes du roi de France (XIVe-XVe siècles)", in: *Écrit et pouvoir dans les chancelleries médiévales: Espace français, espace anglais,* ed. Kouky FIANU and DeLloyd J. GUTH (Louvain-la-Neuve, 1997), pp. 100-131.

GUYOTJEANNIN, Olivier, and Olivier MATTÉONI, "Ecrire, décrire, ordonner: Les actes et la légitimité du pouvoir à la fin du Moyen Âge", in: *La légitimité implicite: Actes des conférences organisées à Rome en 2010 et en 2011 par SAS en collaboration avec l'École française de Rome*, ed. Jean-Philippe GENET (Paris, 2015), pp. 299-315.

GYARMATI, Sándor, "The great linen register of Bardejov", *Annual of Medieval Studies at CEU* 14 (2014), pp. 117-132.

GYÖNGYÖSSY, Márton, *Pénzgazdálkodás és monetáris politika a késő középkori Magyarországon* [Money economy and monetary policy in late medieval Hungary] (Budapest, 2003).

HAJNAL, István, "Die Kanzlei König Bélas IV", *Ungarische Rundschau* 5 (1916-1917), pp. 26-62; Hungarian version: *Turul* 32 (1914), pp. 1-42.

HAJNAL, István, "Írásbeliség, intellektuális réteg és európai fejlődés" [Literacy, intellectual stratum and European development], in: *Évkönyv Károlyi Árpád születése nyolcvanadik fordulójának ünnepére* [Yearbook on the eighteenth anniversary of Árpád Károlyi's birth] (Budapest, 1933), pp. 183-214.

HAJNAL, István, "Le rôle social de l'écriture et l'évolution européenne", *Revue de l'Institut de Sociologie* (Bruxelles), 14.1-2 (1934), pp. 23-53, 253-282.

HAJNAL, István, "Racionális fejlődés és írásbeliség" [Rational development and literacy], in: *A Bécsi Történetkutató Intézet Évkönyvve* [Yearbook of the Hungarian Historical Institute in Vienna] (Wien, 1932), pp. 1-6.

HAJNAL, István, *L'enseignement de l'écriture aux universités médiévales* (Budapest, 1954: *Studia Historica Academiae Scientiarum Hungaricae*; second revised edn. 1959).
HAJNAL, István, *Technika, művelődés* [Technology, culture], ed. and commentary Ferenc GLATZ (Budapest, 1993).
HAJNIK, Imre, *A királyi könyvek a vegyes házakbeli királyok korszakában* [The 'royal books' in the period between 1301 and 1526] (Budapest, 1879: *Értekezések a történelmi tudományok köréből*).
HALAGA, Ondrej, "A kassai városi könyvek, 1394-1797" [The municipal books of Košice], *Levéltári Híradó* 7 (1957), pp. 518-549.
HALAGA, Ondrej, *Košické mestské knihy (1394-1737)* [The municipal books of Košice (1394-1737)] (Košice, 1956).
Hatalom, adó, jog: Gazdaságtörténeti tanulmányok a magyar középkorról [Power, tax, law: Studies on the economic history of medieval Hungary], ed. Boglárka WEISZ and István KÁDAS (Budapest, 2017).
HAVERKAMP, Eva, "Jewish Images on Christian coins: Economy and symbolism in medieval Germany", in: *Jews and Christians in Medieval Europe: The Historiographical Legacy of Bernhard Blumenkranz,* ed. Philippe BUC, Martha KEIL, and John TOLAN (Turnhout, 2016), pp. 189-226.
HÁZI, Jenő, "A soproni magyar-latin szójegyzék" [The Hungarian-Latin glossary from Sopron], *Magyar Nyelv* 20 (1923), pp. 149-168.
HÁZI, Jenő, "A soproni virágének" [The flower-song of Sopron], *Magyar Nyelv* 25 (1929), pp. 88-90.
HÁZI, Jenő, "A városi kancellária kialakulása Sopronban" [The emergence of the town chancery in Sopron], *Soproni Szemle* 10 (1956), pp. 202-215.
HEAD, Randolph, "Knowing like a State: The transformation of political knowledge in Swiss archives, 1450-1770", *The Journal of Modern History* 75 (2003), pp. 745-782.
HELMHOLZ, Richard H., *The Spirit of Classical Canon Law* (Athens and London, 2010).
HIRSCHFELDER, Gunther, *Die Kölner Handelsbeziehungen im Spätmittelalter* (Köln, 1994).
HLAVÁČEK, Ivan, "Dreisprachigkeit im Bereich der Böhmischen Krone: Zum Phänomen der Sprachbenutzung im böhmischen diplomatischen Material bis zur Hussitischen Revolution", in: *The Development of Literate Mentalities*, pp. 289-310.
HOLČÍK, Štefan P., *Bratislavská radnica* [The Town Hall of Pressburg] (Bratislava, 1990).
HORVÁTH, Iván, "Magyar versek: mi veszett el?" [Hungarian poems: What has been lost?], in: *Ghesaurus: Tanulmányok Szentmártoni Szabó Géza hatvanadik születésnapjára* [Ghesaurus: Studies for Géza Szentmártoni Szabó's sixtieth birthday], ed. István CSÖRSZ RUMEN (Budapest, 2010), pp. 83-98.

HORVÁTH, Iván, *Ómagyar szövegemlékek mint textológiai tárgyak* [Old Hungarian texts as objects of textology] (Budapest, 2015: *Információtörténeti Műhely*).

HOSKING, Geoffrey, "Trust and distrust: A suitable theme for historians?" *Transactions of the Royal Historical Society* 16 (2006), pp. 95-115.

HOSKING, Geoffrey, *Trust: A History* (Oxford, 2014).

HOUBEN, Hubert, *Roger II of Sicily: A Ruler between East and West* (Cambridge, 2002).

HUDSON, Anne. "Outline of a theory of diglossia", in: *Focus on Diglossia*, ed. Joshua A. FISHMAN, *International Journal of the Sociology of Language*, Special Issue No. 157 (Berlin and New York, 2002), pp. 1-48.

HUNYADI, Zsolt, "Administering the law: Hungary's *loca credibilia*", in: *Custom and Law in Central Europe*, ed. Martyn RADY (Cambridge, 2003: *Faculty of Law, Occasional Papers* No. 6), pp. 25-35.

HUNYADI, Zsolt, "*Extra et intra muros*: Military-religious orders and medieval Hungarian towns (c. 1150-1350)", in: *Les ordres religieux militaires dans la ville médiévale (1100-1350)*, ed. Damien CARRAZ (Clermont-Ferrand, 2014), pp. 139-158.

HUNYADI, Zsolt, "The Knights of St. John and the Hungarian private legal literacy up to the mid-fourteenth century", in: *'The Man of Many Devices ...'*, pp. 507-519.

HUNYADI, Zsolt, "Uses of literacy by the Templars and Hospitallers in the medieval kingdom of Hungary", in: *Die Rolle der Schriftlichkeit in den geistlichen Ritterorden des Mittelalters: innere Organisation, Sozialstruktur, Politik*, ed. Roman CZAJA and Jürgen SARNOWSKY (Toruń, 2009: *Ordines Militares – Colloquia Torunensia Historica* 15), pp. 39-51.

HUSZÁR, Lajos, *A budai pénzverés története a középkorban* [The history of minting in medieval Buda] (Budapest, 1958).

In medio regni Hungariae: Régészeti, művészettörténeti és történeti kutatások "az ország közepén" [Archaeological, art historical and historical researches 'in the middle of the kingdom'], ed. Elek BENKŐ and Krisztina OROSZ (Budapest, 2015).

INCZE, János, "'Bound by pledge': Bártfa (Bardejov) and king Sigismund's policy of pledging towns", *Annual of Medieval Studies at CEU* 19 (2013), pp. 83-94.

INCZE, János, "The pledge policy of king Sigismund of Luxembourg in Hungary (1387-1437)", in: *Money and Finance in Central Europe*, pp. 87-109.

IRSIGLER, Franz, "Die Bedeutung Ungarns für die europäische Wirtschaft im Spätmittelalter", in: *Sigismund von Luxemburg*, pp. 25-34.

IRSIGLER, Franz, "Papierhandel in Mitteleuropa, 14.-16. Jahrhundert", in: *Miscellanea Franz Irsigler: Festgabe zum 65. Geburtstag,* ed. Volker HENN and Michel PAULY (Trier, 2006), pp. 309-348.

IRSIGLER, Franz, "Was machte eine mittelalterliche Siedlung zur Stadt?" in: *Miscellanea Franz Irsigler: Festgabe zum 65. Geburtstag,* ed. Volker HENN and Michel PAULY (Trier, 2006), pp. 472-486.

ISENMANN, Eberhard, *Die deutsche Stadt im Mittelalter 1150-1550* (Wien, Köln, and Weimar, 2012).

ISTVÁNYI, Géza, "A megyei írásbeliség első korszaka" [The first period of county literacy], *Századok* 71 (1937), pp. 517-552.

ISTVÁNYI, Géza, *A magyarnyelvű írásbeliség kialakulása* [The formation of Hungarian literacy] (Budapest, 1934).

IVÁNYI, Béla, "A középkori Eperjes magyarsága" [Hungarians in medieval Prešov], *Szegedi Füzetek* 1 (1934), pp. 85-97, 169-175, 263-274.

IVÁNYI, Béla, "Das Deutschtum der Stadt Eperies im Mittelalter", *Südost-Forschungen* 5 (1940), pp. 361-402.

IVÁNYi, Béla, "Eperjes középkori festői" [Medieval painters at Eperjes], *Muzeumi és Könyvtári Értesítő* 11 (1917), pp. 88-116.

IVÁNYI, Béla, "Eperjes város végrendeleti könyve, 1474-1513" [The testamentary book of Prešov], *Történelmi Tár* 10 (1909), pp. 438-449.

IVÁNYI, Béla, *A középkori Vasvár* [Vasvár in the Middle Ages] (Vasvár, 1992).

IVÁNYI, Béla, *Debrecen és a budai jog* [Debrecen and the law of Buda] (Debrecen, 1924).

JAKÓ, Zsigmond, "Az oklevélírások fejlődése Erdélyben a XIV-XV. században" [The development of diplomatic scripts in Transylvania in the fourteenth and fifteenth centuries], *Levéltári Hiradó* 8 (1958), pp. 123-162.

JAKÓ, Zsigmond, and Radu MANOLESCU, *A latin írás története* [The history of Latin script] (Budapest, 1987).

JAKÓ, Sigismund, and Radu MANOLESCU, *Scrierea latină în evul mediu* [Latin script in the Middle Ages] (București, 1971).

JANECZEK, Andrzej, "Urban communes, ethnic communities, and language use in late medieval Red Ruthenian towns", in: *Uses of the Written Word*, pp. 19-35.

JANKÓ, Ferenc, József KÜCSÁN, and Katalin SZENDE, *Sopron* (Sopron, 2010: *Hungarian Atlas of Historic Towns* 1).

JARITZ, Gerhard, "Österreichische Bürgertestamente als Quellen zur Erforschung städtischer Lebensformen des Spätmittelalters", *Jahrbuch für Geschichte des Feudalismus* 8 (1984), pp. 249-264.

JOHANEK, Peter, "Das Gedächtnis der Stadt – Stadtchronistik im Mittelalter", in: *Handbuch Chroniken des Mittelalters*, ed. Gerhard WOLF and Norbert H. OTT (Berlin, 2016), pp. 337-398.

JOHANEK, Peter, "Geschichtsschreibung und Geschichtsüberlieferung in Augsburg am Ausgang des Mittelalters", in: *Literarisches Leben in Augsburg während des 15. Jahrhunderts*, ed. Johannes JANOTA and Werner WILLIAMS-KRAPP (Tübingen, 1996), pp. 160-182.

JOHNSTONE, Stephen, "*Pistis* and citizens in ancient Greece", in: *Trust and Happiness in the History of European Political Thought*, ed. László KONTLER and Mark SOMOS (Leiden, 2018), pp. 371-390.

JOHNSTONE, Stephen, *A History of Trust in Ancient Greece* (Chicago, 2011).

JUCKER, Michael, "Trust and mistrust in letters: Late medieval diplomacy and its communication practices", in: *Strategies of Writing*, pp. 213-236.

JUCKER, Michael, "Urban literacy and urban secrecy? Some new approaches to an old problem", in: *Writing and the Administration of Medieval Towns*, pp. 231-241.

JUREK, Tomasz, "Die Rechtskraft von Urkunden im mittelalterlichen Polen", in: *The Development of Literate Mentalities*, pp. 59-91.

KEIL, Martha, "Juden in Grenzgemeinden: Wiener Neustadt und Ödenburg im Spätmittelalter", in: *Studien zur Geschichte der Juden in Österreich*, 2, ed. Martha KEIL and Eleonore LAPPIN (Berlin and Bodenheim – Mainz, 1998), pp. 9-33.

KEIL, Martha, "Mobilität und Sittsamkeit: Jüdische Frauen im Wirtschaftsleben des spätmittelalterlichen Aschkenas", in: *Wirtschaftsgeschichte der mittelalterlichen Juden*, pp. 153-180.

KEIL, Martha, "Heilige Worte – Schriften des Abscheus: Der Umgang mit Büchern als Paradigma des jüdisch-christlichen Spannungsverhältnisses", in: *Text als Realie* (Wien, 2003: *Sitzungsberichte der Österreichische Akademie der Wissenschaften, Phil.-Hist. Kl.* 704), pp. 49-61.

KEJŘ, Jiří, *Die mittelalterlichen Städte in den böhmischen Ländern: Gründung – Verfassung – Entwicklung* (Köln, Weimar, and Wien, 2010: *Städteforschung A*, 78).

KEJŘ, Jiří, "Die Urkunde als Beweismittel im Gerichtsverfahren im mittelalterlichen Böhmen", in: *The Development of Literate Mentalities*, pp. 51-58.

KENYERES, István, "The fate of the medieval archives of Buda and Pest", in: *Medieval Buda in Context*, pp. 52-68.

KIRÁLY, János, *Pozsony város joga a középkorban* [The law of the town of Pressburg in the Middle Ages] (Budapest, 1894).

KIRST, Jozef, "The oldest coat of arms in Europe awarded to a city", in: *Košice in the Coordinates of European History*, ed. Mária HAJDUOVÁ and Martin BARTOŠ (Košice, 2013), pp. 66-73.

KISS, András, "A kolozsvári városi levéltár első levéltári segédlete" [The first finding aid of the municipal archives of Cluj], *Levéltári Közlemények* 66 (1995), pp. 197-219.

KISS, Etele, "Ötvösség és fémművesség Magyarországon a tatárjárás idején" [Goldsmithing and metalworking in Hungary at the time of the Mongol invasion], in: *A tatárjárás (1241-42): Kiállítás a Magyar Nemzeti Múzeumban*, ed. Ágnes RITOÓK and Éva GARAM (Budapest, 2007), pp. 60-68.

KISS, Farkas Gábor, "Az első, részben magyar nyelvű nyomtatvány (Melanchthon: *Elementa Latinae grammatices*, Krakkó, Vietor, 1526)" [The first, partially Hungarian printed volume], in: *MONOKgraphia: Tanulmányok Monok István 60. születésnapjára* [Studies on István Monok's sixtieth birthday], ed. Judit NYERGES, Attila VERÓK, and Edina ZVARA (Budapest, 2016), pp. 375-379.

KISS, Farkas Gábor, "Latin és népnyelv a késő-középkori magyarországi domonkos kolostorokban: Leonhard Huntpichler: *Directio pedagogorum*" [Latin and vernacular in late medieval Dominican friaries in Hungary], *Irodalomtörténeti Közlemények* 120 (2016), pp. 225-247.

KISS, József Géza, and Róbert ÚJSZÁSZI, "Megjegyzések a késő Árpád-kori pénzek jegyrendszereinek kérdéseivel kapcsolatban" [Remarks on the marking system of the late Árpád age coins], *Numizmatikai Közlöny* 112-113 (2013-2014), pp. 43-60.

KLAIĆ, Nada, *Zagreb u srednjem vijeku: Povijest Zagreba,* 1 [Zagreb in the Middle Ages: History of Zagreb, 1] (Zagreb, 1982).

KLEIN, Karl Kurt, "Luxemburg und Siebenbürgen: Aus den Vorarbeiten zum Siebenbürgisch-Deutschen Sprachatlas", in: *Luxemburg und Siebenbürgen,* ed. Karl Kurt KLEIN (Köln and Graz, 1966), pp. 1-111.

KLUGE, Mathias Franc, *Die Macht des Gedächtnisses: Entstehung und Wandel kommunaler Schriftkultur im spätmittelalterlichen Augsburg* (Leiden, 2014: *Studies in Medieval and Reformation Traditions*).

Kódexek a középkori Magyarországon [Codices in medieval Hungary] (Exhibition catalogue), ed. András VIZKELETY (Budapest, 1986).

KOHN, Renate, "Versuch einer Nutzungs- und Ausstattungsgeschichte des Kapellenkomplexes aus historischer Sicht", in: *Die Virgilkapelle in Wien: Baugeschichte und Nutzung,* ed. Michaela KRONBERGER (Wien, 2016) pp. 167-171.

KOHN, Sámuel, *A zsidók története Magyarországon: A legrégibb időktől a mohácsi vészig: 68 kiadatlan okirattal* [The history of Jews in Hungary: From the oldest times to the battle of Mohács: with 68 unpublished documents] (Budapest, 1884).

KOLMER, Lothar, *Promissorische Eide im Mittelalter* (Kallmünz Opf., 1989: *Regensburger historische Forschungen* 12).

B. KOROKNAY, Éva, "A soproni metszett kötéstábla" [The engraved book cover from Sopron], *Soproni Szemle* 16 (1962), pp. 164-167.

KOROMPAY, Klára, "Naissance des premiers textes hongrois", in: *Les hongrois et l'Europe: Conquête et integration*, ed. Sándor Csernus, and Klára KOROMPAY (Szeged and Paris, 1999), pp. 368-371.

KOSÁRY, Domokos, *Bevezetés Magyarország történetének forrásaiba és irodalmába, 1, Általános rész, 3, Megyei levéltárak és forrásközlések* [Introduction to the sources and literature of the history of Hungary, 1, General Part, 3, County archives and source publications] (Budapest, 2008).

KOSÁRY, Domokos, Krisztina KULCSÁR, and Orsolya SZAKÁLY, *Bevezetés Magyarország történetének forrásaiba és irodalmába, 1, Általános rész, 4, Városi levéltárak és forrásközlések.* [Introduction to the sources and literature of the history of Hungary, 1, General Part, 4, Municipal archives and source publications] (Budapest, 2015).

KOSZTA, László, "A magyar székeskáptalanok kanonokjai és a hiteleshelyi tevékenység 1200-1350 között" [The canons of the cathedral chapters in Hungary and the activity of the places of authentication between 1200 and 1350] in: *Loca credibilia: Hiteleshelyek a középkori Magyarországon* [*Loca credibilia*: Places of authentication in medieval Hungary], ed. Irén BILKEI and Tamás FEDELES (Pécs, 2009), pp. 65-85.

KOSZTA, László, "Byzantine archiepiscopal ecclesiastical system in Hungary?" in: *A Kárpát-medence, a magyarság és Bizánc – The Carpathian Basin, the Hungarians and Byzantium*, ed. Terézia OLAJOS, Szilvia KOVÁCS, and Pál SZABÓ (Szeged, 2014: *Acta Universitatis Szegediensis Opuscula Byzantina* 11), pp. 127-143.

KOSZTA, László, "Püspöki székhely és városfejlődés" [Episcopal seats and urban development], in: *Kelet és Nyugat között: Történeti tanulmányok Kristó Gyula tiszteletére* [Between East and West: Historical studies in honour of Gyula Kristó], ed. László KOSZTA (Szeged, 1995), pp. 233-272.

KOSZTA, László, *A kalocsai érseki tartomány kialakulása* [The formation of the archiepiscopal province of Kalocsa] (Pécs, 2013); English summary: pp. 146-150.

KOVALOVSZKI, Júlia, *Gothic and Renaissance Furniture* (Budapest, 1980).

KOVÁTS, Ferenc, "A pozsonyi zsidókönyvtöredék, 1498-1503" [The fragment of a *Judenbuch* from Pressburg, 1498-1503], in: *Emlékkönyv Dr. Gróf Klebelsberg Kunó negyedszázados kultúrpolitikai működésének emlékére* [Festschrift for Count Dr. Kunó Klebelsberg on the twenty-fifth anniversary of his activity in the field of cultural policy], ed. Imre LUKINICH (Budapest, 1925), pp. 331-346.

KOVÁTS, Ferenc, "Pozsony városának háztartása a XV. században" [The accounts of the city of Pressburg in the fifteenth century], *Magyar Gazdaságtörténeti Szemle* 9 (1902), pp. 433-466.

KOVÁTS, Ferenc, *Preßburger Grundbuchführung und Liegenschaftsrecht im Spätmittelalter (1439-1517)* (Weimar, 1918).

KÖRMENDY, Adrienne, "Mittelalterliche *aedificatio terrae* im Lichte der ungarischen Historiographie", in: *Historiographical Approaches to the Medieval Colonization of East Central Europe,* ed. Jan PISKORSKI (Boulder, 2002: *East European Monographs* 611), pp. 145-177.

KRAUSS, Samuel, *Die Wiener Geserah vom Jahre 1421* (Wien, 1920).

KREKIĆ, Bariša, "On the Latino-Slavic cultural symbiosis in late medieval and renaissance Dalmatia and Dubrovnik", *Viator: Medieval and Renaissance Studies* 26 (1995), pp. 321-333.

KRISTÓ, Gyula, *Magyar historiográfia*, 1, *Történetírás a középkori Magyarországon* [Hungarian historiography, 1, Historical writing in medieval Hungary] (Budapest, 2002).

KRISTÓ, Gyula, *Nem magyar népek a középkori Magyarországon* [Non-Hungarian peoples in medieval Hungary] (Budapest, 2003).

KUBINYI, András. "A budai és pesti polgárok családi összeköttetései a Jagelló korban" [Family connections of the burghers of Buda and Pest in the Jagellonian period

(1490-1526)], *Levéltári Közlemények* 37 (1966), pp. 227-291, reprinted in: ID., *Tanulmányok Budapest középkori történetéről*, pp. 513-570.

KUBINYI, András, "A budai jogkönyvről: Ismertetés Mollay Károly monográfiájáról" [On the Ofner Stadtrecht: Review of Károly Mollay's monograph], *Tanulmányok Budapest Múltjából* 14 (1961), pp. 643-645.

KUBINYI, András, "A királyi kancellária és udvari kápolna Magyarországon a XII. század közepén" [The royal chancery and the court chapel in Hungary in the mid-twelfth century], *Levéltári Közlemények* 46 (1975), pp. 59-121.

KUBINYI, András, "'A magyar várostörténet első fejezete'" ['The first chapter of Hungarian urban history'] *Társadalomtörténeti Tanulmányok: Studia Miskolcinensia* 2, ed. Csaba FAZEKAS (Miskolc, 1996), pp. 36-46.

KUBINYI, András, "A magyarországi zsidóság története a középkorban" [The history of Jews in Hungary in the Middle Ages], *Soproni Szemle* 48 (1995), pp. 2-27.

KUBINYI, András, "A városi rend kialakulásának gazdasági feltételei és a főváros kereskedelme a XV. század végén" [The economic conditions of the formation of towns as an estate and the trade of the capital at the end of the fifteenth century], *Tanulmányok Budapest Múltjából* 15 (1963), pp. 189-226.

KUBINYI, András, "A városok az országos politikában, különös tekintettel Sopronra" [The towns in national politics, with special regard to Sopron], in: *A város térben és időben: Sopron kapcsolatrendszerének változásai* [The town in space and time: Changes in the relational network of Sopron], ed. Éva TURBULY (Sopron, 2002), pp. 29-53.

KUBINYI, András, "Buda város pecséthasználatának kialakulása" [The emergence of the use of seals in the town of Buda], *Tanulmányok Budapest Múltjából* 14 (1961), pp. 109-146.

KUBINYI, András, "Buda, medieval capital of Hungary", in: *Medieval Buda in Context*, pp. 366-383.

KUBINYI, András, "Budafelhévíz topográfiája és gazdasági fejlődése" [Topography and economic development of Budafelhévíz], *Tanulmányok Budapest Múltjából* 16 (1964), pp. 85-180; reprinted in: ID., *Tanulmányok Budapest középkori történetéről*, pp. 115-182.

KUBINYI, András. "Budai Kakas János és történeti feljegyzései" [János Kakas of Buda and his historical notes], *Tanulmányok Budapest Múltjából* 18 (1971), pp. 59-79.

KUBINYI, András, "Deutsche und Nicht-Deutsche in den Städten des mittelalterlichen ungarischen Königreichs", in: *Internationales kulturhistorisches Symposion Mogersdorf* (Eisenstadt, 1996), pp. 145-177.

KUBINYI, András, "Die Anfänge des städtischen Handwerks in Ungarn", in: *La formation et le développement des métiers au moyen âge*, ed. László GEREVICH (Budapest, 1977), pp. 139-153.

KUBINYI, András, *Die Anfänge Ofens* (Wiesbaden, 1972: *Osteuropastudien der Hochschulen des Landes Hessen, Reihe* 1, 60).

KUBINYI, András, "Die Zusammensetzung des städtischen Rates im mittelalterlichen Königreich Ungarn", *Südostdeutsches Archiv* 34-35 (1991-1992), pp. 23-42.

KUBINYI, András, "Ethnische Minderheiten in den ungarischen Städten des Mittelalters", in: *Städtische Randgruppen und Minderheiten,* ed. Bernd KIRCHGÄSSNER, Fritz REUTER (Sigmaringen, 1986), pp. 183-199.

KUBINYI, András, "Les Cotta de Tolède et la colonie espagnole à Bude aux 15ᵉ et 16ᵉ siècles", in: *Mélanges offerts à Szabolcs de Vajay*, ed. Ghellinck VAERNEWYCK, Xavier D'ADHÉMAR DE PANAT, and Pierre D'BRIÈRE (Braga, 1971), pp. 381-390.

KUBINYI, András, "Städtische Bürger und Universitätsstudium in Ungarn am Ende des Mittelalters", in: *Stadt und Universität im Mittelalter und in der frühen Neuzeit*, ed. Erich MASCHKE and Jürgen SYDOW (Sigmaringen, 1977: *Stadt in der Geschichte* 3), pp. 161-175.

KUBINYI, András, "Székesfehérvár középkori oklevéladása és pecsétei" [The medieval charter-issuing activity and seals of Székesfehérvár], in: *Székesfehérvár évszázadai* [Centuries of Székesfehérvár] 2, ed. Alán KRALOVÁNSZKY (Székesfehérvár, 1972), pp. 151-168.

KUBINYI, András, *Tanulmányok Budapest középkori történetéről* [Studies on the medieval History of Budapest] (Budapest, 2009).

KUBINYI, András, "Városhálózat a késő középkori Kárpát-medencében" [The urban network of the Carpathian Basin in the late Middle Ages], *Történelmi Szemle* 46 (2004), pp. 1-30.

KUBINYI, András. "Stadt und Kirche in Ungarn im Mittelalter", in: *Stadt und Kirche*, ed. Franz-Heinz HYE (Linz, 1995: Beiträge zur Geschichte der Städte Mitteleuropas, Bd. 13), pp. 179-197.

KUBINYI, András, "Zur Frage der Toleranz im mittelalterlichen Königreich Ungarn", in: *Toleranz*, ed. Alexander PATSCHOVSKY and Hajo ZIMMERMANN (Sigmaringen, 1998: *Vorträge und Forschungen* 45), pp. 187-206.

KÜMIN, Beat, *The Communal Age in Western Europe, c.1100-1800* (Basingstoke and New York, 2013).

KUMOROVITZ, Lajos Bernát, "A leleszi konvent országos levéltárának története" [The history of the public archives of the convent of Leles], *Levéltári Közlemények* 10 (1932), pp. 223-255.

KUMOROVITZ, Lajos Bernát, "Szent László király vásár-törvénye és Kálmán király pecsétes cartulája" [St. Ladislas's law on fairs and king Coloman's sealed cartula], in: *Athleta Patriae: Tanulmányok Szent László történetéhez* [*Athleta patriae*: Studies on St. Ladislas's history], ed. László MEZEY (Budapest, 1980), pp. 85-109.

KURLANSKY, Mark, *Paper: Paging through History* (London and New York, 2016).

LACKO, Richard, "Kremnická mestská kniha z rokov 1426-1700" [The town book of Kremnica from 1426-1700], *Slovenská archivistika* 19.2 (1984), pp. 96-114.

LADÁNYI, Erzsébet, *Az önkormányzat intézményei és elméleti alapvetése az európai és hazai városfejlődés korai szakaszában* [The institutions of self-governance and their theoretical basis in the early period of Hungarian urban development] (Budapest, 1996).

LAKATOS, Bálint, "Entry 'Petrus Niger'", in: *Magyar Művelődéstörténeti Lexikon* [Lexicon of Hungarian cultural history], ed. Péter KŐSZEGHY, 8 (Budapest, 2009), pp. 223-224.

LAKATOS, Bálint Péter, *Hivatali írásbeliség és ügyintézés a késő középkori magyarországi mezővárosokban, okleveleik tükrében* [Official literacy and administration in late medieval market owns of Hungary as reflected in their charters], 2 vols. (unpublished PhD dissertation, ELTE Budapest, 2013; vol. 2 *Adattár* [Gazetteer].

LAKATOS, Bálint, "Ingatlanforgalmi ügyek a késő középkori magyarországi mezővárosokban és falvakban" [Sales contracts of real estates in late medieval Hungarian market towns and villages], *Acta Universitatis Szegediensis: Acta Historica* 135 (2013), pp. 139-164.

LAKATOS, Bálint, "Kismarton város két oklevele (1461, 1502): Városi szervezet és oklevéladás" [Two charters of the town of Eisenstadt (1461, 1502). Urban governance and charter-issuing], *Soproni Szemle* 71 (2017), pp. 286-306.

LAKATOS, Bálint, *Mezővárosi oklevelek: Települési önkormányzat és írásbeliség a késő középkori Magyarországon, 1301-1526* [Documents from market towns: Local self-governance and literacy in Late Medieval Hungary] (Budapest, 2018: *Magyar történelmi emlékek: Adattárak – Monumenta Hungariae historica: Elenchi*, forthcoming).

Language Change and Social Networks, ed. Kees DE BOT and Saskia STOESSEL (Berlin and New York, 2002: *International Journal of the Sociology of Language* 153).

LANTSCHNER, Patrick, *The Logic of Political Conflict in Medieval Cities: Italy and the Southern Low Countries, 1370-1440* (Oxford, 2015).

LASZLOVSZKY, József, "Frühstädtische Siedlungsentwicklung in Ungarn", in: *Burg – Burgstadt – Stadt: Zur Genese mittelalterlicher nichtagrarischer Zentren in Ostmitteleuropa*, ed. Hansjörgen BRACHMANN (Berlin, 1995), pp. 307-315.

Latinská epigrafia: Dejiny a metodika výskumu historických nápisov zo Slovenska [Latin epigraphy: The history and methodology of the research on historical inscriptions in Slovakia], ed. Juraj ŠEDIVÝ *et al.* (Bratislava, 2014).

LEHOTSKÁ, Darina, "K počiatkom vedenia mestských kníh na Slovensku. Najstaršia bratislavská mestská kniha 1364-1538" [The beginnings of keeping municipal books in Slovakia: The oldest town book of Pressburg, 1364-1538], *Historické štúdie* 5 (1959), pp. 325-347.

LEHOTSKÁ, Darina, "Vývoj Bratislavskej mestskej kancelárie do roku 1526" [The development of the municipal chancery of Pressburg up to 1526], *Historické štúdie* 4 (1958), pp. 222-274.

Lexicon latinitatis medii aevi Hungarie, ed. I. BORONKAI, K. SZOVÁK *et al.*, 6 vols. (Budapest, 1987-2017).

Lexikon stredovekých miest na Slovensku [Lexicon of medieval towns in Slovakia], ed. Martin ŠTEFÁNIK and Jan LUKAČKA (Bratislava, 2010).

LISKOVÁ, Henrieta, "Mesto Banská Bystrica a jeho obyvatelia na základe záznamov v najstaršej mestskej knihe" [The town of Banská Bystrica and its inhabitants in the first preserved town book from 1386-1399], in: *Minulosť a prítomnosť Banskej Bystrice pri príležitosti 750. výročia mesta* [Past and present of Banská Bystrica on the occasion of the 750th anniversary of the town], ed. Imrich NAGY, 2 vols. (Banská Bystrica, 2005), 1, pp. 53-69.

LOHRMANN, Klaus, *Die Wiener Juden im Mittelalter* (Berlin, Wien, 2000).

LUHMANN, Niklas, *Trust and Power* (Chichester, 1979).

LUHMANN, Niklas, *Vertrauen: Ein Mechanismus der Reduktion sozialer Komplexität* (Stuttgart, 1968).

LUPESCU MAKÓ, Mária, "'*Item lego ...*': Gifts for the soul in late medieval Transylvania", *Annual of Medieval Studies at CEU* 7 (2001), pp. 161-185.

LUPESCU MAKÓ, Mária, "Between sacred and profane: The trial by hot iron ceremony based on the 'Regestrum Varadiense'", *Mediævalia Transilvanica* 3 (1999), pp. 5-26.

LUPESCU MAKÓ, Mária, "Der Ausgleich von Klausenburg 1458", in: *Klausenburg: Wege einer Stadt und ihrer Menschen in Europa*, ed. Ulrich BURGER and Rudolf GRÄF (Cluj-Napoca, 2007), pp. 39-50.

LUPESCU MAKÓ, Mária, "Spoken and written words in testaments: Orality and literacy in last wills of medieval Transylvanian burghers", in: *Uses of the Written Word*, pp. 271-297.

MACŮREK, Josef, "K otázce české listiny a české kanceláře na dvoře uherském v 2. pol. 15 století" [On the question of Czech charters and Czech chancellors in the Hungarian court in the second half of the fifteenth century], *Historický Časopis* 6 (1958), pp. 560-569.

MADAS, Edit, "*Fragmenta codicum in bibliothecis Hungariae* (Egy középkori forrásterület rendszeres feltárásáról)" [The systematic exploration of a group of medieval sources], *Aetas* 23 (2008), pp. 101-115.

MADAS, Edit, "Írás, könyv és könyvhasználat a középkori Magyarországon, 1000-1526" [Writing, books and their uses in medieval Hungary] in: Edit MADAS and István MONOK, *A könyvkultúra Magyarországon a kezdetektől 1800-ig* [Book culture in Hungary from its beginnings to 1800] (Budapest, 2003), pp. 11-88.

MADAS, Edit, "La naissance du Hongrois écrit", in: *The Development of Literate Mentalities*, pp. 311-319.

MAGDOŠKO, Drahoslav, *Samospráva mesta Košice v stredoveku* [The local government of Košice in the Middle Ages] (Košice, 2017).

MAGOCSI, Paul Robert, *Historical Atlas of Central Europe*; Cartographic design by Geoffrey J. MATTHEWS (Seattle, 1993).

'Magyaroknak eleiről': Ünnepi tanulmányok a hatvan esztendős Makk Ferenc tiszteletére ['On the forebears of the Hungarians': Studies in honour of Ferenc Makk's sixtieth birthday], ed. Ferenc PITI (Szeged, 2000).

Magyarországi művészet 1300-1470 körül, ed. Ernő MAROSI, 2 vols. (Budapest, 1987).

MAJOROSSY, Judit, "A foglalkozás topográfiája: A társadalmi tértől a személyes térig: a társadalmi mobilitás térbeli elemei a 15. századi Pozsonyban" [The topography of profession: From social space to personal space: Spatial elements of social mobility in fifteenth-century Bratislava], *Korall* 45 (2011), pp. 102-135.

MAJOROSSY, Judit, "A Krisztus Teste konfraternitás helye a középkori pozsonyi polgárok életében" [The role of the Corpus Christi confraternity in the life of the medieval Pressburg burghers], in: *Bártfától Pozsonyig*, pp. 253-291.

MAJOROSSY, Judit, "Archives of the dead: Administration of last wills in medieval Hungarian towns", *Medium Aevum Quotidianum* 48 (2003), pp. 13-28.

MAJOROSSY, Judit, *Church in Town: Urban Religious Life in Late Medieval Pressburg in the Mirror of Last Wills* (unpublished PhD Dissertation, to be published in 2018 by CEU Press – *CEU Medievalia*).

MAJOROSSY, Judit, "From the judge's house to the town's house: Town halls in medieval Hungary", in: *Rathäuser als multifunktionale Räume der Repräsentation, der Parteiungen und des Geheimnisses*, ed. Susanne C. PILS, Martin SCHEUTZ, Christoph SONNLECHNER, and Stefan SPEVAK (Innsbruck, 2012: *Forschungen und Beiträge zur Wiener Stadtgeschichte* 55), pp. 155-210.

MAJOROSSY, Judit, "Late medieval confraternities in Pressburg", in: *Pfarreien im Mittelalter: Deutschland, Polen, Tschechien und Ungarn im Vergleich*, ed. Natalie KRUPPA (Göttingen, 2008), pp. 339-362.

MAJOROSSY, Judit, and Katalin SZENDE, "Hospitals in medieval and early modern Hungary", in: *Europäisches Spitalwesen: Institutionelle Fürsorge in Mittelalter und Früher Neuzeit*, ed. Martin SCHEUTZ, Andrea SOMMERLECHNER, Herwig WEIGL, and Alfred Stephan WEIß (Wien and München, 2008: *MIÖG Ergänzungsband* 51), pp. 409-454.

MAJOROSSY, Judit, and Katalin SZENDE, "*Libri civitatum*: Városkönyvek a középkori Magyar Királyság közigazgatásában" [*Libri civitatum*: Town books in the administration of the medieval kingdom of Hungary], in: *Tiszteletkör: Történeti tanulmányok Draskóczy István egyetemi tanár 60. születésnapjára* [Circle of honour: Historical studies for the sixtieth birthday of Professor István Draskóczy], ed. Gábor MIKÓ, Bence PÉTERFI, and András VADAS (Budapest, 2012), pp. 319-330.

MAJOROSSY, Judit, and Katalin SZENDE, "Městské knihy ve středověkých uherských městech se zvláštním zřetelem na bratislavskou knihu *Protocollum Testamentorum*" [Municipal books in the towns of medieval Hungary, with special regard to the *Protocollum Testamentorum* of Pressburg], in: *Stav a perspektivy*, pp. 199-212.

MAJOROSSY, Judit, and Katalin SZENDE, "Sources for the hospitals in medieval and early modern Hungary", in: *Quellen zur Geschichte des Spitals und der institutio-*

nellen Fürsorge in Mittelalter und Neuzeit, ed. Martin SCHEUTZ, Andrea SOMMERLECHNER, Herwig WEIGL, and Alfred Stephan WEIß (Wien, 2010: *Quelleneditionen des Instituts für Österreichische Geschichtsforschung* 3), pp. 323-368.

MAKKAI, László, *Magyar-román közös múlt* [Hungarian-Romanian common past] (Budapest, 1948; reprinted Budapest, 1989).

MÁLYUSZ, Elemér, *A középkori magyarság település- és nemzetiségpolitikája* [Settlement- and ethnic policy of the Hungarians in the Middle Ages], ed. István SOÓS (Budapest, 2002).

MÁNDOKY KONGUR, István, "A kun miatyánk" [The Cuman *pater noster*], *Szolnok Megyei Múzeumi Évkönyv* 1973, pp. 117-125.

MAREK, Miloš, *Archivum familiae Majténi: Stredoveké dejiny rodiny Majténiovcov a listiny z jej archívu* [The medieval history of the Majtényi family and documents from their archive] (Trnava and Kraków, 2013: *Fontes rerum Slovacarum* 3).

MARSINA, Richard, "Mestské knihy na Slovensku v stredoveku" [Town books in Slovakia in the Middle Ages], in: *Stav a perspektivy*, pp. 107-116.

MARSINA, Richard, "Výsady pre žilinských Slovákov z roku 1381" [Privileges for the Slovaks of Žilina in 1381], in: *Národnostný vývoj*, pp. 13-40.

MCLEOD, Claire, "Trust", in: *The Stanford Encyclopedia of Philosophy*, https://plato.stanford.edu/entries/trust/. First published 20 February 2006; substantive revision 3 August 2015.

Medieval Buda in Context, ed. Balázs NAGY, Martyn RADY, Katalin SZENDE, and András VADAS (Leiden, 2016).

Medieval Multilingualism: The Francophone World and its Neighbours, ed. Chistopher KLEINHENZ and Keith BUSBY (Turnhout, 2011).

Medium Regni: Medieval Hungarian Royal Seats, ed. Gergely Buzás (Budapest, 1999).

MELICH, János, "Magyar-horvát glosszák" [Hungarian-Croatian glosses], *Nyelvtudományi Közlemények* 28 (1898), p. 33.

MERSIOWSKY, Mark, *Die Anfänge territorialer Rechnungslegung im deutschen Nordwesten: Spätmittelalterliche Rechnungen, Verwaltungspraxis, Hof und Territorium* (Stuttgart, 2000: *Residenzenforschung* 9).

MERTANOVÁ, Štefánia, *Ius tavernicale: Studie o procese rmovania práva tavernickych miest v etapach vyvoja tavernickeho súdu v Uhorsku (15-17. stor.)* [*Ius tavernicale*: A study on the development of the law of tavernical towns in the period of the formation of the tavernical court] (Bratislava, 1985).

MEYER, Andreas, "The Curia: The apostolic chancery", in: *A Companion to the Medieval Papacy: Growth of an Ideology and Institution*, ed. Keith David SISSON and Atria LARSON (Leiden, 2016), pp. 249-258.

MEZEY, László, "Anfänge der Privaturkunde in Ungarn und der glaubwürdigen Orte", *Archiv für Diplomatik* 18 (1972), pp. 290-302.

MIHELIĆ, Darja, "Siegel erzählen: Fallbeispiel: Mittelalterliche Städte auf slowenischem Gebiet", in: *Bild und Wahrnehmung der Stadt*, ed. OPLL, pp. 97-117.

MIKÓ, Árpád, "A bártfai városháza: Adalékok a Jagelló-kori reneszánsz történetéhez Felső-Magyarországon" [The town hall of Bardejov: Data on the history of the Renaissance in the Jagellonian era in Upper Hungary], *Művészettörténeti Értesítő* 53 (2004), pp. 19-52.

MIKÓ, Gábor, "A középkori magyar királyok ismeretlen lajstroma Monoszlóy András könyvtárából" [An unknown list of medieval kings from András Monoszlóy's library], *Acta Universitatis Szegedinensis: Acta Historica* 135 (2013), pp. 125-138.

MITCHELL, Paul, "Early stone houses in Vienna", *Fontes Urbis Medii Aevi* 3 (2006), pp. 18-25.

MITTEIS, Heinrich, and Hans LIEBERICH, *Deutsche Rechtsgeschichte,* thirteenth edn. (München, 1974).

MOLLAY, Károly, "A három középkori városháza" [The three medieval town halls] *Soproni Szemle* 31 (1977), pp. 234-247.

MOLLAY, Károly, "Gugelweit János, a Soproni virágének lejegyzője" [Hans Gugelweit, the man who noted down the 'flower song of Sopron'] *Soproni Szemle* 3 (1939), pp. 78-80.

MOLLAY, Károly, *Német-magyar nyelvi érintkezések a XVI. század végéig* [German-Hungarian language contacts until the end of the sixteenth century] (Budapest, 1982).

MOLLAY, Károly, "Többnyelvűség a középkori Sopronban – a latin nyelv" [Multilingualism in medieval Sopron – The Latin language] *Soproni Szemle* 21 (1967), pp. 155-171, 205-223, 317-333; *Soproni Szemle* 22 (1968), pp. 37-58, 130-150.

MOLLAY, Károly, "Ungarisch – Deutsch" in: *Sprachgeschichte: Ein Handbuch zur Geschichte der deutschen Sprache und ihrer Erforschung,* ed. Werner BESCH, Oskar REICHMANN, and Stefan SONDEREGGER (Berlin and New York, 1984), pp. 893-897.

MOLNÁR, Antal, *A zágrábi püspökség és a magyarországi katolikus egyház a 17. században* [The bishopric of Zagreb and the Hungarian Catholic Church in the seventeenth century] (Budapest, 2012, *METEM Könyvek* 77).

Money and Finance in Central Europe during the Later Middle Ages, ed. Roman ZAORAL (Basingstoke, 2016).

MORDOVIN, Maxim, "Late medieval and early modern cloth seals in the collection of the Hungarian National Museum", *Archeologiai Értesítő* 139 (2014), pp. 193-237.

MORGAN SPALTER, Anne, and Andries VAN DAM, "Digital visual literacy", in: *Digital Literacies in the Age of Sight and Sound* (= *Theory into Practice* 47.2 (2008)), pp. 93-101.

MOSTERT, Marco, "Forgery and trust", in *Strategies of Writing*, pp. 37-60.

Multilingualism in Medieval Britain (c. 1066-1520): Sources and Analysis, ed. Judith JEFFERSON and Ad PUTTER (Turnhout, 2013).

Multilingualism in the Middle Ages, ed. Albrecht CLASSEN (Berlin, 2016).

NÄGLER, Thomas, *Die Ansiedlung der Siebenbürger Sachsen* (Bucharest, 1979).

NAGY, Balázs, "The towns of medieval Hungary in the reports of contemporary travellers", in: *Segregation, Integration, Assimilation*, pp. 169-178.

Národnostný vývoj miest na Slovensku do roku 1918 [Ethnic development in the towns of Slovakia until 1918], ed. Richard MARSINA (Martin, 1984).

Neidhartrezeption in Wort und Bild, ed. Gertrud BLASCHITZ (Krems, 2000: *Medium Aevum Quotidianum, Sonderband* 11).

NÉMETH, András, "Learning and preaching in Central Europe: The evidence of a late medieval Rhyming Decalogue", *Annual of Medieval Studies at CEU* 11 (2005), pp. 77-96.

NÉMETH, Gábor, "Mezővárosi önkormányzat és társadalmi meghatározói a 16-17. századi Abaúj és Zemplén megyében" [Self-government and its social determinants in Abaúj and Zemplén counties in the sixteenth and seventeenth centuries], *Agrártörténeti Szemle* 32 (1988), pp. 306-338.

NÉMETH, István H., "Az archontológia és a várostörténet: Karrierek és hatalmi csoportok a kora újkori városokban (XVI-XVIII. század)" [Archontology and urban history: Careers and power groups in early medieval towns (sixteenth-seventeenth centuries)], *Fons: Forráskutatás és történeti segédtudományok* 11 (2004), pp. 197-218.

NÉMETH, István H., *Várospolitika és gazdaságpolitika a 16-17. századi Magyarországon: A felső-magyarországi városszövetség* [Urban policy and economic policy in Hungary in the sixteenth and seventeenth centuries: The alliance of Upper Hungarian towns], 2 vols. (Budapest, 2004).

NÉMETH, János, "Lateinische Relikte und Graphemverwendung im Geschäftsbuch des Krämers Paul Moritz: Ein Beitrag zum Frühneuhochdeutschen in Ungarn", *Neuphilologische Mitteilungen* 104 (2003), pp. 437-454.

NÉMETH, János. "Die Sprache des Ödenburger Gerichtsbuches", in: *Gerichtsbuch – Bírósági könyv*, pp. 47-67.

NÉMETH, János, "Die Sprache des Zunftbuches und der Zunfturkunden der Fleischer zu Ofen", in: *Zunftbuch und Privilegien*, pp. 159-168.

NEUMANN, Tibor, "'Minden időkben kegyelmes uratok kívánunk lenni': A királyi városok adóztatása a 15. század végén" ['We always wish to be your gracious lord': Taxation of royal towns at the end of the fifteenth century], in: *Hatalom, adó, jog*, pp. 13-106.

NEW, Elizabeth, "Seals and status in medieval English towns", in: *Good Impressions*, pp. 35-42.

NIEDERSTÄTTER, Alois, "Das Stadtsiegel: Medium kommunaler Selbstdarstellung: Eine Annäherung anhand von Beispielen aus dem Habsburgisch-österreichischen Alpen- und Donauraum", in: *Bild und Wahrnehmung der Stadt*, ed. OPLL, pp. 143-156.

NUSSBÄCHER, Gernot, "Din activitatea arhivistică a lui Christian Pomarius" [The activity of Christian Pomarius as archivist], *Revista Arhivelor* 1965, No. 2, pp. 169-180.

NYÉKHELYI, Dóra B., *Középkori kútlelet a budavári Szent György téren* [Finds from a medieval well on the St. George Square at Buda], (Budapest, 2003: *Monumenta Historica Budapestinensia* 12).

OPLL, Ferdinand, "Das älteste Wiener Rathaus", *Jahrbuch des Vereins für Geschichte der Stadt Wien* 46 (1990), pp. 107-122.

OPLL, Ferdinand, *Das große Wiener Stadtbuch, genannt 'Eisenbuch'* (Wien, 1999).

OPLL, Ferdinand, "Preßburg und Wien im Mittelalter: Unterschiede, Parallelen und Begegnungen", in: *Städte im Donauraum*, pp. 97-120.

Oral History of the Middle Ages: The Spoken Word in Context, ed. Gerhard JARITZ and Michael RICHTER (Budapest and Krems, 2001: *Medium Aevum Quotidianum: Sonderband* 11 – CEU *Medievalia* 3).

PACH, Zsigmond Pál, "Hungary and the Levantine trade in the fourteenth-seventeenth centuries", *Acta Orientalia Academiae Scientiarum Hungaricae* 60.1 (2007), pp. 9-31.

PAKUCS-WILLCOCKS, Mária, *Sibiu-Hermannstadt: Oriental Trade in Sixteenth-century Transylvania* (Köln, Weimar, and Wien, 2007: *Städteforschung A* 73).

PÁLFFY, Ilona, "Városi levéltáraink kezdetei" [The beginnings of municipal archives in Hungary], *Levéltári Közlemények* 18-19 (1940-1941), pp. 351-379.

PÁLOSFALVI, Tamás, *The Noble Elite in the County of Körös (Križevci), 1400-1526* (Budapest, 2014).

Papier im mittelalterlichen Europa: Herstellung und Gebrauch, ed. Carla MEYER, Sandra SCHULTZ, and Bernd SCHNEIDMÜLLER (Berlin, 2015).

PAPP, László, *A hiteleshelyek története és működése az újkorban* [The history and activity of the places of authentication in modern times] (Budapest, 1936).

PAPP, Szilárd, "Die neue Residenz Sigismunds in Preßburg", in: *Sigismundus rex et imperator*, pp. 239-245.

PAPSONOVÁ, Mária, "Das Silleiner Rechtsbuch (1378-1524) im Spiegel der Forschung", *Brücken, N.F.* 5 (Berlin, Prag, and Prešov, 1997), pp. 255-267.

PAVLICOVÁ, S. and TŘIKAČ, J., "The documentary clerical agenda of Prague's municipal offices during the Middle Ages", in: *The Development of Literate Mentalities*, pp. 183-197.

PERGER, Richard, "Wohntürme im mittelalterlichen Wien", *Beiträge zur Mittelalterarchäologie in Österreich* 8 (1992), pp. 103-115.

PERGER, Richard, *Die Wiener Ratsbürger. Ein Handbuch* (Wien, 1988).

PÉTER, Katalin, "Az egyszerű ember, az oklevelek és a levéltárak a 16-17. századi Magyarországon – háromszáz éves visszatekintéssel" [The common people, the charters and the archives in Hungary in the sixteenth and seventeenth centuries – with hindsight to the preceding three hundred years], *Történelmi Szemle* 53 (2011), pp. 335-349.

PETER, Thomas, "Judenbücher als Quellengattung und die Znaimer Judenbücher", in: *Räume und Wege: Jüdische Geschichte im Alten Reich 1300-1800*, ed. Rolf KIEẞLING *et al.* (Berlin, 2007), pp. 307-334.

PETROVICS, István, "A középkori Pécs polgárai" [The burghers of medieval Pécs], in: *Pécs szerepe a Mohács előtti Magyarországon* [The role of Pécs in Hungary before the Battle of Mohács] ed. Márta FONT (Pécs 2001), pp. 163-196.

PETROVICS, István, "A város története a 14. század közepétől 1526-ig" [The history of Pécs from the mid-fourteenth century to 1526], in: *Pécs története, 2, A püspökség alapításától a török hódításig* [The history of Pécs, 2, From the foundation of the bishopric to the Ottoman conquest], ed. Márta FONT (Pécs, 2015), pp. 173-288.

PETROVICS, István, "Foreign ethnic groups in the towns of southern Hungary in the Middle Ages", in: *Segregation, Integration, Assimilation*, pp. 67-88.

PETROVICS, István, "The cities and towns of medieval Hungary as economic and cultural centres and places of coexistence: The case of Pécs", *Colloquia* 18 (2011), pp. 5-26.

PETROVICS, István, "The fading glory of a former royal seat: The case of medieval Temesvár", in: *'The Man of Many Devices ...'*, pp. 527-538.

PEYER, Hans Conrad, *Leinwandgewerbe und Fernhandel der Stadt St. Gallen von den Anfängen bis 1520*, 2 vols. (St. Gallen, 1959-1960).

PIEKALSKI, Jerzy, "Die Rolle der Wohntürme bei der Entwicklung städtischen Wohnens im 12. und 13. Jahrhundert im Mitteleuropa", *Offa* 63-64 (2006-2007), pp. 173-196.

PIIRAINEN, Ilpo Tapani, and Sona POLLÁKOVÁ, *Die Chroniken der frühen Neuzeit aus der Zips* (Levoča, 2013).

PITZ, Ernst, *Schrift- und Aktenwesen der städtischen Verwaltung im Spätmittelalter: Köln – Nürnberg – Lübeck* (Köln, 1959).

PLANITZ, Hans, *Grundlagen des deutschen Arrestprozesses* (Leipzig, 1922).

POHL-RESL, Brigitte, *Rechnen mit der Ewigkeit: Das Wiener Bürgerspital im Mittelalter* (München, 1996).

POLLÁK, Miksa, *A zsidók története Sopronban a legrégibb időktől a mai napig* [The history of Jews in Sopron from the oldest times to the present] (Budapest, 1896).

Power, Profit, and Urban Land: Landownership in Medieval and Early Modern Northern European Towns, ed. Finn-Einar ELIASSEN and Geir Atle ERSLAND (Aldershot, 1996).

Pragmatic Literacy, East and West, 1200-1330, ed. Richard H. BRITNELL (Woodbridge, 1997).

Pragmatische Schriftlichkeit im Mittelalter: Erscheinungsformen und Entwicklungsstufen: Akten des Internationalen Kolloquiums, 17.-19. Mai 1989, ed. Hagen KELLER, Klaus GRUBMÜLLER, and Nikolaus SATUBACH (München, 1992).

PREVENIER, Walter, "Urban chanceries in the Low Countries from the twelfth to the fourteenth century: The European context", in: *Stadt, Kanzlei und Kultur im Über-*

gang zur Frühen Neuzeit – City Culture and Urban Chanceries in an Era of Change, ed. Rudolf SUNTRUP and Jan R. VEENSTRA (Frankfurt am Main, 2004), pp. 3-13.

PRICE, David H., *Johannes Reuchlin and the Campaign to Destroy Jewish Books* (Oxford, 2010).

PROKOPP, Gyula, "Az esztergomi prímási levéltár 15. századi leltára" [The fifteenth-century inventory of the archbishop's archives in Esztergom], *Levéltári Közlemények* 37 (1966), pp. 113-137.

RÁBIK, Vladimir, "*Libri beneficiorum* farnosti sv. Mikuláša v Trnave z rokov 1481-1495" [The Book of church benefices of the St. Nicholas parish in Trnava 1481-1495, in: *Stav a perspektivy*. pp. 327-336.

RÁBIK, Vladimir, "Pôsobnosť pisárov a notárov v Trnave v stredoveku" [The activity of scribes and notaries in Trnava], in: *Mestská kniha príjmov trnavskej farnosti sv. Mikuláša z roku 1495* [The book of benefices of the St. Nicholas parish in Trnava from 1495], ed. Vladimir RÁBIK (Trnava, 2006), pp. 79-89.

RÁCZ, György, "Az Árpádok sávozott címere egyes főúri pecséteken a XIII-XIV. században" [The use of the Árpádian coat of arms in some seals of noble families in the thirteenth-fourteenth centuries], *Levéltári Közlemények* 63 (1992), pp. 123-135.

RÁCZ, György, "Az első megyei papíroklevelek" [The first paper document in the counties], in: *Erősségénél fogva várépítésre való: Tanulmányok a 70 éves Németh Péter tiszteletére* [Due to its strength it is apt for building castles: Studies in honour of Péter Németh's seventieth birthday], ed. Juan CABELLO and Norbert C. TÓTH (Nyíregyháza, 2011), pp. 307-313.

RÁCZ, György, "Gentilis és Károly: Levélírás Pozsonyban – koronázás Fehérvárott: A papír megjelenése Magyarországon" [Gentilis and Charles: Letter from Pressburg – Coronation at Fehérvár: The appearance of paper in Hungary], in: *Károly Róbert és Székesfehérvár*, ed. Terézia KERNY and András SMOHAY (Székesfehérvár, 2011), pp. 32-43.

RÁDÓCZY, Gyula, "Héber betűjeles Árpád-kori pénzek" [Árpádian-age coins marked with Hebrew letters], *Numizmatikai Közlöny* 70-71 (1971-1972), pp. 33-37.

RADY, Martyn, *Custom and Law in Hungary* (Oxford, 2015).

RADY, Martyn, *Medieval Buda: A Study of Municipal Government and Jurisdiction in the Kingdom of Hungary* (Boulder, 1985: *East European Monographs* 182).

RADY, Martyn, "The government of medieval Buda", in: *Medieval Buda in Context*, pp. 303-321.

REES JONES, Sarah, "Emotions, speech, and the art of politics in fifteenth-century York: House Books, mystery plays and Richard duke of Gloucester", *Urban History* 44 (2017), pp. 586-603.

REYNOLDS, Susan, *Kingdoms and Communities in Western Europe, 900-1300* (Oxford, 1984).

REYNOLDS, Susan, "Trust in medieval society and politics", in: EAD., *The Middle Ages without Feudalism: Essays in Criticism and Comparison on the Medieval West* (Ashgate, 2012), No. IX.

RICHTER, Michael, *Sprache und Gesellschaft im Mittelalter: Untersuchungen zur mündlichen Kommunikation in England von der Mitte des elften bis zum Beginn des vierzehnten Jahrhunderts* (Stuttgart, 1979).

RODENBURG, Nora Maria, *Seal and deal: Cloth production and trade between the Netherlands and Scania during the late Middle Ages and Early Modern Times* (MA Thesis, Lund University, 2011).

ROHÁČ, Juraj, "Entstehung der Amtsbücher in der Slowakei", in: *La diplomatique urbaine en Europe au moyen âge,* ed. Therèse DE HEMPTINE, Walter PREVENIER (Louvain, Apeldoorn 2000), pp. 407-417.

ROMAINE, Suzanne, *Bilingualism* (Oxford, 1989: *Language in Society* 13).

ROMHÁNYI, Beatrix F., "Egy régi-új forrás az erdélyi domonkosok történetéhez" [A rediscovered source on the history of the Dominicans in Transylvania], *Communicationes Archaeologicae Hungariae* 2004, pp. 235-247.

ROMHÁNYI, Beatrix F., *Kolostorok és társaskáptalanok a középkori Magyarországon* [Monasteries and collegiate chapters in medieval Hungary] (Budapest, 1999).

ROMSICS, Ignác, *Clio bűvöletében: Magyar történetírás a 19-20. században – nemzetközi kitekintéssel* [Enchanted by Clio: Hungarian historiography in the nineteenth and twentieth centuries, in an international perspective] (Budapest, 2011).

RÓZSA, Zoltán, and Beáta TUGYA, "Kik voltak az első Orosháza lakói?" [Who were the inhabitants of the first Orosháza?], *Mozaikok Orosháza és vidéke múltjából* 6 (2012), pp. 17-31.

SARBAK, Gábor, "A pannonhalmi *Liber Ruber*" [The *Liber Ruber* of Pannonhalma], in: *Mons Sacer 996-1996: Pannonhalma 1000 éve* [*Mons Sacer*: Thousand years of Pannonhalma], ed. Imre TAKÁCS, 3 vols. (Pannonhalma, 1996), 1, pp. 401-421.

SARKADI NAGY, Emese, *Local Workshops – Foreign Connections: Late Medieval Altarpieces from Transylvania* (Ostfildern, 2012).

SÁROSI, Edit, *Deserting Villages, Emerging Market Towns: Settlement Dynamics and Land Management in the Great Hungarian Plain, 1300-1700* (Budapest, 2016).

SCHENDL, Herbert, "Linguistic aspects of code-switching in medieval English texts", in: *Multilingualism in Later Medieval Britain*, ed. D.A. TROTTER (Cambridge, 2000), pp. 80-88.

SCHLÖGL, Rudolf, "Historiker, Max Weber und Niklas Luhmann: Zum schwierigen (aber möglicherweise produktiven) Verhältnis von Geschichtswissenschaft und Systemtheorie", *Soziale Systeme: Zeitschrift für soziologische Theorie* 7 (2001), pp. 23-45.

SCHMIDT-WIEGAND, Ruth, "Rechtsbücher als Ausdruck pragmatischer Schriftlichkeit. Eine Bilanz", *Frühmittelalterliche Studien* 37 (2003), pp. 435-475.

SCHNEIDER, Reinhard, "Schriftlichkeit und Mündlichkeit im Bereich der Kapitularien", in: *Recht und Schrift im Mittelalter*, ed. Peter CLASSEN (Sigmaringen, 1977: *Vorträge und Forschungen* 23).

SCHRECKENBERG, Heinz, *Die christlichen Adversus-Judaeos-Texte und ihr literarisches und historisches Umfeld (13-20. Jh.)* (Frankfurt am Main, 1994).

SCHULTE, Petra, "Friedrich Barbarossa, die italienischen Kommunen und das politische Konzept der Treue", *Frühmittelalterliche Studien* 38 (2004), pp. 153-172.

SCHULTE, Petra, *"Scripturae publicae creditur": das Vertrauen in Notariatsurkunden im kommunalen Italien des 12. und 13. Jahrhunderts* (Tübingen, 2003: *Bibliothek des Deutschen Historischen Instituts in Rom* 101).

SCOTT, Tom, "Kleine Städte, keine Städte: Das sogenannte 'urbane Netz' in Südwestdeutschland im ausgehenden Mittelalter", in: *Minderstädte – Kümmerformen – Gefreite Dörfer*, ed. Herbert KNITTLER (Linz, 2006), pp. 181-200.

Scris i societate în Transilvania secolelor XIII-XVII [Writing and society in Transylvania, thirteenth-seventeenth centuries], ed. Susana ANDEA (Cluj-Napoca, [2015]).

ŠEDIVÝ, Juraj, "Deutschsprachige Beurkundung im Donaugebiet des mittelalterlichen Königreichs Ungarn", in: *Urkunden und ihre Erforschung: Zum Gedenken an Heinrich Appelt,* ed. Werner MALECZEK (Wien, 2014: *Veröffentlichungen des Instituts für Österreichische Geschichtsforschung* 62), pp. 247-265.

ŠEDIVÝ, Juraj, "Die Anfänge der Beurkundung im mittelalterlichen Pressburg (Bratislava)", in: *Wege zur Urkunde, Wege der Urkunde, Wege der Forschung: Beiträge zur europäischen Diplomatik des Mittelalters*, ed. Karel HRUZA and Paul HEROLD (Wien, Köln, and Weimar, 2005), pp. 81-115.

ŠEDIVÝ, Juraj, "Forschungen der mittelalterlichen lateinischen Schrift in der Slowakischen Republik", in: *The History of Written Culture*, pp. 19-32.

ŠEDIVÝ, Juraj, *Mittelalterliche Schriftkultur im Pressburger Kollegiatkapitel* (Bratislava, 2007).

ŠEDIVÝ, Juraj, "Najstarší patriciát v stredovekej Bratislave: šľachtici alebo mešťania?" [The oldest patriciate of medieval Pressburg: nobles or burghers?], *Forum Historiae* 2008.1 online journal, http://forumhistoriae.sk/-/najstarsi-patriciat-v-stredovekej-bratislave-slachtici-alebo-mestania.

ŠEDIVÝ, Juraj, "Písmo na stredovekých zvonoch z územia Slovenska" [Inscriptions on medieval bells of the territory of Slovakia], *Monument revue* 4 (2015), No. 2, pp. 26-34.

ŠEDIVÝ, Juraj, "Stredoveká písomná kultúra na Spiši" [Medieval written culture in Spiš], in: *Historia Scepusii*, 1, ed. Martin HOMZA and Stanisław SROKA (Bratislava and Kraków, 2009), pp. 483-520.

Segregation, Integration, Assimilation: Religious and Ethnic Groups in the Medieval Towns of Central and Eastern Europe, ed. Derek KEENE, Balázs NAGY, and Katalin SZENDE (Farnham, 2009).

SELIGMAN, Adam B., *The Problem of Trust* (Princeton, 1997).

Sigismund von Luxemburg: Ein Kaiser in Mitteleuropa, ed. Michel PAULY and François REINERT (Mainz, 2006).

Sigismundus rex et imperator: Kunst und Kultur zur Zeit Sigismund von Luxemburg, 1387-1437: Ausstellungskatalog, ed. Imre TAKÁCS (Mainz, 2006).

SIMMS, Anngret, "Paradigm shift: From town foundation to town formation", in: *Städteatlanten: Vier Jahrzehnte Atlasarbeit in Europa*, ed. Wilfried EHBRECHT (Köln, Weimar, and Wien, 2013), pp. 217-233.

SIMONYI, Zsigmond, "Az Ábel-féle szójegyzék" [The word list found by Ábel], *Nyelvtudományi Közlemények*, 31 (1901), pp. 225-227.

SKORKA, Renáta, "The formation of the guild system", in: *The History of Handicraft in Hungary*, ed. János SZULOVSZKY (Budapest, 2012), pp. 109-150.

ŠKREBLIN, Bruno, "Ethnic groups in Zagreb's Gradec in the late Middle Ages", *Review of Croatian History* 9 (2013), pp. 25-59.

SOLYMOSI, László, *A földesúri járadékok új rendszere a 13. századi Magyarországon* [The new system of seigniorial revenues in thirteenth-century Hungary] (Budapest, 1998).

SOLYMOSI, László, "A székesfehérvári káptalan hiteleshelyi működésének főbb sajátosságai az Árpád-korban" [The main characteristics of the Chapter of Székesfehérvár as a place of authentication in the Árpádian period], in: *A székesfehérvári Boldogasszony bazilika történeti jelentősége* [The historical significance of the basilica of the Blessed Virgin in Székesfehérvár], ed. Gábor FARKAS (Székesfehérvár, 1996), pp. 178-201.

SOLYMOSI, László, "Debrecen 1361. évi kiváltságlevele" [The charter of privilege of Debrecen from 1361], in: *Debrecen város 650 éves: Várostörténeti tanulmányok* [650 years of Debrecen as a town], ed. Attila BÁRÁNY, Klára PAPP, and Tamás SZÁLKAI (Debrecen, 2011), pp. 9-22.

SOLYMOSI, László, "Die glaubwürdigen Orte (*loca credibilia*) Ungarns im 14.-15. Jahrhundert", *Archiv für Dipomatik* 62 (2011), pp. 175-190.

SOLYMOSI, László, "Muttersprache und rechtliche Schriftlichkeit im mittelalterlichen Königreich Ungarn", *Archiv für Diplomatik* 59 (2013), pp. 133-163.

SOPKO, Július, "Kódexy stredoslovenských banských miest" [The codices of mining towns in central Slovakia], *Historické štúdie* 19 (1974), pp. 149-179.

SOPKO, Július, *Kroniky stredovekého Slovenska* [Chronicles of medieval Slovakia] (Budmerice, 1995).

SOPKO, Július, "Pisári a vzník Žilinskej knihy" [The scribes and the genesis of the Žilina book], in: *Národnostný vývoj*, pp. 41-71.

SPEKNER, Enikő, *Hogyan lett Buda a középkori Magyarország fővárosa? A budai királyi székhely története a 12. század végétől a 14. század közepéig* [How did Buda become the capital of medieval Hungary? The history of the Buda seat from the end of the twelfth to the mid-fourteenth century] (Budapest, 2015: *Monumenta historica Budapestinensia*, 17).

SPIRITZA, Juraj, "Testament Liebharda Egkenfeldera, bratislavského mestského notára v rokoch 1441-1456" [The last will of Liebhart Egkenfelder, town notary of Pressburg], *Zborník Slovenskeho Narodneho Múzea História* 7 (1967), pp. 165-182.
Städte im Donauraum, ed. Richard MARSINA (Bratislava, 1993).
Stav a perspektivy zpřístupňování středověkých a raně novověkých městských knih [The state and perspectives of accessing medieval and early modern municipal books], ed. Ludmila SULITKOVÁ, Michaela HRUBÁ, and Vilém ZÁBRANSKÝ (Ustí nad Labem, 2010).
ŠTEFÁNIK, Martin, "Die Anfänge der slowakischen Bergstädte: Das Beispiel Neusohl", in: *Stadt und Bergbau*, ed. K.-H. KAUFHOLD and Peter JOHANEK (Köln, Weimar, and Wien, 2004: *Städteforschung A* 64), pp. 295-312.
ŠTEFANIK, Martin, "Die Pivilegierung der Kremnitzer Bevölkerung unter besonderer Berücksichtigung der Münzer-Privilegien und ihre sozioökonomischen Zusammenhänge (1328-1526)", in: *Montanregion als Sozialregion,* ed. Angelika WESTERMANN (Husum, 2012), pp. 437-456.
ŠTEFÁNIK, Martin, "Kriminalität im mittelalterlichen Preßburg, Aechtbuch: Das erste mittelalterliche Gerichtsbuch der Stadt Bratislava-Preßburg aus den Jahren 1435-1519", *Wiener Geschichtsblätter* 65.1 (2010), pp. 47-60.
ŠTEFÁNIK, Martin, "The Kremnica town book of accounts: The economy of a mining and mint town in the kingdom of Hungary", in: *Money and Finance in Central Europe*, pp. 42-56.
Strategies of Writing: Studies on Text and Trust in the Middle Ages, ed. Petra SCHULTE, Marco MOSTERT, and Irene VAN RENSWOUDE (Turnhout, 2008: USML 13).
ŠVECOVÁ, Adriana, "Die Stadtrechtsbücher in der mittelalterlichen Slowakei und Ungarn als Beispiel des eigenen selbstbewusstseins im Rahmen der europäischen Rechtskultur", *Krakowskie Studia z Historii Państwa i Prawa* 9 (2016), pp. 327-343.
SZABÓ, András Péter, "Caspar Hain lőcsei krónikája – egy kompiláció forrásai" [The chronicle of Caspar Hain at Levoča – The sources of a compilation], in: *Clio inter arma: Tanulmányok a 16-18. századi magyarországi történetírásról* [*Clio inter arma*: Studies on Hungarian historiography in the sixteenth-eighteenth centuries], ed. Gergely TÓTH (Budapest, 2014), pp. 169-202.
SZAKÁLY, Ferenc, "A szekszárdi konvent hiteleshelyi és oklevéladó működése 1526-ig" [The work of the Szekszárd convent as place of authentication and issuer of charters up to 1526], *Tanulmányok Tolna megye történetéből* 1 (1968), pp. 9-60.
SZEGEDI, Edit, "A városi történetírás kezdetei Brassóban" [The beginnings of urban historiography in Brașov], in: *Erdélyi várostörténeti tanulmányok* [Studies on the urban history of Transylvania], ed. Judit PÁL and János FLEISZ (Csíkszereda, 2001), pp. 98-118.
SZEGHYOVÁ, Blanka, "The topography of justice: Symbols, rituals, and the representation of urban justice in early modern Hungary", in: *Faces of Community: Images,*

Symbols and Performances in East Central European Towns (1400-1700), ed. Kateřina HORNÍČKOVÁ (Lanham MD, 2018), pp. 65-90.

SZÉKELY, György, "Wallons et italiens en Europe Centrale aux XIe-XVIe siècles", *Annales Universitatis Scientiarum Budapestinensis de Rolando Eötvös Nominatae: Sectio Historica* 6 (1964), pp. 3-71.

SZELESTEI NAGY, László, "Liebhard Eghenvelder egy kódexe az Esztergomi Ferences Könyvtárban" [One of Liebhard Eghenvelder's codices in the Franciscan library of Esztergom], *Magyar Könyvszemle* 93 (1977), pp. 271-274.

SZENDE, Katalin, "A magyar városi írasbeliség kezdetei" [The beginnings of urban literacy in Hungary], in: *Arcana tabularii: Tanulmányok Solymosi László tiszteletére* [*Arcana tabularii*: Studies in honour of László Solymosi], ed. Attila BÁRÁNY, Gábor DRESKA, and Kornél SZOVÁK (Budapest and Debrecen, 2014), pp. 435-458.

SZENDE, Katalin, "*Alter alterius lingua loquatur?* Mehrsprachigkeit zwischen Konsens und Konflikt – Zum Sprachgebrauch in den mittelalterlichen Städten Ungarns", in: *Mittelalterliche Stadtsprachen*, ed. Susanne EHRICH and Maria SELIG (Regensburg, 2016: *Forum Mittelalter, Studien* 11), pp. 77-91.

SZENDE, Katalin, "Between hatred and affection: Towns and Sigismund in Hungary and the Empire", in: *Sigismund von Luxemburg*, pp. 199-210.

SZENDE, Katalin, "Beziehungen zwischen Preßburg und Ödenburg im späten Mittelalter", in: *Städte im Donauraum*, pp. 135-148.

SZENDE, Katalin, "'*In geschribn pergament einbunden*': A könyvkötéshez felhasznált kódextöredékek társadalom- és kultúrtörténeti összefüggései Sopronban [Fragments of codices used for bookbinding in Sopron in social and cultural context], *Magyar Könyvszemle* 123 (2007), pp. 278-310.

SZENDE, Katalin, "'Innen-' und 'Außensicht': Das Bild der ungarischen Städte vom Spätmittelalter bis zur Mitte des 16. Jahrhunderts" in: *Bild und Wahrnehmung*, ed. OPLL, pp. 241-264.

SZENDE, Katalin, "Integration through language: The multilingual character of late medieval Hungarian towns", in: *Segregation, Integration, Assimilation*, pp. 205-234.

SZENDE, Katalin, "Laws, loans, literates: Trust in writing in the context of Jewish-Christian contacts in medieval Hungary", in: *Religious Cohabitation in Medieval Towns*, ed. Stéphane BOISSELLIER and John TOLAN (Turnhout, 2014), pp. 243-271.

SZENDE, Katalin, "*Nundinae seu forum annuale*: Sokadalomtartási engedélyek Nagy Lajos várospolitikájában" [*Nundinae seu forum annuale*: Grants to hold annual fairs in the urban policy of Louis the Great], in: *Hatalom, adó, jog*, pp. 231-262.

SZENDE, Katalin, *Otthon a városban: Társadalom és anyagi kultúra a középkori Sopronban, Pozsonyban és Eperjesen* [At home in town: Society and material culture in medieval Sopron, Pressburg, and Prešov] (Budapest, 2004: *Társadalom- és Művelődéstörténeti Tanulmányok* 32).

SZENDE, Katalin, "Polgárnak lenni: A polgárjog megszerzésének elvei és gyakorlata a késő-középkori Sopronban" [To be a burgher: Principles and practice of acquiring burghers' right in late medieval Sopron], in: *Urbs: Magyar Várostörténeti Évkönyv* 1 (2006), pp. 85-107.

SZENDE, Katalin, "Power and identity: Royal privileges to the towns of medieval Hungary in the thirteenth century", in: *Urban Liberties and Civic Participation from the Middle Ages to Modern Times,* ed. Michel PAULY and Alexander LEE (Trier, 2015: *Beiträge zur Landes- und Kulturgeschichte* 9), pp. 27-67.

SZENDE, Katalin, "Scapegoats or competitors? The expulsion of Jews from Hungarian towns on the aftermath of the battle of Mohács (1526)", in: *Expulsion and Diaspora Formation: Religious and Ethnic Identities in Flux from Antiquity to the Seventeenth Century*, ed. John TOLAN (Turnhout, 2015), pp. 51-83.

SZENDE, Katalin, "Some aspects of urban landownership in western Hungary", in: *Power, Profit, and Urban Land*, pp. 141-166.

SZENDE, Katalin, "Spitalbesitz und Konfessionalisierung: Drei Inventare des Ödenburger (Soproner) Spitals aus den Jahren 1574, 1577 und 1585", in: *Stadt, Handwerk, Armut: Eine Quellensammlung zur Geschichte der Frühen Neuzeit: Festschrift für Helmut Bräuer*, ed. Katrin KELLER, Gerald DIESENER, and Gabriele VIERTEL (Leipzig, 2008), pp. 70-88.

SZENDE, Katalin, "Testaments and testimonies: Orality and literacy in composing last wills in late medieval Hungary", in: *Oral History of the Middle Ages*, pp. 49-66.

SZENDE, Katalin, "The uses of archives in medieval Hungary", in: *The Development of Literate Mentalities in East Central Europe*, pp. 107-142.

SZENDE, Katalin, "Towns along the way: Changing patterns of long-distance trade and the urban network of medieval Hungary", in: *Towns and Communication: Volume 2: Communication between Towns,* ed. Hubert HOUBEN and Kristjan TOOMASPOEG (Lecce, 2011), pp. 161-225.

SZENDE, Katalin, "Towns and the written word in medieval Hungary", in: *Writing and the Administration,* pp. 123-148.

SZENDE, Katalin, "Traders, 'court Jews', town Jews: The changing roles of Hungary's Jewish population in the light of royal policy between the eleventh and the fourteenth centuries", in: *Intricate Interfaith Networks in the Middle Ages: Quotidian Jewish-Christian Contacts*, ed. Ephraim SHOHAM-STEINER (Turnhout, 2016), pp. 119-151.

SZENDE, Katalin, "Von der Gespanschaftsburg zur Stadt: Warum, wie – oder warum nicht? Ein möglicher Weg der Stadtentwicklung im mittelalterlichen Ungarn", in: *Stadtgründung und Stadtwerdung: Beiträge von Archäologie und Stadtgeschichtsforschung,* ed. Ferdinand OPLL and Christoph SONNLECHNER (Wien, 2011), pp. 375-405.

SZENDE, Katalin, "Was there a bourgeoisie in medieval Hungary?", in: *The Man of Many Devices*, pp. 445-459.

SZENDE, Katalin, and András Végh, "Royal power and urban space in medieval Hungary", in: *Medieval Urban Form in Comparative Perspective: The Contribution of the Historic Towns Atlas*, ed. Anngret SIMMS and Howard B. CLARKE (Farnham, 2015), pp. 255-286.

SZENTPÉTERY, Imre, *Magyar oklevéltan* [Hungarian diplomatics] (Budapest, 1930).

SZŰCS, Jenő, *Az utolsó Árpádok* [The last Árpádians] (Budapest, 1993).

SZŰCS, Jenő, *Városok és kézművesség a XV. századi Magyarországon* [Towns and craftsmanship in fifteenth-century Hungary] (Budapest, 1955).

TAKÁCS, Imre, "Königshof und Hofkunst in Ungarn in der späten Anjouzeit", in: *Sigismundus rex et imperator*, pp. 68-86.

TEKE, Zsuzsa, "Kassa külkereskedelme az 1393-1405. évi bírói könyv bejegyzései alapján" [The foreign trade of Košice as reflected in the entries of the court protocol, 1393-1405], *Századok* 137 (2003), pp. 381-404.

TEKE, Zsuzsa, "Operatori economici fiorentini in Ungheria nel tardo Trecento e primo Quattrocento", *Archivio Storico Italiano* 153 (1995), pp. 697-707.

The Development of Literate Mentalities in East Central Europe, ed. Marco MOSTERT and Anna ADAMSKA (Turnhout, 2004: USML 9).

The History of Written Culture in the 'Carpatho-Danubian' Region, ed. Hana PÁTKOVÁ, Pavel SPUNAR, and Juraj ŠEDIVÝ (Bratislava, Praha, 2003).

The Man of Many Devices, Who Wandered Full Many Ways ... Festschrift in Honor of János M. Bak, ed. Balázs NAGY and Marcell SEBŐK (Budapest, 1999).

The Medieval Royal Town at Visegrád: Royal Centre, Urban Settlement, Churches, ed. József LASZLOVSZKY, Gergely BUZÁS, and Orsolya MÉSZÁROS (Budapest, 2014).

THOMASON, Sarah G., *Language Contact* (Washington, 2001).

TILLY, Charles, "Cities, states, and trust networks: Chapter 1 of Cities and States in World History". *Theory and Society: Renewal and Critique in Social Theory*, 39 (3), 2010.

TILLY, Charles, *Trust and Rule* (Cambridge, 2005).

TOCH, Michael, "Economic activities of German Jews in the Middle Ages", in: *Wirtschaftsgeschichte der mittelalterlichen Juden*, pp. 181-210.

TONK, Sándor, *Erdélyiek egyetemjárása a középkorban* [University attendance of Transylvanians in the Middle Ages] (Bucharest, 1979).

TÖRÖK, Gyöngyi, "Középkori magyarországi könyvfestészet" [Book illumination in medieval Hungary], in: *Kódexek*, pp. 35-46.

TÓTH, István György, *Literacy and Written Culture in Early Modern Central Europe* (Budapest, 2000).

TÓTH, Norbert C., "Az esztergom-szentistváni prépostság második vizitációja" [The second visitation of the provostry of Esztergom-Szentistván], *Egyháztörténeti Szemle* 15.1 (2014), pp. 3-23.

TRINGLI, István, "Megyék a középkori Magyarországon" [Counties in medieval Hungary], in: *Honoris causa: Tanulmányok Engel Pál tiszteletére* [*Honoris causa*:

Studies in honour of Pál Engel], ed. Tibor NEUMANN and György RÁCZ (Budapest and Piliscsaba, 2009), pp. 487-518.

TRINGLI, István, "Vásártér és vásári jog a középkori Magyarországon" [Marketplace and market law in medieval Hungary], *Századok* 144 (2010), pp. 1291-1344.

Trust and Happiness in the History of European Political Thought, ed. László KONTLER and Mark SOMOS (Leiden, 2018).

UHRIN, Dorottya, "Szent Katalin és Borbála, a felvidéki bányavárosok védőszentjei" [St. Catherine and Barbara, patron saints of the Upper Hungarian mining towns], in: *Hatalom, adó, jog,* pp. 369-386.

ULIČNÝ, Ferdinand, "K výskumu národnostnej štruktúry stredovekých miest na Slovensku" [Data on the ethnic structure of medieval towns in Slovakia], in: *Národnostný vývoj*, pp. 153-162.

Uses of the Written Word in Medieval Towns, ed. Marco MOSTERT and Anna ADAMSKA (Turnhout, 2015: USML 28).

VÁRADI, Zoltán, *Románkori, korai gótikus és gótikus feliratok a Dunántúlon* [Romanesque, early Gothic and Gothic inscriptions in Transdanubia], 2 vols (Szekszárd, 1999-2000).

VARGA, Lívia, and Pál LŐVEI, "Funerary art in medieval Hungary", *Acta Historiae Artium* 35 (1992), pp. 115-167.

VATTAI, Erzsébet F., "Az esztergomi latinok kettős pecsétje" [The double seal of the *Latini* of Esztergom], *Archaeologiai Értesítő* 90 (1963), pp. 39-45.

VÉGH, András, "A budai plébániák határjárásainak helyrajzi elemzése" [Topographical analysis of the perambulations of the Buda parishes], in: *Quasi liber et pictura: Tanulmányok Kubinyi András hetvenedik születésnapjára: Studies in Honour of András Kubinyi on his Seventieth Birthday*, ed. Gyöngyi KOVÁCS (Budapest, 2004), pp. 641-654.

VÉGH, András, *Buda, Part 1, up to 1686* (Budapest, 2015: *Hungarian Atlas of Historic Towns* 4).

VÉGH, András, "Buda, the multi-ethnic capital of medieval Hungary", in: *Segregation, Integration, Assimilation*, pp. 89-100.

VÉGH, András, *Buda város középkori helyrajza* [The topography of medieval Buda], 2 vols. (Budapest, 2006-2008: *Monumenta Historica Budapestinensia* 15-16)

VÉGH, András, "The remains of the first Jewish quarter of Buda in the light of recent excavations", in: *Régészeti kutatások Magyarországon 2005 – Archaeological Investigations in Hungary 2005,* ed. Júlia KISFALUDI (Budapest, 2006), pp. 125-148.

Verschriftung und Verschriftlichung: Aspekte des Medienwechsels in verschiedenen Kulturen und Epochen, ed. Christine EHLER and Ulrike SCHAEFER (Tübingen, 1998: *ScriptOralia* 94).

VESZPRÉMY, László, "On the margins of book and charter palaeography, the dating of some Hungarian manuscripts from the eleventh to the thirteenth century", in: *Dat-*

ing Undated Medieval Charters, ed. M. GERVERS (Woodbridge, 2000), pp. 193-206.

VESZPRÉMY, László, "Zum Stand der paläographischen Forschungen in Ungarn", in: *The History of Written Culture*, pp. 33-51.

VIZKELETY, András, "Die deutsche Sprache und das deutsche Schrifttum im ungarischen Mittelalter", in: *The Development of Literate Mentalities*, pp. 277-287.

VODRÁŽKOVÁ, Lenka, and Václav BOK, "Prag", in: *Schreiborte des deutschen Mittelalters: Skriptorien – Werke – Mäzene*, ed. Martin SCHUBERT (Berlin, 2013), pp. 425-459.

VON STROMER, Wolfgang, "Die erste Papiermühle in Mitteleuropa: Ulman Stromeirs 'Hadermühle' Nürnberg 1390-1453, an der Wiege der Massenmedien", in: *Produzione e commercio della carta e del libro secc. XIII-XVIII.* ed. Simonetta CAVACIOCCHI (Firenze, 1992), pp. 297-311.

VON STROMER, Wolfgang, "Große Innovation der Papierfabrikation in Spätmittelalter und Frühneuzeit", *Technikgeschichte* 6 (1993), pp. 1-6.

WALLACE, David, "Constance", in: *Europe, 1348-1418: A Literary History*, ed. David WALLACE (Oxford, 2016), pp. 655-682.

WEINELT, Herbert, *Das Stadtbuch von Zipser Neudorf und seine Sprache: Forschungen zum Volkstum einer ostdeutschen Volksinselstadt* (München, 1940: *Veröffentlichungen des Südostinstituts* 20).

WEISZ, Boglárka, "A bányaváros mint önálló várostípus a 14. században" [Mining towns as a separate town type in the fourteenth century], *Bányászattörténeti Közlemények* 19 (2015), pp. 31-57.

WEISZ, Boglárka, "Mining town privileges in Angevin Hungary", *The Hungarian Historical Review* 2 (2013), pp. 288-312.

WEISZ, Boglárka, "Zsidó kamaraispánok az Árpád-korban" [Jewish counts of the chamber in the Árpádian period], in: *Tanulmányok a középkori magyar történelemről* [Studies on medieval Hungarian history], ed. Sarolta HOMONNAI, Ferenc PITI, and Ildikó TÓTH (Szeged, 1999), pp. 151-161.

WEISZ, Boglárka, "Zsidók a budai jogkönyvben" [Jews in the *Ofner Stadtrecht*] in: *'Magyaroknak eleiről'*, pp. 681-694.

WELTECKE, Dorothea, "Gab es 'Vertrauen' im Mittelalter? Methodische Überlegungen", in: *Vertrauen: Historische Annäherungen*, ed. Ute FREVERT (Göttingen, 2003), pp. 67-89.

WELTECKE, Dorothea, "Trust: Some methodological reflections", in: *Strategies of Writing*, pp. 379-391.

WENNINGER, Markus J., "Juden als Münzmeister, Zollpächter und fürstliche Finanzbeamte im mittelalterlichen Aschkenas", in: *Wirtschaftsgeschichte der mittelalterlichen Juden*, pp. 121-138.

WENZEL, Edith, "Alt-Jiddisch oder Mittelhochdeutsch?" in: *Grenzen und Grenzüberschreitungen: Kulturelle Kontakte zwischen Juden und Christen im Mittelalter* ed. E. WENZEL (= *Aschkenas* 14.1 (2004)), pp. 31-49.

WIEDL, Birgit, "Jews and the city: Parameters of Jewish urban life in late medieval Austria", in: *Urban Space in the Middle Ages and Early Modern Times*, ed. Albrecht CLASSEN (Berlin, 2009), pp. 273-307.

Wirtschaftsgeschichte der mittelalterlichen Juden, ed. Michael TOCH (München, 2008).

WORM, Peter, "From subscription to seal: The growing importance of seals as signs of authenticity in early medieval royal charters", in: *Strategies of Writing,* pp. 63-83.

WRIGHT, Laura, "Bills, accounts, inventories: Everyday trilingual activities in the business world of later medieval England", in: *Multilingualism in Later Medieval Britain*, ed. David A. TROTTER (Cambridge, 2000), pp. 149-156.

WRIGHT, Laura C., "The records of Hanseatic merchants: Ignorant, sleepy or degenerate?" *Multilingua* 16.4 (Berlin, 1997), pp. 337-349.

Writing and the Administration of Medieval Towns, ed. Marco MOSTERT and Anna ADAMSKA (Turnhout, 2015: USML 27).

ZEHETMAYER, Roman, "Notare und Schreibpersonal in steirischen Städten im 13. Jahrhundert", in: *Rutengänge: Studien zur geschichtlichen Landeskunde: Festgabe für Walter Brunner zum 70. Geburtstag* (Graz, 2010), pp. 47-59.

ZUPKA, Dušan, "Communication in a town: Urban rituals and literacy in the medieval kingdom of Hungary", in: *Uses of the Written Word*, pp. 341-373.

ZSOLDOS, Attila, "Városlakók a királyi család szolgálatában" [Urban burghers in the service of the royal family], *Történelmi Szemle* 47 (2005), pp. 193-206.

ZSOLDOS, Attila, *Székesfehérvár története az Árpád-korban* [History of Székesfehérvár in the Árpádian period] (Székesfehérvár, 2016).

Index

Aachen, 262
account books, 55, 148, 156-164, 170, 172, 174-175, 189, 194, 198, 217, 225-228, 244, 284, 296, 313, 331
Achilles, parish priest of Sárospatak, 126
Achilles, provost of Fehérvár, 97
Adamska, Anna, 21-22, 234
Adriatic Sea, 35, 123
al-Andalus (region), 140
Alba Iulia (Gyulafehérvár), 75
Albert, king of Hungary and duke of Austria, 116, 127, 158 n., 220, 257, 270, 274-275
aldermen, *see*: magistrates
Alexander de Villa Dei, grammarian, 127, 312
Alexander the Great, ancient Macedon ruler, 127
Alps (mountains), 144, 240, 332
Andrew II, king of Hungary, 89, 91
Andrew III, king of Hungary, 112
Angevin, dynasty, 36, 75, 94, 141, 291
Arany, Krisztina, 217 n.
archives, 45, 50-54, 67-69, 165, 169-174, 287-321; cabinet, 302-304
Arlinghaus, Franz-Josef, 12, 20, 120
Arthur, mythical king, 127, 196
Augsburg, 330
Austria, 33 n., 50, 116, 208, 214, 253, 255, 263 n., 267, 278, 283-284
authenticity, 1-2, 16, 68-69, 72-75, 87-88, 95-98, 136-138, 219, 280-284
autonomy, 14-15, 20-21, 27, 34, 61-63, 67-68, 93-95, 119, 123, 185, 200, 318-320
Babenberg, dynasty, 89
Bač (Bács), 75
Baia Mare, 94, 123, 130, 299
Baier, Annette, 9
Balkans (peninsula), 37, 208
Banská Bystrica, 36, 58, 69, 92, 124, 149, 153, 173 n., 225, 232, 326
Banská Štiavnica, 36, 69, 111, 124 n., 130, 131 n., 149 n., 151-153, 155, 157, 173, 326
Bardejov, 32, 37, 52, 56, 113 n., 125-126, 129, 131, 142, 144 n., 145 n., 162-164, 172, 174, 224, 293, 298, 299-304, 326
Bartoszewicz, Agnieszka, 22, 189, 323, 331
Baumgartner (Pomarius), Christian, notary of Sibiu and Braşov, 305
Beatrix of Aragon, queen-consort to Matthias Corvinus and Wladislas II, 217
Béla III, king of Hungary, 253, 290
Béla IV, king of Hungary, 27, 77, 81, 91, 97, 123, 158, 255-257, 283, 316
Benda, Judit, 47
Benedictines, *see*: religious orders
Benkő, Elek, 57
Beregovo, 32, 69
Bergen (Norway), 319 n.
Bertényi, Iván, 89
Bertrand, Paul, 18-19, 137-138, 145 n.
Bertrandon de la Broquière, traveller and diplomat, 216, 280
Bihač (Bihács), 69, 111
bilingualism, *see*: multilingualism
binding, bookbinders, 56, 156, 183-184, 306-314
biscriptality, *see*: palaeography

bishop's seat, 26, 74-77, 133
Bistrița, 149, 175, 214, 218, 228, 305, 326
Black Sea, 144
Blockmans, Wim, 14-16, 185, 199
Bohemia, 22, 33, 65, 101, 119, 124 n., 189, 198, 208, 212, 255, 280
Boniface IX, Pope, 231
Borsa, Iván, 50
Bosnia, 106
Brașov, 37, 54, 69, 125, 175, 195-196, 211, 214, 218, 223, 302, 305, 326
Braunschweig, 119
Britain, 20
British Isles, 21
Britnell, Richard H., 21
Brno (Brünn), 22
Bruck an der Leitha, 275
Bruges (Brugge, Brügge), 330
Buda (part of present-day Budapest), 3, 26, 33-35, 37, 43-49, 53, 55, 57, 66-67, 69, 82-85, 88-89, 91-92, 95, 97, 101, 104, 106-107, 109-110, 115 n., 116, 119 n., 122-123, 127, 133, 135-136, 138, 142, 144, 149, 158, 162, 167, 170, 174, 177-178, 186-188, 191, 198, 207, 209, 214, 216-220, 222, 228, 230-231, 245, 255, 259-260, 280, 281, 282-283, 291, 299, 315-316, 320 n., 326
Budapest, 3, 25, 56, 166 n., 188 n., 302
burgage, *see*: plot
Burzenland (Țara Bârsei, Barcaság; region), 175
Bzovík (Bozók), 122
canon law, *see*: law
Caransebe (Karánsebes), 215 n.
Carpathian Basin, 2, 21, 23, 25, 33 n., 37, 42, 50, 55, 57, 116-117, 123, 141, 168, 181, 189, 205, 208, 213, 215, 219, 250, 281, 323, 329
Carpathians (mountains), 37, 69
Cenad, 75
Central Europe, 12, 16, 21-22, 50, 119, 160, 164, 198, 234, 271, 282, 287
chamberlain, *see*: magistrates
chancery / writing office, municipal, 58-59, 66-68, 80-84, 117-134, 170-171, 185-186, 197-198, 280-281, 283, 290-293, 307-308, 313-315, 325-332; papal, 290; royal, 1 n., 27, 106, 130, 133, 136, 142, 158, 170, 195, 198, 280, 290-291, 315
chapter, cathedral, 69, 72-76, 123-124, 131; collegiate, 48, 56, 72, 76, 79-80, 83, 109, 182, 244-245, 263, 290, 293
Charles I (Robert), king of Hungary, 36, 64, 79, 94, 98-99, 106, 123, 130, 256, 290, 311
Charles VI, king of France, 216
charter (letter) of privilege, 27, 32-33, 36-37, 45, 53, 62-70, 84-86, 95, 97, 102-104, 110, 121-122, 130, 142, 256-259, 261-262, 272, 289-290, 304, 307, 311, 314-316
Chartier, Roger, 18
chirograph, 74, 82-84, 288
chronicles, *see*: historiography
church building, sacristy, 193-194, 289-290, 292-293
Cistercians, *see*: religious orders
Clanchy, Michael, 17
Classen, Peter, 17
clergy (*see also*: parish), 63, 67, 73-77, 130, 133, 171, 189, 252, 328, 330
clerks, *see*: notaries of towns
Cluj, 37, 54 n., 58, 85, 92, 99, 119 n., 124-125, 136, 175, 185, 214, 218, 220, 224, 231, 299 n., 305, 326
Cluj-Manaștur (Kolozsmonostor; part of present-day Cluj), 289
coats of arms, *see*: heraldry
code-switching, 236-237
Colinus, notary from Gelnica, 123
Cologne (Köln), 119, 136-137
Coloman (the Learned), king of Hungary, 251 n., 252 n.
confraternities, 150, 162, 185, 189, 207
correspondence *see*: missives
council, councillor (in towns), *see*: magistrates
counties, literacy of, 63-64, 67, 73, 77, 79, 93, 98, 141-142, 152, 215, 224; noble, 51, 136, 211, 222, 291; royal, 26, 28-29, 84, 314
court cases, courts of justice, 15-16, 73, 81, 99-100, 115-118, 123, 133, 140, 142, 153, 156, 167-168, 173-174, 191, 210, 216, 218, 222, 226, 231, 238, 262-265, 282, 290,

293, 302, 316; civil cases, 169, 173; criminal cases, 152, 154, 169-170, 172-173
Cracow (Kraków), 37, 126, 131, 136, 153, 169, 198, 210, 233, 235
credit contract, 117 n., 154, 169, 179, 260, 262, 269, 271-277, 278, 281-282, 284
Croatia, 44, 55, 215
Croatian language, *see*: Slavic languages
Cromer, Leonhard, notary of Košice, 131 n., 132, 166 n.
Csepreg, 212, 213 n.
Csukovits, Enikő, 152
Cumans, Cuman language, 215, 240-242
customary law, *see*: law
Czech language, *see*: Slavic languages
Czibner, Christian, notary of Prešov, 210
Dalmatia, 35, 44, 62, 123, 145, 215-216
Danube (river), 26, 34-35, 79, 95, 101, 123, 161, 206, 255
Debrecen, 106 n., 200
Dej, 69
Devín (Theben, Dévény), 273
diet (of Hungary), 37, 98, 225, 245
diglossia, 236-238, 246
Dilcher, Gerhard, 18
Diósy, Gergely, notary of Cluj, 305
diplomatics, 16, 57, 84
documents, *see*: probative value
Dominicans, *see*: religious orders
Dráva (river), 113
Dresinger, Thomas, councillor of Sopron, 273, 274
Dubica (Kozarska Dubica), 68-69, 117
Dubrovnik (Ragusa), 20, 216
Duranti, Luciana, 333
East Central Europe, 16, 21, 55, 65, 217, 275, 312
Eastern Europe, 32, 35
Ebner, Matthias, burgher of Nuremberg and Kremnica, 153
Eger, 75, 118, 242
Egkenfelder, Liebhart, notary of Pressburg, 127-128, 129 n., 165
Eisenstadt (Kismarton), 117
Elizabeth Piast, queen-consort to king Charles I, 94, 130
Emeric (Saint), prince, 73
Emeric, king of Hungary, 89
Empfängerausfertigung, 80, 122, 211, 212 n., 245 n.
epigraphy, 48, 50, 56-57, 194, 254
Ernest of Habsburg, ruler of Inner Austrian duchies 152
Ernst, Konrad, burgher of Vienna and notary of Sopron, 127, 154, 159, 170, 214, 224, 269, 295
Esztergom, 25-26, 61, 69, 75, 81, 86, 88-92, 95, 101, 108, 110, 111 n., 113, 130, 215, 283, 284 n., 289-290, 293, 324, 326-327
evictio (warranty), 109, 117, 169, 176, 276
Fabriano, 141
fair, 37, 119-120, 123, 130 n., 241, 307
Far East, 21
Fehérvár, *see*: Székesfehérvár
Felhévíz (part of present-day Budapest), 145
Flanders, 330
Flins, Niklas, councillor of Pressburg, 104
Flóra, Ágnes, 100, 121
Florence (Firenze), 318
forgeries, 16, 69, 109, 117, 186, 190, 258, 285, 319, 321
France, 21, 138, 216
Frederick II the Quarrelsome, duke of Austria and Styria, 255-256
Fügedi, Erik, 86
Gabriel de Zömlen, *literatus*, 258
Garai, Hungarian noble family, 264
Garai, Miklós, palatine of Hungary, 264
Gelnica, 123, 124 n., 130, 154, 328
Gembický, Juraj, 57
Geneva (Genève, Genf), 144
Gentile da Montefiore, cardinal and papal legate in Hungary, 141
German language, 47-48, 56, 66, 80, 85, 113, 138, 143, 148, 152, 159, 165, 168, 171, 173, 175, 186-187, 192, 194, 200, 208 n., 210-228, 231-245, 266, 277-278, 280-282, 312, 316, 328-329, 331
Germans, *see*: *hospes*
Germany, 52, 206
Geuenich, Dieter, 148
Ghent (Gent, Gand), 110, 330

Giddens, Anthony, 9-10, 13
Glagolitic script, *see*: palaeography
Goda, Károly, 172
Goldner, Johannes, notary of Sibiu, 125
Gömör County, 224
Gönc, 224
Goody, Jack, 12
Gradec (part of present-day Zagreb), 105-106, 122-124, 126, 129-131, 167, 174, 176, 179, 190, 198, 246, 326, 328
Granasztói, György, 207 n.
grant of arms, *see*: heraldry
Greff, Mathias, judge of Buda, 167
Grüngrass, Lucas, burgher of Braşov, chronicler, 196
Gugelweit, Hans, notary of Sopron, 243
guilds (of craftsmen), 54-55, 133, 138, 169-171, 174, 185-189, 199, 214, 223, 228, 238-239, 308, 330-331
Guyotjeannin, Olivier, 18
Gyarmati, Sándor, 163-164
Győr, 69, 75, 77 n., 78, 124, 159, 200, 283
Hainburg, 136, 275, 276
Hajnal, István, 11-12, 44
Házi, Jenő, 52, 58, 77, 118
Hebrew language and script, 48, 217, 237-238, 242, 254, 265-266, 273-278, 280-284, 306-308, 313; *see also*: palaeography
Hedwig (Jadwiga), daughter of king Louis I, queen of Poland, 96-97
Hegyalja (region), 224
Hegyi, Géza, 55
Heiligenkreuz, 211-212, 245
Heinrich von Mügeln, chronicler, 192 n.
Heinrich, notary of Prague, 119
Henc, burgher of Fehérvár, 81
heraldry, heraldic symbols, 52, 88-89, 92-94, 101-102
Heyden, Sebald, theologian, cantor, 233
historiography, 46, 189-196, 212, 242, 331
Holy Roman Empire, 16, 35, 101, 119, 136, 198, 206, 286
Hosking, Geoffrey, 13, 323
hospes (settler), 26, 32-33, 62 n., 63-66, 68-69, 99, 105, 107, 110-112, 115, 205, 208-209, 213, 218, 256-257, 260, 327-328, 330; Germans (*Saxones, Teutonici*), 52, 69, 96, 125, 175, 192, 195-196, 208, 211, 245; *Latini*, 33, 75, 85-87, 89, 91-92, 216, 327
hospital, 46, 111, 140, 162, 171
Hronsky Benadík (Garamszentbenedek), 122
Huber, Wolfgang, printer at Nuremberg, 312
Huszár, Lajos, 57
Iberian Peninsula, 263
information retrieval, 137-138, 311
Innocent III, Pope, 137
Irsigler, Franz, 144
Ismaelitae, *see*: Muslims
Isserlein, rabbi of Wiener Neustadt, 281
Italian dialects, 210, 216-217, 240
Italy, 16, 50, 144-145, 216, 332
iudex, iudex regius, *see*: judge
iudex Iudaeorum, *see*: Jews
Iványi, Béla, 52
Jacob, judge of Pressburg, 295
Jakó, Zsigmond, 54, 141
Janecek, Andrzej, 22
Jews, *iudex Iudaeorum*, *praefectus Iudaeorum*, 48-49, 80-81, 117 n., 135, 143, 208-209, 216-217, 237-238, 242, 249-286, 295, 308, 313, 316; from France, 216, 280; from Regensburg, 33-34, 250; from Spain, 280
Jihlava (Iglau), 36, 119
Johannes filius Cantus, notary of Buda, 122
John I Albert, king of Poland, 156
Judenbuch, 278-280, 285
Judenprivileg, 81
judge (in towns: *iudex*, *iudex regius*, *villicus*), 34, 63, 79, 83 n., 85-87, 98, 103-106, 109-110, 112-115, 117, 122, 127, 130, 133, 135, 142, 152-153, 155, 157-158, 165-167, 169, 172, 176-178, 181, 185, 190, 194, 199, 210-211, 213, 220-221, 227, 246, 256, 260-265, 271, 292-295, 305, 317, 321
Juding, Niklas, councillor of Sopron, 264
Jurek, Tomasz, 22
Kalocsa, 26, 75
Kaltenstein *see*: Levél
Kaptol (part of present-day Zagreb), 123
Kassariel, Jewish burgher of Sopron, 237, 273-274
Katz, Chajjim, Jewish inhabitant of Buda, 48-

49, 280
Kecskemét, 200
Kejř, Jiři, 22
Keller, Hagen, 17-18
Kežmarok, 58 n., 69, 125, 194
Kiss, Etele, 91
Klingenbach, 110
Klostermarienberg (Borsmonostor), 110, 212 n.
Kluge, Mathias Franc, 330
Knights Hospitaller, *see*: religious orders
Knights of St. Stephen, *see*: religious orders
Kolín, 119
Koloman, Hungarian prince and king of Halych, 85
Komárno (Révkomárom, Komárom), 92
Königsberg (Kaliningrad), 94, 214
Konstanz, 194
Körmend, 255
Körmendi, Tamás, 94
Kosáry, Domokos, 50-51
Košice, 32, 37, 69, 94, 97, 100, 101 n., 104, 125, 132-133, 136, 153, 156, 161, 165-166, 169, 172, 186, 190, 224, 227, 232, 299, 305, 326
Kőszeg, 33, 55, 59, 212, 264
Kovács, András W., 55
Kováts, Ferenc, 269-270, 277 n.
Krapina (Korpona), 92
Kras, Paweł, 22
Kremnica, 36, 65, 69, 93-94, 123, 124 n., 130, 140, 144 n., 153, 157, 160, 173, 225, 244, 321 n., 326
Kreusl, Hans, notary of Kremnica, 244
Kromer, Niklas, notary of Trnava, 127
Krupina (Korpona), 66, 69, 122 n., 129, 168, 219, 245
Kubinyi, András, 4, 42, 44, 67, 88-89, 93, 204, 205 n., 228
Kulm, 332
Kumorovitz, Lajos Bernát, 53, 252
Kutná Hora (Kuttenberg), 65
Ladislas I (Saint), king of Hungary, 251 n., 252 n.
Ladislas V (Postumus), king of Hungary and Bohemia, 257 n.
Ladislaus of Naples, king of Naples and pretender to the Hungarian throne, 107
Lakatos, Bálint, 304
language, *see*: Cumans, German language, Italian dialects, Hebrew language and script, Latin language, Slavic languages, vernacular languages, Yiddish language
language maintenance, 241, 243
Latin language, 10, 23, 54, 56, 72, 75 n., 116, 127, 138, 152, 168, 171, 186 n., 188, 194, 204, 210-214, 216-217, 220, 222, 224-229, 232-233, 235-241, 243-246, 252, 254, 266, 278 n., 280, 282-283, 304, 306-307, 312, 316, 326-328, 330-331
Latini, see: *hospes*
law, 17-18, 35-36, 37 n., 45, 54, 73, 78, 98, 104, 131, 135-136, 138, 140, 144 n., 148, 154, 165, 170, 173-174, 185-188, 192, 199, 222, 232, 239, 245, 252-253, 259-266, 278, 330, 332; canon law, 13, 86, 87 n., 133; customary law, 18, 32, 35, 98, 109 n., 167, 176, 198, 258, 272, 316; Magdeburg law, 32, 33 n., 35, 66, 168, 198-199, 223, 332; mining law, 36, 52, 65, 156, 173
layout (columns, marginal notes), 18, 138, 143-144, 164, 184, 233, 276, 316, 319
Lehotská, Darina, 53, 58
Leles (Lelesz), 288-289
Lesser Poland, 136, 198
Levant, 37, 42 n., 55
Levél (Kaltenstein), 212
Levoča, 31, 149, 190 n., 191, 193-195, 232
library, 56, 127, 165, 194, 304, 307
Liège (Luik, Lüttich), 242, 330
Linz, 119
List, Stefan, mayor of Pressburg, 178
literacy, *see*: counties, vernacular languages
literatus, *see*: Gabriel de Zömlen
Litoměřice (Leitmeritz), 119
Litovel (Littau), 168
liturgical books, 46, 48, 59, 127
Livonia, 144
loca credibilia (*locus credibilis*, places of authentication), 72-75, 77-83, 109, 112, 115, 117-118, 121, 123-124, 133, 136-137, 141-142, 171, 175, 185-186, 197-199, 219, 244-245, 257, 283, 288-289, 292, 298-299, 307,

319, 327
Louis I (the Great), king of Hungary and Poland, 36-37, 66, 94, 97, 99, 106, 130, 165, 212 n., 219, 290, 311
Louis II, king of Hungary and Bohemia, 37, 258 n.
Lővei, Pál, 56
Low Countries, 16, 118, 144, 198, 332
Lower Austria, 136, 211, 273
Lübeck, 21, 119, 332
Ľubietová, 124, 130
Lucerne (Luzern), 292
Luhmann, Niklas, 9-10, 120
Luther, Martin, reformer, 239
Mabillon, Jean, Benedictine monk and scholar, 16
Madas, Edit, 205
Magdeburg, 32, 33 n., 35, 66, 116, 168, 198-199, 223, 332
Magdeburg law, *see*: law
Magdoško, Drahoslav, 161
magister tavernicorum (master of the royal treasury), 37, 130, 159-160, 165-166, 174, 186, 200, 222, 308
magistrates (aldermen, chamberlain, council, councillors), 15, 18, 34, 63, 78, 80-83, 85-86, 90, 93, 102, 104-108, 110-112, 114-119, 121-124, 127, 133, 135, 148-149, 154, 158-162, 165-166, 168-171, 173-174, 176-178, 184, 186-191, 199-200, 210-211, 217-221, 223-225, 229-230, 236, 245, 261-266, 273-274, 278, 283-284, 286, 292-293, 296, 298, 313-314, 316, 319-320, 324, 330-331; *see also*: judge, mayor
Magyi, János, notary of Pest, 186
Mainz, 250
Marchegg, 295
market, 26, 63-64, 76, 145, 161-162, 167, 241, 260, 307
market towns, *see*: seigniorial towns
Martin (Turócszentmárton), 66
Mary the Virgin, Saint, 94
Mary, queen of Hungary, 107
Matthias Corvinus, king of Hungary, 37, 113 n., 118 n., 138, 178, 186, 206, 217, 257, 266
mayor, 90, 112, 178, 181, 190, 196, 210, 214, 215 n., 218 n., 224, 235, 263, 265, 295, 305, 311
media change, 12, 332
Mediterranean, 35, 123, 140
medium regni, 26, 69, 115
Medvedgrad (Medvevár; part of present-day Zagreb), 106
Melanchthon, Philip, Lutheran reformer, 233
Mendel, Jewish family at Buda, 283
Merhell, rabbi at Sopron, 274
Mersiowsky, Mark, 157
mining (activity, town), 16, 36-39, 44, 69, 85, 94, 123-125, 130, 133, 153-154, 160, 173, 200, 239, 245, 326-329
mining law, *see*: law
minting, 34, 57, 156, 170, 253-254
Miskolc, 200, 214
missives, 101, 112-113, 145, 149, 213, 215, 224, 291, 302, 317
Moldavia, 223
Mollay, Károly (Karl), 58, 204, 296 n.
monastery, monks, 26, 68 n., 111, 140, 178, 290, 330
Moravia, 33 n., 119, 126, 136, 168, 240, 280
Moritz, Paul, town judge and merchant at Sopron, 227
Most (Brüx), 119
Mostert, Marco, 19-21, 319-320
Muhi, 6
multilingualism (bilingualism), 204-205, 210, 234-237, 246, 278 n., 280
Muslims (*Ismaelitae*), 250 n., 263
Myser, Johannes, mayor of Szeged, 215 n.
Naples (kingdom), 291
Németh, János, 227-228
Németi (part of present-day Satu Mare), 112
Nicopolis (Nikopol), 107
Niger, Petrus, Domincan friar, theologian, 282 n.
Nitra, 75, 252
Nitra County, 57
nobility, 15, 37, 63, 67, 73, 118, 141, 239, 267, 260, 271, 293
notaries of towns (clerks, scribes), 58-59, 72, 74-75, 79-81, 103-105, 119, 121-133, 135, 138, 140, 145 n., 152, 154, 156, 159, 161,

164-170, 172-176, 179, 184, 186, 188-189, 196-200, 210, 213-214, 219-221, 223-224, 226, 239, 243-244, 264, 269, 283, 287, 292-293, 295, 299, 302 n., 305, 307-308, 311-312, 314-315, 317, 319-321, 324 n., 325-328, 331; payment of 126, 130-132, 161, 260
notary public, 133, 138, 186
Nová Baňa, 93-94, 122-123, 127
Novgorod, 20
Nuremberg (Nürnberg), 35, 136, 144-146, 153, 312
Nyitra County, 215
oath, 14-15, 85, 97, 127, 155, 157, 160, 256, 260, 264, 321
Óbuda (part of present-day Budapest), 3, 25-26, 43-44, 83, 94, 326
Ofner Stadtrecht (law book of Buda), 35, 83, 84 n., 103, 108, 116, 127, 131-132, 145-135, 138, 152, 165-166, 184, 191, 221-223, 259, 283-284, 306 n., 315, 320 n., 321
Oláh, Nicholas, archbishop of Esztergom, chronicler, 215
Olomouc (Olmütz), 136, 168
Opava (Troppau), 149
Oradea, 6, 37, 73, 75, 162, 302
orality, 11, 15, 19, 181, 230, 252
Oraştie (Szászváros), 215 n.
Orthodox (clergy, religion), 223, 240
Ottokar II Přemysl, king of Bohemia, 255
Ottoman conquest / occupation, 55, 69, 74, 188, 197, 208, 259
Pakucs-Willcocks, Mária, 55
palaeography, scripts,16, 19, 50, 57, 59, 122 n., 145, 210, 223, 237, 241; biscriptality, 237; Cyrillic script 210, 223, Glagolitic script, 215, 240, 246; Hebrew script, 237-238, 254, 266 n., 273, 276, 280-282
paper (production, trade, watermarks), 2, 48, 56 n., 84, 112, 138, 140-147, 158, 183, 191, 197-198, 244, 271, 291-292, 299, 307, 311-313, 318
parchment, 48, 84, 140-142, 144 n., 165, 243-244, 271, 276, 304, 307-309, 311, 313-314
parish church, 56, 62, 76, 79-80, 103-105, 122, 142 n., 150, 179, 193-195, 207 n., 226, 230-233, 292-293, 304, 307, 318; priest, 63, 79 n., 80, 103, 105, 111, 121-122, 125-126, 153, 171-172, 190, 194, 226, 230-232, 265, 292, 308; rights 14, 133, 232
Passau, 35
Patak *see*: Sárospatak
patron saint, 94
Pécs, 75-76, 191, 329
Pécsvárad, 75
Pero, judge of Sopron, 110
Pest (part of present-day Budapest), 3, 23, 34, 37, 43-44, 53, 89, 91, 95, 107, 108 n., 110, 122-123, 133, 186, 188, 224, 315, 326-328.
Peter, apothecary at Buda, 122
Peter, painter at Pressburg, 296
Piirainen, Ilpo Tapani, 53
Piti, Ferenc, 55
places of authentication, *see*: *loca credibilia*
plot (burgage), 63, 67, 75, 107, 143, 144, 176, 179, 266-267, 280, 294
Poland, 21-22, 32, 136, 156, 191, 198, 215 n., 331
Polish language, *see*: Slavic languages
praefectus Iudaeorum, *see*: Jews
Prague (Praha), 22, 119, 137, 156, 293
Premonstratensians, *see*: religious orders
Prešov, 32, 37, 52, 126, 164, 172, 185, 210, 222, 225-226, 232, 296, 299-301, 313, 326
Pressburg, 2-4, 33, 37, 48, 56, 58-59, 69, 74 n., 77-80, 92, 95, 97, 101-102, 104, 108-109, 112, 114-115, 118-119, 122, 014, 127-131, 136, 138-141, 144, 149-150, 158, 160-162, 165, 169-172, 176, 178-180, 182-185, 187-188, 198, 207, 211-212, 224-225, 245, 259, 262-263, 265, 269-280, 281-284, 284, 293-295, 299-300, 320, 326, 328
Prevenier, Walter, 330
priest, *see*: parish church
probative value / power of documents, 22, 61, 74, 100, 115, 136, 178, 188, 325
Procopius, scribe at Prague, 156
Pukanec, 94, 124 n.
Rábik, Vladimír, 158
Rácz, György, 50 n.
Rady, Martyn, 166, 316
Ränes, Stephan, judge of Pressburg, 178

Ransano, Pietro, chronicler, 206, 209
Red Rus', *see*: Ruthenia
Reformation (Lutheranism, Protestantism), 46, 194, 201, 214 n., 231-232, 239, 308
Regensburg, 33-35, 116, 136, 250
Reichersdorffer, Georg, notary of Sibiu, 175
religious orders, Benedictines, 72, 74 n., 75, 136; Cistercians, 111, 211, 212 n.; Dominicans, 122, 232 n., 282; Knights Hospitaller, 72, 77-78, 81, 110, 117 n., 293; Knights of St. Stephen, 72; Premonstratensians, 72, 122 n.
Reuchlin, Johannes, German humanist, 282 n.
Reymarus, notary of Cluj, 125
Reynolds, Susan, 14, 246
Rhine (river), 95
Rhyssus, Johannes, notary of Sibiu, 213
Rodna, 36, 69, 85, 108
Roger (Master), chronicler and Archbishop of Split, 6
Roger II, king of Sicily, 140
Roland *de genere* Rátót, palatine of Hungary, 79
Romaine, Suzanne, 235
Romance languages (*see also*: Italian dialects), 33, 216, 242
Romania, 23, 52, 55
Romanian principalities, 23
Rome (Roma), 207
Rotenburg, Hans von, inhabitant of Buda, 214, 217 n.
royal court, 101, 152, 195, 198-199, 209, 217, 239, 290
Rück, Peter, 318
Rudabánya, 94
Ruedlinus dictus Waldner, burgher of Pressburg and *iudex Iudeorum*, 263
Russia, 21
Ruthenia (Red Rus'), 22, 215
Ruthenian language, *see*: Slavic languages
Sabinov, 32, 126, 232
Šariš County, 57
Sáros County, 215
Sárospatak (Potok, Patak), 108, 126
Sátoraljaújhely, 32, 126
Satu Mare (Szatmárnémeti), 69, 112
Sava (Száva; river), 113, 215
Saxones, *see*: *hospes*
Scheutzlich, Hans, notary of Košice, 156, 305
schools, schooling, 232-233, 239, 320; schoolbooks, 18; 233; schoolmaster, 80, 124, 126, 129, 214, 308
scribes, *see*: notaries of towns
scriptorium (chapter, monastic, seigniorial), 59, 118-119, 211
scripts *see*: palaeography
seals, authentic, 2, 54, 72, 74, 79, 98, 102, 115, 121, 198, 252, 325, 327, 330-332; cloth seal, 95; of ecclesiastic bodies, 54, 69, 81, 87, 95, 97, 109, 176; forged, 150-106, 118, 177, 190, 258, 321; of Jews, 282-283; municipal, 51, 57, 79, 83-84, 87-106, 112, 117, 121, 135, 177, 188, 200, 212, 272, 282, 292, 307, 322, 328; private, 87, 98, 104, 126, 274, 282, 291; royal, 5-6, 87, 97, 106, 123, 315; of the Saxon province of Transylvania, 96, 125, 328; *typarium* (matrix), 88-91, 93-94, 99, 322
Šedivý, Juraj, 48, 56-59, 79-80, 118, 122, 211, 212 n., 245
seigniorial towns, 186, 200, 328
Seligman, Adam B., 9-10
Senj (Zengg), 35
Seraphin, Georgius, notary of Bistriţa, 305
Serbia, 23
settler, *see*: *hospes*
Shalom, rabbi of Wiener Neustadt, 281
Sibiu, 37, 54-55, 59, 69, 85, 96, 111, 125, 175, 195, 208, 211, 213-214, 215 n., 218, 223, 232, 235, 302, 305, 311, 326, 328
Siegfried, notary of Pressburg, 80, 124, 130
Sighişoara, 214, 218, 232
Sigismund of Luxemburg, king of Hungary, Bohemia, and Holy Roman emperor, 36, 81, 100-102, 107, 133, 152-153, 170, 191-192, 206, 222, 257-259, 275, 284, 291, 295
Sigismund, a Jew from Sopron, 265
signature, 112, 266, 283
Silesia, 32, 136, 198, 240
Simon, Zsolt, 228
Slavic languages (Croatian, Czech, Polish, Ruthenian, Slovak), 168, 205, 210, 212,

214-215, 219, 223, 232-233, 235, 239-242, 245-246, 263, 329
Slavonia (region), 35, 62, 69, 113, 123, 174, 178, 246
Slovak language, *see*: Slavic languages
Slovakia, 2, 23, 51, 53, 55, 57-58, 113, 123, 149 n.
Smolník, 54, 123, 130, 149, 154
Solymosi, László, 205
Sopron, 4, 33-34, 37, 46, 52, 54-55, 58-59, 66, 69, 77-78, 92, 97-99, 108, 110, 112, 113 n., 114, 117 n., 118, 124, 126-130, 133, 142 n., 143-144, 153, 158-160, 170-172, 174, 179, 185, 187, 190, 196, 204, 208, 210, 211 n., 212-214, 218, 224-227, 237, 238 n., 243, 255-257, 261-269, 274, 279 and n., 281, 283, 293, 295-297, 299-300, 306-313, 315, 317, 320, 326, 328
Sörös, Tamás, vice-notary of Sopron, 224
Spiš (Zips, Szepesség; region), 33, 44, 191-192, 194-195, 224
Spišská Kapitula, 130
Spišská Nová Ves, 52
Spišská Sobota, 58 n., 191
Stary Tekov, 122 n.
Stephen of Harka, burgher of Sopron, 78-79
Stockhaimer, Christoff, burgher of Eisenstadt, 117 n.
Strasbourg, 119
Stromair (Stromer) family, enterpreneurs at Nuremberg, 144, 146
Swiss Federation, 318
Szabó, András Péter, 228
Szeben (district), 213
Székesfehérvár (Fehérvár), 3, 25-26, 66, 69, 80-81, 84, 91-92, 95, 97-99, 116, 133-134, 162, 257, 283, 289-290, 326-327
Szombathely, 113 n., 200
Talkner, Johannes, councillor of Trnava, 158
Tata, 265
tax lists / registers, 144, 148, 152, 156-159, 247, 268, 305-309, 311
Telkibánya, 94, 200 n.
Teschen (Cieszyn), 66, 168, 219
testaments, *see*: wills
Teutonici, *see*: *hospes*
Theben, *see*: Devín
Tilly, Charles, 14
Timişoara, 34
Toch, Michael, 285
Topusko (Topuszkó), 111
Tóth, Norbert C., 55
Tours, 229
town halls, 103, 105, 119, 161, 190, 196, 210, 260, 284, 293-298, 303-304, 306-311, 313, 317, 319, 326-329
trade, 27, 37, 40, 42, 46, 55, 64-65, 119, 129, 131, 141, 162, 175, 188, 216-218, 222, 225-227, 250-252, 255, 258, 260, 293, 302 n., 309, 316, 329
translation, 168, 173, 211-212, 223, 229, 244-245, 281
Transylvania, 23, 33, 36, 44, 50 n., 52, 54-55, 57, 69, 85, 96, 123, 125, 131 n., 141, 149, 174-175, 185, 195-196, 208, 211, 213, 213-214, 218, 223, 228, 245, 255, 326, 328-329
Trenčín, 69, 85, 97, 168
Trencsén County, 66, 215
Tripartitum, 98-99, 109, 258
Trnava, 37, 54, 69, 86, 94, 97, 109-110, 112, 117, 127, 131, 145, 158, 172, 199, 212, 232, 263, 265, 293, 314
Troy (in the borders of present-day Hisarlik), 196
Turán, Tamás, 281
Turda (Torda), 200 n.
Turiec (Turóc), 219
Turóc County, 66
Újhely, *see*: Sátoraljaújhely
Ukraine, 215
Uničov (Mährisch-Neustadt), 126
universitas Saxonum (in Transylvania), 96, 125, 175
university, 42, 44 n., 126, 210, 213 n., 235, 240, 326
Urban von Weyten, altar chaplain at Sopron, 308
Utrecht, 110
Vác, 75, 94
Valentin Gobil, codex illuminator, 155, 157
Valentinus de Chepreg, chaplain of the hospital chapel of Sopron, 171

Valla, Lorenzo, humanist, 16
Váradi, Zoltán, 56
Varaždin, 85, 92
Vasvár, 78, 92, 213 n., 255
Venice (Venezia), 110, 145, 318
vernacular languages and literacy, 46, 80, 159, 168, 175, 200, 204, 210-215, 217, 222-223, 229-246, 280, 304, 325-331; *see also*: German, Hebrew, Hungarian, Italian, Slavic, Yiddish
Veszprém, 72, 75, 289
Veszprémy, László, 55
Vienna (Wien), 35, 88, 119, 126-127, 133, 136-138, 140, 145, 154, 161, 170, 188, 198, 210, 214 n., 231, 235, 237 n., 263, 265, 269-270, 275-276, 295-296, 307
Villach, 119
villicus, *see*: judge
Virovitica, 85
Visegrád, 26, 34, 92, 97, 152, 170
Vizkelety, András, 205, 210
Vrbové (Verbó), 263
Vynohradiv (Nagyszőlős), 32
Wallachia, 106, 223
warranty, *see*: *evictio*
watermarks, *see*: paper
Watertown (Víziváros; part of present-day Budapest), 145
Watt, Ian, 12
Weltecke, Dorothea, 10
Werbőczy, István, Palatine of Hungary 98, 258
Western Europe, 21, 63, 213, 230, 287
Wiedl, Birgit, 267
Wiener Neustadt, 97, 119, 145, 269, 281
William of Habsburg, duke of Austria, 96-97
wills (testaments), 46, 48, 109-110, 122, 127, 129, 138-139, 154, 156, 169-170, 181-185, 196-197, 199, 207, 252, 279, 305, 308, 320, 343
witness, 45, 63, 73-74, 107, 115, 117, 170, 184, 199-200, 222, 251-252, 266, 272, 282-283
Wladislas II, king of Hungary and Bohemia, 37, 258 n.
Władysław Jagiełło, king of Poland, 97
writing office, *see*: chancery
Wrocław (Breslau), 136
Wylhelmus, notary and schoolmaster of Sopron, 124
Wysmułek, Jakub, 22
Yiddish language, 237
York, 196
Ypres, 330
Zagreb, 35, 37, 69, 75, 92, 97, 105-106, 108, 118, 122-123, 131, 137, 153, 158, 167, 174, 176, 178, 215-216, 218, 293, 326-328
Zawkan, Philipp, mayor of Sopron, 311
Ziegler, Arne, 150
Ziegler, Hans, notary of Sopron, 226, 311, 315
Žilina, 66, 125-126, 130, 149 n., 167-169, 173, 219, 223, 245
Zirkendorffer, Hans, burgher of Sopron, 274
Zvolen (Zólyom), 58 n., 126